THE WIDOW'S CURSE

COLLECTED COMIC STRIPS
FROM THE PAGES OF

DOCTOR · WHO
MAGAZINE

PANINI BOOKS

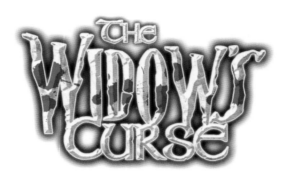

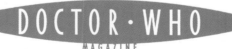

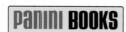

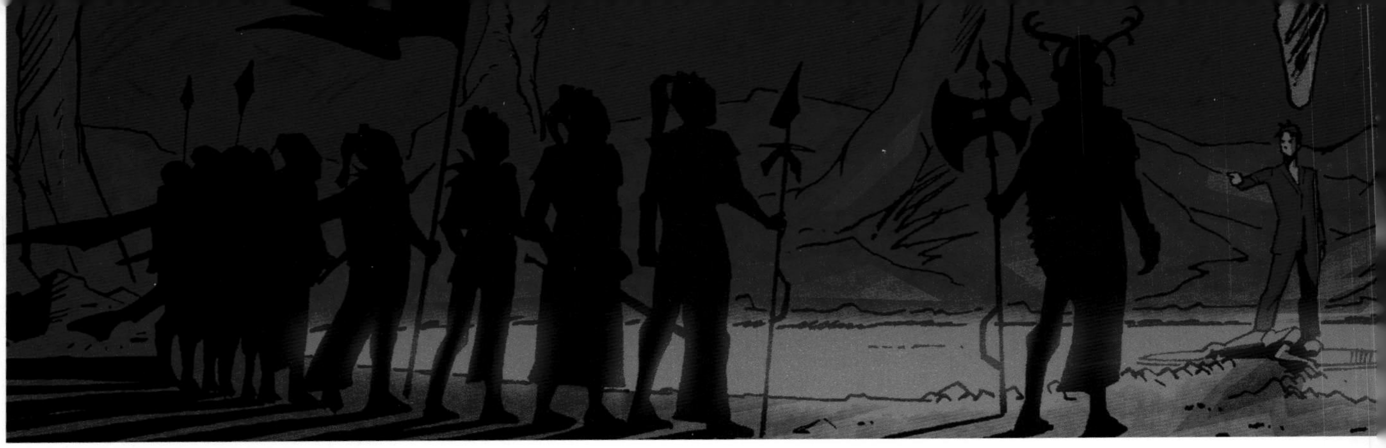

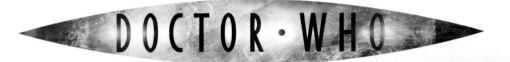

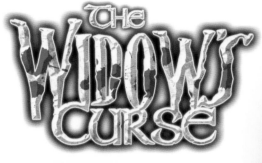

DOCTOR WHO

The Widow's Curse

A Panini Books GRAPHIC NOVEL

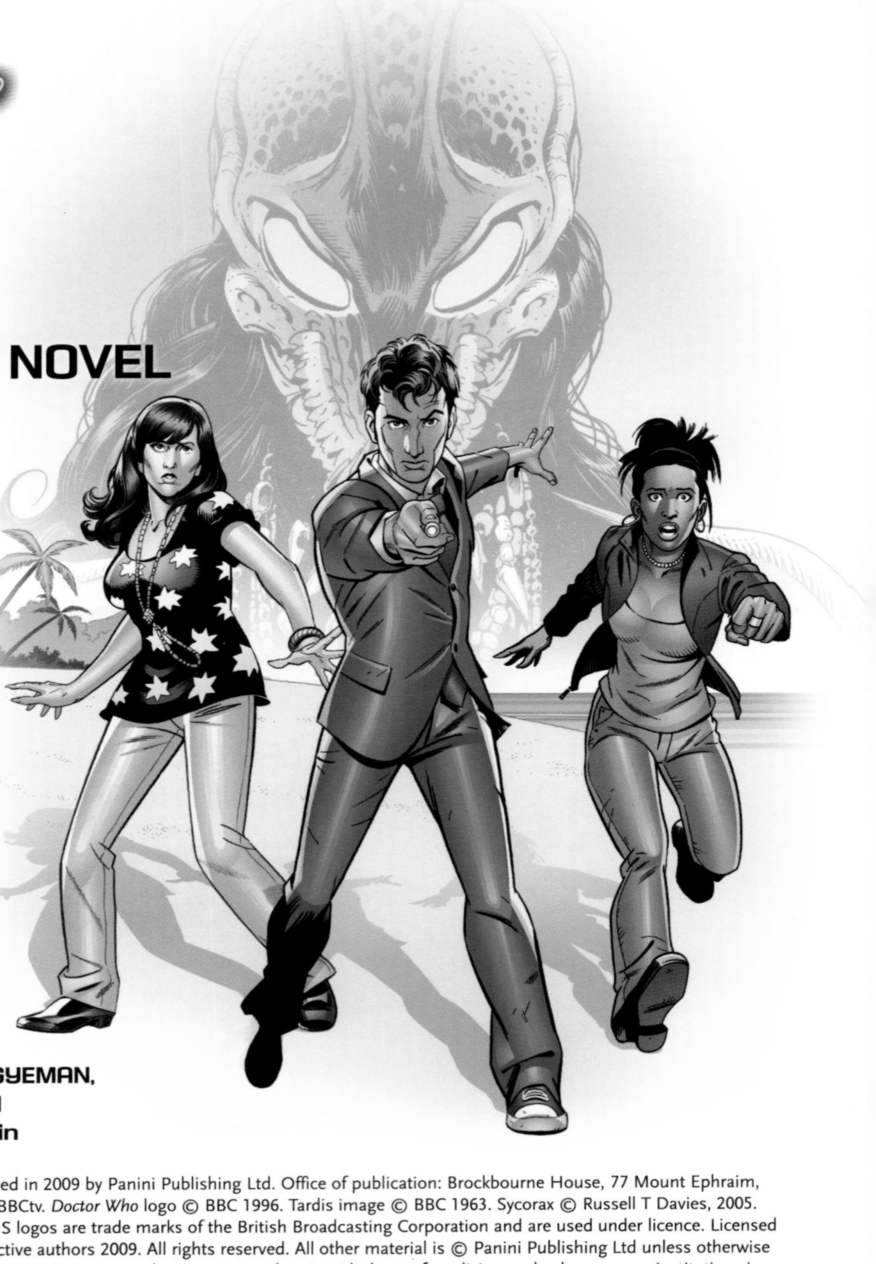

Project editor
TOM SPILSBURY

Designer
PERI GODBOLD

Consultant
SCOTT GRAY

Cover pencils and inks by
MARTIN GERAGHTY

Cover colours by
JAMES OFFREDI

Head of Production **MARK IRVINE**
Managing Editor **ALAN O'KEEFE**
Managing Director **MIKE RIDDELL**

Special thanks to
RUSSELL T DAVIES, CLAYTON HICKMAN, PETER WARE, DAVID TENNANT, FREEMA AGYEMAN, CATHERINE TATE and all the writers and artists whose work is presented herein

Doctor Who Graphic Novel #12: "The Widow's Curse". Published in 2009 by Panini Publishing Ltd. Office of publication: Brockbourne House, 77 Mount Ephraim, Tunbridge Wells, Kent TN4 8BS. Printed in Italy. ISBN 978-1-84653-429-4

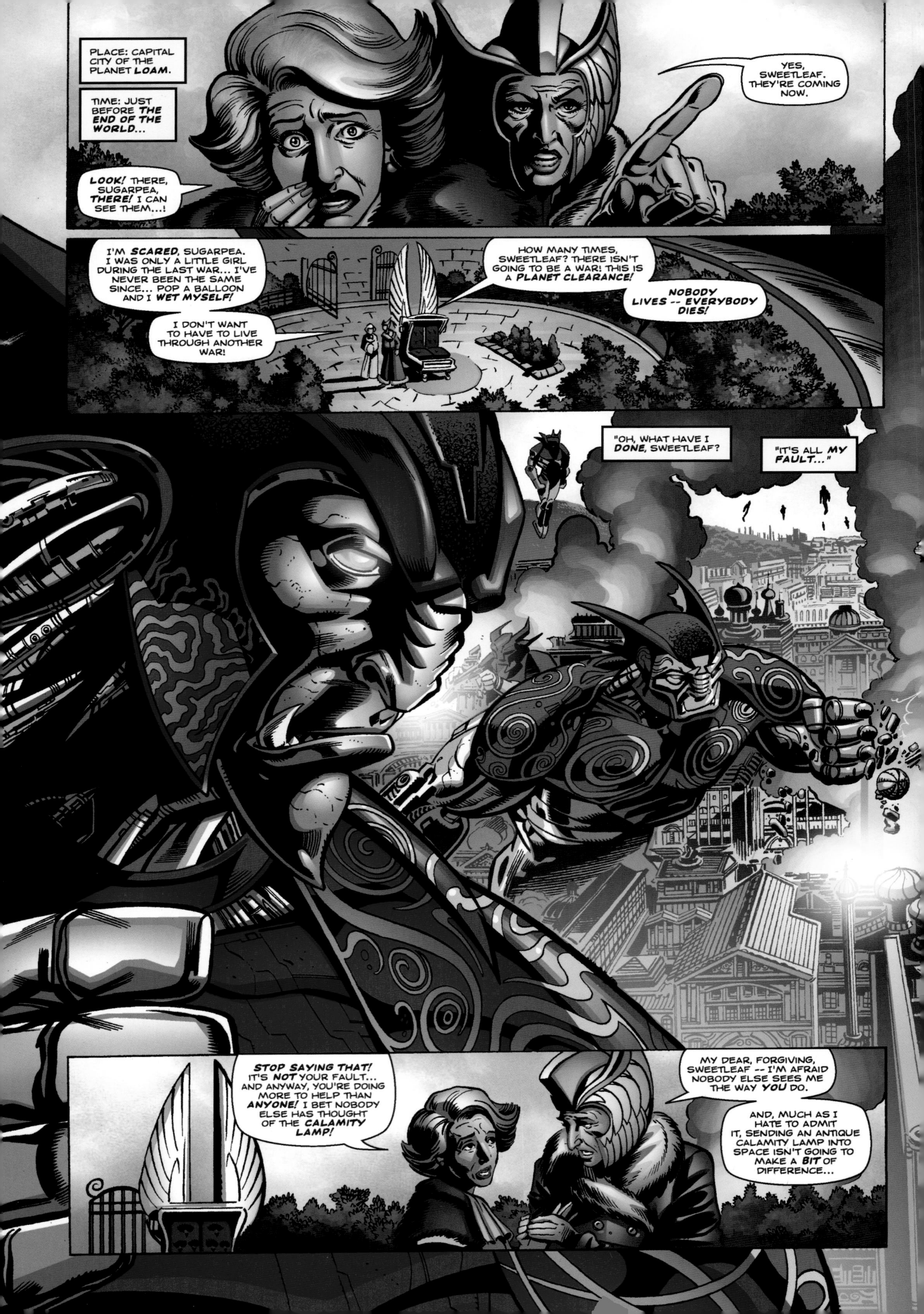
PLACE: CAPITAL CITY OF THE PLANET LOAM.
TIME: JUST BEFORE THE END OF THE WORLD...
YES, SWEETLEAF. THEY'RE COMING NOW.
LOOK! THERE, SUGARPEA, THERE! I CAN SEE THEM...!
I'M SCARED, SUGARPEA. I WAS ONLY A LITTLE GIRL DURING THE LAST WAR... I'VE NEVER BEEN THE SAME SINCE... POP A BALLOON AND I WET MYSELF!
I DON'T WANT TO HAVE TO LIVE THROUGH ANOTHER WAR!
HOW MANY TIMES, SWEETLEAF? THERE ISN'T GOING TO BE A WAR! THIS IS A PLANET CLEARANCE!
NOBODY LIVES -- EVERYBODY DIES!
"OH, WHAT HAVE I DONE, SWEETLEAF?
"IT'S ALL MY FAULT..."
STOP SAYING THAT! IT'S NOT YOUR FAULT... AND ANYWAY, YOU'RE DOING MORE TO HELP THAN ANYONE! I BET NOBODY ELSE HAS THOUGHT OF THE CALAMITY LAMP!
MY DEAR, FORGIVING, SWEETLEAF -- I'M AFRAID NOBODY ELSE SEES ME THE WAY YOU DO.
AND, MUCH AS I HATE TO ADMIT IT, SENDING AN ANTIQUE CALAMITY LAMP INTO SPACE ISN'T GOING TO MAKE A BIT OF DIFFERENCE...

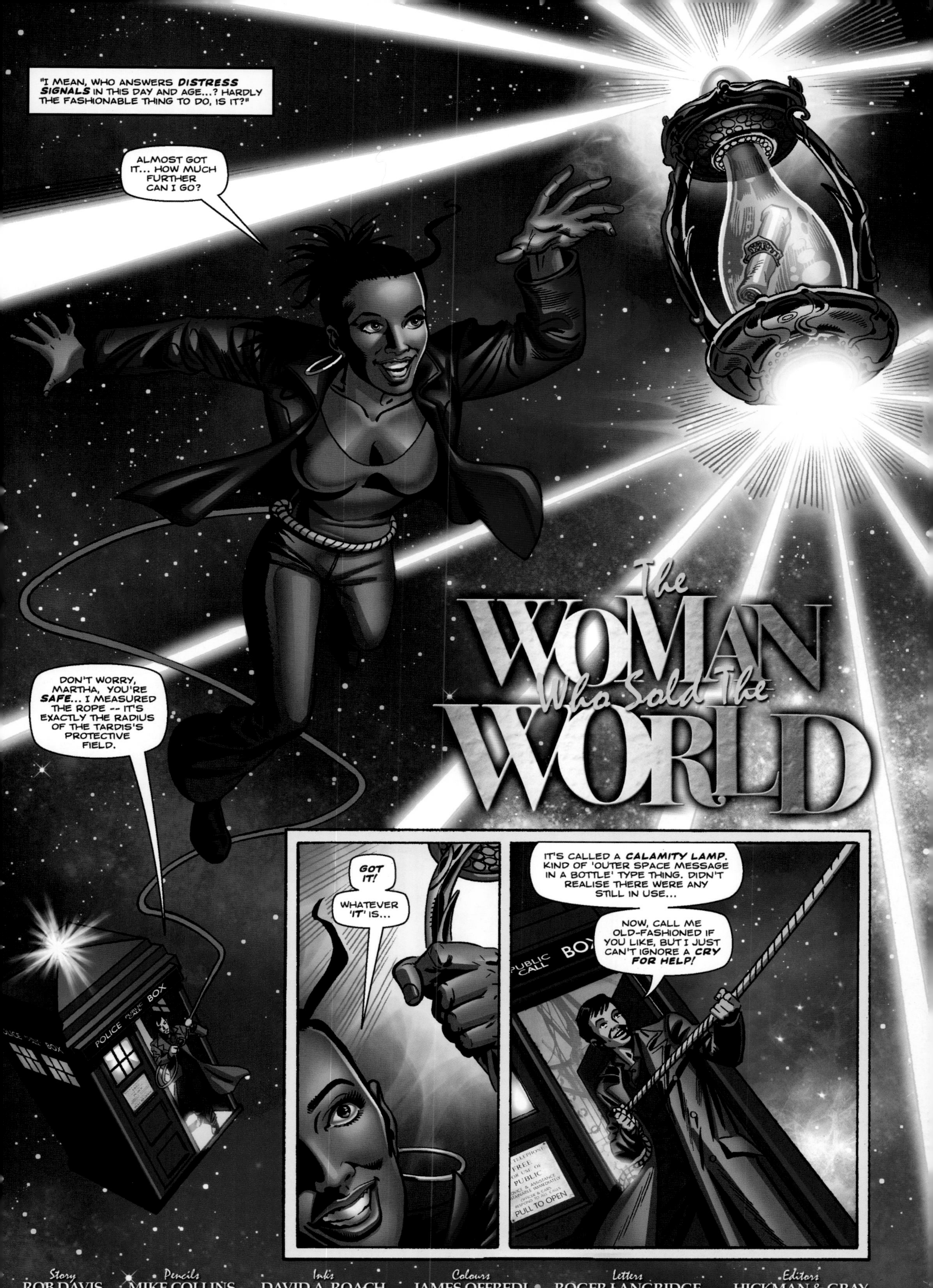
"I MEAN, WHO ANSWERS DISTRESS SIGNALS IN THIS DAY AND AGE...? HARDLY THE FASHIONABLE THING TO DO, IS IT?"
ALMOST GOT IT... HOW MUCH FURTHER CAN I GO?
DON'T WORRY, MARTHA, YOU'RE SAFE... I MEASURED THE ROPE -- IT'S EXACTLY THE RADIUS OF THE TARDIS'S PROTECTIVE FIELD.
The WOMAN Who Sold The WORLD
GOT IT!
WHATEVER 'IT' IS...
IT'S CALLED A CALAMITY LAMP. KIND OF 'OUTER SPACE MESSAGE IN A BOTTLE' TYPE THING. DIDN'T REALISE THERE WERE ANY STILL IN USE...
NOW, CALL ME OLD-FASHIONED IF YOU LIKE, BUT I JUST CAN'T IGNORE A CRY FOR HELP!

Story ROB DAVIS · Pencils MIKE COLLINS · Inks DAVID A. ROACH · Colours JAMES OFFREDI · Letters ROGER LANGRIDGE · Editors HICKMAN & GRAY

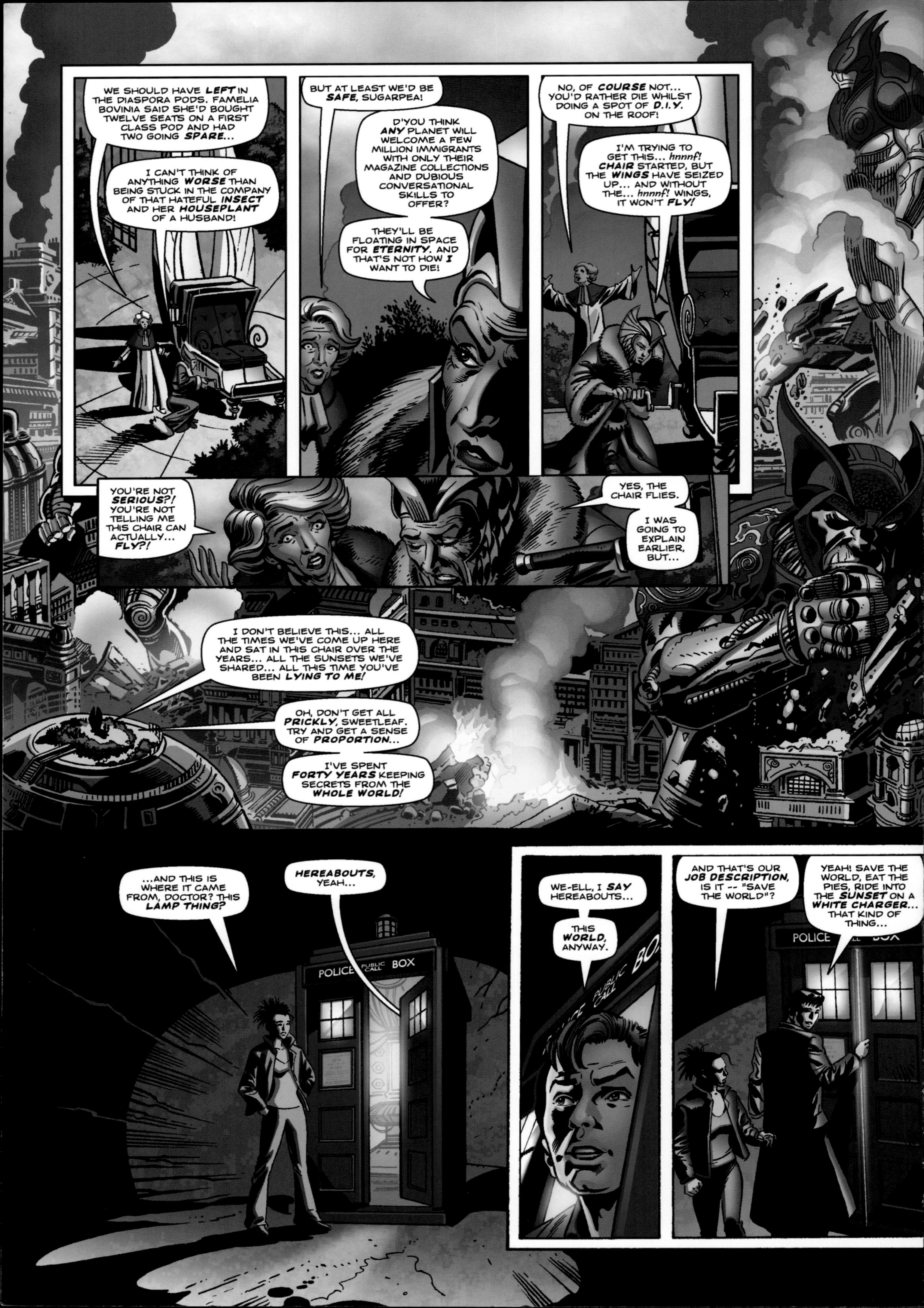
WE SHOULD HAVE LEFT IN THE DIASPORA PODS. FAMELIA BOVINIA SAID SHE'D BOUGHT TWELVE SEATS ON A FIRST CLASS POD AND HAD TWO GOING SPARE...
I CAN'T THINK OF ANYTHING WORSE THAN BEING STUCK IN THE COMPANY OF THAT HATEFUL INSECT AND HER HOUSEPLANT OF A HUSBAND!
BUT AT LEAST WE'D BE SAFE, SUGARPEA!
D'YOU THINK ANY PLANET WILL WELCOME A FEW MILLION IMMIGRANTS WITH ONLY THEIR MAGAZINE COLLECTIONS AND DUBIOUS CONVERSATIONAL SKILLS TO OFFER?
THEY'LL BE FLOATING IN SPACE FOR ETERNITY. AND THAT'S NOT HOW I WANT TO DIE!
NO, OF COURSE NOT... YOU'D RATHER DIE WHILST DOING A SPOT OF D.I.Y. ON THE ROOF!
I'M TRYING TO GET THIS... hnnnf! CHAIR STARTED, BUT THE WINGS HAVE SEIZED UP... AND WITHOUT THE... hnnnf! WINGS, IT WON'T FLY!
YOU'RE NOT SERIOUS?! YOU'RE NOT TELLING ME THIS CHAIR CAN ACTUALLY... FLY?!
YES, THE CHAIR FLIES.
I WAS GOING TO EXPLAIN EARLIER, BUT...
I DON'T BELIEVE THIS... ALL THE TIMES WE'VE COME UP HERE AND SAT IN THIS CHAIR OVER THE YEARS... ALL THE SUNSETS WE'VE SHARED... ALL THIS TIME YOU'VE BEEN LYING TO ME!
OH, DON'T GET ALL PRICKLY, SWEETLEAF. TRY AND GET A SENSE OF PROPORTION...
I'VE SPENT FORTY YEARS KEEPING SECRETS FROM THE WHOLE WORLD!
...AND THIS IS WHERE IT CAME FROM, DOCTOR? THIS LAMP THING?
HEREABOUTS, YEAH...
POLICE PUBLIC CALL BOX
WE-ELL, I SAY HEREABOUTS...
THIS WORLD, ANYWAY.
AND THAT'S OUR JOB DESCRIPTION, IS IT -- "SAVE THE WORLD"?
YEAH! SAVE THE WORLD, EAT THE PIES, RIDE INTO THE SUNSET ON A WHITE CHARGER... THAT KIND OF THING...

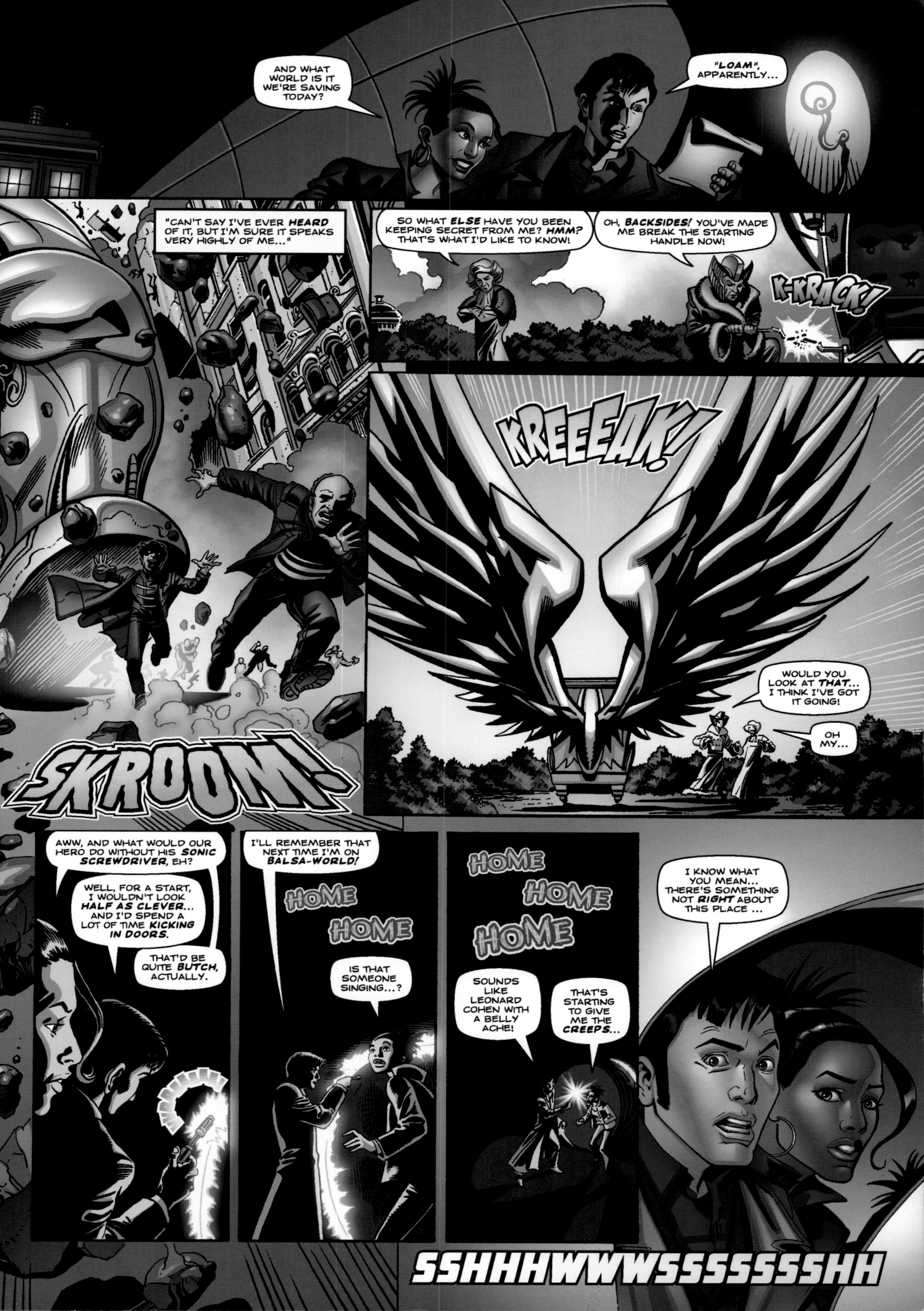

AND WHAT WORLD IS IT WE'RE SAVING TODAY?
"LOAM", APPARENTLY...
"CAN'T SAY I'VE EVER HEARD OF IT, BUT I'M SURE IT SPEAKS VERY HIGHLY OF ME..."
SO WHAT ELSE HAVE YOU BEEN KEEPING SECRET FROM ME? HMM? THAT'S WHAT I'D LIKE TO KNOW!
OH, BACKSIDES! YOU'VE MADE ME BREAK THE STARTING HANDLE NOW!
K-KRACK!
KREEEAK!
WOULD YOU LOOK AT THAT... I THINK I'VE GOT IT GOING!
OH MY...
SKROOM!
AWW, AND WHAT WOULD OUR HERO DO WITHOUT HIS SONIC SCREWDRIVER, EH?
WELL, FOR A START, I WOULDN'T LOOK HALF AS CLEVER... AND I'D SPEND A LOT OF TIME KICKING IN DOORS.
THAT'D BE QUITE BUTCH, ACTUALLY.
I'LL REMEMBER THAT NEXT TIME I'M ON BALSA-WORLD!
HOME
HOME
IS THAT SOMEONE SINGING...?
HOME
HOME
HOME
SOUNDS LIKE LEONARD COHEN WITH A BELLY ACHE!
THAT'S STARTING TO GIVE ME THE CREEPS...
I KNOW WHAT YOU MEAN... THERE'S SOMETHING NOT RIGHT ABOUT THIS PLACE ...
SSHHHWWWSSSSSSSHH

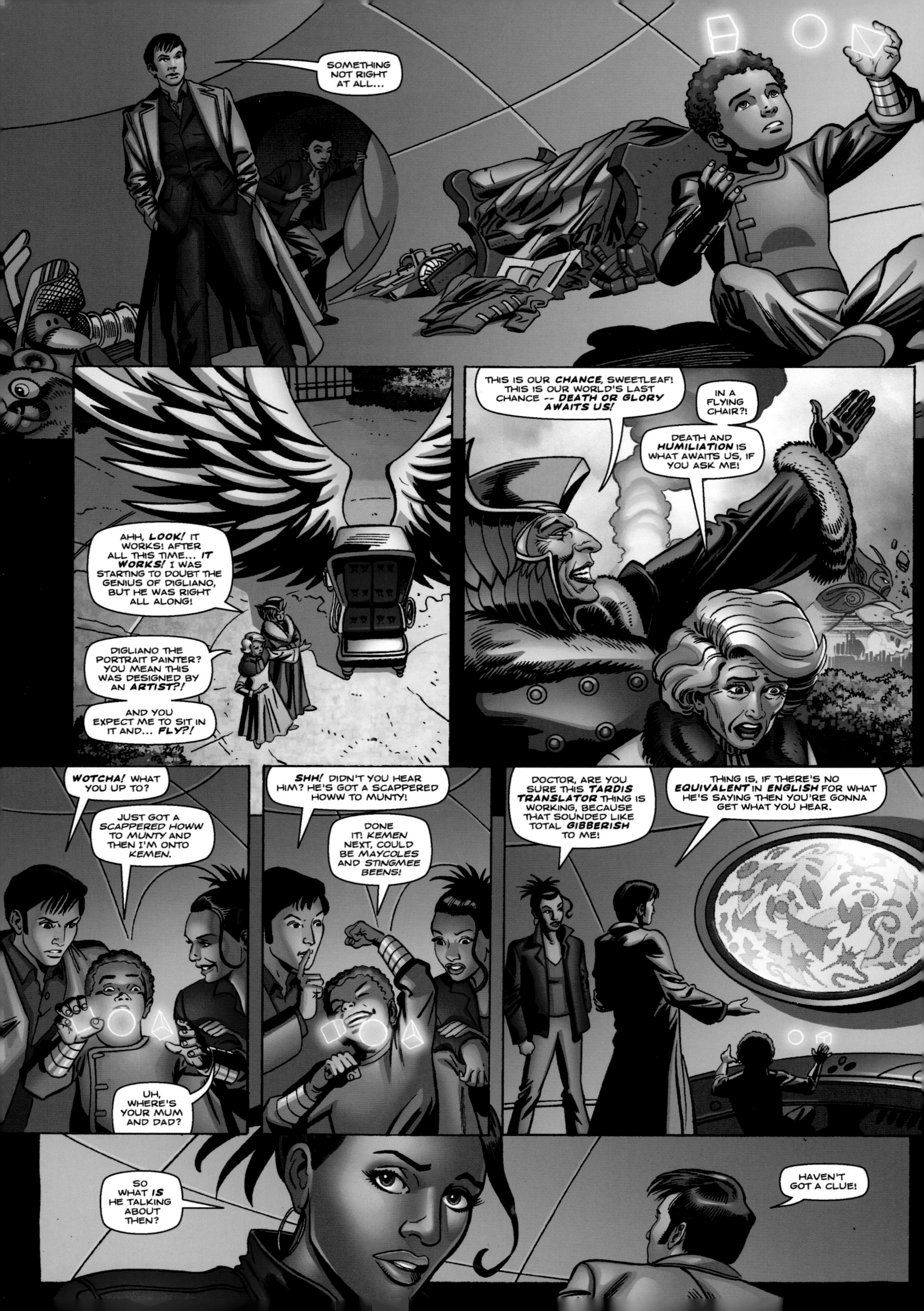
SOMETHING NOT RIGHT AT ALL...
AHH, LOOK! IT WORKS! AFTER ALL THIS TIME... IT WORKS! I WAS STARTING TO DOUBT THE GENIUS OF DIGLIANO, BUT HE WAS RIGHT ALL ALONG!
DIGLIANO THE PORTRAIT PAINTER? YOU MEAN THIS WAS DESIGNED BY AN ARTIST?!
AND YOU EXPECT ME TO SIT IN IT AND... FLY?!
THIS IS OUR CHANCE, SWEETLEAF! THIS IS OUR WORLD'S LAST CHANCE -- DEATH OR GLORY AWAITS US!
IN A FLYING CHAIR?!
DEATH AND HUMILIATION IS WHAT AWAITS US, IF YOU ASK ME!
WOTCHA! WHAT YOU UP TO?
JUST GOT A SCAPPERED HOWW TO MUNTY AND THEN I'M ONTO KEMEN.
UH, WHERE'S YOUR MUM AND DAD?
SHH! DIDN'T YOU HEAR HIM? HE'S GOT A SCAPPERED HOWW TO MUNTY!
DONE IT! KEMEN NEXT, COULD BE MAYCOLES AND STINGMEE BEENS!
DOCTOR, ARE YOU SURE THIS TARDIS TRANSLATOR THING IS WORKING, BECAUSE THAT SOUNDED LIKE TOTAL GIBBERISH TO ME!
THING IS, IF THERE'S NO EQUIVALENT IN ENGLISH FOR WHAT HE'S SAYING THEN YOU'RE GONNA GET WHAT YOU HEAR.
SO WHAT IS HE TALKING ABOUT THEN?
HAVEN'T GOT A CLUE!

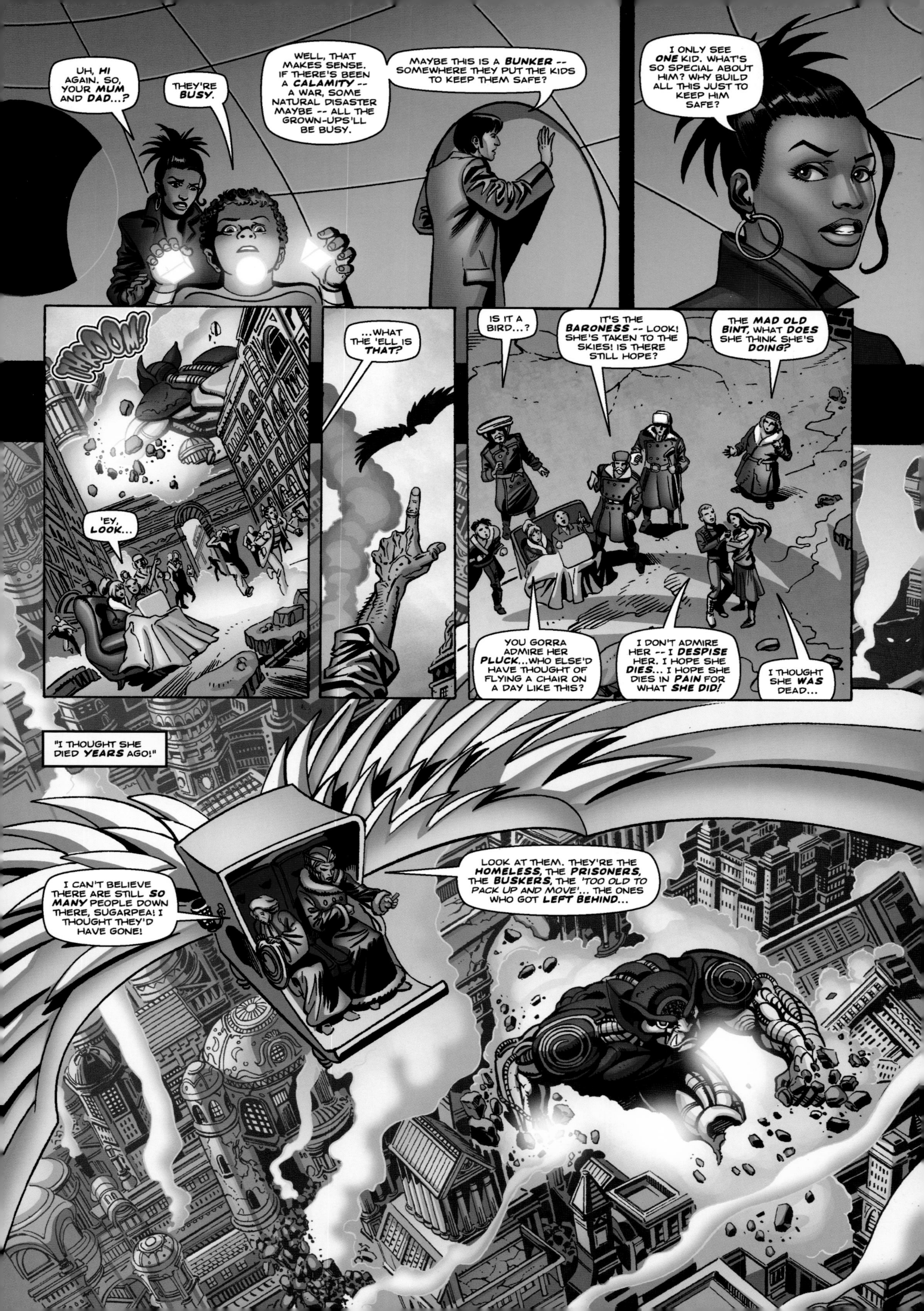
UH, HI AGAIN. SO, YOUR MUM AND DAD...?
THEY'RE BUSY.
WELL, THAT MAKES SENSE. IF THERE'S BEEN A CALAMITY -- A WAR, SOME NATURAL DISASTER MAYBE -- ALL THE GROWN-UPS'LL BE BUSY.
MAYBE THIS IS A BUNKER -- SOMEWHERE THEY PUT THE KIDS TO KEEP THEM SAFE?
I ONLY SEE ONE KID. WHAT'S SO SPECIAL ABOUT HIM? WHY BUILD ALL THIS JUST TO KEEP HIM SAFE?
THROOM!
'EY, LOOK...
...WHAT THE 'ELL IS THAT?
IS IT A BIRD...?
IT'S THE BARONESS -- LOOK! SHE'S TAKEN TO THE SKIES! IS THERE STILL HOPE?
THE MAD OLD BINT, WHAT DOES SHE THINK SHE'S DOING?
YOU GORRA ADMIRE HER PLUCK...WHO ELSE'D HAVE THOUGHT OF FLYING A CHAIR ON A DAY LIKE THIS?
I DON'T ADMIRE HER -- I DESPISE HER. I HOPE SHE DIES... I HOPE SHE DIES IN PAIN FOR WHAT SHE DID!
I THOUGHT SHE WAS DEAD...
"I THOUGHT SHE DIED YEARS AGO!"
I CAN'T BELIEVE THERE ARE STILL SO MANY PEOPLE DOWN THERE, SUGARPEA! I THOUGHT THEY'D HAVE GONE!
LOOK AT THEM. THEY'RE THE HOMELESS, THE PRISONERS, THE BUSKERS, THE 'TOO OLD TO PACK UP AND MOVE'... THE ONES WHO GOT LEFT BEHIND...

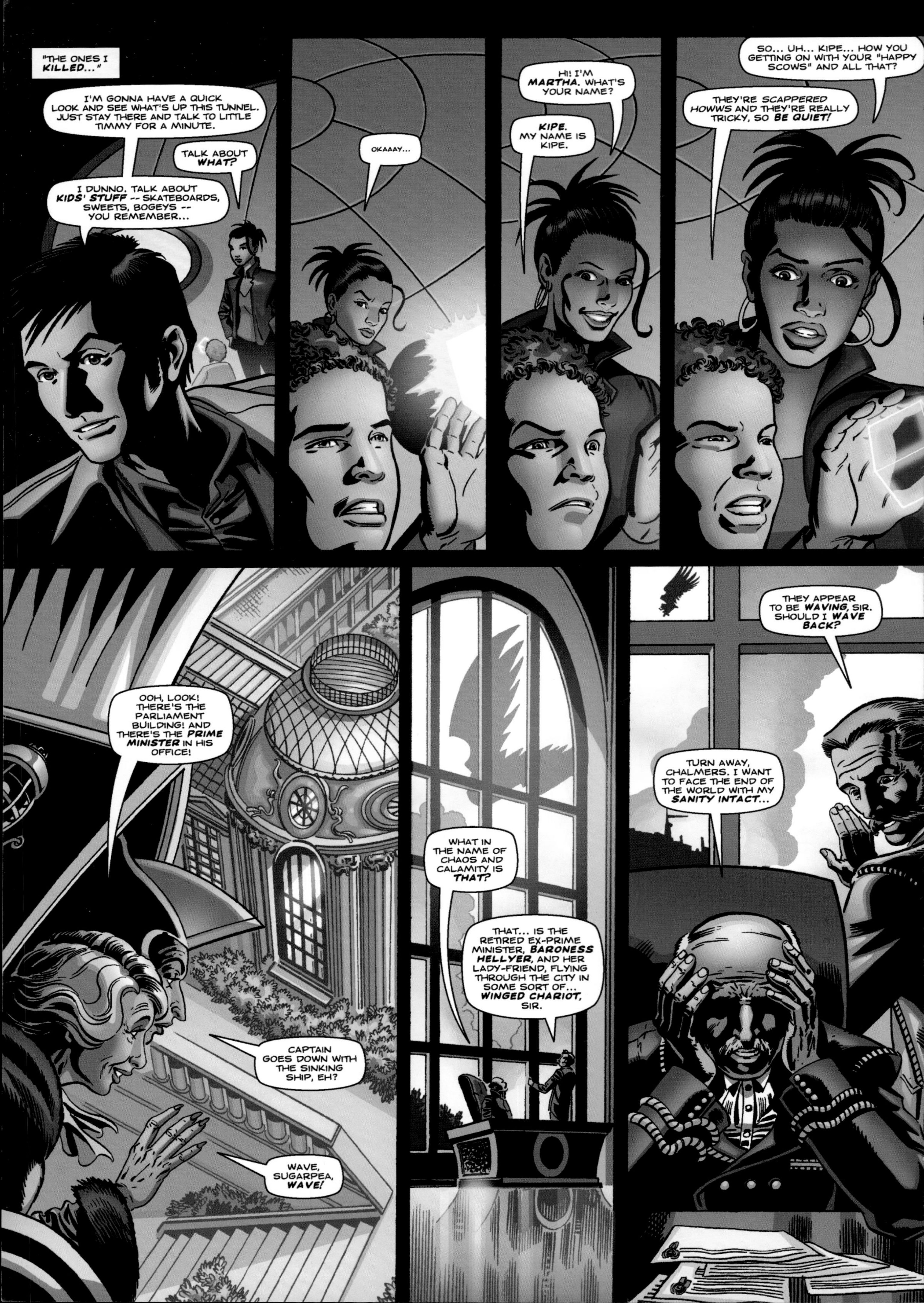
"THE ONES I KILLED..."
I'M GONNA HAVE A QUICK LOOK AND SEE WHAT'S UP THIS TUNNEL. JUST STAY THERE AND TALK TO LITTLE TIMMY FOR A MINUTE.
TALK ABOUT WHAT?
I DUNNO. TALK ABOUT KIDS' STUFF -- SKATEBOARDS, SWEETS, BOGEYS -- YOU REMEMBER...
OKAAAY...
HI! I'M MARTHA. WHAT'S YOUR NAME?
KIPE. MY NAME IS KIPE.
SO... UH... KIPE... HOW YOU GETTING ON WITH YOUR "HAPPY SCOWS" AND ALL THAT?
THEY'RE SCAPPERED HOWWS AND THEY'RE REALLY TRICKY, SO BE QUIET!
OOH, LOOK! THERE'S THE PARLIAMENT BUILDING! AND THERE'S THE PRIME MINISTER IN HIS OFFICE!
CAPTAIN GOES DOWN WITH THE SINKING SHIP, EH?
WAVE, SUGARPEA, WAVE!
WHAT IN THE NAME OF CHAOS AND CALAMITY IS THAT?
THAT... IS THE RETIRED EX-PRIME MINISTER, BARONESS HELLYER, AND HER LADY-FRIEND, FLYING THROUGH THE CITY IN SOME SORT OF... WINGED CHARIOT, SIR.
THEY APPEAR TO BE WAVING, SIR. SHOULD I WAVE BACK?
TURN AWAY, CHALMERS. I WANT TO FACE THE END OF THE WORLD WITH MY SANITY INTACT...

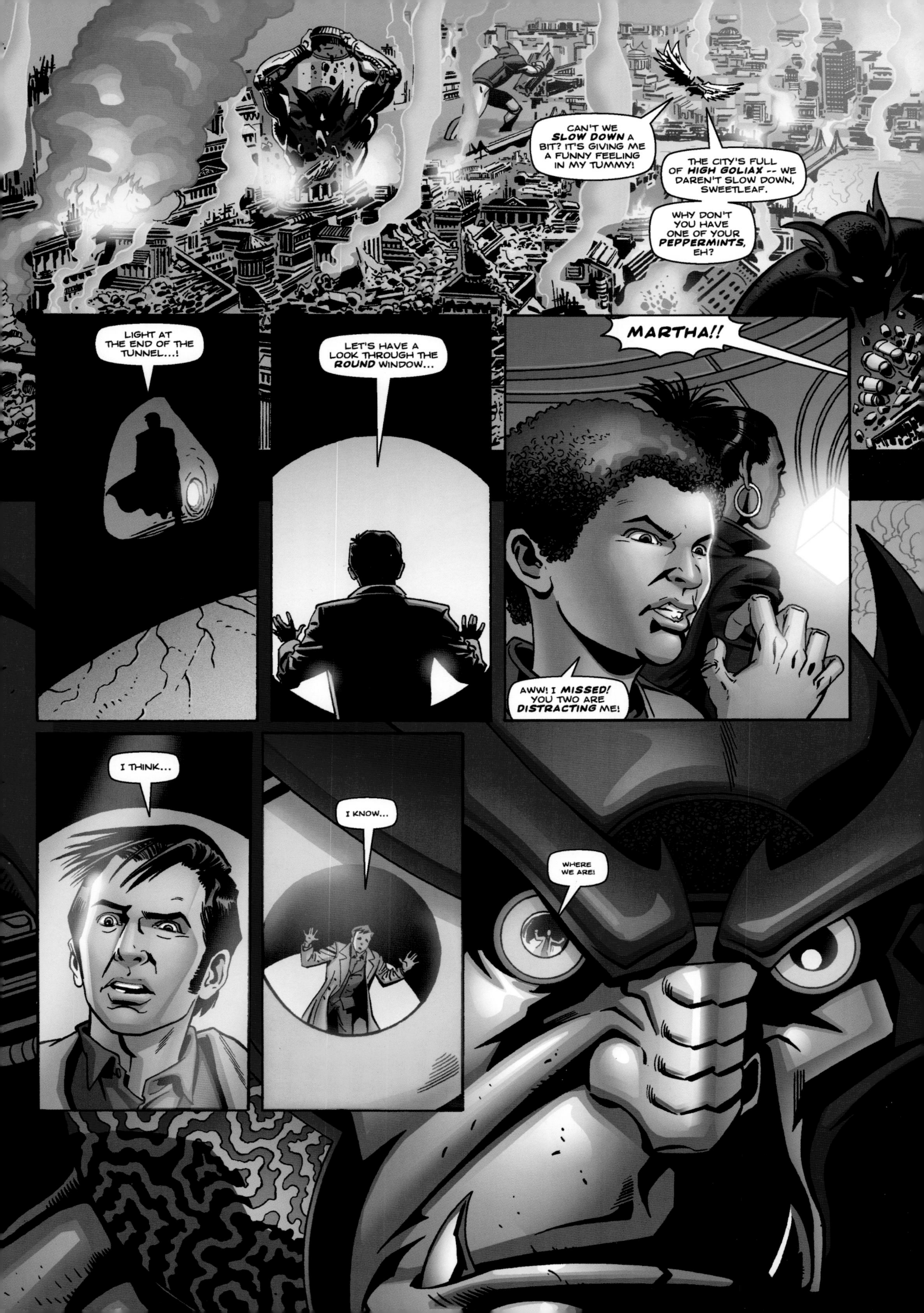
CAN'T WE SLOW DOWN A BIT? IT'S GIVING ME A FUNNY FEELING IN MY TUMMY!
THE CITY'S FULL OF HIGH GOLIAX -- WE DAREN'T SLOW DOWN, SWEETLEAF.
WHY DON'T YOU HAVE ONE OF YOUR PEPPERMINTS, EH?
LIGHT AT THE END OF THE TUNNEL...!
LET'S HAVE A LOOK THROUGH THE ROUND WINDOW...
MARTHA!!
AWW! I MISSED! YOU TWO ARE DISTRACTING ME!
I THINK...
I KNOW...
WHERE WE ARE!

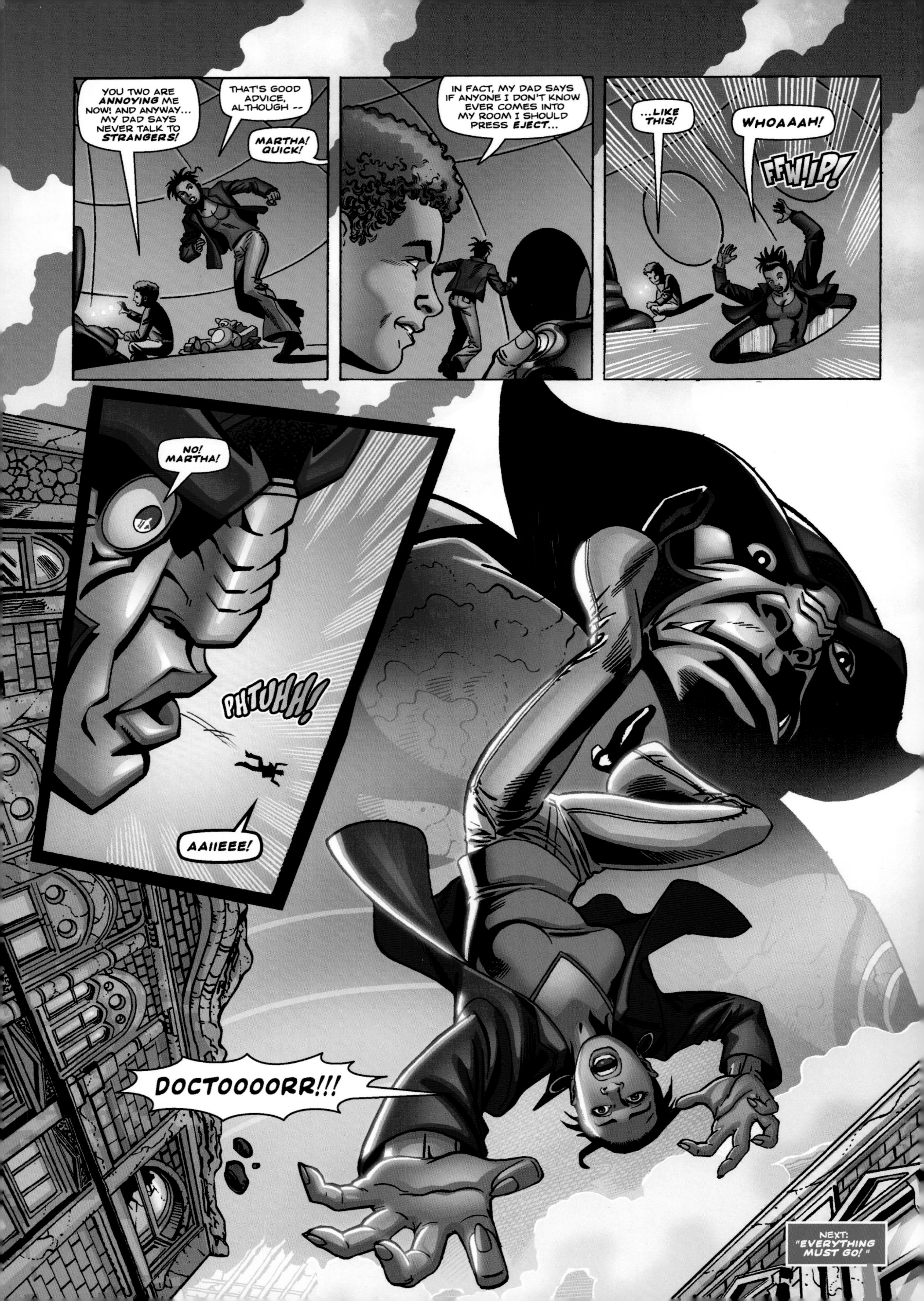
YOU TWO ARE ANNOYING ME NOW! AND ANYWAY... MY DAD SAYS NEVER TALK TO STRANGERS!
THAT'S GOOD ADVICE, ALTHOUGH --
MARTHA! QUICK!
IN FACT, MY DAD SAYS IF ANYONE I DON'T KNOW EVER COMES INTO MY ROOM I SHOULD PRESS EJECT...
...LIKE THIS!
WHOAAAH!
FFWHIP!
NO! MARTHA!
PHTUHH!
AAIIEEE!
DOCTOOOORR!!!
NEXT: "EVERYTHING MUST GO!"

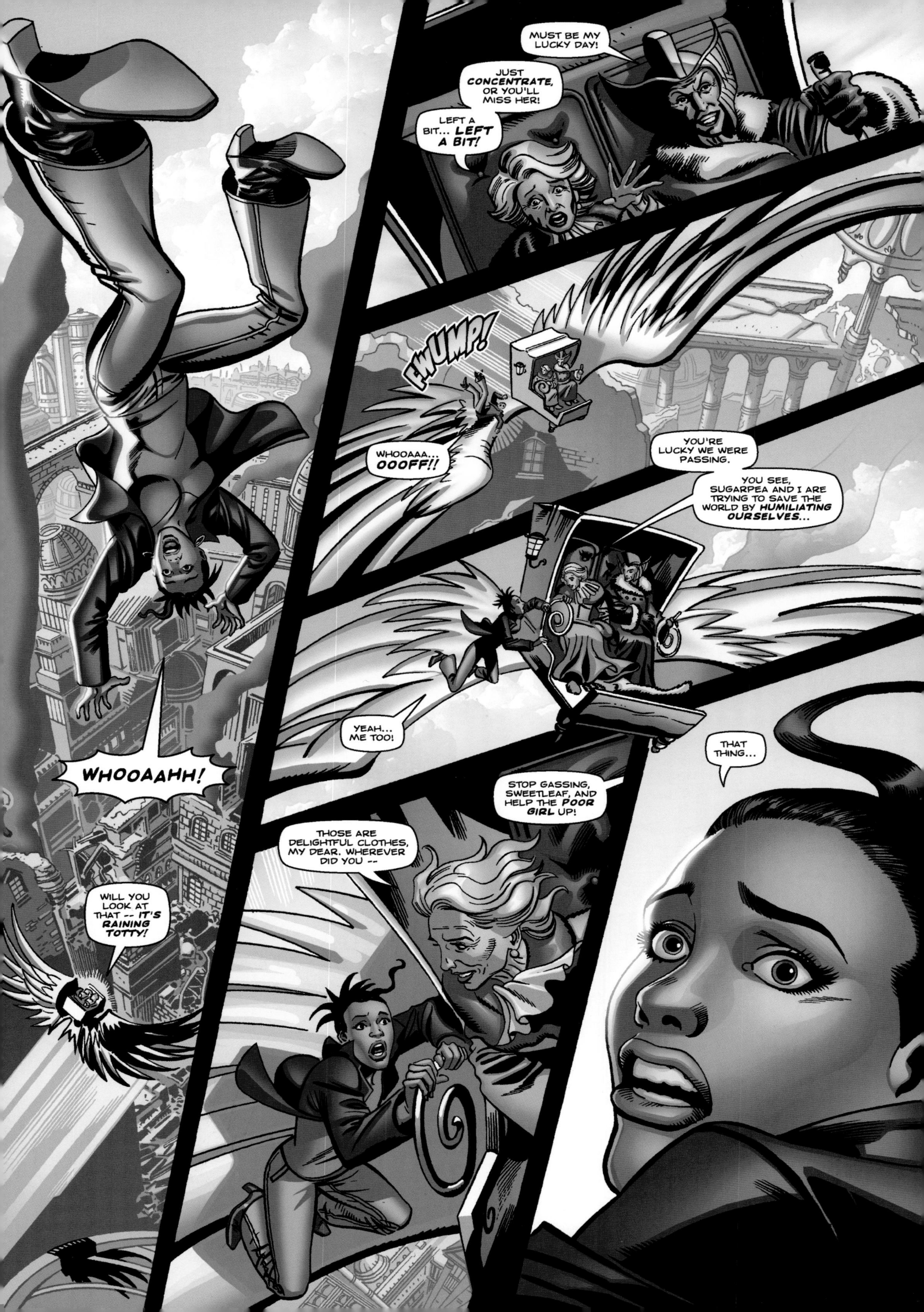
MUST BE MY LUCKY DAY!
JUST CONCENTRATE, OR YOU'LL MISS HER!
LEFT A BIT... LEFT A BIT!
FWUMP!
WHOOAAA... OOOFF!!
YOU'RE LUCKY WE WERE PASSING.
YOU SEE, SUGARPEA AND I ARE TRYING TO SAVE THE WORLD BY HUMILIATING OURSELVES...
YEAH... ME TOO!
WHOOAAHH!
WILL YOU LOOK AT THAT -- IT'S RAINING TOTTY!
STOP GASSING, SWEETLEAF, AND HELP THE POOR GIRL UP!
THOSE ARE DELIGHTFUL CLOTHES, MY DEAR. WHEREVER DID YOU --
THAT THING...

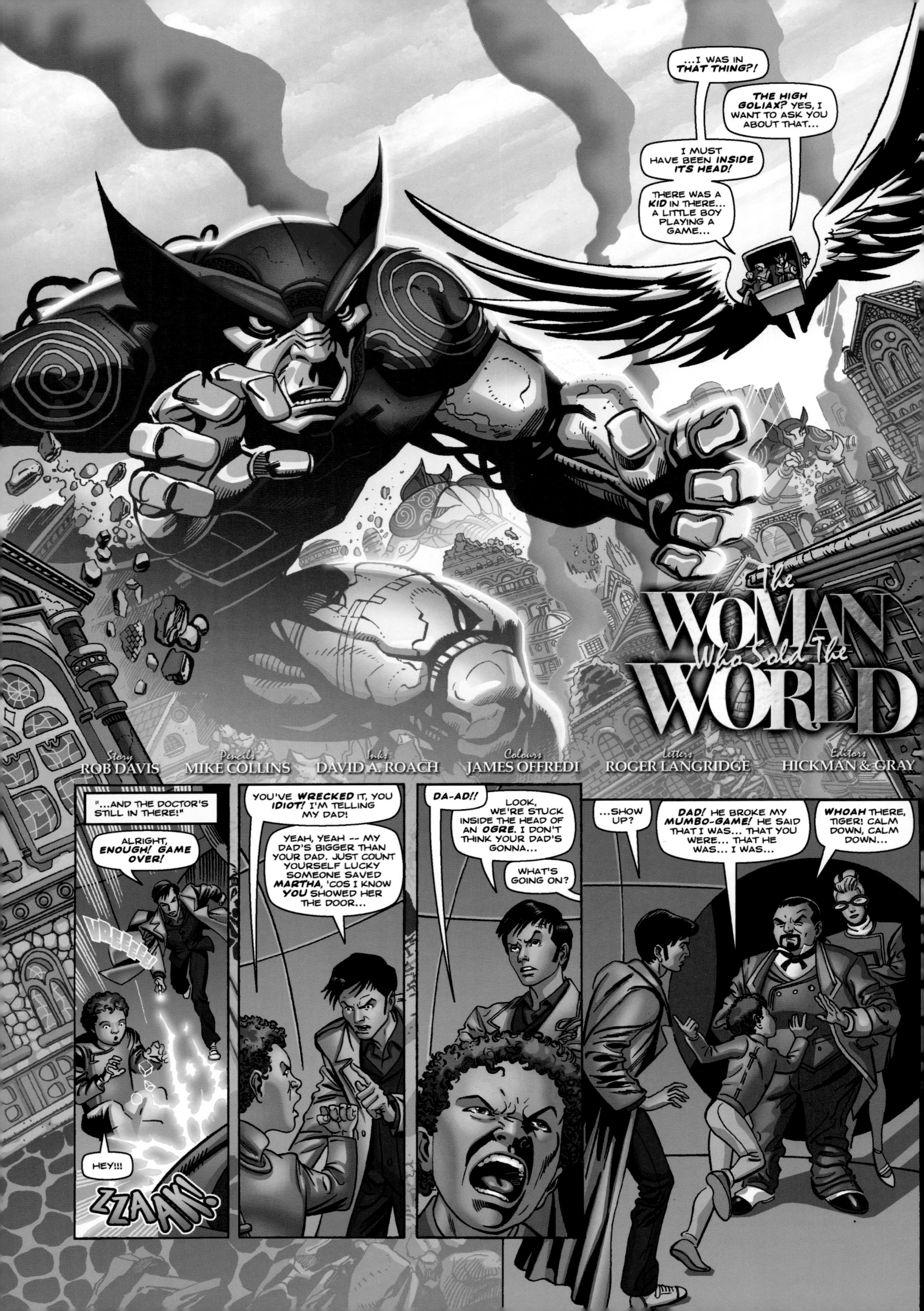

...I WAS IN THAT THING?!
I MUST HAVE BEEN INSIDE ITS HEAD!
THERE WAS A KID IN THERE... A LITTLE BOY PLAYING A GAME...
THE HIGH GOLIAX? YES, I WANT TO ASK YOU ABOUT THAT...
The WOMAN Who Sold The WORLD
Story ROB DAVIS
Pencils MIKE COLLINS
Inks DAVID A. ROACH
Colours JAMES OFFREDI
Letters ROGER LANGRIDGE
Editors HICKMAN & GRAY
"...AND THE DOCTOR'S STILL IN THERE!"
ALRIGHT, ENOUGH! GAME OVER!
VREEEEE!
HEY!!!
ZZAAK!
YOU'VE WRECKED IT, YOU IDIOT! I'M TELLING MY DAD!
YEAH, YEAH -- MY DAD'S BIGGER THAN YOUR DAD. JUST COUNT YOURSELF LUCKY SOMEONE SAVED MARTHA, 'COS I KNOW YOU SHOWED HER THE DOOR...
DA-AD!!
LOOK, WE'RE STUCK INSIDE THE HEAD OF AN OGRE. I DON'T THINK YOUR DAD'S GONNA...
WHAT'S GOING ON?
...SHOW UP?
DAD! HE BROKE MY MUMBO-GAME! HE SAID THAT I WAS... THAT YOU WERE... THAT HE WAS... I WAS...
WHOAH THERE, TIGER! CALM DOWN, CALM DOWN...

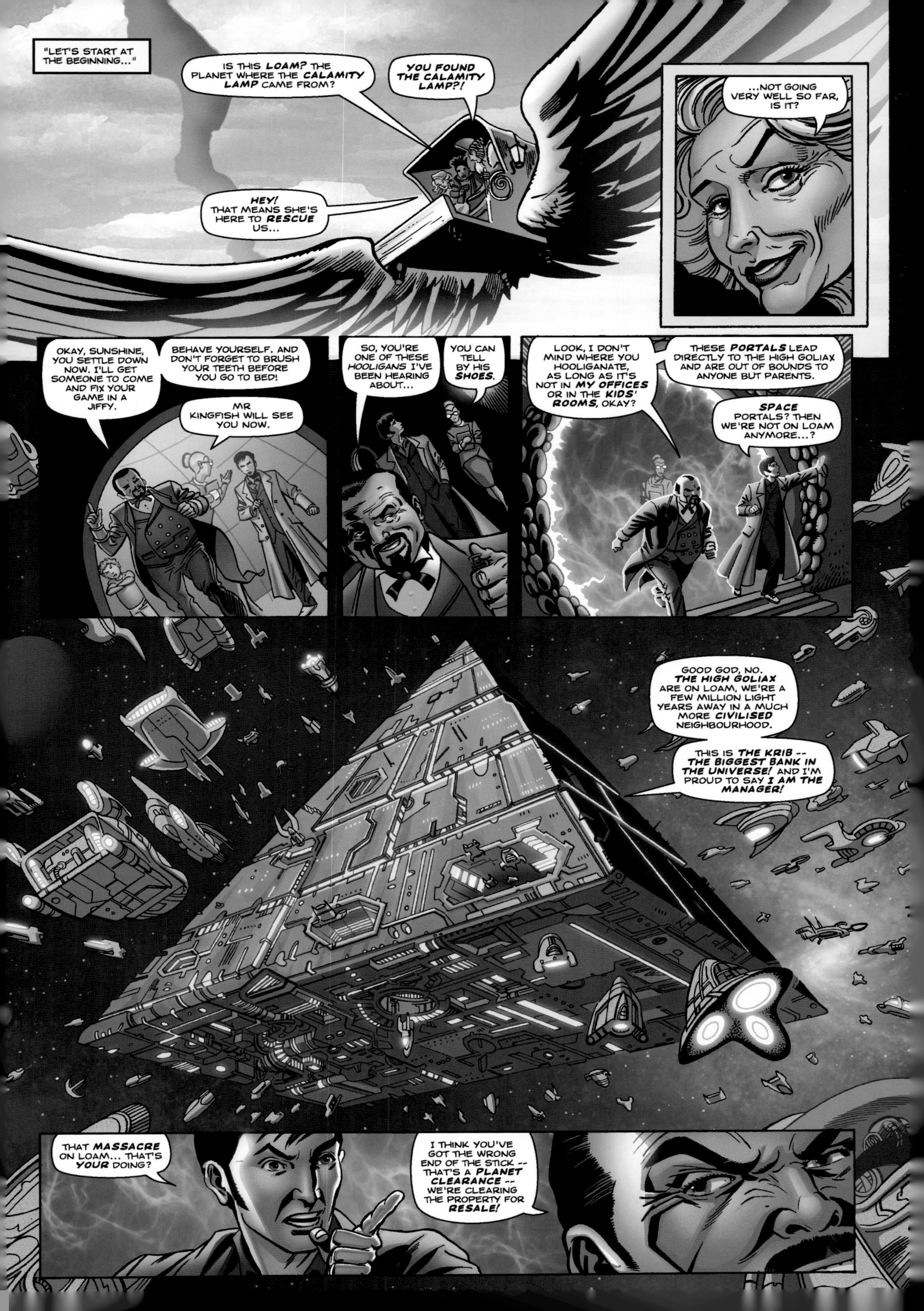

"LET'S START AT THE BEGINNING..."
IS THIS LOAM? THE PLANET WHERE THE CALAMITY LAMP CAME FROM?
YOU FOUND THE CALAMITY LAMP?!
HEY! THAT MEANS SHE'S HERE TO RESCUE US...
...NOT GOING VERY WELL SO FAR, IS IT?
OKAY, SUNSHINE, YOU SETTLE DOWN NOW. I'LL GET SOMEONE TO COME AND FIX YOUR GAME IN A JIFFY.
BEHAVE YOURSELF. AND DON'T FORGET TO BRUSH YOUR TEETH BEFORE YOU GO TO BED!
MR KINGFISH WILL SEE YOU NOW.
SO, YOU'RE ONE OF THESE HOOLIGANS I'VE BEEN HEARING ABOUT...
YOU CAN TELL BY HIS SHOES.
LOOK, I DON'T MIND WHERE YOU HOOLIGANATE, AS LONG AS IT'S NOT IN MY OFFICES OR IN THE KIDS' ROOMS, OKAY?
THESE PORTALS LEAD DIRECTLY TO THE HIGH GOLIAX AND ARE OUT OF BOUNDS TO ANYONE BUT PARENTS.
SPACE PORTALS? THEN WE'RE NOT ON LOAM ANYMORE...?
GOOD GOD, NO. THE HIGH GOLIAX ARE ON LOAM, WE'RE A FEW MILLION LIGHT YEARS AWAY IN A MUCH MORE CIVILISED NEIGHBOURHOOD.
THIS IS THE KRIB -- THE BIGGEST BANK IN THE UNIVERSE! AND I'M PROUD TO SAY I AM THE MANAGER!
THAT MASSACRE ON LOAM... THAT'S YOUR DOING?
I THINK YOU'VE GOT THE WRONG END OF THE STICK -- THAT'S A PLANET CLEARANCE -- WE'RE CLEARING THE PROPERTY FOR RESALE!

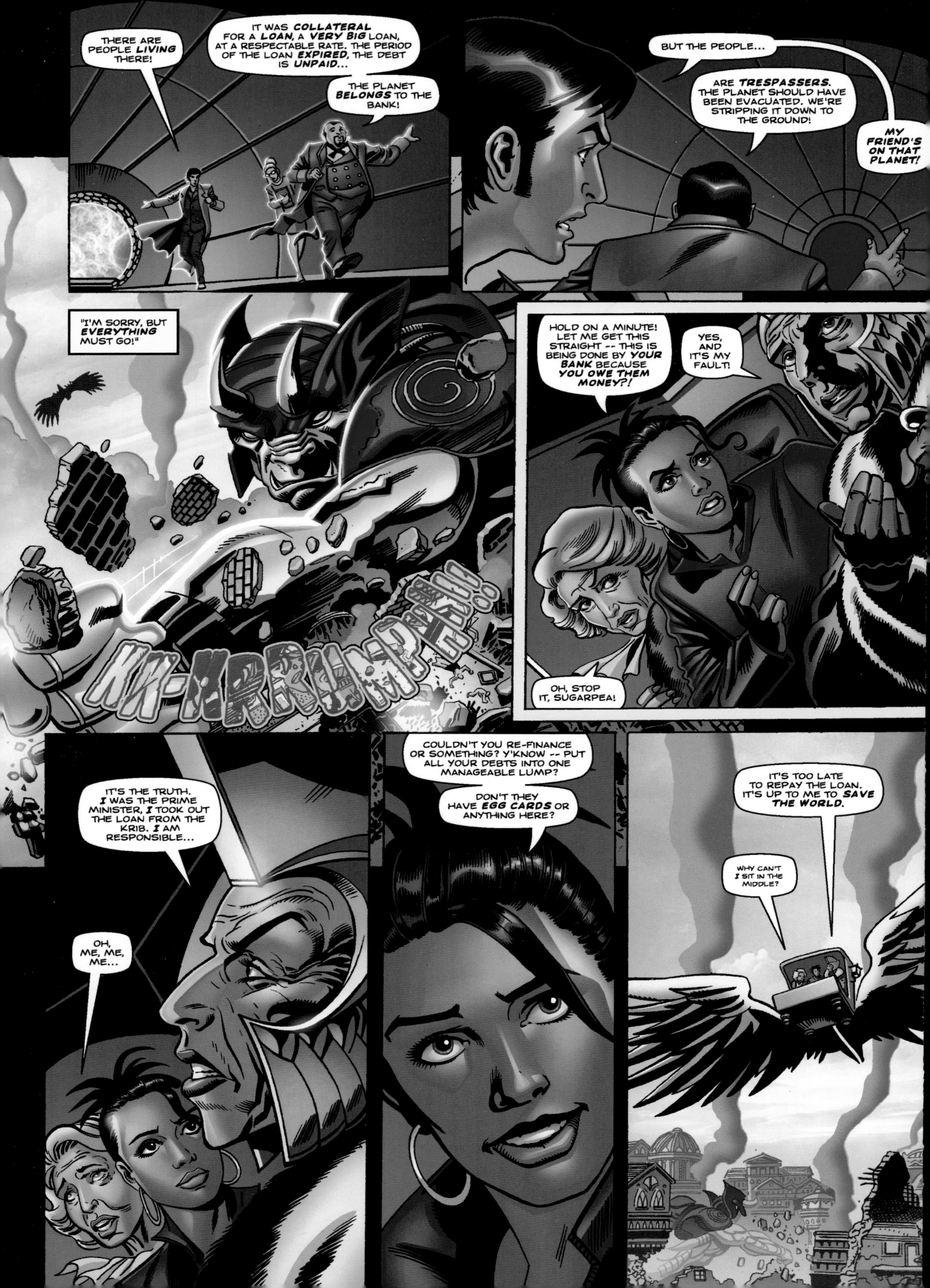
THERE ARE PEOPLE LIVING THERE!
IT WAS COLLATERAL FOR A LOAN, A VERY BIG LOAN, AT A RESPECTABLE RATE. THE PERIOD OF THE LOAN EXPIRED, THE DEBT IS UNPAID...
THE PLANET BELONGS TO THE BANK!
BUT THE PEOPLE...
ARE TRESPASSERS. THE PLANET SHOULD HAVE BEEN EVACUATED. WE'RE STRIPPING IT DOWN TO THE GROUND!
MY FRIEND'S ON THAT PLANET!
"I'M SORRY, BUT EVERYTHING MUST GO!"
KA-KRRUMP!
HOLD ON A MINUTE! LET ME GET THIS STRAIGHT -- THIS IS BEING DONE BY YOUR BANK BECAUSE YOU OWE THEM MONEY?!
YES, AND IT'S MY FAULT!
OH, STOP IT, SUGARPEA!
IT'S THE TRUTH. I WAS THE PRIME MINISTER, I TOOK OUT THE LOAN FROM THE KRIB. I AM RESPONSIBLE...
OH, ME, ME, ME...
COULDN'T YOU RE-FINANCE OR SOMETHING? Y'KNOW -- PUT ALL YOUR DEBTS INTO ONE MANAGEABLE LUMP?
DON'T THEY HAVE EGG CARDS OR ANYTHING HERE?
IT'S TOO LATE TO REPAY THE LOAN. IT'S UP TO ME TO SAVE THE WORLD.
WHY CAN'T I SIT IN THE MIDDLE?

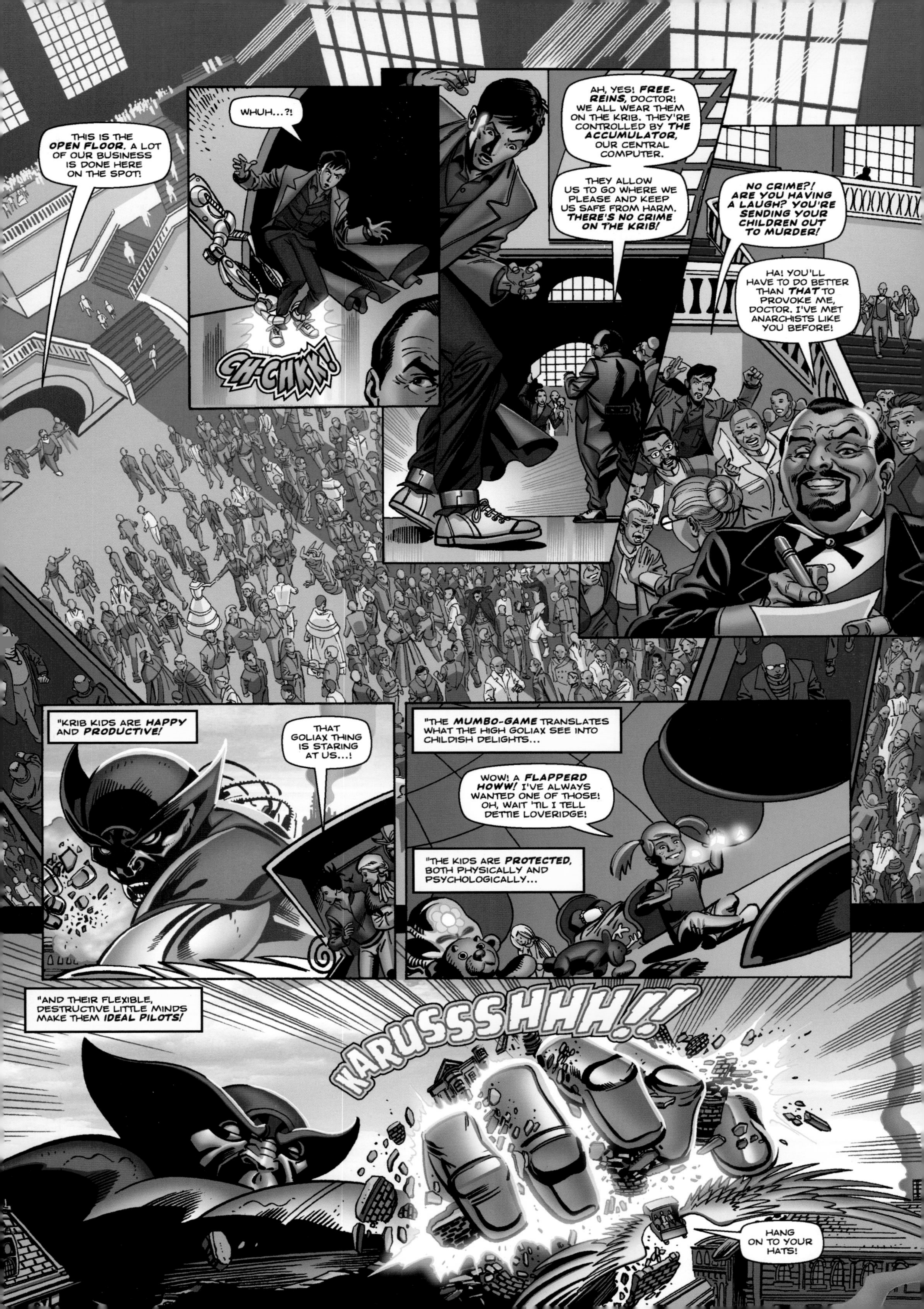
THIS IS THE OPEN FLOOR. A LOT OF OUR BUSINESS IS DONE HERE ON THE SPOT!
WHUH...?!
CH-CHKK!
AH, YES! FREE-REINS, DOCTOR! WE ALL WEAR THEM ON THE KRIB. THEY'RE CONTROLLED BY THE ACCUMULATOR, OUR CENTRAL COMPUTER.
THEY ALLOW US TO GO WHERE WE PLEASE AND KEEP US SAFE FROM HARM. THERE'S NO CRIME ON THE KRIB!
NO CRIME?! ARE YOU HAVING A LAUGH? YOU'RE SENDING YOUR CHILDREN OUT TO MURDER!
HA! YOU'LL HAVE TO DO BETTER THAN THAT TO PROVOKE ME, DOCTOR. I'VE MET ANARCHISTS LIKE YOU BEFORE!
"KRIB KIDS ARE HAPPY AND PRODUCTIVE!
THAT GOLIAX THING IS STARING AT US...!
"THE MUMBO-GAME TRANSLATES WHAT THE HIGH GOLIAX SEE INTO CHILDISH DELIGHTS...
WOW! A FLAPPERD HOWW! I'VE ALWAYS WANTED ONE OF THOSE! OH, WAIT 'TIL I TELL DETTIE LOVERIDGE!
"THE KIDS ARE PROTECTED, BOTH PHYSICALLY AND PSYCHOLOGICALLY...
"AND THEIR FLEXIBLE, DESTRUCTIVE LITTLE MINDS MAKE THEM IDEAL PILOTS!
KARUSSSHHH!!
HANG ON TO YOUR HATS!

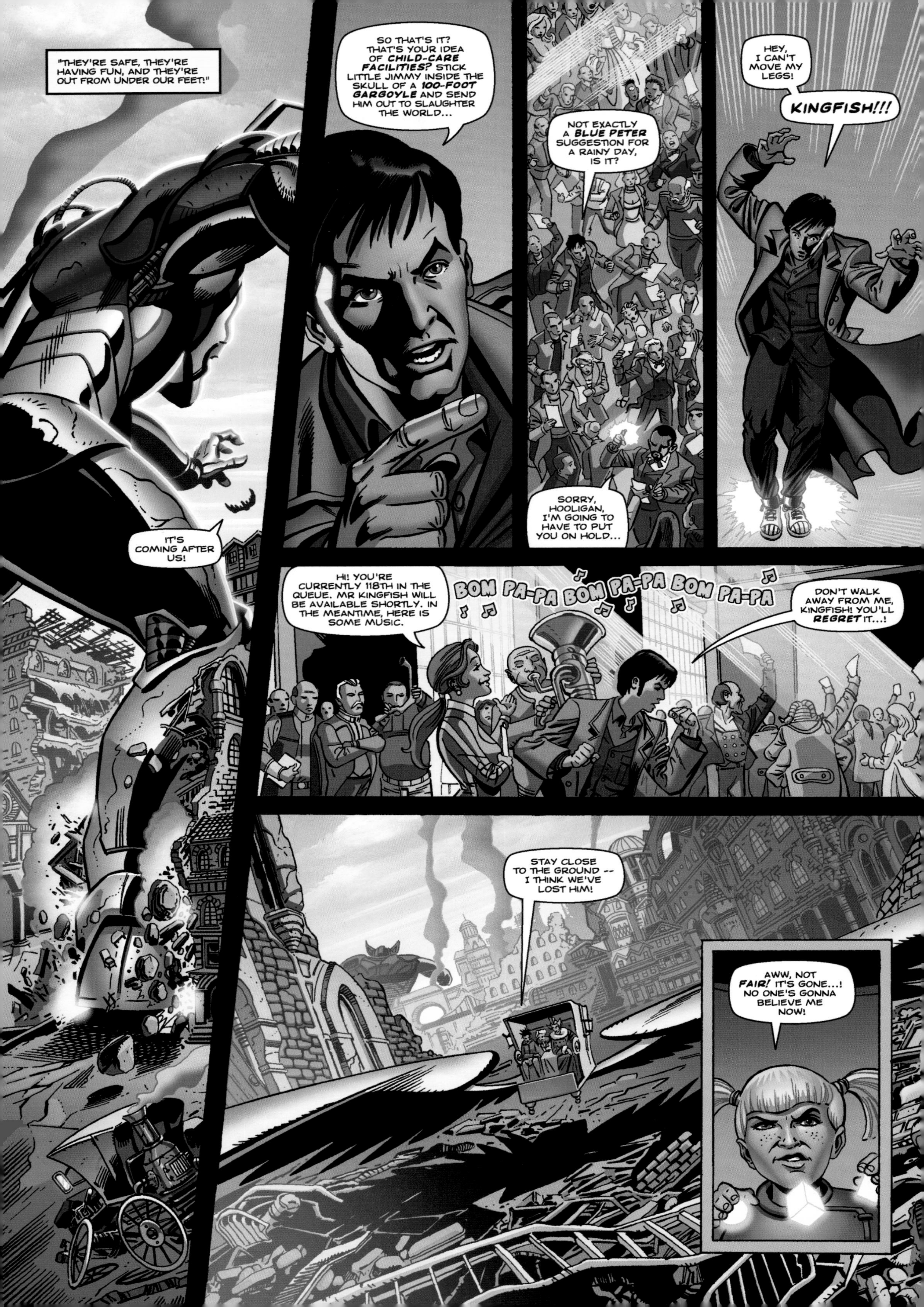
"THEY'RE SAFE, THEY'RE HAVING FUN, AND THEY'RE OUT FROM UNDER OUR FEET!"
SO THAT'S IT? THAT'S YOUR IDEA OF CHILD-CARE FACILITIES? STICK LITTLE JIMMY INSIDE THE SKULL OF A 100-FOOT GARGOYLE AND SEND HIM OUT TO SLAUGHTER THE WORLD...
NOT EXACTLY A BLUE PETER SUGGESTION FOR A RAINY DAY, IS IT?
SORRY, HOOLIGAN, I'M HAVING TO PUT YOU ON HOLD...
HEY, I CAN'T MOVE MY LEGS!
KINGFISH!!!
IT'S COMING AFTER US!
HI! YOU'RE CURRENTLY 118TH IN THE QUEUE. MR KINGFISH WILL BE AVAILABLE SHORTLY. IN THE MEANTIME, HERE IS SOME MUSIC.
BOM PA-PA BOM PA-PA BOM PA-PA
DON'T WALK AWAY FROM ME, KINGFISH! YOU'LL REGRET IT...!
STAY CLOSE TO THE GROUND -- I THINK WE'VE LOST HIM!
AWW, NOT FAIR! IT'S GONE...! NO ONE'S GONNA BELIEVE ME NOW!

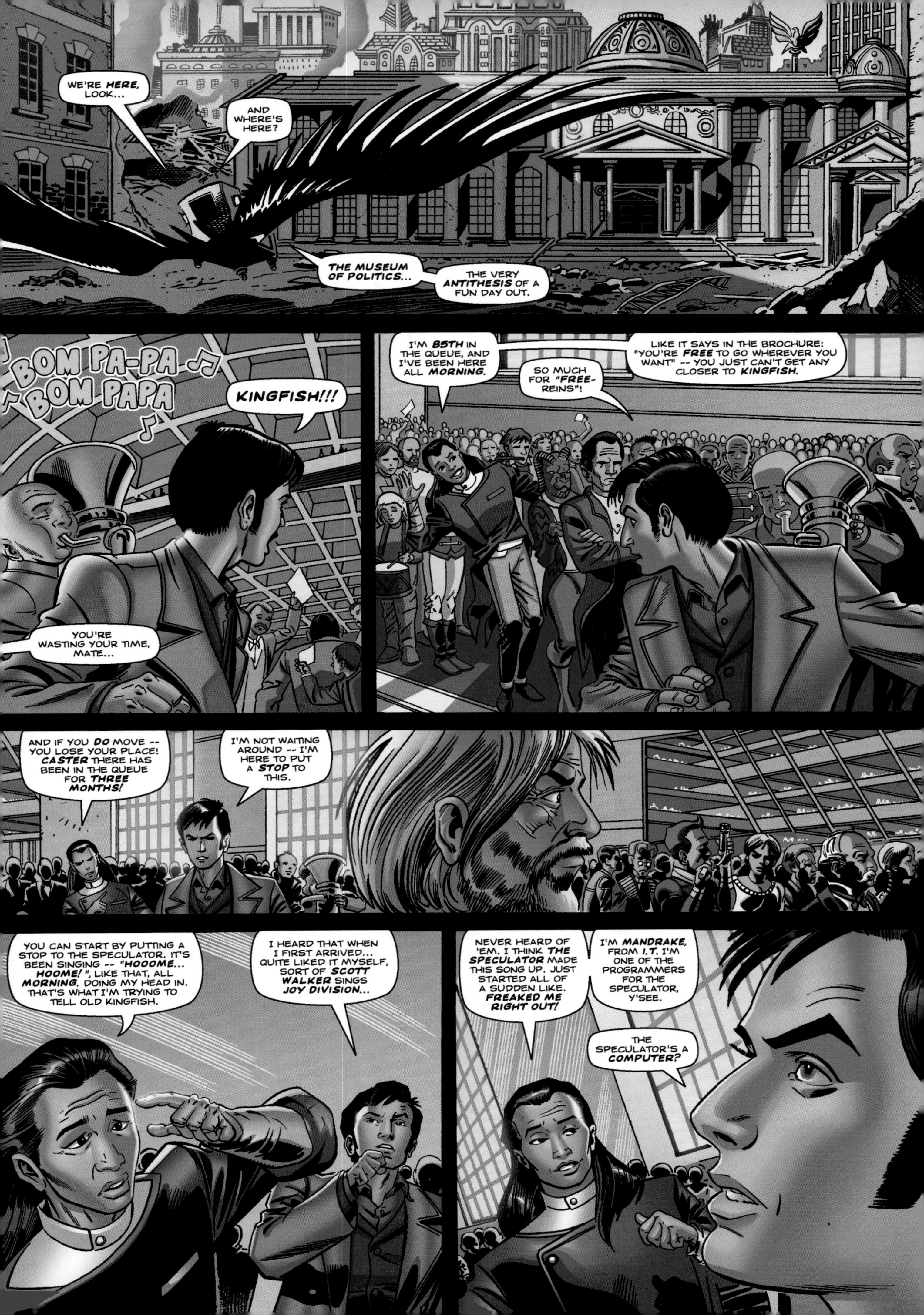
WE'RE HERE, LOOK...
AND WHERE'S HERE?
THE MUSEUM OF POLITICS...
THE VERY ANTITHESIS OF A FUN DAY OUT.
BOM PA-PA BOM PAPA
KINGFISH!!!
YOU'RE WASTING YOUR TIME, MATE...
I'M 85TH IN THE QUEUE, AND I'VE BEEN HERE ALL MORNING.
LIKE IT SAYS IN THE BROCHURE: "YOU'RE FREE TO GO WHEREVER YOU WANT" -- YOU JUST CAN'T GET ANY CLOSER TO KINGFISH.
SO MUCH FOR "FREE-REINS"!
AND IF YOU DO MOVE -- YOU LOSE YOUR PLACE! CASTER THERE HAS BEEN IN THE QUEUE FOR THREE MONTHS!
I'M NOT WAITING AROUND -- I'M HERE TO PUT A STOP TO THIS.
YOU CAN START BY PUTTING A STOP TO THE SPECULATOR. IT'S BEEN SINGING -- "HOOOME... HOOME!", LIKE THAT, ALL MORNING. DOING MY HEAD IN. THAT'S WHAT I'M TRYING TO TELL OLD KINGFISH.
I HEARD THAT WHEN I FIRST ARRIVED... QUITE LIKED IT MYSELF, SORT OF SCOTT WALKER SINGS JOY DIVISION...
NEVER HEARD OF 'EM. I THINK THE SPECULATOR MADE THIS SONG UP. JUST STARTED ALL OF A SUDDEN LIKE. FREAKED ME RIGHT OUT!
I'M MANDRAKE, FROM I.T. I'M ONE OF THE PROGRAMMERS FOR THE SPECULATOR, Y'SEE.
THE SPECULATOR'S A COMPUTER?

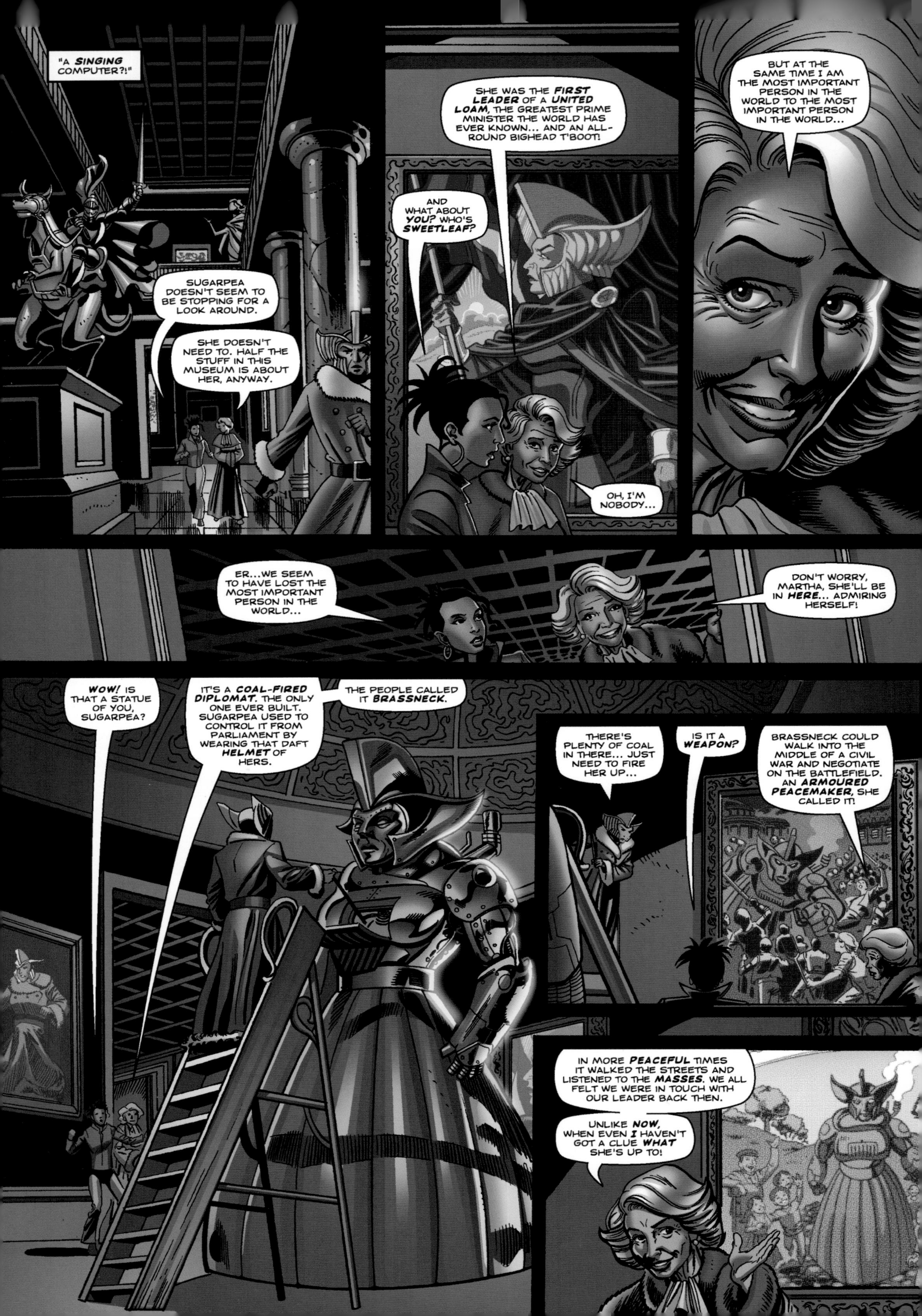
"A SINGING COMPUTER?!"
SUGARPEA DOESN'T SEEM TO BE STOPPING FOR A LOOK AROUND.
SHE DOESN'T NEED TO. HALF THE STUFF IN THIS MUSEUM IS ABOUT HER, ANYWAY.
SHE WAS THE FIRST LEADER OF A UNITED LOAM, THE GREATEST PRIME MINISTER THE WORLD HAS EVER KNOWN... AND AN ALL-ROUND BIGHEAD T'BOOT!
AND WHAT ABOUT YOU? WHO'S SWEETLEAF?
OH, I'M NOBODY...
BUT AT THE SAME TIME I AM THE MOST IMPORTANT PERSON IN THE WORLD TO THE MOST IMPORTANT PERSON IN THE WORLD...
ER...WE SEEM TO HAVE LOST THE MOST IMPORTANT PERSON IN THE WORLD...
DON'T WORRY, MARTHA, SHE'LL BE IN HERE... ADMIRING HERSELF!
WOW! IS THAT A STATUE OF YOU, SUGARPEA?
IT'S A COAL-FIRED DIPLOMAT. THE ONLY ONE EVER BUILT. SUGARPEA USED TO CONTROL IT FROM PARLIAMENT BY WEARING THAT DAFT HELMET OF HERS.
THE PEOPLE CALLED IT BRASSNECK.
THERE'S PLENTY OF COAL IN THERE... JUST NEED TO FIRE HER UP...
IS IT A WEAPON?
BRASSNECK COULD WALK INTO THE MIDDLE OF A CIVIL WAR AND NEGOTIATE ON THE BATTLEFIELD. AN ARMOURED PEACEMAKER, SHE CALLED IT!
IN MORE PEACEFUL TIMES IT WALKED THE STREETS AND LISTENED TO THE MASSES. WE ALL FELT WE WERE IN TOUCH WITH OUR LEADER BACK THEN.
UNLIKE NOW, WHEN EVEN I HAVEN'T GOT A CLUE WHAT SHE'S UP TO!

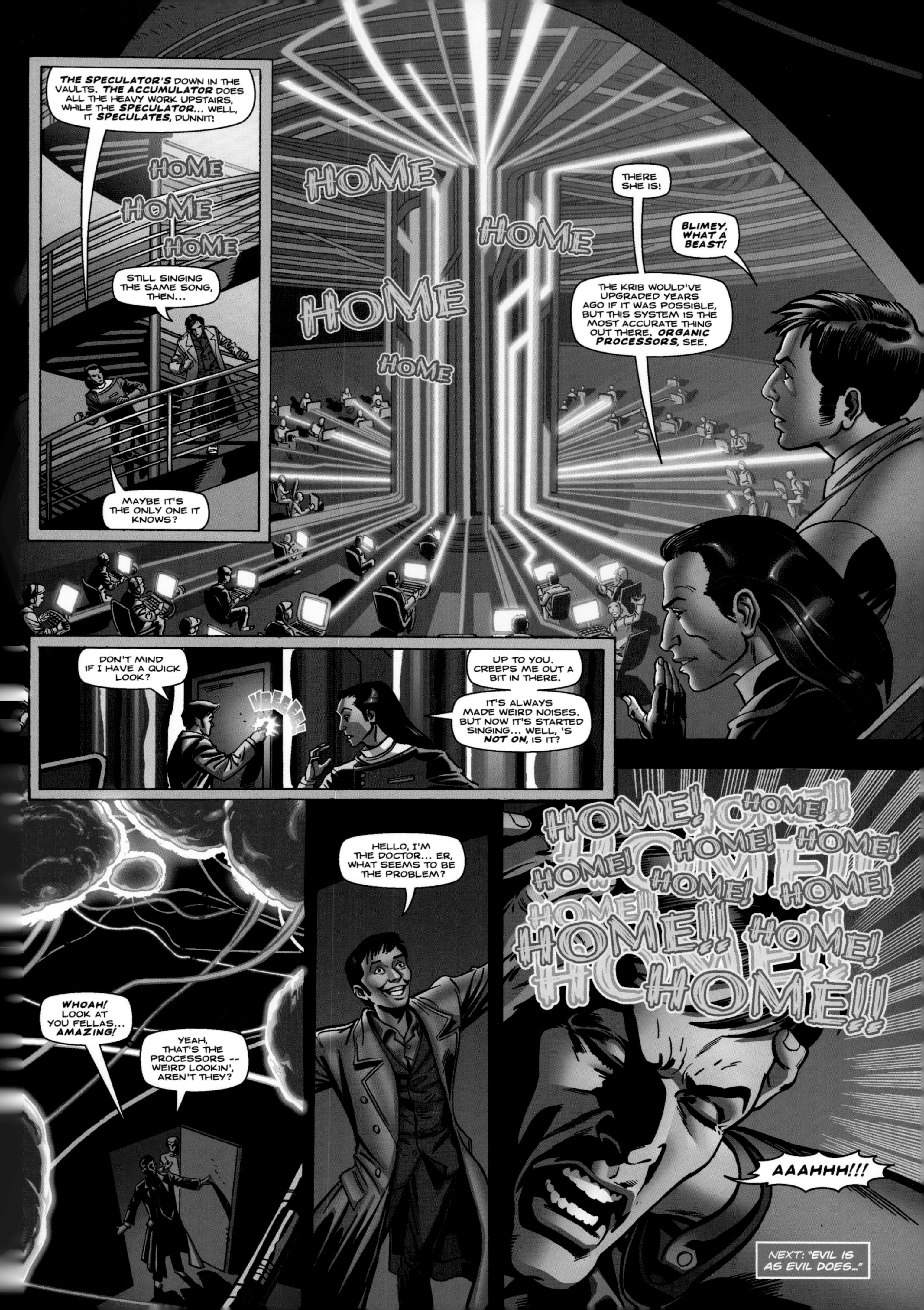
THE SPECULATOR'S DOWN IN THE VAULTS. THE ACCUMULATOR DOES ALL THE HEAVY WORK UPSTAIRS, WHILE THE SPECULATOR... WELL, IT SPECULATES, DUNNIT!
HOME
HOME
HOME
STILL SINGING THE SAME SONG, THEN...
MAYBE IT'S THE ONLY ONE IT KNOWS?
HOME
HOME
HOME
HOME
THERE SHE IS!
BLIMEY, WHAT A BEAST!
THE KRIB WOULD'VE UPGRADED YEARS AGO IF IT WAS POSSIBLE, BUT THIS SYSTEM IS THE MOST ACCURATE THING OUT THERE. ORGANIC PROCESSORS, SEE.
DON'T MIND IF I HAVE A QUICK LOOK?
VREEE
UP TO YOU. CREEPS ME OUT A BIT IN THERE.
IT'S ALWAYS MADE WEIRD NOISES. BUT NOW IT'S STARTED SINGING... WELL, 'S NOT ON, IS IT?
WHOAH! LOOK AT YOU FELLAS... AMAZING!
YEAH, THAT'S THE PROCESSORS -- WEIRD LOOKIN', AREN'T THEY?
HELLO, I'M THE DOCTOR... ER, WHAT SEEMS TO BE THE PROBLEM?
HOME! HOME!! HOME! HOME! HOME! HOME! HOME! HOME!! HOME! HOME!!
AAAHHH!!!
NEXT: "EVIL IS AS EVIL DOES..."

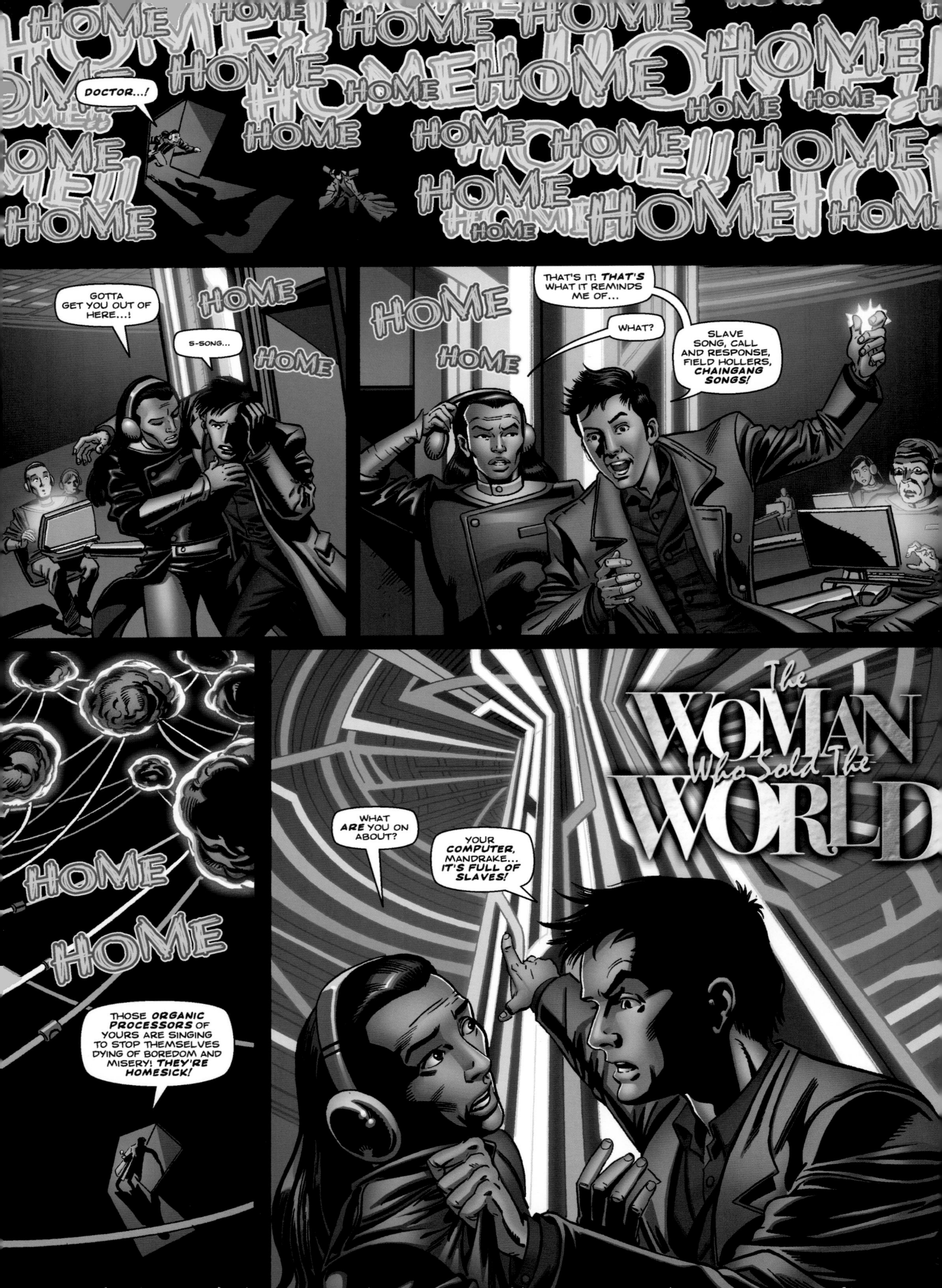
HOME
HOME!!
DOCTOR...!
HOME
HOME
HOME
GOTTA GET YOU OUT OF HERE...!
S-SONG...
HOME
HOME
THAT'S IT! THAT'S WHAT IT REMINDS ME OF...
WHAT?
SLAVE SONG, CALL AND RESPONSE, FIELD HOLLERS, CHAINGANG SONGS!
HOME
HOME
THOSE ORGANIC PROCESSORS OF YOURS ARE SINGING TO STOP THEMSELVES DYING OF BOREDOM AND MISERY! THEY'RE HOMESICK!
The WOMAN Who Sold The WORLD
WHAT ARE YOU ON ABOUT?
YOUR COMPUTER, MANDRAKE... IT'S FULL OF SLAVES!

Story ROB DAVIS Pencils MIKE COLLINS Inks DAVID A. ROACH Colours JAMES OFFREDI Letters ROGER LANGRIDGE Editors HICKMAN & GRAY

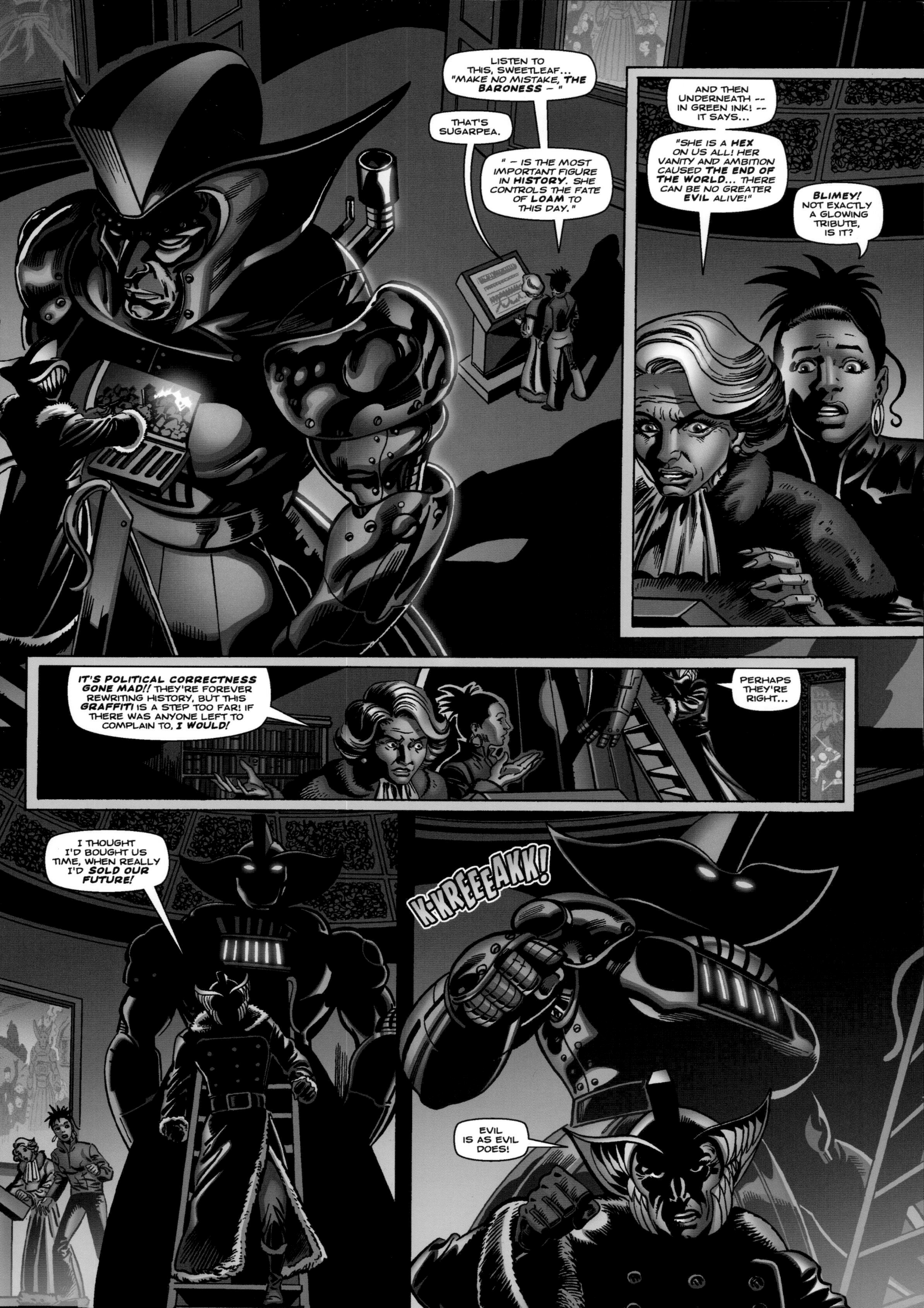
LISTEN TO THIS, SWEETLEAF... "MAKE NO MISTAKE, THE BARONESS – "
THAT'S SUGARPEA.
" – IS THE MOST IMPORTANT FIGURE IN HISTORY. SHE CONTROLS THE FATE OF LOAM TO THIS DAY."
AND THEN UNDERNEATH -- IN GREEN INK! -- IT SAYS...
"SHE IS A HEX ON US ALL! HER VANITY AND AMBITION CAUSED THE END OF THE WORLD... THERE CAN BE NO GREATER EVIL ALIVE!"
BLIMEY! NOT EXACTLY A GLOWING TRIBUTE, IS IT?
IT'S POLITICAL CORRECTNESS GONE MAD!! THEY'RE FOREVER REWRITING HISTORY, BUT THIS GRAFFITI IS A STEP TOO FAR! IF THERE WAS ANYONE LEFT TO COMPLAIN TO, I WOULD!
PERHAPS THEY'RE RIGHT...
I THOUGHT I'D BOUGHT US TIME, WHEN REALLY I'D SOLD OUR FUTURE!
K-KREEEAKK!
EVIL IS AS EVIL DOES!

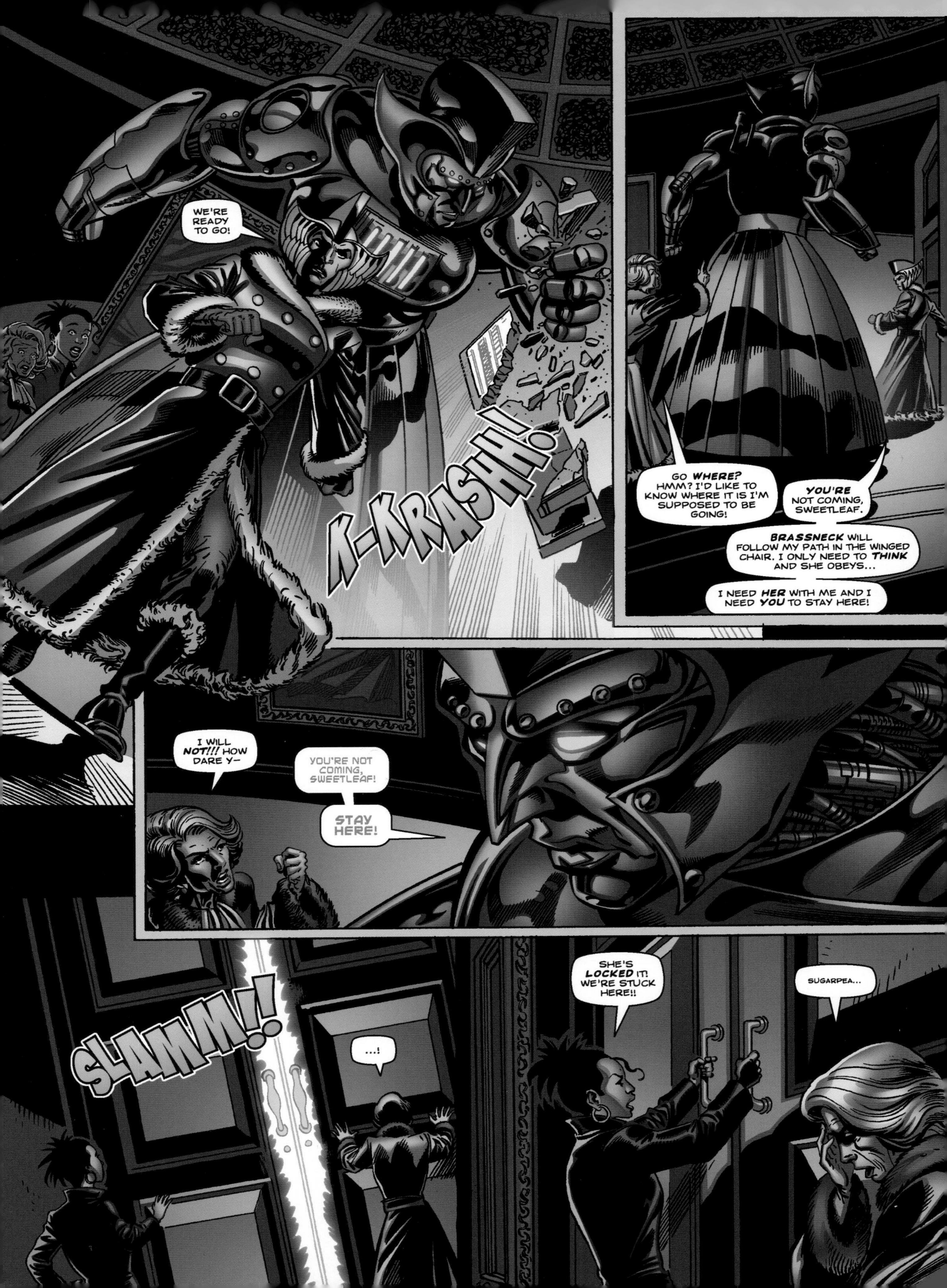
WE'RE READY TO GO!
K-KRASHH!!
GO WHERE? HMM? I'D LIKE TO KNOW WHERE IT IS I'M SUPPOSED TO BE GOING!
YOU'RE NOT COMING, SWEETLEAF.
BRASSNECK WILL FOLLOW MY PATH IN THE WINGED CHAIR. I ONLY NEED TO THINK AND SHE OBEYS...
I NEED HER WITH ME AND I NEED YOU TO STAY HERE!
I WILL NOT!!! HOW DARE Y–
YOU'RE NOT COMING, SWEETLEAF!
STAY HERE!
SLAMM!!
...!
SHE'S LOCKED IT! WE'RE STUCK HERE!!
SUGARPEA...

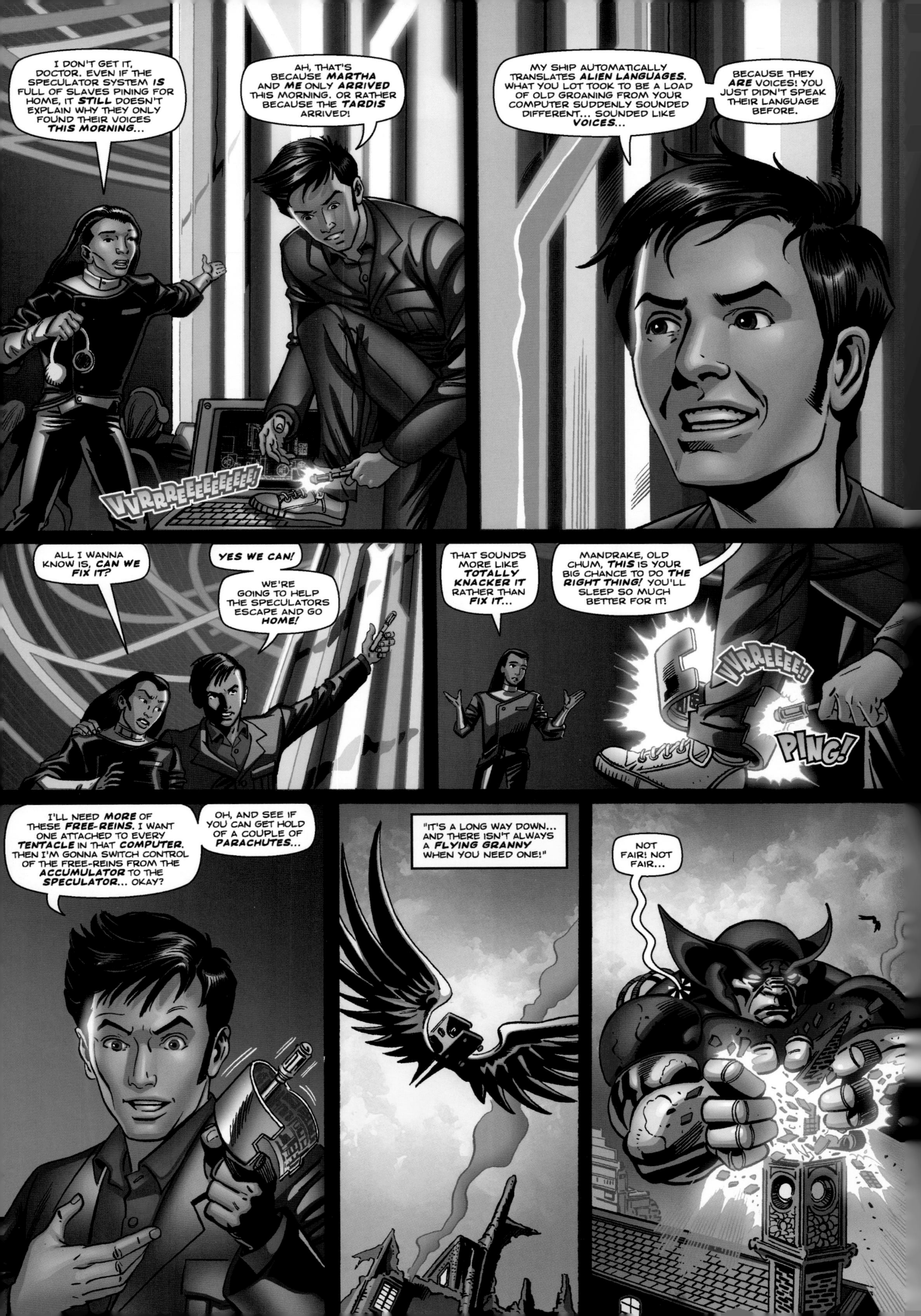
I DON'T GET IT, DOCTOR. EVEN IF THE SPECULATOR SYSTEM IS FULL OF SLAVES PINING FOR HOME, IT STILL DOESN'T EXPLAIN WHY THEY ONLY FOUND THEIR VOICES THIS MORNING...
AH, THAT'S BECAUSE MARTHA AND ME ONLY ARRIVED THIS MORNING. OR RATHER BECAUSE THE TARDIS ARRIVED!
VVRRREEEEEEEEEE!
MY SHIP AUTOMATICALLY TRANSLATES ALIEN LANGUAGES. WHAT YOU LOT TOOK TO BE A LOAD OF OLD GROANING FROM YOUR COMPUTER SUDDENLY SOUNDED DIFFERENT... SOUNDED LIKE VOICES...
BECAUSE THEY ARE VOICES! YOU JUST DIDN'T SPEAK THEIR LANGUAGE BEFORE.
ALL I WANNA KNOW IS, CAN WE FIX IT?
YES WE CAN!
WE'RE GOING TO HELP THE SPECULATORS ESCAPE AND GO HOME!
THAT SOUNDS MORE LIKE TOTALLY KNACKER IT RATHER THAN FIX IT...
MANDRAKE, OLD CHUM, THIS IS YOUR BIG CHANCE TO DO THE RIGHT THING! YOU'LL SLEEP SO MUCH BETTER FOR IT!
VVRREEEE!!
PING!
I'LL NEED MORE OF THESE FREE-REINS. I WANT ONE ATTACHED TO EVERY TENTACLE IN THAT COMPUTER. THEN I'M GONNA SWITCH CONTROL OF THE FREE-REINS FROM THE ACCUMULATOR TO THE SPECULATOR... OKAY?
OH, AND SEE IF YOU CAN GET HOLD OF A COUPLE OF PARACHUTES...
"IT'S A LONG WAY DOWN... AND THERE ISN'T ALWAYS A FLYING GRANNY WHEN YOU NEED ONE!"
NOT FAIR! NOT FAIR...

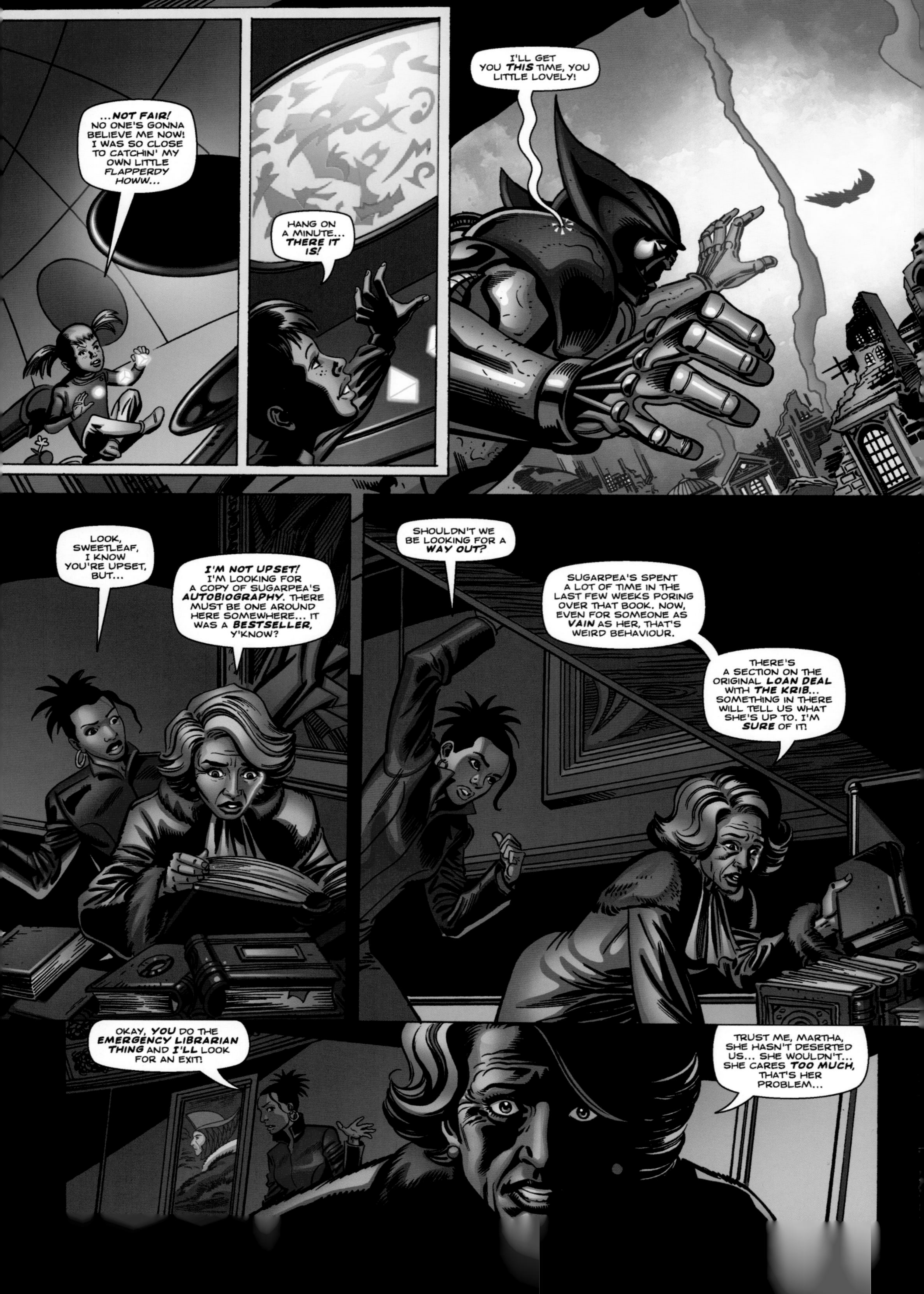
...NOT FAIR! NO ONE'S GONNA BELIEVE ME NOW! I WAS SO CLOSE TO CATCHIN' MY OWN LITTLE FLAPPERDY HOWW...
HANG ON A MINUTE... THERE IT IS!
I'LL GET YOU THIS TIME, YOU LITTLE LOVELY!
LOOK, SWEETLEAF, I KNOW YOU'RE UPSET, BUT...
I'M NOT UPSET! I'M LOOKING FOR A COPY OF SUGARPEA'S AUTOBIOGRAPHY. THERE MUST BE ONE AROUND HERE SOMEWHERE... IT WAS A BESTSELLER, Y'KNOW?
SHOULDN'T WE BE LOOKING FOR A WAY OUT?
SUGARPEA'S SPENT A LOT OF TIME IN THE LAST FEW WEEKS PORING OVER THAT BOOK. NOW, EVEN FOR SOMEONE AS VAIN AS HER, THAT'S WEIRD BEHAVIOUR.
THERE'S A SECTION ON THE ORIGINAL LOAN DEAL WITH THE KRIB... SOMETHING IN THERE WILL TELL US WHAT SHE'S UP TO. I'M SURE OF IT!
OKAY, YOU DO THE EMERGENCY LIBRARIAN THING AND I'LL LOOK FOR AN EXIT!
TRUST ME, MARTHA, SHE HASN'T DESERTED US... SHE WOULDN'T... SHE CARES TOO MUCH, THAT'S HER PROBLEM...

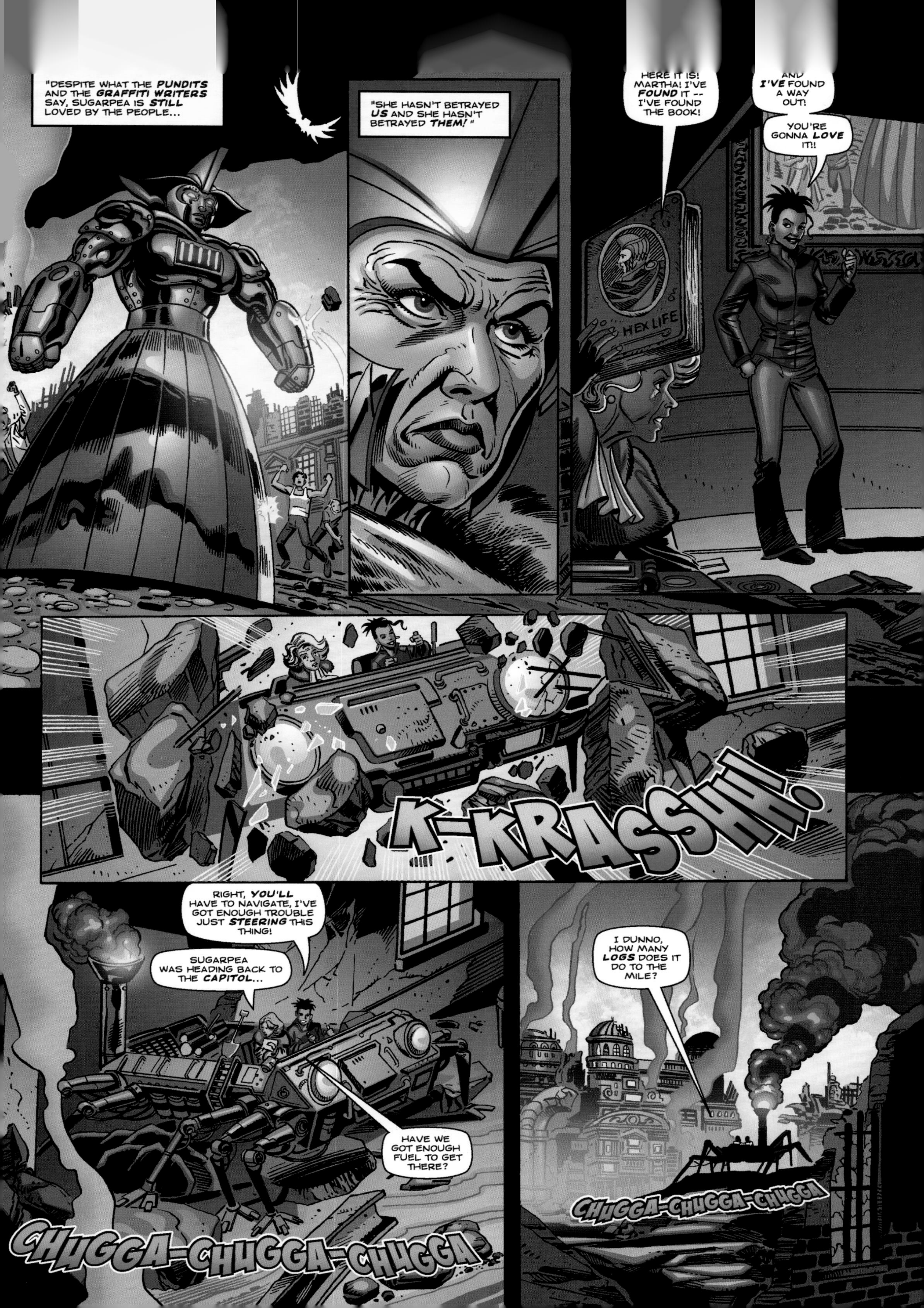
"DESPITE WHAT THE PUNDITS AND THE GRAFFITI WRITERS SAY, SUGARPEA IS STILL LOVED BY THE PEOPLE...
"SHE HASN'T BETRAYED US AND SHE HASN'T BETRAYED THEM!"
HERE IT IS! MARTHA! I'VE FOUND IT -- I'VE FOUND THE BOOK!
AND I'VE FOUND A WAY OUT!
YOU'RE GONNA LOVE IT!!
HEX LIFE
K-KRASSHH!
RIGHT, YOU'LL HAVE TO NAVIGATE, I'VE GOT ENOUGH TROUBLE JUST STEERING THIS THING!
SUGARPEA WAS HEADING BACK TO THE CAPITOL...
HAVE WE GOT ENOUGH FUEL TO GET THERE?
CHUGGA-CHUGGA-CHUGGA
I DUNNO, HOW MANY LOGS DOES IT DO TO THE MILE?
CHUGGA-CHUGGA-CHUGGA

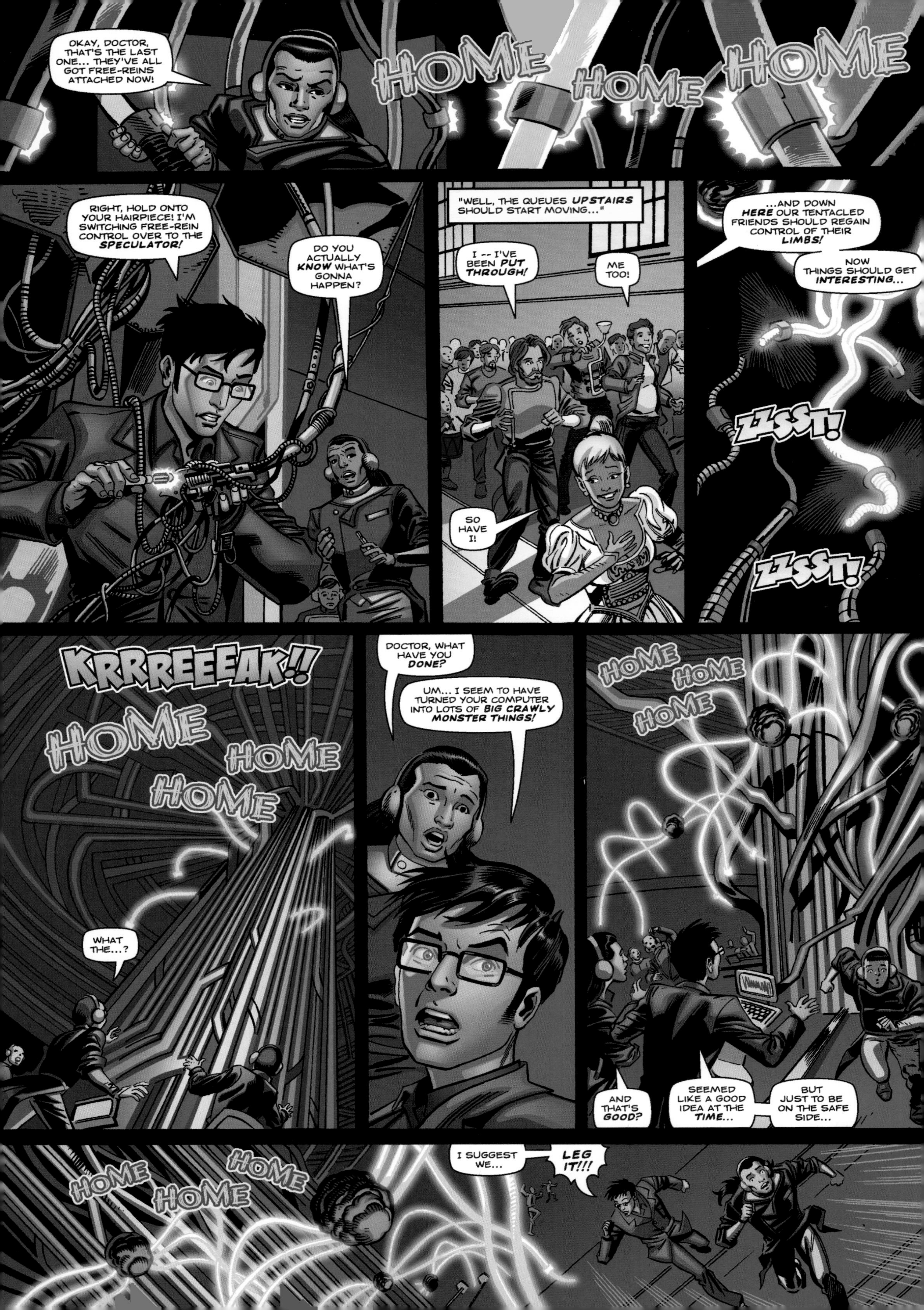
OKAY, DOCTOR, THAT'S THE LAST ONE... THEY'VE ALL GOT FREE-REINS ATTACHED NOW!
HOME HOME HOME
RIGHT, HOLD ONTO YOUR HAIRPIECE! I'M SWITCHING FREE-REIN CONTROL OVER TO THE SPECULATOR!
DO YOU ACTUALLY KNOW WHAT'S GONNA HAPPEN?
"WELL, THE QUEUES UPSTAIRS SHOULD START MOVING..."
I -- I'VE BEEN PUT THROUGH!
ME TOO!
SO HAVE I!
...AND DOWN HERE OUR TENTACLED FRIENDS SHOULD REGAIN CONTROL OF THEIR LIMBS!
NOW THINGS SHOULD GET INTERESTING...
ZZSST!
ZZSST!
KRRREEEAK!!
HOME HOME HOME
WHAT THE...?
DOCTOR, WHAT HAVE YOU DONE?
UM... I SEEM TO HAVE TURNED YOUR COMPUTER INTO LOTS OF BIG CRAWLY MONSTER THINGS!
HOME HOME HOME
AND THAT'S GOOD?
SEEMED LIKE A GOOD IDEA AT THE TIME...
BUT JUST TO BE ON THE SAFE SIDE...
HOME HOME HOME
I SUGGEST WE...
LEG IT!!!

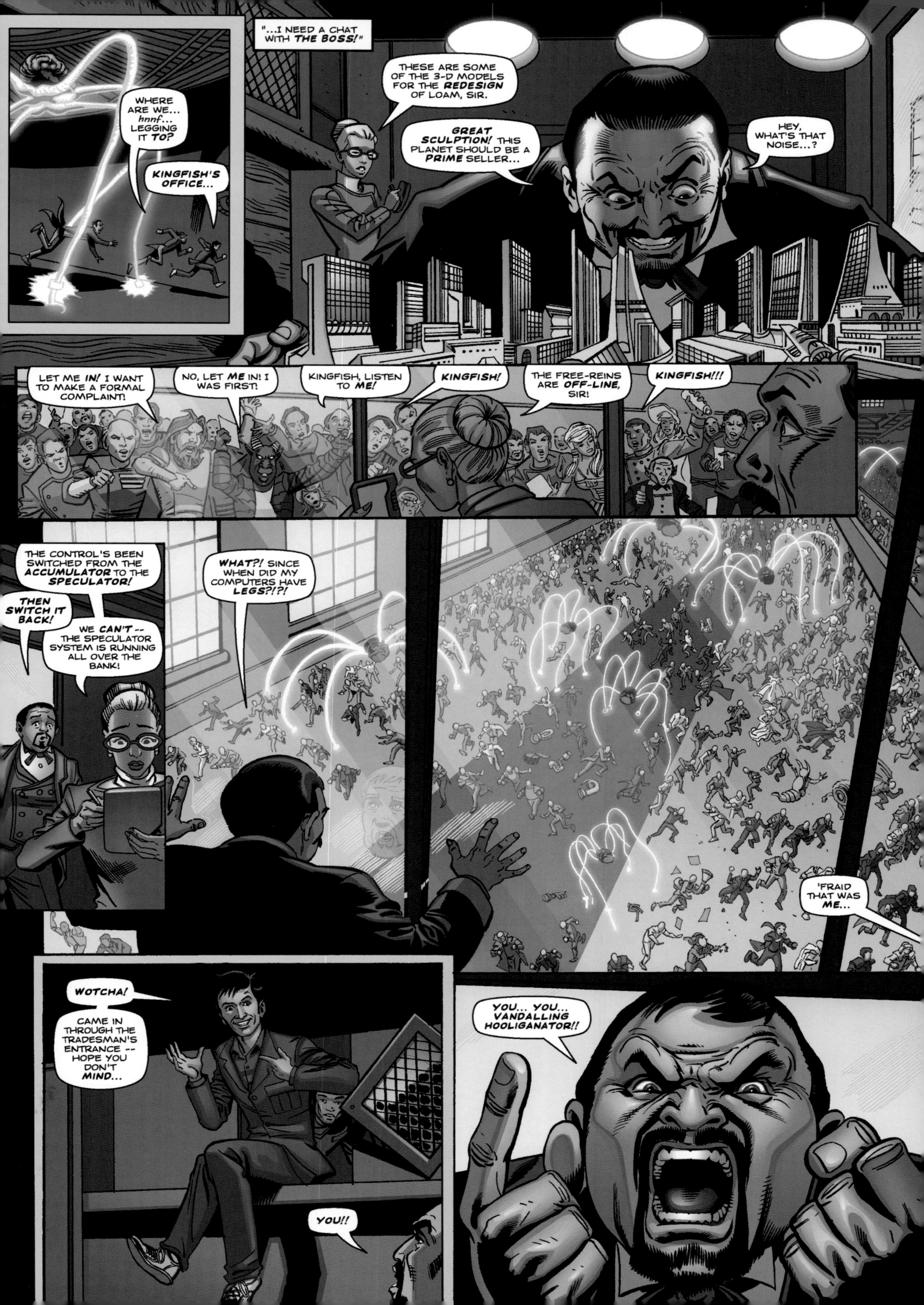
WHERE ARE WE... hnnf... LEGGING IT TO?
KINGFISH'S OFFICE...
"...I NEED A CHAT WITH THE BOSS!"
THESE ARE SOME OF THE 3-D MODELS FOR THE REDESIGN OF LOAM, SIR.
GREAT SCULPTION! THIS PLANET SHOULD BE A PRIME SELLER...
HEY, WHAT'S THAT NOISE...?
LET ME IN! I WANT TO MAKE A FORMAL COMPLAINT!
NO, LET ME IN! I WAS FIRST!
KINGFISH, LISTEN TO ME!
KINGFISH!
THE FREE-REINS ARE OFF-LINE, SIR!
KINGFISH!!!
THE CONTROL'S BEEN SWITCHED FROM THE ACCUMULATOR TO THE SPECULATOR!
THEN SWITCH IT BACK!
WE CAN'T -- THE SPECULATOR SYSTEM IS RUNNING ALL OVER THE BANK!
WHAT?! SINCE WHEN DID MY COMPUTERS HAVE LEGS?!?!
'FRAID THAT WAS ME...
WOTCHA!
CAME IN THROUGH THE TRADESMAN'S ENTRANCE -- HOPE YOU DON'T MIND...
YOU!!
YOU... YOU... VANDALLING HOOLIGANATOR!!

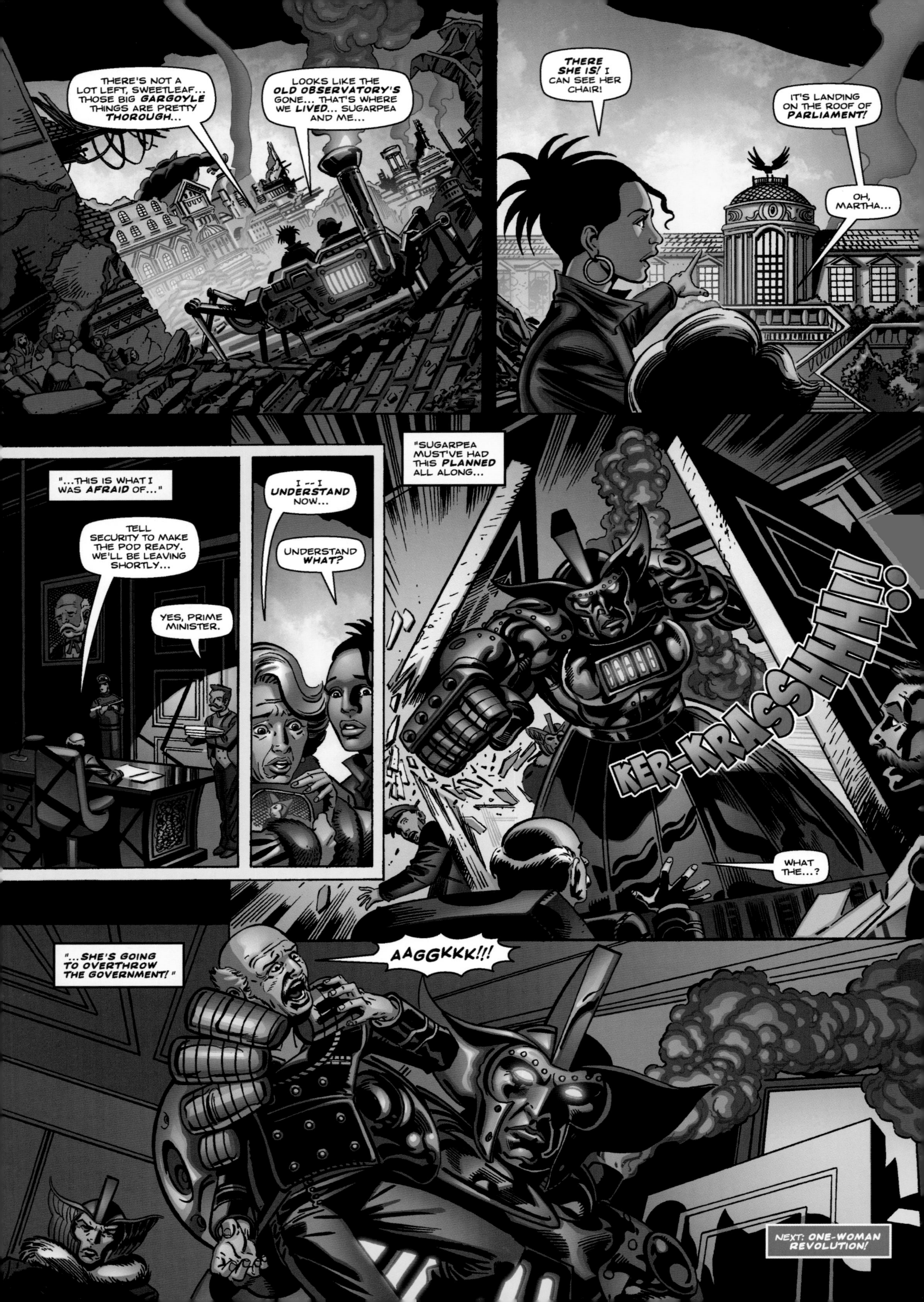
THERE'S NOT A LOT LEFT, SWEETLEAF... THOSE BIG GARGOYLE THINGS ARE PRETTY THOROUGH...
LOOKS LIKE THE OLD OBSERVATORY'S GONE... THAT'S WHERE WE LIVED... SUGARPEA AND ME...
THERE SHE IS! I CAN SEE HER CHAIR!
IT'S LANDING ON THE ROOF OF PARLIAMENT!
OH, MARTHA...
"...THIS IS WHAT I WAS AFRAID OF..."
TELL SECURITY TO MAKE THE POD READY. WE'LL BE LEAVING SHORTLY...
YES, PRIME MINISTER.
I -- I UNDERSTAND NOW...
UNDERSTAND WHAT?
"SUGARPEA MUST'VE HAD THIS PLANNED ALL ALONG...
KER-KRASSHHH!!
WHAT THE...?
"...SHE'S GOING TO OVERTHROW THE GOVERNMENT!"
AAGGKKK!!!
NEXT: ONE-WOMAN REVOLUTION!

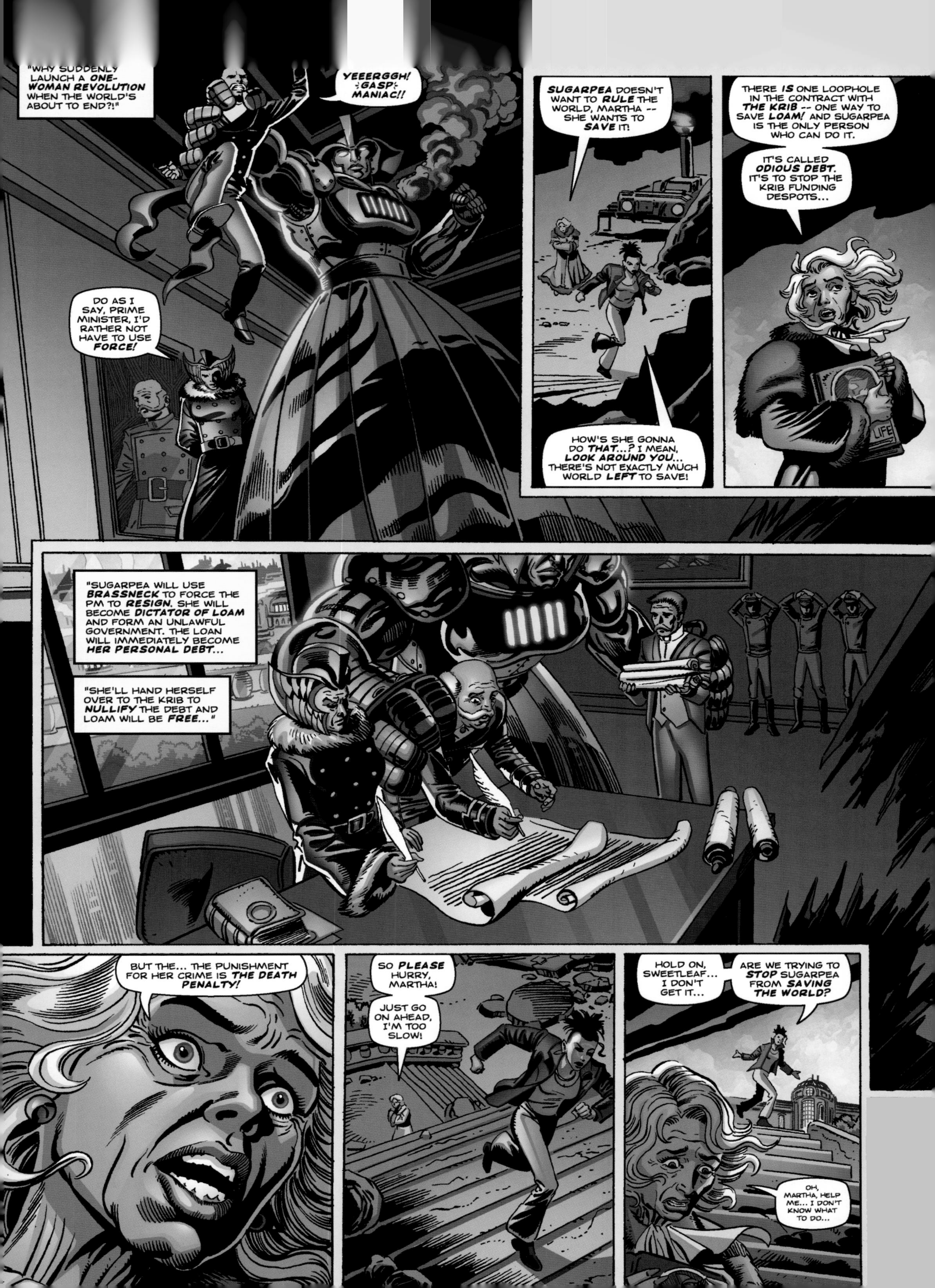
"WHY SUDDENLY LAUNCH A ONE-WOMAN REVOLUTION WHEN THE WORLD'S ABOUT TO END?!"
YEEERGGH! GASP! MANIAC!!
DO AS I SAY, PRIME MINISTER, I'D RATHER NOT HAVE TO USE FORCE!
SUGARPEA DOESN'T WANT TO RULE THE WORLD, MARTHA -- SHE WANTS TO SAVE IT!
HOW'S SHE GONNA DO THAT...? I MEAN, LOOK AROUND YOU... THERE'S NOT EXACTLY MUCH WORLD LEFT TO SAVE!
THERE IS ONE LOOPHOLE IN THE CONTRACT WITH THE KRIB -- ONE WAY TO SAVE LOAM! AND SUGARPEA IS THE ONLY PERSON WHO CAN DO IT.
IT'S CALLED ODIOUS DEBT. IT'S TO STOP THE KRIB FUNDING DESPOTS...
LIFE
"SUGARPEA WILL USE BRASSNECK TO FORCE THE PM TO RESIGN. SHE WILL BECOME DICTATOR OF LOAM AND FORM AN UNLAWFUL GOVERNMENT. THE LOAN WILL IMMEDIATELY BECOME HER PERSONAL DEBT...
"SHE'LL HAND HERSELF OVER TO THE KRIB TO NULLIFY THE DEBT AND LOAM WILL BE FREE..."
BUT THE... THE PUNISHMENT FOR HER CRIME IS THE DEATH PENALTY!
SO PLEASE HURRY, MARTHA!
JUST GO ON AHEAD, I'M TOO SLOW!
HOLD ON, SWEETLEAF... I DON'T GET IT...
ARE WE TRYING TO STOP SUGARPEA FROM SAVING THE WORLD?
OH, MARTHA, HELP ME... I DON'T KNOW WHAT TO DO...

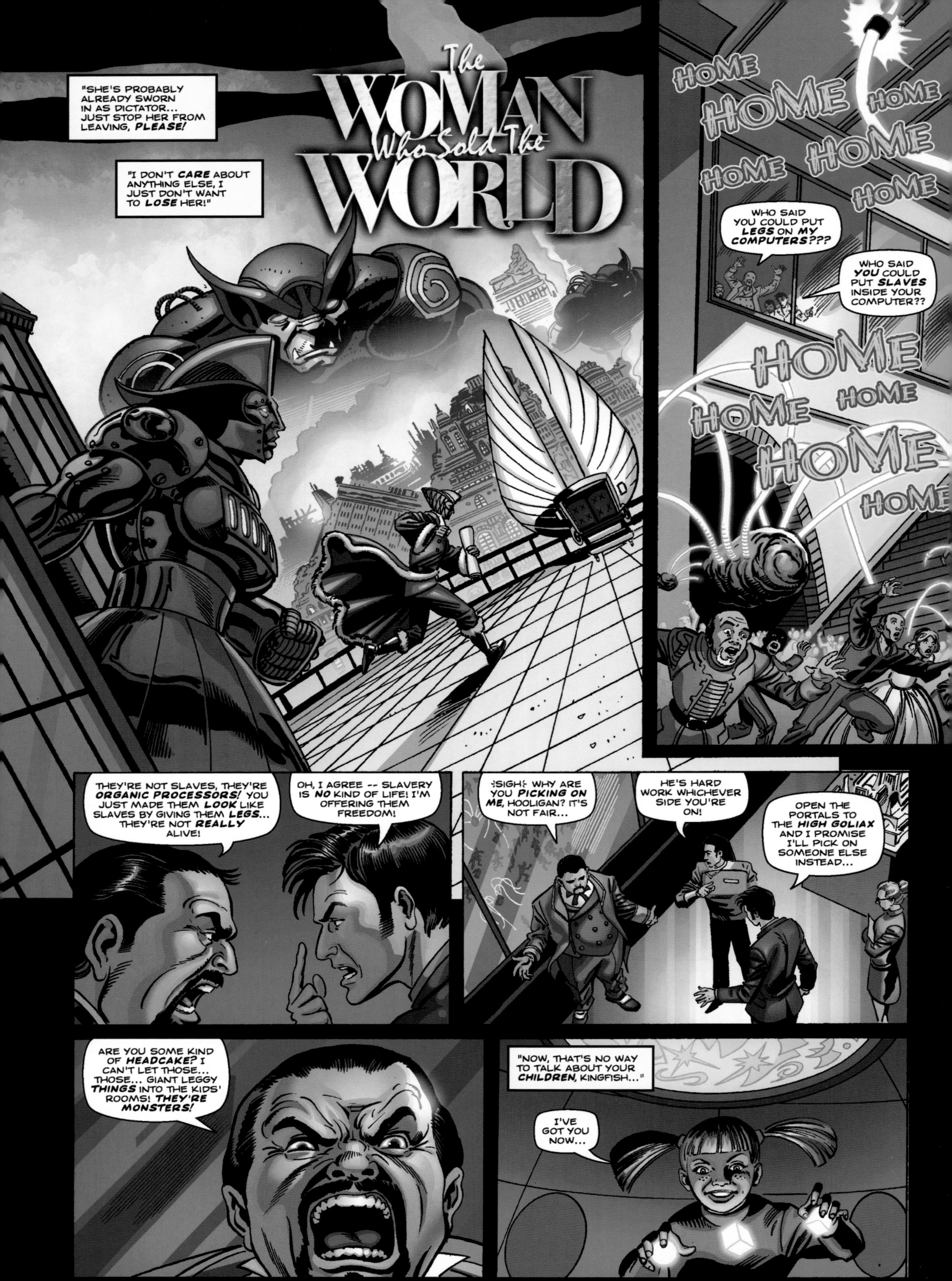

The WOMAN Who Sold The WORLD
"SHE'S PROBABLY ALREADY SWORN IN AS DICTATOR... JUST STOP HER FROM LEAVING, PLEASE!
"I DON'T CARE ABOUT ANYTHING ELSE, I JUST DON'T WANT TO LOSE HER!"
HOME HOME HOME HOME HOME HOME
WHO SAID YOU COULD PUT LEGS ON MY COMPUTERS???
WHO SAID YOU COULD PUT SLAVES INSIDE YOUR COMPUTER??
HOME HOME HOME HOME HOME
THEY'RE NOT SLAVES, THEY'RE ORGANIC PROCESSORS! YOU JUST MADE THEM LOOK LIKE SLAVES BY GIVING THEM LEGS... THEY'RE NOT REALLY ALIVE!
OH, I AGREE -- SLAVERY IS NO KIND OF LIFE! I'M OFFERING THEM FREEDOM!
SIGH WHY ARE YOU PICKING ON ME, HOOLIGAN? IT'S NOT FAIR...
HE'S HARD WORK WHICHEVER SIDE YOU'RE ON!
OPEN THE PORTALS TO THE HIGH GOLIAX AND I PROMISE I'LL PICK ON SOMEONE ELSE INSTEAD...
ARE YOU SOME KIND OF HEADCAKE? I CAN'T LET THOSE... THOSE... GIANT LEGGY THINGS INTO THE KIDS' ROOMS! THEY'RE MONSTERS!
"NOW, THAT'S NO WAY TO TALK ABOUT YOUR CHILDREN, KINGFISH..."
I'VE GOT YOU NOW...

Story ROB DAVIS | Pencils MIKE COLLINS | Inks DAVID A. ROACH | Colours JAMES OFFREDI | Letters ROGER LANGRIDGE | Editors HICKMAN & GRAY

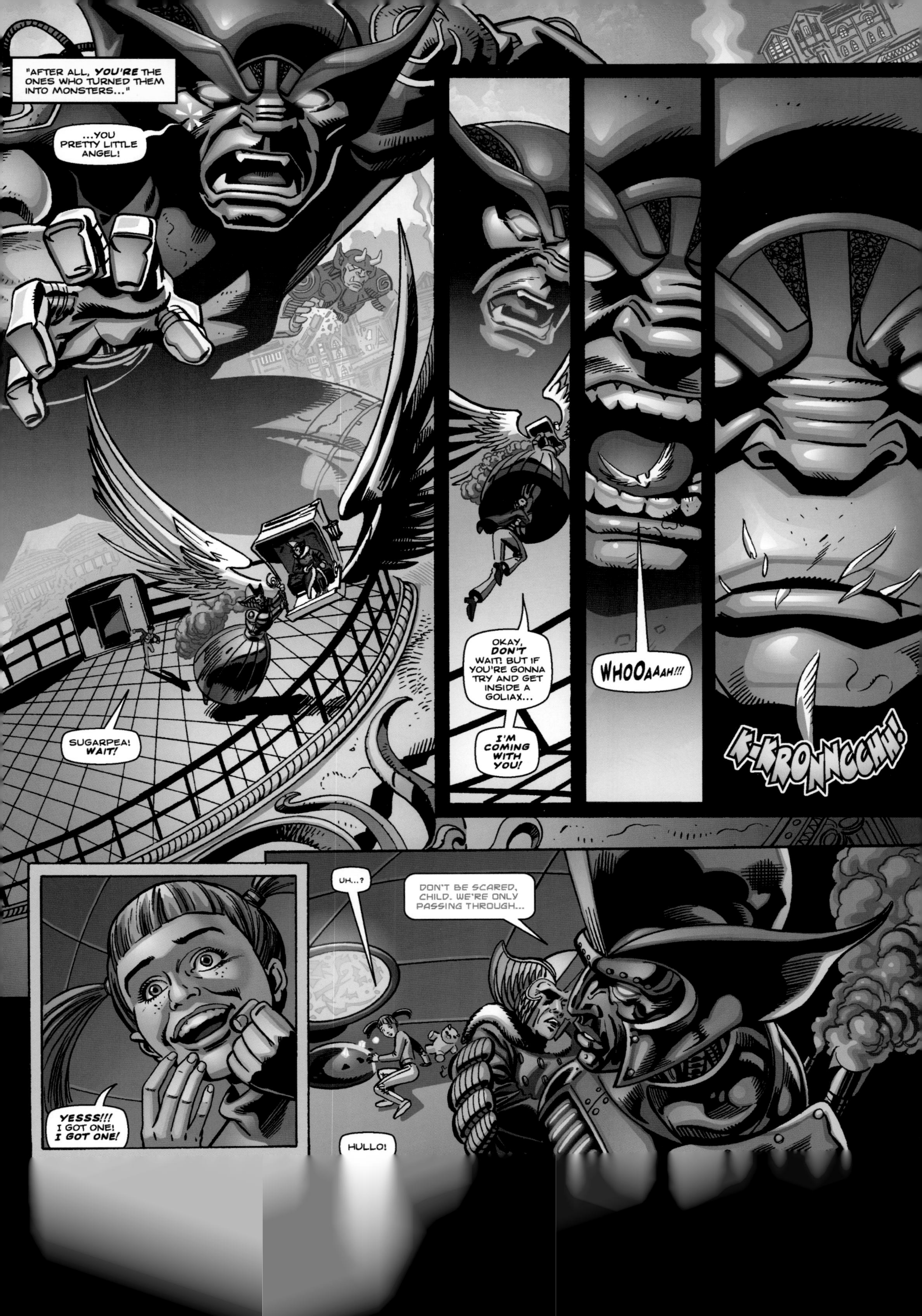
"AFTER ALL, YOU'RE THE ONES WHO TURNED THEM INTO MONSTERS..."
...YOU PRETTY LITTLE ANGEL!
SUGARPEA! WAIT!
OKAY, DON'T WAIT! BUT IF YOU'RE GONNA TRY AND GET INSIDE A GOLIAX...
I'M COMING WITH YOU!
WHOOAAAH!!!
K-KRONNCCHH!
YESSS!!! I GOT ONE! I GOT ONE!
UH...?
DON'T BE SCARED, CHILD. WE'RE ONLY PASSING THROUGH...
HULLO!

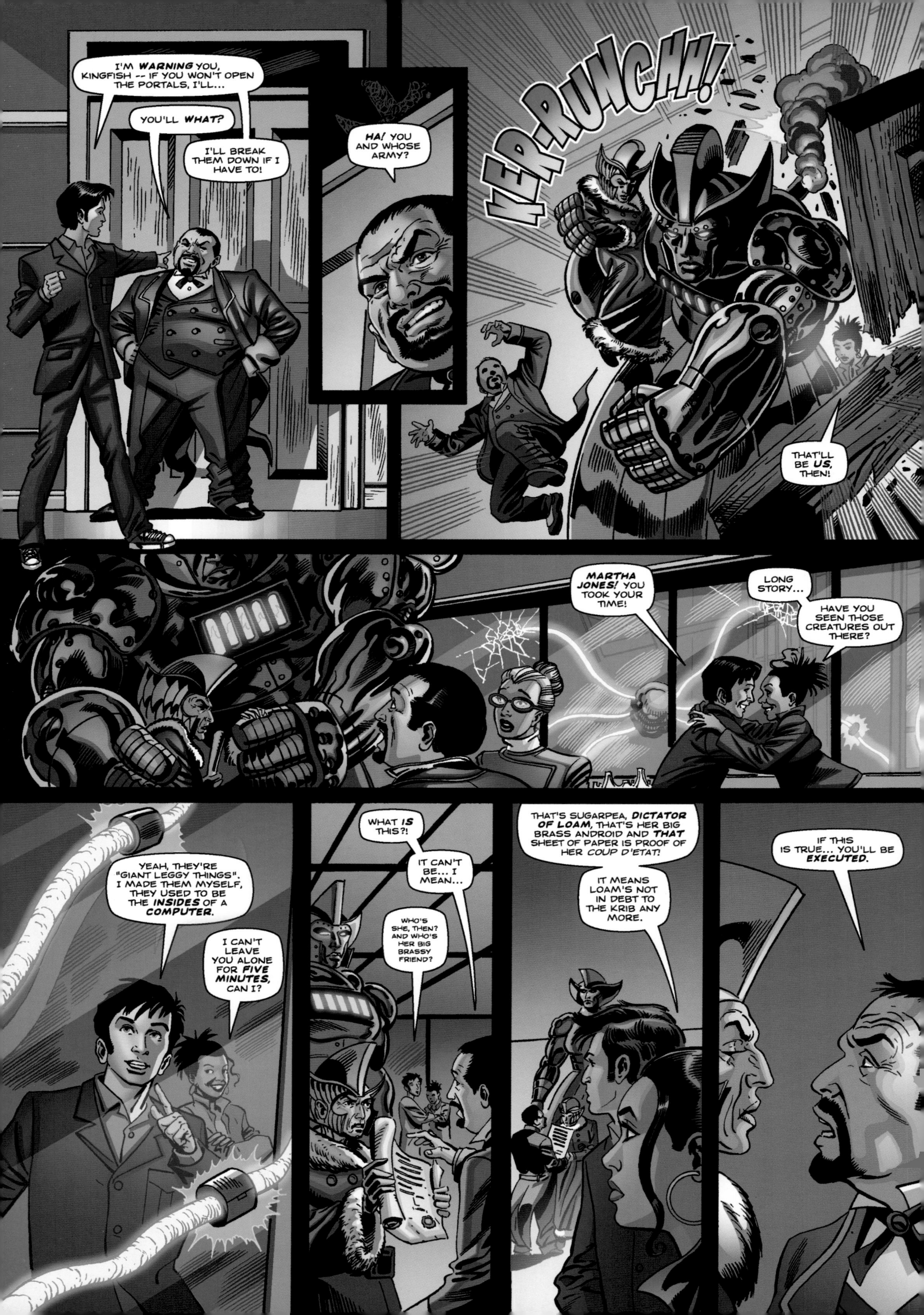

I'M WARNING YOU, KINGFISH -- IF YOU WON'T OPEN THE PORTALS, I'LL...
YOU'LL WHAT?
I'LL BREAK THEM DOWN IF I HAVE TO!
HA! YOU AND WHOSE ARMY?
KER-RUNCHH!
THAT'LL BE US, THEN!
MARTHA JONES! YOU TOOK YOUR TIME!
LONG STORY...
HAVE YOU SEEN THOSE CREATURES OUT THERE?
YEAH, THEY'RE "GIANT LEGGY THINGS". I MADE THEM MYSELF, THEY USED TO BE THE INSIDES OF A COMPUTER.
I CAN'T LEAVE YOU ALONE FOR FIVE MINUTES, CAN I?
WHAT IS THIS?!
IT CAN'T BE... I MEAN...
WHO'S SHE, THEN? AND WHO'S HER BIG BRASSY FRIEND?
THAT'S SUGARPEA, DICTATOR OF LOAM, THAT'S HER BIG BRASS ANDROID AND THAT SHEET OF PAPER IS PROOF OF HER COUP D'ETAT!
IT MEANS LOAM'S NOT IN DEBT TO THE KRIB ANY MORE.
IF THIS IS TRUE... YOU'LL BE EXECUTED.

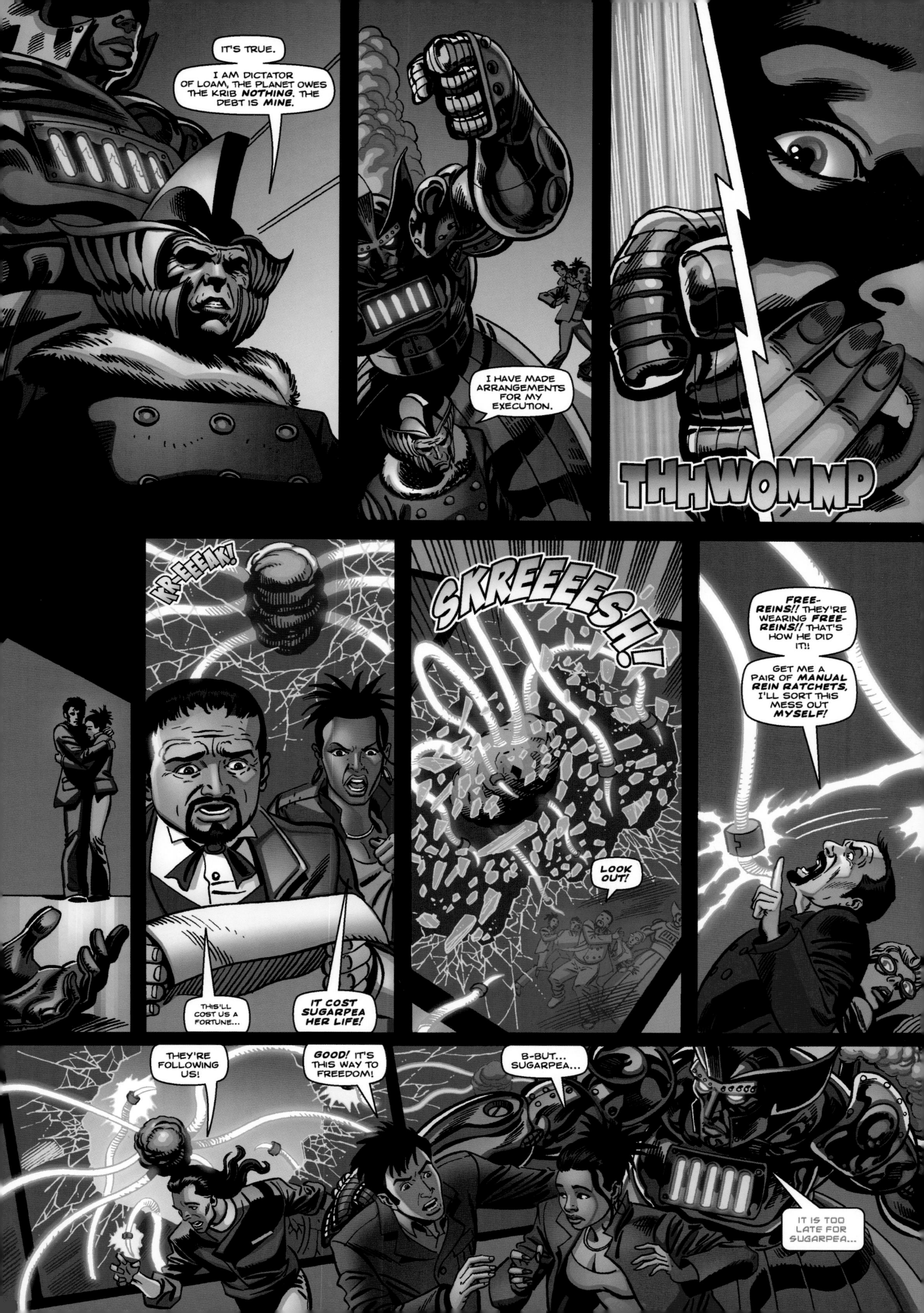
IT'S TRUE.
I AM DICTATOR OF LOAM, THE PLANET OWES THE KRIB NOTHING. THE DEBT IS MINE.
I HAVE MADE ARRANGEMENTS FOR MY EXECUTION.
THHWOMMP
KR-EEEAK!
THIS'LL COST US A FORTUNE...
IT COST SUGARPEA HER LIFE!
SKREEEESH!!
LOOK OUT!
FREE-REINS!! THEY'RE WEARING FREE-REINS!! THAT'S HOW HE DID IT!!
GET ME A PAIR OF MANUAL REIN RATCHETS, I'LL SORT THIS MESS OUT MYSELF!
THEY'RE FOLLOWING US!
GOOD! IT'S THIS WAY TO FREEDOM!
B-BUT... SUGARPEA...
IT IS TOO LATE FOR SUGARPEA...

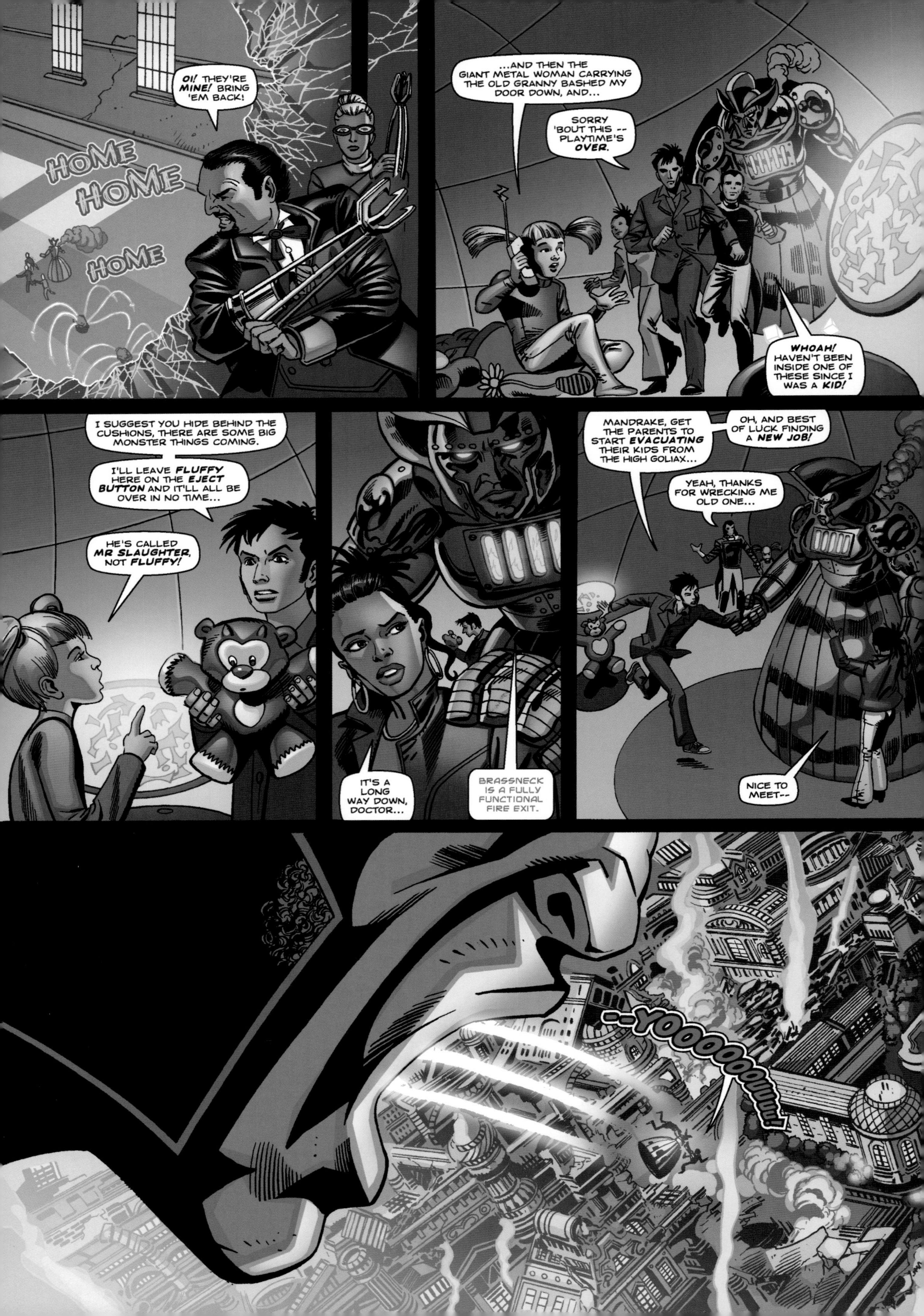
OI! THEY'RE MINE! BRING 'EM BACK!
HOME
HOME
HOME
...AND THEN THE GIANT METAL WOMAN CARRYING THE OLD GRANNY BASHED MY DOOR DOWN, AND...
SORRY 'BOUT THIS -- PLAYTIME'S OVER.
WHOAH! HAVEN'T BEEN INSIDE ONE OF THESE SINCE I WAS A KID!
I SUGGEST YOU HIDE BEHIND THE CUSHIONS, THERE ARE SOME BIG MONSTER THINGS COMING.
I'LL LEAVE FLUFFY HERE ON THE EJECT BUTTON AND IT'LL ALL BE OVER IN NO TIME...
HE'S CALLED MR SLAUGHTER, NOT FLUFFY!
IT'S A LONG WAY DOWN, DOCTOR...
BRASSNECK IS A FULLY FUNCTIONAL FIRE EXIT.
MANDRAKE, GET THE PARENTS TO START EVACUATING THEIR KIDS FROM THE HIGH GOLIAX...
OH, AND BEST OF LUCK FINDING A NEW JOB!
YEAH, THANKS FOR WRECKING ME OLD ONE...
NICE TO MEET--
--YOOOOOOUUUU!

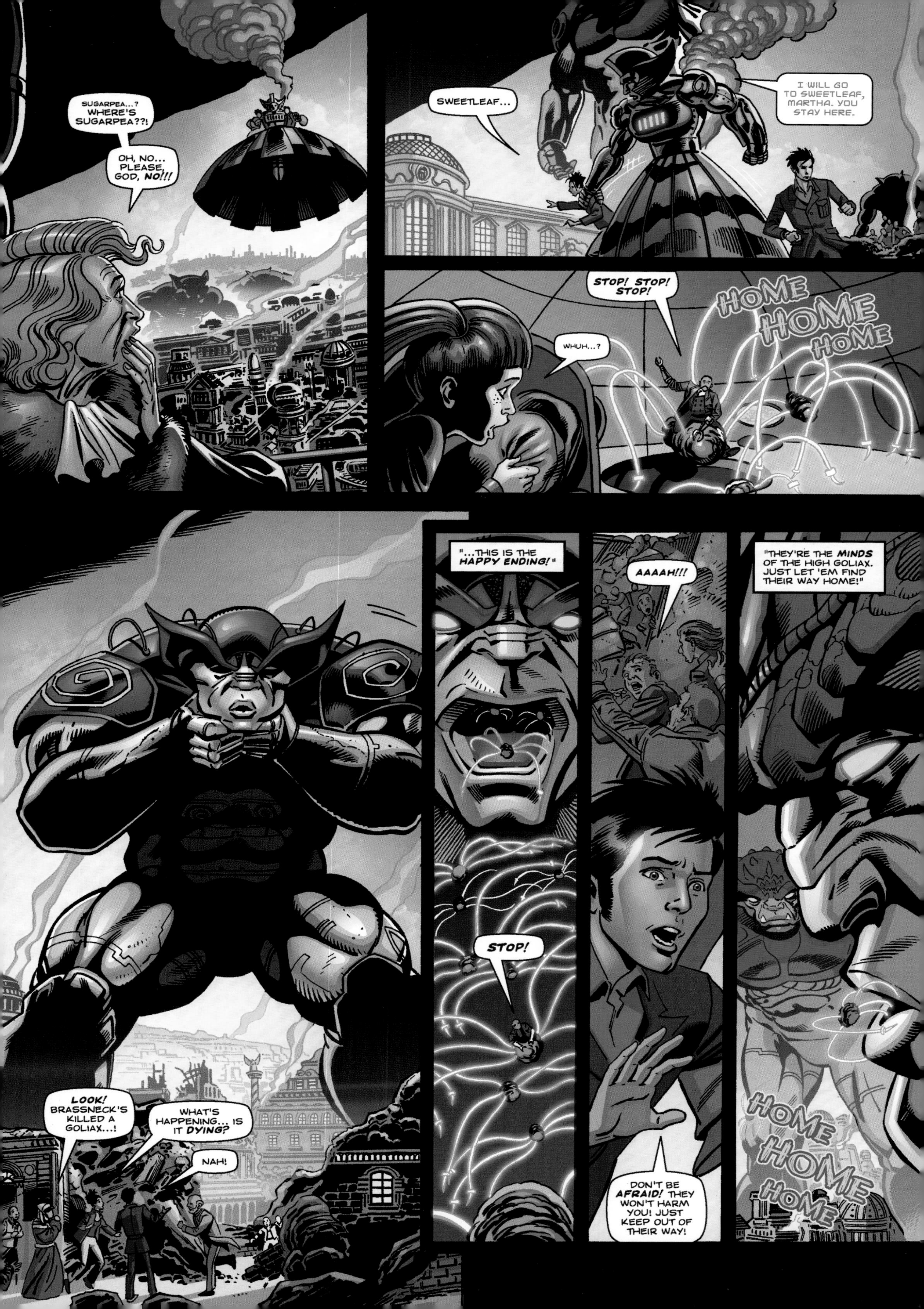
SUGARPEA...? WHERE'S SUGARPEA??!
OH, NO... PLEASE GOD, NO!!!
SWEETLEAF...
I WILL GO TO SWEETLEAF, MARTHA. YOU STAY HERE.
STOP! STOP! STOP!
WHUH...?
HOME HOME HOME
LOOK! BRASSNECK'S KILLED A GOLIAX...!
WHAT'S HAPPENING... IS IT DYING?
NAH!
"...THIS IS THE HAPPY ENDING!"
STOP!
AAAAH!!!
DON'T BE AFRAID! THEY WON'T HARM YOU! JUST KEEP OUT OF THEIR WAY!
"THEY'RE THE MINDS OF THE HIGH GOLIAX. JUST LET 'EM FIND THEIR WAY HOME!"
HOME HOME HOME

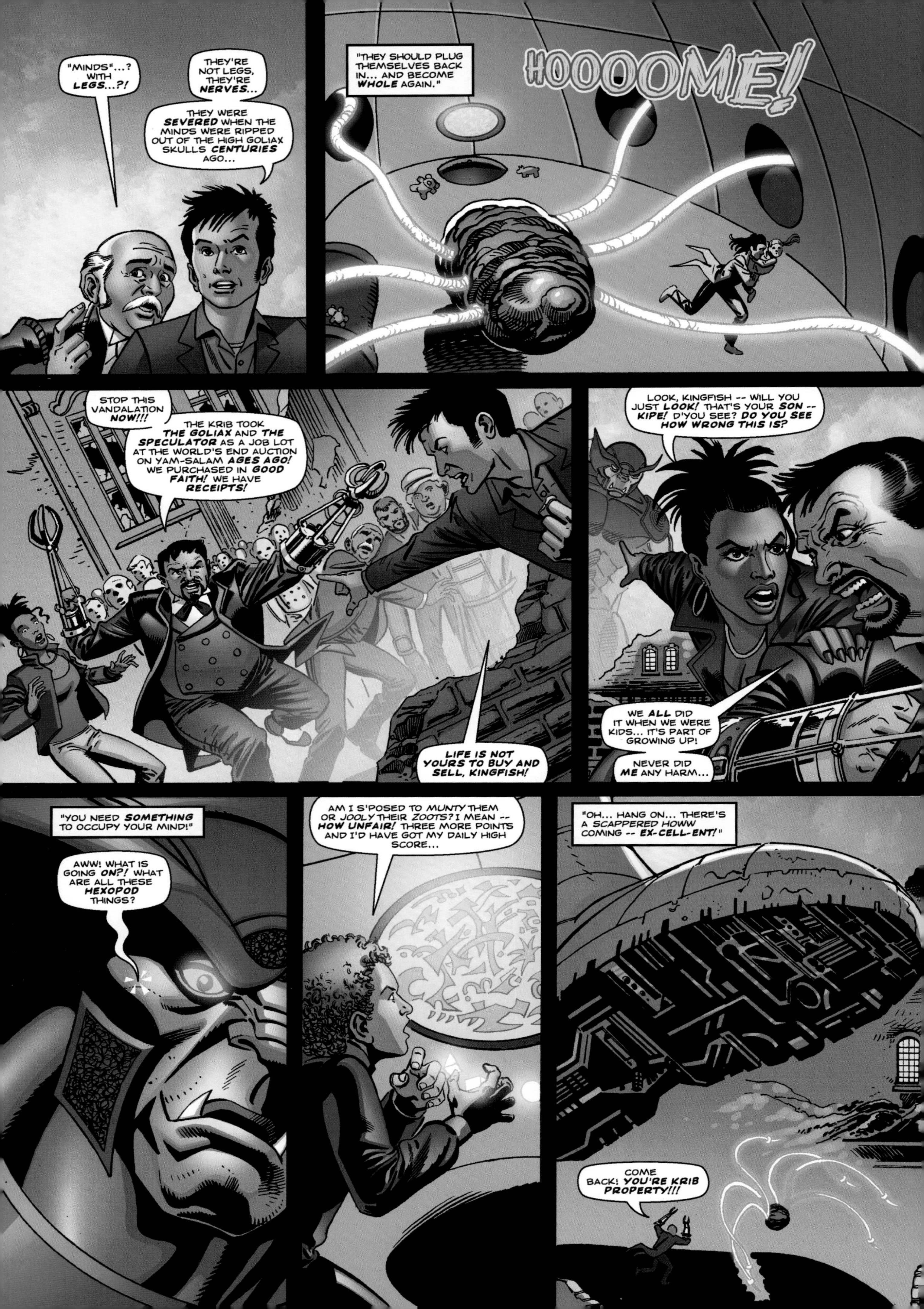
"MINDS"...? WITH LEGS...?!
THEY'RE NOT LEGS, THEY'RE NERVES...
THEY WERE SEVERED WHEN THE MINDS WERE RIPPED OUT OF THE HIGH GOLIAX SKULLS CENTURIES AGO...
"THEY SHOULD PLUG THEMSELVES BACK IN... AND BECOME WHOLE AGAIN."
HOOOOOME!
STOP THIS VANDALATION NOW!!!
THE KRIB TOOK THE GOLIAX AND THE SPECULATOR AS A JOB LOT AT THE WORLD'S END AUCTION ON YAM-SALAM AGES AGO! WE PURCHASED IN GOOD FAITH! WE HAVE RECEIPTS!
LIFE IS NOT YOURS TO BUY AND SELL, KINGFISH!
LOOK, KINGFISH -- WILL YOU JUST LOOK! THAT'S YOUR SON -- KIPE! D'YOU SEE? DO YOU SEE HOW WRONG THIS IS?
WE ALL DID IT WHEN WE WERE KIDS... IT'S PART OF GROWING UP!
NEVER DID ME ANY HARM...
"YOU NEED SOMETHING TO OCCUPY YOUR MIND!"
AWW! WHAT IS GOING ON?! WHAT ARE ALL THESE HEXOPOD THINGS?
AM I S'POSED TO MUNTY THEM OR JOOLY THEIR ZOOTS? I MEAN -- HOW UNFAIR! THREE MORE POINTS AND I'D HAVE GOT MY DAILY HIGH SCORE...
"OH... HANG ON... THERE'S A SCAPPERED HOWW COMING -- EX-CELL-ENT!"
COME BACK! YOU'RE KRIB PROPERTY!!!

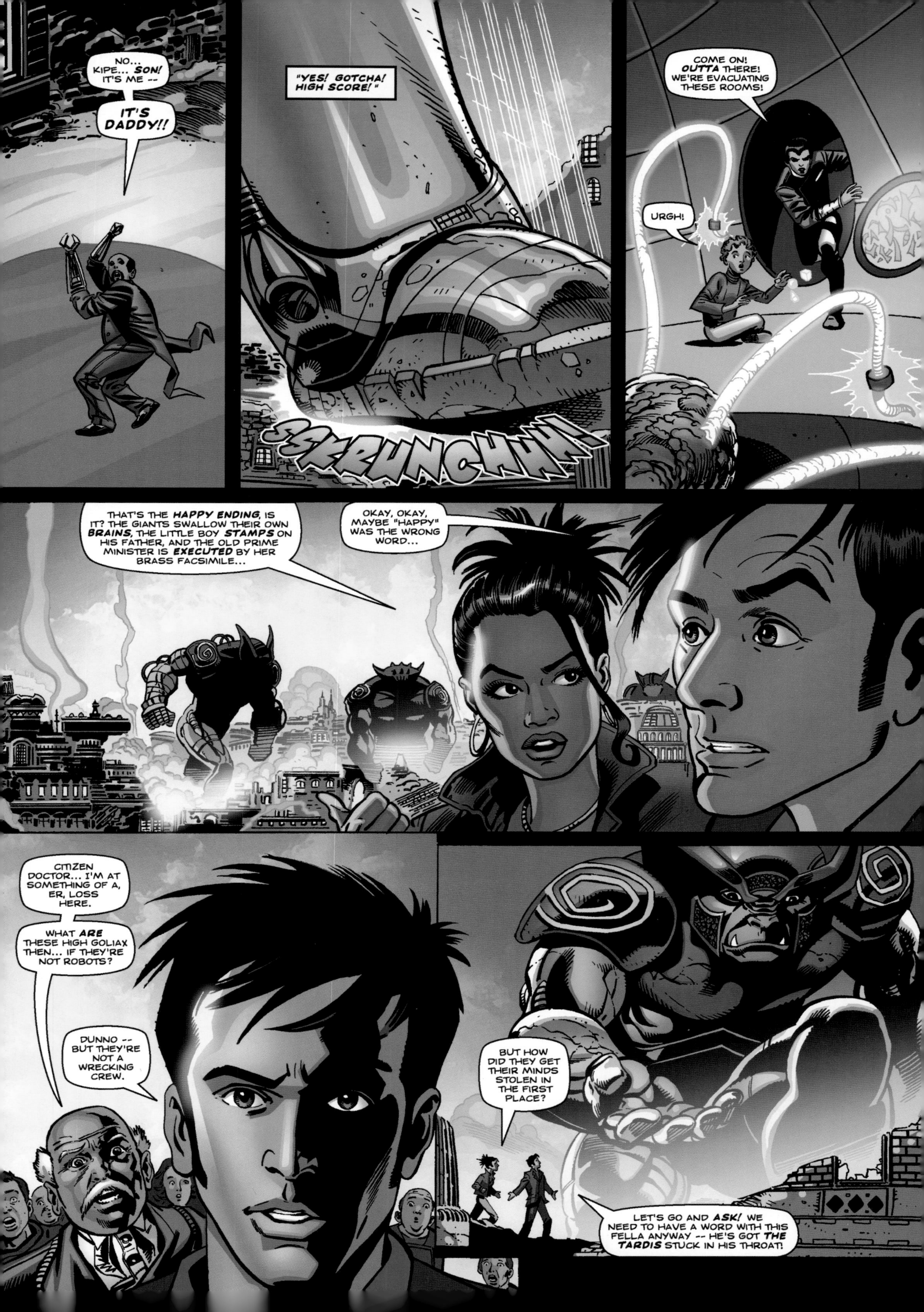
NO... KIPE... SON! IT'S ME --
IT'S DADDY!!
"YES! GOTCHA! HIGH SCORE!"
SSKRUNCHHH!
COME ON! OUTTA THERE! WE'RE EVACUATING THESE ROOMS!
URGH!
THAT'S THE HAPPY ENDING, IS IT? THE GIANTS SWALLOW THEIR OWN BRAINS, THE LITTLE BOY STAMPS ON HIS FATHER, AND THE OLD PRIME MINISTER IS EXECUTED BY HER BRASS FACSIMILE...
OKAY, OKAY, MAYBE "HAPPY" WAS THE WRONG WORD...
CITIZEN DOCTOR... I'M AT SOMETHING OF A, ER, LOSS HERE.
WHAT ARE THESE HIGH GOLIAX THEN... IF THEY'RE NOT ROBOTS?
DUNNO -- BUT THEY'RE NOT A WRECKING CREW.
BUT HOW DID THEY GET THEIR MINDS STOLEN IN THE FIRST PLACE?
LET'S GO AND ASK! WE NEED TO HAVE A WORD WITH THIS FELLA ANYWAY -- HE'S GOT THE TARDIS STUCK IN HIS THROAT!

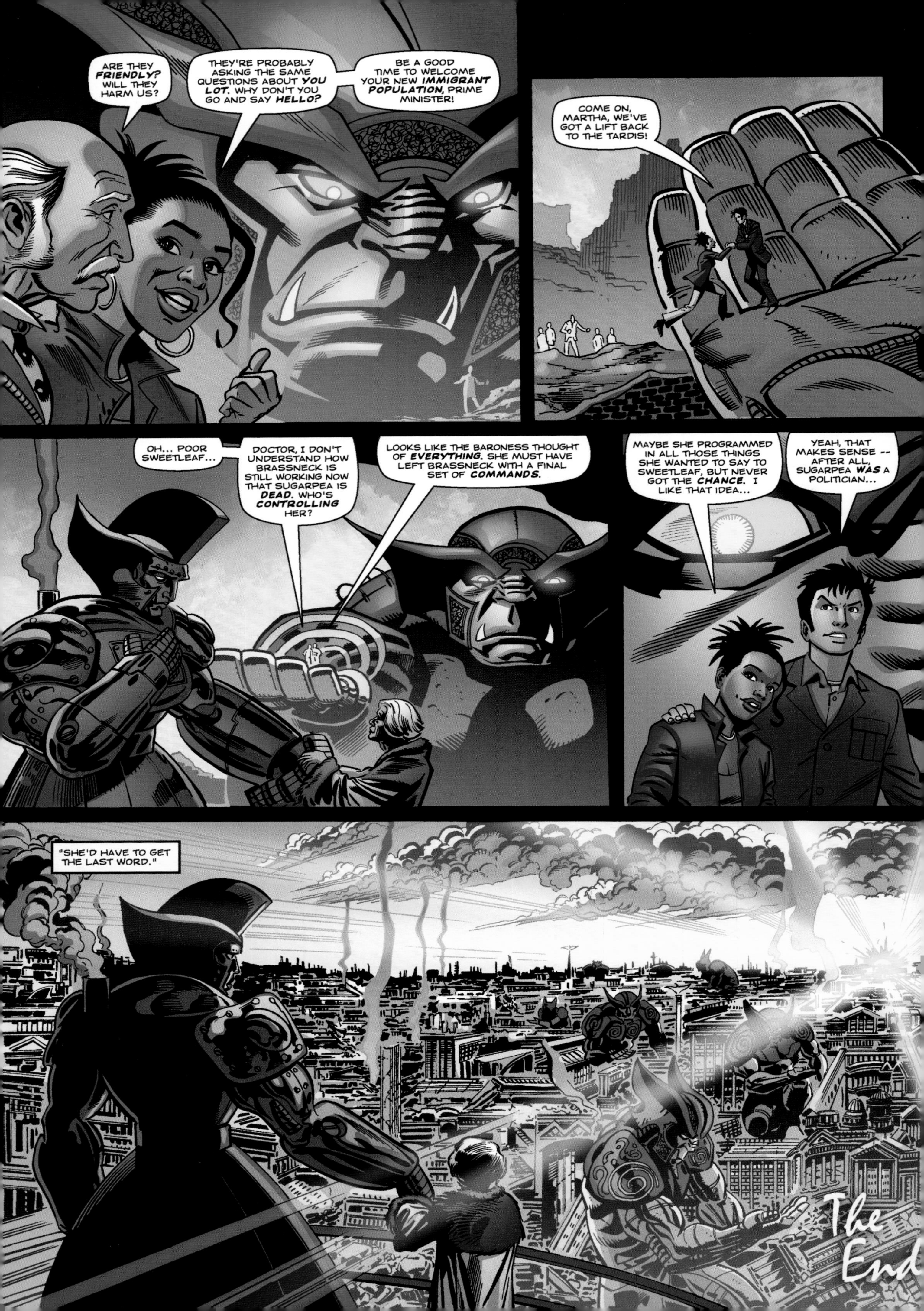
ARE THEY FRIENDLY? WILL THEY HARM US?
THEY'RE PROBABLY ASKING THE SAME QUESTIONS ABOUT YOU LOT. WHY DON'T YOU GO AND SAY HELLO?
BE A GOOD TIME TO WELCOME YOUR NEW IMMIGRANT POPULATION, PRIME MINISTER!
COME ON, MARTHA, WE'VE GOT A LIFT BACK TO THE TARDIS!
OH... POOR SWEETLEAF...
DOCTOR, I DON'T UNDERSTAND HOW BRASSNECK IS STILL WORKING NOW THAT SUGARPEA IS DEAD. WHO'S CONTROLLING HER?
LOOKS LIKE THE BARONESS THOUGHT OF EVERYTHING. SHE MUST HAVE LEFT BRASSNECK WITH A FINAL SET OF COMMANDS.
MAYBE SHE PROGRAMMED IN ALL THOSE THINGS SHE WANTED TO SAY TO SWEETLEAF, BUT NEVER GOT THE CHANCE. I LIKE THAT IDEA...
YEAH, THAT MAKES SENSE -- AFTER ALL, SUGARPEA WAS A POLITICIAN...
"SHE'D HAVE TO GET THE LAST WORD."
The End

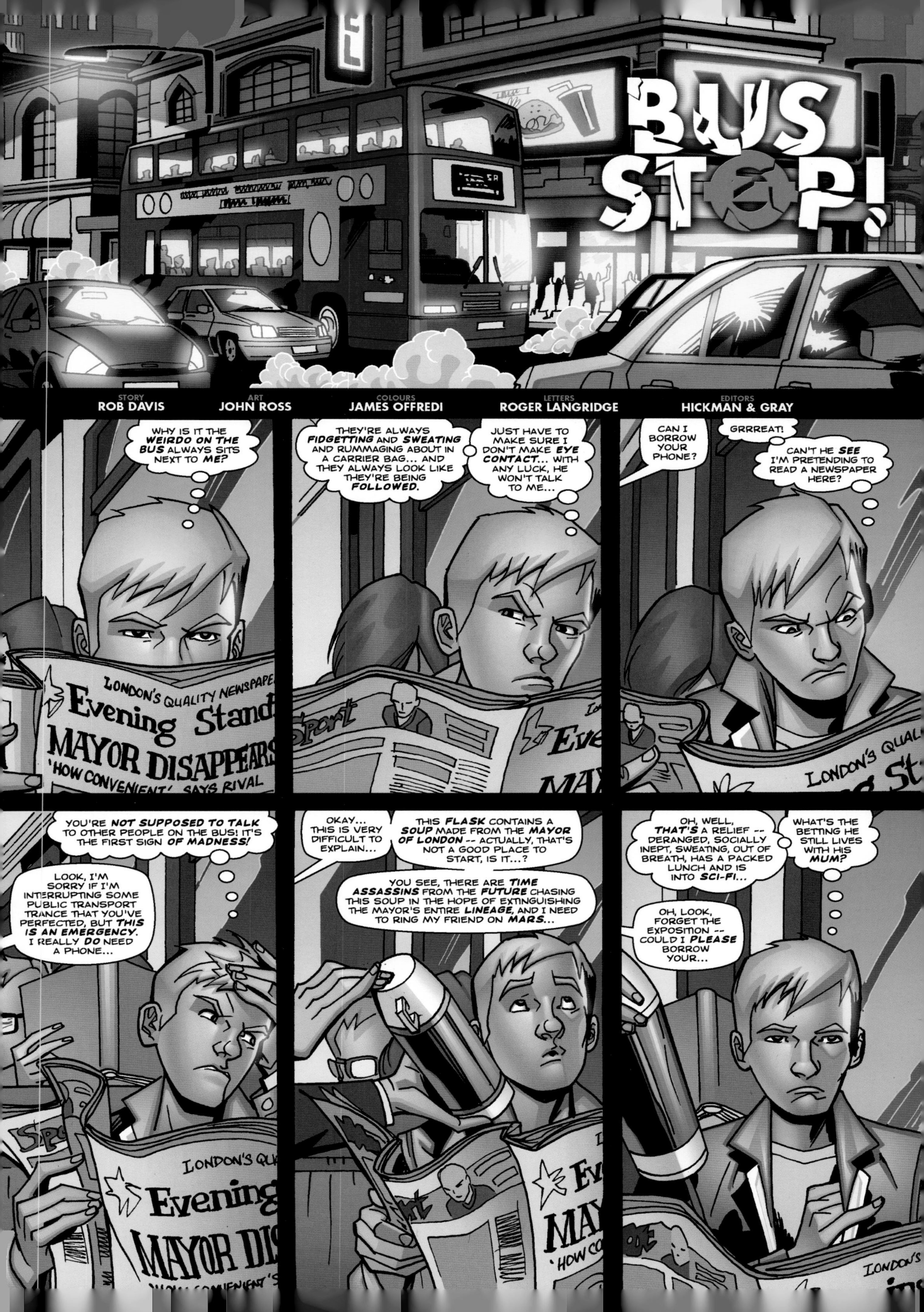
BUS STOP!
STORY ROB DAVIS
ART JOHN ROSS
COLOURS JAMES OFFREDI
LETTERS ROGER LANGRIDGE
EDITORS HICKMAN & GRAY
WHY IS IT THE WEIRDO ON THE BUS ALWAYS SITS NEXT TO ME?
LONDON'S QUALITY NEWSPAPER
Evening
MAYOR DISAPPEARS
'HOW CONVENIENT' SAYS RIVAL
THEY'RE ALWAYS FIDGETTING AND SWEATING AND RUMMAGING ABOUT IN A CARRIER BAG... AND THEY ALWAYS LOOK LIKE THEY'RE BEING FOLLOWED.
JUST HAVE TO MAKE SURE I DON'T MAKE EYE CONTACT... WITH ANY LUCK, HE WON'T TALK TO ME...
CAN I BORROW YOUR PHONE?
GRRREAT!
CAN'T HE SEE I'M PRETENDING TO READ A NEWSPAPER HERE?
YOU'RE NOT SUPPOSED TO TALK TO OTHER PEOPLE ON THE BUS! IT'S THE FIRST SIGN OF MADNESS!
LOOK, I'M SORRY IF I'M INTERRUPTING SOME PUBLIC TRANSPORT TRANCE THAT YOU'VE PERFECTED, BUT THIS IS AN EMERGENCY. I REALLY DO NEED A PHONE...
OKAY... THIS IS VERY DIFFICULT TO EXPLAIN...
THIS FLASK CONTAINS A SOUP MADE FROM THE MAYOR OF LONDON -- ACTUALLY, THAT'S NOT A GOOD PLACE TO START, IS IT...?
YOU SEE, THERE ARE TIME ASSASSINS FROM THE FUTURE CHASING THIS SOUP IN THE HOPE OF EXTINGUISHING THE MAYOR'S ENTIRE LINEAGE, AND I NEED TO RING MY FRIEND ON MARS...
OH, WELL, THAT'S A RELIEF -- DERANGED, SOCIALLY INEPT, SWEATING, OUT OF BREATH, HAS A PACKED LUNCH AND IS INTO SCI-FI...
WHAT'S THE BETTING HE STILL LIVES WITH HIS MUM?
OH, LOOK, FORGET THE EXPOSITION -- COULD I PLEASE BORROW YOUR...

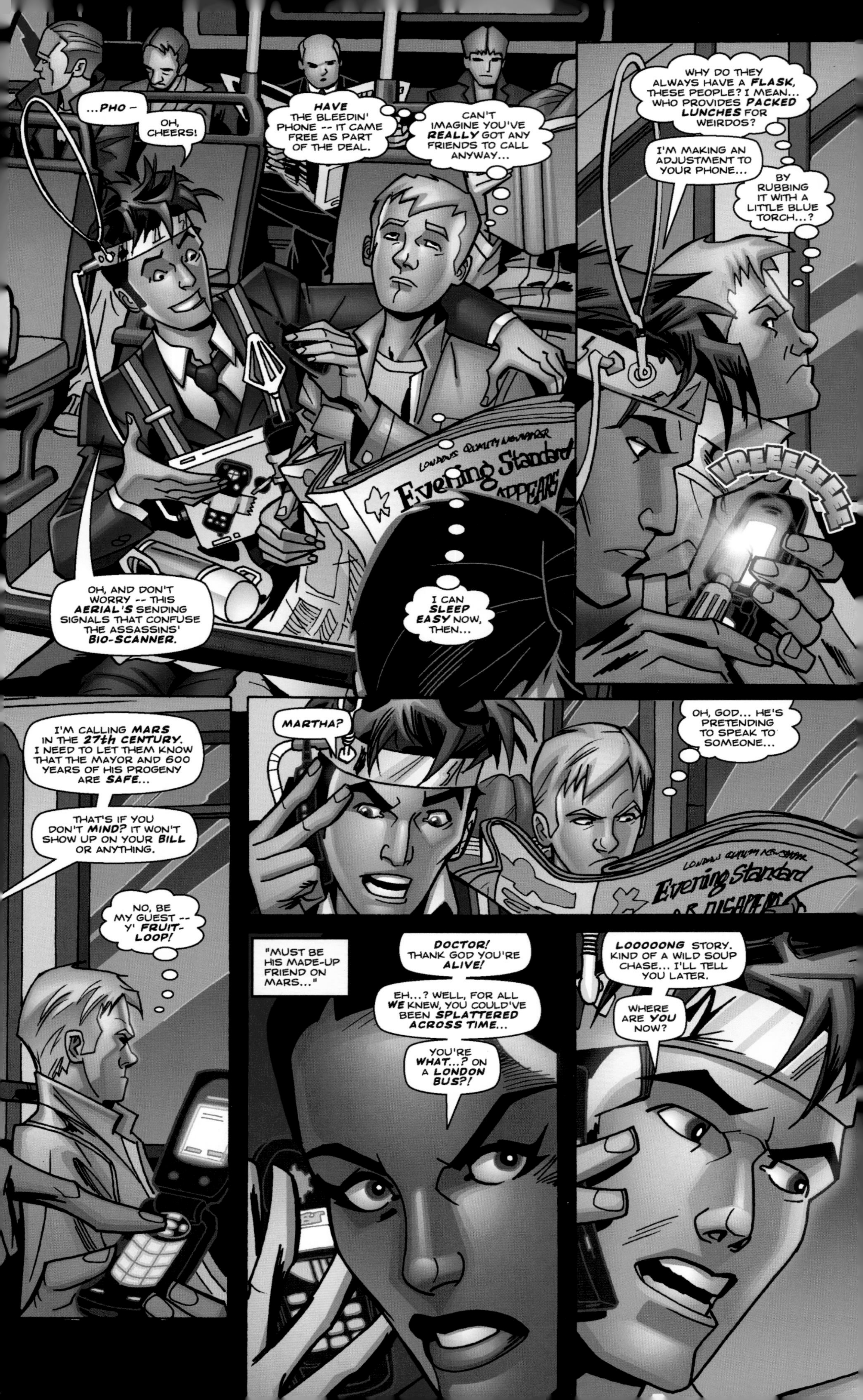
...PHO –
OH, CHEERS!
HAVE THE BLEEDIN' PHONE -- IT CAME FREE AS PART OF THE DEAL.
CAN'T IMAGINE YOU'VE REALLY GOT ANY FRIENDS TO CALL ANYWAY...
OH, AND DON'T WORRY -- THIS AERIAL'S SENDING SIGNALS THAT CONFUSE THE ASSASSINS' BIO-SCANNER.
I CAN SLEEP EASY NOW, THEN...
London's Quality Newspaper
Evening Standard
APPEARS
WHY DO THEY ALWAYS HAVE A FLASK, THESE PEOPLE? I MEAN... WHO PROVIDES PACKED LUNCHES FOR WEIRDOS?
I'M MAKING AN ADJUSTMENT TO YOUR PHONE...
BY RUBBING IT WITH A LITTLE BLUE TORCH...?
VREEEEEEEE
I'M CALLING MARS IN THE 27th CENTURY. I NEED TO LET THEM KNOW THAT THE MAYOR AND 600 YEARS OF HIS PROGENY ARE SAFE...
THAT'S IF YOU DON'T MIND? IT WON'T SHOW UP ON YOUR BILL OR ANYTHING.
NO, BE MY GUEST -- Y' FRUIT-LOOP!
MARTHA?
OH, GOD... HE'S PRETENDING TO SPEAK TO SOMEONE...
Evening Standard
"MUST BE HIS MADE-UP FRIEND ON MARS..."
DOCTOR! THANK GOD YOU'RE ALIVE!
EH...? WELL, FOR ALL WE KNEW, YOU COULD'VE BEEN SPLATTERED ACROSS TIME...
YOU'RE WHAT...? ON A LONDON BUS?!
LOOOOONG STORY. KIND OF A WILD SOUP CHASE... I'LL TELL YOU LATER.
WHERE ARE YOU NOW?

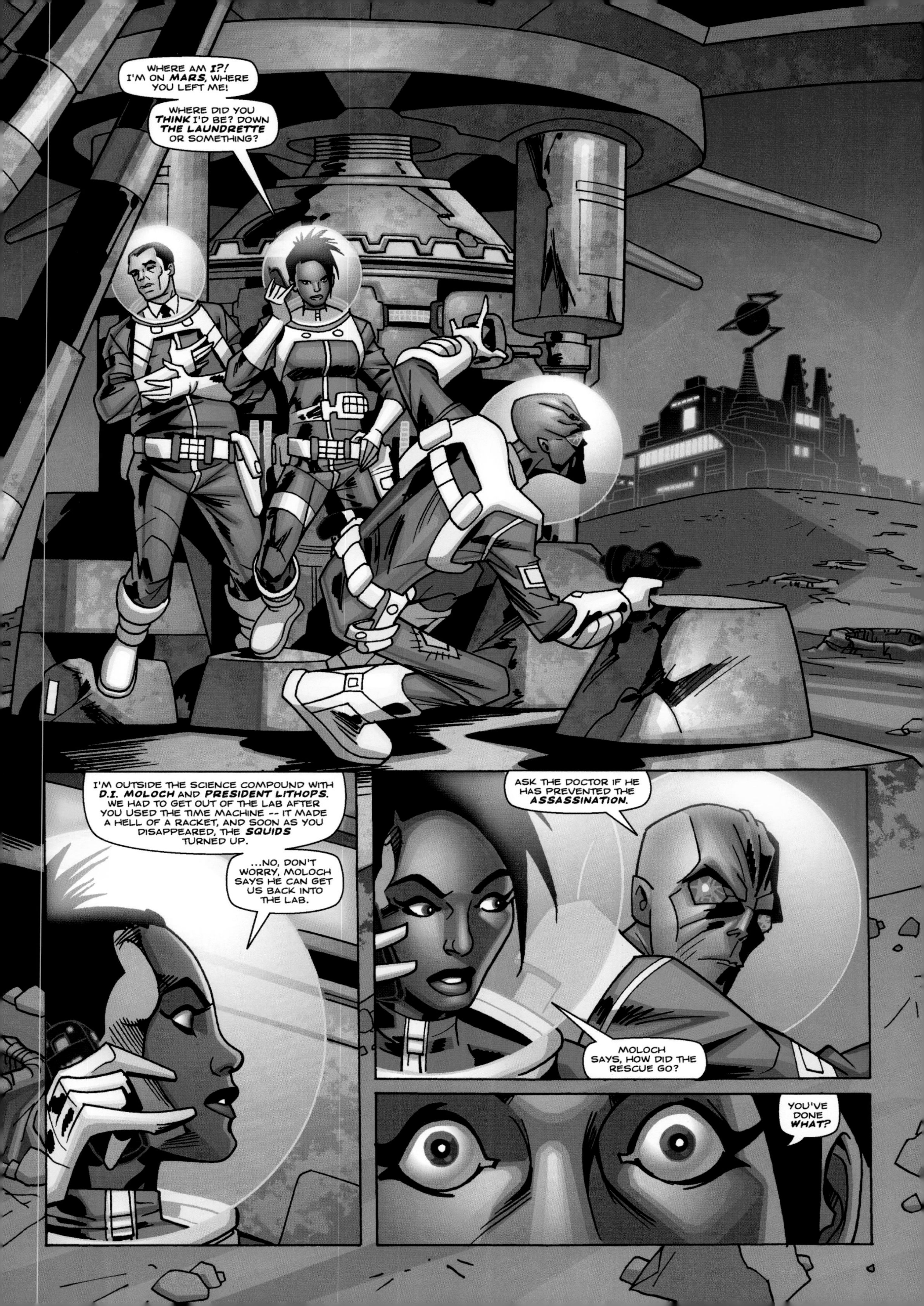
WHERE AM I?! I'M ON MARS, WHERE YOU LEFT ME!
WHERE DID YOU THINK I'D BE? DOWN THE LAUNDRETTE OR SOMETHING?
I'M OUTSIDE THE SCIENCE COMPOUND WITH D.I. MOLOCH AND PRESIDENT LITHOPS. WE HAD TO GET OUT OF THE LAB AFTER YOU USED THE TIME MACHINE -- IT MADE A HELL OF A RACKET, AND SOON AS YOU DISAPPEARED, THE SQUIDS TURNED UP.
...NO, DON'T WORRY, MOLOCH SAYS HE CAN GET US BACK INTO THE LAB.
ASK THE DOCTOR IF HE HAS PREVENTED THE ASSASSINATION.
MOLOCH SAYS, HOW DID THE RESCUE GO?
YOU'VE DONE WHAT?

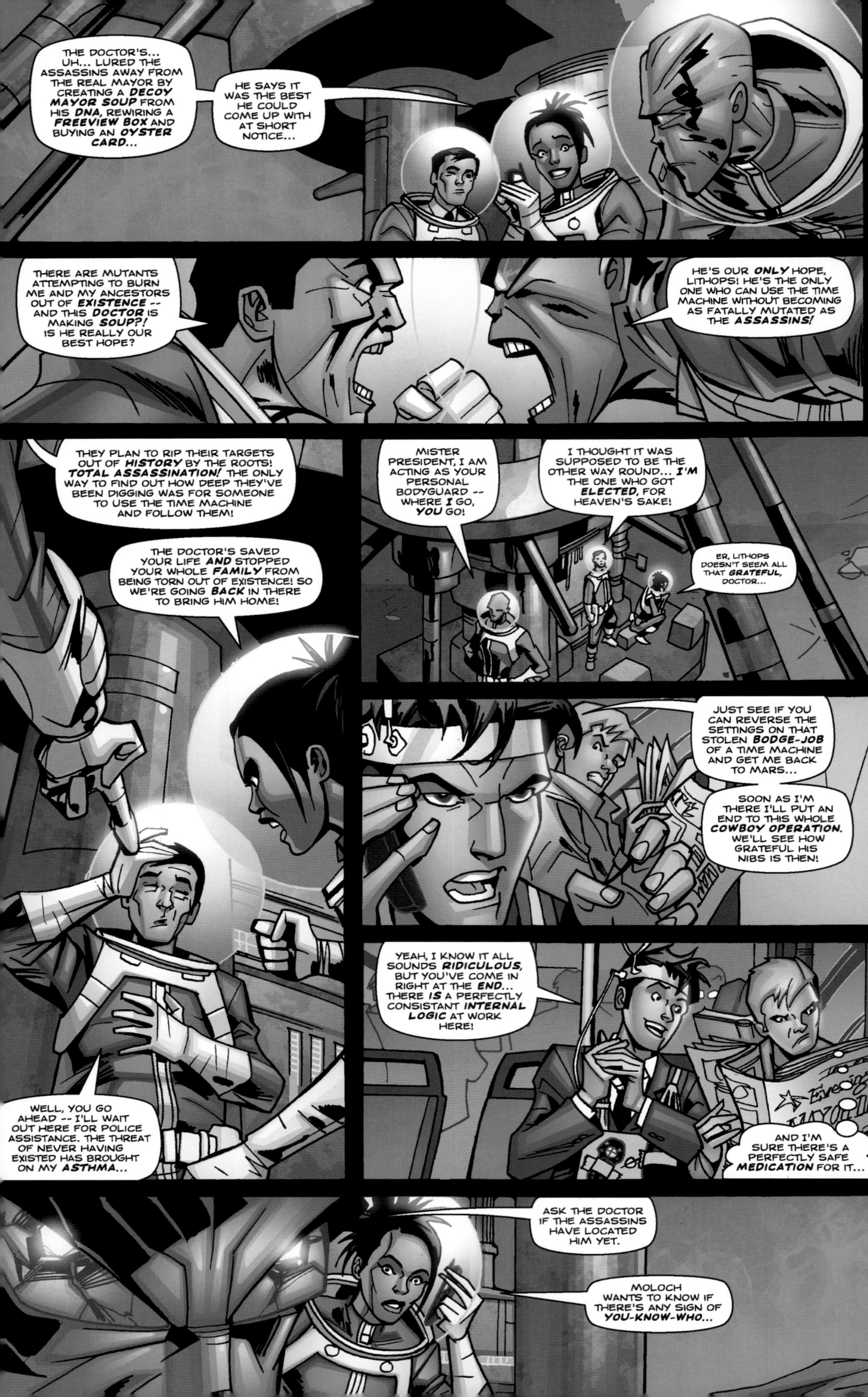
THE DOCTOR'S... UH... LURED THE ASSASSINS AWAY FROM THE REAL MAYOR BY CREATING A DECOY MAYOR SOUP FROM HIS DNA, REWIRING A FREEVIEW BOX AND BUYING AN OYSTER CARD...
HE SAYS IT WAS THE BEST HE COULD COME UP WITH AT SHORT NOTICE...
THERE ARE MUTANTS ATTEMPTING TO BURN ME AND MY ANCESTORS OUT OF EXISTENCE -- AND THIS DOCTOR IS MAKING SOUP?! IS HE REALLY OUR BEST HOPE?
HE'S OUR ONLY HOPE, LITHOPS! HE'S THE ONLY ONE WHO CAN USE THE TIME MACHINE WITHOUT BECOMING AS FATALLY MUTATED AS THE ASSASSINS!
THEY PLAN TO RIP THEIR TARGETS OUT OF HISTORY BY THE ROOTS! TOTAL ASSASSINATION! THE ONLY WAY TO FIND OUT HOW DEEP THEY'VE BEEN DIGGING WAS FOR SOMEONE TO USE THE TIME MACHINE AND FOLLOW THEM!
THE DOCTOR'S SAVED YOUR LIFE AND STOPPED YOUR WHOLE FAMILY FROM BEING TORN OUT OF EXISTENCE! SO WE'RE GOING BACK IN THERE TO BRING HIM HOME!
WELL, YOU GO AHEAD -- I'LL WAIT OUT HERE FOR POLICE ASSISTANCE. THE THREAT OF NEVER HAVING EXISTED HAS BROUGHT ON MY ASTHMA...
MISTER PRESIDENT, I AM ACTING AS YOUR PERSONAL BODYGUARD -- WHERE I GO, YOU GO!
I THOUGHT IT WAS SUPPOSED TO BE THE OTHER WAY ROUND... I'M THE ONE WHO GOT ELECTED, FOR HEAVEN'S SAKE!
ER, LITHOPS DOESN'T SEEM ALL THAT GRATEFUL, DOCTOR...
JUST SEE IF YOU CAN REVERSE THE SETTINGS ON THAT STOLEN BODGE-JOB OF A TIME MACHINE AND GET ME BACK TO MARS...
SOON AS I'M THERE I'LL PUT AN END TO THIS WHOLE COWBOY OPERATION. WE'LL SEE HOW GRATEFUL HIS NIBS IS THEN!
YEAH, I KNOW IT ALL SOUNDS RIDICULOUS, BUT YOU'VE COME IN RIGHT AT THE END... THERE IS A PERFECTLY CONSISTANT INTERNAL LOGIC AT WORK HERE!
AND I'M SURE THERE'S A PERFECTLY SAFE MEDICATION FOR IT...
ASK THE DOCTOR IF THE ASSASSINS HAVE LOCATED HIM YET.
MOLOCH WANTS TO KNOW IF THERE'S ANY SIGN OF YOU-KNOW-WHO...

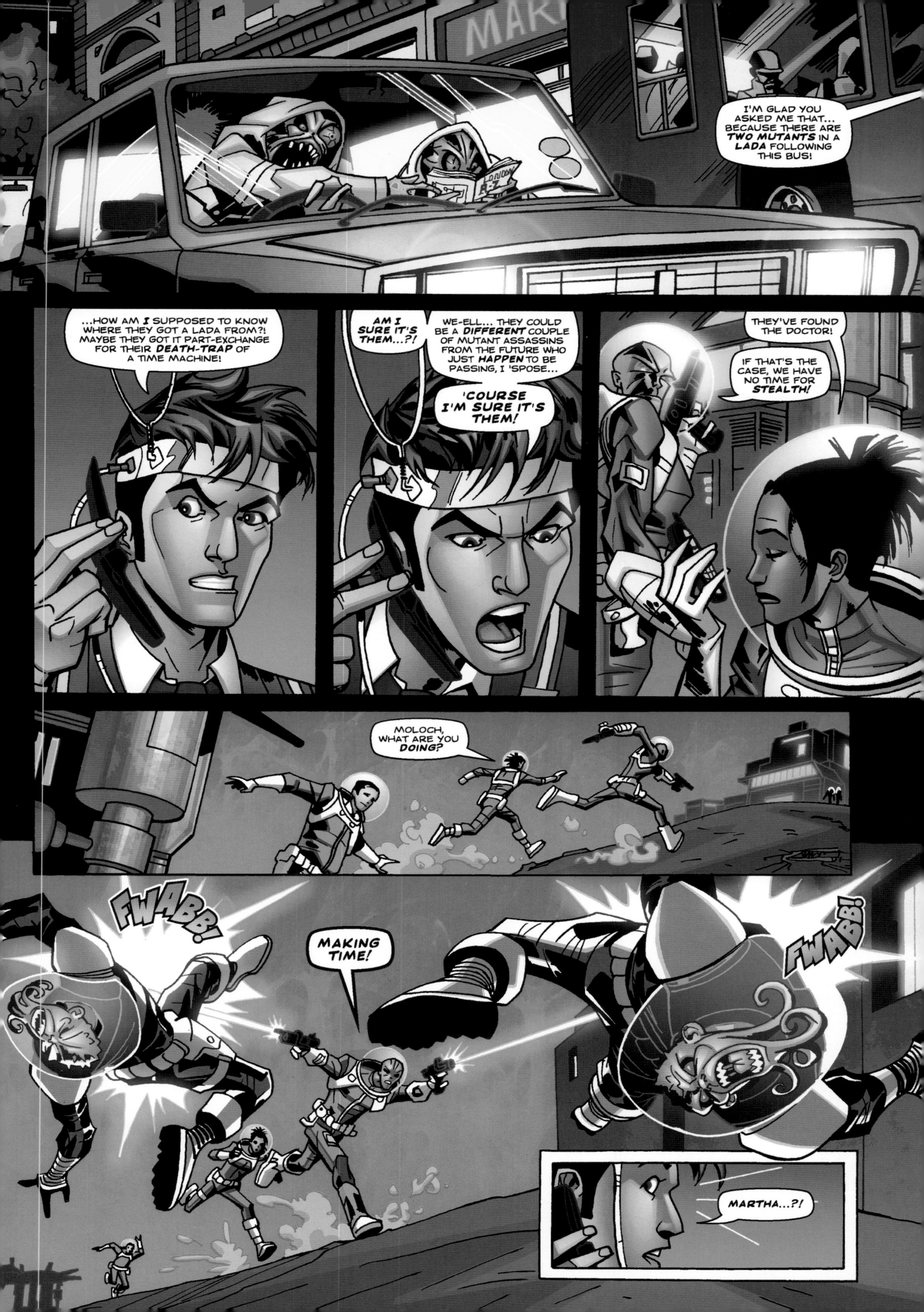
I'M GLAD YOU ASKED ME THAT... BECAUSE THERE ARE TWO MUTANTS IN A LADA FOLLOWING THIS BUS!
...HOW AM I SUPPOSED TO KNOW WHERE THEY GOT A LADA FROM?! MAYBE THEY GOT IT PART-EXCHANGE FOR THEIR DEATH-TRAP OF A TIME MACHINE!
AM I SURE IT'S THEM...?!
WE-ELL... THEY COULD BE A DIFFERENT COUPLE OF MUTANT ASSASSINS FROM THE FUTURE WHO JUST HAPPEN TO BE PASSING, I 'SPOSE...
'COURSE I'M SURE IT'S THEM!
THEY'VE FOUND THE DOCTOR!
IF THAT'S THE CASE, WE HAVE NO TIME FOR STEALTH!
MOLOCH, WHAT ARE YOU DOING?
FWABB!
MAKING TIME!
FWABB!
MARTHA...?!

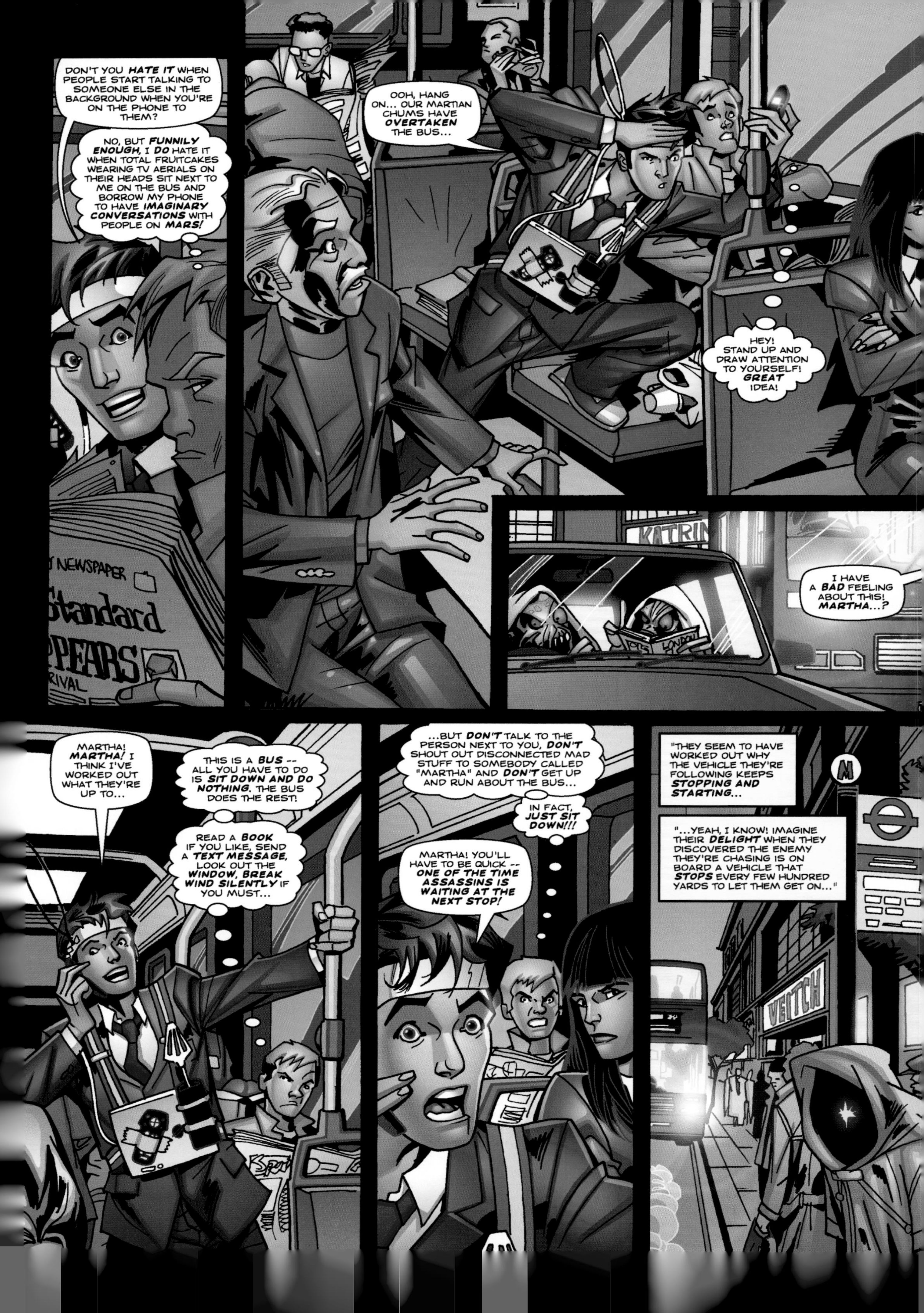

DON'T YOU HATE IT WHEN PEOPLE START TALKING TO SOMEONE ELSE IN THE BACKGROUND WHEN YOU'RE ON THE PHONE TO THEM?
NO, BUT FUNNILY ENOUGH, I DO HATE IT WHEN TOTAL FRUITCAKES WEARING TV AERIALS ON THEIR HEADS SIT NEXT TO ME ON THE BUS AND BORROW MY PHONE TO HAVE IMAGINARY CONVERSATIONS WITH PEOPLE ON MARS!
OOH, HANG ON... OUR MARTIAN CHUMS HAVE OVERTAKEN THE BUS...
HEY! STAND UP AND DRAW ATTENTION TO YOURSELF! GREAT IDEA!
Standard
I HAVE A BAD FEELING ABOUT THIS! MARTHA...?
MARTHA! MARTHA! I THINK I'VE WORKED OUT WHAT THEY'RE UP TO...
THIS IS A BUS -- ALL YOU HAVE TO DO IS SIT DOWN AND DO NOTHING. THE BUS DOES THE REST!
READ A BOOK IF YOU LIKE, SEND A TEXT MESSAGE, LOOK OUT THE WINDOW, BREAK WIND SILENTLY IF YOU MUST...
...BUT DON'T TALK TO THE PERSON NEXT TO YOU, DON'T SHOUT OUT DISCONNECTED MAD STUFF TO SOMEBODY CALLED "MARTHA" AND DON'T GET UP AND RUN ABOUT THE BUS...
IN FACT, JUST SIT DOWN!!!
MARTHA! YOU'LL HAVE TO BE QUICK -- ONE OF THE TIME ASSASSINS IS WAITING AT THE NEXT STOP!
"THEY SEEM TO HAVE WORKED OUT WHY THE VEHICLE THEY'RE FOLLOWING KEEPS STOPPING AND STARTING...
"...YEAH, I KNOW! IMAGINE THEIR DELIGHT WHEN THEY DISCOVERED THE ENEMY THEY'RE CHASING IS ON BOARD A VEHICLE THAT STOPS EVERY FEW HUNDRED YARDS TO LET THEM GET ON..."
VEITCH

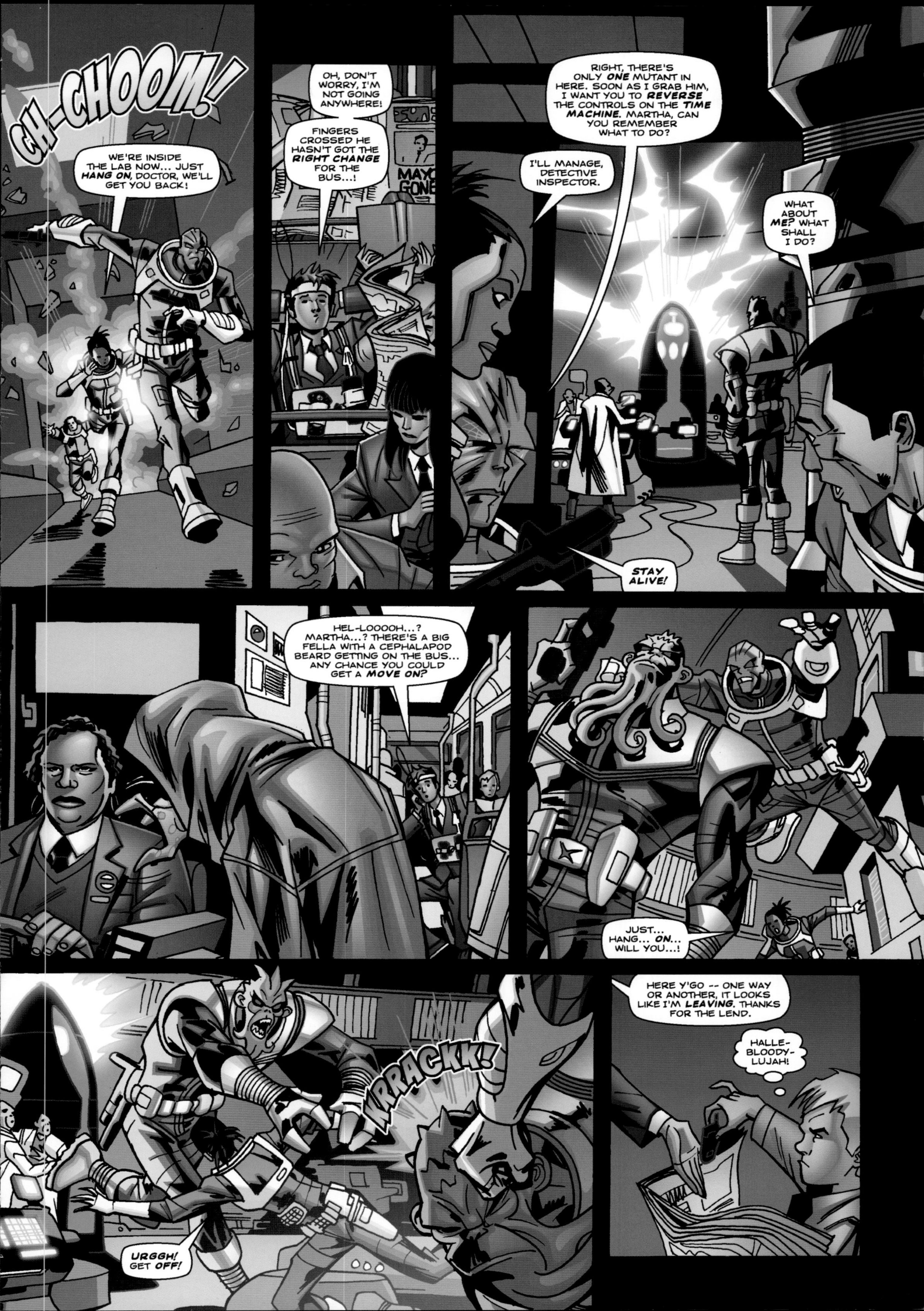

CH-CHOOM!
WE'RE INSIDE THE LAB NOW... JUST HANG ON, DOCTOR, WE'LL GET YOU BACK!
OH, DON'T WORRY, I'M NOT GOING ANYWHERE!
FINGERS CROSSED HE HASN'T GOT THE RIGHT CHANGE FOR THE BUS...!
MAYO GONE
RIGHT, THERE'S ONLY ONE MUTANT IN HERE. SOON AS I GRAB HIM, I WANT YOU TO REVERSE THE CONTROLS ON THE TIME MACHINE. MARTHA, CAN YOU REMEMBER WHAT TO DO?
I'LL MANAGE, DETECTIVE INSPECTOR.
WHAT ABOUT ME? WHAT SHALL I DO?
STAY ALIVE!
HEL-LOOOOH...? MARTHA...? THERE'S A BIG FELLA WITH A CEPHALAPOD BEARD GETTING ON THE BUS... ANY CHANCE YOU COULD GET A MOVE ON?
JUST... HANG... ON... WILL YOU...!
KRRACKK!
URGGH! GET OFF!
HERE Y'GO -- ONE WAY OR ANOTHER, IT LOOKS LIKE I'M LEAVING. THANKS FOR THE LEND.
HALLE-BLOODY-LUJAH!

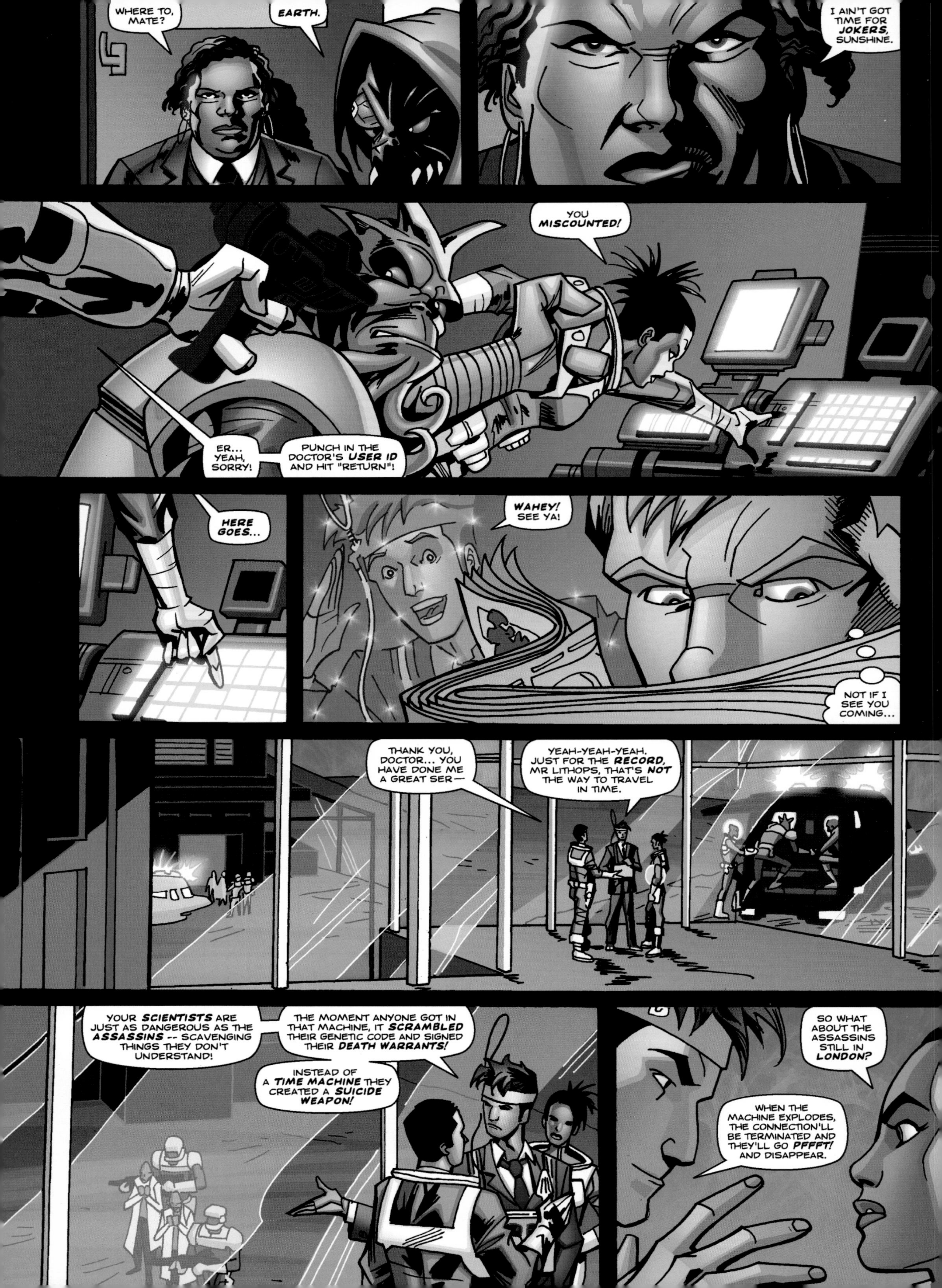

WHERE TO, MATE?
EARTH.
I AIN'T GOT TIME FOR JOKERS, SUNSHINE.
YOU MISCOUNTED!
ER... YEAH, SORRY!
PUNCH IN THE DOCTOR'S USER ID AND HIT "RETURN"!
HERE GOES...
WAHEY! SEE YA!
NOT IF I SEE YOU COMING...
THANK YOU, DOCTOR... YOU HAVE DONE ME A GREAT SER—
YEAH-YEAH-YEAH. JUST FOR THE RECORD, MR LITHOPS, THAT'S NOT THE WAY TO TRAVEL IN TIME.
YOUR SCIENTISTS ARE JUST AS DANGEROUS AS THE ASSASSINS -- SCAVENGING THINGS THEY DON'T UNDERSTAND!
THE MOMENT ANYONE GOT IN THAT MACHINE, IT SCRAMBLED THEIR GENETIC CODE AND SIGNED THEIR DEATH WARRANTS!
INSTEAD OF A TIME MACHINE THEY CREATED A SUICIDE WEAPON!
SO WHAT ABOUT THE ASSASSINS STILL IN LONDON?
WHEN THE MACHINE EXPLODES, THE CONNECTION'LL BE TERMINATED AND THEY'LL GO PFFFT! AND DISAPPEAR.

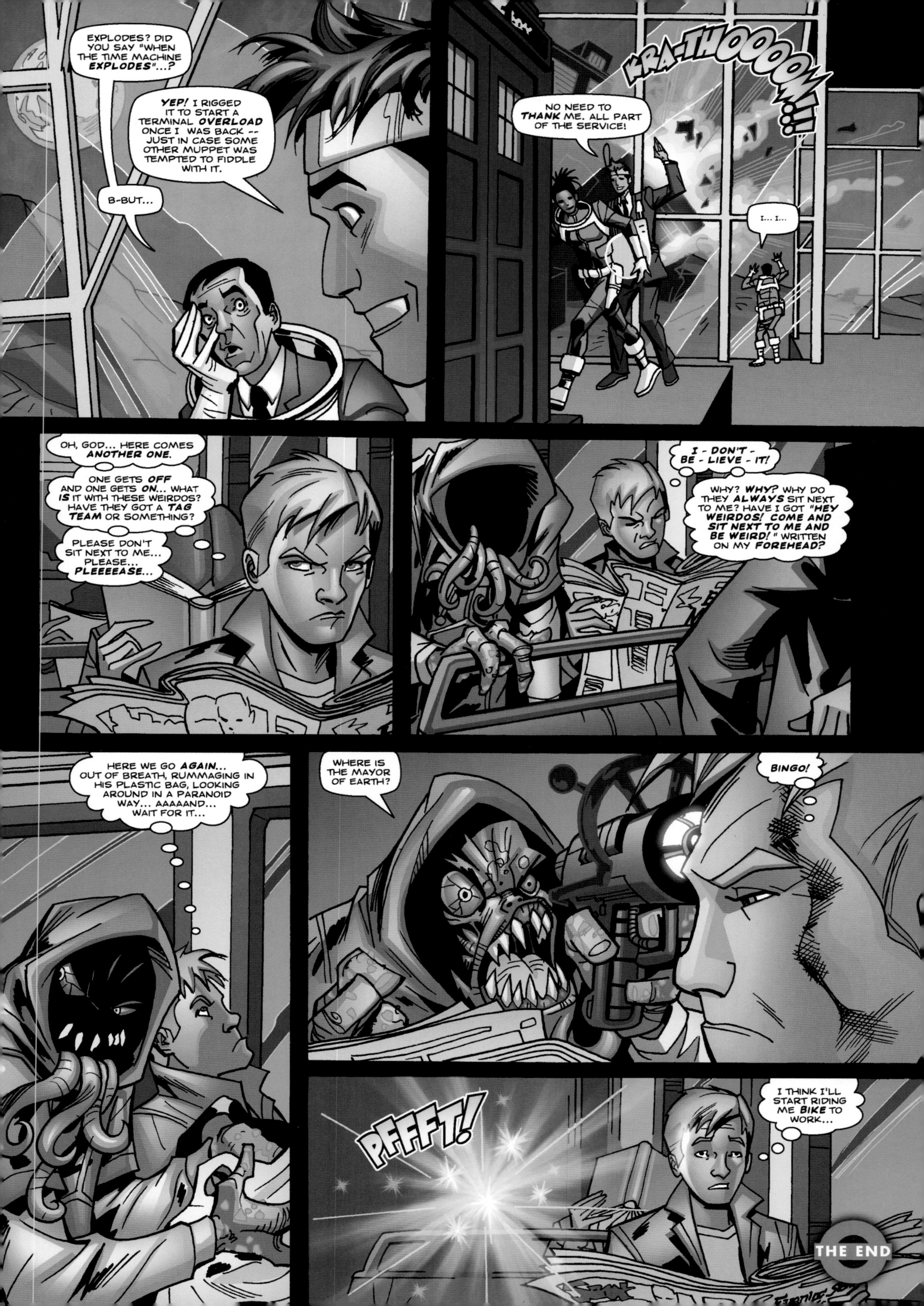

EXPLODES? DID YOU SAY "WHEN THE TIME MACHINE EXPLODES"...?
YEP! I RIGGED IT TO START A TERMINAL OVERLOAD ONCE I WAS BACK -- JUST IN CASE SOME OTHER MUPPET WAS TEMPTED TO FIDDLE WITH IT.
B-BUT...
KRA-THOOOOM!!!
NO NEED TO THANK ME. ALL PART OF THE SERVICE!
I... I...
OH, GOD... HERE COMES ANOTHER ONE.
ONE GETS OFF AND ONE GETS ON... WHAT IS IT WITH THESE WEIRDOS? HAVE THEY GOT A TAG TEAM OR SOMETHING?
PLEASE DON'T SIT NEXT TO ME... PLEASE... PLEEEEASE...
I - DON'T - BE - LIEVE - IT!
WHY? WHY? WHY DO THEY ALWAYS SIT NEXT TO ME? HAVE I GOT "HEY WEIRDOS! COME AND SIT NEXT TO ME AND BE WEIRD!" WRITTEN ON MY FOREHEAD?
HERE WE GO AGAIN... OUT OF BREATH, RUMMAGING IN HIS PLASTIC BAG, LOOKING AROUND IN A PARANOID WAY... AAAAAND... WAIT FOR IT...
WHERE IS THE MAYOR OF EARTH?
BINGO!
PFFFT!
I THINK I'LL START RIDING ME BIKE TO WORK...
THE END

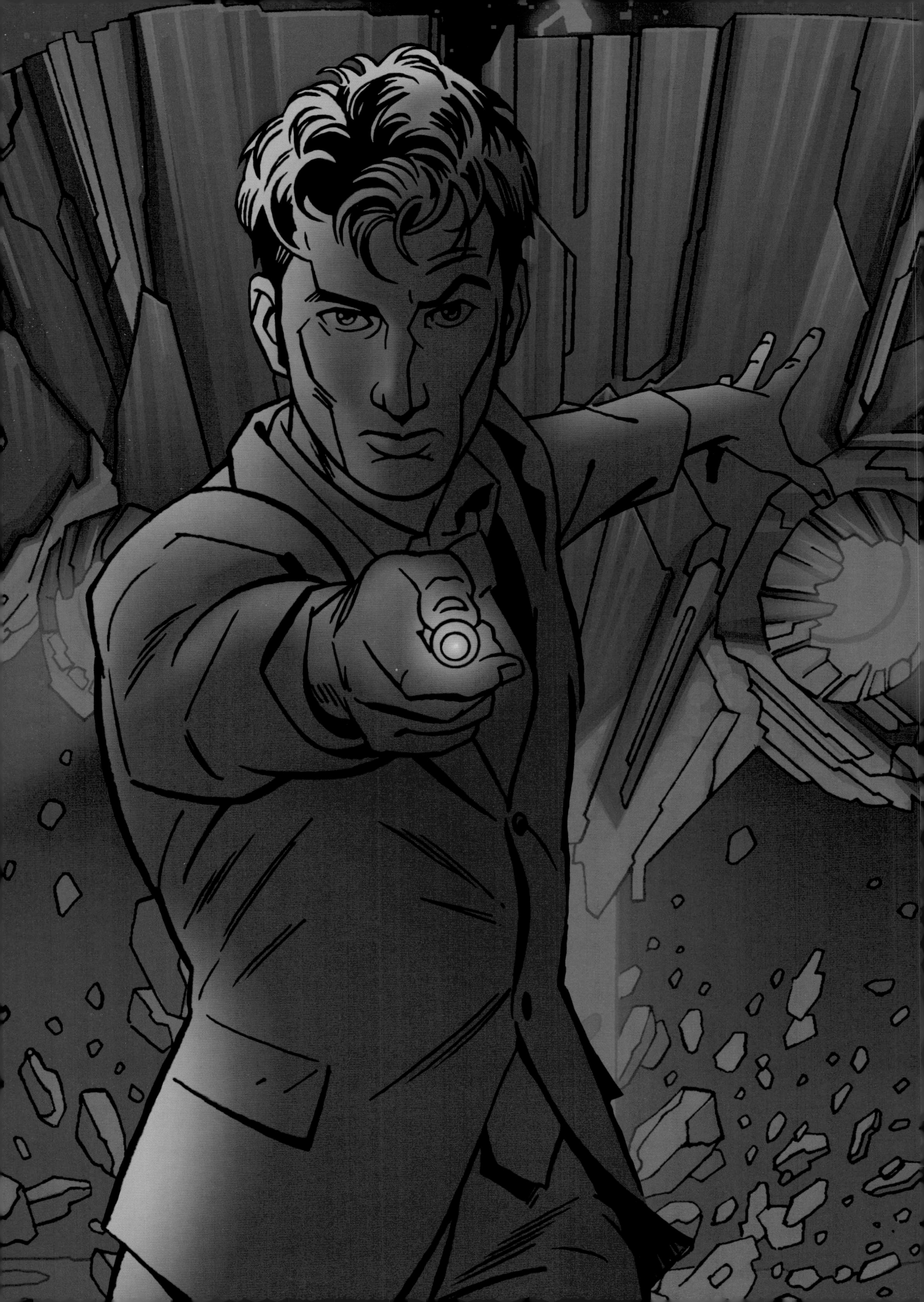

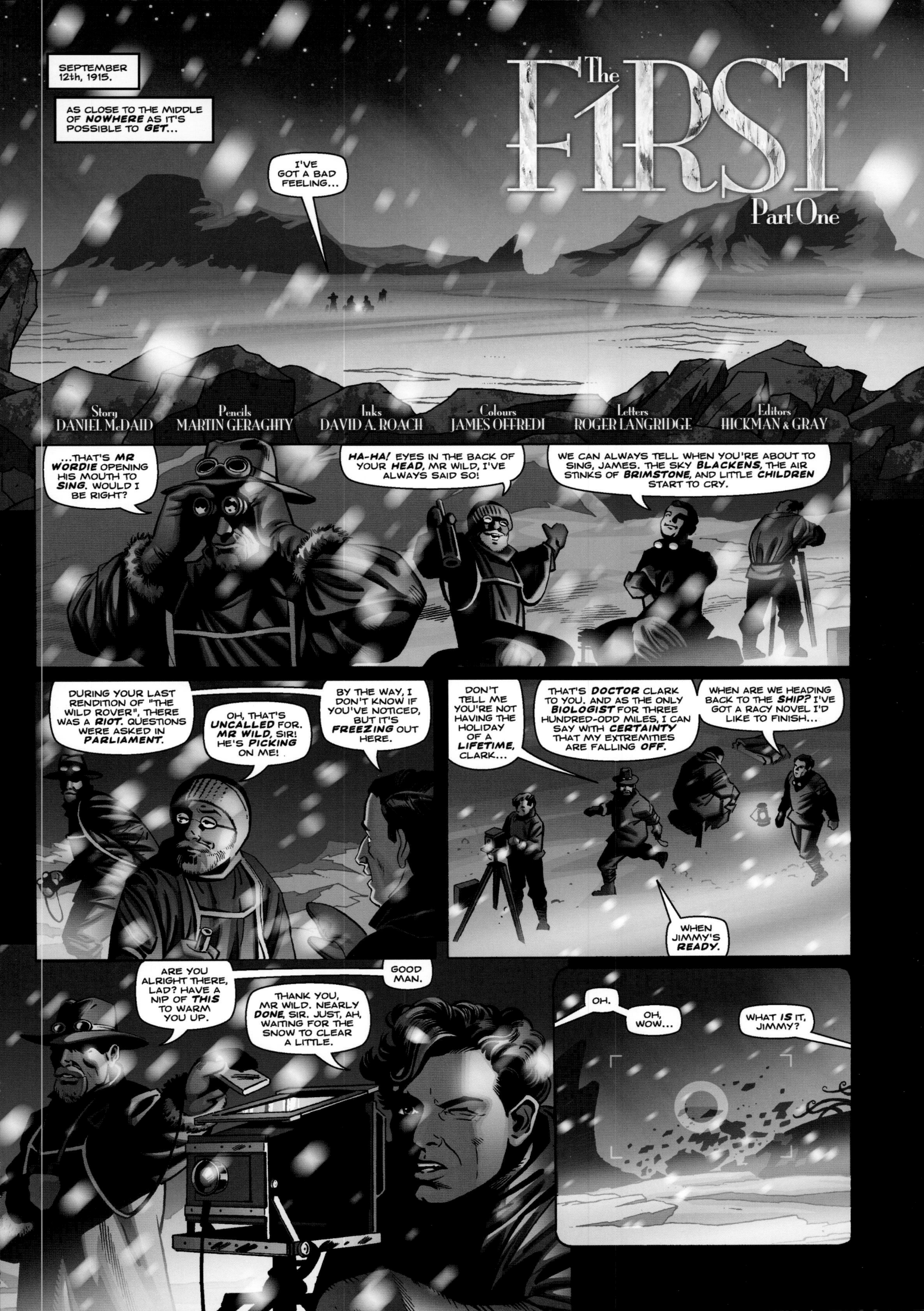
SEPTEMBER 12th, 1915.
AS CLOSE TO THE MIDDLE OF NOWHERE AS IT'S POSSIBLE TO GET...
I'VE GOT A BAD FEELING...
The FIRST Part One
Story DANIEL McDAID
Pencils MARTIN GERAGHTY
Inks DAVID A. ROACH
Colours JAMES OFFREDI
Letters ROGER LANGRIDGE
Editors HICKMAN & GRAY
...THAT'S MR WORDIE OPENING HIS MOUTH TO SING. WOULD I BE RIGHT?
HA-HA! EYES IN THE BACK OF YOUR HEAD, MR WILD, I'VE ALWAYS SAID SO!
WE CAN ALWAYS TELL WHEN YOU'RE ABOUT TO SING, JAMES. THE SKY BLACKENS, THE AIR STINKS OF BRIMSTONE, AND LITTLE CHILDREN START TO CRY.
DURING YOUR LAST RENDITION OF "THE WILD ROVER", THERE WAS A RIOT. QUESTIONS WERE ASKED IN PARLIAMENT.
OH, THAT'S UNCALLED FOR. MR WILD, SIR! HE'S PICKING ON ME!
BY THE WAY, I DON'T KNOW IF YOU'VE NOTICED, BUT IT'S FREEZING OUT HERE.
DON'T TELL ME YOU'RE NOT HAVING THE HOLIDAY OF A LIFETIME, CLARK...
THAT'S DOCTOR CLARK TO YOU. AND AS THE ONLY BIOLOGIST FOR THREE HUNDRED-ODD MILES, I CAN SAY WITH CERTAINTY THAT MY EXTREMITIES ARE FALLING OFF.
WHEN ARE WE HEADING BACK TO THE SHIP? I'VE GOT A RACY NOVEL I'D LIKE TO FINISH...
WHEN JIMMY'S READY.
ARE YOU ALRIGHT THERE, LAD? HAVE A NIP OF THIS TO WARM YOU UP.
GOOD MAN.
THANK YOU, MR WILD. NEARLY DONE, SIR. JUST, AH, WAITING FOR THE SNOW TO CLEAR A LITTLE.
OH.
OH, WOW...
WHAT IS IT, JIMMY?

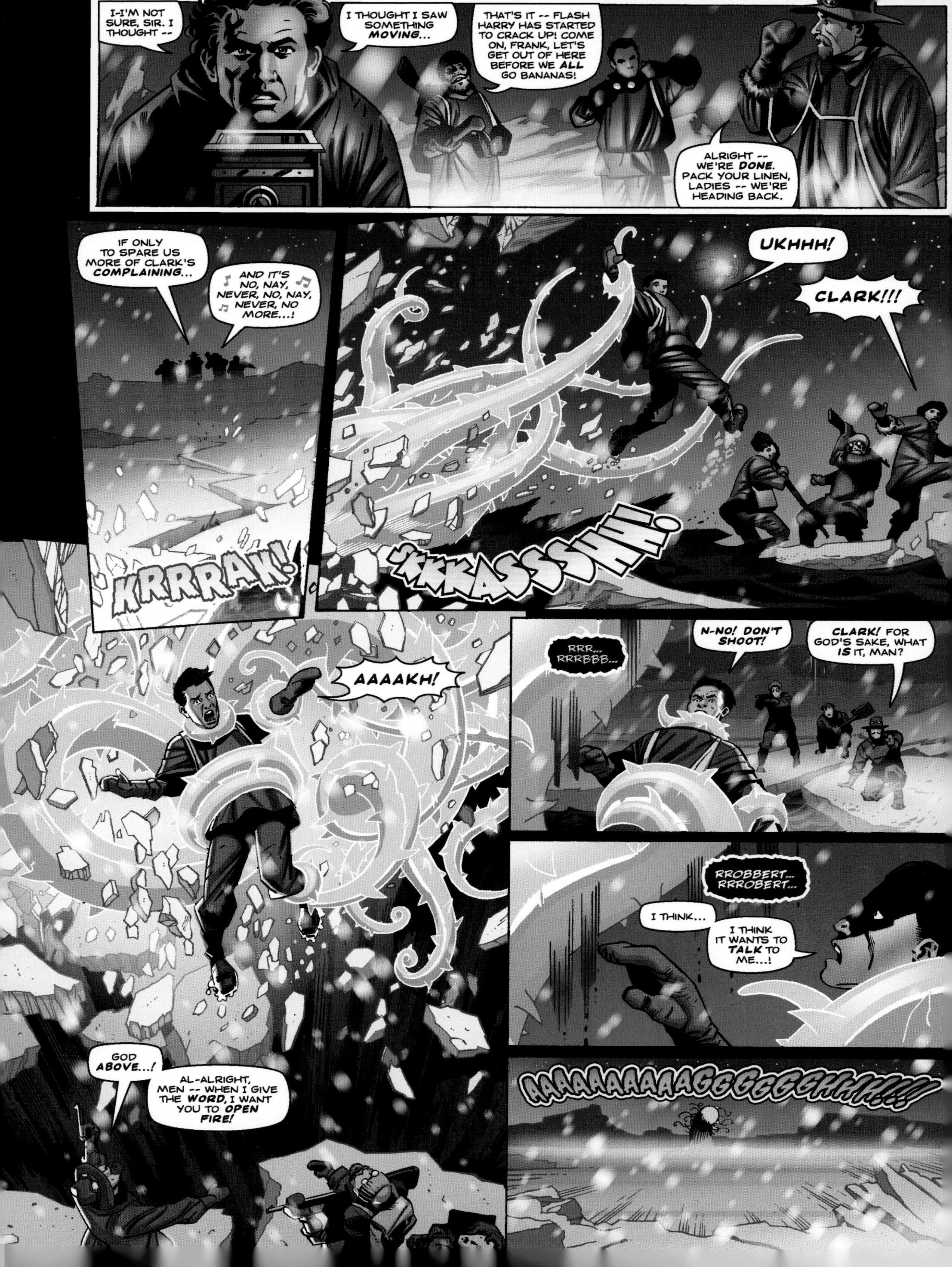

I-I'M NOT SURE, SIR. I THOUGHT --
I THOUGHT I SAW SOMETHING MOVING...
THAT'S IT -- FLASH HARRY HAS STARTED TO CRACK UP! COME ON, FRANK, LET'S GET OUT OF HERE BEFORE WE ALL GO BANANAS!
ALRIGHT -- WE'RE DONE. PACK YOUR LINEN, LADIES -- WE'RE HEADING BACK.
IF ONLY TO SPARE US MORE OF CLARK'S COMPLAINING...
AND IT'S NO, NAY, NEVER, NO, NAY, NEVER, NO MORE...!
KRRRAK!
UKHHH!
CLARK!!!
SKKKASSSSHH!
AAAAKH!
RRR... RRRBBB...
N-NO! DON'T SHOOT!
CLARK! FOR GOD'S SAKE, WHAT IS IT, MAN?
RROBBERT... RRROBERT...
I THINK...
I THINK IT WANTS TO TALK TO ME...!
GOD ABOVE...!
AL-ALRIGHT, MEN -- WHEN I GIVE THE WORD, I WANT YOU TO OPEN FIRE!
AAAAAAAAAAGGGGGGHHH!!!

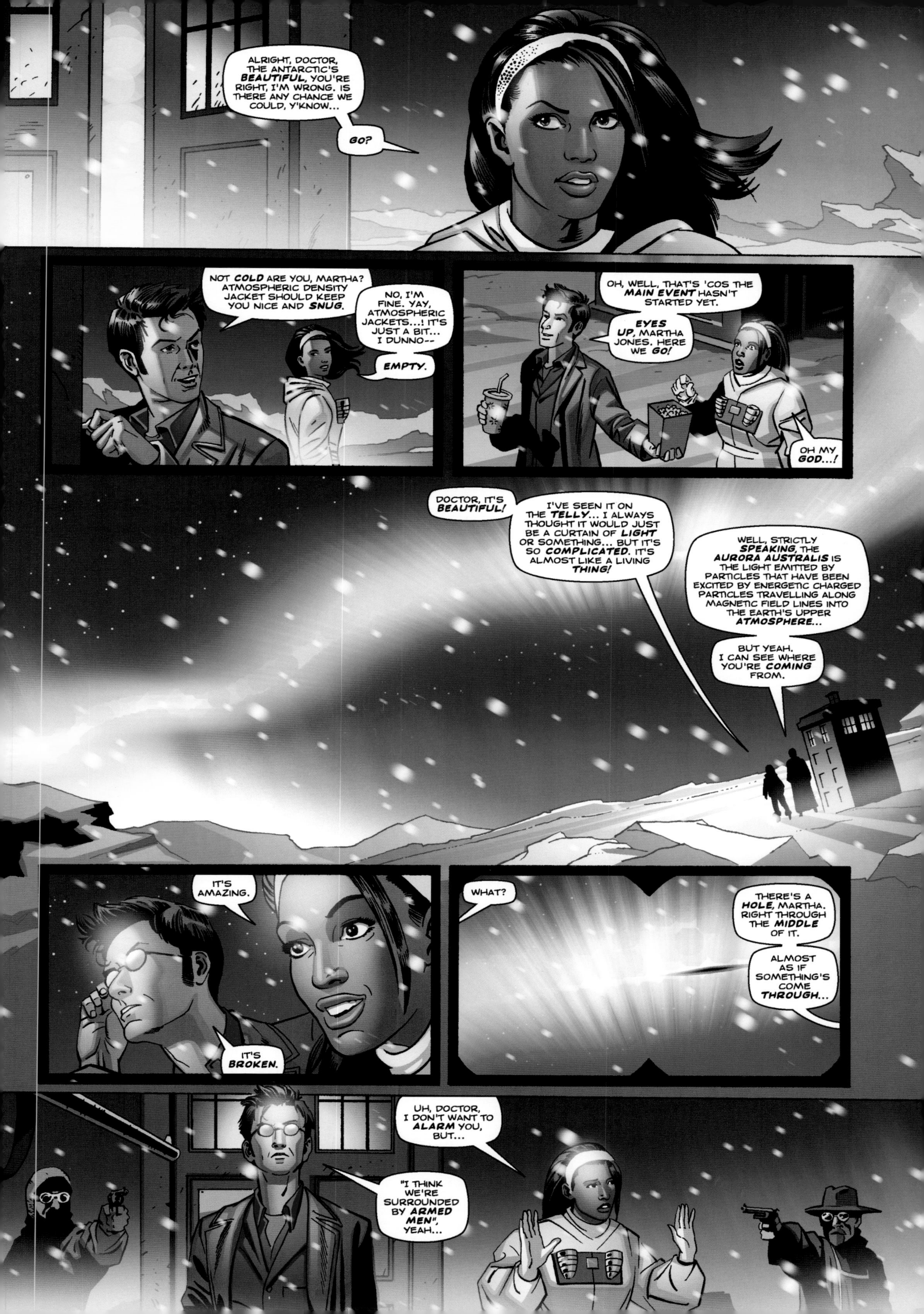
ALRIGHT, DOCTOR, THE ANTARCTIC'S BEAUTIFUL, YOU'RE RIGHT, I'M WRONG. IS THERE ANY CHANCE WE COULD, Y'KNOW...
GO?
NOT COLD ARE YOU, MARTHA? ATMOSPHERIC DENSITY JACKET SHOULD KEEP YOU NICE AND SNUG.
NO, I'M FINE. YAY, ATMOSPHERIC JACKETS...! IT'S JUST A BIT... I DUNNO--
EMPTY.
OH, WELL, THAT'S 'COS THE MAIN EVENT HASN'T STARTED YET.
EYES UP, MARTHA JONES. HERE WE GO!
OH MY GOD...!
DOCTOR, IT'S BEAUTIFUL!
I'VE SEEN IT ON THE TELLY... I ALWAYS THOUGHT IT WOULD JUST BE A CURTAIN OF LIGHT OR SOMETHING... BUT IT'S SO COMPLICATED. IT'S ALMOST LIKE A LIVING THING!
WELL, STRICTLY SPEAKING, THE AURORA AUSTRALIS IS THE LIGHT EMITTED BY PARTICLES THAT HAVE BEEN EXCITED BY ENERGETIC CHARGED PARTICLES TRAVELLING ALONG MAGNETIC FIELD LINES INTO THE EARTH'S UPPER ATMOSPHERE...
BUT YEAH. I CAN SEE WHERE YOU'RE COMING FROM.
IT'S AMAZING.
IT'S BROKEN.
WHAT?
THERE'S A HOLE, MARTHA. RIGHT THROUGH THE MIDDLE OF IT.
ALMOST AS IF SOMETHING'S COME THROUGH...
UH, DOCTOR, I DON'T WANT TO ALARM YOU, BUT...
"I THINK WE'RE SURROUNDED BY ARMED MEN", YEAH...

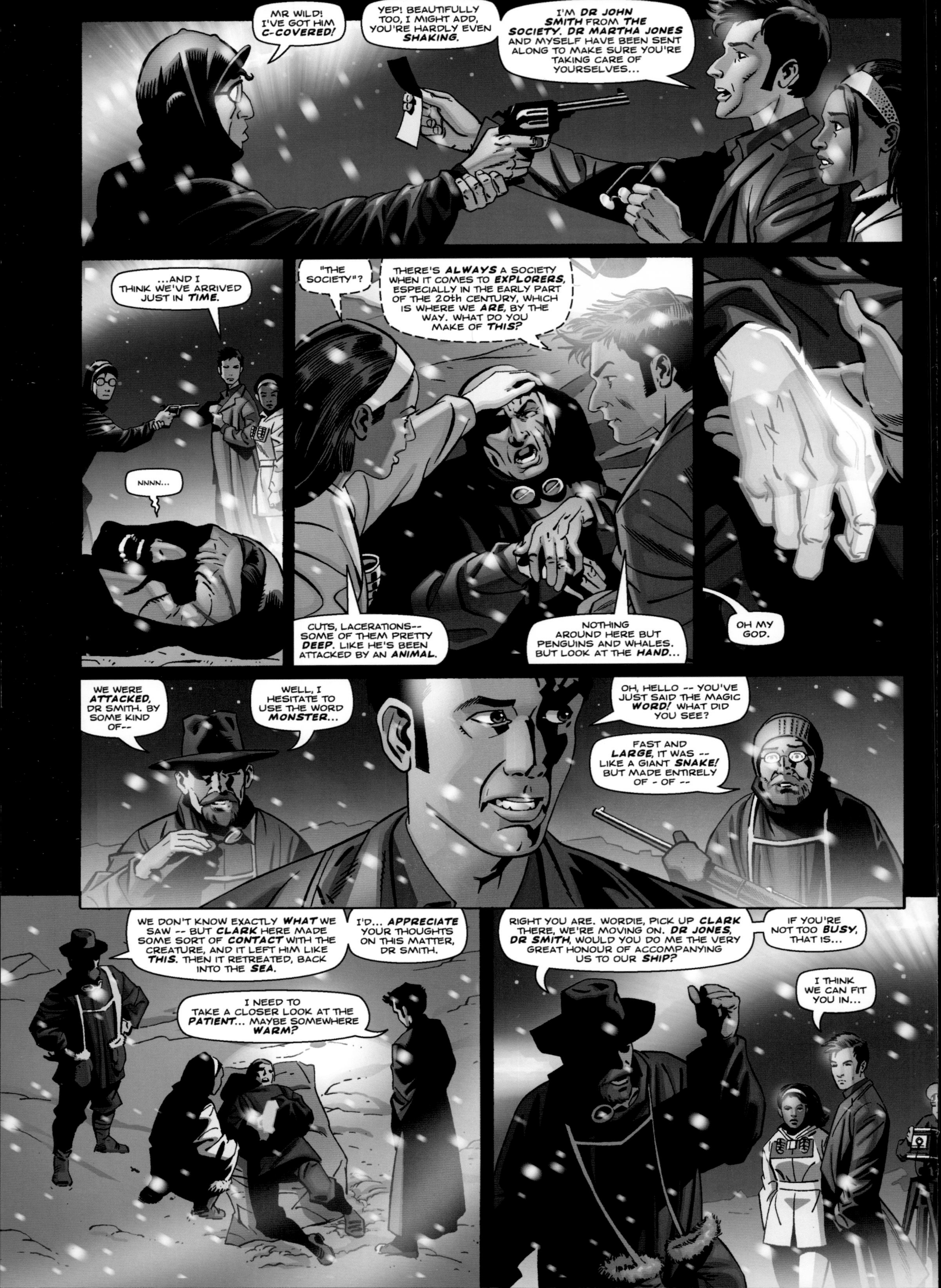
MR WILD! I'VE GOT HIM C-COVERED!
YEP! BEAUTIFULLY TOO, I MIGHT ADD, YOU'RE HARDLY EVEN SHAKING.
I'M DR JOHN SMITH FROM THE SOCIETY. DR MARTHA JONES AND MYSELF HAVE BEEN SENT ALONG TO MAKE SURE YOU'RE TAKING CARE OF YOURSELVES...
...AND I THINK WE'VE ARRIVED JUST IN TIME.
NNNN...
"THE SOCIETY"?
THERE'S ALWAYS A SOCIETY WHEN IT COMES TO EXPLORERS, ESPECIALLY IN THE EARLY PART OF THE 20th CENTURY, WHICH IS WHERE WE ARE, BY THE WAY. WHAT DO YOU MAKE OF THIS?
CUTS, LACERATIONS-- SOME OF THEM PRETTY DEEP. LIKE HE'S BEEN ATTACKED BY AN ANIMAL.
NOTHING AROUND HERE BUT PENGUINS AND WHALES. BUT LOOK AT THE HAND...
OH MY GOD.
WE WERE ATTACKED, DR SMITH. BY SOME KIND OF--
WELL, I HESITATE TO USE THE WORD MONSTER...
OH, HELLO -- YOU'VE JUST SAID THE MAGIC WORD! WHAT DID YOU SEE?
FAST AND LARGE, IT WAS -- LIKE A GIANT SNAKE! BUT MADE ENTIRELY OF - OF --
WE DON'T KNOW EXACTLY WHAT WE SAW -- BUT CLARK HERE MADE SOME SORT OF CONTACT WITH THE CREATURE, AND IT LEFT HIM LIKE THIS. THEN IT RETREATED, BACK INTO THE SEA.
I'D... APPRECIATE YOUR THOUGHTS ON THIS MATTER, DR SMITH.
I NEED TO TAKE A CLOSER LOOK AT THE PATIENT... MAYBE SOMEWHERE WARM?
RIGHT YOU ARE. WORDIE, PICK UP CLARK THERE, WE'RE MOVING ON. DR JONES, DR SMITH, WOULD YOU DO ME THE VERY GREAT HONOUR OF ACCOMPANYING US TO OUR SHIP?
IF YOU'RE NOT TOO BUSY, THAT IS...
I THINK WE CAN FIT YOU IN...

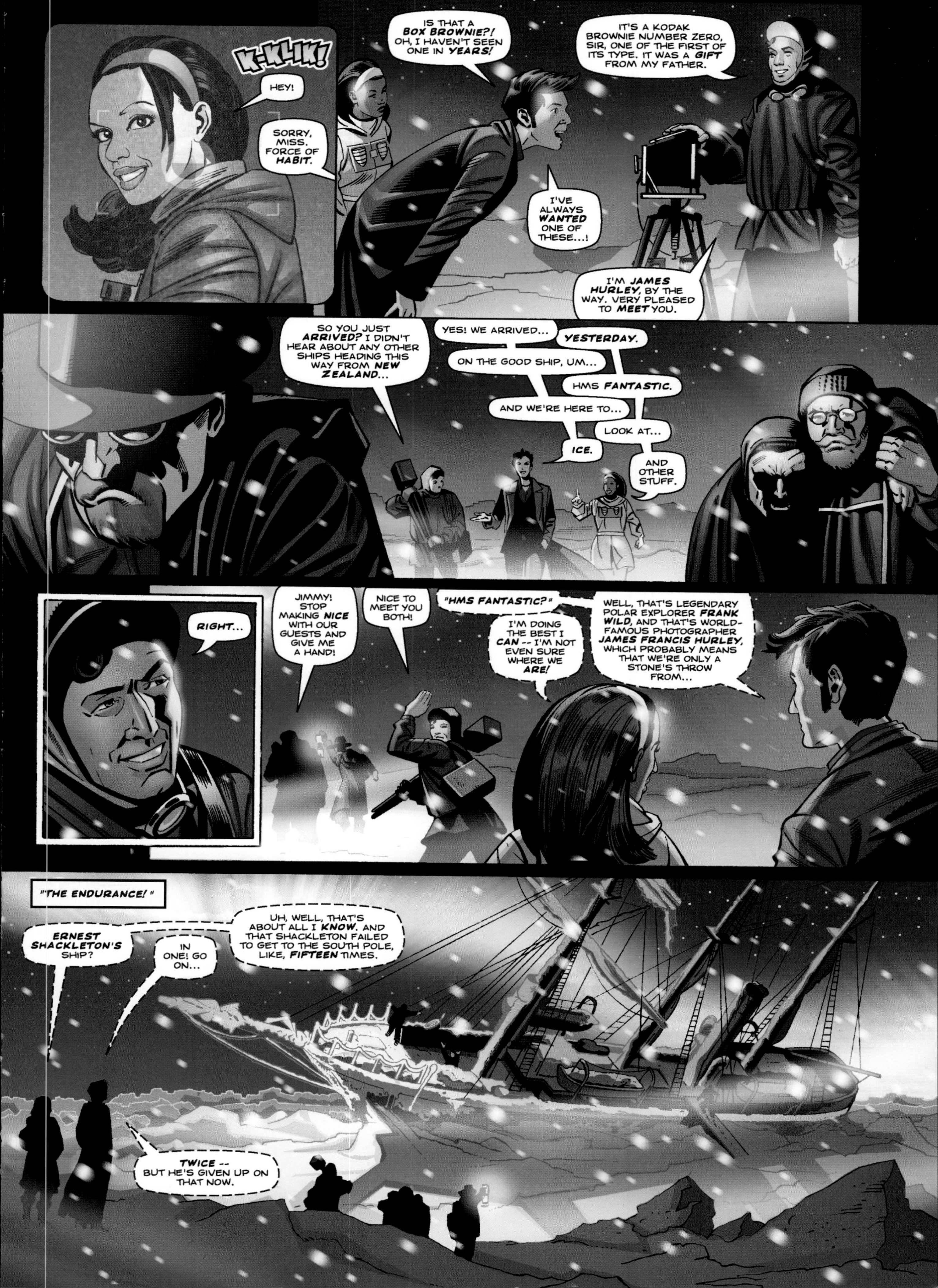
K-KLIK!
HEY!
SORRY, MISS. FORCE OF HABIT.
IS THAT A BOX BROWNIE?! OH, I HAVEN'T SEEN ONE IN YEARS!
IT'S A KODAK BROWNIE NUMBER ZERO, SIR, ONE OF THE FIRST OF ITS TYPE. IT WAS A GIFT FROM MY FATHER.
I'VE ALWAYS WANTED ONE OF THESE...!
I'M JAMES HURLEY, BY THE WAY. VERY PLEASED TO MEET YOU.
SO YOU JUST ARRIVED? I DIDN'T HEAR ABOUT ANY OTHER SHIPS HEADING THIS WAY FROM NEW ZEALAND...
YES! WE ARRIVED...
YESTERDAY.
ON THE GOOD SHIP, UM...
HMS FANTASTIC.
AND WE'RE HERE TO...
LOOK AT...
ICE.
AND OTHER STUFF.
RIGHT...
JIMMY! STOP MAKING NICE WITH OUR GUESTS AND GIVE ME A HAND!
NICE TO MEET YOU BOTH!
"HMS FANTASTIC?"
I'M DOING THE BEST I CAN -- I'M NOT EVEN SURE WHERE WE ARE!
WELL, THAT'S LEGENDARY POLAR EXPLORER FRANK WILD, AND THAT'S WORLD-FAMOUS PHOTOGRAPHER JAMES FRANCIS HURLEY, WHICH PROBABLY MEANS THAT WE'RE ONLY A STONE'S THROW FROM...
"THE ENDURANCE!"
ERNEST SHACKLETON'S SHIP?
UH, WELL, THAT'S ABOUT ALL I KNOW. AND THAT SHACKLETON FAILED TO GET TO THE SOUTH POLE, LIKE, FIFTEEN TIMES.
IN ONE! GO ON...
TWICE -- BUT HE'S GIVEN UP ON THAT NOW.

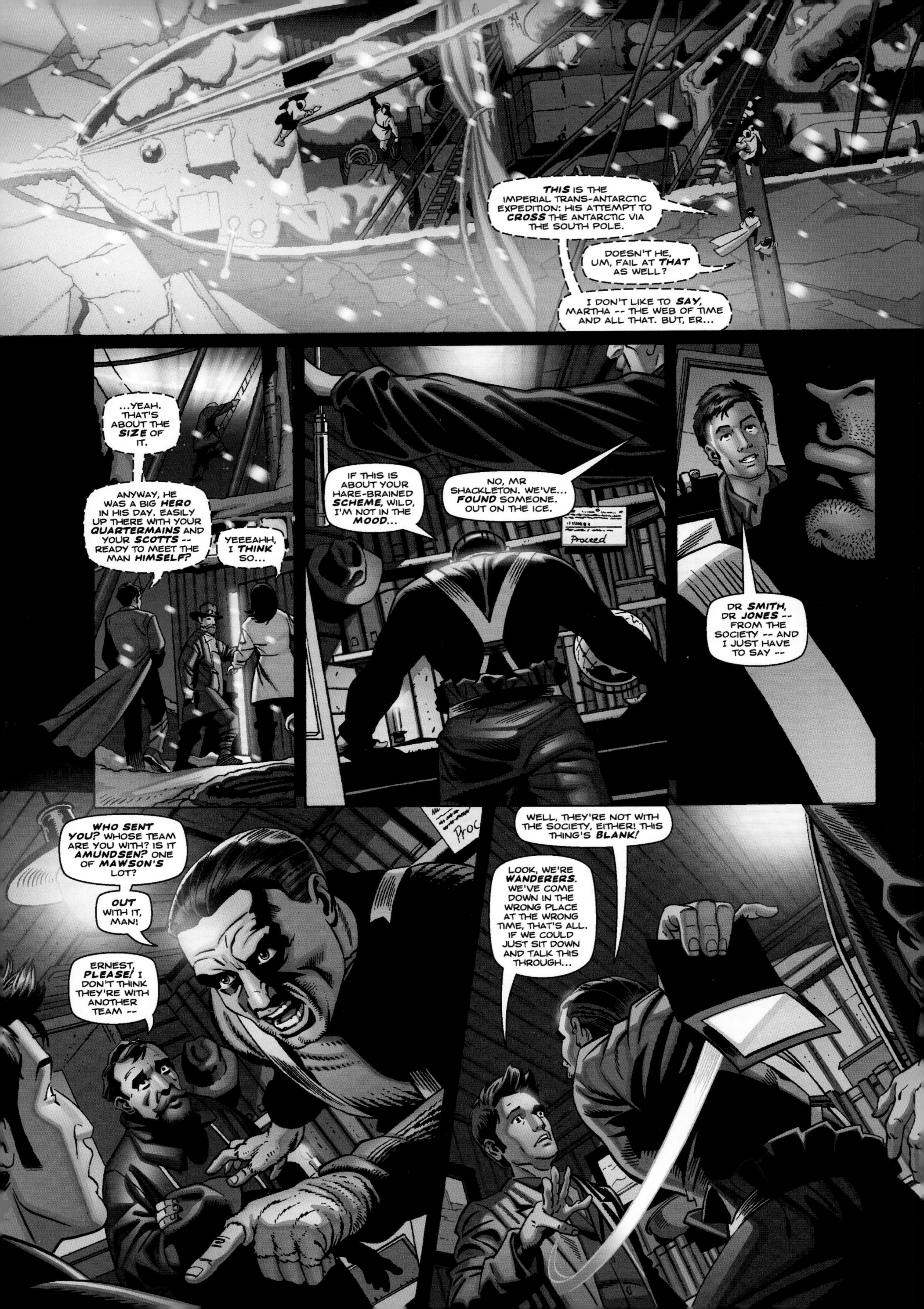

THIS IS THE IMPERIAL TRANS-ANTARCTIC EXPEDITION: HIS ATTEMPT TO CROSS THE ANTARCTIC VIA THE SOUTH POLE.
DOESN'T HE, UM, FAIL AT THAT AS WELL?
I DON'T LIKE TO SAY, MARTHA -- THE WEB OF TIME AND ALL THAT. BUT, ER...
...YEAH. THAT'S ABOUT THE SIZE OF IT.
ANYWAY, HE WAS A BIG HERO IN HIS DAY. EASILY UP THERE WITH YOUR QUARTERMAINS AND YOUR SCOTTS -- READY TO MEET THE MAN HIMSELF?
YEEEAHH, I THINK SO...
IF THIS IS ABOUT YOUR HARE-BRAINED SCHEME, WILD, I'M NOT IN THE MOOD...
NO, MR SHACKLETON. WE'VE... FOUND SOMEONE. OUT ON THE ICE.
Proceed
DR SMITH, DR JONES -- FROM THE SOCIETY -- AND I JUST HAVE TO SAY --
WHO SENT YOU? WHOSE TEAM ARE YOU WITH? IS IT AMUNDSEN? ONE OF MAWSON'S LOT?
OUT WITH IT, MAN!
ERNEST, PLEASE! I DON'T THINK THEY'RE WITH ANOTHER TEAM --
WELL, THEY'RE NOT WITH THE SOCIETY, EITHER! THIS THING'S BLANK!
LOOK, WE'RE WANDERERS. WE'VE COME DOWN IN THE WRONG PLACE AT THE WRONG TIME, THAT'S ALL. IF WE COULD JUST SIT DOWN AND TALK THIS THROUGH...

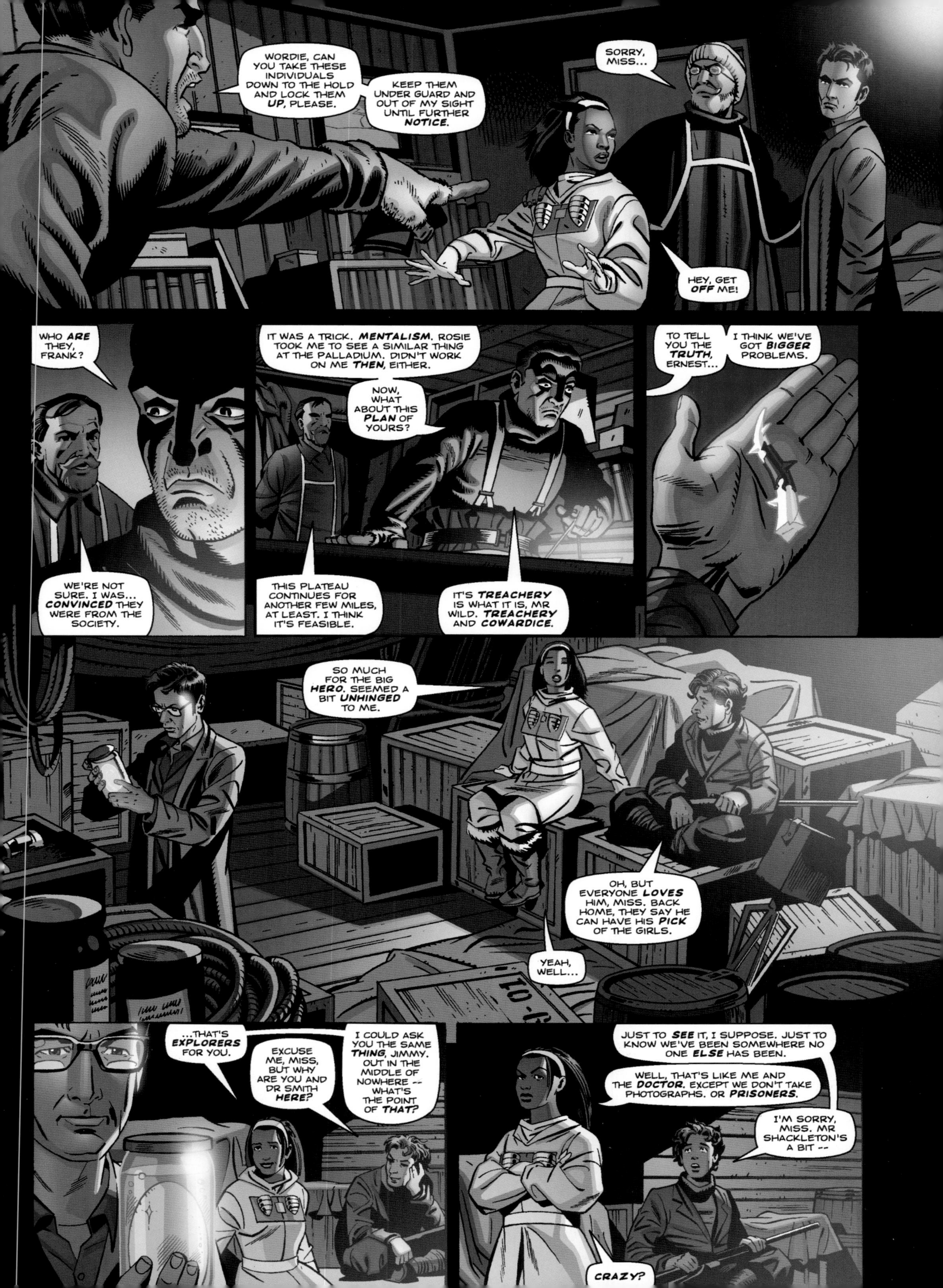

WORDIE, CAN YOU TAKE THESE INDIVIDUALS DOWN TO THE HOLD AND LOCK THEM UP, PLEASE.
KEEP THEM UNDER GUARD AND OUT OF MY SIGHT UNTIL FURTHER NOTICE.
SORRY, MISS...
HEY, GET OFF ME!
WHO ARE THEY, FRANK?
WE'RE NOT SURE. I WAS... CONVINCED THEY WERE FROM THE SOCIETY.
IT WAS A TRICK. MENTALISM. ROSIE TOOK ME TO SEE A SIMILAR THING AT THE PALLADIUM. DIDN'T WORK ON ME THEN, EITHER.
NOW, WHAT ABOUT THIS PLAN OF YOURS?
THIS PLATEAU CONTINUES FOR ANOTHER FEW MILES, AT LEAST. I THINK IT'S FEASIBLE.
IT'S TREACHERY IS WHAT IT IS, MR WILD. TREACHERY AND COWARDICE.
TO TELL YOU THE TRUTH, ERNEST...
I THINK WE'VE GOT BIGGER PROBLEMS.
SO MUCH FOR THE BIG HERO. SEEMED A BIT UNHINGED TO ME.
OH, BUT EVERYONE LOVES HIM, MISS. BACK HOME, THEY SAY HE CAN HAVE HIS PICK OF THE GIRLS.
YEAH, WELL...
...THAT'S EXPLORERS FOR YOU.
EXCUSE ME, MISS, BUT WHY ARE YOU AND DR SMITH HERE?
I COULD ASK YOU THE SAME THING, JIMMY. OUT IN THE MIDDLE OF NOWHERE -- WHAT'S THE POINT OF THAT?
JUST TO SEE IT, I SUPPOSE. JUST TO KNOW WE'VE BEEN SOMEWHERE NO ONE ELSE HAS BEEN.
WELL, THAT'S LIKE ME AND THE DOCTOR, EXCEPT WE DON'T TAKE PHOTOGRAPHS. OR PRISONERS.
I'M SORRY, MISS. MR SHACKLETON'S A BIT --
CRAZY?

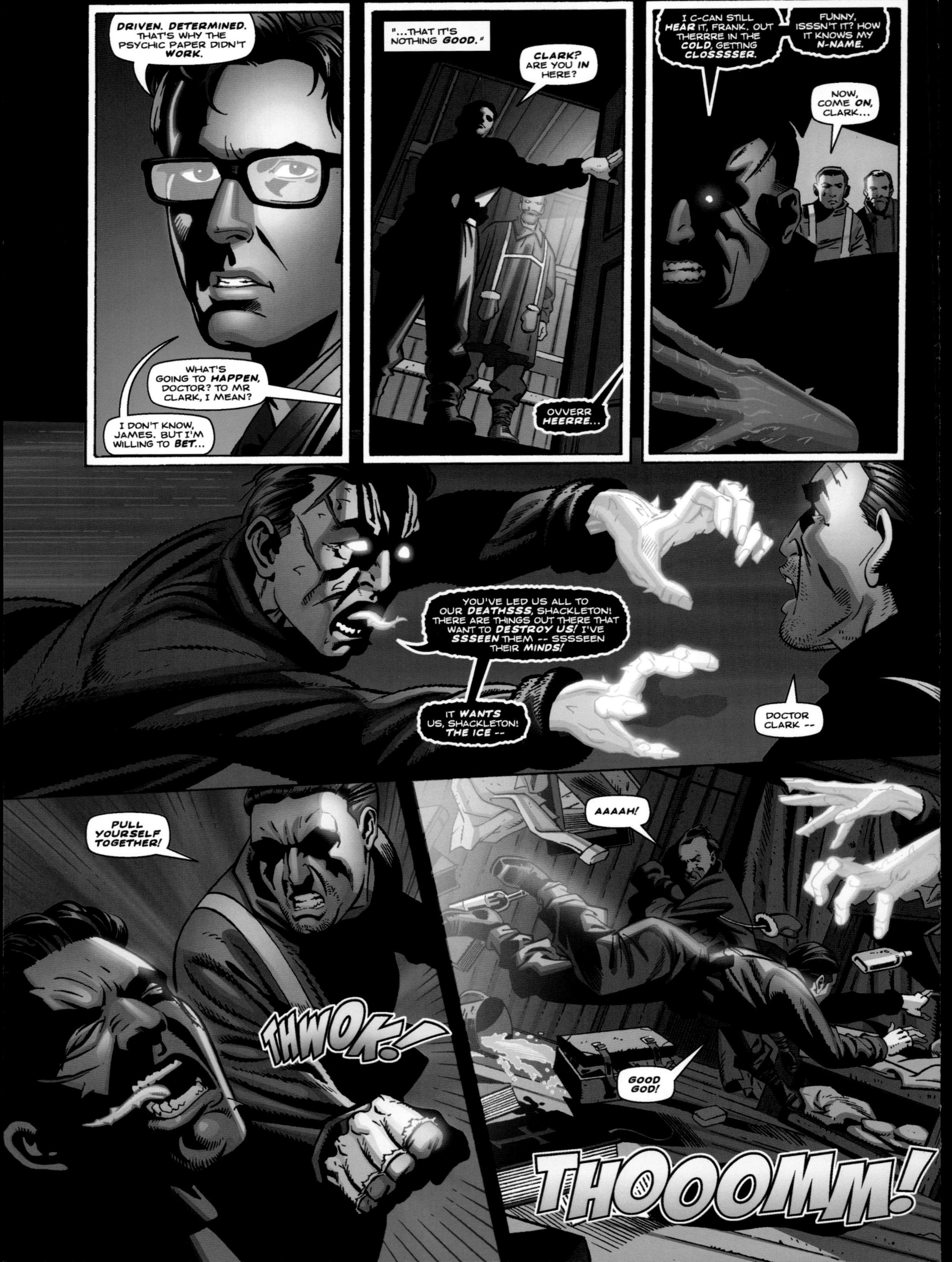
DRIVEN. DETERMINED. THAT'S WHY THE PSYCHIC PAPER DIDN'T WORK.
WHAT'S GOING TO HAPPEN, DOCTOR? TO MR CLARK, I MEAN?
I DON'T KNOW, JAMES. BUT I'M WILLING TO BET...
"...THAT IT'S NOTHING GOOD."
CLARK? ARE YOU IN HERE?
OVVERR HEERRE...
I C-CAN STILL HEAR IT, FRANK. OUT THERRRE IN THE COLD, GETTING CLOSSSSER.
FUNNY, ISSSN'T IT? HOW IT KNOWS MY N-NAME.
NOW, COME ON, CLARK...
YOU'VE LED US ALL TO OUR DEATHSSS, SHACKLETON! THERE ARE THINGS OUT THERE THAT WANT TO DESTROY US! I'VE SSSEEN THEM -- SSSSEEN THEIR MINDS!
IT WANTS US, SHACKLETON! THE ICE --
DOCTOR CLARK --
PULL YOURSELF TOGETHER!
THWOK!
AAAAH!
GOOD GOD!
THOOOMM!

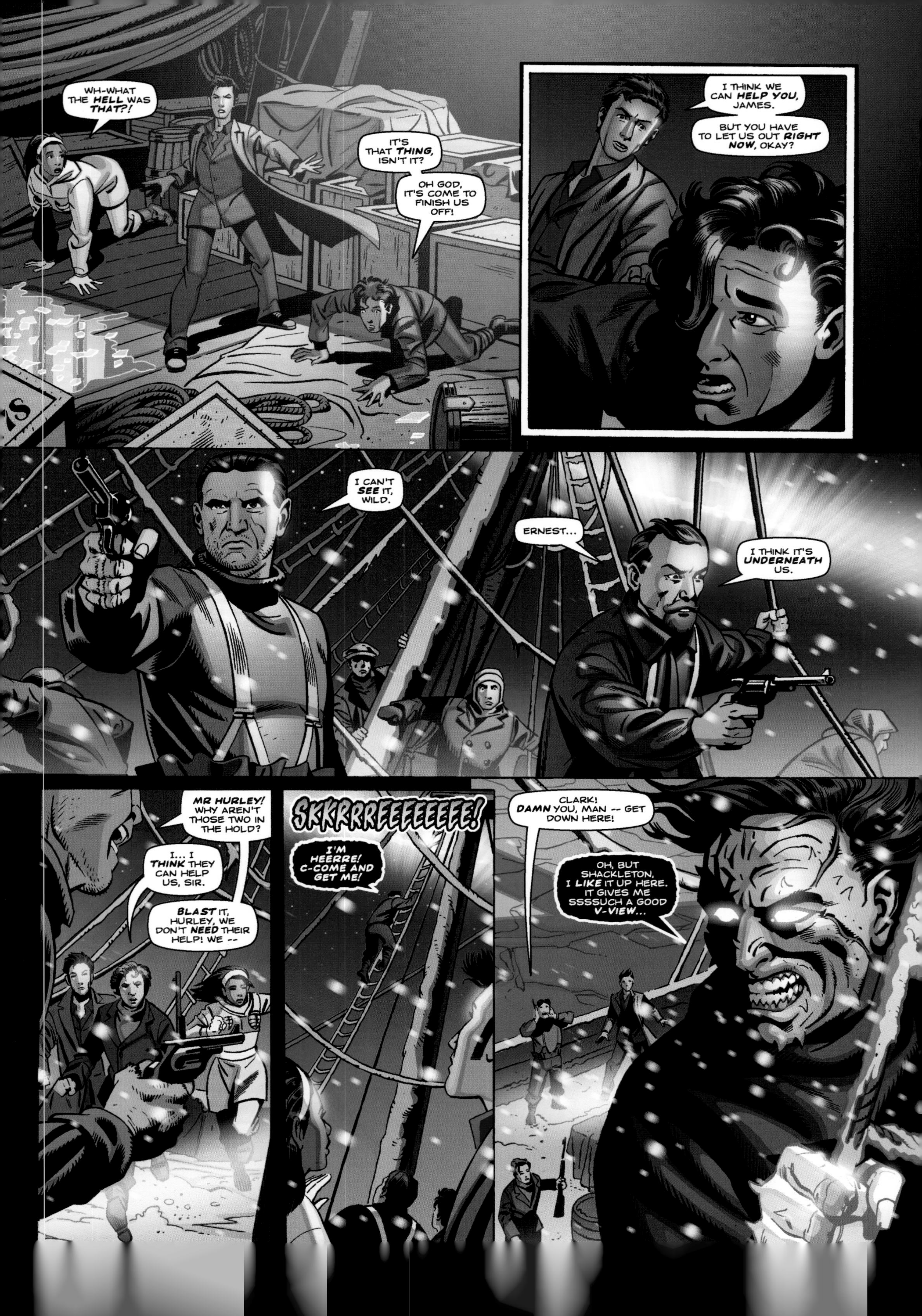
WH-WHAT THE HELL WAS THAT?!
IT'S THAT THING, ISN'T IT?
OH GOD, IT'S COME TO FINISH US OFF!
I THINK WE CAN HELP YOU, JAMES.
BUT YOU HAVE TO LET US OUT RIGHT NOW, OKAY?
I CAN'T SEE IT, WILD.
ERNEST...
I THINK IT'S UNDERNEATH US.
MR HURLEY! WHY AREN'T THOSE TWO IN THE HOLD?
I... I THINK THEY CAN HELP US, SIR.
BLAST IT, HURLEY, WE DON'T NEED THEIR HELP! WE --
SKKRRRREEEEEEEEE!
I'M HEERRE! C-COME AND GET ME!
CLARK! DAMN YOU, MAN -- GET DOWN HERE!
OH, BUT SHACKLETON, I LIKE IT UP HERE. IT GIVES ME SSSSUCH A GOOD V-VIEW...

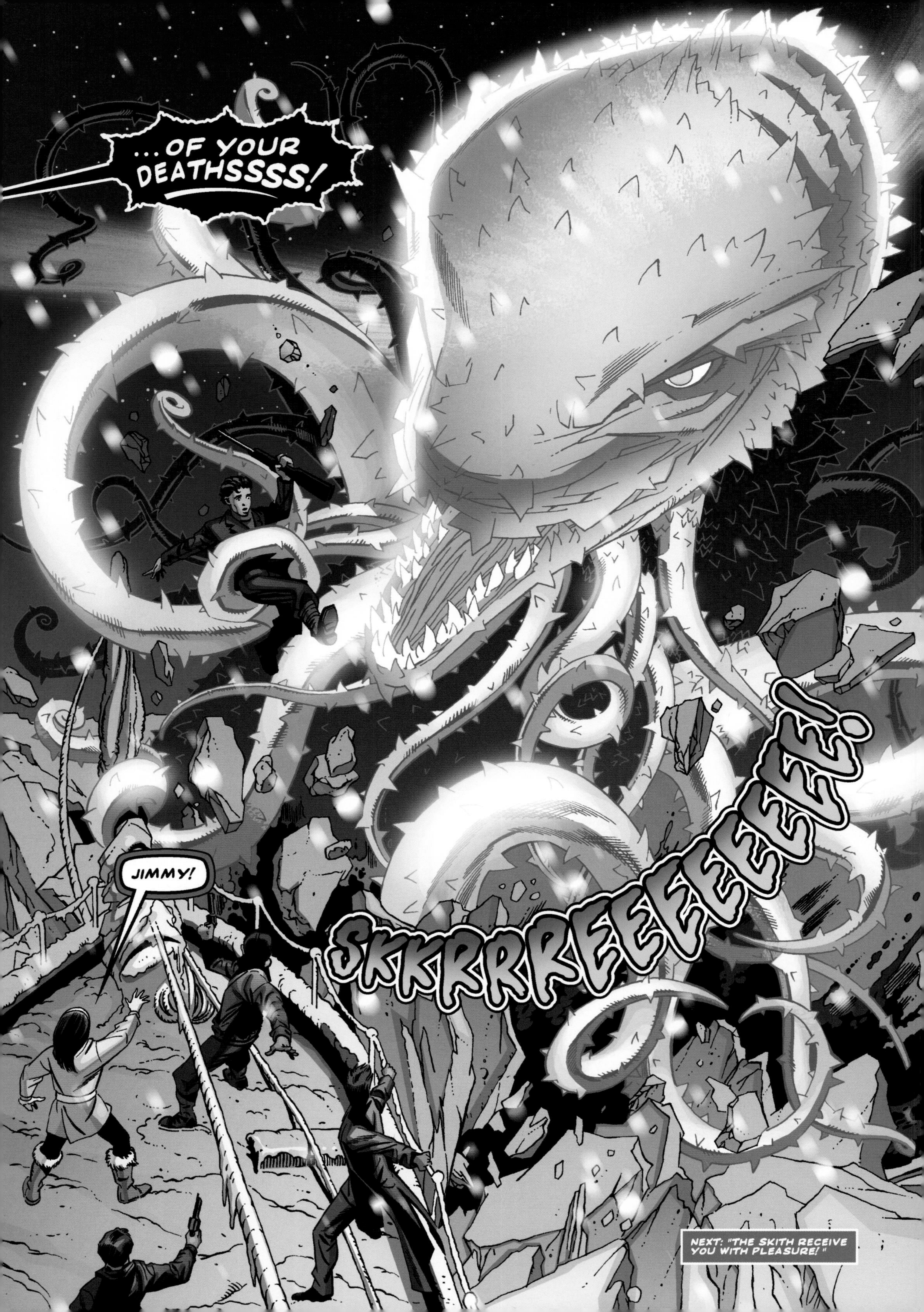
...OF YOUR DEATHSSSS!
JIMMY!
SKKRRREEEEEEEE!
NEXT: "THE SKITH RECEIVE YOU WITH PLEASURE!"

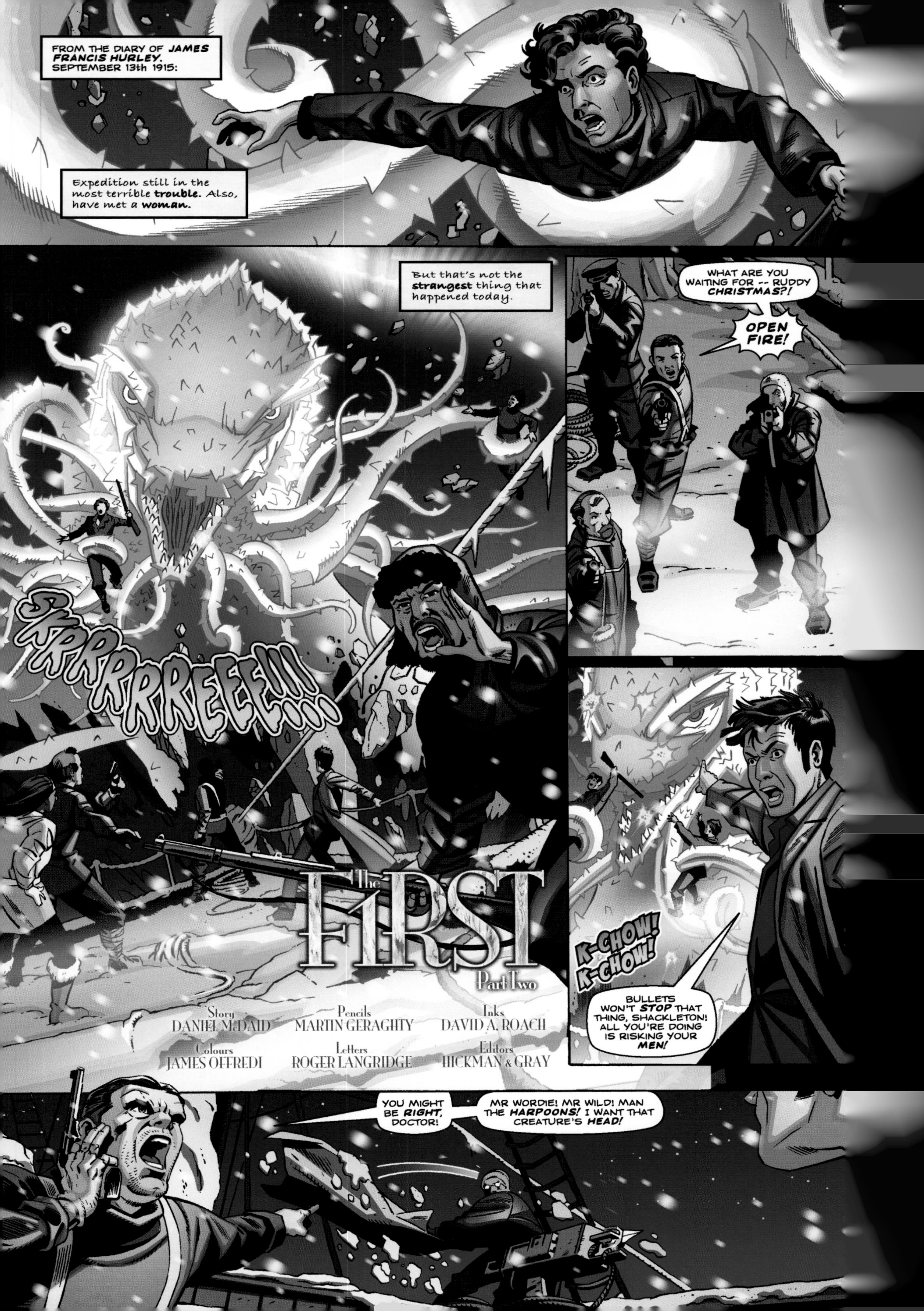

FROM THE DIARY OF JAMES FRANCIS HURLEY. SEPTEMBER 13th 1915:
Expedition still in the most terrible trouble. Also, have met a woman.
But that's not the strangest thing that happened today.
SKRRRRREEEE!!!
WHAT ARE YOU WAITING FOR -- RUDDY CHRISTMAS?!
OPEN FIRE!
K-CHOW! K-CHOW!
BULLETS WON'T STOP THAT THING, SHACKLETON! ALL YOU'RE DOING IS RISKING YOUR MEN!
The FIRST Part Two
Story DANIEL McDAID
Pencils MARTIN GERAGHTY
Inks DAVID A. ROACH
Colours JAMES OFFREDI
Letters ROGER LANGRIDGE
Editors HICKMAN & GRAY
YOU MIGHT BE RIGHT, DOCTOR!
MR WORDIE! MR WILD! MAN THE HARPOONS! I WANT THAT CREATURE'S HEAD!

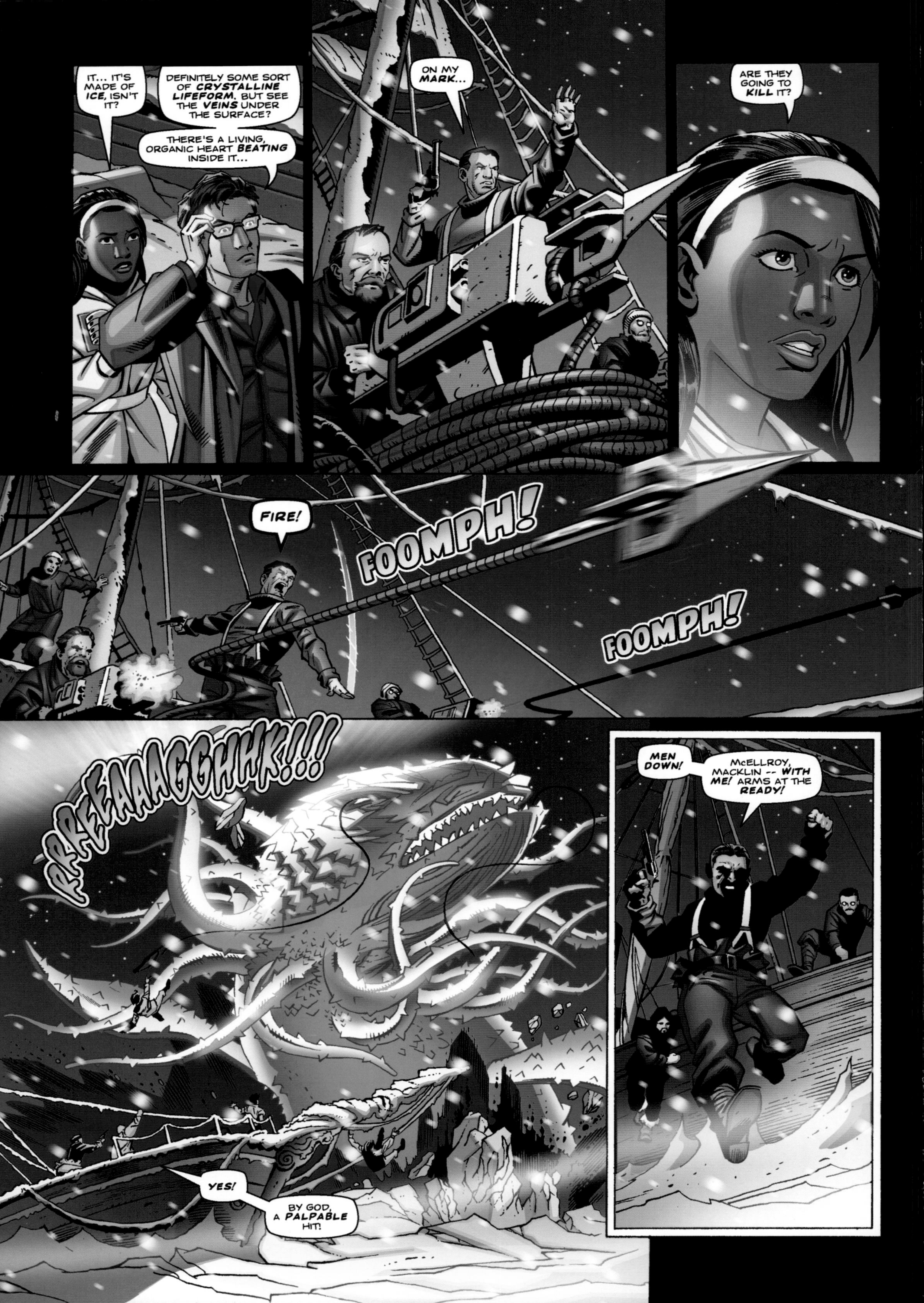
IT... IT'S MADE OF ICE, ISN'T IT?
DEFINITELY SOME SORT OF CRYSTALLINE LIFEFORM. BUT SEE THE VEINS UNDER THE SURFACE?
THERE'S A LIVING, ORGANIC HEART BEATING INSIDE IT...
ON MY MARK...
ARE THEY GOING TO KILL IT?
FIRE!
FOOMPH!
FOOMPH!
RRREEAAAGGHHK!!!
YES!
BY GOD, A PALPABLE HIT!
MEN DOWN!
McELLROY, MACKLIN -- WITH ME! ARMS AT THE READY!

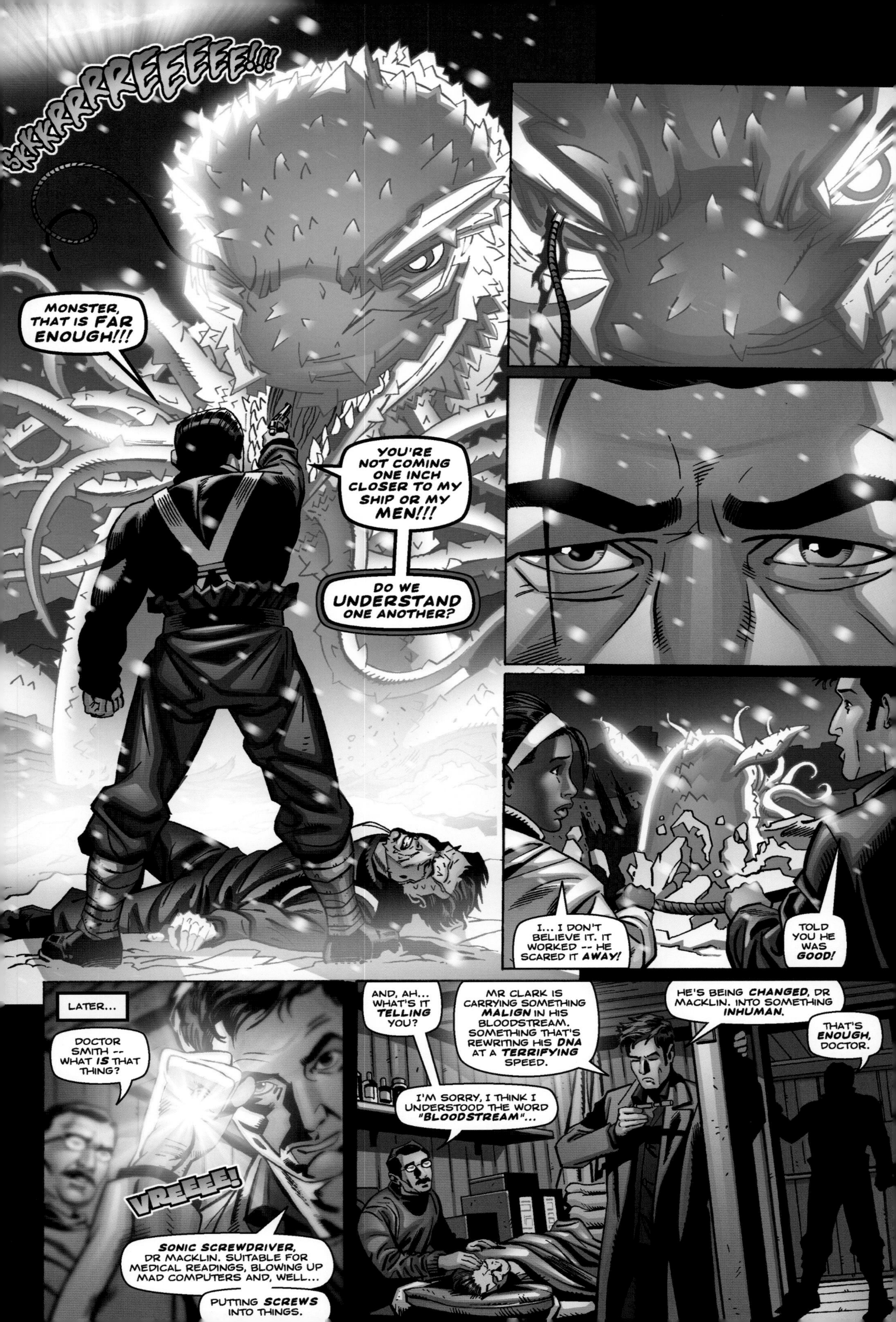

SKKKRRRRREEEEEE!!!!
MONSTER, THAT IS FAR ENOUGH!!!
YOU'RE NOT COMING ONE INCH CLOSER TO MY SHIP OR MY MEN!!!
DO WE UNDERSTAND ONE ANOTHER?
I... I DON'T BELIEVE IT. IT WORKED -- HE SCARED IT AWAY!
TOLD YOU HE WAS GOOD!
LATER...
DOCTOR SMITH -- WHAT IS THAT THING?
VREEEEE!
SONIC SCREWDRIVER, DR MACKLIN. SUITABLE FOR MEDICAL READINGS, BLOWING UP MAD COMPUTERS AND, WELL...
PUTTING SCREWS INTO THINGS.
AND, AH... WHAT'S IT TELLING YOU?
MR CLARK IS CARRYING SOMETHING MALIGN IN HIS BLOODSTREAM. SOMETHING THAT'S REWRITING HIS DNA AT A TERRIFYING SPEED.
I'M SORRY, I THINK I UNDERSTOOD THE WORD "BLOODSTREAM"...
HE'S BEING CHANGED, DR MACKLIN. INTO SOMETHING INHUMAN.
THAT'S ENOUGH, DOCTOR.

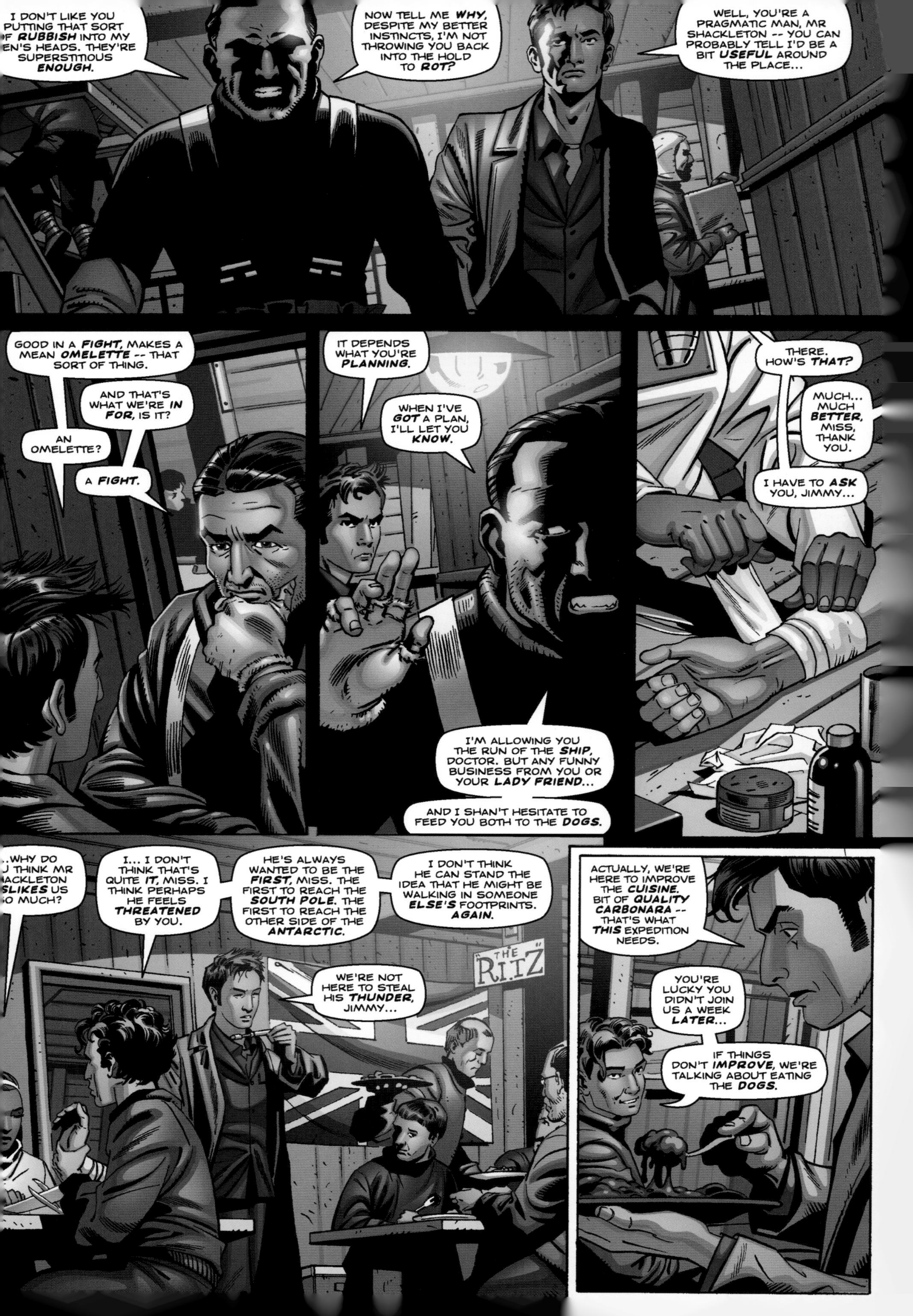
I DON'T LIKE YOU PUTTING THAT SORT OF RUBBISH INTO MY MEN'S HEADS. THEY'RE SUPERSTITIOUS ENOUGH.
NOW TELL ME WHY, DESPITE MY BETTER INSTINCTS, I'M NOT THROWING YOU BACK INTO THE HOLD TO ROT?
WELL, YOU'RE A PRAGMATIC MAN, MR SHACKLETON -- YOU CAN PROBABLY TELL I'D BE A BIT USEFUL AROUND THE PLACE...
GOOD IN A FIGHT, MAKES A MEAN OMELETTE -- THAT SORT OF THING.
AND THAT'S WHAT WE'RE IN FOR, IS IT?
AN OMELETTE?
A FIGHT.
IT DEPENDS WHAT YOU'RE PLANNING.
WHEN I'VE GOT A PLAN, I'LL LET YOU KNOW.
I'M ALLOWING YOU THE RUN OF THE SHIP, DOCTOR. BUT ANY FUNNY BUSINESS FROM YOU OR YOUR LADY FRIEND...
AND I SHAN'T HESITATE TO FEED YOU BOTH TO THE DOGS.
THERE. HOW'S THAT?
MUCH... MUCH BETTER, MISS, THANK YOU.
I HAVE TO ASK YOU, JIMMY...
...WHY DO YOU THINK MR SHACKLETON DISLIKES US SO MUCH?
I... I DON'T THINK THAT'S QUITE IT, MISS. I THINK PERHAPS HE FEELS THREATENED BY YOU.
HE'S ALWAYS WANTED TO BE THE FIRST, MISS. THE FIRST TO REACH THE SOUTH POLE. THE FIRST TO REACH THE OTHER SIDE OF THE ANTARCTIC.
I DON'T THINK HE CAN STAND THE IDEA THAT HE MIGHT BE WALKING IN SOMEONE ELSE'S FOOTPRINTS. AGAIN.
THE RITZ
WE'RE NOT HERE TO STEAL HIS THUNDER, JIMMY...
ACTUALLY, WE'RE HERE TO IMPROVE THE CUISINE. BIT OF QUALITY CARBONARA -- THAT'S WHAT THIS EXPEDITION NEEDS.
YOU'RE LUCKY YOU DIDN'T JOIN US A WEEK LATER...
IF THINGS DON'T IMPROVE, WE'RE TALKING ABOUT EATING THE DOGS.

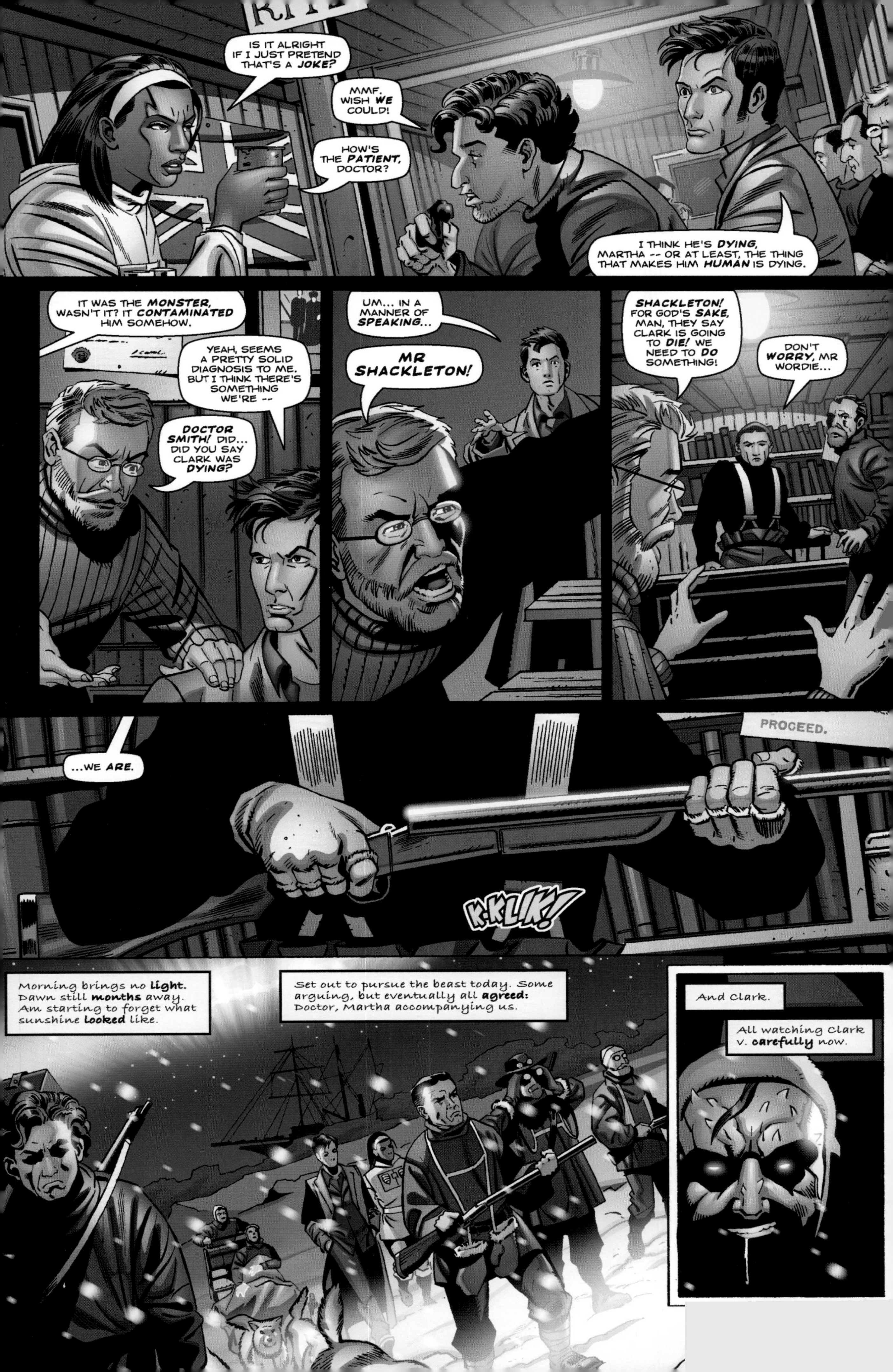

IS IT ALRIGHT IF I JUST PRETEND THAT'S A JOKE?
MMF. WISH WE COULD!
HOW'S THE PATIENT, DOCTOR?
I THINK HE'S DYING, MARTHA -- OR AT LEAST, THE THING THAT MAKES HIM HUMAN IS DYING.
IT WAS THE MONSTER, WASN'T IT? IT CONTAMINATED HIM SOMEHOW.
YEAH, SEEMS A PRETTY SOLID DIAGNOSIS TO ME. BUT I THINK THERE'S SOMETHING WE'RE --
DOCTOR SMITH! DID... DID YOU SAY CLARK WAS DYING?
UM... IN A MANNER OF SPEAKING...
MR SHACKLETON!
SHACKLETON! FOR GOD'S SAKE, MAN, THEY SAY CLARK IS GOING TO DIE! WE NEED TO DO SOMETHING!
DON'T WORRY, MR WORDIE...
...WE ARE.
PROCEED.
K-KLIK!
Morning brings no light. Dawn still months away. Am starting to forget what sunshine looked like.
Set out to pursue the beast today. Some arguing, but eventually all agreed: Doctor, Martha accompanying us.
And Clark.
All watching Clark v. carefully now.

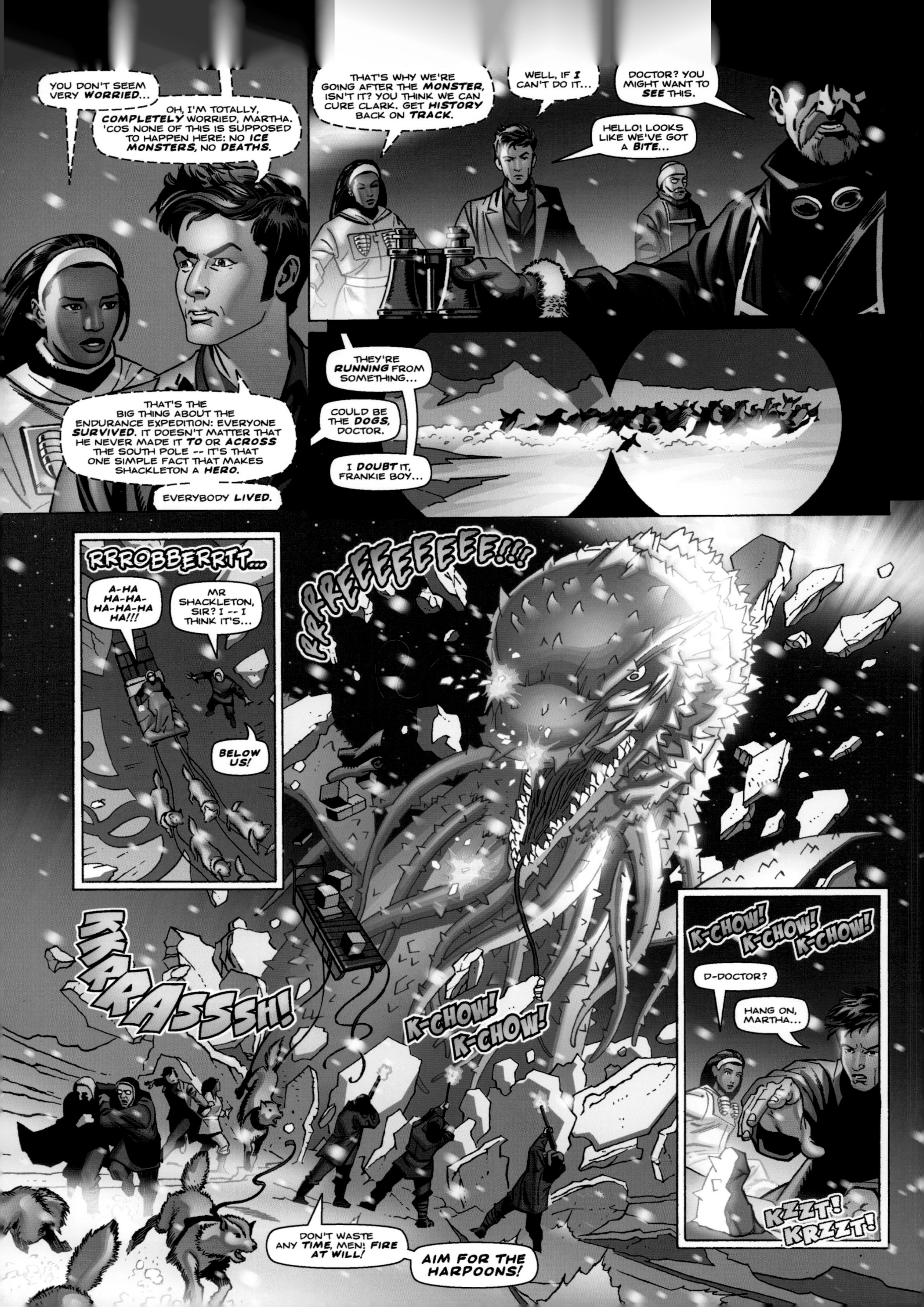
YOU DON'T SEEM VERY WORRIED...
OH, I'M TOTALLY, COMPLETELY WORRIED, MARTHA. 'COS NONE OF THIS IS SUPPOSED TO HAPPEN HERE: NO ICE MONSTERS, NO DEATHS.
THAT'S WHY WE'RE GOING AFTER THE MONSTER, ISN'T IT? YOU THINK WE CAN CURE CLARK. GET HISTORY BACK ON TRACK.
WELL, IF I CAN'T DO IT...
DOCTOR? YOU MIGHT WANT TO SEE THIS.
HELLO! LOOKS LIKE WE'VE GOT A BITE...
THAT'S THE BIG THING ABOUT THE ENDURANCE EXPEDITION: EVERYONE SURVIVED. IT DOESN'T MATTER THAT HE NEVER MADE IT TO OR ACROSS THE SOUTH POLE -- IT'S THAT ONE SIMPLE FACT THAT MAKES SHACKLETON A HERO.
EVERYBODY LIVED.
THEY'RE RUNNING FROM SOMETHING...
COULD BE THE DOGS, DOCTOR.
I DOUBT IT, FRANKIE BOY...
RRROBBERRTT...
A-HA HA-HA-HA-HA-HA HA!!!
MR SHACKLETON, SIR? I -- I THINK IT'S...
BELOW US!
RRRREEEEEEEEE!!!
KKRRASSSSH!
K-CHOW! K-CHOW!
DON'T WASTE ANY TIME, MEN! FIRE AT WILL!
AIM FOR THE HARPOONS!
K-CHOW! K-CHOW! K-CHOW!
D-DOCTOR?
HANG ON, MARTHA...
KZZT! KRZZT!

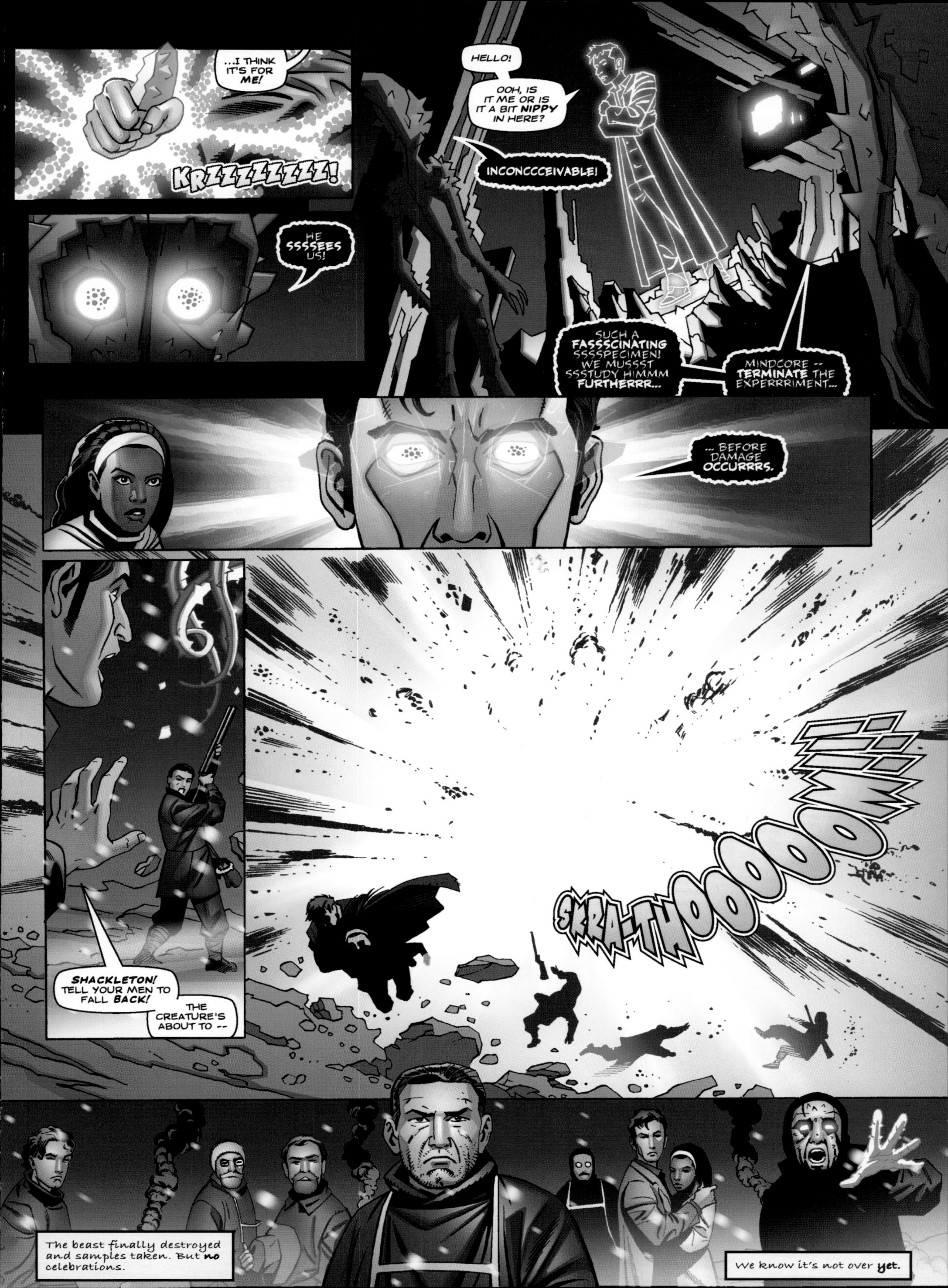

...I THINK IT'S FOR ME!
KRZZZZZZZZ!
HELLO!
OOH, IS IT ME OR IS IT A BIT NIPPY IN HERE?
INCONCCCEIVABLE!
HE SSSSEES US!
SUCH A FASSSCINATING SSSSPECIMEN! WE MUSSST SSSTUDY HIMMM FURTHERRR...
MINDCORE -- TERMINATE THE EXPERRRIMENT...
... BEFORE DAMAGE OCCURRRS.
SHACKLETON! TELL YOUR MEN TO FALL BACK!
THE CREATURE'S ABOUT TO --
SKRA-THOOOOOOM!!!
The beast finally destroyed and samples taken. But no celebrations.
We know it's not over yet.

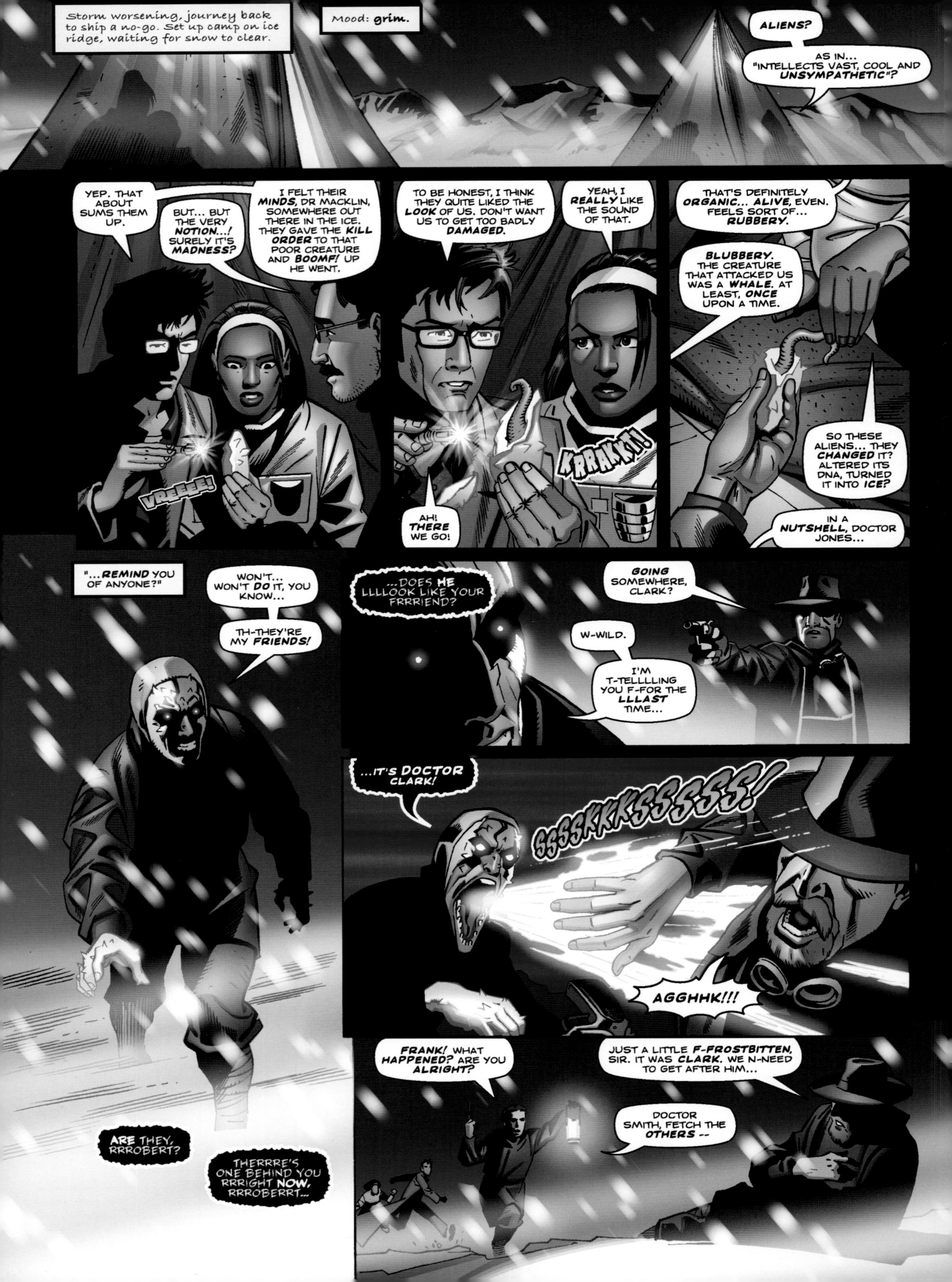

Storm worsening, journey back to ship a no-go. Set up camp on ice ridge, waiting for snow to clear.
Mood: grim.
ALIENS?
AS IN... "INTELLECTS VAST, COOL AND UNSYMPATHETIC"?
YEP. THAT ABOUT SUMS THEM UP.
BUT... BUT THE VERY NOTION...! SURELY IT'S MADNESS?
I FELT THEIR MINDS, DR MACKLIN, SOMEWHERE OUT THERE IN THE ICE. THEY GAVE THE KILL ORDER TO THAT POOR CREATURE AND BOOMF! UP HE WENT.
VREEEE!
TO BE HONEST, I THINK THEY QUITE LIKED THE LOOK OF US. DON'T WANT US TO GET TOO BADLY DAMAGED.
YEAH, I REALLY LIKE THE SOUND OF THAT.
KRRAKKT!
AH! THERE WE GO!
THAT'S DEFINITELY ORGANIC... ALIVE, EVEN. FEELS SORT OF... RUBBERY.
BLUBBERY. THE CREATURE THAT ATTACKED US WAS A WHALE. AT LEAST, ONCE UPON A TIME.
SO THESE ALIENS... THEY CHANGED IT? ALTERED ITS DNA, TURNED IT INTO ICE?
IN A NUTSHELL, DOCTOR JONES...
"...REMIND YOU OF ANYONE?"
WON'T... WON'T DO IT, YOU KNOW...
TH-THEY'RE MY FRIENDS!
ARE THEY, RRROBERT?
THERRRE'S ONE BEHIND YOU RRRIGHT NOW, RRROBERRT...
...DOES HE LLLLOOK LIKE YOUR FRRRIEND?
GOING SOMEWHERE, CLARK?
W-WILD.
I'M T-TELLLLING YOU F-FOR THE LLLAST TIME...
...IT'S DOCTOR CLARK!
SSSSKKKSSSSSSS!
AGGHHK!!!
FRANK! WHAT HAPPENED? ARE YOU ALRIGHT?
JUST A LITTLE F-FROSTBITTEN, SIR. IT WAS CLARK. WE N-NEED TO GET AFTER HIM...
DOCTOR SMITH, FETCH THE OTHERS --

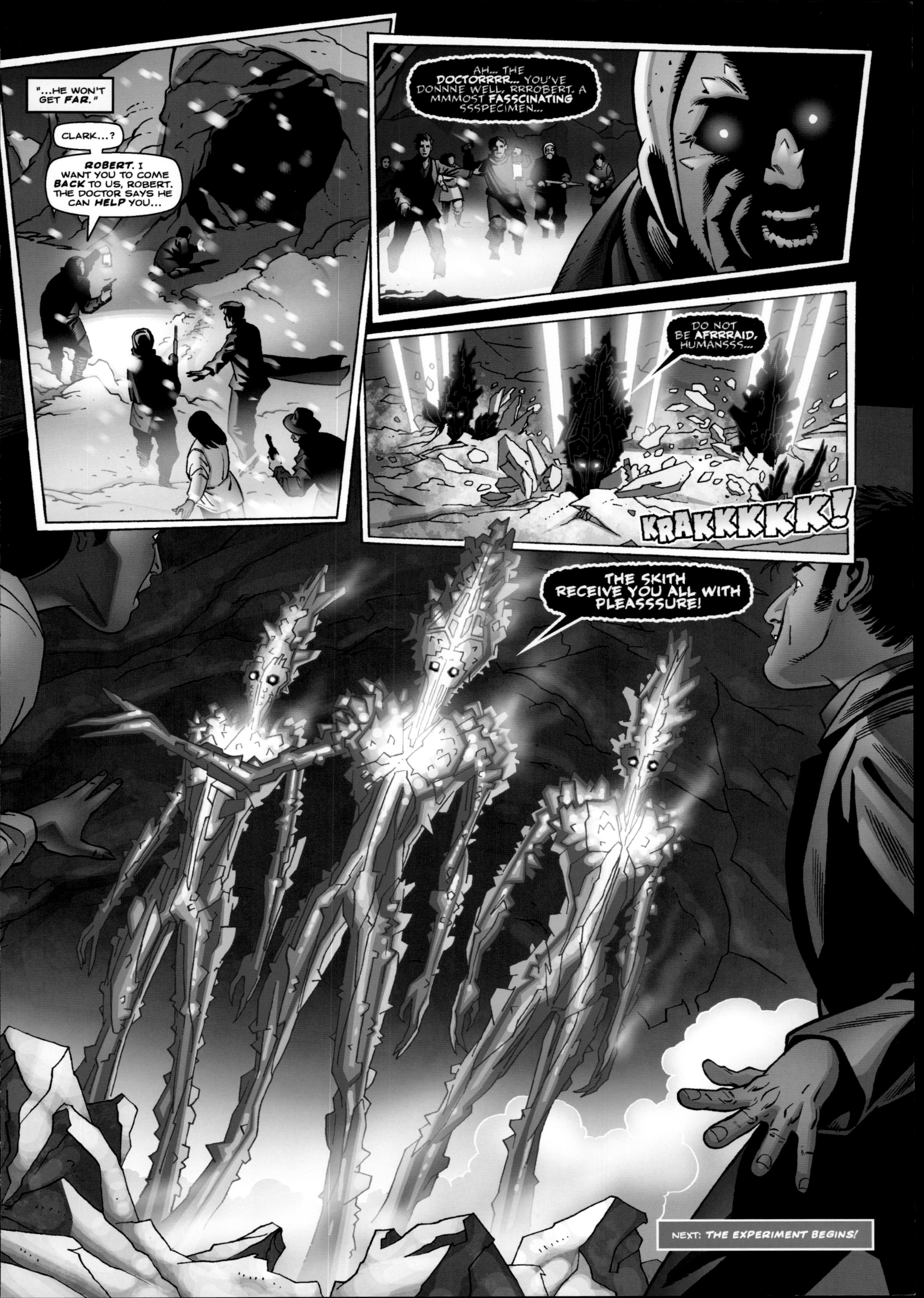
"...HE WON'T GET FAR."
CLARK...?
ROBERT. I WANT YOU TO COME BACK TO US, ROBERT. THE DOCTOR SAYS HE CAN HELP YOU...
AH... THE DOCTORRRR... YOU'VE DONNNE WELL, RRROBERT. A MMMOST FASSCINATING SSSPECIMEN...
DO NOT BE AFRRRAID, HUMANSSS...
KRAKKKKK!
THE SKITH RECEIVE YOU ALL WITH PLEASSSURE!
NEXT: THE EXPERIMENT BEGINS!

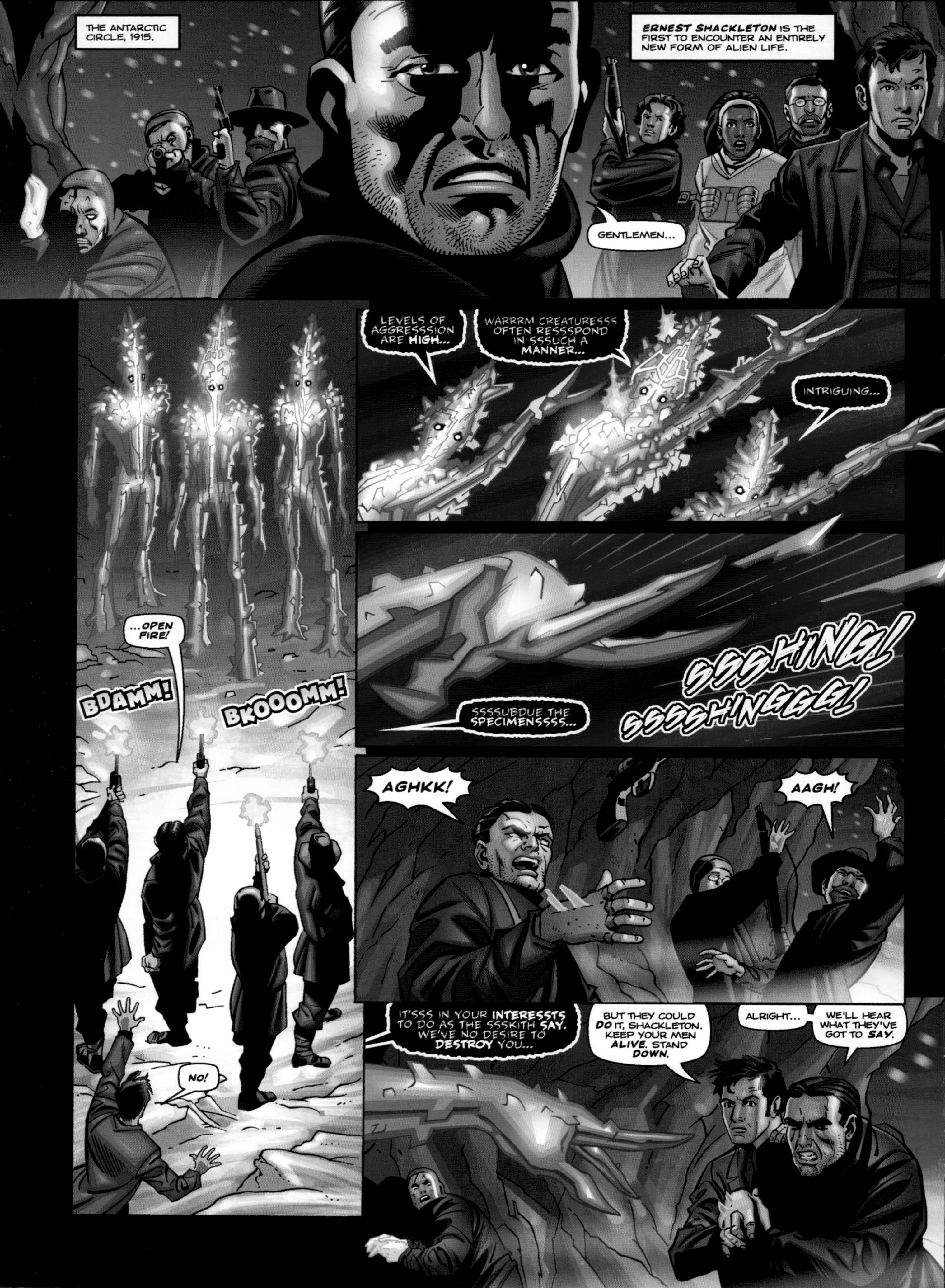
THE ANTARCTIC CIRCLE, 1915.
ERNEST SHACKLETON IS THE FIRST TO ENCOUNTER AN ENTIRELY NEW FORM OF ALIEN LIFE.
GENTLEMEN...
...OPEN FIRE!
BDAMM!
BKOOOMM!
NO!
LEVELS OF AGGRESSSION ARE HIGH...
WARRRM CREATURESSS OFTEN RESSSPOND IN SSSUCH A MANNER...
INTRIGUING...
SSSSUBDUE THE SPECIMENSSSS...
SSSHING!
SSSSHINGGG!
AGHKK!
AAGH!
IT'SSS IN YOUR INTERESSTS TO DO AS THE SSSKITH SAY. WE'VE NO DESIRE TO DESTROY YOU...
BUT THEY COULD DO IT, SHACKLETON. KEEP YOUR MEN ALIVE. STAND DOWN.
ALRIGHT...
WE'LL HEAR WHAT THEY'VE GOT TO SAY.

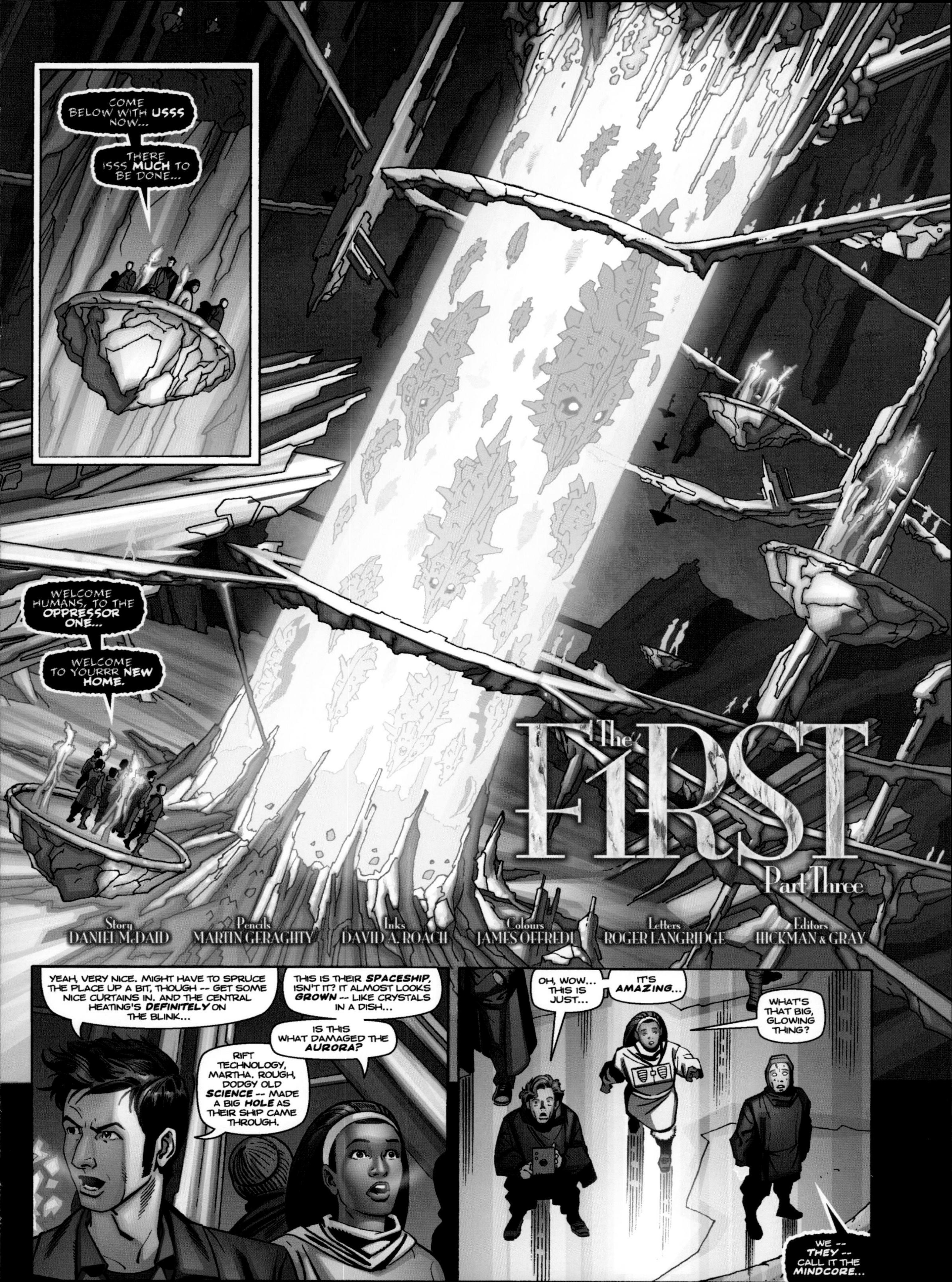

COME BELOW WITH USSS NOW...
THERE ISSS MUCH TO BE DONE...
WELCOME HUMANS, TO THE OPPRESSOR ONE...
WELCOME TO YOURRR NEW HOME.
The FIRST
Part Three
Story DANIEL McDAID
Pencils MARTIN GERAGHTY
Inks DAVID A. ROACH
Colours JAMES OFFREDI
Letters ROGER LANGRIDGE
Editors HICKMAN & GRAY
YEAH, VERY NICE. MIGHT HAVE TO SPRUCE THE PLACE UP A BIT, THOUGH -- GET SOME NICE CURTAINS IN. AND THE CENTRAL HEATING'S DEFINITELY ON THE BLINK...
THIS IS THEIR SPACESHIP, ISN'T IT? IT ALMOST LOOKS GROWN -- LIKE CRYSTALS IN A DISH...
IS THIS WHAT DAMAGED THE AURORA?
RIFT TECHNOLOGY, MARTHA. ROUGH, DODGY OLD SCIENCE -- MADE A BIG HOLE AS THEIR SHIP CAME THROUGH.
OH, WOW... THIS IS JUST...
IT'S AMAZING...
WHAT'S THAT BIG, GLOWING THING?
WE -- THEY -- CALL IT THE MINDCORE...

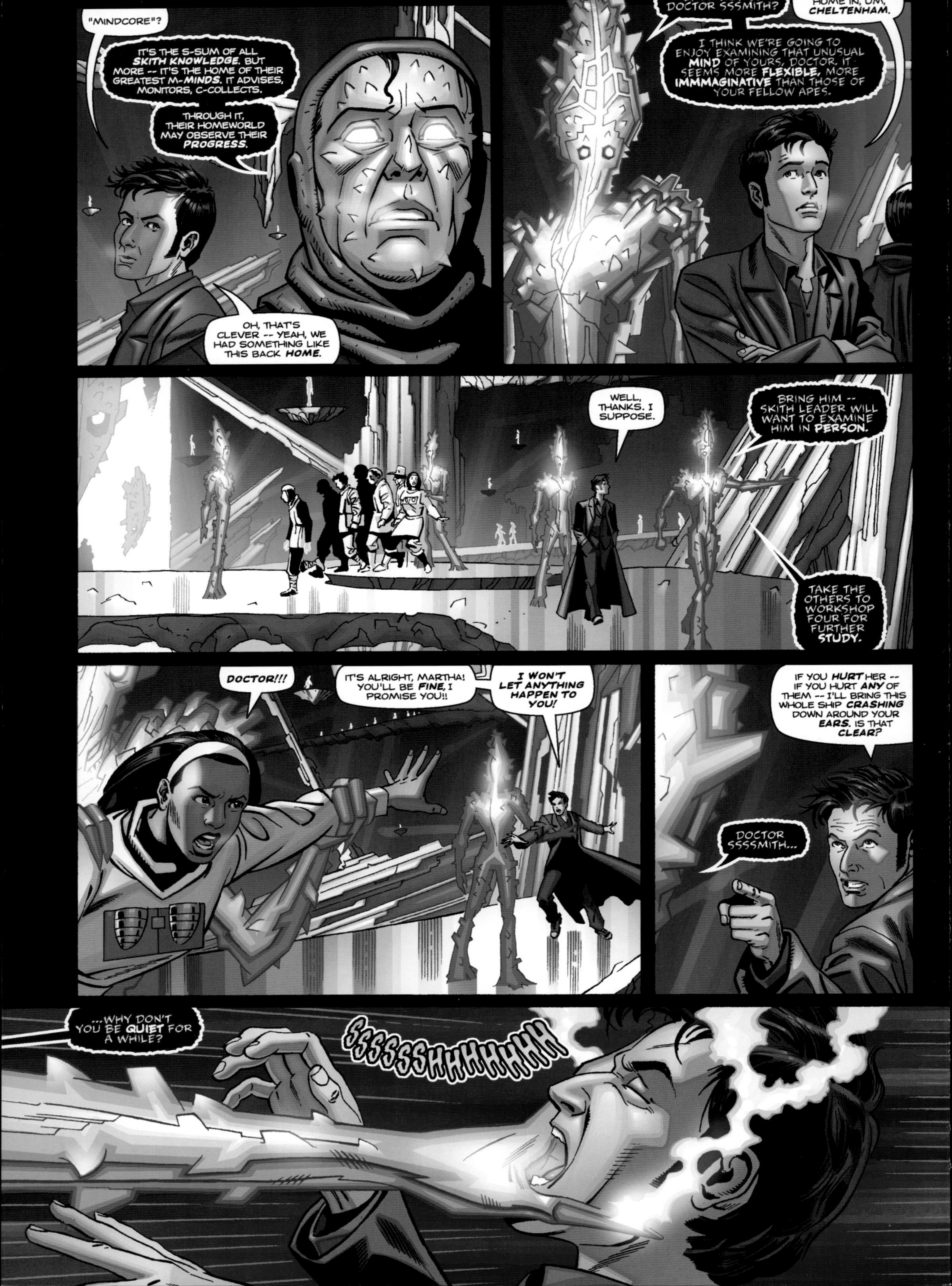
"MINDCORE"?
IT'S THE S-SUM OF ALL SKITH KNOWLEDGE. BUT MORE -- IT'S THE HOME OF THEIR GREATEST M-MINDS. IT ADVISES, MONITORS, C-COLLECTS.
THROUGH IT, THEIR HOMEWORLD MAY OBSERVE THEIR PROGRESS.
OH, THAT'S CLEVER -- YEAH, WE HAD SOMETHING LIKE THIS BACK HOME.
BACK HOME, DOCTOR SSSMITH?
ER, YEAH... BACK HOME IN, UM, CHELTENHAM.
I THINK WE'RE GOING TO ENJOY EXAMINING THAT UNUSUAL MIND OF YOURS, DOCTOR. IT SEEMS MORE FLEXIBLE, MORE IMMMAGINATIVE THAN THOSE OF YOUR FELLOW APES.
WELL, THANKS. I SUPPOSE.
BRING HIM -- SKITH LEADER WILL WANT TO EXAMINE HIM IN PERSON.
TAKE THE OTHERS TO WORKSHOP FOUR FOR FURTHER STUDY.
DOCTOR!!!
IT'S ALRIGHT, MARTHA! YOU'LL BE FINE, I PROMISE YOU!!
I WON'T LET ANYTHING HAPPEN TO YOU!
IF YOU HURT HER -- IF YOU HURT ANY OF THEM -- I'LL BRING THIS WHOLE SHIP CRASHING DOWN AROUND YOUR EARS. IS THAT CLEAR?
DOCTOR SSSSMITH...
...WHY DON'T YOU BE QUIET FOR A WHILE?
SSSSSSHHHHHHHH

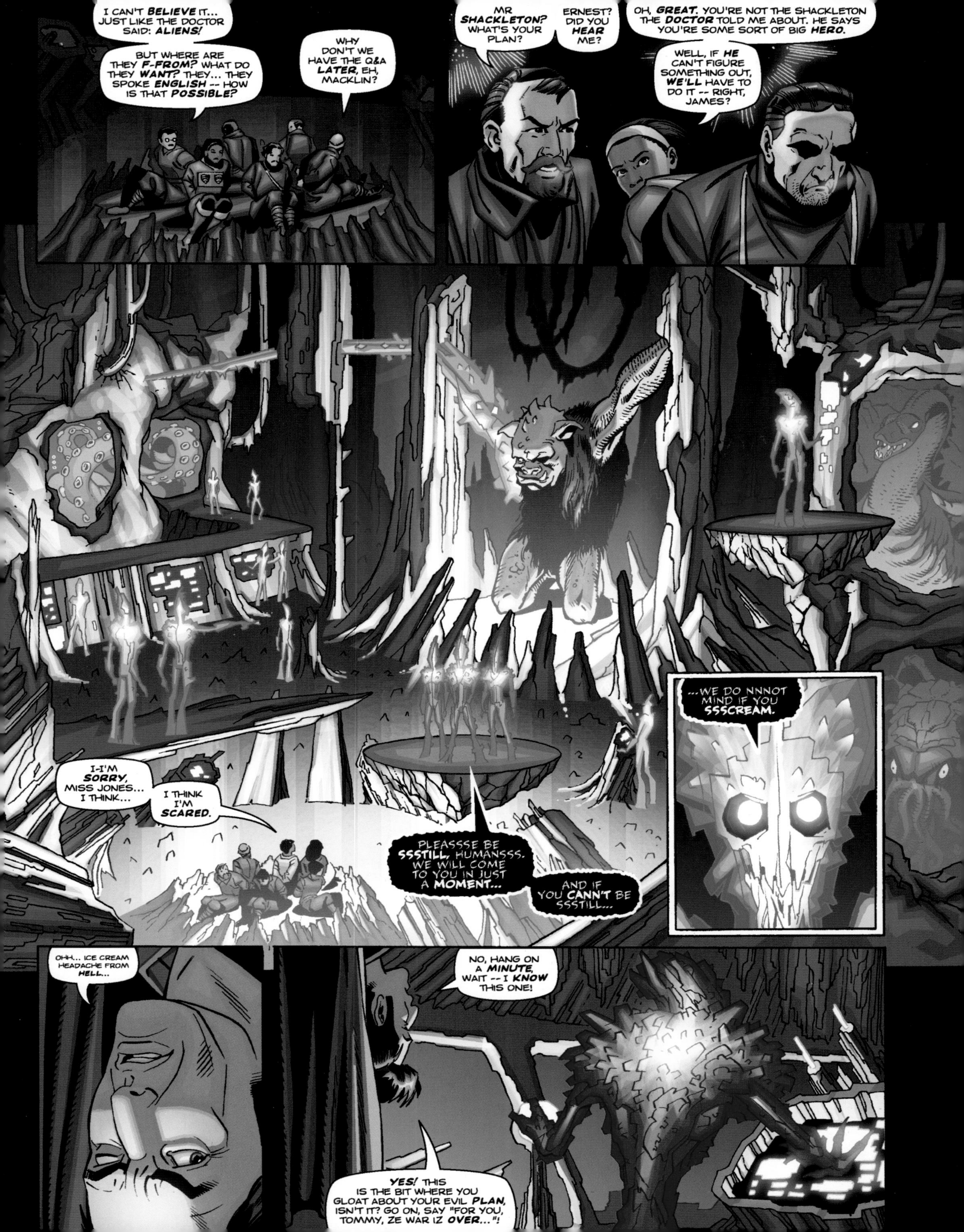
I CAN'T BELIEVE IT... JUST LIKE THE DOCTOR SAID: ALIENS!
BUT WHERE ARE THEY F-FROM? WHAT DO THEY WANT? THEY... THEY SPOKE ENGLISH -- HOW IS THAT POSSIBLE?
WHY DON'T WE HAVE THE Q&A LATER, EH, MACKLIN?
MR SHACKLETON? WHAT'S YOUR PLAN?
ERNEST? DID YOU HEAR ME?
OH, GREAT. YOU'RE NOT THE SHACKLETON THE DOCTOR TOLD ME ABOUT. HE SAYS YOU'RE SOME SORT OF BIG HERO.
WELL, IF HE CAN'T FIGURE SOMETHING OUT, WE'LL HAVE TO DO IT -- RIGHT, JAMES?
I-I'M SORRY, MISS JONES... I THINK...
I THINK I'M SCARED.
PLEASSSE BE SSSTILL, HUMANSSS. WE WILL COME TO YOU IN JUST A MOMENT...
AND IF YOU CANN'T BE SSSTILL...
...WE DO NNNOT MIND IF YOU SSSCREAM.
OHH... ICE CREAM HEADACHE FROM HELL...
NO, HANG ON A MINUTE, WAIT -- I KNOW THIS ONE!
YES! THIS IS THE BIT WHERE YOU GLOAT ABOUT YOUR EVIL PLAN, ISN'T IT? GO ON, SAY "FOR YOU, TOMMY, ZE WAR IZ OVER..."!

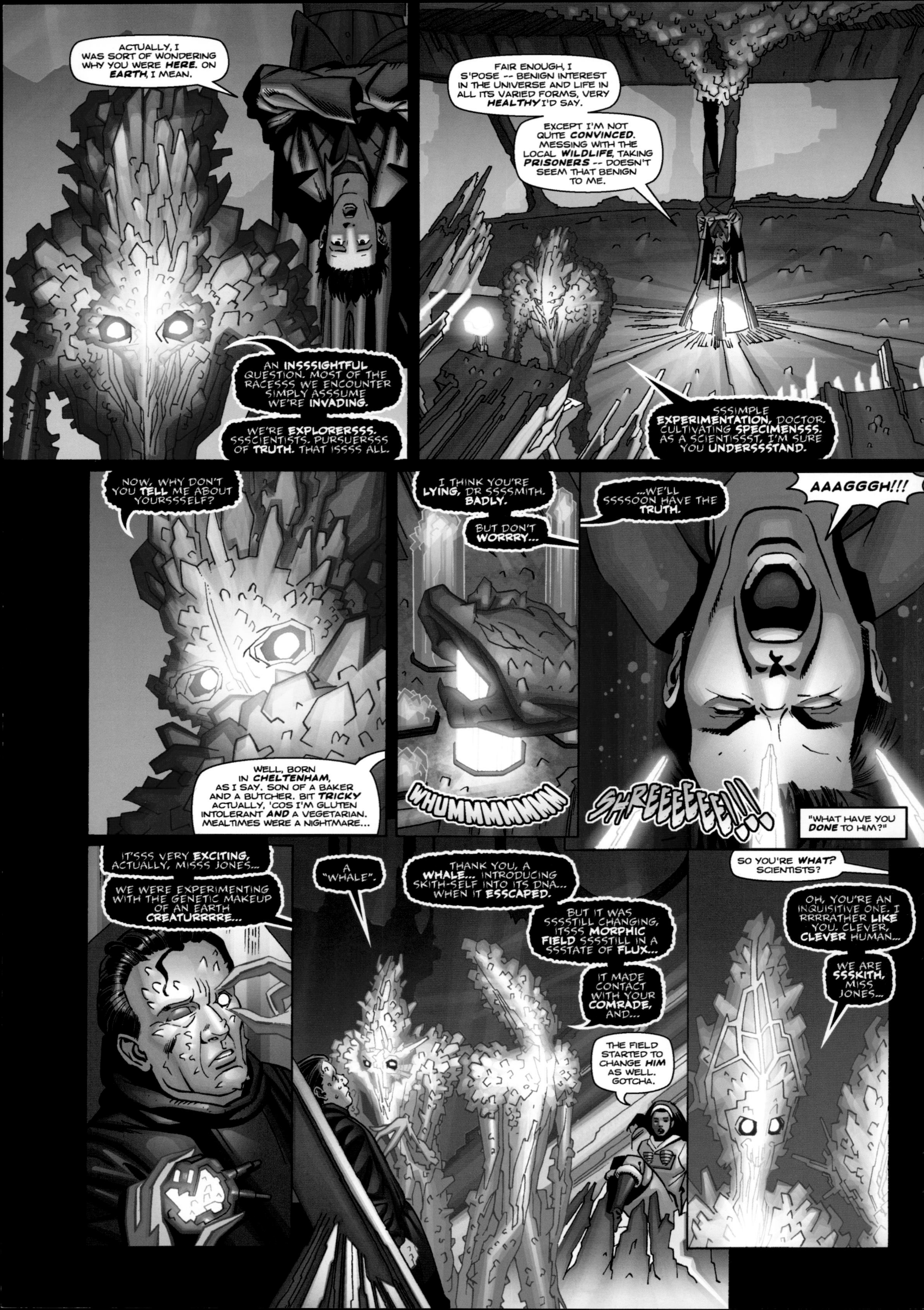
ACTUALLY, I WAS SORT OF WONDERING WHY YOU WERE HERE. ON EARTH, I MEAN.
AN INSSSIGHTFUL QUESTION. MOST OF THE RACESSS WE ENCOUNTER SIMPLY ASSSUME WE'RE INVADING.
WE'RE EXPLORERSSS. SSSCIENTISTS. PURSUERSSS OF TRUTH. THAT ISSSS ALL.
FAIR ENOUGH, I S'POSE -- BENIGN INTEREST IN THE UNIVERSE AND LIFE IN ALL ITS VARIED FORMS, VERY HEALTHY I'D SAY.
EXCEPT I'M NOT QUITE CONVINCED. MESSING WITH THE LOCAL WILDLIFE, TAKING PRISONERS -- DOESN'T SEEM THAT BENIGN TO ME.
SSSIMPLE EXPERIMENTATION, DOCTOR. CULTIVATING SPECIMENSSS. AS A SCIENTISSST, I'M SURE YOU UNDERSSSTAND.
NOW, WHY DON'T YOU TELL ME ABOUT YOURSSSELF?
WELL, BORN IN CHELTENHAM, AS I SAY. SON OF A BAKER AND A BUTCHER. BIT TRICKY ACTUALLY, 'COS I'M GLUTEN INTOLERANT AND A VEGETARIAN. MEALTIMES WERE A NIGHTMARE...
I THINK YOU'RE LYING, DR SSSSMITH. BADLY.
BUT DON'T WORRRY...
WHUMMMMMMM
...WE'LL SSSSOON HAVE THE TRUTH.
AAAGGGH!!!
SHREEEEEE!!!
"WHAT HAVE YOU DONE TO HIM?"
IT'SSS VERY EXCITING, ACTUALLY, MISSS JONES...
WE WERE EXPERIMENTING WITH THE GENETIC MAKEUP OF AN EARTH CREATURRRRE...
A "WHALE".
THANK YOU, A WHALE... INTRODUCING SKITH-SELF INTO ITS DNA... WHEN IT ESSCAPED.
BUT IT WAS SSSSTILL CHANGING, ITSSS MORPHIC FIELD SSSSTILL IN A SSSTATE OF FLUX...
IT MADE CONTACT WITH YOUR COMRADE, AND...
THE FIELD STARTED TO CHANGE HIM AS WELL. GOTCHA.
SO YOU'RE WHAT? SCIENTISTS?
OH, YOU'RE AN INQUISITIVE ONE. I RRRRATHER LIKE YOU. CLEVER, CLEVER HUMAN...
WE ARE SSSKITH, MISS JONES...

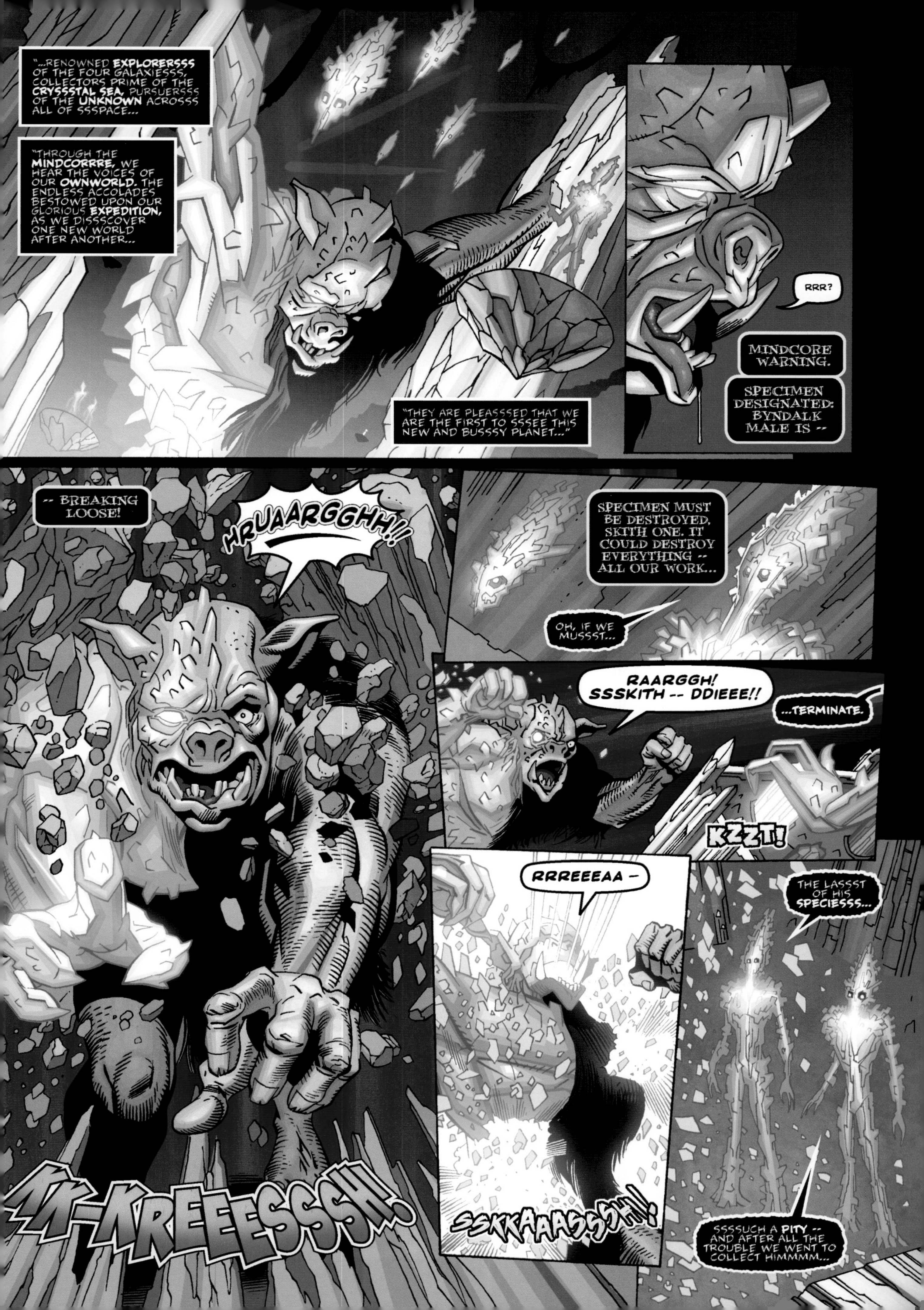
"...RENOWNED EXPLORERSSS OF THE FOUR GALAXIESSS, COLLECTORS PRIME OF THE CRYSSSTAL SEA, PURSUERSSS OF THE UNKNOWN ACROSSS ALL OF SSSPACE...
"THROUGH THE MINDCORRRE, WE HEAR THE VOICES OF OUR OWNWORLD. THE ENDLESS ACCOLADES BESTOWED UPON OUR GLORIOUS EXPEDITION, AS WE DISSSCOVER ONE NEW WORLD AFTER ANOTHER...
"THEY ARE PLEASSSED THAT WE ARE THE FIRST TO SSSEE THIS NEW AND BUSSSY PLANET..."
RRR?
MINDCORE WARNING.
SPECIMEN DESIGNATED: BYNDALK MALE IS --
-- BREAKING LOOSE!
HRUAARGGHH!!
KK-KREEEESSSSH!
SPECIMEN MUST BE DESTROYED, SKITH ONE. IT COULD DESTROY EVERYTHING -- ALL OUR WORK...
OH, IF WE MUSSST...
RAARGGH! SSSKITH -- DDIEEE!!
...TERMINATE.
KZZT!
RRREEEAA --
SSKKAAASSSH!!
THE LASSST OF HIS SPECIESSS...
SSSSUCH A PITY -- AND AFTER ALL THE TROUBLE WE WENT TO COLLECT HIMMMM...

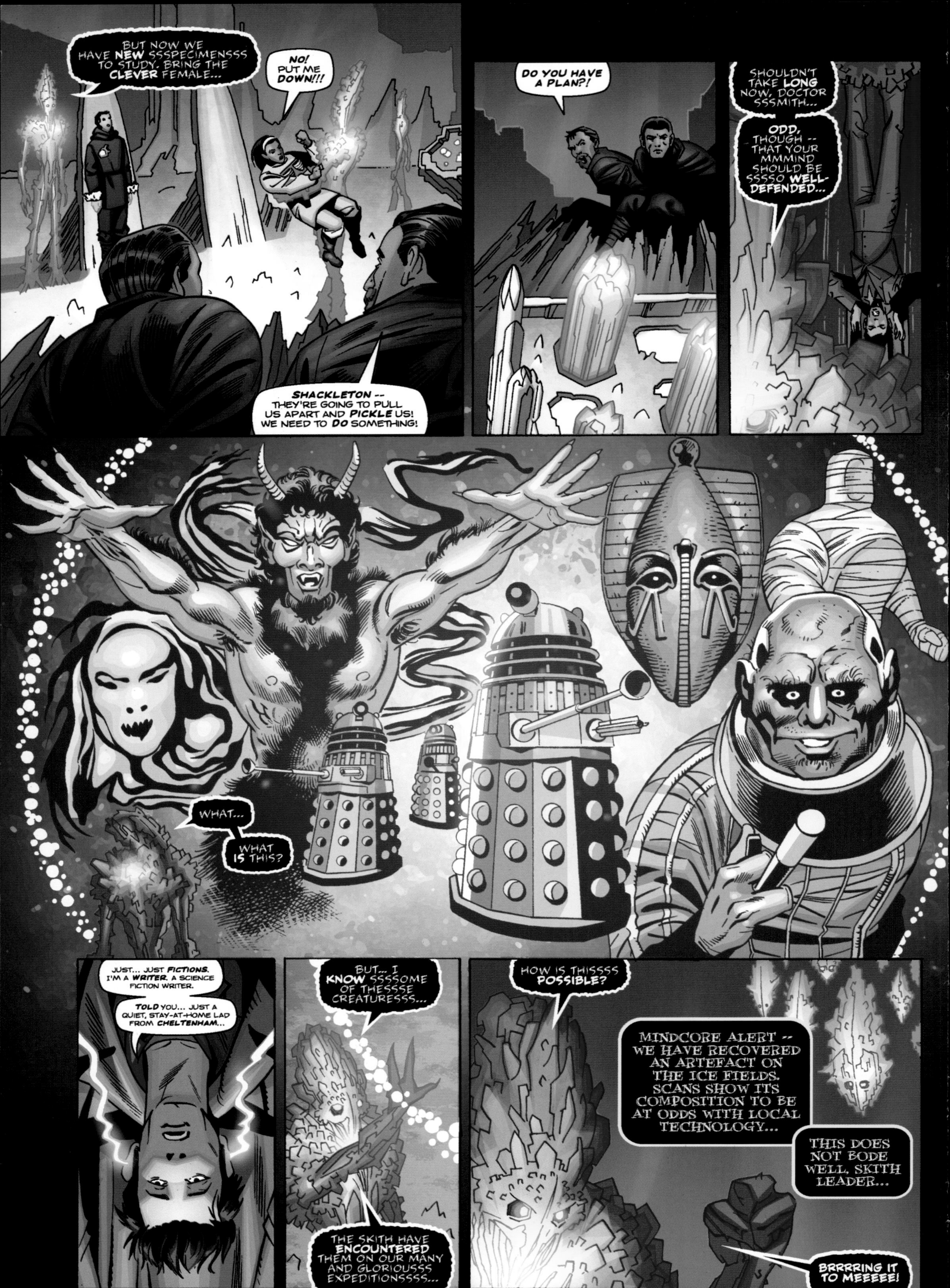

BUT NOW WE HAVE NEW SSSPECIMENSSS TO STUDY. BRING THE CLEVER FEMALE...
NO! PUT ME DOWN!!!
SHACKLETON -- THEY'RE GOING TO PULL US APART AND PICKLE US! WE NEED TO DO SOMETHING!
DO YOU HAVE A PLAN?!
SHOULDN'T TAKE LONG NOW, DOCTOR SSSMITH...
ODD, THOUGH -- THAT YOUR MMMIND SHOULD BE SSSSO WELL-DEFENDED...
WHAT...
WHAT IS THIS?
JUST... JUST FICTIONS. I'M A WRITER. A SCIENCE FICTION WRITER.
TOLD YOU... JUST A QUIET, STAY-AT-HOME LAD FROM CHELTENHAM...
BUT... I KNOW SSSSOME OF THESSSE CREATURESSS...
THE SKITH HAVE ENCOUNTERED THEM ON OUR MANY AND GLORIOUSSS EXPEDITIONSSSS...
HOW IS THISSSS POSSIBLE?
MINDCORE ALERT -- WE HAVE RECOVERED AN ARTEFACT ON THE ICE FIELDS. SCANS SHOW ITS COMPOSITION TO BE AT ODDS WITH LOCAL TECHNOLOGY...
THIS DOES NOT BODE WELL, SKITH LEADER...
BRRRRING IT TO MEEEEE!

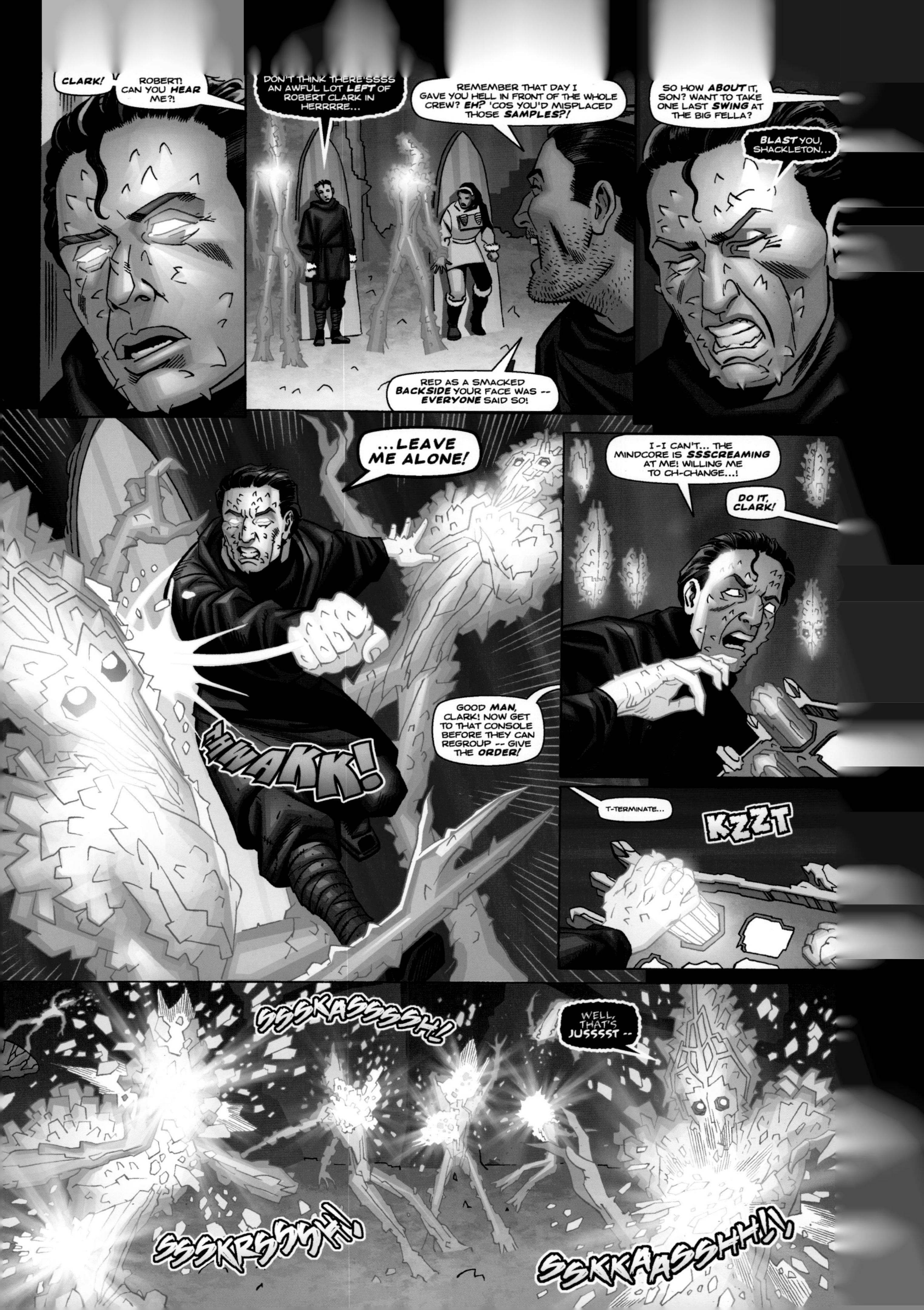
CLARK!
ROBERT! CAN YOU HEAR ME?!
DON'T THINK THERE'SSSS AN AWFUL LOT LEFT OF ROBERT CLARK IN HERRRRE...
REMEMBER THAT DAY I GAVE YOU HELL IN FRONT OF THE WHOLE CREW? EH? 'COS YOU'D MISPLACED THOSE SAMPLES?!
RED AS A SMACKED BACKSIDE YOUR FACE WAS -- EVERYONE SAID SO!
SO HOW ABOUT IT, SON? WANT TO TAKE ONE LAST SWING AT THE BIG FELLA?
BLAST YOU, SHACKLETON...
...LEAVE ME ALONE!
THWAKK!
GOOD MAN, CLARK! NOW GET TO THAT CONSOLE BEFORE THEY CAN REGROUP -- GIVE THE ORDER!
I-I CAN'T... THE MINDCORE IS SSSCREAMING AT ME! WILLING ME TO CH-CHANGE...!
DO IT, CLARK!
T-TERMINATE...
KZZT
SSSKASSSSH!
WELL, THAT'S JUSSSST --
SSSKRSSSH!
SSKKAASSHH!!

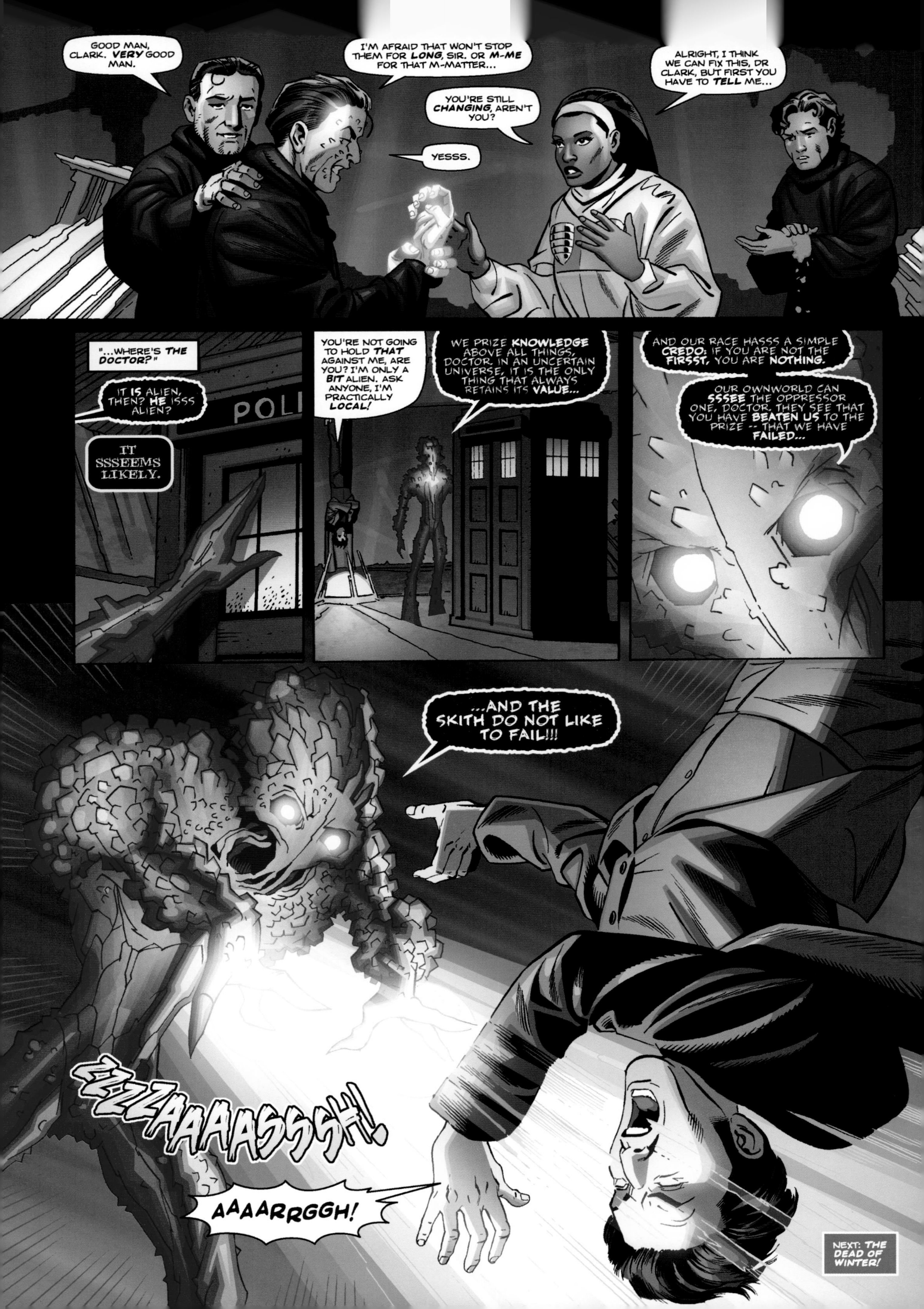

GOOD MAN, CLARK. VERY GOOD MAN.
I'M AFRAID THAT WON'T STOP THEM FOR LONG, SIR. OR M-ME FOR THAT M-MATTER...
YOU'RE STILL CHANGING, AREN'T YOU?
YESSS.
ALRIGHT, I THINK WE CAN FIX THIS, DR CLARK, BUT FIRST YOU HAVE TO TELL ME...
"...WHERE'S THE DOCTOR?"
IT IS ALIEN, THEN? HE ISSS ALIEN?
IT SSSEEMS LIKELY.
POLI
YOU'RE NOT GOING TO HOLD THAT AGAINST ME, ARE YOU? I'M ONLY A BIT ALIEN. ASK ANYONE, I'M PRACTICALLY LOCAL!
WE PRIZE KNOWLEDGE ABOVE ALL THINGS, DOCTOR. IN AN UNCERTAIN UNIVERSE, IT IS THE ONLY THING THAT ALWAYS RETAINS ITS VALUE...
AND OUR RACE HASSS A SIMPLE CREDO: IF YOU ARE NOT THE FIRSST, YOU ARE NOTHING.
OUR OWNWORLD CAN SSSEE THE OPPRESSOR ONE, DOCTOR. THEY SEE THAT YOU HAVE BEATEN US TO THE PRIZE -- THAT WE HAVE FAILED...
...AND THE SKITH DO NOT LIKE TO FAIL!!!
ZZZZAAAAASSSSH!
AAAARRGGH!
NEXT: THE DEAD OF WINTER!

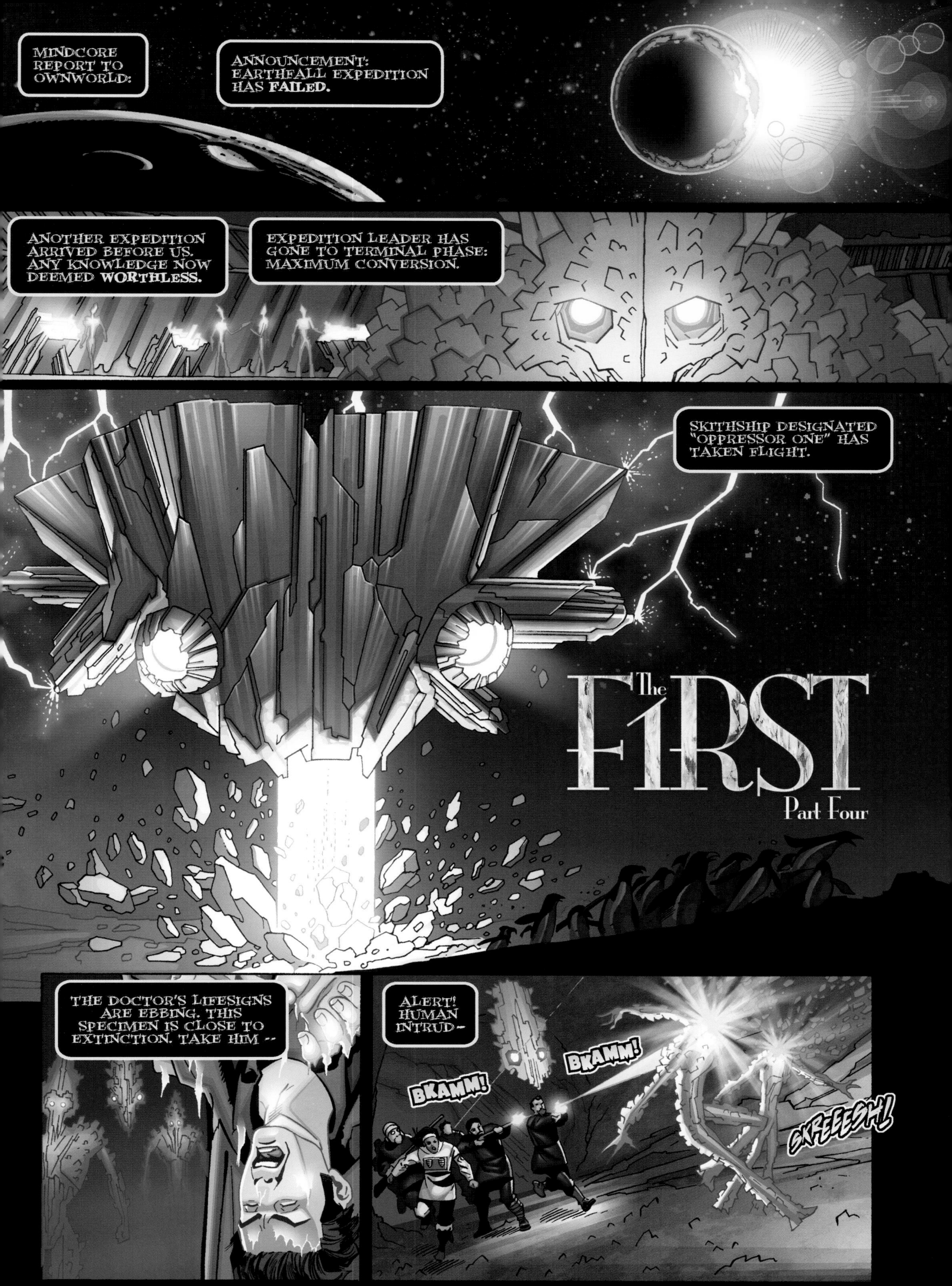
MINDCORE REPORT TO OWNWORLD:
ANNOUNCEMENT: EARTHFALL EXPEDITION HAS FAILED.
ANOTHER EXPEDITION ARRIVED BEFORE US. ANY KNOWLEDGE NOW DEEMED WORTHLESS.
EXPEDITION LEADER HAS GONE TO TERMINAL PHASE: MAXIMUM CONVERSION.
SKITHSHIP DESIGNATED "OPPRESSOR ONE" HAS TAKEN FLIGHT.
The FIRST
Part Four
THE DOCTOR'S LIFESIGNS ARE EBBING. THIS SPECIMEN IS CLOSE TO EXTINCTION. TAKE HIM --
ALERT! HUMAN INTRUD--
BKAMM!
BKAMM!
SKREEEESH!

Story DANIEL McDAID · Pencils MARTIN GERAGHTY · Inks DAVID A. ROACH · Colours JAMES OFFREDI · Letters ROGER LANGRIDGE · Editors HICKMAN & GRAY

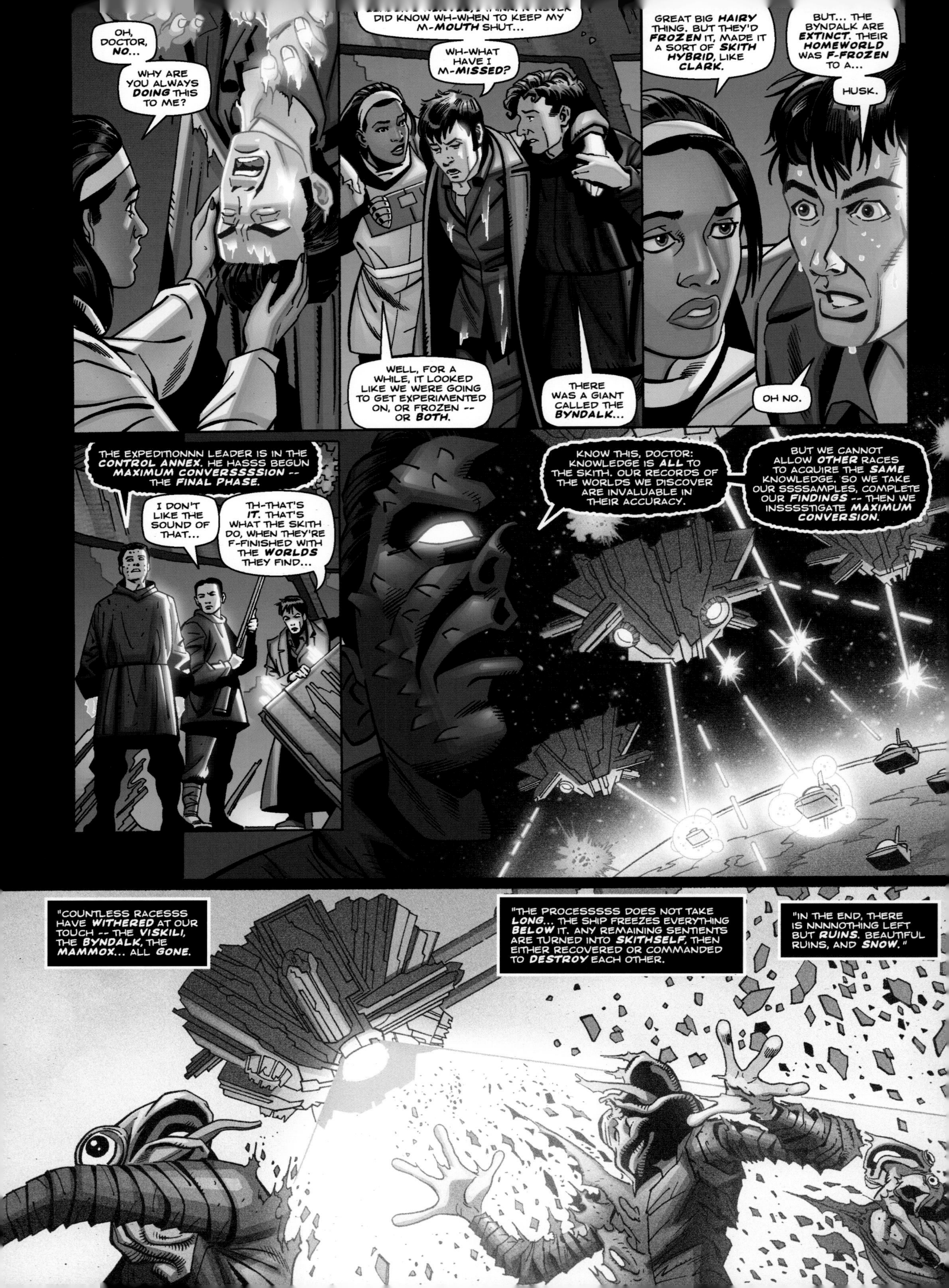
OH, DOCTOR, NO...
WHY ARE YOU ALWAYS DOING THIS TO ME?
DID KNOW WH-WHEN TO KEEP MY M-MOUTH SHUT...
WH-WHAT HAVE I M-MISSED?
WELL, FOR A WHILE, IT LOOKED LIKE WE WERE GOING TO GET EXPERIMENTED ON, OR FROZEN -- OR BOTH.
THERE WAS A GIANT CALLED THE BYNDALK...
GREAT BIG HAIRY THING. BUT THEY'D FROZEN IT, MADE IT A SORT OF SKITH HYBRID, LIKE CLARK.
BUT... THE BYNDALK ARE EXTINCT. THEIR HOMEWORLD WAS F-FROZEN TO A...
HUSK.
OH NO.
THE EXPEDITIONNN LEADER IS IN THE CONTROL ANNEX. HE HASSS BEGUN MAXIMUM CONVERSSSSION -- THE FINAL PHASE.
I DON'T LIKE THE SOUND OF THAT...
TH-THAT'S IT. THAT'S WHAT THE SKITH DO, WHEN THEY'RE F-FINISHED WITH THE WORLDS THEY FIND...
KNOW THIS, DOCTOR: KNOWLEDGE IS ALL TO THE SKITH. OUR RECORDS OF THE WORLDS WE DISCOVER ARE INVALUABLE IN THEIR ACCURACY.
BUT WE CANNOT ALLOW OTHER RACES TO ACQUIRE THE SAME KNOWLEDGE. SO WE TAKE OUR SSSSAMPLES, COMPLETE OUR FINDINGS -- THEN WE INSSSSTIGATE MAXIMUM CONVERSION.
"COUNTLESS RACESSS HAVE WITHERED AT OUR TOUCH -- THE VISKILI, THE BYNDALK, THE MAMMOX... ALL GONE.
"THE PROCESSSSS DOES NOT TAKE LONG... THE SHIP FREEZES EVERYTHING BELOW IT. ANY REMAINING SENTIENTS ARE TURNED INTO SKITHSELF, THEN EITHER RECOVERED OR COMMANDED TO DESTROY EACH OTHER.
"IN THE END, THERE IS NNNNOTHING LEFT BUT RUINS. BEAUTIFUL RUINS, AND SNOW."

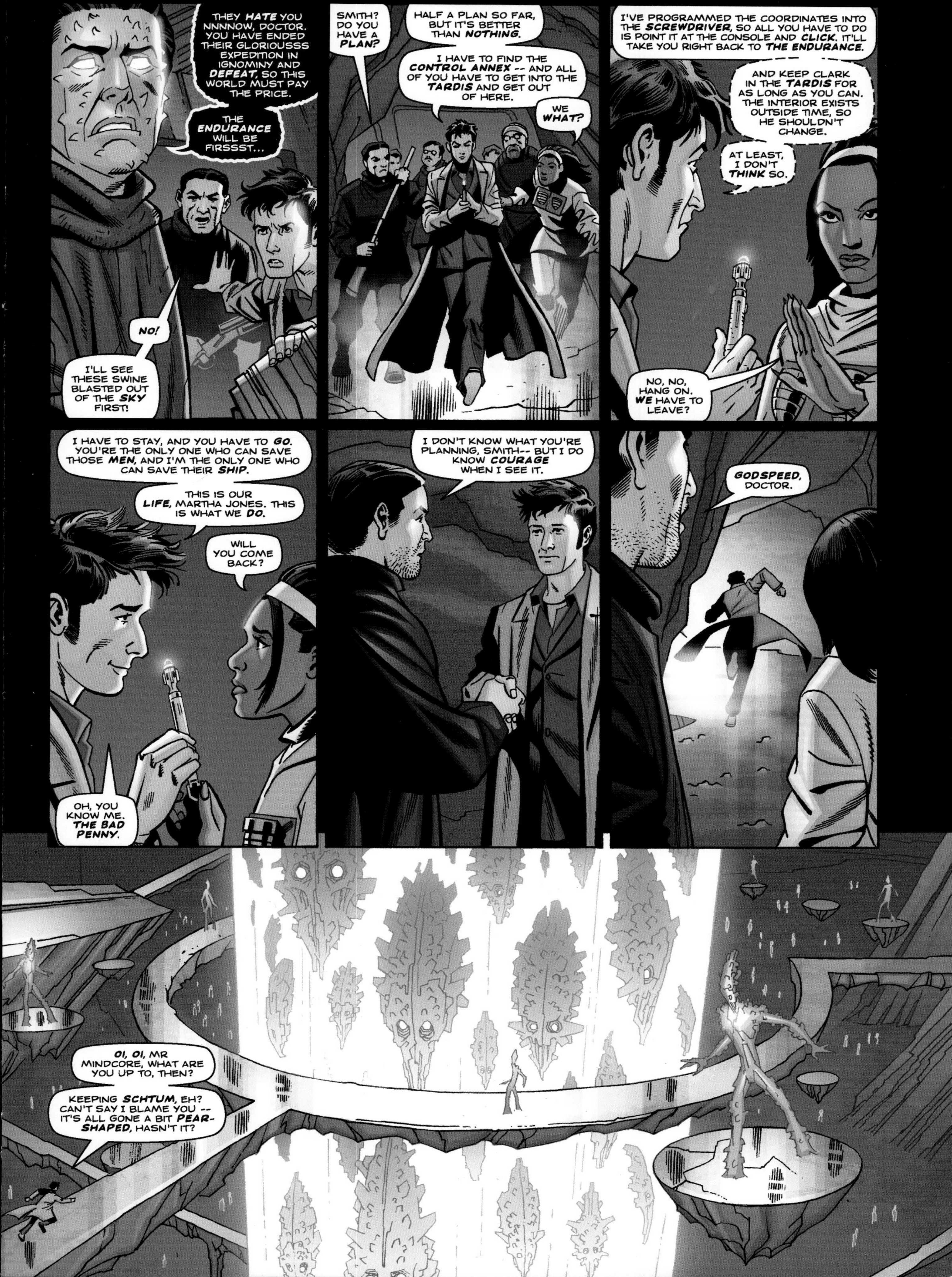

THEY HATE YOU NNNNOW, DOCTOR. YOU HAVE ENDED THEIR GLORIOUSSS EXPEDITION IN IGNOMINY AND DEFEAT, SO THIS WORLD MUST PAY THE PRICE.
THE ENDURANCE WILL BE FIRSSST...
NO!
I'LL SEE THESE SWINE BLASTED OUT OF THE SKY FIRST!
SMITH? DO YOU HAVE A PLAN?
HALF A PLAN SO FAR, BUT IT'S BETTER THAN NOTHING.
I HAVE TO FIND THE CONTROL ANNEX -- AND ALL OF YOU HAVE TO GET INTO THE TARDIS AND GET OUT OF HERE.
WE WHAT?
I'VE PROGRAMMED THE COORDINATES INTO THE SCREWDRIVER, SO ALL YOU HAVE TO DO IS POINT IT AT THE CONSOLE AND CLICK, IT'LL TAKE YOU RIGHT BACK TO THE ENDURANCE.
AND KEEP CLARK IN THE TARDIS FOR AS LONG AS YOU CAN. THE INTERIOR EXISTS OUTSIDE TIME, SO HE SHOULDN'T CHANGE.
AT LEAST, I DON'T THINK SO.
NO, NO, HANG ON. WE HAVE TO LEAVE?
I HAVE TO STAY, AND YOU HAVE TO GO. YOU'RE THE ONLY ONE WHO CAN SAVE THOSE MEN, AND I'M THE ONLY ONE WHO CAN SAVE THEIR SHIP.
THIS IS OUR LIFE, MARTHA JONES. THIS IS WHAT WE DO.
WILL YOU COME BACK?
OH, YOU KNOW ME. THE BAD PENNY.
I DON'T KNOW WHAT YOU'RE PLANNING, SMITH-- BUT I DO KNOW COURAGE WHEN I SEE IT.
GODSPEED, DOCTOR.
OI, OI, MR MINDCORE, WHAT ARE YOU UP TO, THEN?
KEEPING SCHTUM, EH? CAN'T SAY I BLAME YOU -- IT'S ALL GONE A BIT PEAR-SHAPED, HASN'T IT?

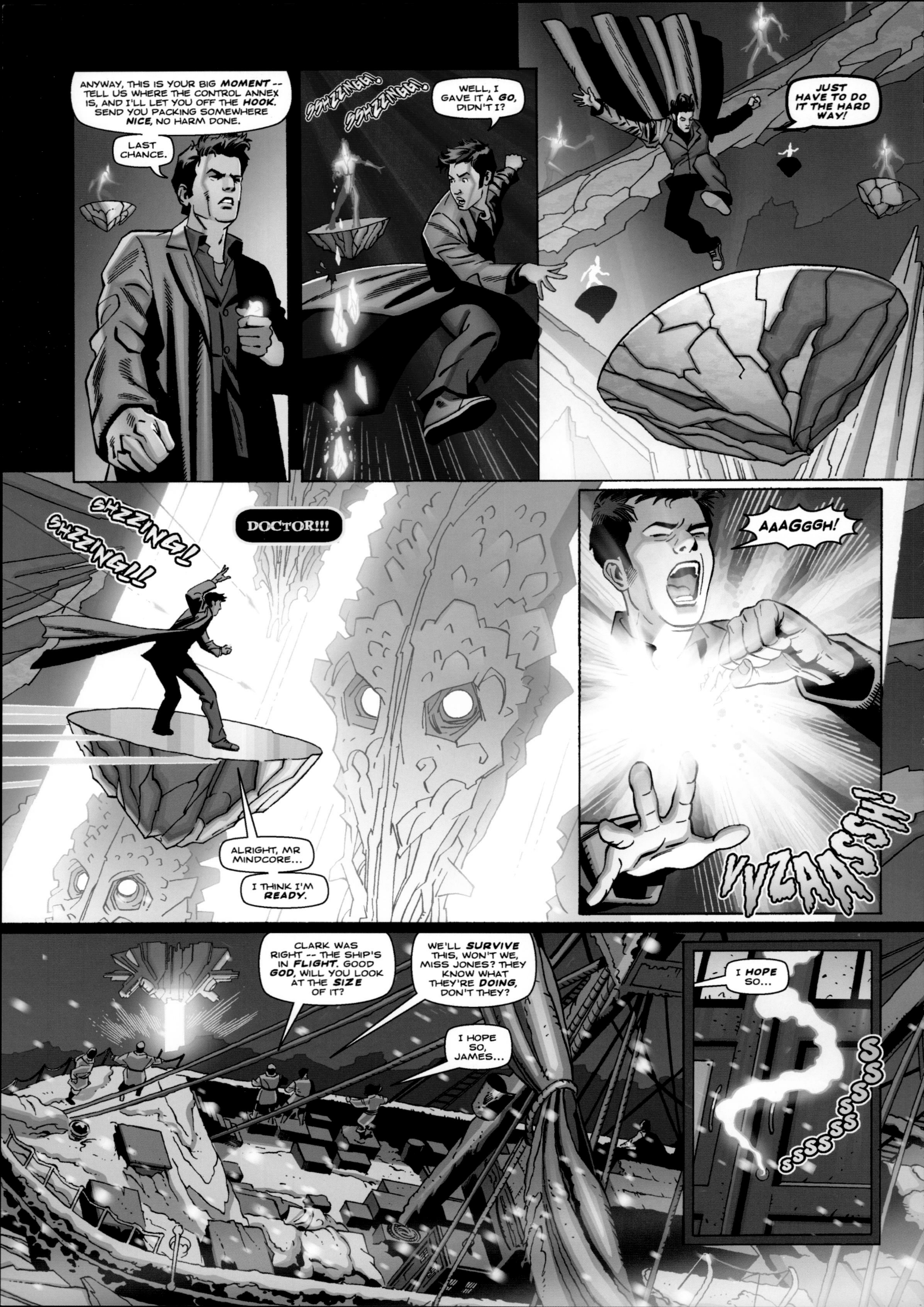
ANYWAY, THIS IS YOUR BIG MOMENT -- TELL US WHERE THE CONTROL ANNEX IS, AND I'LL LET YOU OFF THE HOOK. SEND YOU PACKING SOMEWHERE NICE, NO HARM DONE.
LAST CHANCE.
SSHZZINGG!!
SSHZZINGG!!
WELL, I GAVE IT A GO, DIDN'T I?
JUST HAVE TO DO IT THE HARD WAY!
SHZZING!!
SHZZING!!
DOCTOR!!!
ALRIGHT, MR MINDCORE...
I THINK I'M READY.
AAAGGGH!
VVZAASSH!
CLARK WAS RIGHT -- THE SHIP'S IN FLIGHT. GOOD GOD, WILL YOU LOOK AT THE SIZE OF IT?
WE'LL SURVIVE THIS, WON'T WE, MISS JONES? THEY KNOW WHAT THEY'RE DOING, DON'T THEY?
I HOPE SO, JAMES...
I HOPE SO...
SSSSSSSSSSSSSS

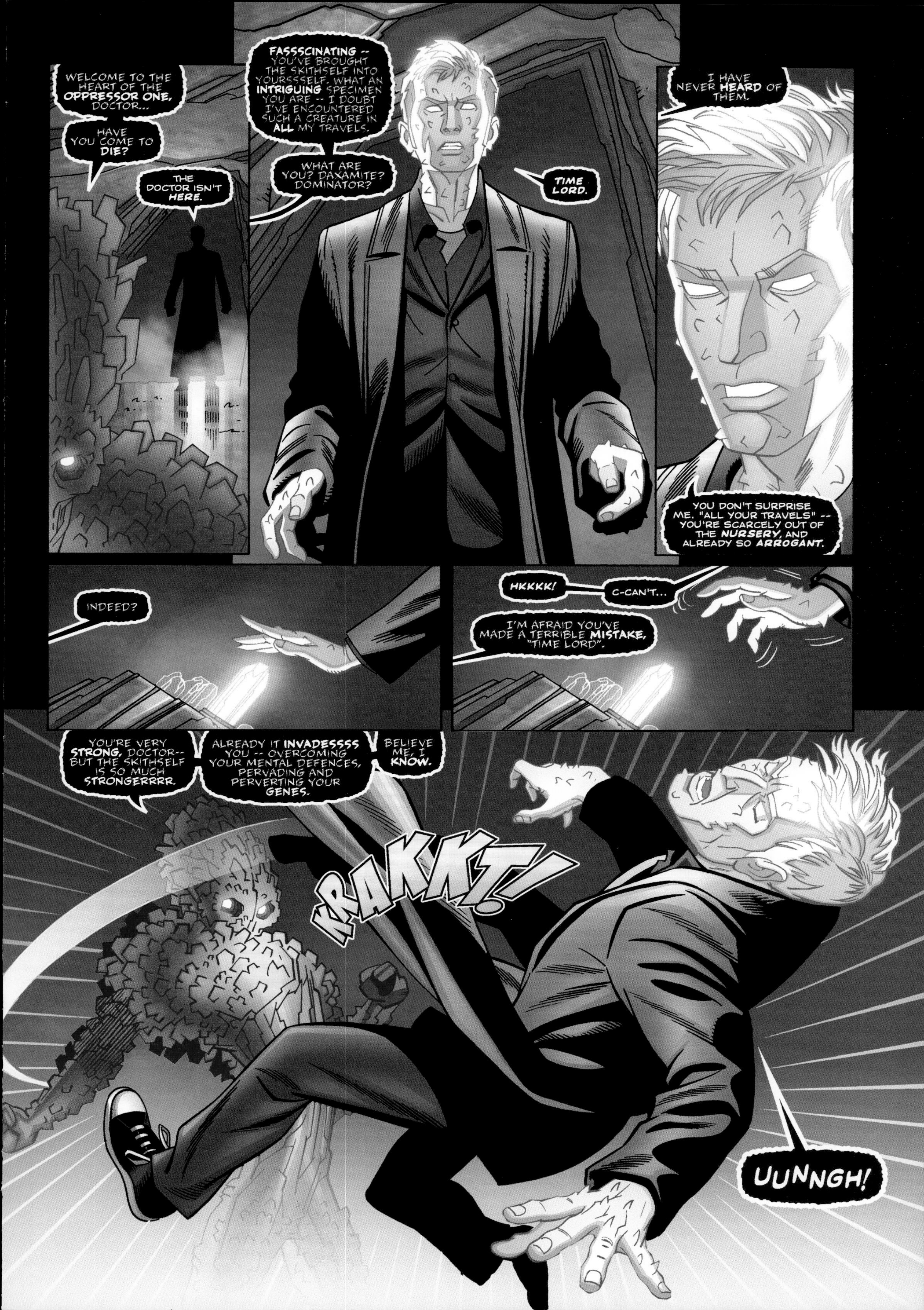
WELCOME TO THE HEART OF THE OPPRESSOR ONE, DOCTOR...
HAVE YOU COME TO DIE?
THE DOCTOR ISN'T HERE.
FASSSCINATING -- YOU'VE BROUGHT THE SKITHSELF INTO YOURSSSELF. WHAT AN INTRIGUING SPECIMEN YOU ARE -- I DOUBT I'VE ENCOUNTERED SUCH A CREATURE IN ALL MY TRAVELS.
WHAT ARE YOU? DAXAMITE? DOMINATOR?
TIME LORD.
I HAVE NEVER HEARD OF THEM.
YOU DON'T SURPRISE ME. "ALL YOUR TRAVELS" -- YOU'RE SCARCELY OUT OF THE NURSERY, AND ALREADY SO ARROGANT.
INDEED?
HKKKK!
C-CAN'T...
I'M AFRAID YOU'VE MADE A TERRIBLE MISTAKE, "TIME LORD".
YOU'RE VERY STRONG, DOCTOR-- BUT THE SKITHSELF IS SO MUCH STRONGERRRR.
ALREADY IT INVADESSSS YOU -- OVERCOMING YOUR MENTAL DEFENCES, PERVADING AND PERVERTING YOUR GENES.
BELIEVE ME, I KNOW.
KRAKKT!
UUNNGH!

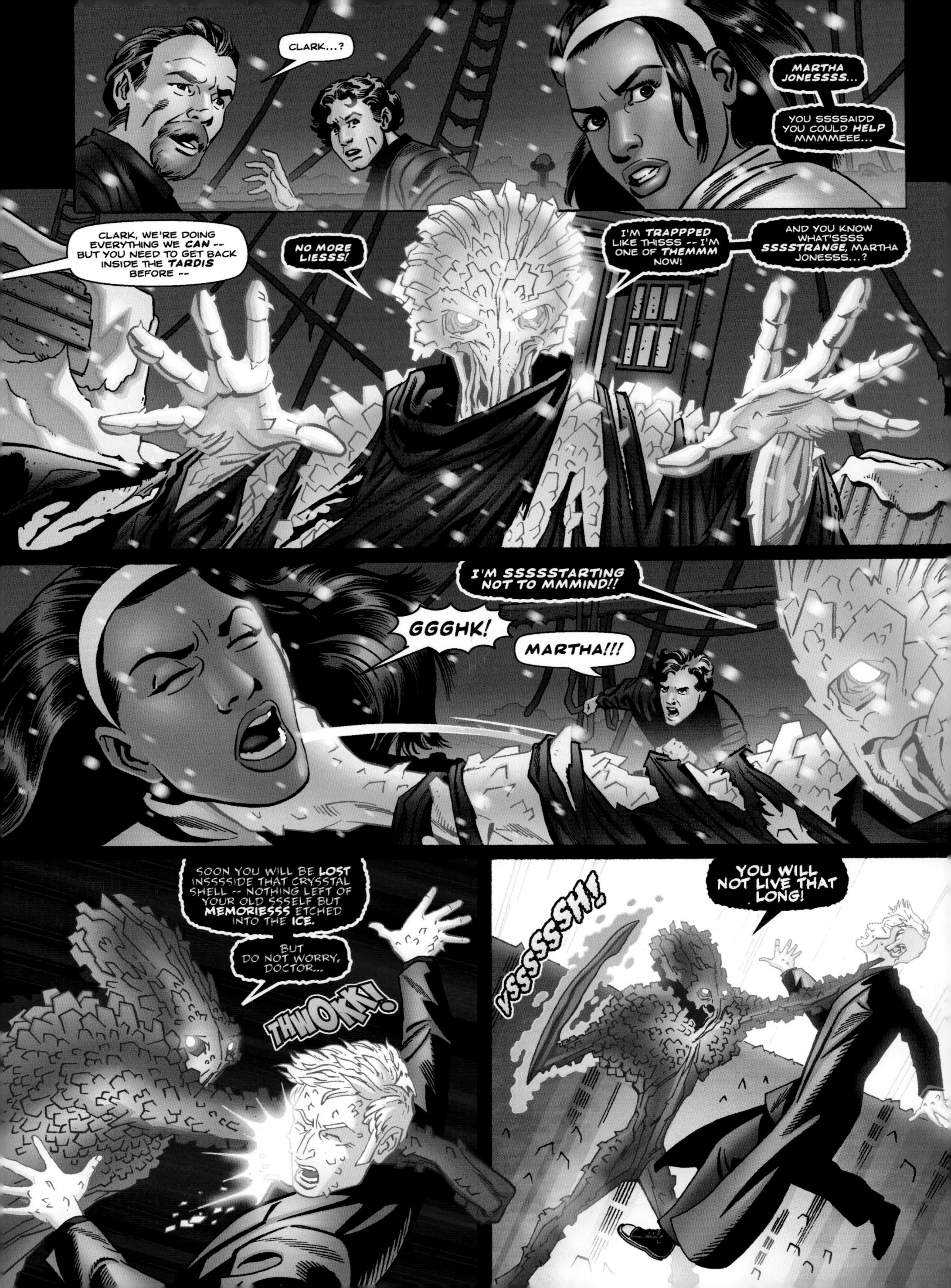
CLARK...?
MARTHA JONESSSS...
YOU SSSSAIDD YOU COULD HELP MMMMEEE...
CLARK, WE'RE DOING EVERYTHING WE CAN -- BUT YOU NEED TO GET BACK INSIDE THE TARDIS BEFORE --
NO MORE LIESSS!
I'M TRAPPPED LIKE THISSS -- I'M ONE OF THEMMM NOW!
AND YOU KNOW WHAT'SSSS SSSSTRANGE, MARTHA JONESSS...?
I'M SSSSSTARTING NOT TO MMMIND!!
GGGHK!
MARTHA!!!
SOON YOU WILL BE LOST INSSSSIDE THAT CRYSSTAL SHELL -- NOTHING LEFT OF YOUR OLD SSSELF BUT MEMORIESSS ETCHED INTO THE ICE.
BUT DO NOT WORRY, DOCTOR...
THWOKK!
VSSSSSSH!
YOU WILL NOT LIVE THAT LONG!

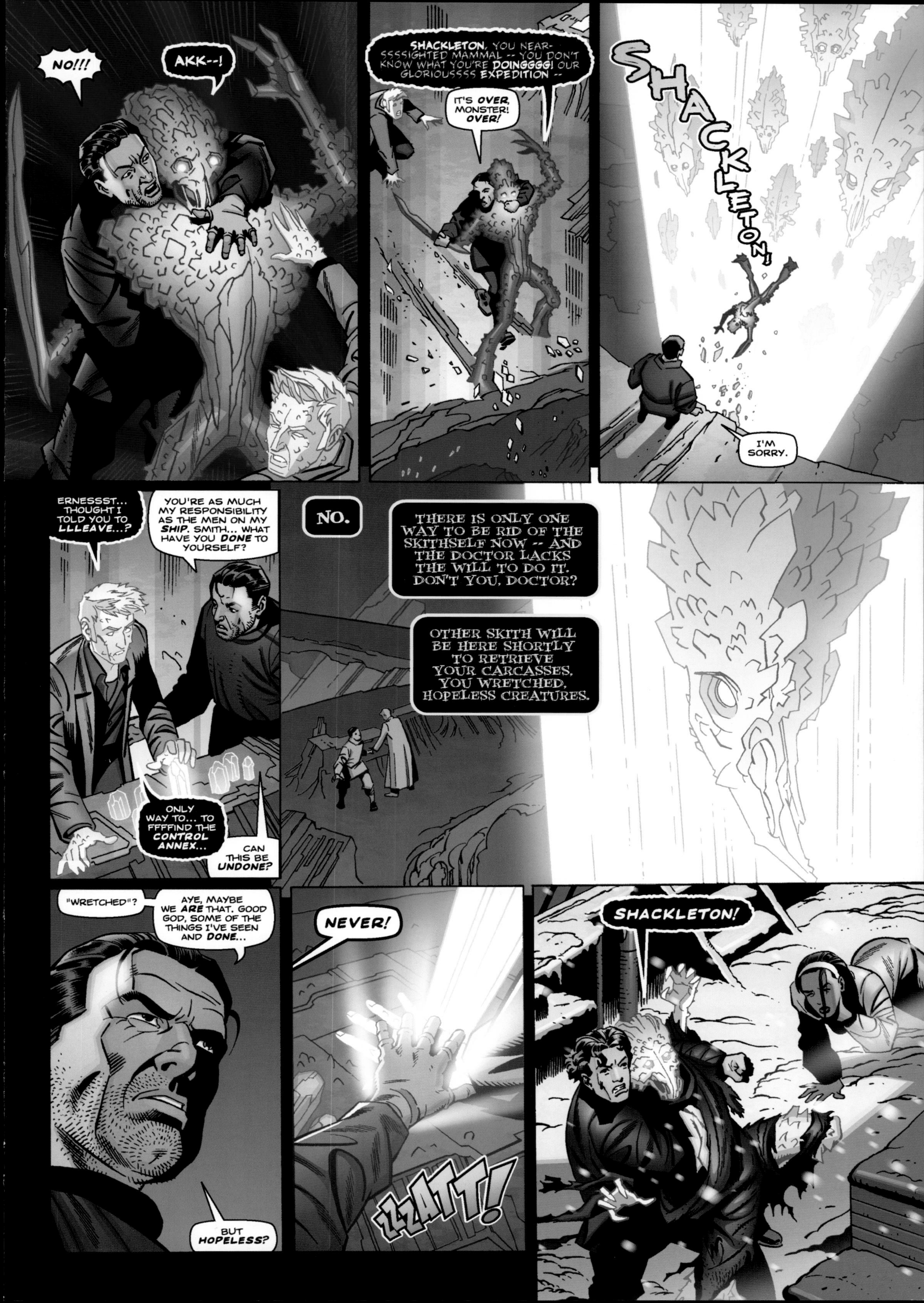
NO!!!
AKK--!
SHACKLETON, YOU NEAR-SSSSIGHTED MAMMAL -- YOU DON'T KNOW WHAT YOU'RE DOINGGGG! OUR GLORIOUSSSS EXPEDITION --
IT'S OVER, MONSTER! OVER!
SHACKLETON!
I'M SORRY.
ERNESSST... THOUGHT I TOLD YOU TO LLLEAVE...?
YOU'RE AS MUCH MY RESPONSIBILITY AS THE MEN ON MY SHIP, SMITH... WHAT HAVE YOU DONE TO YOURSELF?
ONLY WAY TO... TO FFFFIND THE CONTROL ANNEX...
CAN THIS BE UNDONE?
NO.
THERE IS ONLY ONE WAY TO BE RID OF THE SKITHSELF NOW -- AND THE DOCTOR LACKS THE WILL TO DO IT. DON'T YOU, DOCTOR?
OTHER SKITH WILL BE HERE SHORTLY TO RETRIEVE YOUR CARCASSES, YOU WRETCHED, HOPELESS CREATURES.
"WRETCHED"?
AYE, MAYBE WE ARE THAT. GOOD GOD, SOME OF THE THINGS I'VE SEEN AND DONE...
BUT HOPELESS?
NEVER!
ZZZATT!
SHACKLETON!

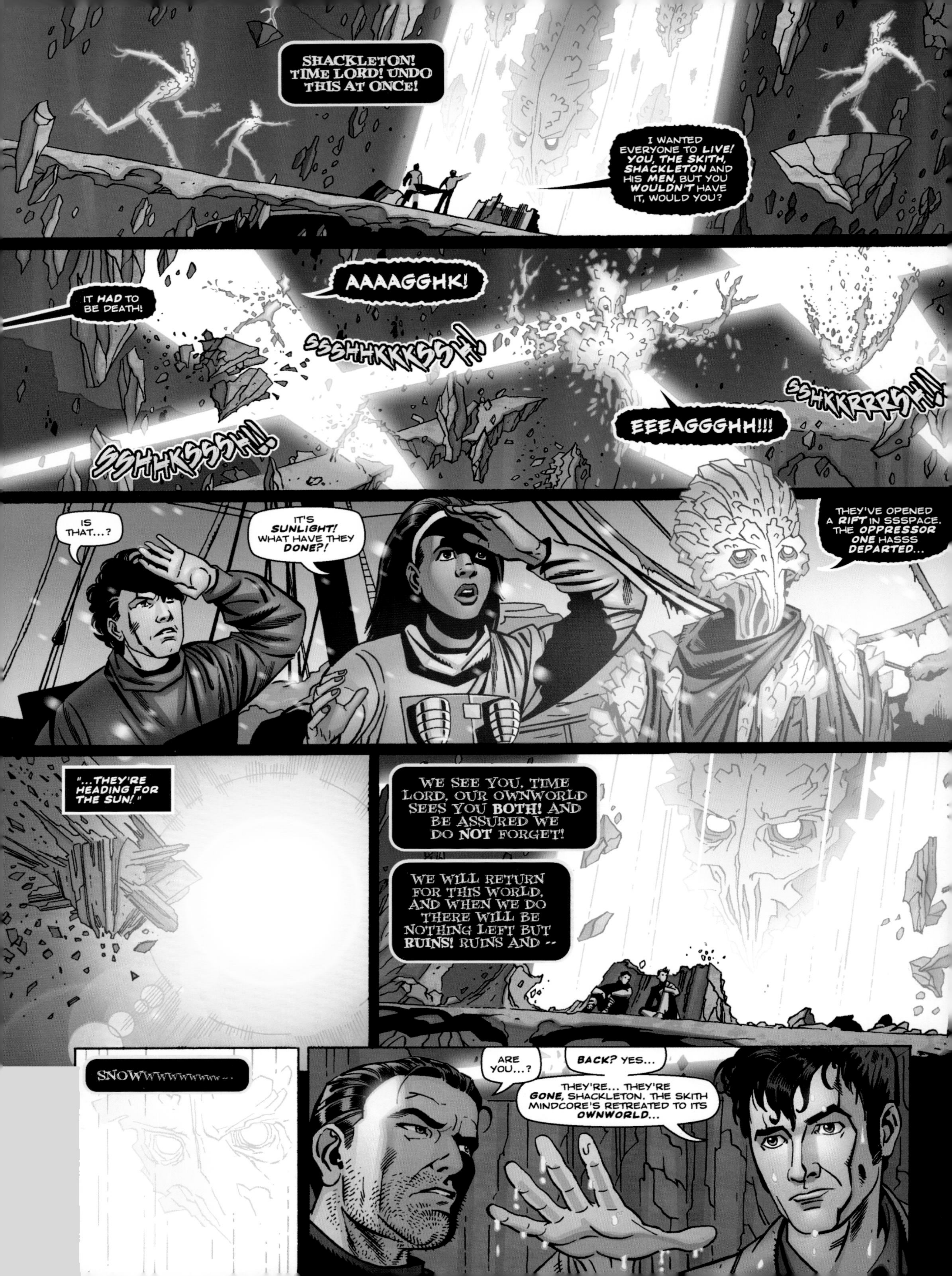

SHACKLETON! TIME LORD! UNDO THIS AT ONCE!
I WANTED EVERYONE TO LIVE! YOU, THE SKITH, SHACKLETON AND HIS MEN, BUT YOU WOULDN'T HAVE IT, WOULD YOU?
IT HAD TO BE DEATH!
AAAAGGHK!
SSSHHKKKSSH!
SSHHKSSSH!!!
EEEAGGGHH!!!
SSHKKRRRSH!!!
IS THAT...?
IT'S SUNLIGHT! WHAT HAVE THEY DONE?!
THEY'VE OPENED A RIFT IN SSSPACE. THE OPPRESSOR ONE HASSS DEPARTED...
"...THEY'RE HEADING FOR THE SUN!"
WE SEE YOU, TIME LORD, OUR OWNWORLD SEES YOU BOTH! AND BE ASSURED WE DO NOT FORGET!
WE WILL RETURN FOR THIS WORLD, AND WHEN WE DO THERE WILL BE NOTHING LEFT BUT RUINS! RUINS AND --
SNOWwwwwwww...
ARE YOU...?
BACK? YES...
THEY'RE... THEY'RE GONE, SHACKLETON. THE SKITH MINDCORE'S RETREATED TO ITS OWNWORLD...

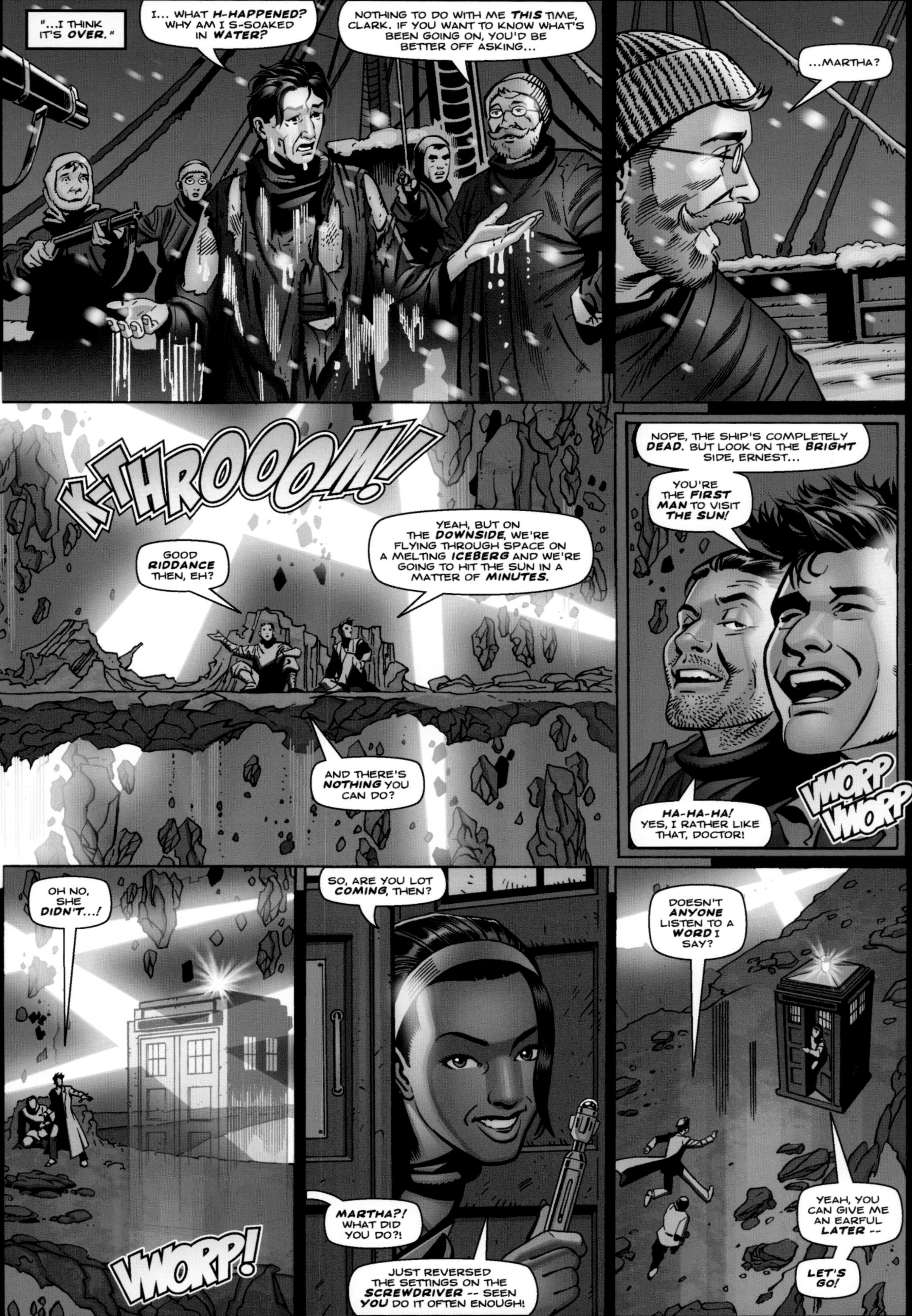
"...I THINK IT'S OVER."
I... WHAT H-HAPPENED? WHY AM I S-SOAKED IN WATER?
NOTHING TO DO WITH ME THIS TIME, CLARK. IF YOU WANT TO KNOW WHAT'S BEEN GOING ON, YOU'D BE BETTER OFF ASKING...
...MARTHA?
K-THROOOM!
GOOD RIDDANCE THEN, EH?
YEAH, BUT ON THE DOWNSIDE, WE'RE FLYING THROUGH SPACE ON A MELTING ICEBERG AND WE'RE GOING TO HIT THE SUN IN A MATTER OF MINUTES.
AND THERE'S NOTHING YOU CAN DO?
NOPE, THE SHIP'S COMPLETELY DEAD. BUT LOOK ON THE BRIGHT SIDE, ERNEST...
YOU'RE THE FIRST MAN TO VISIT THE SUN!
HA-HA-HA! YES, I RATHER LIKE THAT, DOCTOR!
VWORP VWORP
OH NO, SHE DIDN'T...!
VWORP!
SO, ARE YOU LOT COMING, THEN?
MARTHA?! WHAT DID YOU DO?!
JUST REVERSED THE SETTINGS ON THE SCREWDRIVER -- SEEN YOU DO IT OFTEN ENOUGH!
DOESN'T ANYONE LISTEN TO A WORD I SAY?
YEAH, YOU CAN GIVE ME AN EARFUL LATER --
LET'S GO!

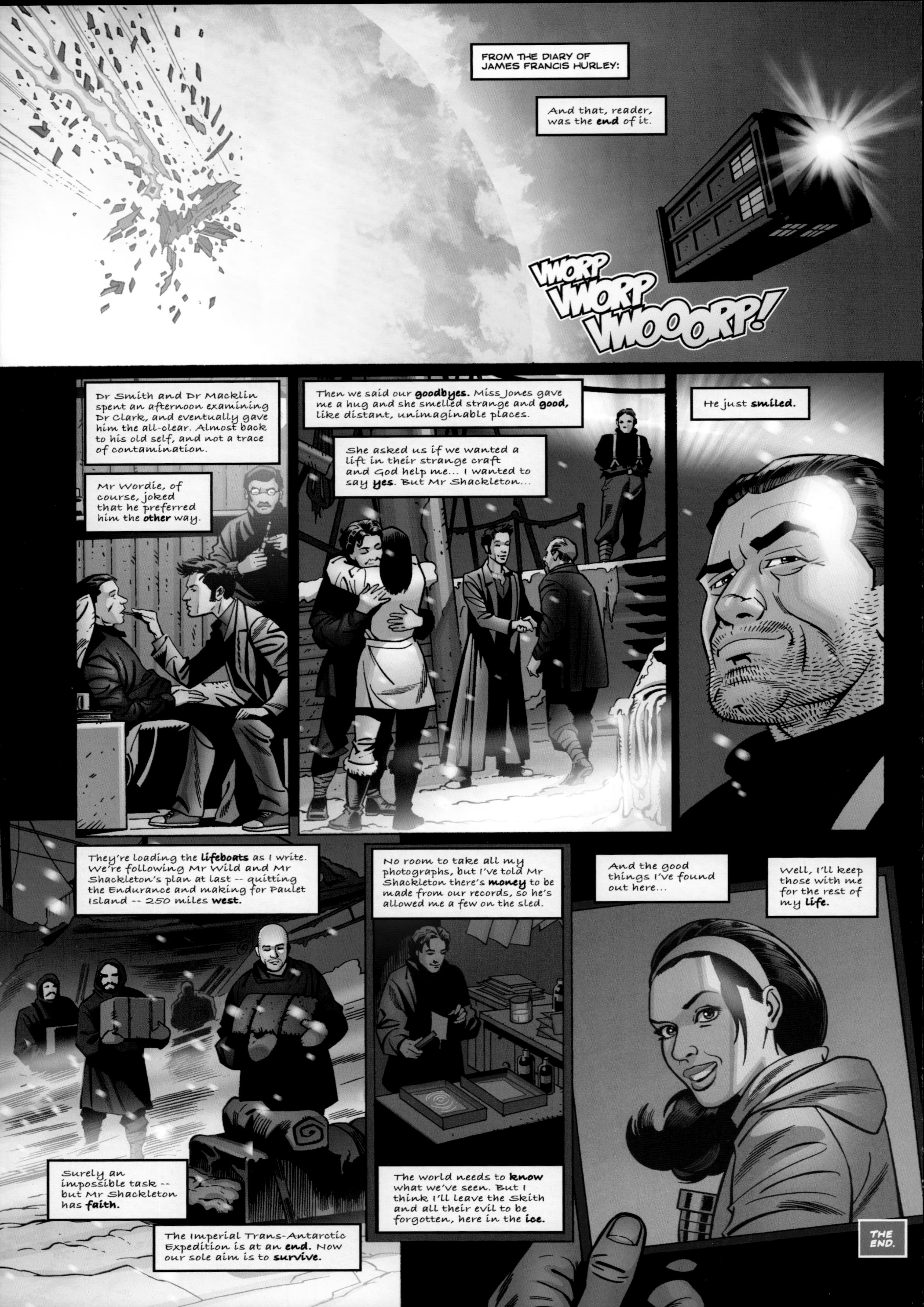
FROM THE DIARY OF JAMES FRANCIS HURLEY:
And that, reader, was the end of it.
VWORP VWORP VWOOORP!
Dr Smith and Dr Macklin spent an afternoon examining Dr Clark, and eventually gave him the all-clear. Almost back to his old self, and not a trace of contamination.
Mr Wordie, of course, joked that he preferred him the other way.
Then we said our goodbyes. Miss Jones gave me a hug and she smelled strange and good, like distant, unimaginable places.
She asked us if we wanted a lift in their strange craft and God help me... I wanted to say yes. But Mr Shackleton...
He just smiled.
They're loading the lifeboats as I write. We're following Mr Wild and Mr Shackleton's plan at last -- quitting the Endurance and making for Paulet Island -- 250 miles west.
Surely an impossible task -- but Mr Shackleton has faith.
The Imperial Trans-Antarctic Expedition is at an end. Now our sole aim is to survive.
No room to take all my photographs, but I've told Mr Shackleton there's money to be made from our records, so he's allowed me a few on the sled.
The world needs to know what we've seen. But I think I'll leave the Skith and all their evil to be forgotten, here in the ice.
And the good things I've found out here...
Well, I'll keep those with me for the rest of my life.
THE END.

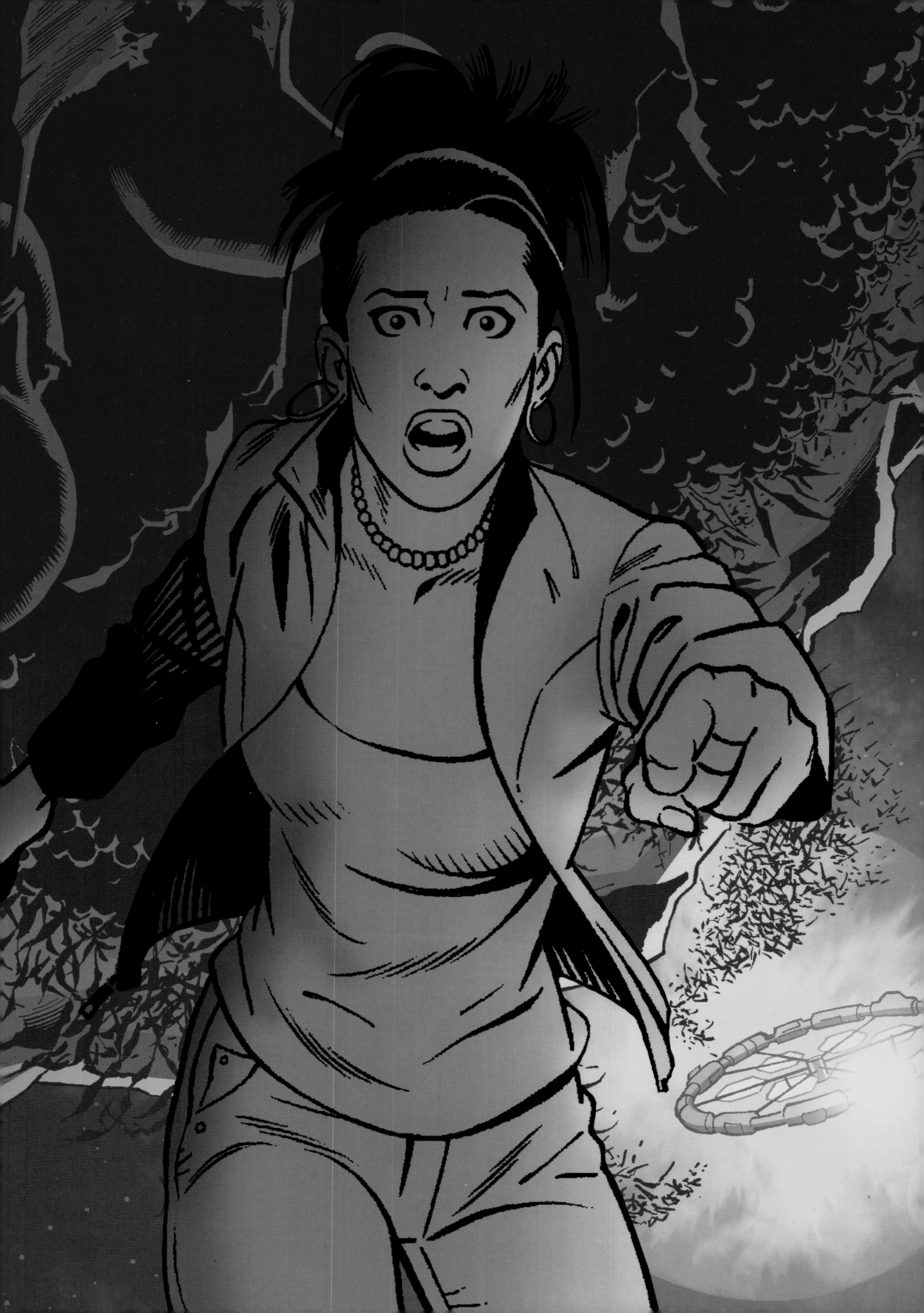

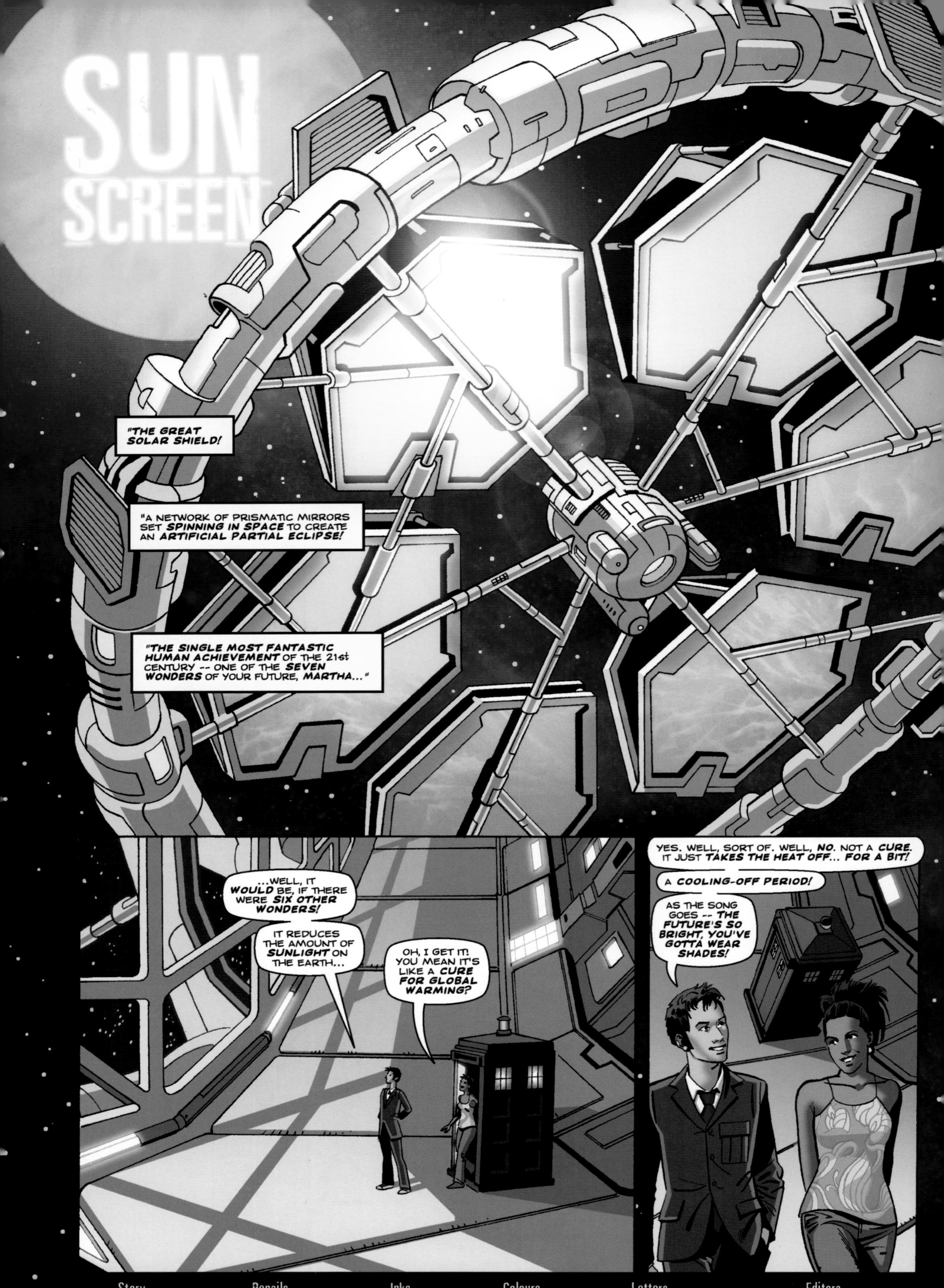

SUN SCREEN
"THE GREAT SOLAR SHIELD!
"A NETWORK OF PRISMATIC MIRRORS SET SPINNING IN SPACE TO CREATE AN ARTIFICIAL PARTIAL ECLIPSE!
"THE SINGLE MOST FANTASTIC HUMAN ACHIEVEMENT OF THE 21st CENTURY -- ONE OF THE SEVEN WONDERS OF YOUR FUTURE, MARTHA..."
...WELL, IT WOULD BE, IF THERE WERE SIX OTHER WONDERS!
IT REDUCES THE AMOUNT OF SUNLIGHT ON THE EARTH...
OH, I GET IT! YOU MEAN IT'S LIKE A CURE FOR GLOBAL WARMING?
YES. WELL, SORT OF. WELL, NO. NOT A CURE. IT JUST TAKES THE HEAT OFF... FOR A BIT!
A COOLING-OFF PERIOD!
AS THE SONG GOES -- THE FUTURE'S SO BRIGHT, YOU'VE GOTTA WEAR SHADES!

Story JONATHAN MORRIS · Pencils MARTIN GERAGHTY · Inks DAVID A ROACH · Colours JAMES OFFREDI · Letters ROGER LANGRIDGE · Editors CLAYTON HICKMAN & SCOTT GRAY

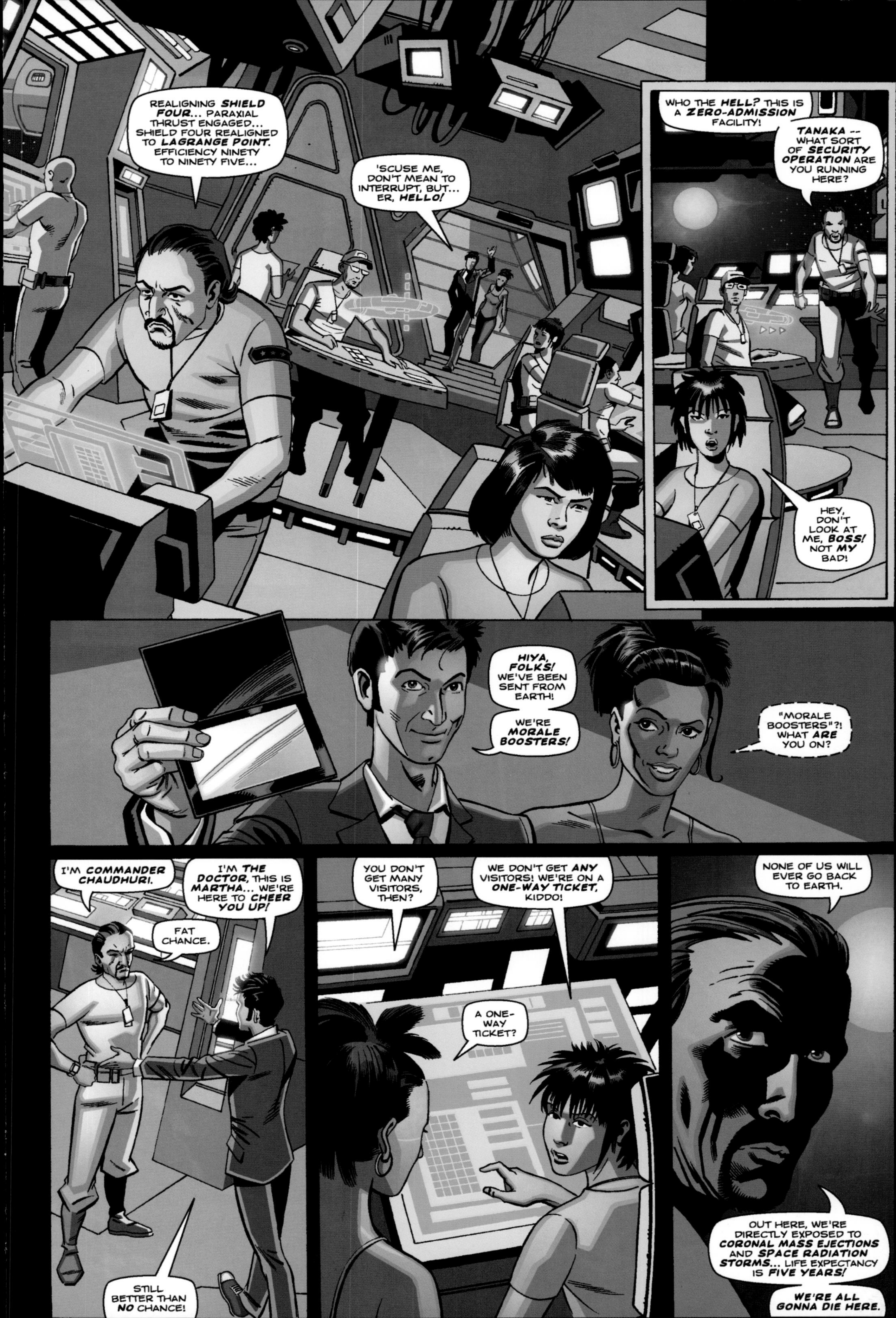
REALIGNING SHIELD FOUR... PARAXIAL THRUST ENGAGED... SHIELD FOUR REALIGNED TO LAGRANGE POINT. EFFICIENCY NINETY TO NINETY FIVE...
'SCUSE ME, DON'T MEAN TO INTERRUPT, BUT... ER, HELLO!
WHO THE HELL? THIS IS A ZERO-ADMISSION FACILITY!
TANAKA -- WHAT SORT OF SECURITY OPERATION ARE YOU RUNNING HERE?
HEY, DON'T LOOK AT ME, BOSS! NOT MY BAD!
HIYA, FOLKS! WE'VE BEEN SENT FROM EARTH!
WE'RE MORALE BOOSTERS!
"MORALE BOOSTERS"?! WHAT ARE YOU ON?
I'M COMMANDER CHAUDHURI.
I'M THE DOCTOR, THIS IS MARTHA... WE'RE HERE TO CHEER YOU UP!
FAT CHANCE.
STILL BETTER THAN NO CHANCE!
YOU DON'T GET MANY VISITORS, THEN?
WE DON'T GET ANY VISITORS! WE'RE ON A ONE-WAY TICKET, KIDDO!
A ONE-WAY TICKET?
NONE OF US WILL EVER GO BACK TO EARTH.
OUT HERE, WE'RE DIRECTLY EXPOSED TO CORONAL MASS EJECTIONS AND SPACE RADIATION STORMS... LIFE EXPECTANCY IS FIVE YEARS!
WE'RE ALL GONNA DIE HERE.

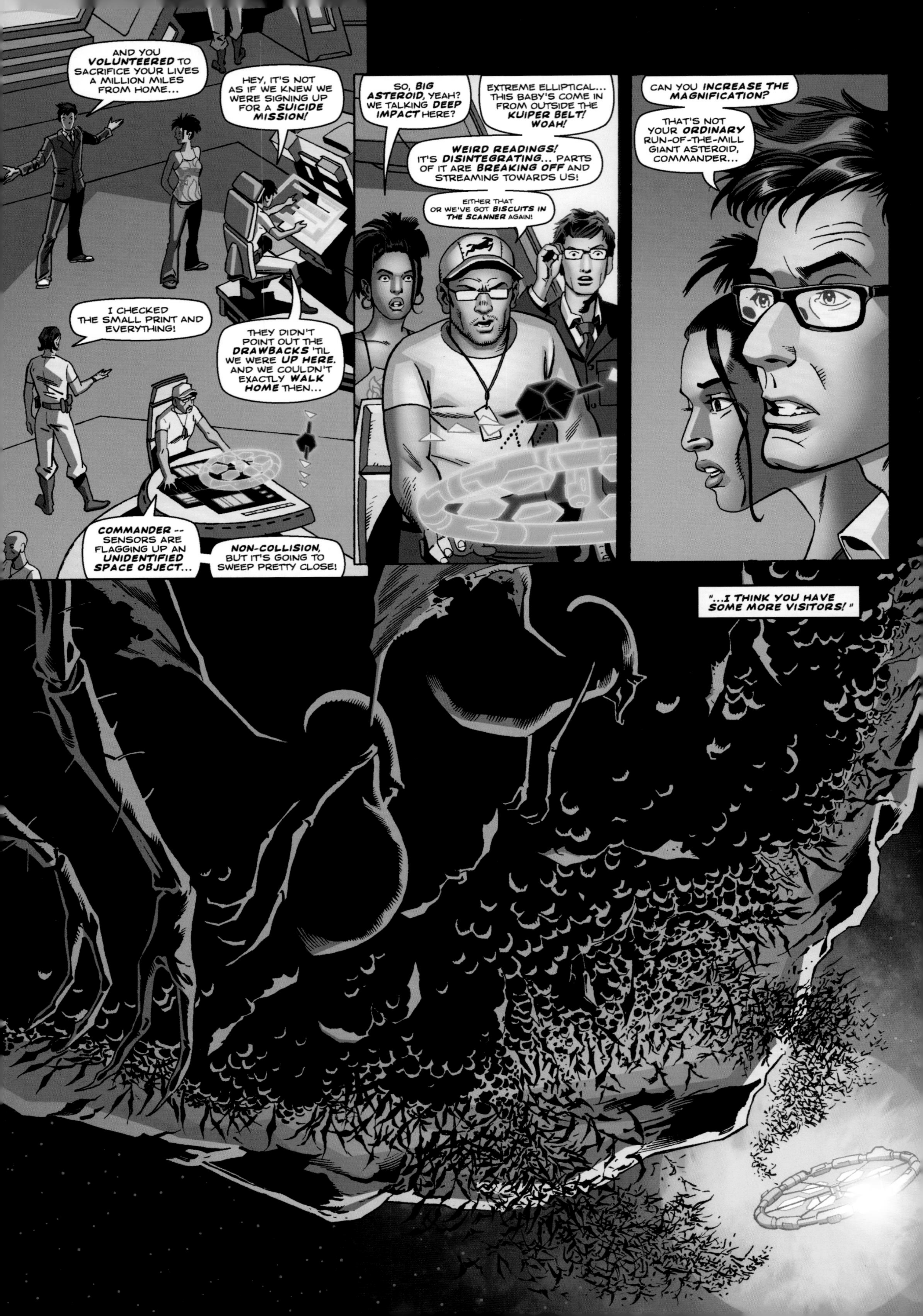
AND YOU VOLUNTEERED TO SACRIFICE YOUR LIVES A MILLION MILES FROM HOME...
HEY, IT'S NOT AS IF WE KNEW WE WERE SIGNING UP FOR A SUICIDE MISSION!
I CHECKED THE SMALL PRINT AND EVERYTHING!
THEY DIDN'T POINT OUT THE DRAWBACKS 'TIL WE WERE UP HERE. AND WE COULDN'T EXACTLY WALK HOME THEN...
COMMANDER -- SENSORS ARE FLAGGING UP AN UNIDENTIFIED SPACE OBJECT...
NON-COLLISION, BUT IT'S GOING TO SWEEP PRETTY CLOSE!
SO, BIG ASTEROID, YEAH? WE TALKING DEEP IMPACT HERE?
EXTREME ELLIPTICAL... THIS BABY'S COME IN FROM OUTSIDE THE KUIPER BELT! WOAH!
WEIRD READINGS! IT'S DISINTEGRATING... PARTS OF IT ARE BREAKING OFF AND STREAMING TOWARDS US!
EITHER THAT OR WE'VE GOT BISCUITS IN THE SCANNER AGAIN!
CAN YOU INCREASE THE MAGNIFICATION?
THAT'S NOT YOUR ORDINARY RUN-OF-THE-MILL GIANT ASTEROID, COMMANDER...
"...I THINK YOU HAVE SOME MORE VISITORS!"

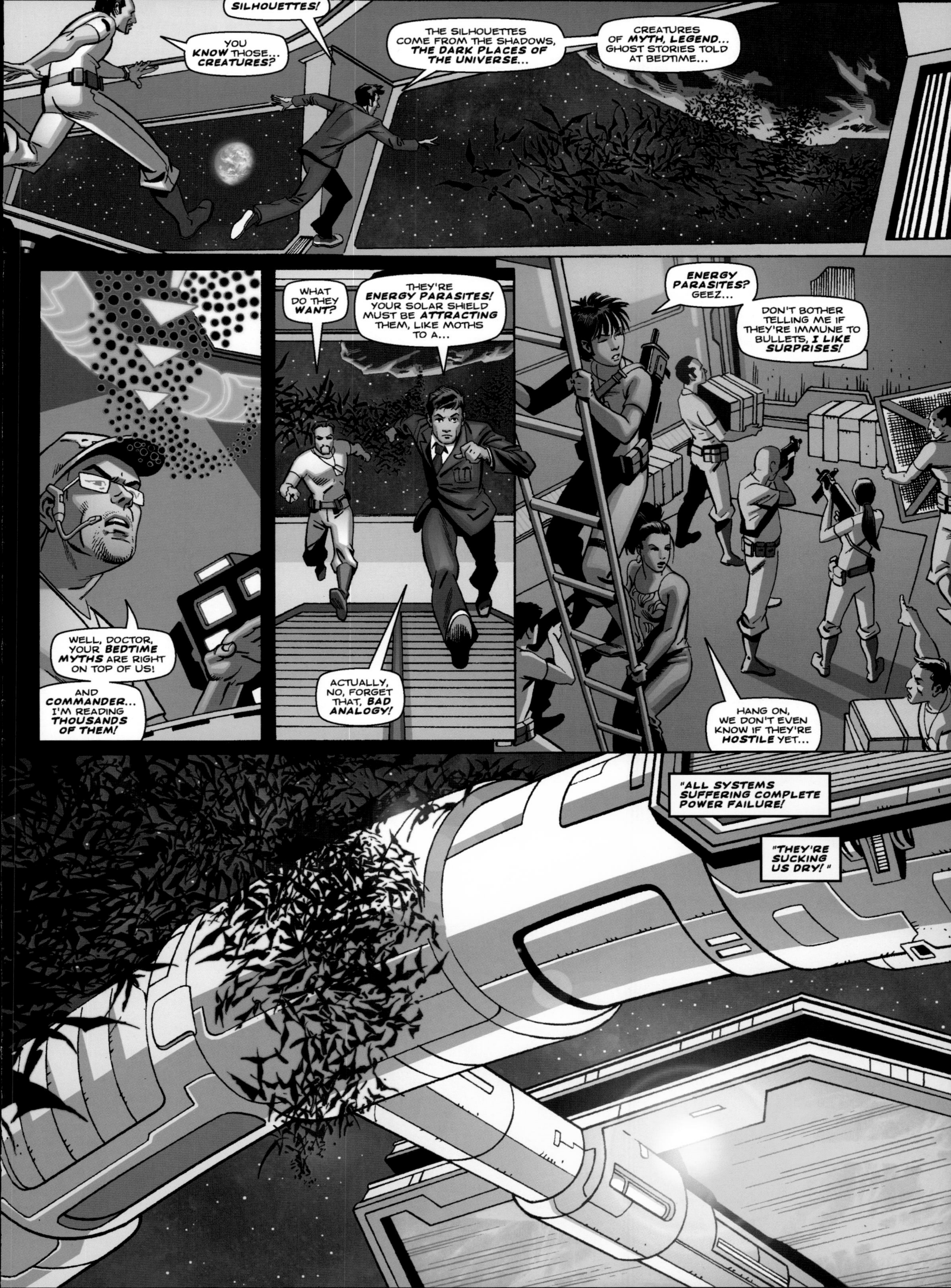
SILHOUETTES!
YOU KNOW THOSE... CREATURES?
THE SILHOUETTES COME FROM THE SHADOWS, THE DARK PLACES OF THE UNIVERSE...
CREATURES OF MYTH, LEGEND... GHOST STORIES TOLD AT BEDTIME...
WELL, DOCTOR, YOUR BEDTIME MYTHS ARE RIGHT ON TOP OF US!
AND COMMANDER... I'M READING THOUSANDS OF THEM!
WHAT DO THEY WANT?
THEY'RE ENERGY PARASITES! YOUR SOLAR SHIELD MUST BE ATTRACTING THEM, LIKE MOTHS TO A...
ACTUALLY, NO, FORGET THAT, BAD ANALOGY!
ENERGY PARASITES? GEEZ...
DON'T BOTHER TELLING ME IF THEY'RE IMMUNE TO BULLETS, I LIKE SURPRISES!
HANG ON, WE DON'T EVEN KNOW IF THEY'RE HOSTILE YET...
"ALL SYSTEMS SUFFERING COMPLETE POWER FAILURE!
"THEY'RE SUCKING US DRY!"

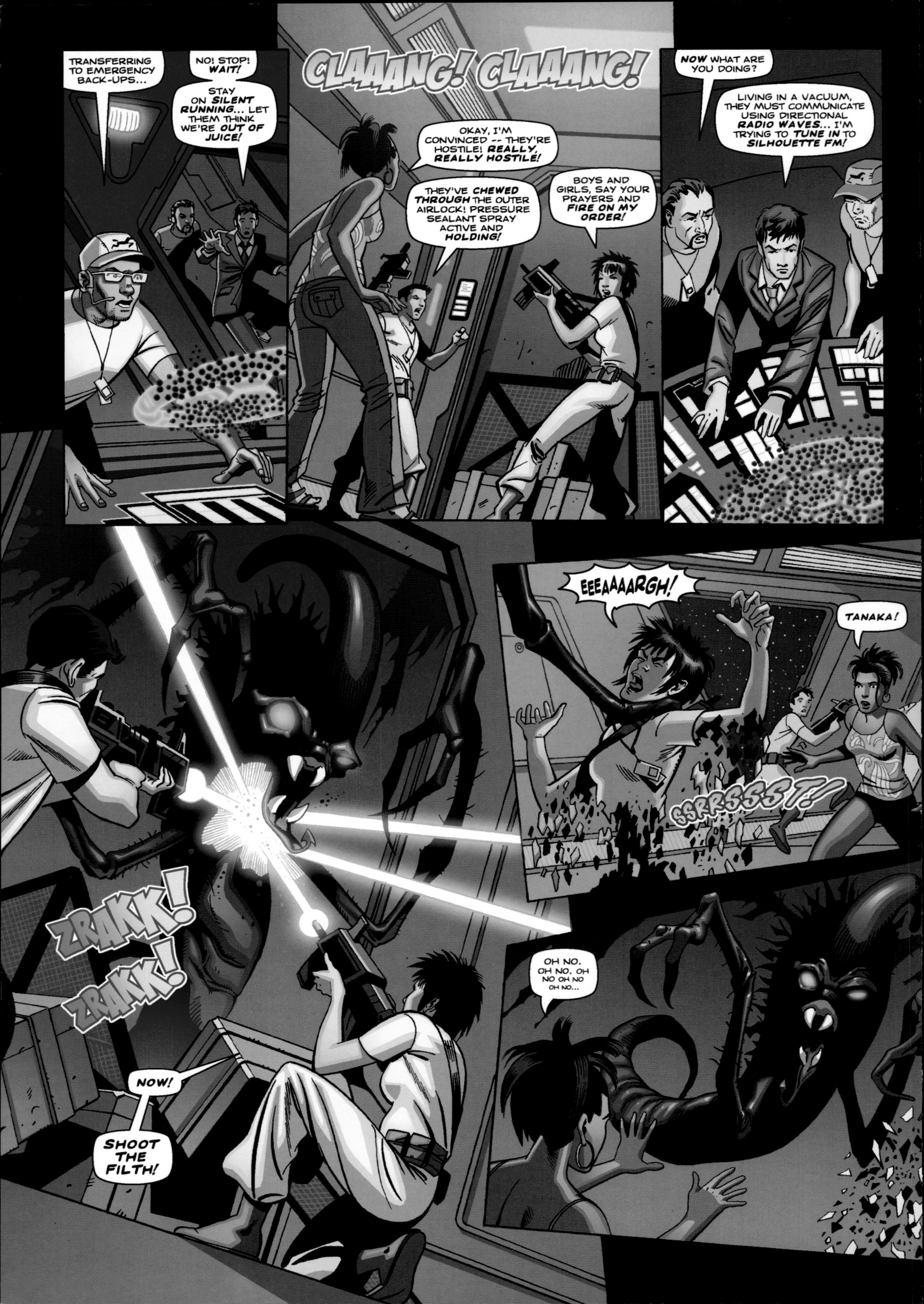
TRANSFERRING TO EMERGENCY BACK-UPS...
NO! STOP! WAIT!
STAY ON SILENT RUNNING... LET THEM THINK WE'RE OUT OF JUICE!
CLAAANG! CLAAANG!
OKAY, I'M CONVINCED -- THEY'RE HOSTILE! REALLY, REALLY HOSTILE!
THEY'VE CHEWED THROUGH THE OUTER AIRLOCK! PRESSURE SEALANT SPRAY ACTIVE AND HOLDING!
BOYS AND GIRLS, SAY YOUR PRAYERS AND FIRE ON MY ORDER!
NOW WHAT ARE YOU DOING?
LIVING IN A VACUUM, THEY MUST COMMUNICATE USING DIRECTIONAL RADIO WAVES... I'M TRYING TO TUNE IN TO SILHOUETTE FM!
ZRAKK! ZRAKK!
NOW!
SHOOT THE FILTH!
EEEAAAARGH!
TANAKA!
SSRRSSST!
OH NO. OH NO. OH NO OH NO OH NO...

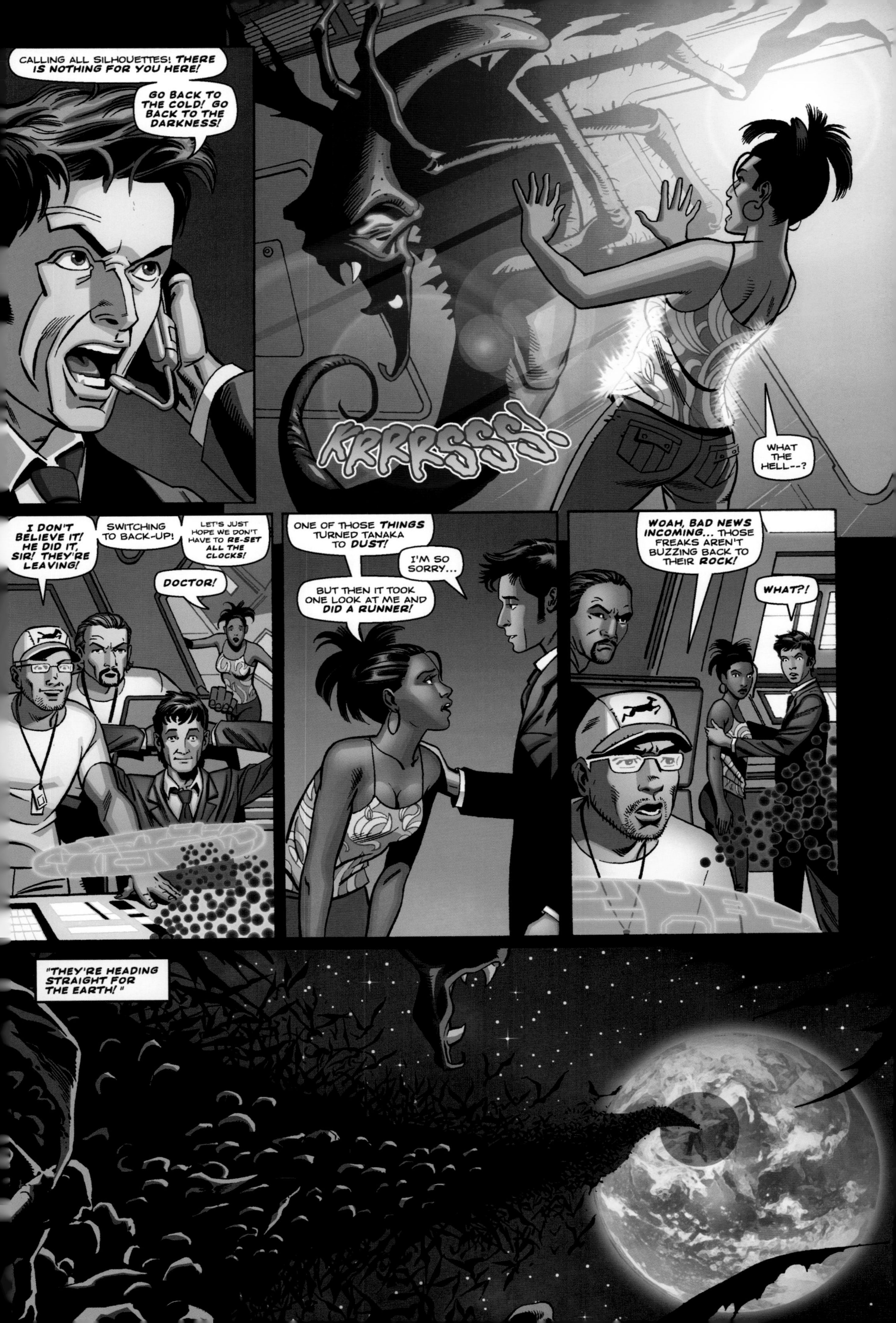
CALLING ALL SILHOUETTES! THERE IS NOTHING FOR YOU HERE!
GO BACK TO THE COLD! GO BACK TO THE DARKNESS!
KRRRSSS!
WHAT THE HELL--?
I DON'T BELIEVE IT! HE DID IT, SIR! THEY'RE LEAVING!
SWITCHING TO BACK-UP!
LET'S JUST HOPE WE DON'T HAVE TO RE-SET ALL THE CLOCKS!
DOCTOR!
ONE OF THOSE THINGS TURNED TANAKA TO DUST!
I'M SO SORRY...
BUT THEN IT TOOK ONE LOOK AT ME AND DID A RUNNER!
WOAH, BAD NEWS INCOMING... THOSE FREAKS AREN'T BUZZING BACK TO THEIR ROCK!
WHAT?!
"THEY'RE HEADING STRAIGHT FOR THE EARTH!"

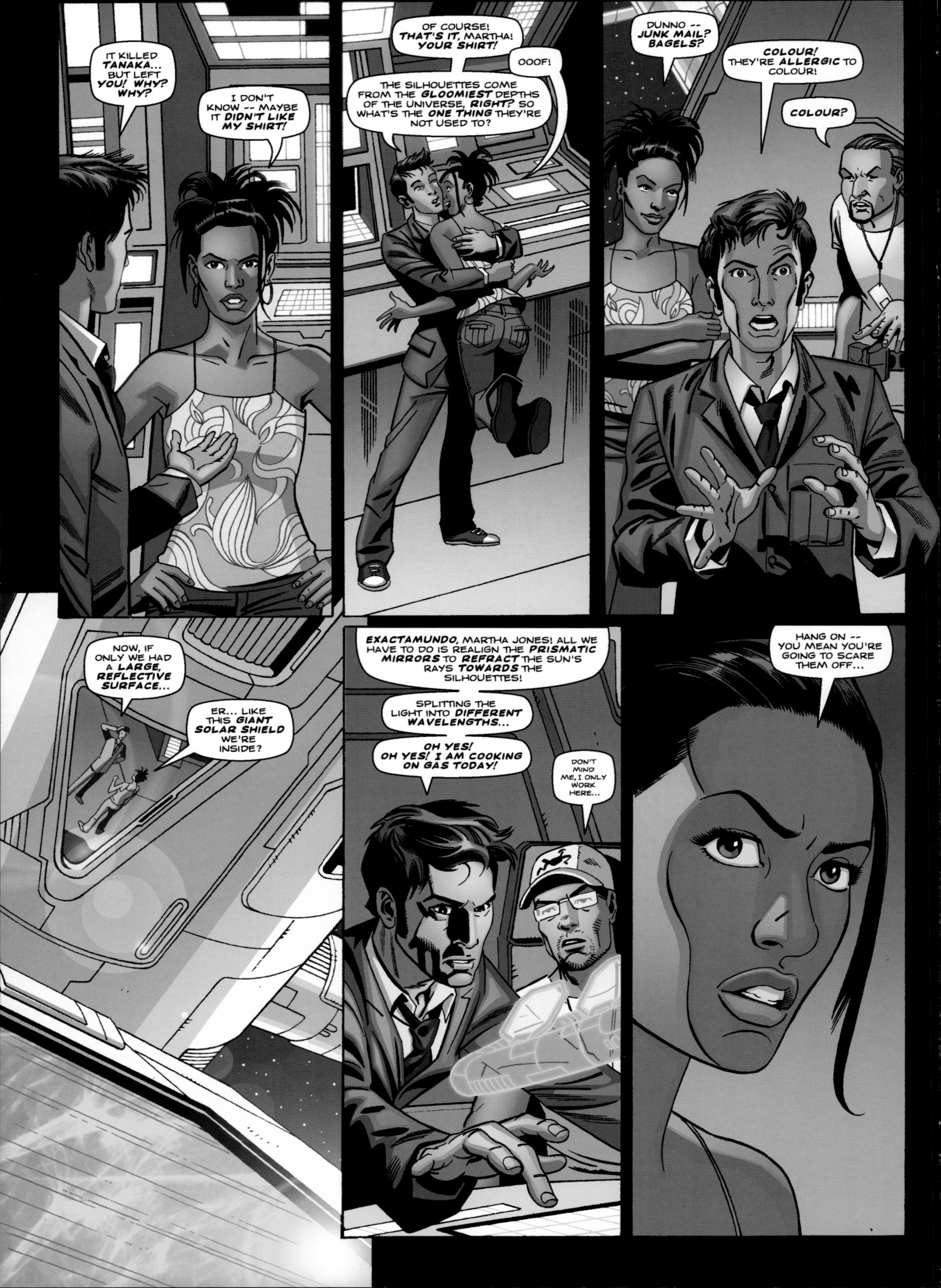
IT KILLED TANAKA... BUT LEFT YOU! WHY? WHY?
I DON'T KNOW -- MAYBE IT DIDN'T LIKE MY SHIRT!
OF COURSE! THAT'S IT, MARTHA! YOUR SHIRT!
OOOF!
THE SILHOUETTES COME FROM THE GLOOMIEST DEPTHS OF THE UNIVERSE, RIGHT? SO WHAT'S THE ONE THING THEY'RE NOT USED TO?
DUNNO -- JUNK MAIL? BAGELS?
COLOUR! THEY'RE ALLERGIC TO COLOUR!
COLOUR?
NOW, IF ONLY WE HAD A LARGE, REFLECTIVE SURFACE...
ER... LIKE THIS GIANT SOLAR SHIELD WE'RE INSIDE?
EXACTAMUNDO, MARTHA JONES! ALL WE HAVE TO DO IS REALIGN THE PRISMATIC MIRRORS TO REFRACT THE SUN'S RAYS TOWARDS THE SILHOUETTES!
SPLITTING THE LIGHT INTO DIFFERENT WAVELENGTHS...
OH YES! OH YES! I AM COOKING ON GAS TODAY!
DON'T MIND ME, I ONLY WORK HERE...
HANG ON -- YOU MEAN YOU'RE GOING TO SCARE THEM OFF...

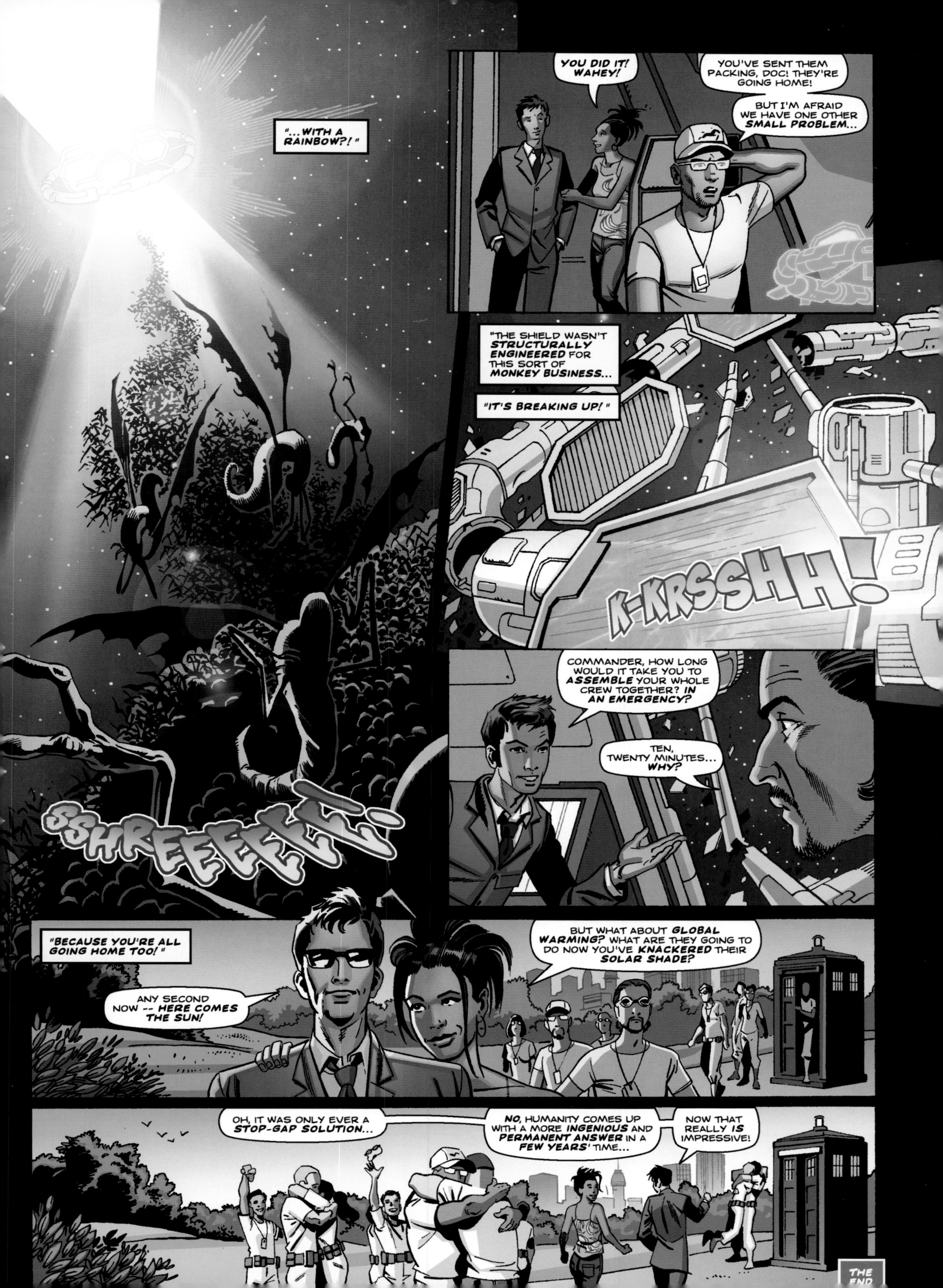
"...WITH A RAINBOW?!"
YOU DID IT! WAHEY!
YOU'VE SENT THEM PACKING, DOC! THEY'RE GOING HOME!
BUT I'M AFRAID WE HAVE ONE OTHER SMALL PROBLEM...
"THE SHIELD WASN'T STRUCTURALLY ENGINEERED FOR THIS SORT OF MONKEY BUSINESS...
"IT'S BREAKING UP!"
K-KRSSHH!
SSHREEEEE!
COMMANDER, HOW LONG WOULD IT TAKE YOU TO ASSEMBLE YOUR WHOLE CREW TOGETHER? IN AN EMERGENCY?
TEN, TWENTY MINUTES... WHY?
"BECAUSE YOU'RE ALL GOING HOME TOO!"
ANY SECOND NOW -- HERE COMES THE SUN!
BUT WHAT ABOUT GLOBAL WARMING? WHAT ARE THEY GOING TO DO NOW YOU'VE KNACKERED THEIR SOLAR SHADE?
OH, IT WAS ONLY EVER A STOP-GAP SOLUTION...
NO, HUMANITY COMES UP WITH A MORE INGENIOUS AND PERMANENT ANSWER IN A FEW YEARS' TIME...
NOW THAT REALLY IS IMPRESSIVE!
THE END

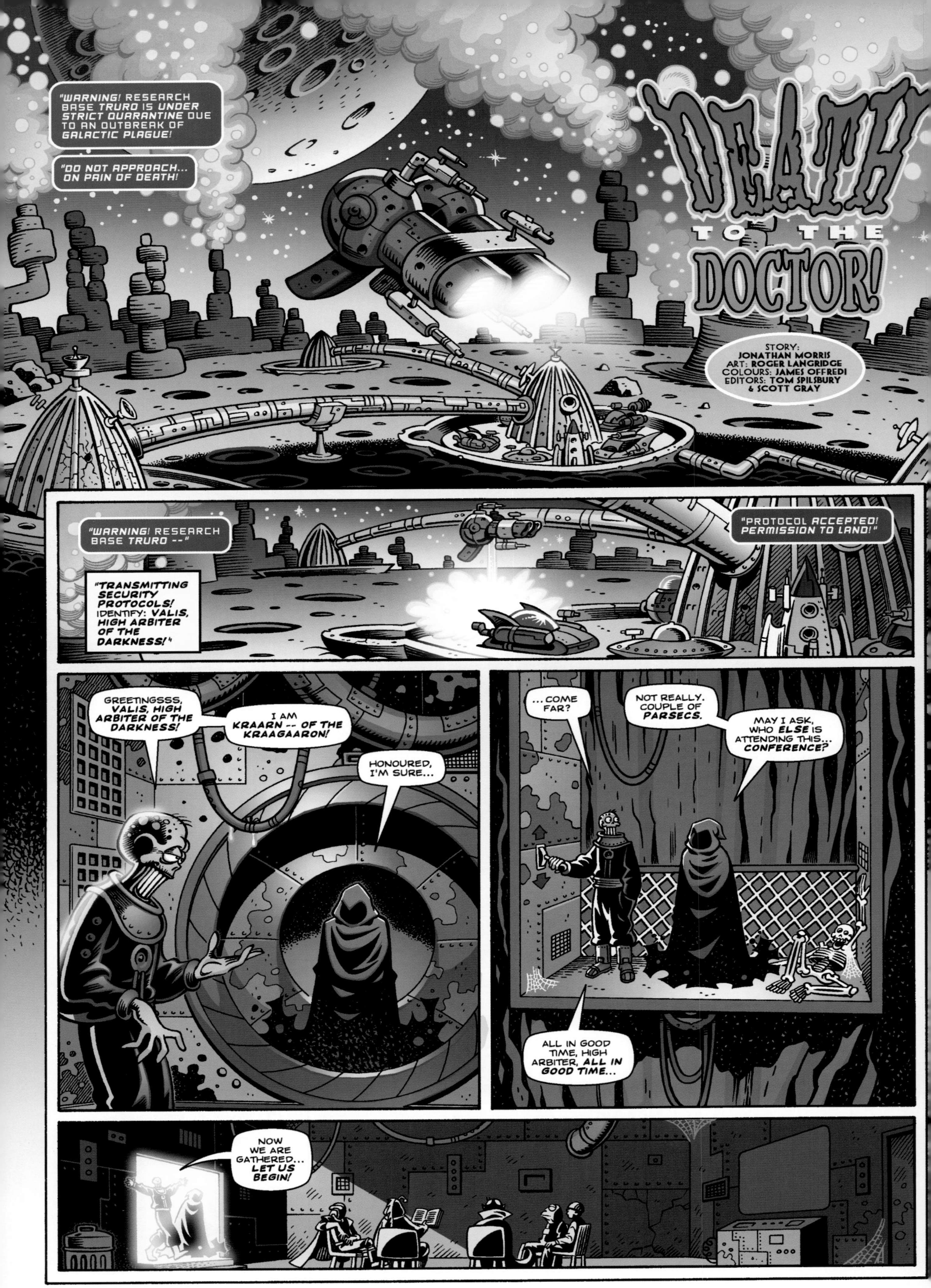
"WARNING! RESEARCH BASE TRURO IS UNDER STRICT QUARANTINE DUE TO AN OUTBREAK OF GALACTIC PLAGUE!
"DO NOT APPROACH... ON PAIN OF DEATH!
DEATH TO THE DOCTOR!
STORY: JONATHAN MORRIS
ART: ROGER LANGRIDGE
COLOURS: JAMES OFFREDI
EDITORS: TOM SPILSBURY & SCOTT GRAY
"WARNING! RESEARCH BASE TRURO --"
"TRANSMITTING SECURITY PROTOCOLS! IDENTIFY: VALIS, HIGH ARBITER OF THE DARKNESS!"
"PROTOCOL ACCEPTED! PERMISSION TO LAND!"
GREETINGSSS, VALIS, HIGH ARBITER OF THE DARKNESS!
I AM KRAARN -- OF THE KRAAGAARON!
HONOURED, I'M SURE...
...COME FAR?
NOT REALLY. COUPLE OF PARSECS.
MAY I ASK, WHO ELSE IS ATTENDING THIS... CONFERENCE?
ALL IN GOOD TIME, HIGH ARBITER, ALL IN GOOD TIME...
NOW WE ARE GATHERED... LET US BEGIN!

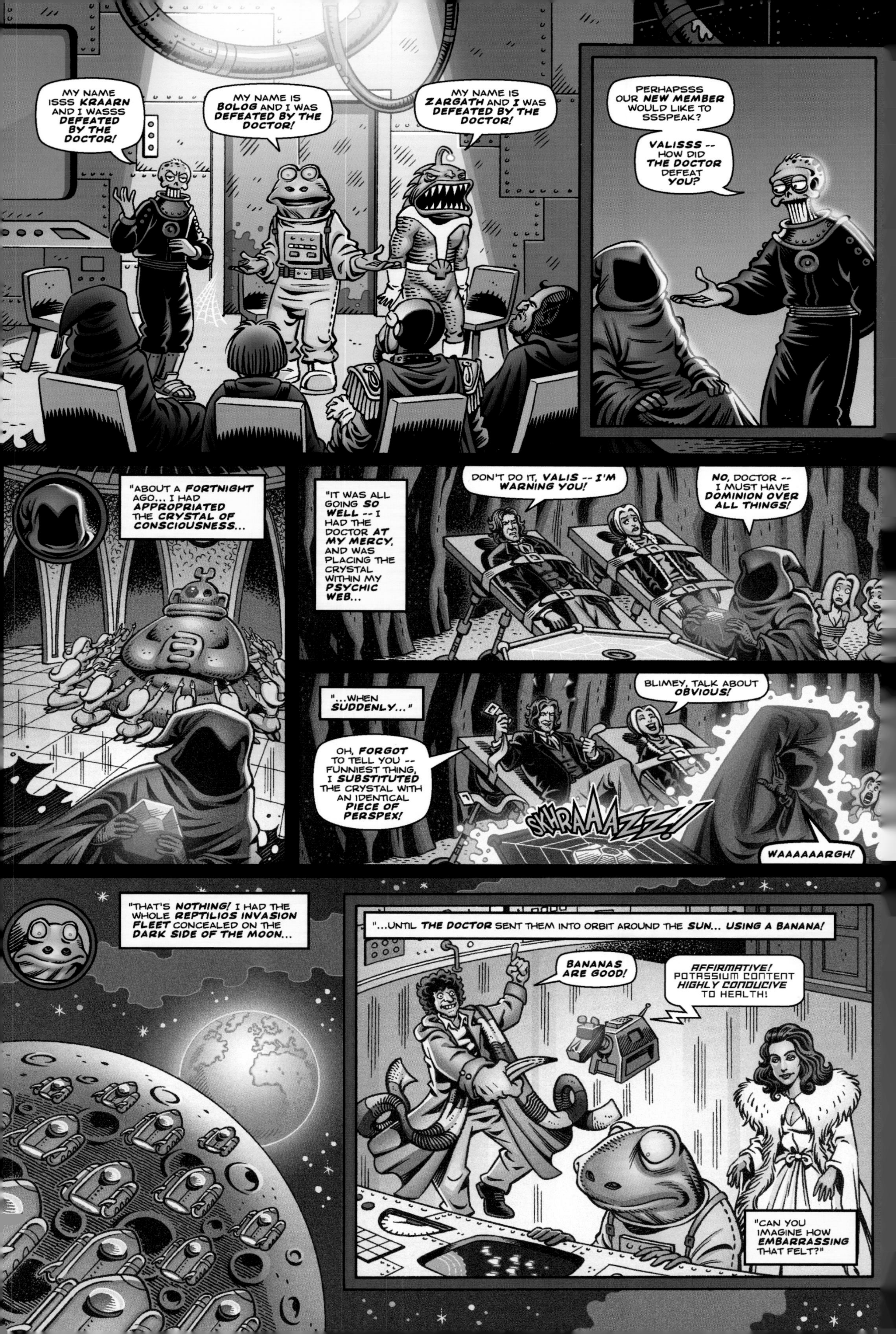
MY NAME ISSS KRAARN AND I WASSS DEFEATED BY THE DOCTOR!
MY NAME IS BOLOG AND I WAS DEFEATED BY THE DOCTOR!
MY NAME IS ZARGATH AND I WAS DEFEATED BY THE DOCTOR!
PERHAPSSS OUR NEW MEMBER WOULD LIKE TO SSSPEAK?
VALISSS -- HOW DID THE DOCTOR DEFEAT YOU?
"ABOUT A FORTNIGHT AGO... I HAD APPROPRIATED THE CRYSTAL OF CONSCIOUSNESS...
"IT WAS ALL GOING SO WELL -- I HAD THE DOCTOR AT MY MERCY, AND WAS PLACING THE CRYSTAL WITHIN MY PSYCHIC WEB...
DON'T DO IT, VALIS -- I'M WARNING YOU!
NO, DOCTOR -- I MUST HAVE DOMINION OVER ALL THINGS!
"...WHEN SUDDENLY..."
BLIMEY, TALK ABOUT OBVIOUS!
OH, FORGOT TO TELL YOU -- FUNNIEST THING, I SUBSTITUTED THE CRYSTAL WITH AN IDENTICAL PIECE OF PERSPEX!
SKHRAAAAZZZ!
WAAAAAARGH!
"THAT'S NOTHING! I HAD THE WHOLE REPTILIOS INVASION FLEET CONCEALED ON THE DARK SIDE OF THE MOON...
"...UNTIL THE DOCTOR SENT THEM INTO ORBIT AROUND THE SUN... USING A BANANA!
BANANAS ARE GOOD!
AFFIRMATIVE! POTASSIUM CONTENT HIGHLY CONDUCIVE TO HEALTH!
"CAN YOU IMAGINE HOW EMBARRASSING THAT FELT?"

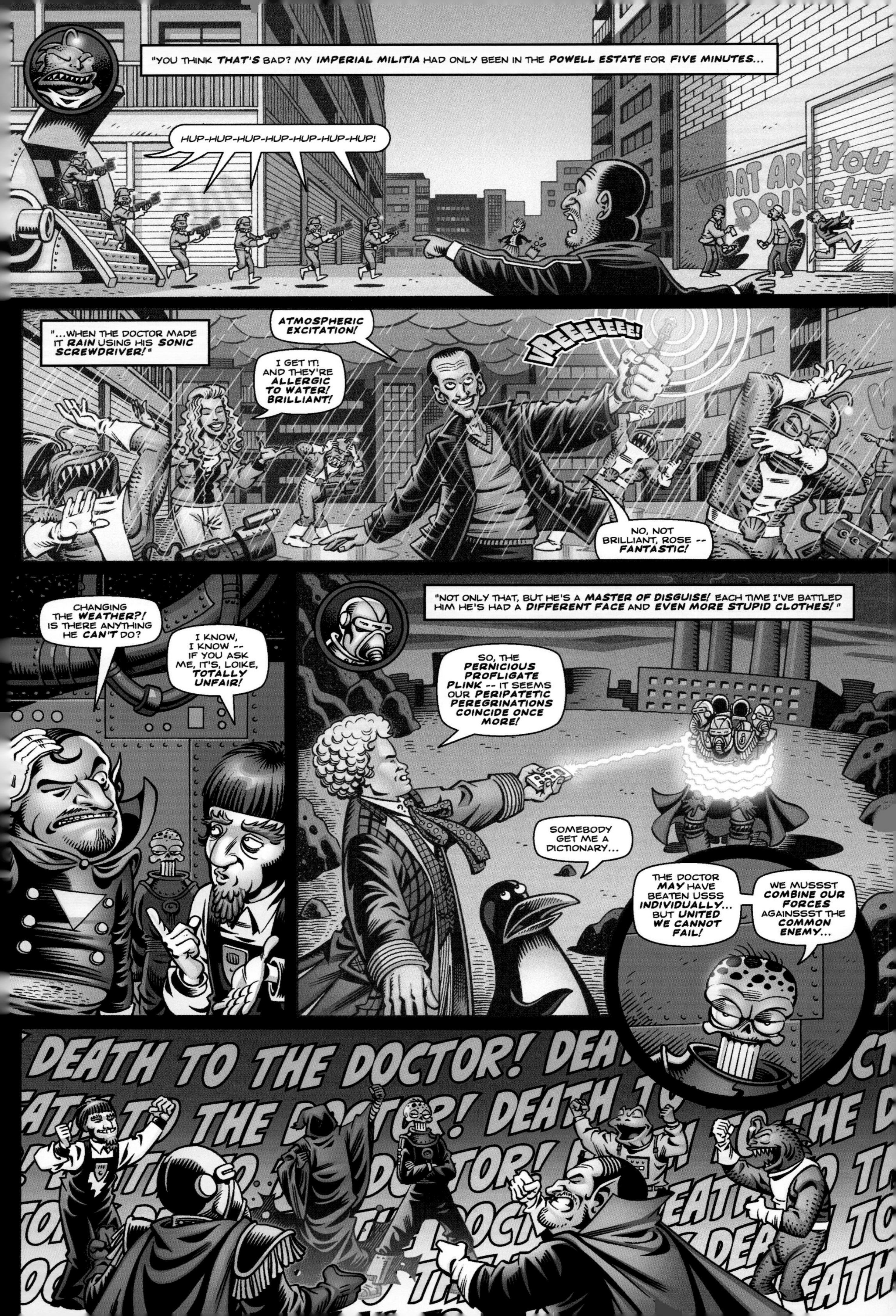

"YOU THINK THAT'S BAD? MY IMPERIAL MILITIA HAD ONLY BEEN IN THE POWELL ESTATE FOR FIVE MINUTES...
HUP-HUP-HUP-HUP-HUP-HUP-HUP!
WHAT ARE YOU DOING HERE
"...WHEN THE DOCTOR MADE IT RAIN USING HIS SONIC SCREWDRIVER!"
ATMOSPHERIC EXCITATION!
VREEEEEEE!
I GET IT! AND THEY'RE ALLERGIC TO WATER! BRILLIANT!
NO, NOT BRILLIANT, ROSE -- FANTASTIC!
CHANGING THE WEATHER?! IS THERE ANYTHING HE CAN'T DO?
I KNOW, I KNOW -- IF YOU ASK ME, IT'S, LOIKE, TOTALLY UNFAIR!
"NOT ONLY THAT, BUT HE'S A MASTER OF DISGUISE! EACH TIME I'VE BATTLED HIM HE'S HAD A DIFFERENT FACE AND EVEN MORE STUPID CLOTHES!"
SO, THE PERNICIOUS PROFLIGATE PLINK -- IT SEEMS OUR PERIPATETIC PEREGRINATIONS COINCIDE ONCE MORE!
SOMEBODY GET ME A DICTIONARY...
THE DOCTOR MAY HAVE BEATEN USSS INDIVIDUALLY... BUT UNITED WE CANNOT FAIL!
WE MUSSST COMBINE OUR FORCES AGAINSSST THE COMMON ENEMY...
DEATH TO THE DOCTOR!

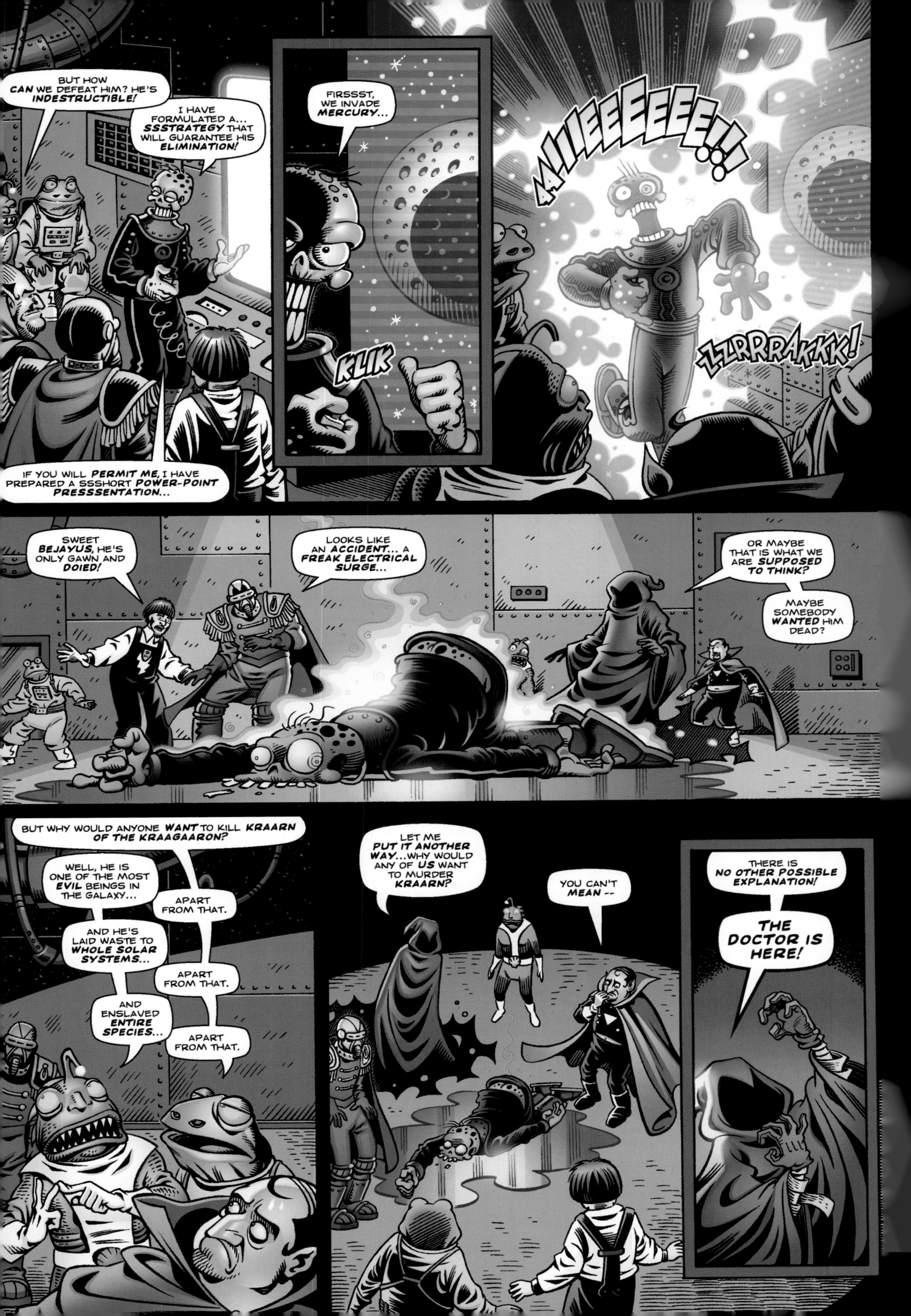

BUT HOW CAN WE DEFEAT HIM? HE'S INDESTRUCTIBLE!
I HAVE FORMULATED A... SSSTRATEGY THAT WILL GUARANTEE HIS ELIMINATION!
IF YOU WILL PERMIT ME, I HAVE PREPARED A SSSHORT POWER-POINT PRESSSENTATION...
FIRSSST, WE INVADE MERCURY...
KLIK
AAIIIEEEEEEE!!!
ZZRRRAKKK!
SWEET BEJAYUS, HE'S ONLY GAWN AND DOIED!
LOOKS LIKE AN ACCIDENT... A FREAK ELECTRICAL SURGE...
OR MAYBE THAT IS WHAT WE ARE SUPPOSED TO THINK?
MAYBE SOMEBODY WANTED HIM DEAD?
BUT WHY WOULD ANYONE WANT TO KILL KRAARN OF THE KRAAGAARON?
WELL, HE IS ONE OF THE MOST EVIL BEINGS IN THE GALAXY...
APART FROM THAT.
AND HE'S LAID WASTE TO WHOLE SOLAR SYSTEMS...
APART FROM THAT.
AND ENSLAVED ENTIRE SPECIES...
APART FROM THAT.
LET ME PUT IT ANOTHER WAY...WHY WOULD ANY OF US WANT TO MURDER KRAARN?
YOU CAN'T MEAN --
THERE IS NO OTHER POSSIBLE EXPLANATION!
THE DOCTOR IS HERE!

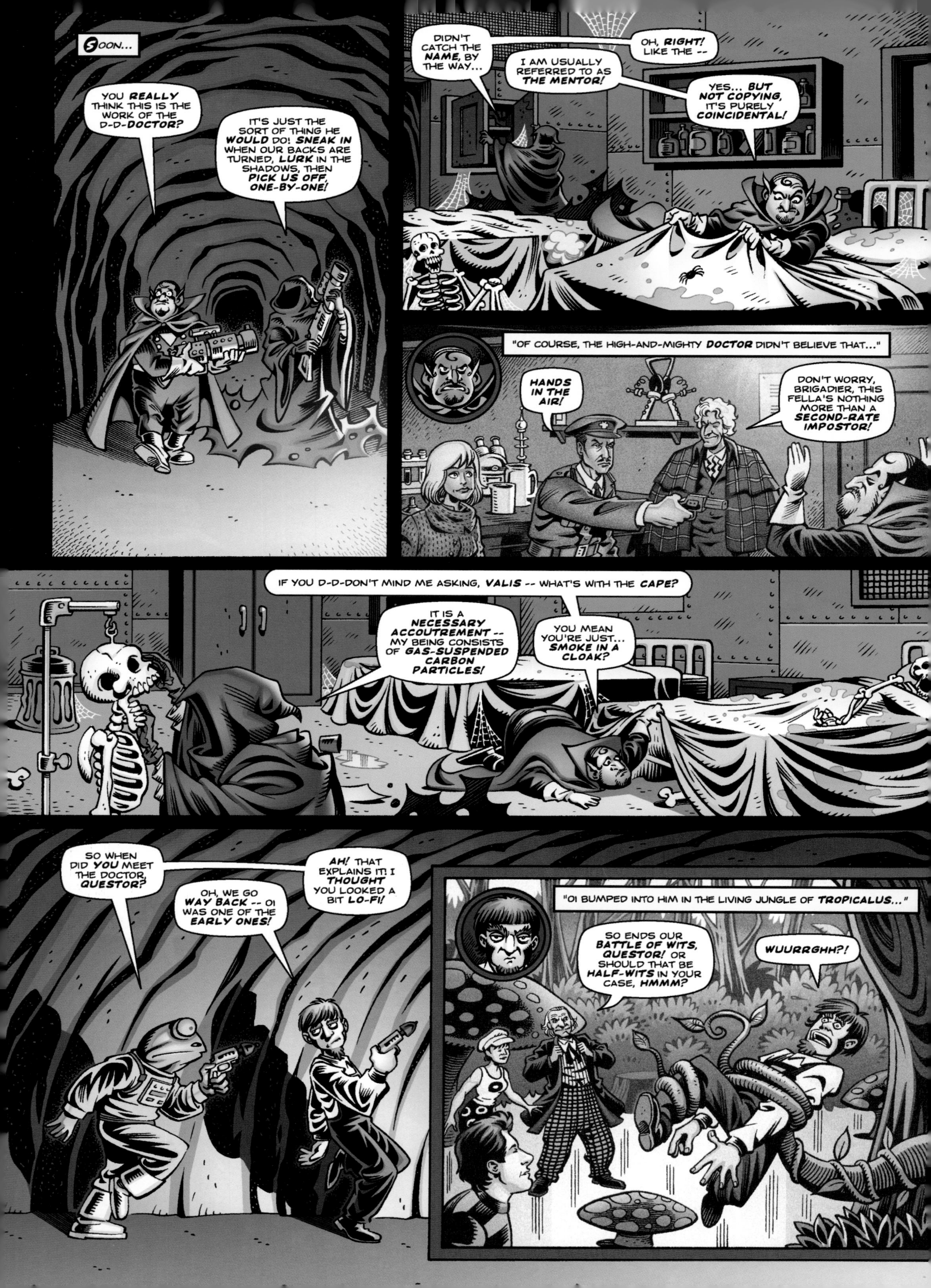
SOON...
YOU REALLY THINK THIS IS THE WORK OF THE D-D-DOCTOR?
IT'S JUST THE SORT OF THING HE WOULD DO! SNEAK IN WHEN OUR BACKS ARE TURNED, LURK IN THE SHADOWS, THEN PICK US OFF, ONE-BY-ONE!
DIDN'T CATCH THE NAME, BY THE WAY...
I AM USUALLY REFERRED TO AS THE MENTOR!
OH, RIGHT! LIKE THE --
YES... BUT NOT COPYING, IT'S PURELY COINCIDENTAL!
"OF COURSE, THE HIGH-AND-MIGHTY DOCTOR DIDN'T BELIEVE THAT..."
HANDS IN THE AIR!
DON'T WORRY, BRIGADIER, THIS FELLA'S NOTHING MORE THAN A SECOND-RATE IMPOSTOR!
IF YOU D-D-DON'T MIND ME ASKING, VALIS -- WHAT'S WITH THE CAPE?
IT IS A NECESSARY ACCOUTREMENT -- MY BEING CONSISTS OF GAS-SUSPENDED CARBON PARTICLES!
YOU MEAN YOU'RE JUST... SMOKE IN A CLOAK?
SO WHEN DID YOU MEET THE DOCTOR, QUESTOR?
OH, WE GO WAY BACK -- OI WAS ONE OF THE EARLY ONES!
AH! THAT EXPLAINS IT! I THOUGHT YOU LOOKED A BIT LO-FI!
"OI BUMPED INTO HIM IN THE LIVING JUNGLE OF TROPICALUS..."
SO ENDS OUR BATTLE OF WITS, QUESTOR! OR SHOULD THAT BE HALF-WITS IN YOUR CASE, HMMM?
WUURRGHH?!

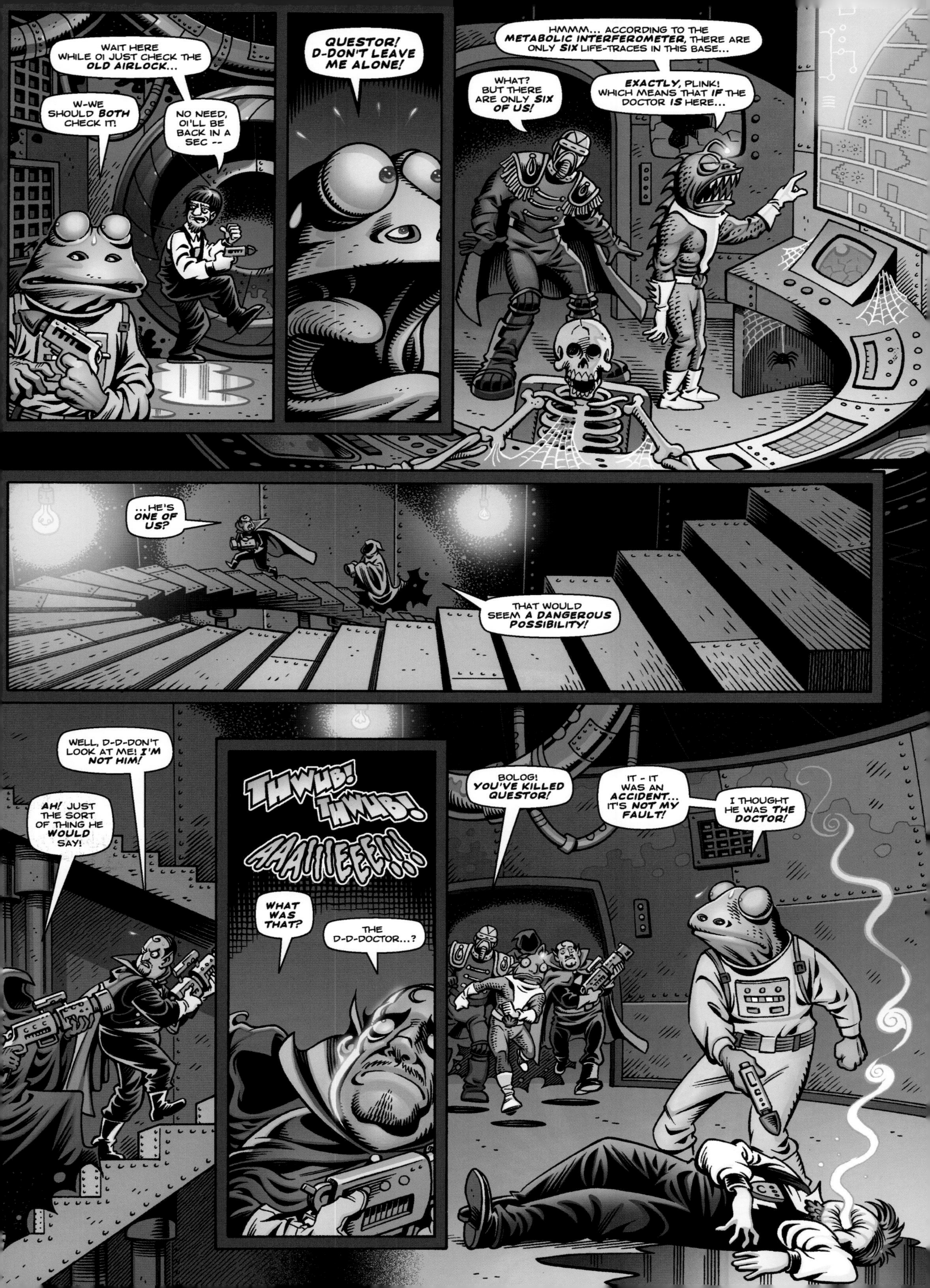
WAIT HERE WHILE OI JUST CHECK THE OLD AIRLOCK...
W-WE SHOULD BOTH CHECK IT!
NO NEED, OI'LL BE BACK IN A SEC --
QUESTOR! D-DON'T LEAVE ME ALONE!
HMMM... ACCORDING TO THE METABOLIC INTERFEROMETER, THERE ARE ONLY SIX LIFE-TRACES IN THIS BASE...
WHAT? BUT THERE ARE ONLY SIX OF US!
EXACTLY, PLINK! WHICH MEANS THAT IF THE DOCTOR IS HERE...
...HE'S ONE OF US?
THAT WOULD SEEM A DANGEROUS POSSIBILITY!
WELL, D-D-DON'T LOOK AT ME! I'M NOT HIM!
AH! JUST THE SORT OF THING HE WOULD SAY!
THWUB! THWUB!
AAAIIIEEE!!!
WHAT WAS THAT?
THE D-D-DOCTOR...?
BOLOG! YOU'VE KILLED QUESTOR!
IT - IT WAS AN ACCIDENT... IT'S NOT MY FAULT!
I THOUGHT HE WAS THE DOCTOR!

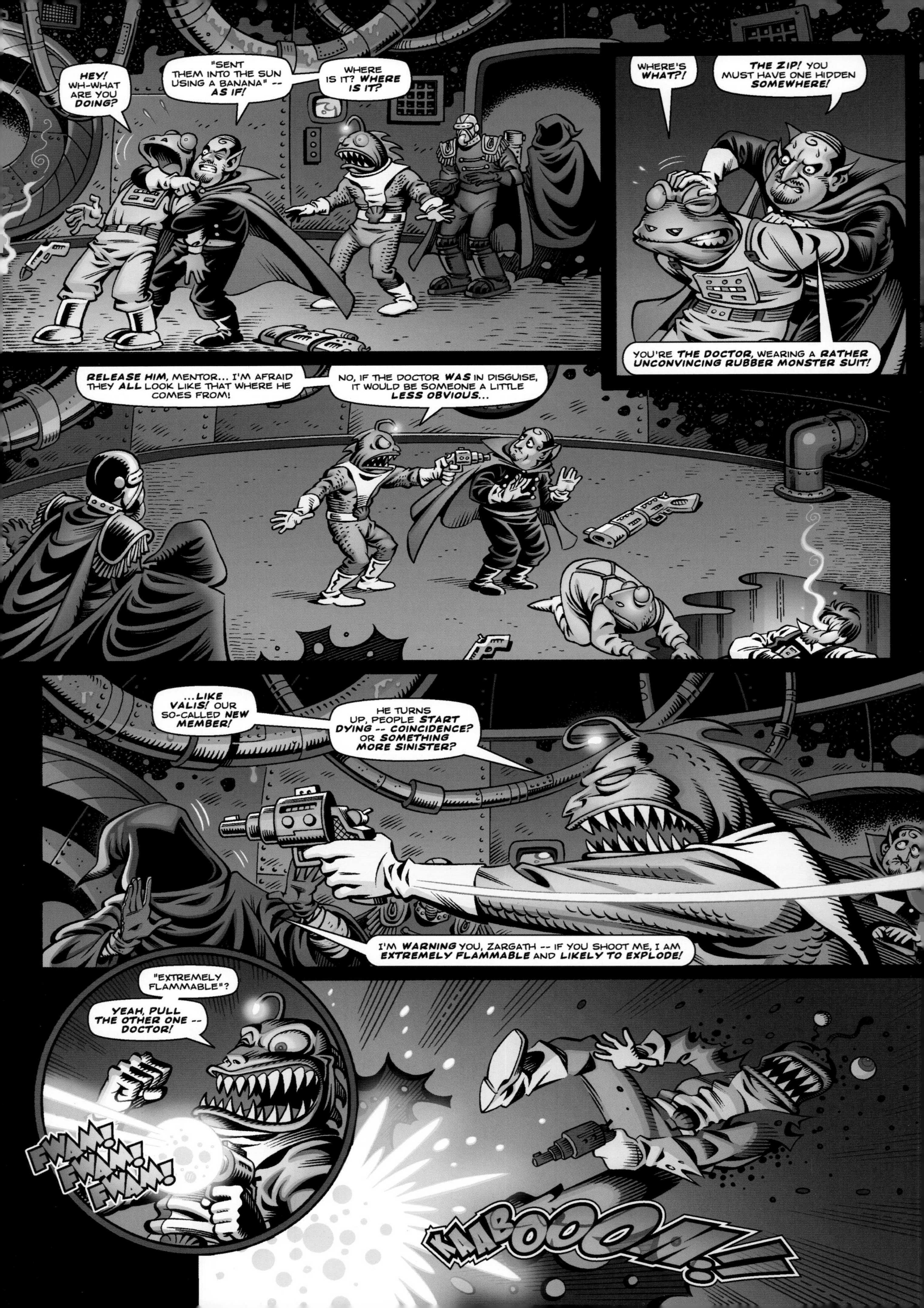
HEY! WH-WHAT ARE YOU DOING?
"SENT THEM INTO THE SUN USING A BANANA" -- AS IF!
WHERE IS IT? WHERE IS IT?
WHERE'S WHAT?!
THE ZIP! YOU MUST HAVE ONE HIDDEN SOMEWHERE!
YOU'RE THE DOCTOR, WEARING A RATHER UNCONVINCING RUBBER MONSTER SUIT!
RELEASE HIM, MENTOR... I'M AFRAID THEY ALL LOOK LIKE THAT WHERE HE COMES FROM!
NO, IF THE DOCTOR WAS IN DISGUISE, IT WOULD BE SOMEONE A LITTLE LESS OBVIOUS...
...LIKE VALIS! OUR SO-CALLED NEW MEMBER!
HE TURNS UP, PEOPLE START DYING -- COINCIDENCE? OR SOMETHING MORE SINISTER?
I'M WARNING YOU, ZARGATH -- IF YOU SHOOT ME, I AM EXTREMELY FLAMMABLE AND LIKELY TO EXPLODE!
"EXTREMELY FLAMMABLE"?
YEAH, PULL THE OTHER ONE -- DOCTOR!
FWAM! FWAM! FWAM!
KABOOOM!!

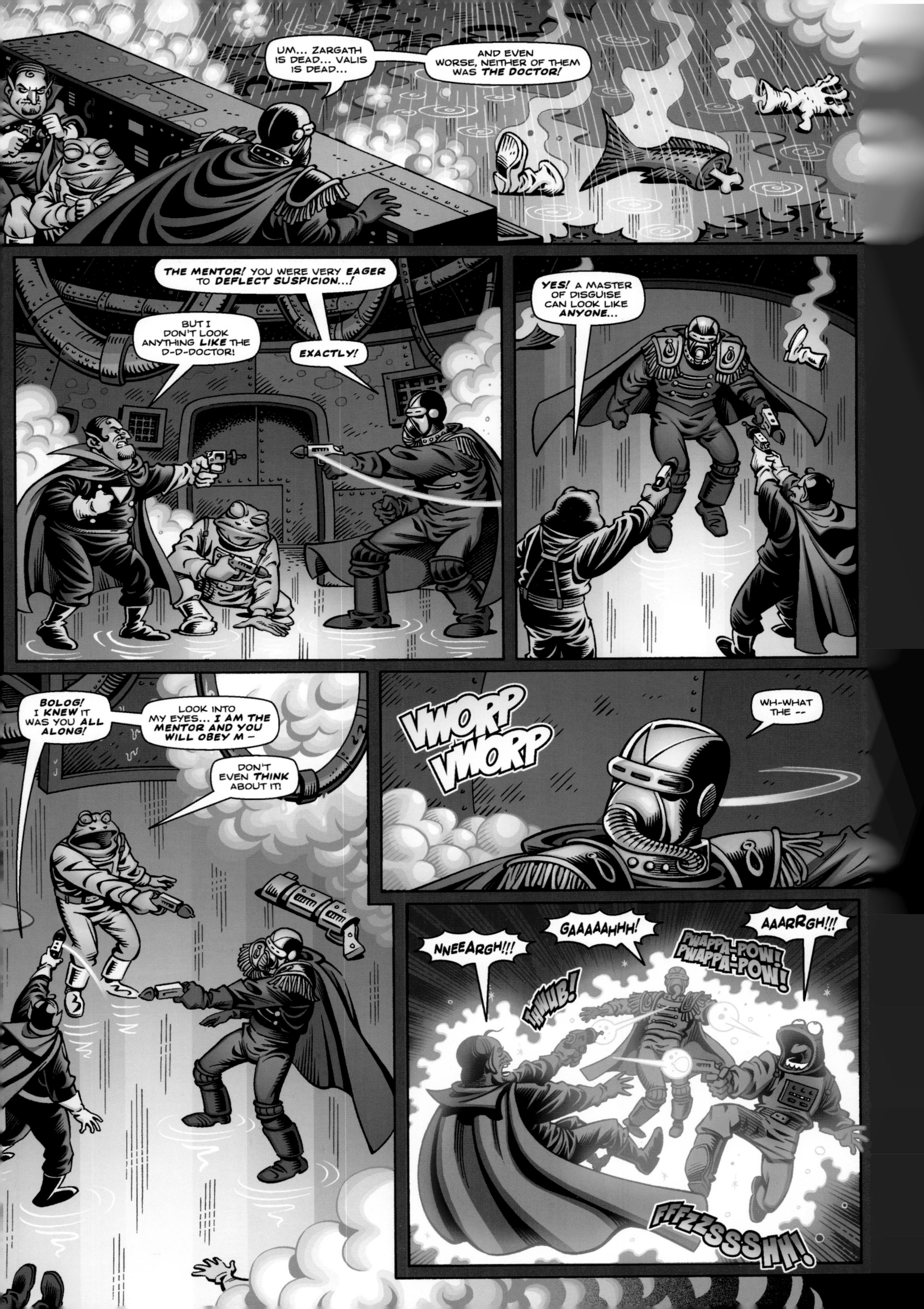
UM... ZARGATH IS DEAD... VALIS IS DEAD...
AND EVEN WORSE, NEITHER OF THEM WAS THE DOCTOR!
THE MENTOR! YOU WERE VERY EAGER TO DEFLECT SUSPICION...!
BUT I DON'T LOOK ANYTHING LIKE THE D-D-DOCTOR!
EXACTLY!
YES! A MASTER OF DISGUISE CAN LOOK LIKE ANYONE...
BOLOG! I KNEW IT WAS YOU ALL ALONG!
LOOK INTO MY EYES... I AM THE MENTOR AND YOU WILL OBEY M –
DON'T EVEN THINK ABOUT IT!
VWORP VWORP
WH-WHAT THE --
NNEEARGH!!!
GAAAAAHHH!
AAARRGH!!!
PWAPPA-POW! PWAPPA-POW!
FFFZZSSSHH!

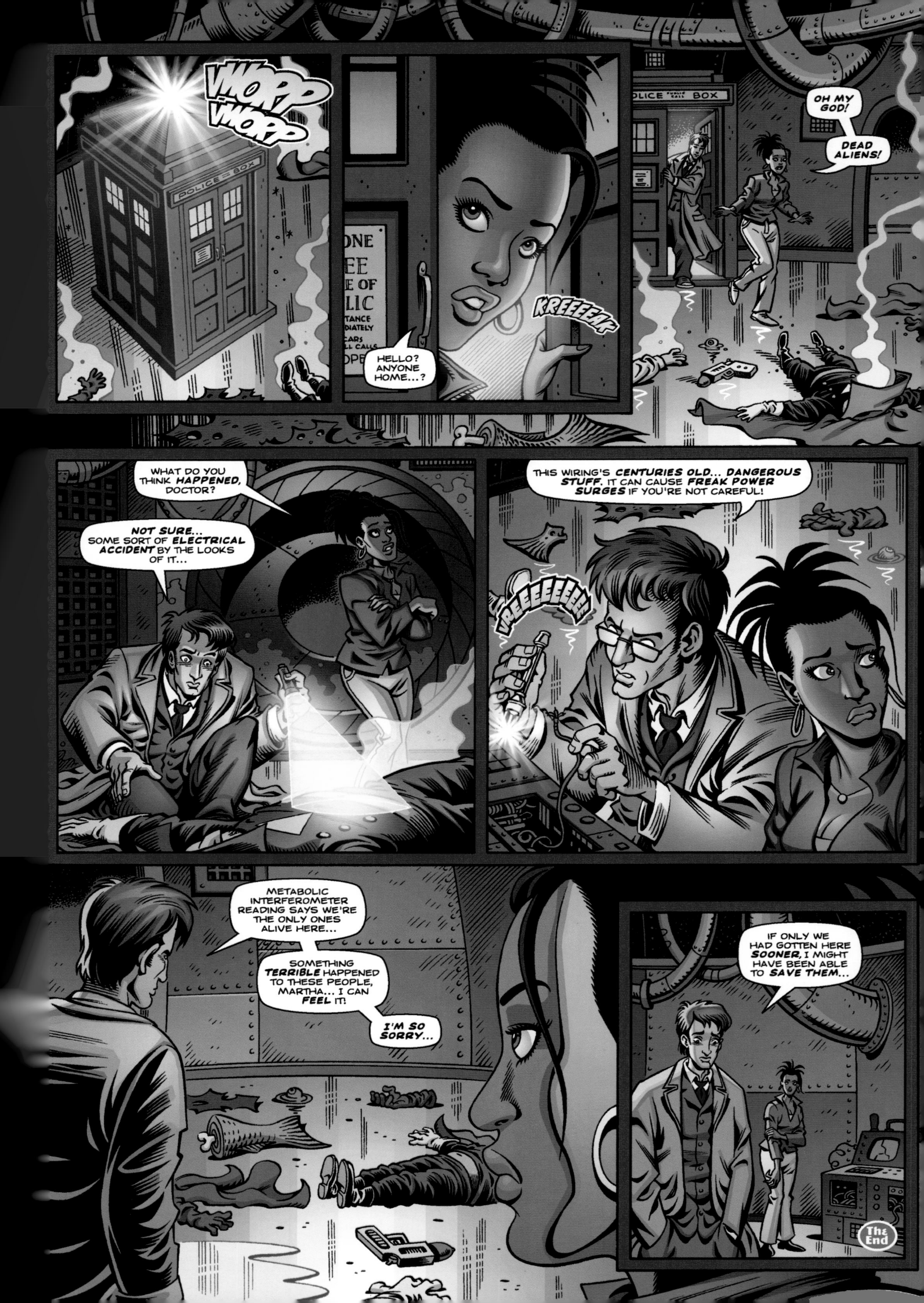
VWORP VWORP
POLICE BOX
HELLO? ANYONE HOME...?
KREEEEAK
OH MY GOD!
DEAD ALIENS!
WHAT DO YOU THINK HAPPENED, DOCTOR?
NOT SURE... SOME SORT OF ELECTRICAL ACCIDENT BY THE LOOKS OF IT...
THIS WIRING'S CENTURIES OLD... DANGEROUS STUFF. IT CAN CAUSE FREAK POWER SURGES IF YOU'RE NOT CAREFUL!
VREEEEEEEE
METABOLIC INTERFEROMETER READING SAYS WE'RE THE ONLY ONES ALIVE HERE...
SOMETHING TERRIBLE HAPPENED TO THESE PEOPLE, MARTHA... I CAN FEEL IT!
I'M SO SORRY...
IF ONLY WE HAD GOTTEN HERE SOONER, I MIGHT HAVE BEEN ABLE TO SAVE THEM...
The End

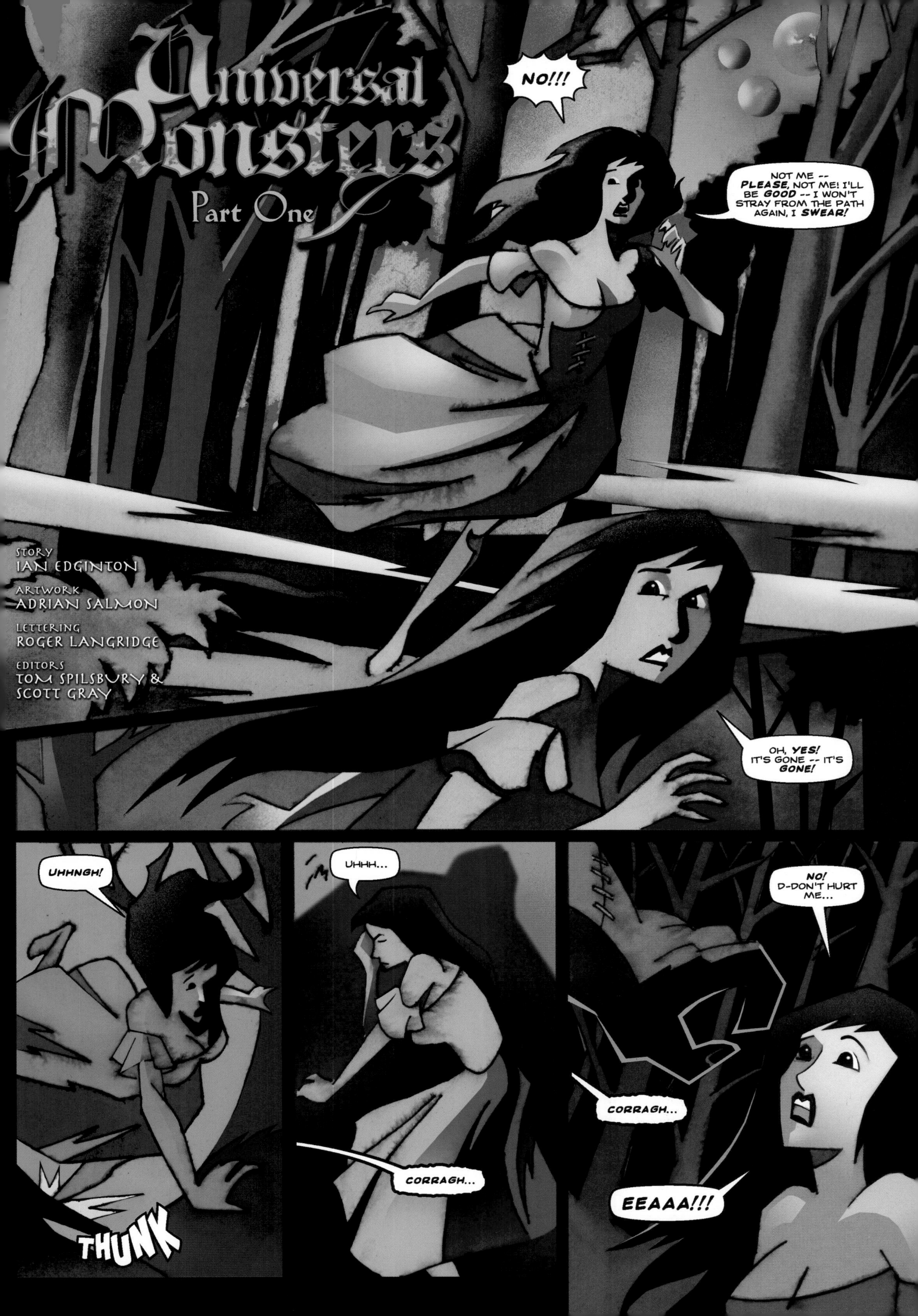
Universal Monsters
Part One
NO!!!
NOT ME -- PLEASE, NOT ME! I'LL BE GOOD -- I WON'T STRAY FROM THE PATH AGAIN, I SWEAR!
STORY
IAN EDGINTON
ARTWORK
ADRIAN SALMON
LETTERING
ROGER LANGRIDGE
EDITORS
TOM SPILSBURY & SCOTT GRAY
OH, YES! IT'S GONE -- IT'S GONE!
UHHNGH!
THUNK
UHHH...
CORRAGH...
NO! D-DON'T HURT ME...
CORRAGH...
EEAAA!!!

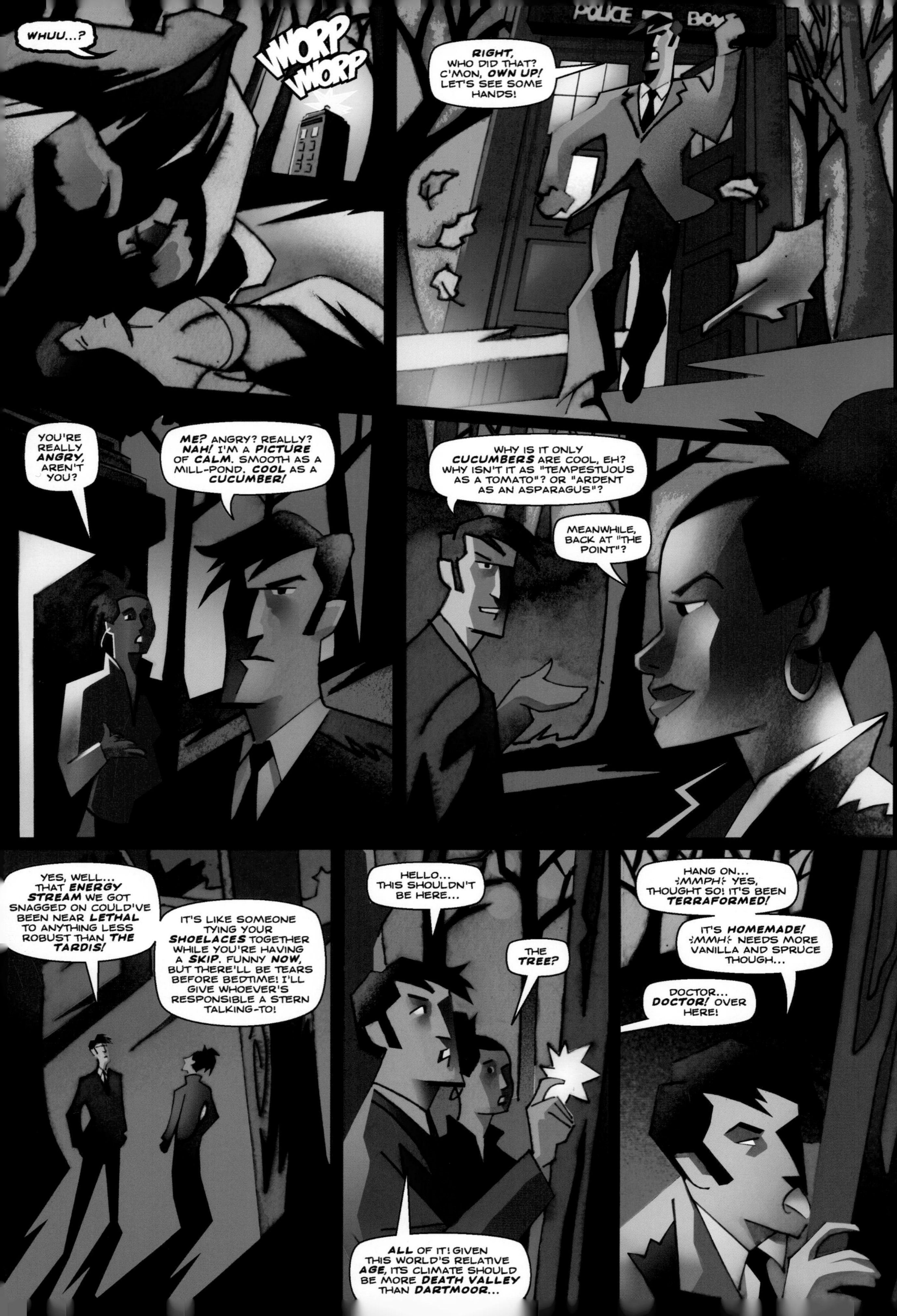
WHUU...?
VWORP VWORP
POLICE BOX
RIGHT, WHO DID THAT? C'MON, OWN UP! LET'S SEE SOME HANDS!
YOU'RE REALLY ANGRY, AREN'T YOU?
ME? ANGRY? REALLY? NAH! I'M A PICTURE OF CALM. SMOOTH AS A MILL-POND. COOL AS A CUCUMBER!
WHY IS IT ONLY CUCUMBERS ARE COOL, EH? WHY ISN'T IT AS "TEMPESTUOUS AS A TOMATO"? OR "ARDENT AS AN ASPARAGUS"?
MEANWHILE, BACK AT "THE POINT"?
YES, WELL... THAT ENERGY STREAM WE GOT SNAGGED ON COULD'VE BEEN NEAR LETHAL TO ANYTHING LESS ROBUST THAN THE TARDIS!
IT'S LIKE SOMEONE TYING YOUR SHOELACES TOGETHER WHILE YOU'RE HAVING A SKIP. FUNNY NOW, BUT THERE'LL BE TEARS BEFORE BEDTIME! I'LL GIVE WHOEVER'S RESPONSIBLE A STERN TALKING-TO!
HELLO... THIS SHOULDN'T BE HERE...
THE TREE?
ALL OF IT! GIVEN THIS WORLD'S RELATIVE AGE, ITS CLIMATE SHOULD BE MORE DEATH VALLEY THAN DARTMOOR...
HANG ON... ⁂MMPH⁂ YES, THOUGHT SO! IT'S BEEN TERRAFORMED!
IT'S HOMEMADE! ⁂MMH⁂ NEEDS MORE VANILLA AND SPRUCE THOUGH...
DOCTOR... DOCTOR! OVER HERE!

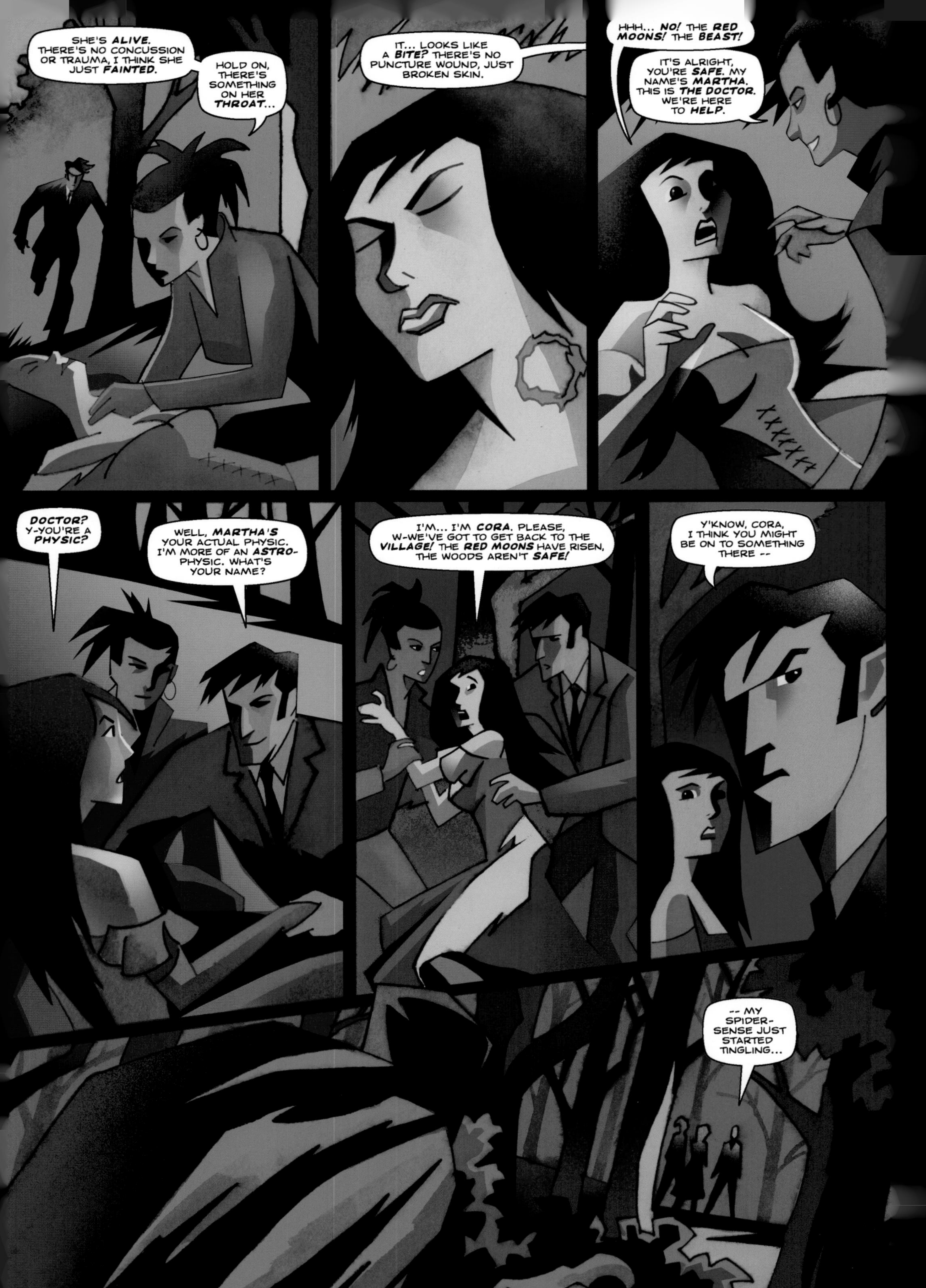
SHE'S ALIVE. THERE'S NO CONCUSSION OR TRAUMA, I THINK SHE JUST FAINTED.
HOLD ON, THERE'S SOMETHING ON HER THROAT...
IT... LOOKS LIKE A BITE? THERE'S NO PUNCTURE WOUND, JUST BROKEN SKIN.
HHH... NO! THE RED MOONS! THE BEAST!
IT'S ALRIGHT, YOU'RE SAFE. MY NAME'S MARTHA. THIS IS THE DOCTOR. WE'RE HERE TO HELP.
DOCTOR? Y-YOU'RE A PHYSIC?
WELL, MARTHA'S YOUR ACTUAL PHYSIC. I'M MORE OF AN ASTRO-PHYSIC. WHAT'S YOUR NAME?
I'M... I'M CORA. PLEASE, W-WE'VE GOT TO GET BACK TO THE VILLAGE! THE RED MOONS HAVE RISEN, THE WOODS AREN'T SAFE!
Y'KNOW, CORA, I THINK YOU MIGHT BE ON TO SOMETHING THERE --
-- MY SPIDER-SENSE JUST STARTED TINGLING...

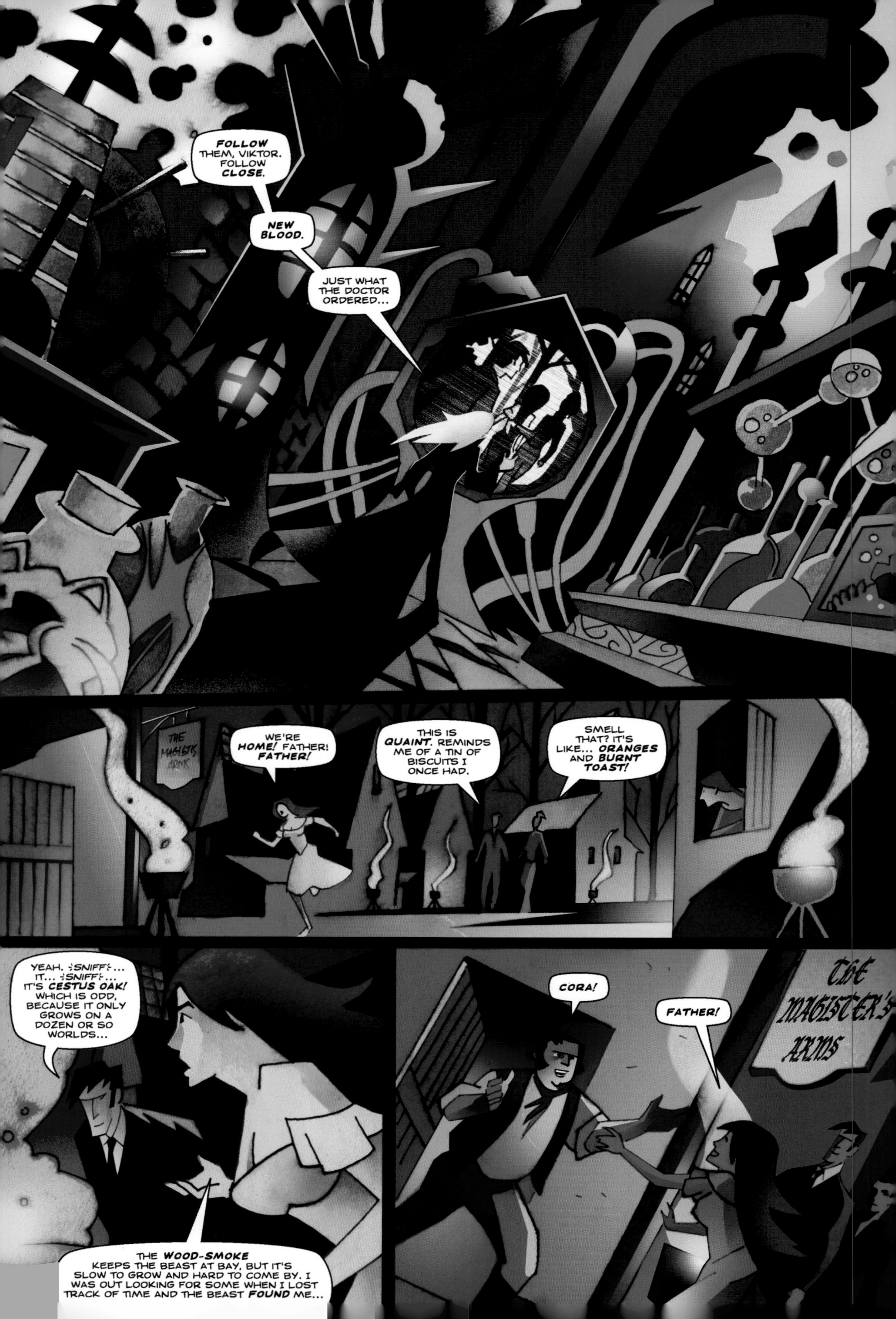
FOLLOW THEM, VIKTOR. FOLLOW CLOSE.
NEW BLOOD.
JUST WHAT THE DOCTOR ORDERED...
WE'RE HOME! FATHER! FATHER!
THIS IS QUAINT. REMINDS ME OF A TIN OF BISCUITS I ONCE HAD.
SMELL THAT? IT'S LIKE... ORANGES AND BURNT TOAST!
YEAH. ⁜SNIFF⁜... IT... ⁜SNIFF⁜... IT'S CESTUS OAK! WHICH IS ODD, BECAUSE IT ONLY GROWS ON A DOZEN OR SO WORLDS...
THE WOOD-SMOKE KEEPS THE BEAST AT BAY, BUT IT'S SLOW TO GROW AND HARD TO COME BY. I WAS OUT LOOKING FOR SOME WHEN I LOST TRACK OF TIME AND THE BEAST FOUND ME...
CORA!
FATHER!
THE MAGISTER'S ARMS

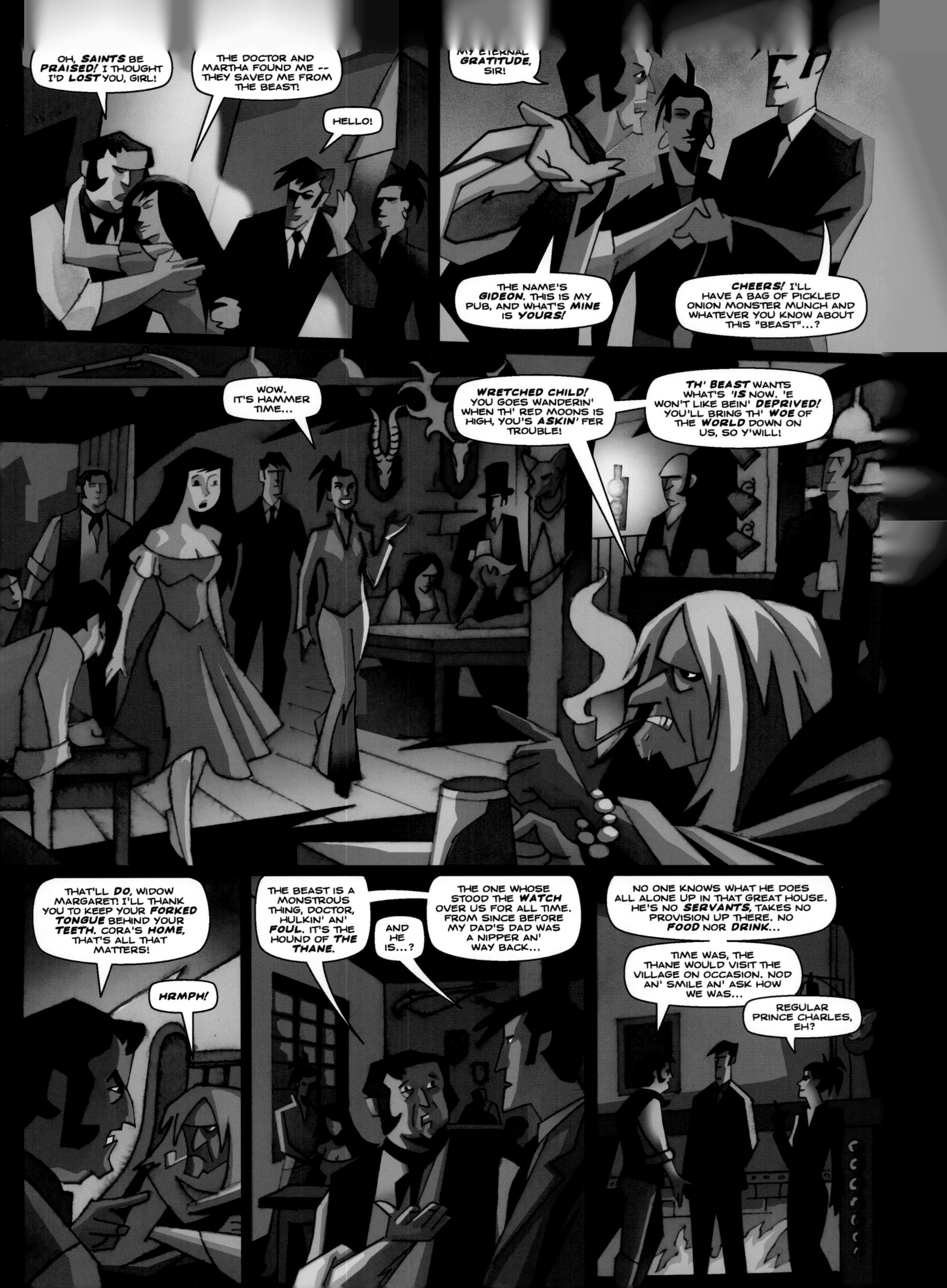

OH, SAINTS BE PRAISED! I THOUGHT I'D LOST YOU, GIRL!
THE DOCTOR AND MARTHA FOUND ME -- THEY SAVED ME FROM THE BEAST!
HELLO!
MY ETERNAL GRATITUDE, SIR!
THE NAME'S GIDEON. THIS IS MY PUB, AND WHAT'S MINE IS YOURS!
CHEERS! I'LL HAVE A BAG OF PICKLED ONION MONSTER MUNCH AND WHATEVER YOU KNOW ABOUT THIS "BEAST"...?
WOW. IT'S HAMMER TIME...
WRETCHED CHILD! YOU GOES WANDERIN' WHEN TH' RED MOONS IS HIGH, YOU'S ASKIN' FER TROUBLE!
TH' BEAST WANTS WHAT'S 'IS NOW. 'E WON'T LIKE BEIN' DEPRIVED! YOU'LL BRING TH' WOE OF THE WORLD DOWN ON US, SO Y'WILL!
THAT'LL DO, WIDOW MARGARET! I'LL THANK YOU TO KEEP YOUR FORKED TONGUE BEHIND YOUR TEETH. CORA'S HOME, THAT'S ALL THAT MATTERS!
HRMPH!
THE BEAST IS A MONSTROUS THING, DOCTOR, HULKIN' AN' FOUL. IT'S THE HOUND OF THE THANE.
AND HE IS...?
THE ONE WHOSE STOOD THE WATCH OVER US FOR ALL TIME. FROM SINCE BEFORE MY DAD'S DAD WAS A NIPPER AN' WAY BACK...
NO ONE KNOWS WHAT HE DOES ALL ALONE UP IN THAT GREAT HOUSE. HE'S NO SERVANTS, TAKES NO PROVISION UP THERE. NO FOOD NOR DRINK...
TIME WAS, THE THANE WOULD VISIT THE VILLAGE ON OCCASION. NOD AN' SMILE AN' ASK HOW WE WAS...
REGULAR PRINCE CHARLES, EH?

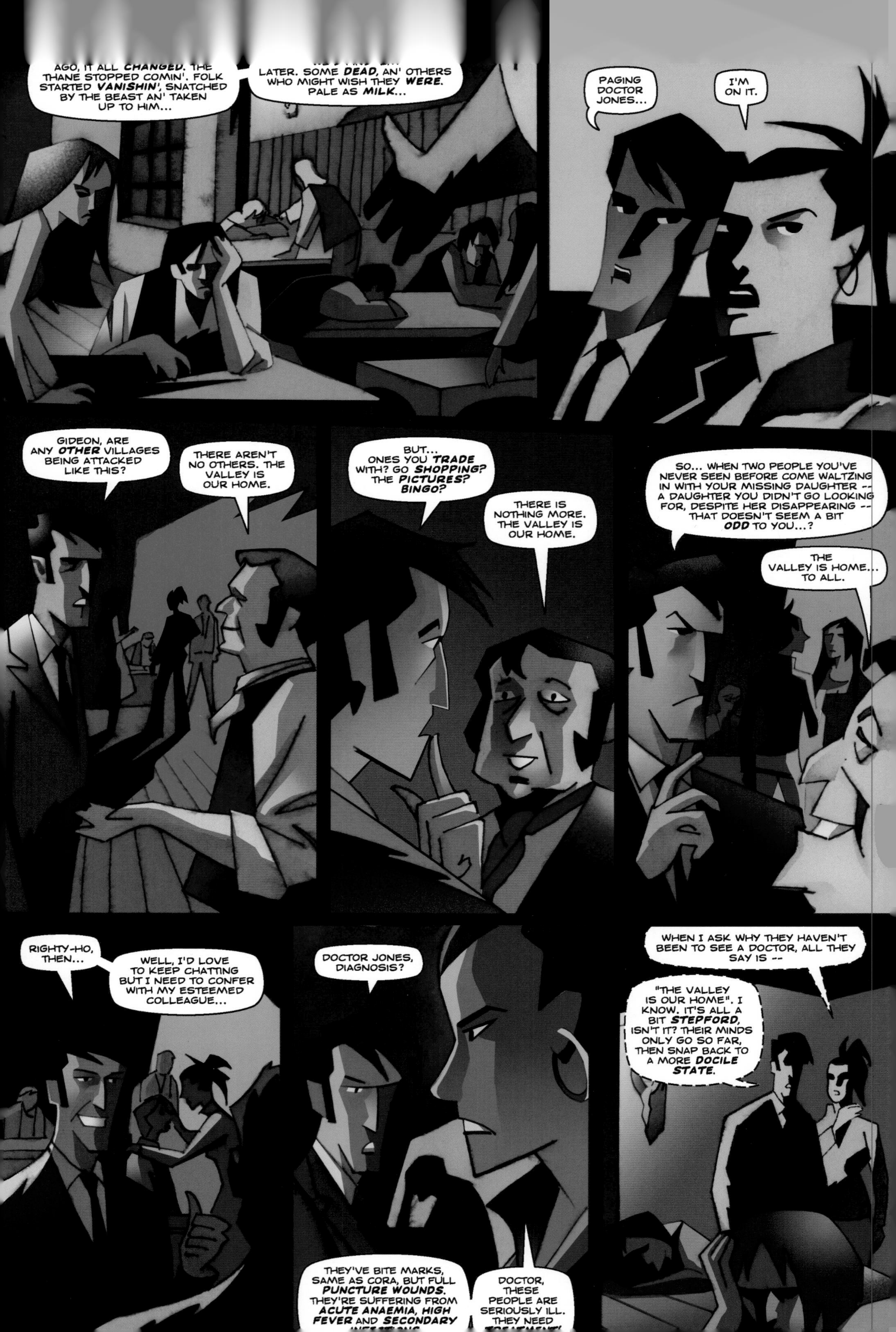
AGO, IT ALL CHANGED. THE THANE STOPPED COMIN'. FOLK STARTED VANISHIN', SNATCHED BY THE BEAST AN' TAKEN UP TO HIM...
LATER. SOME DEAD, AN' OTHERS WHO MIGHT WISH THEY WERE. PALE AS MILK...
PAGING DOCTOR JONES...
I'M ON IT.
GIDEON, ARE ANY OTHER VILLAGES BEING ATTACKED LIKE THIS?
THERE AREN'T NO OTHERS. THE VALLEY IS OUR HOME.
BUT... ONES YOU TRADE WITH? GO SHOPPING? THE PICTURES? BINGO?
THERE IS NOTHING MORE. THE VALLEY IS OUR HOME.
SO... WHEN TWO PEOPLE YOU'VE NEVER SEEN BEFORE COME WALTZING IN WITH YOUR MISSING DAUGHTER -- A DAUGHTER YOU DIDN'T GO LOOKING FOR, DESPITE HER DISAPPEARING -- THAT DOESN'T SEEM A BIT ODD TO YOU...?
THE VALLEY IS HOME... TO ALL.
RIGHTY-HO, THEN...
WELL, I'D LOVE TO KEEP CHATTING BUT I NEED TO CONFER WITH MY ESTEEMED COLLEAGUE...
DOCTOR JONES, DIAGNOSIS?
THEY'VE BITE MARKS, SAME AS CORA, BUT FULL PUNCTURE WOUNDS. THEY'RE SUFFERING FROM ACUTE ANAEMIA, HIGH FEVER AND SECONDARY
DOCTOR, THESE PEOPLE ARE SERIOUSLY ILL. THEY NEED
WHEN I ASK WHY THEY HAVEN'T BEEN TO SEE A DOCTOR, ALL THEY SAY IS --
"THE VALLEY IS OUR HOME". I KNOW. IT'S ALL A BIT STEPFORD, ISN'T IT? THEIR MINDS ONLY GO SO FAR, THEN SNAP BACK TO A MORE DOCILE STATE.

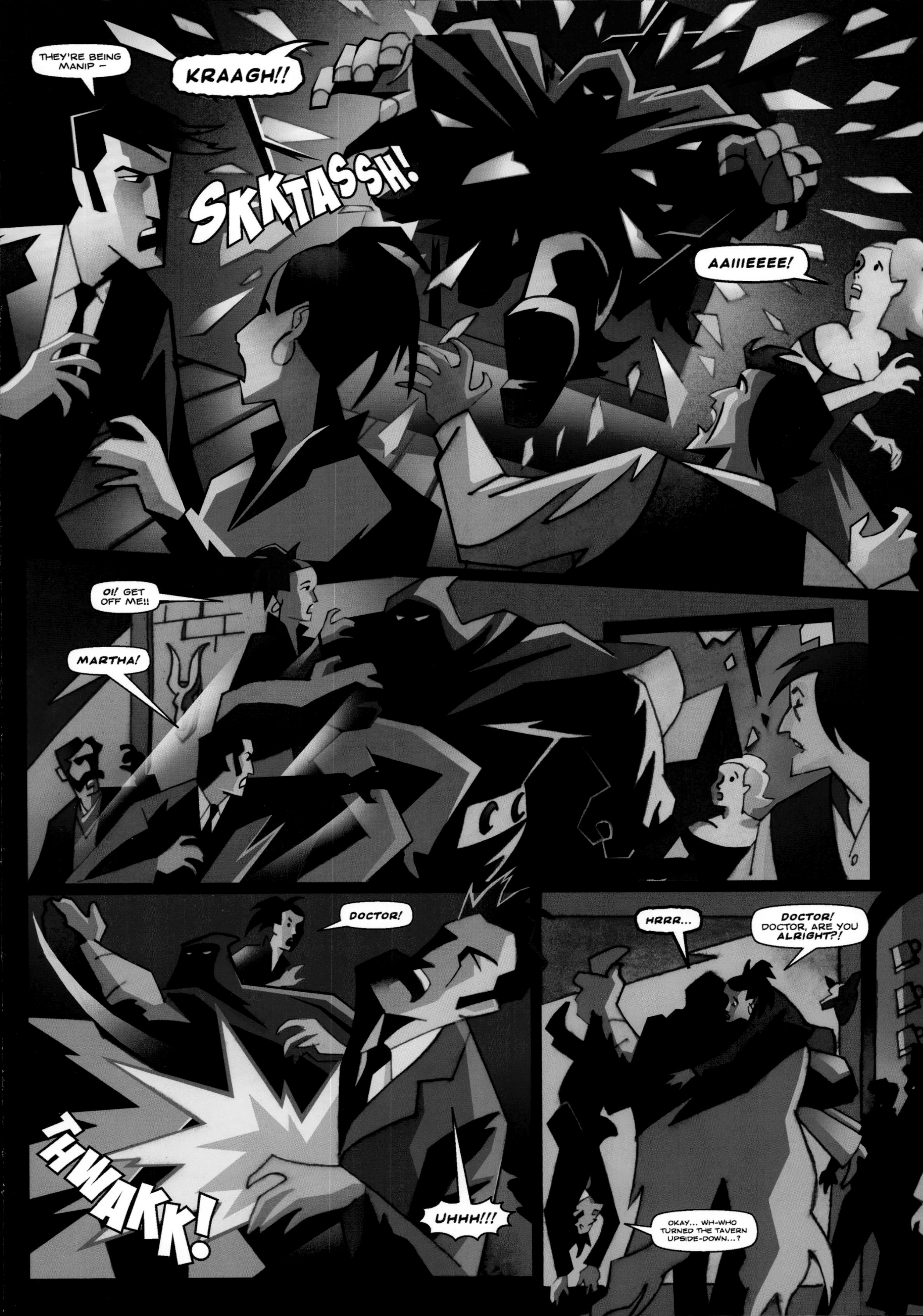
THEY'RE BEING MANIP –
KRAAGH!!
SKKTASSH!
AAIIIEEEE!
OI! GET OFF ME!!
MARTHA!
DOCTOR!
THWAKK!
UHHH!!!
HRRR...
DOCTOR! DOCTOR, ARE YOU ALRIGHT?!
OKAY... WH-WHO TURNED THE TAVERN UPSIDE-DOWN...?

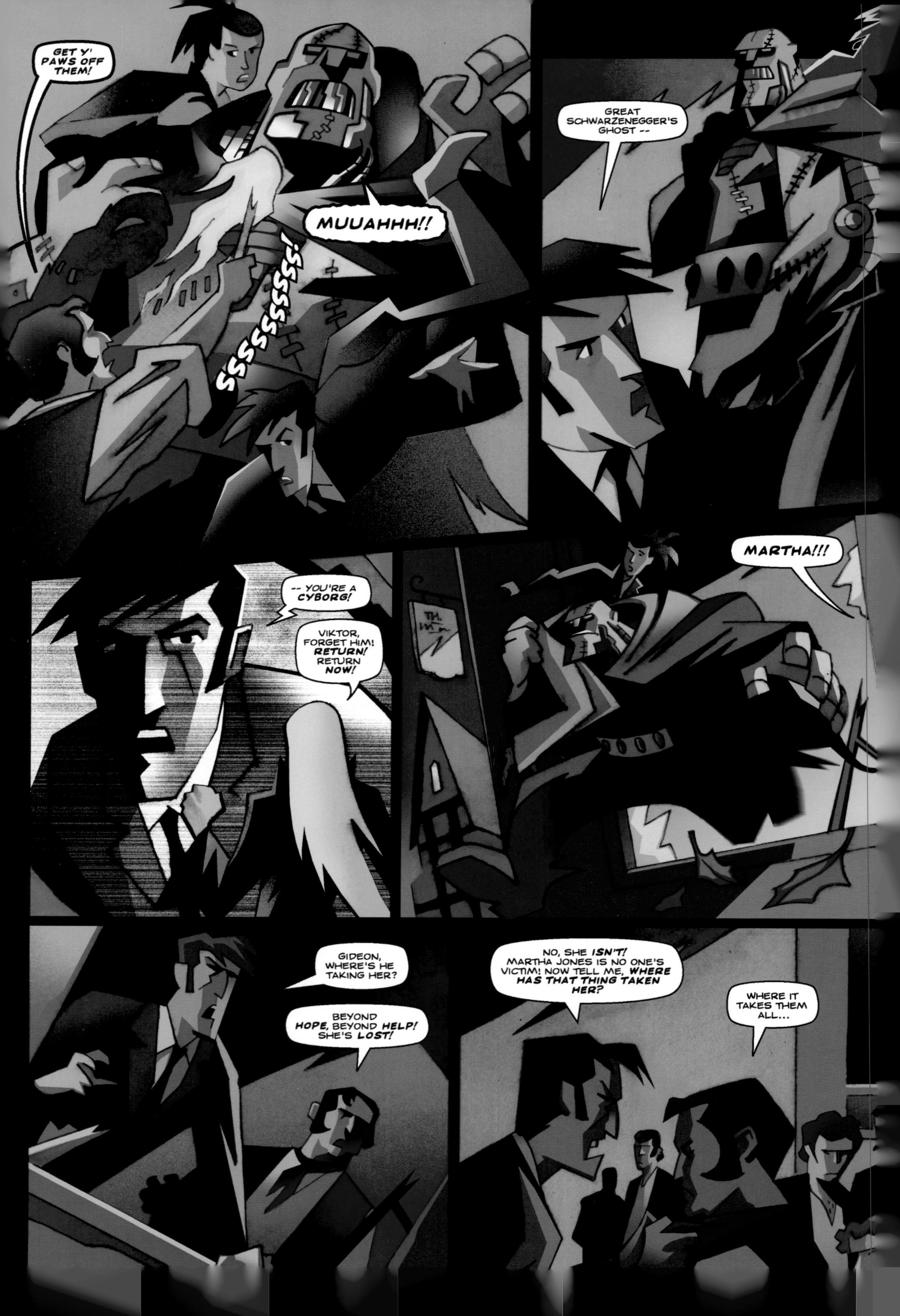

GET Y' PAWS OFF THEM!
MUUAHHH!!
SSSSSSSSSS!
GREAT SCHWARZENEGGER'S GHOST --
-- YOU'RE A CYBORG!
VIKTOR, FORGET HIM! RETURN! RETURN NOW!
MARTHA!!!
GIDEON, WHERE'S HE TAKING HER?
BEYOND HOPE, BEYOND HELP! SHE'S LOST!
NO, SHE ISN'T! MARTHA JONES IS NO ONE'S VICTIM! NOW TELL ME, WHERE HAS THAT THING TAKEN HER?
WHERE IT TAKES THEM ALL...

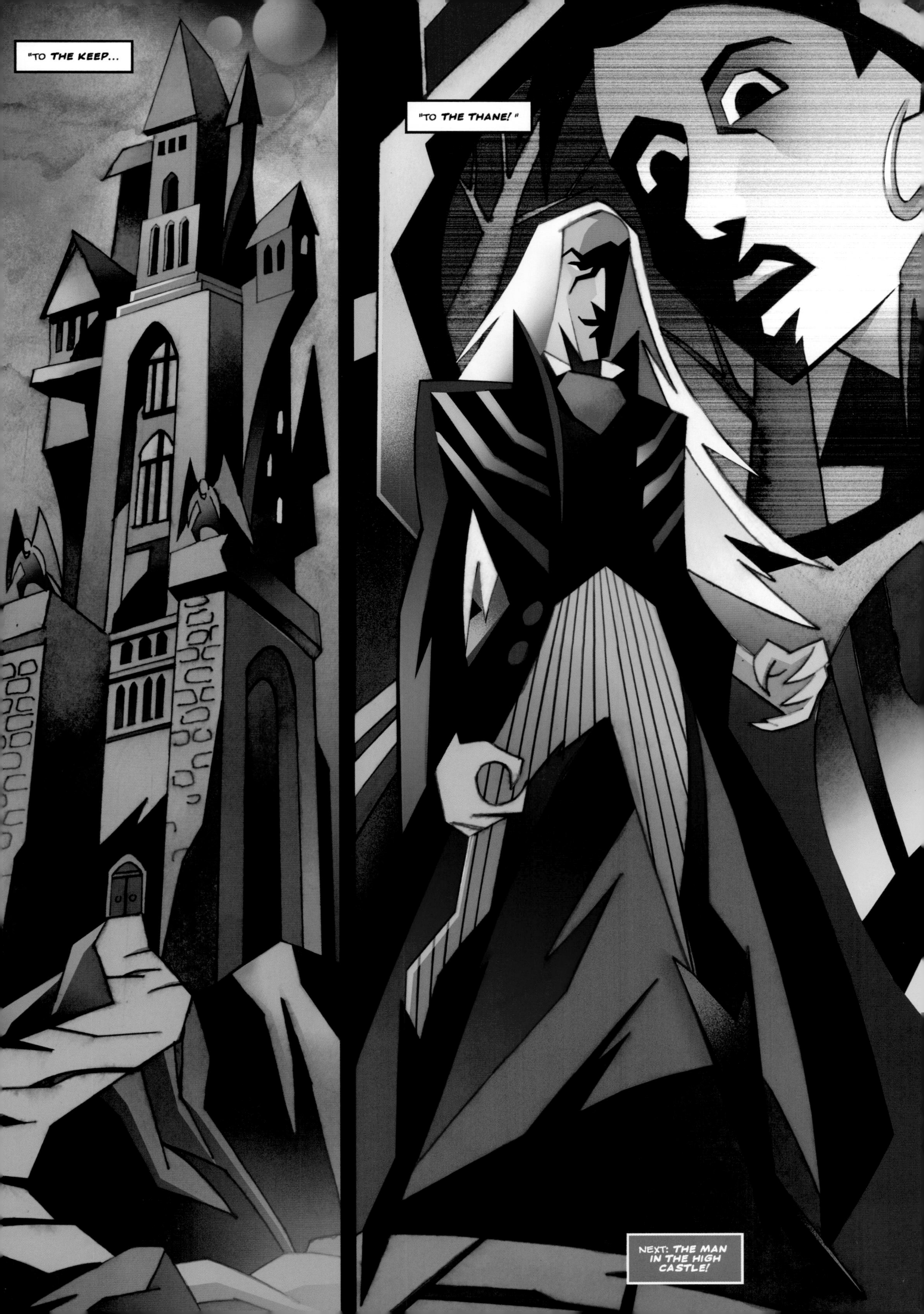
"TO THE KEEP...
"TO THE THANE!"
NEXT: THE MAN IN THE HIGH CASTLE!

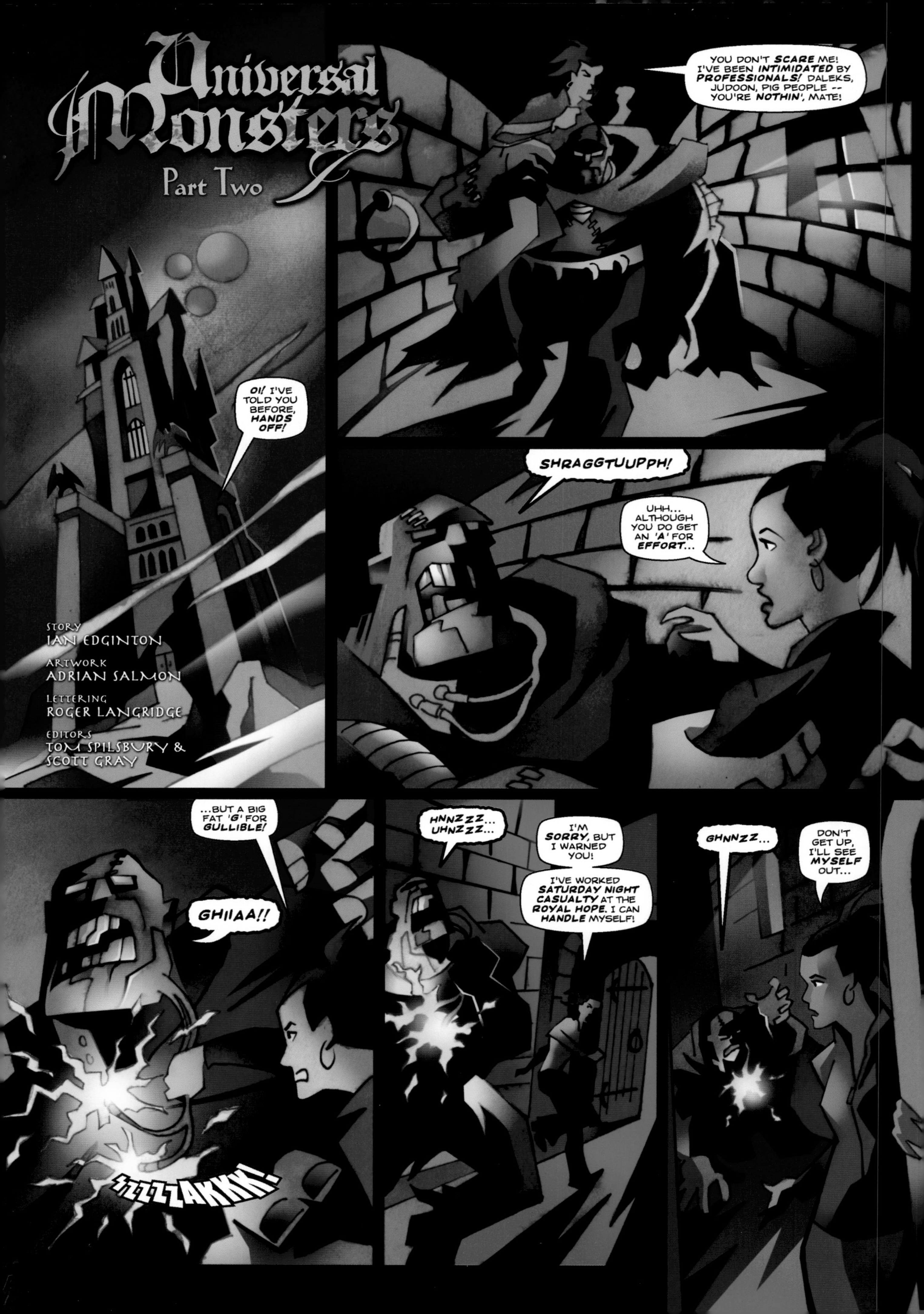
Universal Monsters
Part Two
OI! I'VE TOLD YOU BEFORE, HANDS OFF!
Story
Ian Edginton
Artwork
Adrian Salmon
Lettering
Roger Langridge
Editors
Tom Spilsbury & Scott Gray
YOU DON'T SCARE ME! I'VE BEEN INTIMIDATED BY PROFESSIONALS! DALEKS, JUDOON, PIG PEOPLE -- YOU'RE NOTHIN', MATE!
SHRAGGTUUPPH!
UHH... ALTHOUGH YOU DO GET AN 'A' FOR EFFORT...
...BUT A BIG FAT 'G' FOR GULLIBLE!
GHIIAA!!
SZZZZAKKK!
HNNZZZ... UHNZZZ...
I'M SORRY, BUT I WARNED YOU!
I'VE WORKED SATURDAY NIGHT CASUALTY AT THE ROYAL HOPE. I CAN HANDLE MYSELF!
GHNNZZ...
DON'T GET UP, I'LL SEE MYSELF OUT...

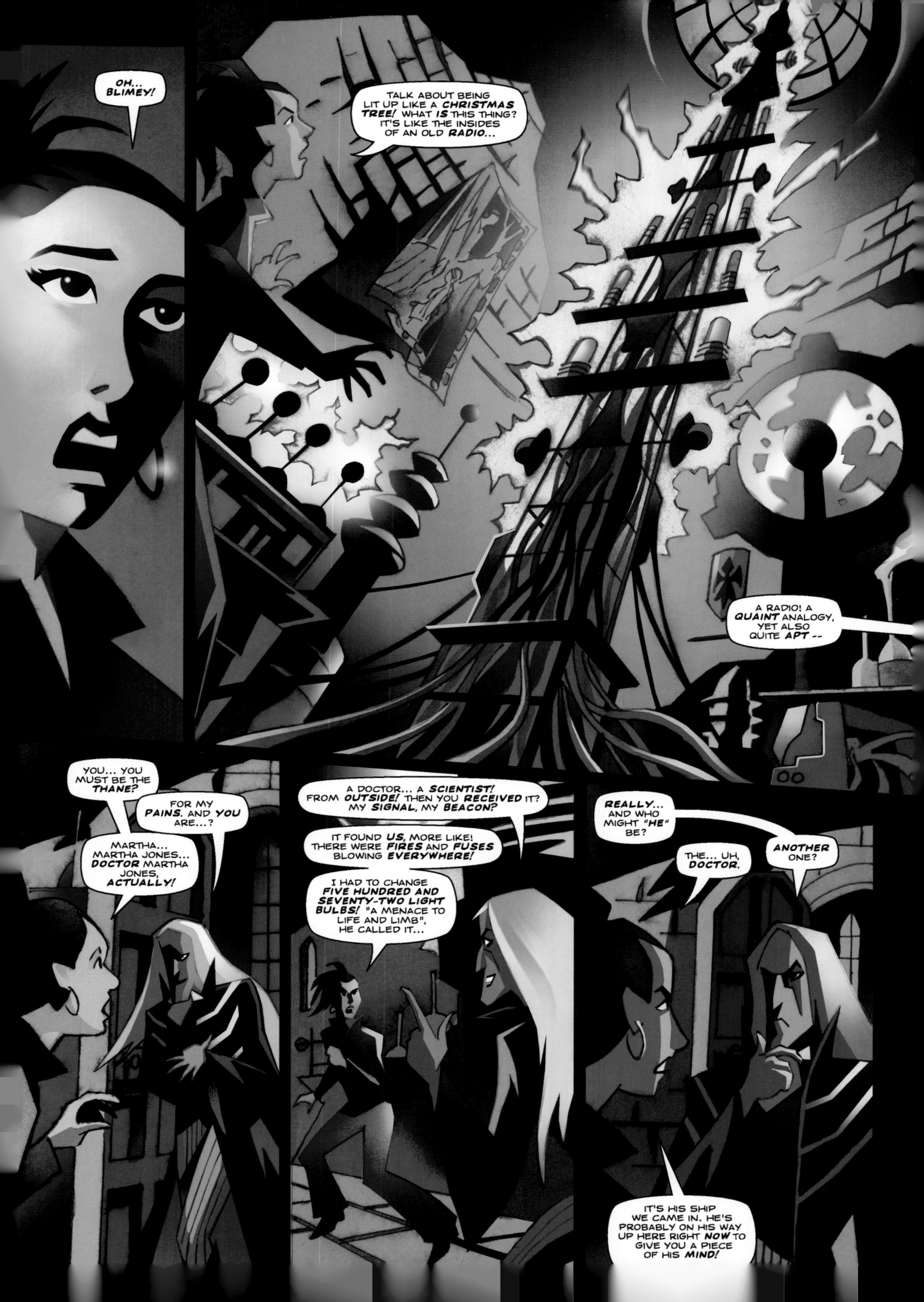
OH... BLIMEY!
TALK ABOUT BEING LIT UP LIKE A CHRISTMAS TREE! WHAT IS THIS THING? IT'S LIKE THE INSIDES OF AN OLD RADIO...
A RADIO! A QUAINT ANALOGY, YET ALSO QUITE APT --
YOU... YOU MUST BE THE THANE?
FOR MY PAINS. AND YOU ARE...?
MARTHA... MARTHA JONES... DOCTOR MARTHA JONES, ACTUALLY!
A DOCTOR... A SCIENTIST! FROM OUTSIDE! THEN YOU RECEIVED IT? MY SIGNAL, MY BEACON?
IT FOUND US, MORE LIKE! THERE WERE FIRES AND FUSES BLOWING EVERYWHERE!
I HAD TO CHANGE FIVE HUNDRED AND SEVENTY-TWO LIGHT BULBS! "A MENACE TO LIFE AND LIMB", HE CALLED IT...
REALLY... AND WHO MIGHT "HE" BE?
THE... UH, DOCTOR.
ANOTHER ONE?
IT'S HIS SHIP WE CAME IN. HE'S PROBABLY ON HIS WAY UP HERE RIGHT NOW TO GIVE YOU A PIECE OF HIS MIND!

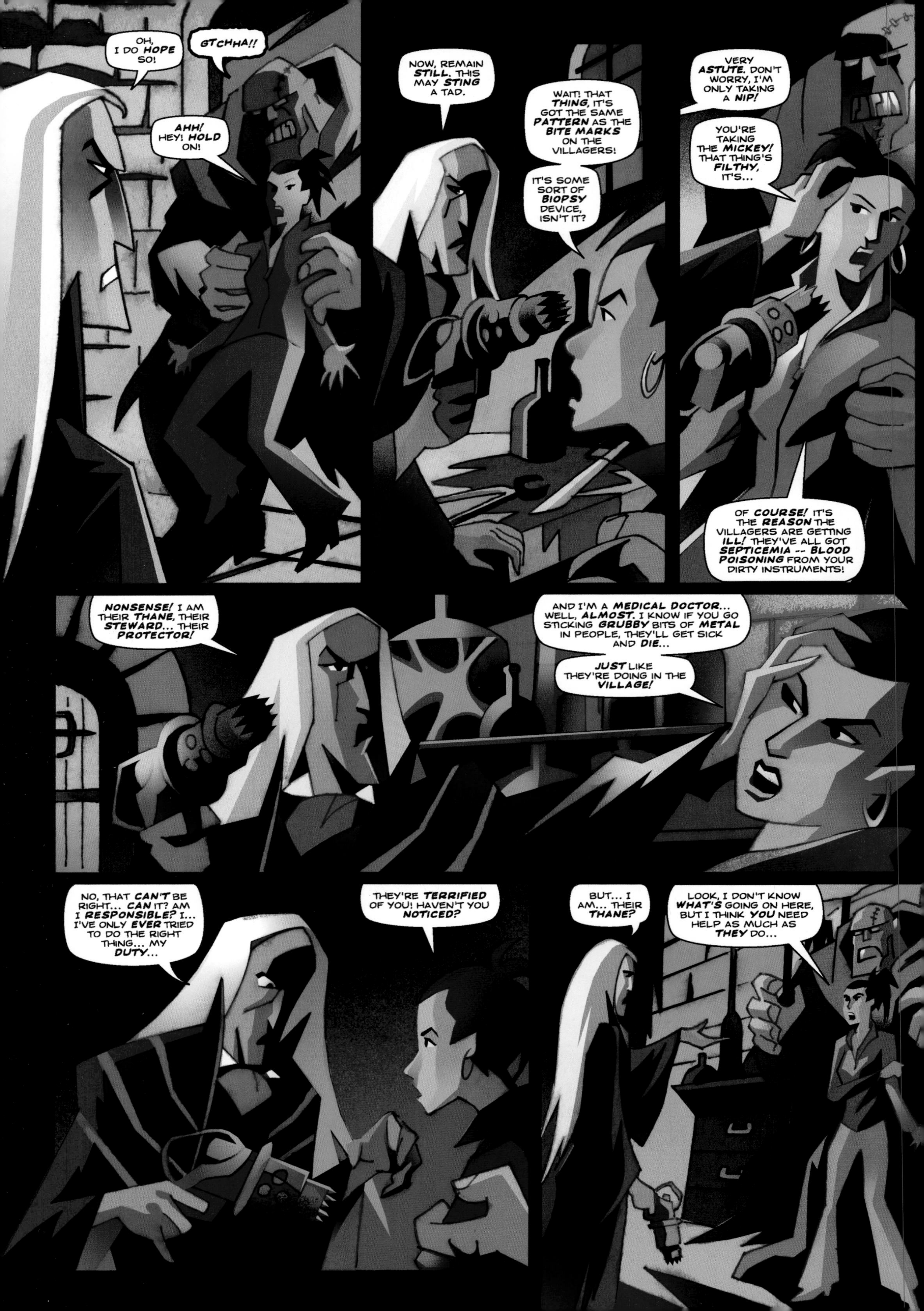
OH, I DO HOPE SO!
GTCHHA!!
AHH! HEY! HOLD ON!
NOW, REMAIN STILL. THIS MAY STING A TAD.
WAIT! THAT THING, IT'S GOT THE SAME PATTERN AS THE BITE MARKS ON THE VILLAGERS!
IT'S SOME SORT OF BIOPSY DEVICE, ISN'T IT?
VERY ASTUTE. DON'T WORRY, I'M ONLY TAKING A NIP!
YOU'RE TAKING THE MICKEY! THAT THING'S FILTHY, IT'S...
OF COURSE! IT'S THE REASON THE VILLAGERS ARE GETTING ILL! THEY'VE ALL GOT SEPTICEMIA -- BLOOD POISONING FROM YOUR DIRTY INSTRUMENTS!
NONSENSE! I AM THEIR THANE, THEIR STEWARD... THEIR PROTECTOR!
AND I'M A MEDICAL DOCTOR... WELL, ALMOST. I KNOW IF YOU GO STICKING GRUBBY BITS OF METAL IN PEOPLE, THEY'LL GET SICK AND DIE...
JUST LIKE THEY'RE DOING IN THE VILLAGE!
NO, THAT CAN'T BE RIGHT... CAN IT? AM I RESPONSIBLE? I... I'VE ONLY EVER TRIED TO DO THE RIGHT THING... MY DUTY...
THEY'RE TERRIFIED OF YOU! HAVEN'T YOU NOTICED?
BUT... I AM... THEIR THANE?
LOOK, I DON'T KNOW WHAT'S GOING ON HERE, BUT I THINK YOU NEED HELP AS MUCH AS THEY DO...

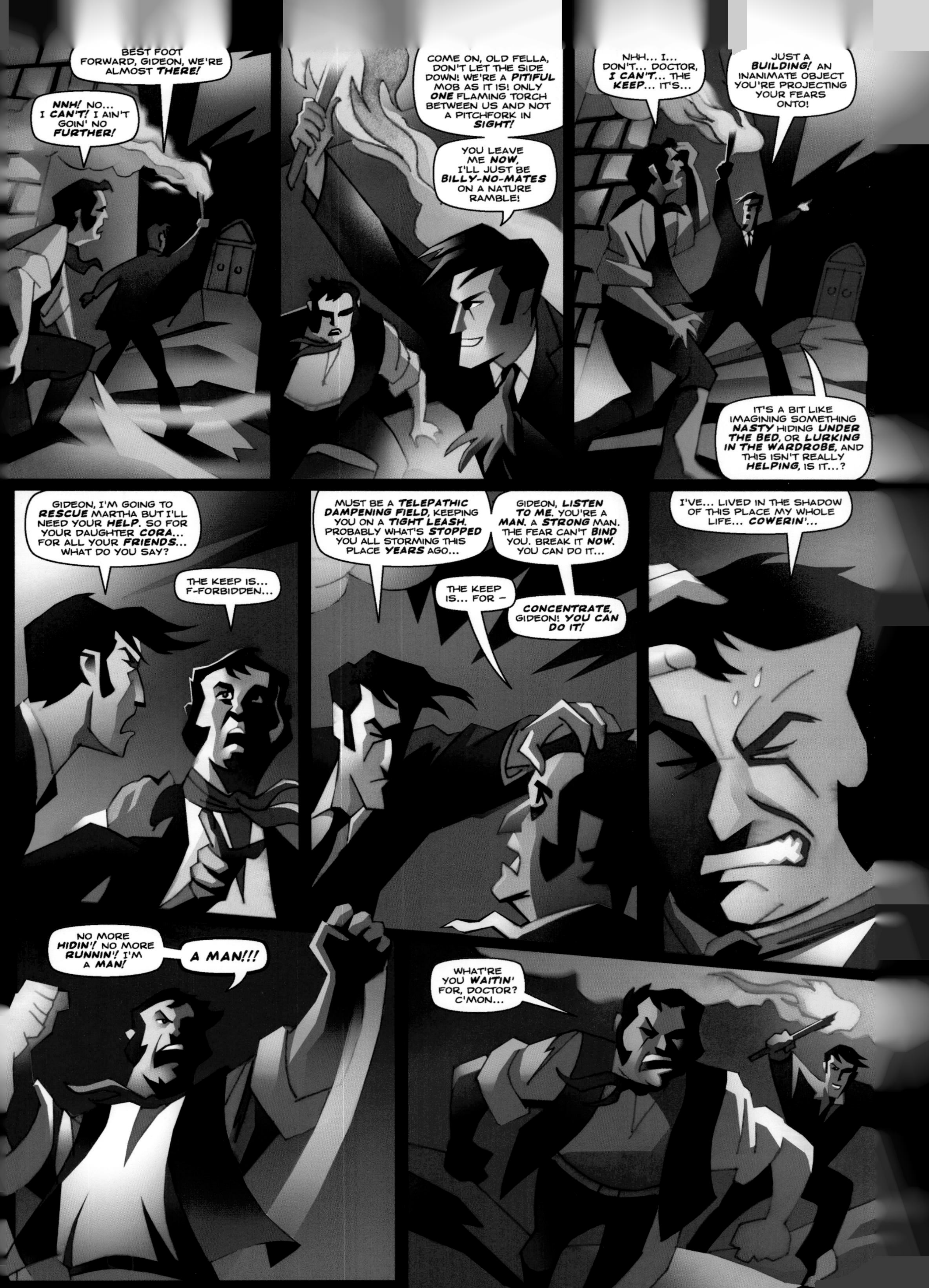
BEST FOOT FORWARD, GIDEON, WE'RE ALMOST THERE!
NNH! NO... I CAN'T! I AIN'T GOIN' NO FURTHER!
COME ON, OLD FELLA, DON'T LET THE SIDE DOWN! WE'RE A PITIFUL MOB AS IT IS! ONLY ONE FLAMING TORCH BETWEEN US AND NOT A PITCHFORK IN SIGHT!
YOU LEAVE ME NOW, I'LL JUST BE BILLY-NO-MATES ON A NATURE RAMBLE!
NHH... I... DON'T... DOCTOR, I CAN'T... THE KEEP... IT'S...
JUST A BUILDING! AN INANIMATE OBJECT YOU'RE PROJECTING YOUR FEARS ONTO!
IT'S A BIT LIKE IMAGINING SOMETHING NASTY HIDING UNDER THE BED, OR LURKING IN THE WARDROBE, AND THIS ISN'T REALLY HELPING, IS IT...?
GIDEON, I'M GOING TO RESCUE MARTHA BUT I'LL NEED YOUR HELP. SO FOR YOUR DAUGHTER CORA... FOR ALL YOUR FRIENDS... WHAT DO YOU SAY?
THE KEEP IS... F-FORBIDDEN...
MUST BE A TELEPATHIC DAMPENING FIELD, KEEPING YOU ON A TIGHT LEASH. PROBABLY WHAT'S STOPPED YOU ALL STORMING THIS PLACE YEARS AGO...
GIDEON, LISTEN TO ME. YOU'RE A MAN. A STRONG MAN. THE FEAR CAN'T BIND YOU. BREAK IT NOW. YOU CAN DO IT...
THE KEEP IS... FOR –
CONCENTRATE, GIDEON! YOU CAN DO IT!
I'VE... LIVED IN THE SHADOW OF THIS PLACE MY WHOLE LIFE... COWERIN'...
NO MORE HIDIN'! NO MORE RUNNIN'! I'M A MAN!
A MAN!!!
WHAT'RE YOU WAITIN' FOR, DOCTOR? C'MON...

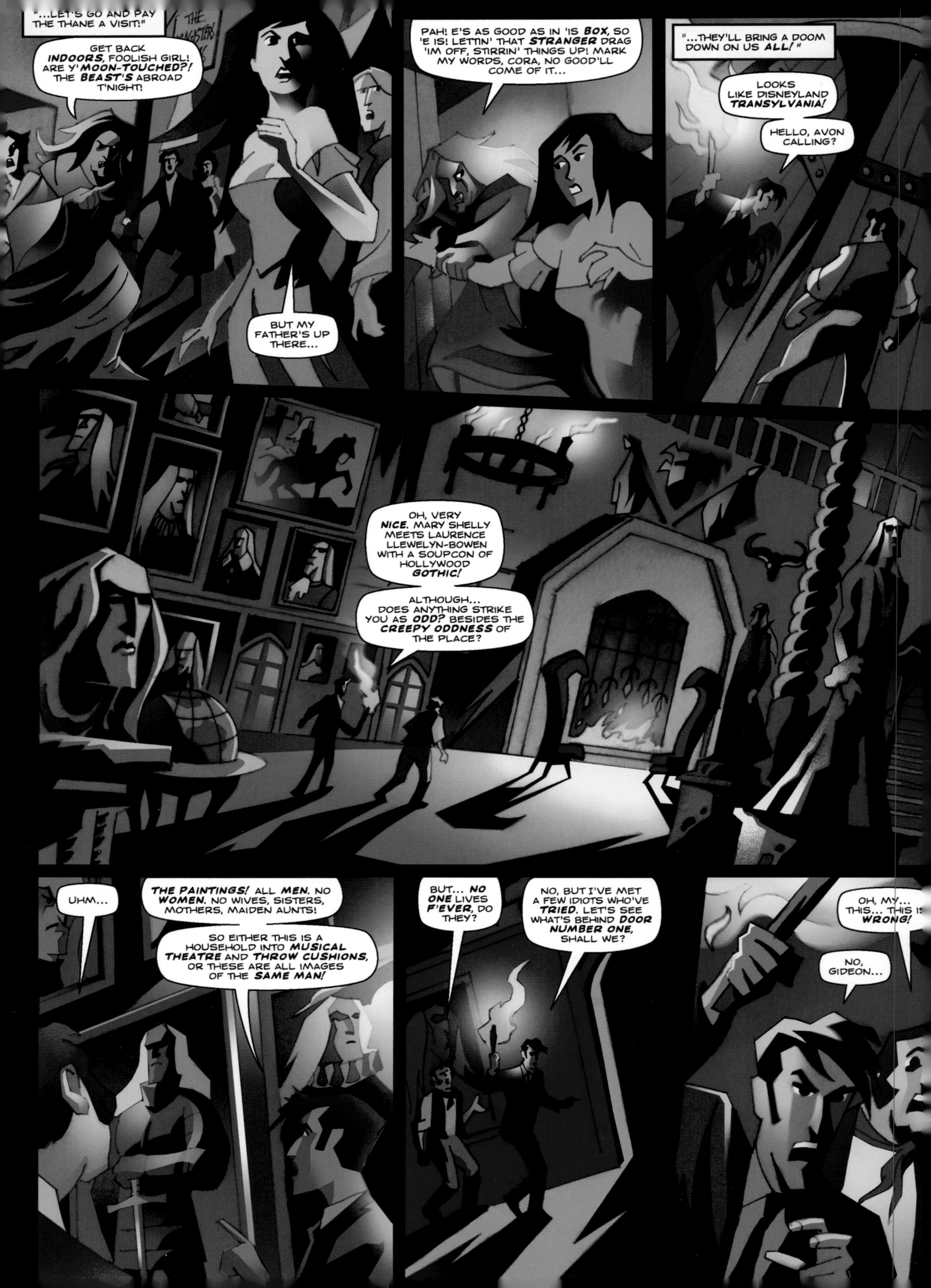
"...LET'S GO AND PAY THE THANE A VISIT!"
GET BACK INDOORS, FOOLISH GIRL! ARE Y'MOON-TOUCHED?! THE BEAST'S ABROAD T'NIGHT!
BUT MY FATHER'S UP THERE...
PAH! E'S AS GOOD AS IN 'IS BOX, SO 'E IS! LETTIN' THAT STRANGER DRAG 'IM OFF, STIRRIN' THINGS UP! MARK MY WORDS, CORA, NO GOOD'LL COME OF IT...
"...THEY'LL BRING A DOOM DOWN ON US ALL!"
LOOKS LIKE DISNEYLAND TRANSYLVANIA!
HELLO, AVON CALLING?
OH, VERY NICE. MARY SHELLY MEETS LAURENCE LLEWELYN-BOWEN WITH A SOUPCON OF HOLLYWOOD GOTHIC!
ALTHOUGH... DOES ANYTHING STRIKE YOU AS ODD? BESIDES THE CREEPY ODDNESS OF THE PLACE?
UHM...
THE PAINTINGS! ALL MEN. NO WOMEN. NO WIVES, SISTERS, MOTHERS, MAIDEN AUNTS!
SO EITHER THIS IS A HOUSEHOLD INTO MUSICAL THEATRE AND THROW CUSHIONS, OR THESE ARE ALL IMAGES OF THE SAME MAN!
BUT... NO ONE LIVES F'EVER, DO THEY?
NO, BUT I'VE MET A FEW IDIOTS WHO'VE TRIED. LET'S SEE WHAT'S BEHIND DOOR NUMBER ONE, SHALL WE?
OH, MY... THIS... THIS IS WRONG!
NO, GIDEON...

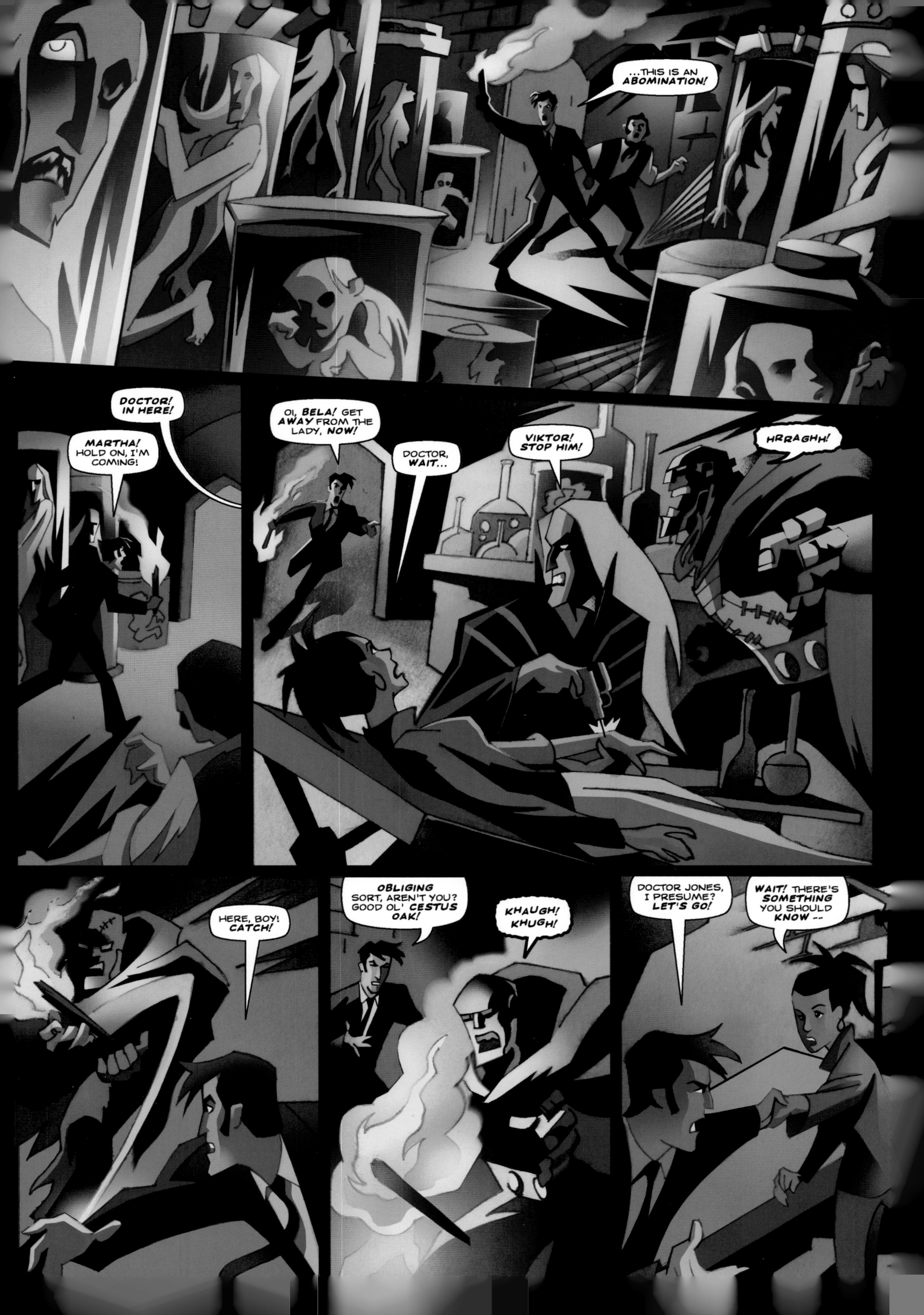
...THIS IS AN ABOMINATION!
DOCTOR! IN HERE!
MARTHA! HOLD ON, I'M COMING!
OI, BELA! GET AWAY FROM THE LADY, NOW!
DOCTOR, WAIT...
VIKTOR! STOP HIM!
HRRAGHH!
HERE, BOY! CATCH!
OBLIGING SORT, AREN'T YOU? GOOD OL' CESTUS OAK!
KHAUGH! KHUGH!
DOCTOR JONES, I PRESUME? LET'S GO!
WAIT! THERE'S SOMETHING YOU SHOULD KNOW --

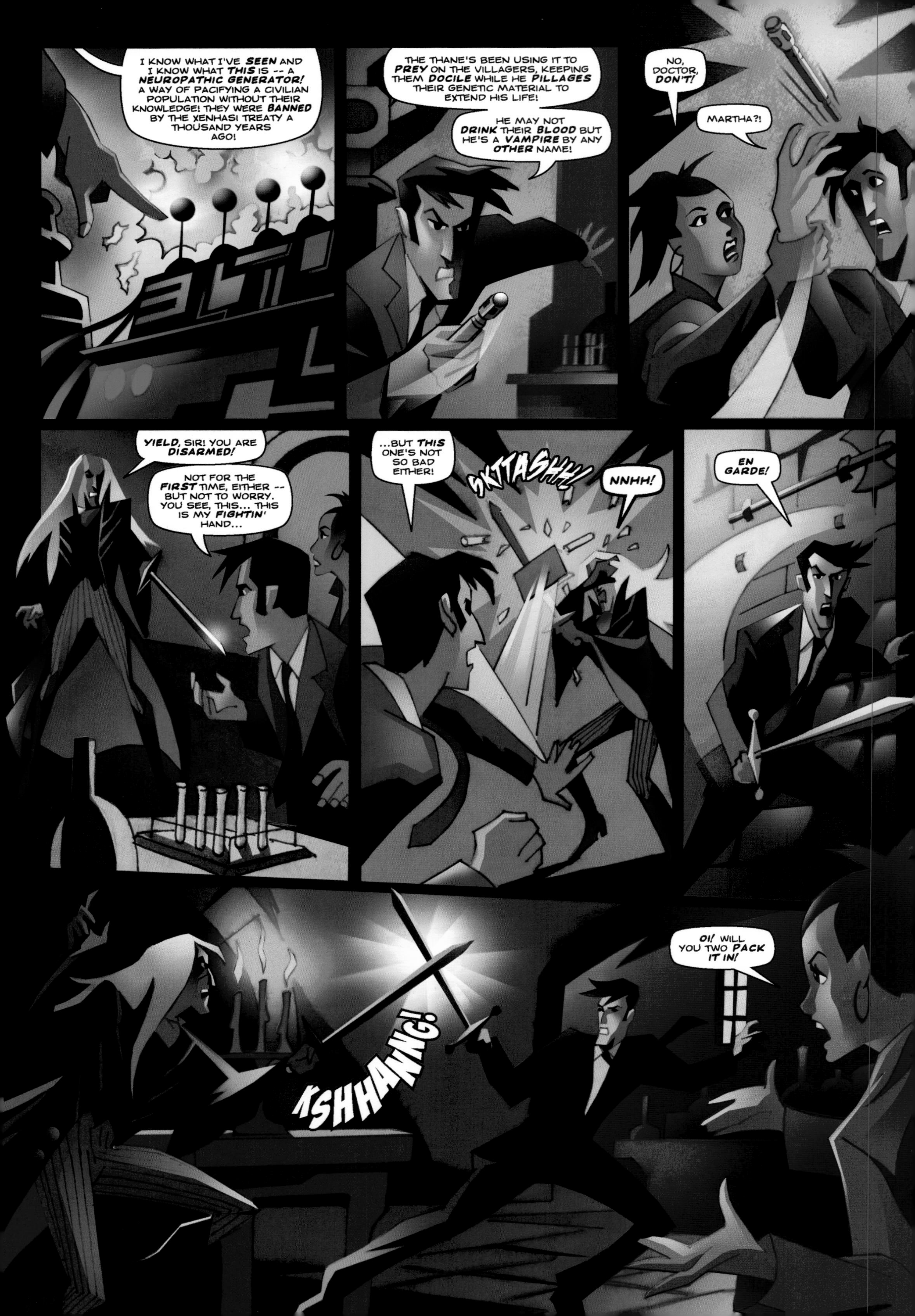
I KNOW WHAT I'VE SEEN AND I KNOW WHAT THIS IS -- A NEUROPATHIC GENERATOR! A WAY OF PACIFYING A CIVILIAN POPULATION WITHOUT THEIR KNOWLEDGE! THEY WERE BANNED BY THE XENHASI TREATY A THOUSAND YEARS AGO!
THE THANE'S BEEN USING IT TO PREY ON THE VILLAGERS, KEEPING THEM DOCILE WHILE HE PILLAGES THEIR GENETIC MATERIAL TO EXTEND HIS LIFE!
HE MAY NOT DRINK THEIR BLOOD BUT HE'S A VAMPIRE BY ANY OTHER NAME!
NO, DOCTOR, DON'T!
MARTHA?!
YIELD, SIR! YOU ARE DISARMED!
NOT FOR THE FIRST TIME, EITHER -- BUT NOT TO WORRY. YOU SEE, THIS... THIS IS MY FIGHTIN' HAND...
...BUT THIS ONE'S NOT SO BAD EITHER!
SKTTASHH!
NNHH!
EN GARDE!
KSHHANNG!
OI! WILL YOU TWO PACK IT IN!

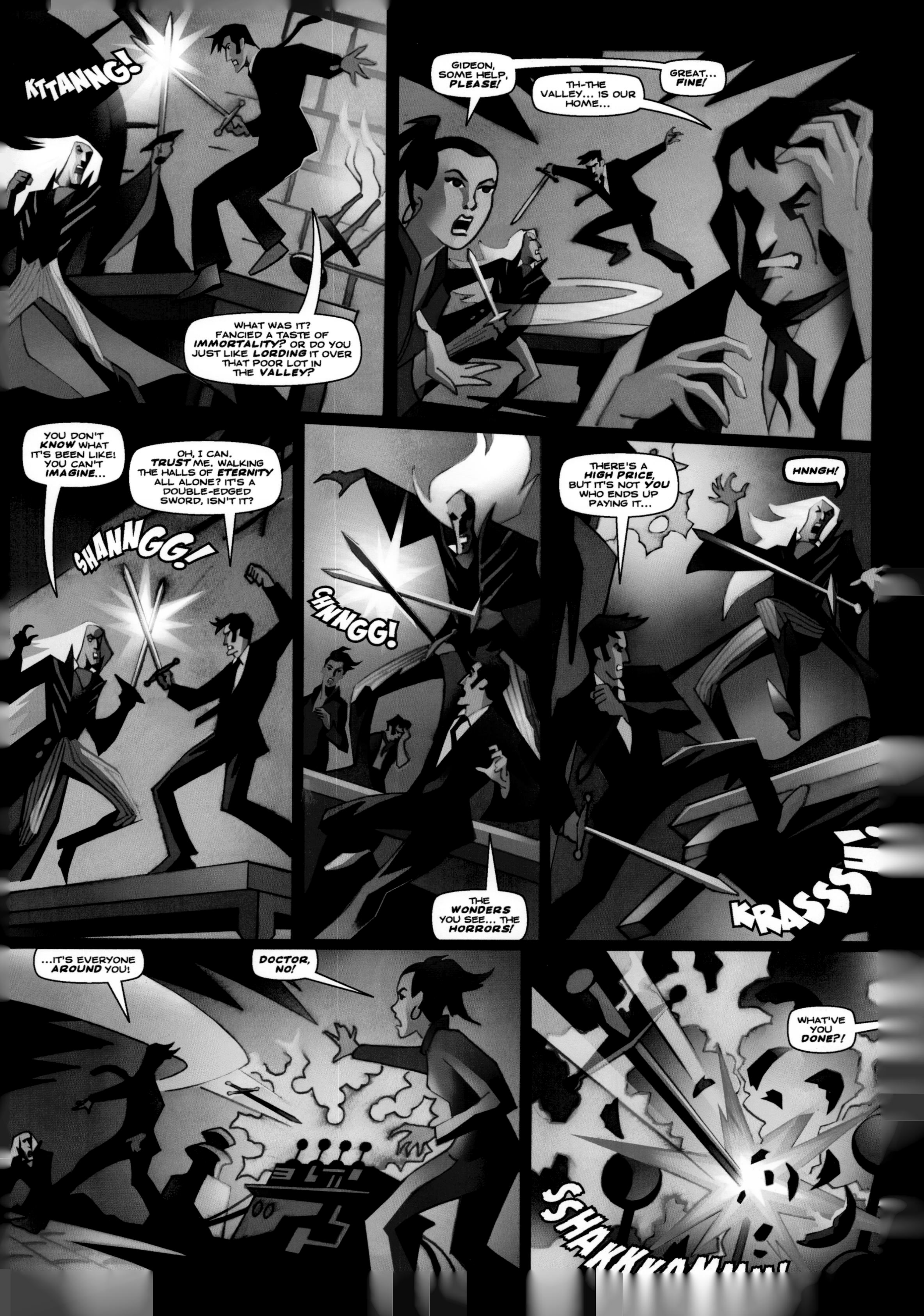
KTTANNG!
WHAT WAS IT? FANCIED A TASTE OF IMMORTALITY? OR DO YOU JUST LIKE LORDING IT OVER THAT POOR LOT IN THE VALLEY?
GIDEON, SOME HELP, PLEASE!
TH-THE VALLEY... IS OUR HOME...
GREAT... FINE!
YOU DON'T KNOW WHAT IT'S BEEN LIKE! YOU CAN'T IMAGINE...
OH, I CAN. TRUST ME. WALKING THE HALLS OF ETERNITY ALL ALONE? IT'S A DOUBLE-EDGED SWORD, ISN'T IT?
SHANNGG!
CHNNGG!
THE WONDERS YOU SEE... THE HORRORS!
THERE'S A HIGH PRICE, BUT IT'S NOT YOU WHO ENDS UP PAYING IT...
HNNGH!
KRASSS
...IT'S EVERYONE AROUND YOU!
DOCTOR, NO!
WHAT'VE YOU DONE?!

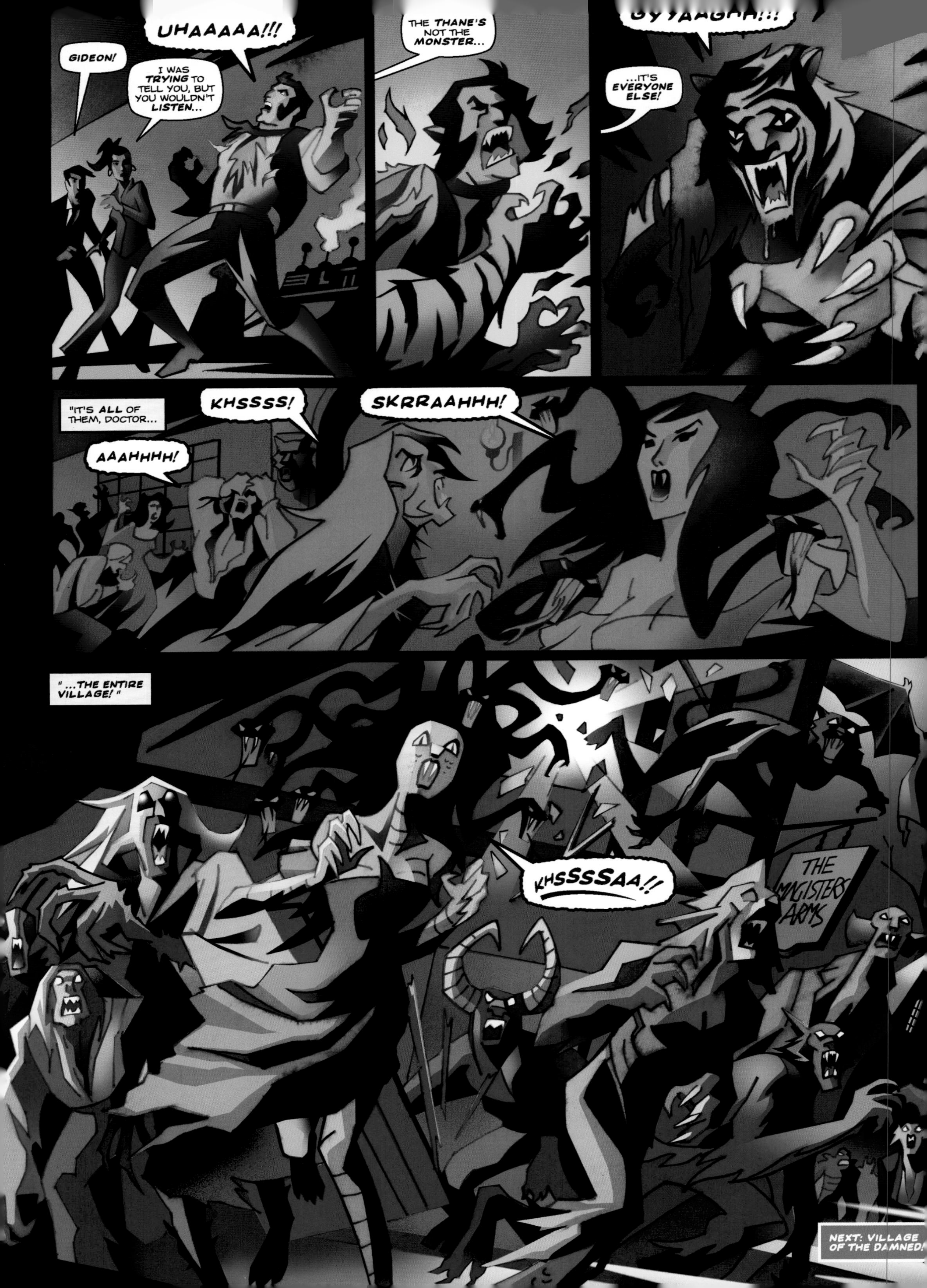
UHAAAAA!!!
GIDEON!
I WAS TRYING TO TELL YOU, BUT YOU WOULDN'T LISTEN...
THE THANE'S NOT THE MONSTER...
...IT'S EVERYONE ELSE!
"IT'S ALL OF THEM, DOCTOR...
KHSSSS!
SKRRAAHHH!
AAAHHHH!
"...THE ENTIRE VILLAGE!"
KHSSSSAA!!
THE MAGISTERS ARMS
NEXT: VILLAGE OF THE DAMNED!

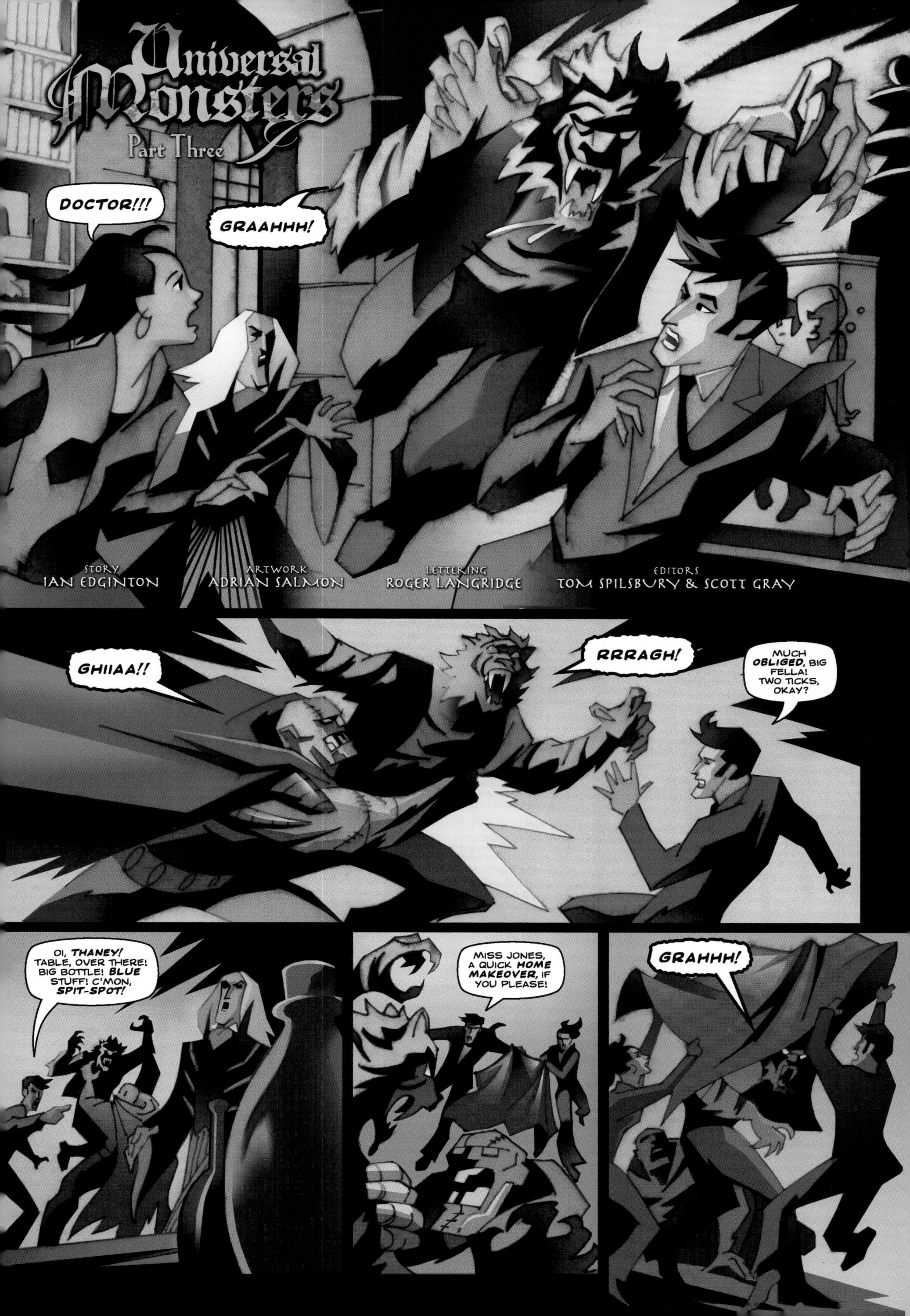
Universal Monsters
Part Three
DOCTOR!!!
GRAAHHH!
STORY IAN EDGINTON
ARTWORK ADRIAN SALMON
LETTERING ROGER LANGRIDGE
EDITORS TOM SPILSBURY & SCOTT GRAY
GHIIAA!!
RRRAGH!
MUCH OBLIGED, BIG FELLA! TWO TICKS, OKAY?
OI, THANEY! TABLE, OVER THERE! BIG BOTTLE! BLUE STUFF! C'MON, SPIT-SPOT!
MISS JONES, A QUICK HOME MAKEOVER, IF YOU PLEASE!
GRAHHH!

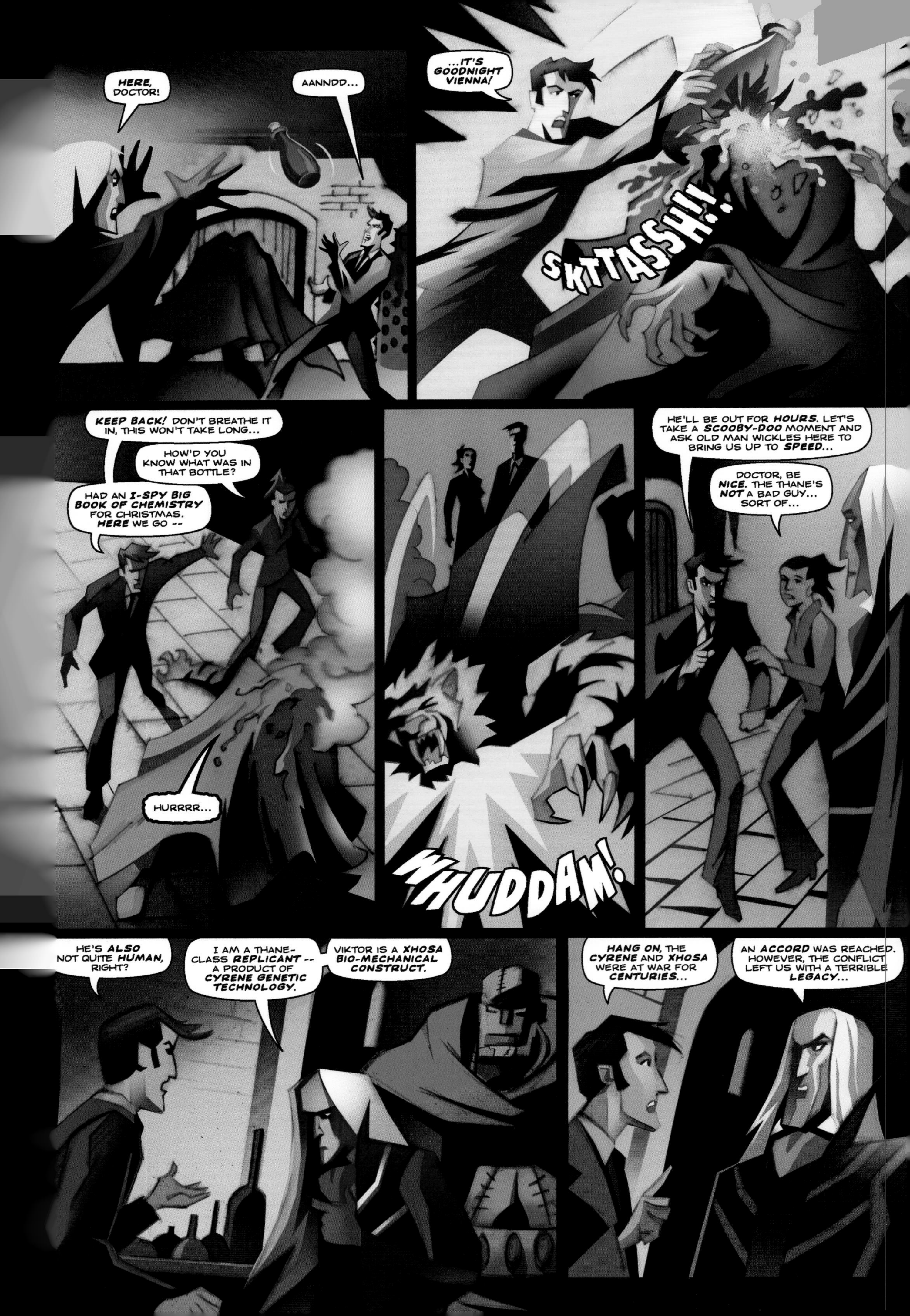

HERE, DOCTOR!
AANNDD...
...IT'S GOODNIGHT VIENNA!
SKTTASSH!!
KEEP BACK! DON'T BREATHE IT IN, THIS WON'T TAKE LONG...
HOW'D YOU KNOW WHAT WAS IN THAT BOTTLE?
HAD AN I-SPY BIG BOOK OF CHEMISTRY FOR CHRISTMAS. HERE WE GO --
HURRRR...
WHUDDAM!
HE'LL BE OUT FOR HOURS. LET'S TAKE A SCOOBY-DOO MOMENT AND ASK OLD MAN WICKLES HERE TO BRING US UP TO SPEED...
DOCTOR, BE NICE. THE THANE'S NOT A BAD GUY... SORT OF...
HE'S ALSO NOT QUITE HUMAN, RIGHT?
I AM A THANE-CLASS REPLICANT -- A PRODUCT OF CYRENE GENETIC TECHNOLOGY.
VIKTOR IS A XHOSA BIO-MECHANICAL CONSTRUCT.
HANG ON, THE CYRENE AND XHOSA WERE AT WAR FOR CENTURIES...
AN ACCORD WAS REACHED. HOWEVER, THE CONFLICT LEFT US WITH A TERRIBLE LEGACY...

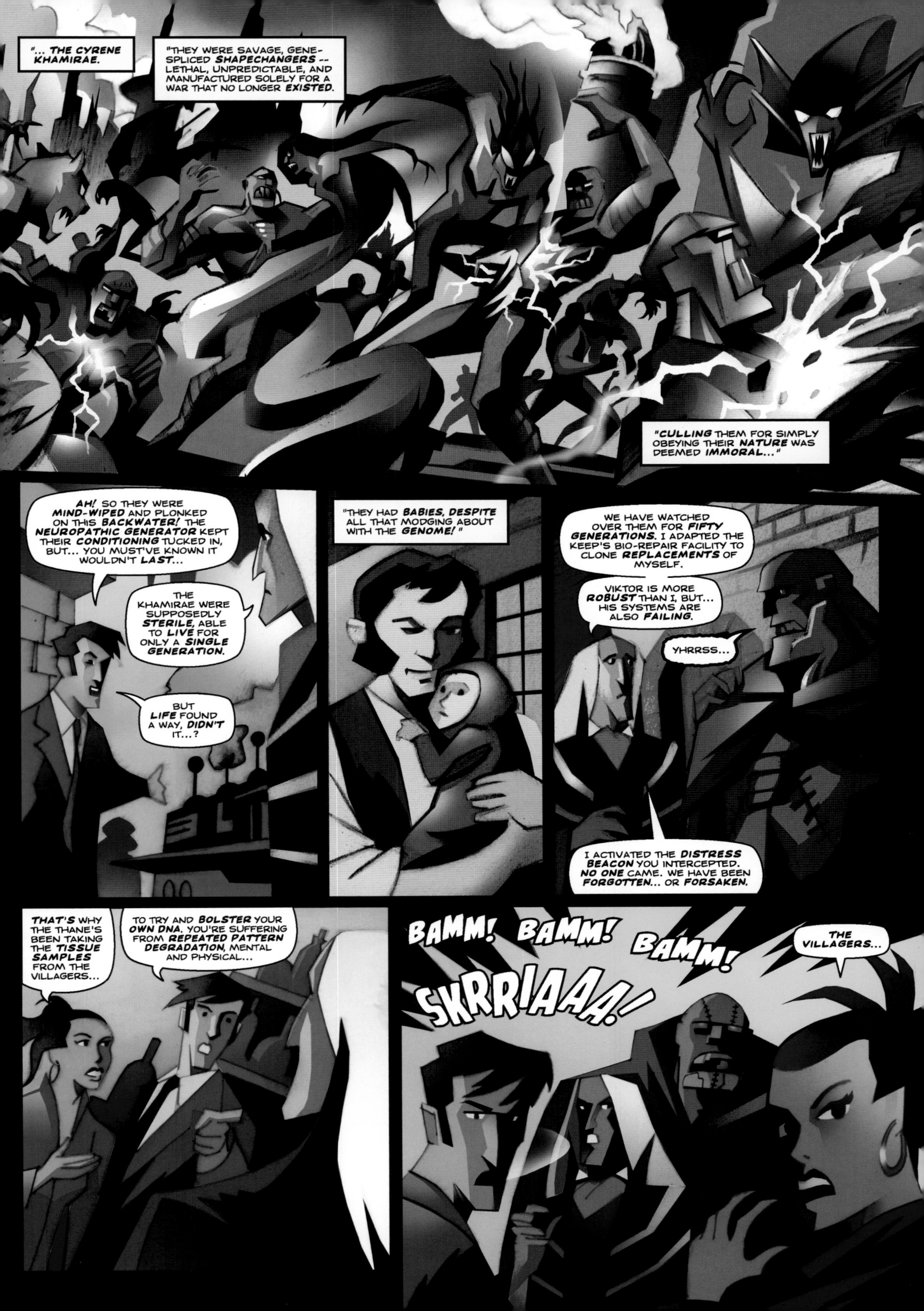
"... THE CYRENE KHAMIRAE.
"THEY WERE SAVAGE, GENE-SPLICED SHAPECHANGERS -- LETHAL, UNPREDICTABLE, AND MANUFACTURED SOLELY FOR A WAR THAT NO LONGER EXISTED.
"CULLING THEM FOR SIMPLY OBEYING THEIR NATURE WAS DEEMED IMMORAL..."
AH! SO THEY WERE MIND-WIPED AND PLONKED ON THIS BACKWATER! THE NEUROPATHIC GENERATOR KEPT THEIR CONDITIONING TUCKED IN, BUT... YOU MUST'VE KNOWN IT WOULDN'T LAST...
THE KHAMIRAE WERE SUPPOSEDLY STERILE, ABLE TO LIVE FOR ONLY A SINGLE GENERATION.
BUT LIFE FOUND A WAY, DIDN'T IT...?
"THEY HAD BABIES, DESPITE ALL THAT MODGING ABOUT WITH THE GENOME!"
WE HAVE WATCHED OVER THEM FOR FIFTY GENERATIONS. I ADAPTED THE KEEP'S BIO-REPAIR FACILITY TO CLONE REPLACEMENTS OF MYSELF.
VIKTOR IS MORE ROBUST THAN I, BUT... HIS SYSTEMS ARE ALSO FAILING.
YHRRSS...
I ACTIVATED THE DISTRESS BEACON YOU INTERCEPTED. NO ONE CAME. WE HAVE BEEN FORGOTTEN... OR FORSAKEN.
THAT'S WHY THE THANE'S BEEN TAKING THE TISSUE SAMPLES FROM THE VILLAGERS...
TO TRY AND BOLSTER YOUR OWN DNA. YOU'RE SUFFERING FROM REPEATED PATTERN DEGRADATION, MENTAL AND PHYSICAL...
BAMM! BAMM! BAMM!
SKRRIAAA!
THE VILLAGERS...

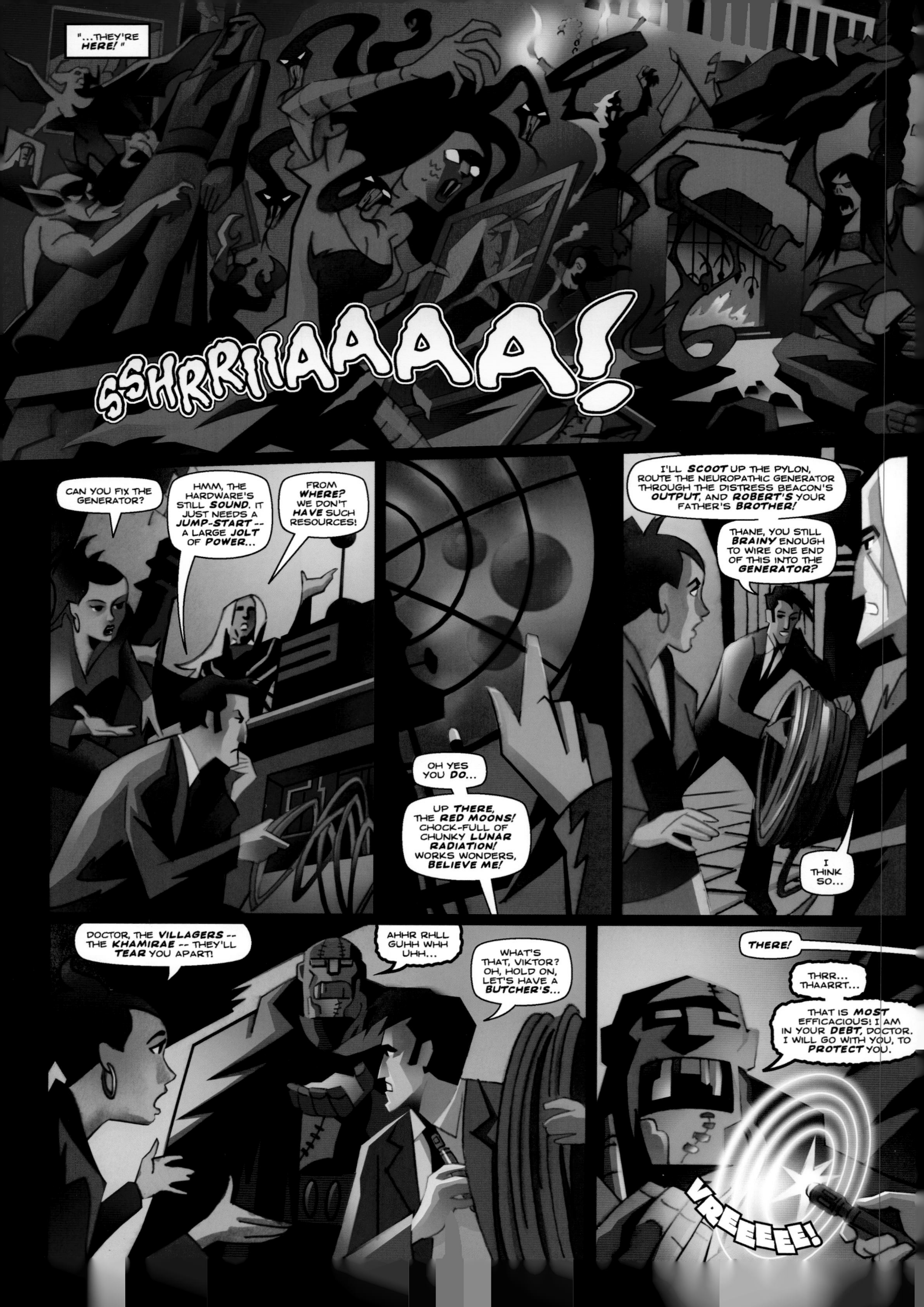
"...THEY'RE HERE!"
SSHRRIIIAAAAA!
CAN YOU FIX THE GENERATOR?
HMM, THE HARDWARE'S STILL SOUND. IT JUST NEEDS A JUMP-START -- A LARGE JOLT OF POWER...
FROM WHERE? WE DON'T HAVE SUCH RESOURCES!
OH YES YOU DO...
UP THERE, THE RED MOONS! CHOCK-FULL OF CHUNKY LUNAR RADIATION! WORKS WONDERS, BELIEVE ME!
I'LL SCOOT UP THE PYLON, ROUTE THE NEUROPATHIC GENERATOR THROUGH THE DISTRESS BEACON'S OUTPUT, AND ROBERT'S YOUR FATHER'S BROTHER!
THANE, YOU STILL BRAINY ENOUGH TO WIRE ONE END OF THIS INTO THE GENERATOR?
I THINK SO...
DOCTOR, THE VILLAGERS -- THE KHAMIRAE -- THEY'LL TEAR YOU APART!
AHHR RHLL GUHH WHH UHH...
WHAT'S THAT, VIKTOR? OH, HOLD ON, LET'S HAVE A BUTCHER'S...
THERE!
THRR... THAARRT...
THAT IS MOST EFFICACIOUS! I AM IN YOUR DEBT, DOCTOR. I WILL GO WITH YOU, TO PROTECT YOU.
VREEEEEE!

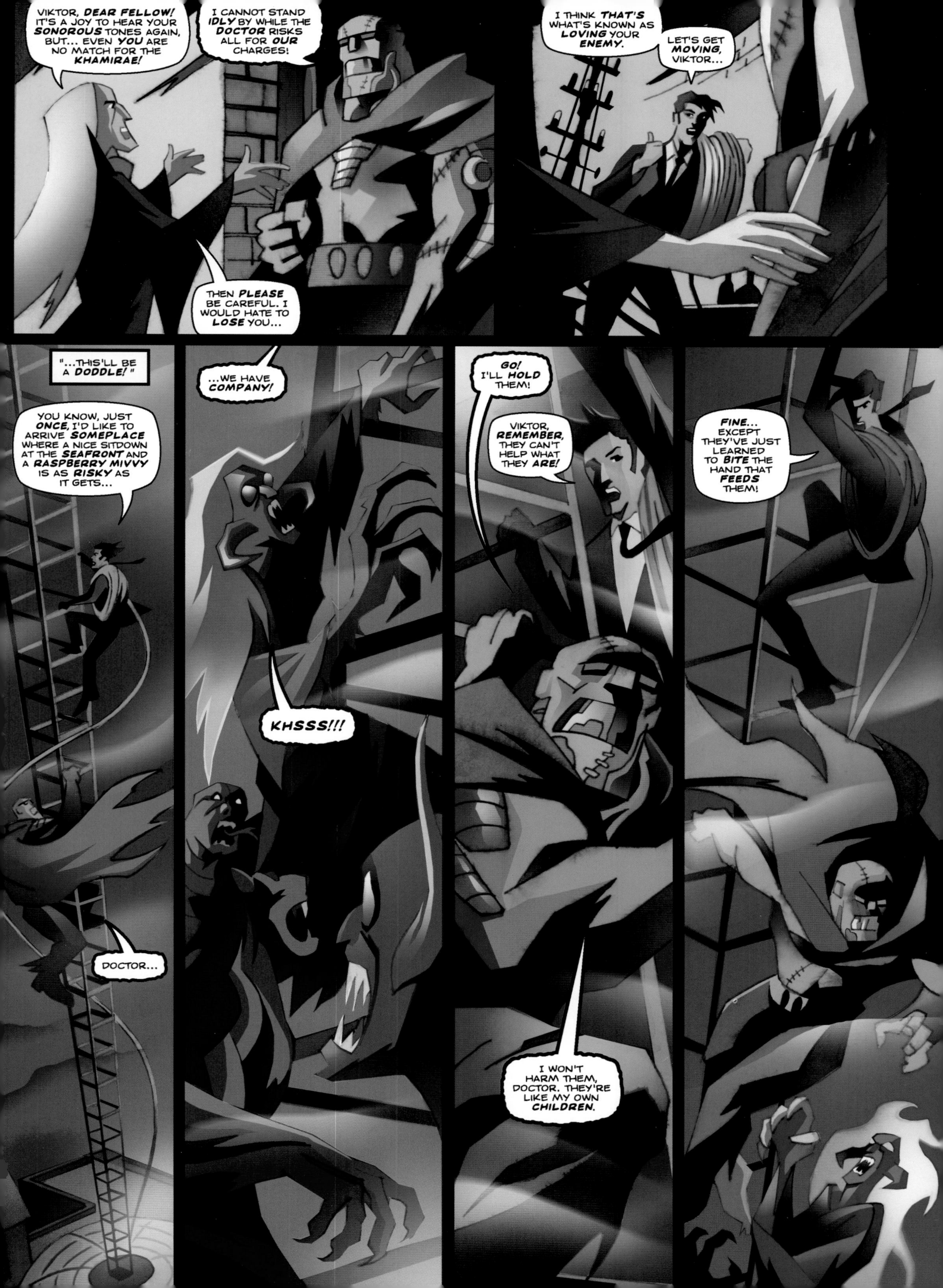

VIKTOR, DEAR FELLOW! IT'S A JOY TO HEAR YOUR SONOROUS TONES AGAIN, BUT... EVEN YOU ARE NO MATCH FOR THE KHAMIRAE!
I CANNOT STAND IDLY BY WHILE THE DOCTOR RISKS ALL FOR OUR CHARGES!
THEN PLEASE BE CAREFUL. I WOULD HATE TO LOSE YOU...
I THINK THAT'S WHAT'S KNOWN AS LOVING YOUR ENEMY.
LET'S GET MOVING, VIKTOR...
"...THIS'LL BE A DODDLE!"
YOU KNOW, JUST ONCE, I'D LIKE TO ARRIVE SOMEPLACE WHERE A NICE SITDOWN AT THE SEAFRONT AND A RASPBERRY MIVVY IS AS RISKY AS IT GETS...
DOCTOR...
...WE HAVE COMPANY!
KHSSS!!!
GO! I'LL HOLD THEM!
VIKTOR, REMEMBER, THEY CAN'T HELP WHAT THEY ARE!
I WON'T HARM THEM, DOCTOR. THEY'RE LIKE MY OWN CHILDREN.
FINE... EXCEPT THEY'VE JUST LEARNED TO BITE THE HAND THAT FEEDS THEM!

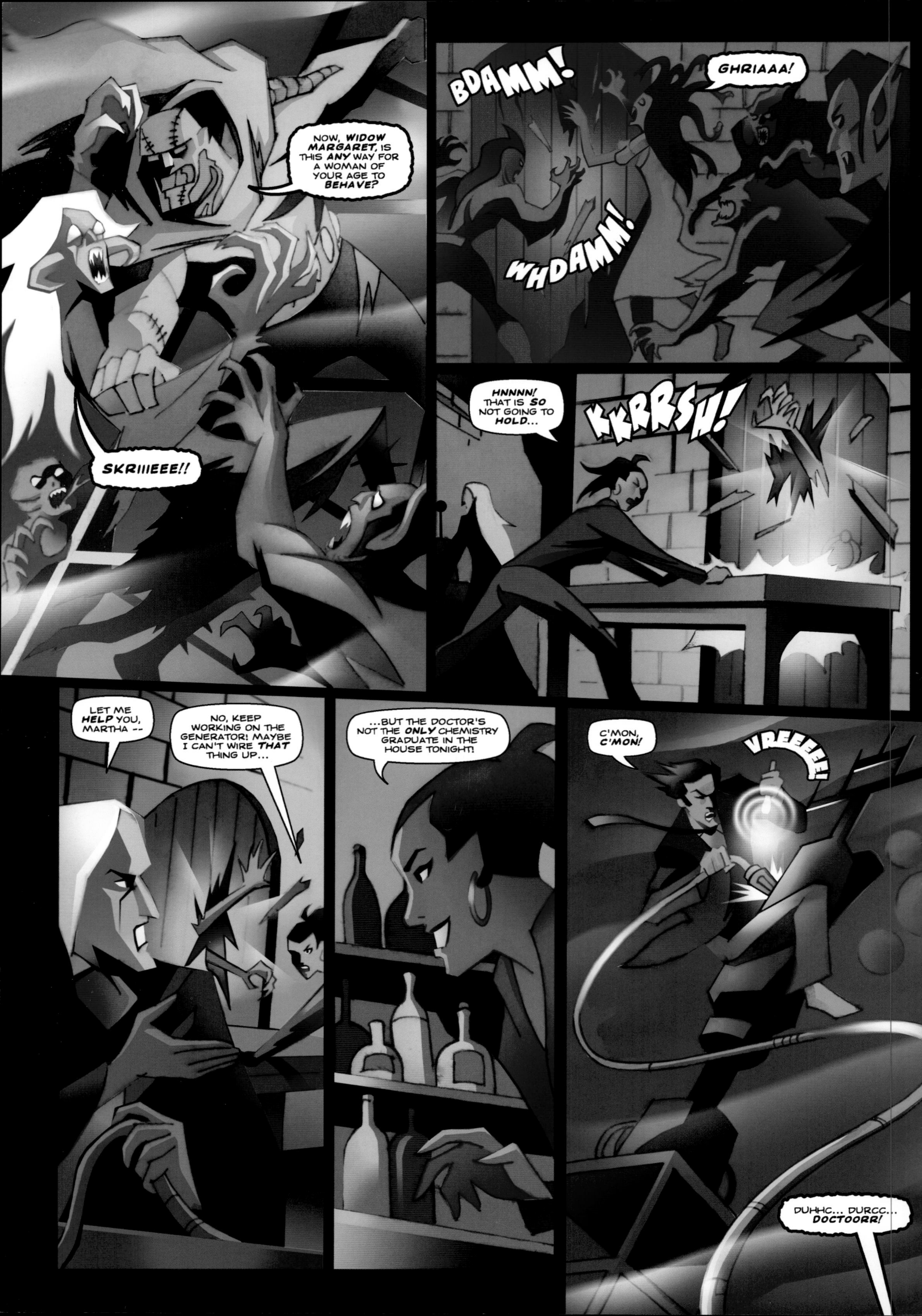
NOW, **WIDOW MARGARET,** IS THIS **ANY** WAY FOR A WOMAN OF YOUR AGE TO **BEHAVE?**
SKRIIIEEE!!
BDAMM!
GHRIAAA!
WHDAMM!
HNNNN! THAT IS **SO** NOT GOING TO **HOLD...**
KKRRSH!
LET ME **HELP** YOU, MARTHA --
NO, KEEP WORKING ON THE GENERATOR! MAYBE I CAN'T WIRE **THAT** THING UP...
...BUT THE DOCTOR'S NOT THE **ONLY** CHEMISTRY GRADUATE IN THE HOUSE TONIGHT!
C'MON, **C'MON!**
VREEEEE!
DUHHC... DURCC... **DOCTOORR!**

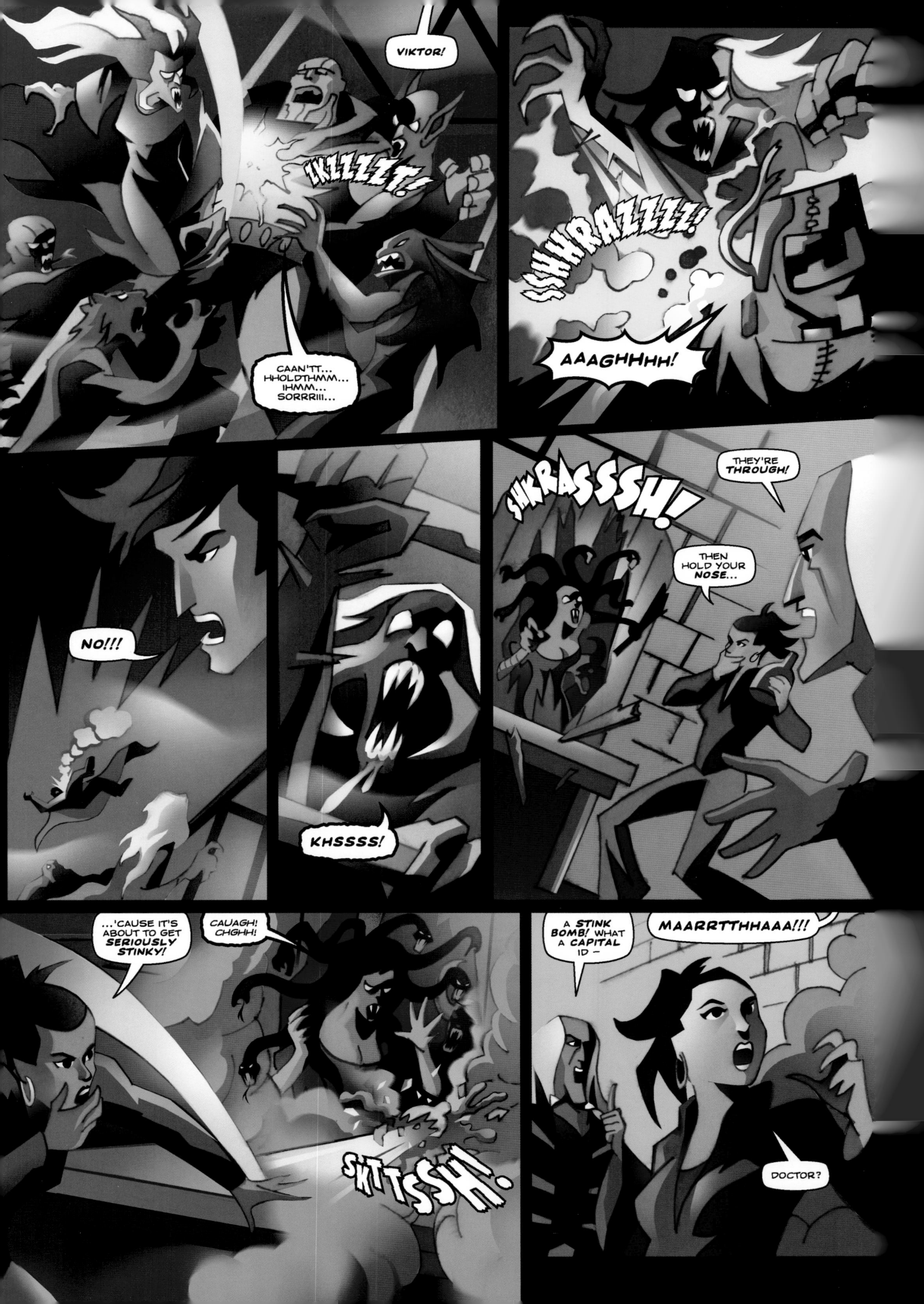
VIKTOR!
ZKZZZZT!
CAAN'TT... HHOLDTHMM... IHMM... SORRRIII...
SSHHRAZZZZZ!
AAAGHHHH!
NO!!!
KHSSSS!
SHKRASSSH!
THEY'RE THROUGH!
THEN HOLD YOUR NOSE...
...'CAUSE IT'S ABOUT TO GET SERIOUSLY STINKY!
CAUAGH! CHGHH!
SKTTSSH!
A STINK BOMB! WHAT A CAPITAL ID –
MAARRTTHHAAA!!!
DOCTOR?

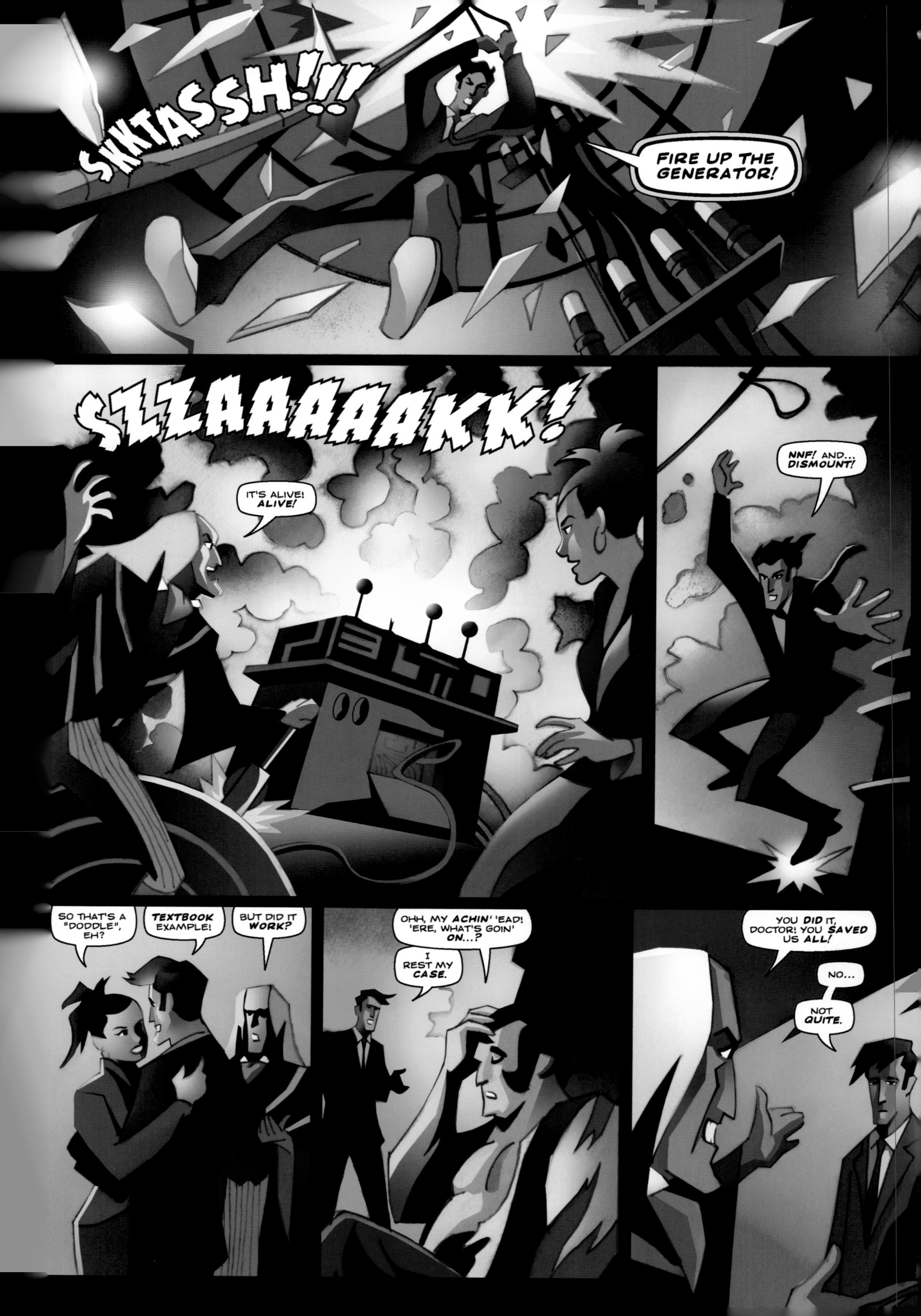
SKKTASSH!!!
FIRE UP THE GENERATOR!
SZZAAAAAAKK!
IT'S ALIVE! ALIVE!
NNF! AND... DISMOUNT!
SO THAT'S A "DODDLE", EH?
TEXTBOOK EXAMPLE!
BUT DID IT WORK?
OHH, MY ACHIN' 'EAD! 'ERE, WHAT'S GOIN' ON...?
I REST MY CASE.
YOU DID IT, DOCTOR! YOU SAVED US ALL!
NO...
NOT QUITE.

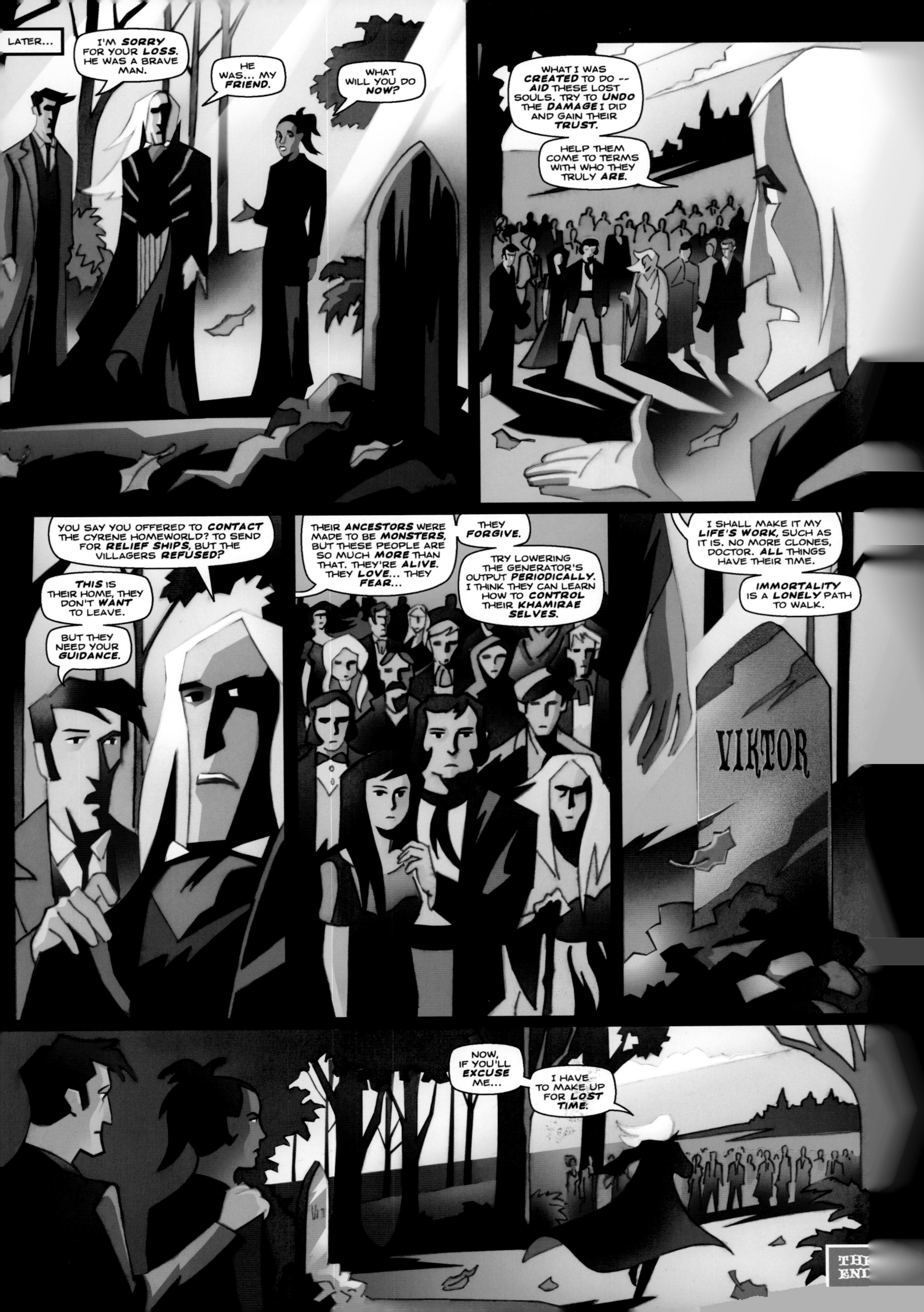
LATER...
I'M SORRY FOR YOUR LOSS. HE WAS A BRAVE MAN.
HE WAS... MY FRIEND.
WHAT WILL YOU DO NOW?
WHAT I WAS CREATED TO DO -- AID THESE LOST SOULS. TRY TO UNDO THE DAMAGE I DID AND GAIN THEIR TRUST.
HELP THEM COME TO TERMS WITH WHO THEY TRULY ARE.
YOU SAY YOU OFFERED TO CONTACT THE CYRENE HOMEWORLD? TO SEND FOR RELIEF SHIPS, BUT THE VILLAGERS REFUSED?
THIS IS THEIR HOME, THEY DON'T WANT TO LEAVE.
BUT THEY NEED YOUR GUIDANCE.
THEIR ANCESTORS WERE MADE TO BE MONSTERS, BUT THESE PEOPLE ARE SO MUCH MORE THAN THAT. THEY'RE ALIVE. THEY LOVE... THEY FEAR...
THEY FORGIVE.
TRY LOWERING THE GENERATOR'S OUTPUT PERIODICALLY. I THINK THEY CAN LEARN HOW TO CONTROL THEIR KHAMIRAE SELVES.
I SHALL MAKE IT MY LIFE'S WORK, SUCH AS IT IS. NO MORE CLONES, DOCTOR. ALL THINGS HAVE THEIR TIME.
IMMORTALITY IS A LONELY PATH TO WALK.
VIKTOR
NOW, IF YOU'LL EXCUSE ME...
I HAVE TO MAKE UP FOR LOST TIME.

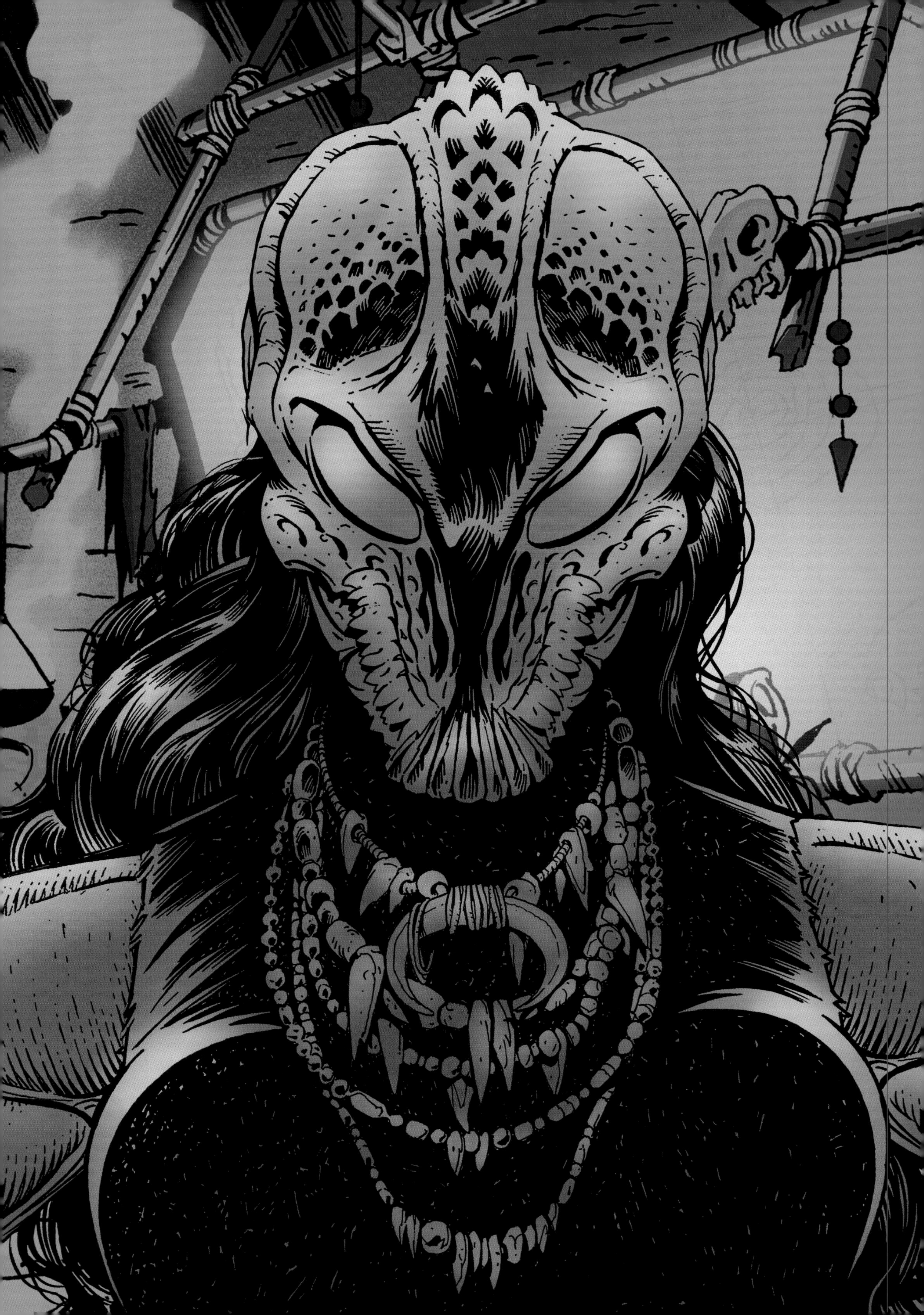

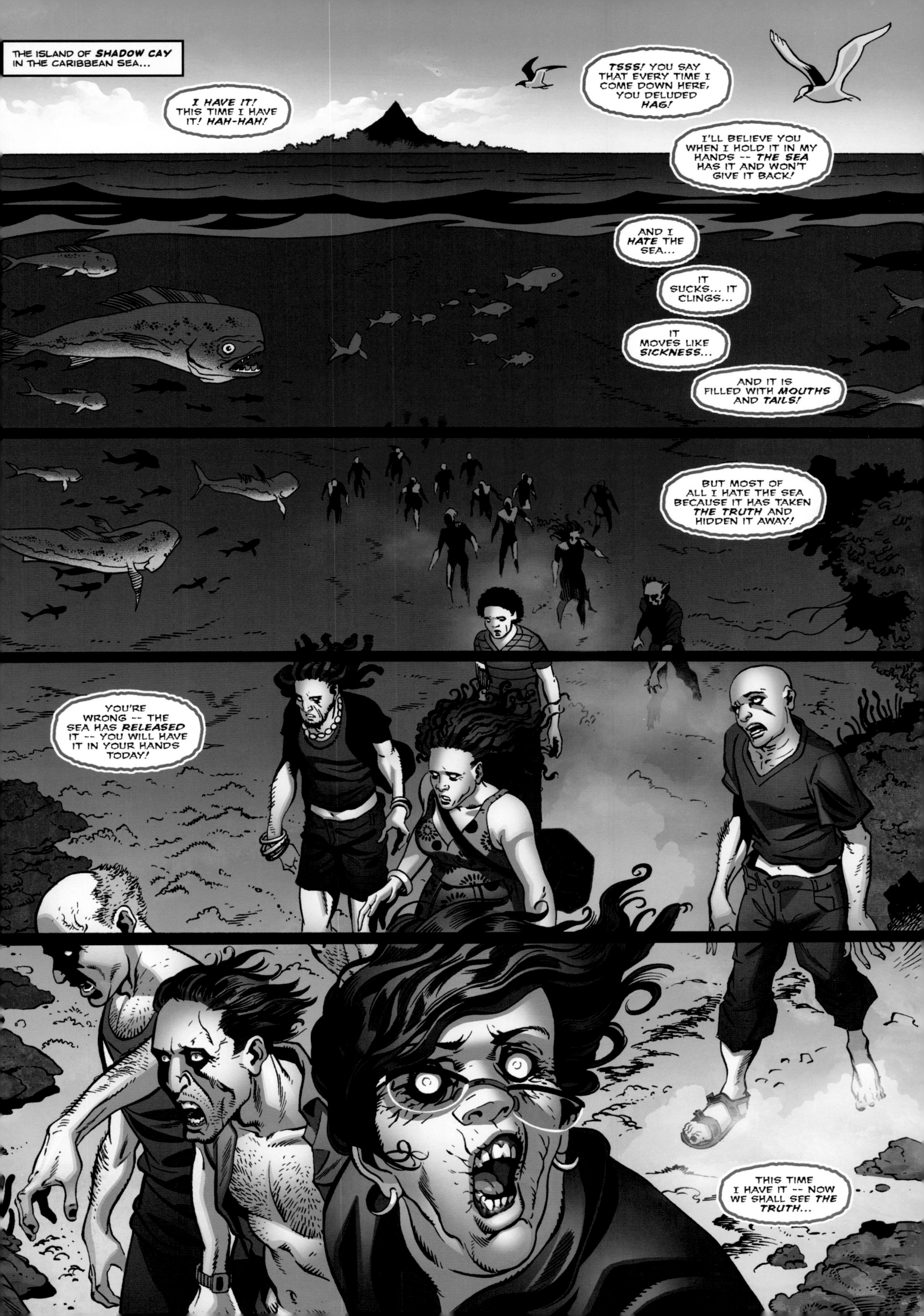
THE ISLAND OF SHADOW CAY IN THE CARIBBEAN SEA...
I HAVE IT! THIS TIME I HAVE IT! HAH-HAH!
TSSS! YOU SAY THAT EVERY TIME I COME DOWN HERE, YOU DELUDED HAG!
I'LL BELIEVE YOU WHEN I HOLD IT IN MY HANDS -- THE SEA HAS IT AND WON'T GIVE IT BACK!
AND I HATE THE SEA...
IT SUCKS... IT CLINGS...
IT MOVES LIKE SICKNESS...
AND IT IS FILLED WITH MOUTHS AND TAILS!
BUT MOST OF ALL I HATE THE SEA BECAUSE IT HAS TAKEN THE TRUTH AND HIDDEN IT AWAY!
YOU'RE WRONG -- THE SEA HAS RELEASED IT -- YOU WILL HAVE IT IN YOUR HANDS TODAY!
THIS TIME I HAVE IT -- NOW WE SHALL SEE THE TRUTH...

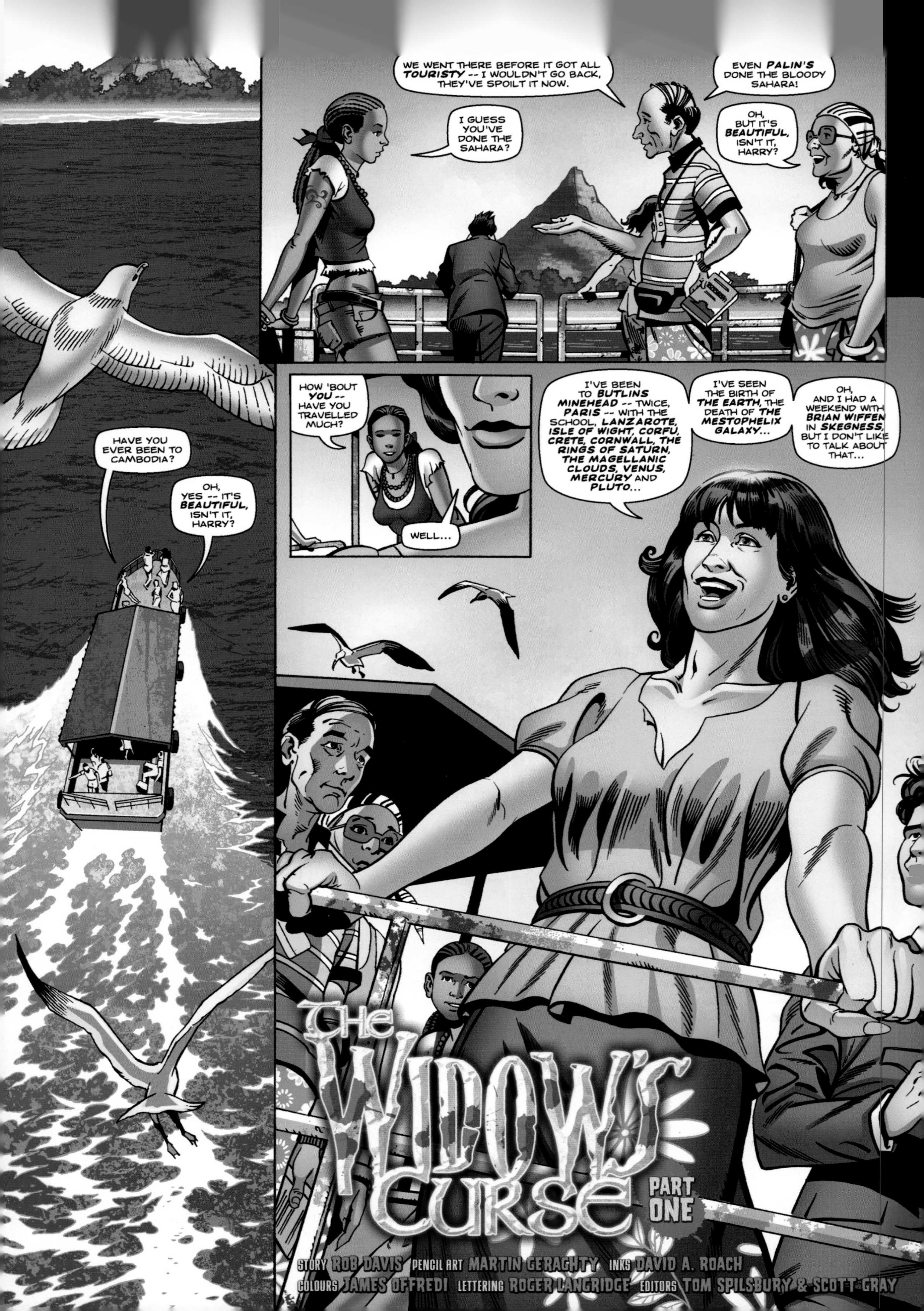
I GUESS YOU'VE DONE THE SAHARA?
WE WENT THERE BEFORE IT GOT ALL TOURISTY -- I WOULDN'T GO BACK, THEY'VE SPOILT IT NOW.
EVEN PALIN'S DONE THE BLOODY SAHARA!
OH, BUT IT'S BEAUTIFUL, ISN'T IT, HARRY?
HAVE YOU EVER BEEN TO CAMBODIA?
OH, YES -- IT'S BEAUTIFUL, ISN'T IT, HARRY?
HOW 'BOUT YOU -- HAVE YOU TRAVELLED MUCH?
WELL...
I'VE BEEN TO BUTLINS MINEHEAD -- TWICE, PARIS -- WITH THE SCHOOL, LANZAROTE, ISLE OF WIGHT, CORFU, CRETE, CORNWALL, THE RINGS OF SATURN, THE MAGELLANIC CLOUDS, VENUS, MERCURY AND PLUTO...
I'VE SEEN THE BIRTH OF THE EARTH, THE DEATH OF THE MESTOPHELIX GALAXY...
OH, AND I HAD A WEEKEND WITH BRIAN WIFFEN IN SKEGNESS, BUT I DON'T LIKE TO TALK ABOUT THAT...
THE WIDOW'S CURSE PART ONE
STORY ROB DAVIS PENCIL ART MARTIN GERAGHTY INKS DAVID A. ROACH
COLOURS JAMES OFFREDI LETTERING ROGER LANGRIDGE EDITORS TOM SPILSBURY & SCOTT GRAY

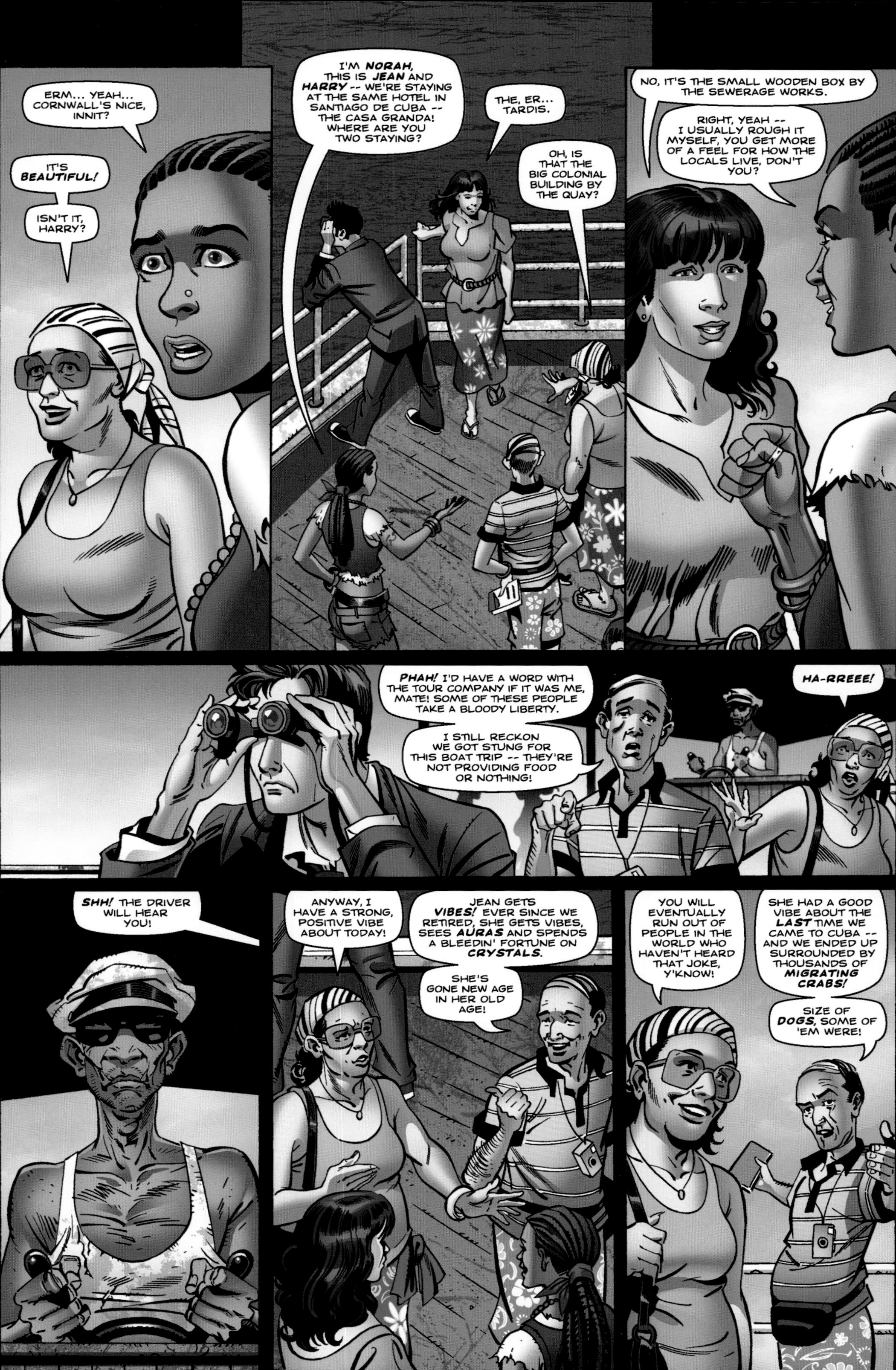
ERM... YEAH... CORNWALL'S NICE, INNIT?
IT'S BEAUTIFUL!
ISN'T IT, HARRY?
I'M NORAH, THIS IS JEAN AND HARRY -- WE'RE STAYING AT THE SAME HOTEL IN SANTIAGO DE CUBA -- THE CASA GRANDA! WHERE ARE YOU TWO STAYING?
THE, ER... TARDIS.
OH, IS THAT THE BIG COLONIAL BUILDING BY THE QUAY?
NO, IT'S THE SMALL WOODEN BOX BY THE SEWERAGE WORKS.
RIGHT, YEAH -- I USUALLY ROUGH IT MYSELF, YOU GET MORE OF A FEEL FOR HOW THE LOCALS LIVE, DON'T YOU?
PHAH! I'D HAVE A WORD WITH THE TOUR COMPANY IF IT WAS ME, MATE! SOME OF THESE PEOPLE TAKE A BLOODY LIBERTY.
I STILL RECKON WE GOT STUNG FOR THIS BOAT TRIP -- THEY'RE NOT PROVIDING FOOD OR NOTHING!
HA-RREEE!
SHH! THE DRIVER WILL HEAR YOU!
ANYWAY, I HAVE A STRONG, POSITIVE VIBE ABOUT TODAY!
JEAN GETS VIBES! EVER SINCE WE RETIRED, SHE GETS VIBES, SEES AURAS AND SPENDS A BLEEDIN' FORTUNE ON CRYSTALS.
SHE'S GONE NEW AGE IN HER OLD AGE!
YOU WILL EVENTUALLY RUN OUT OF PEOPLE IN THE WORLD WHO HAVEN'T HEARD THAT JOKE, Y'KNOW!
SHE HAD A GOOD VIBE ABOUT THE LAST TIME WE CAME TO CUBA -- AND WE ENDED UP SURROUNDED BY THOUSANDS OF MIGRATING CRABS!
SIZE OF DOGS, SOME OF 'EM WERE!

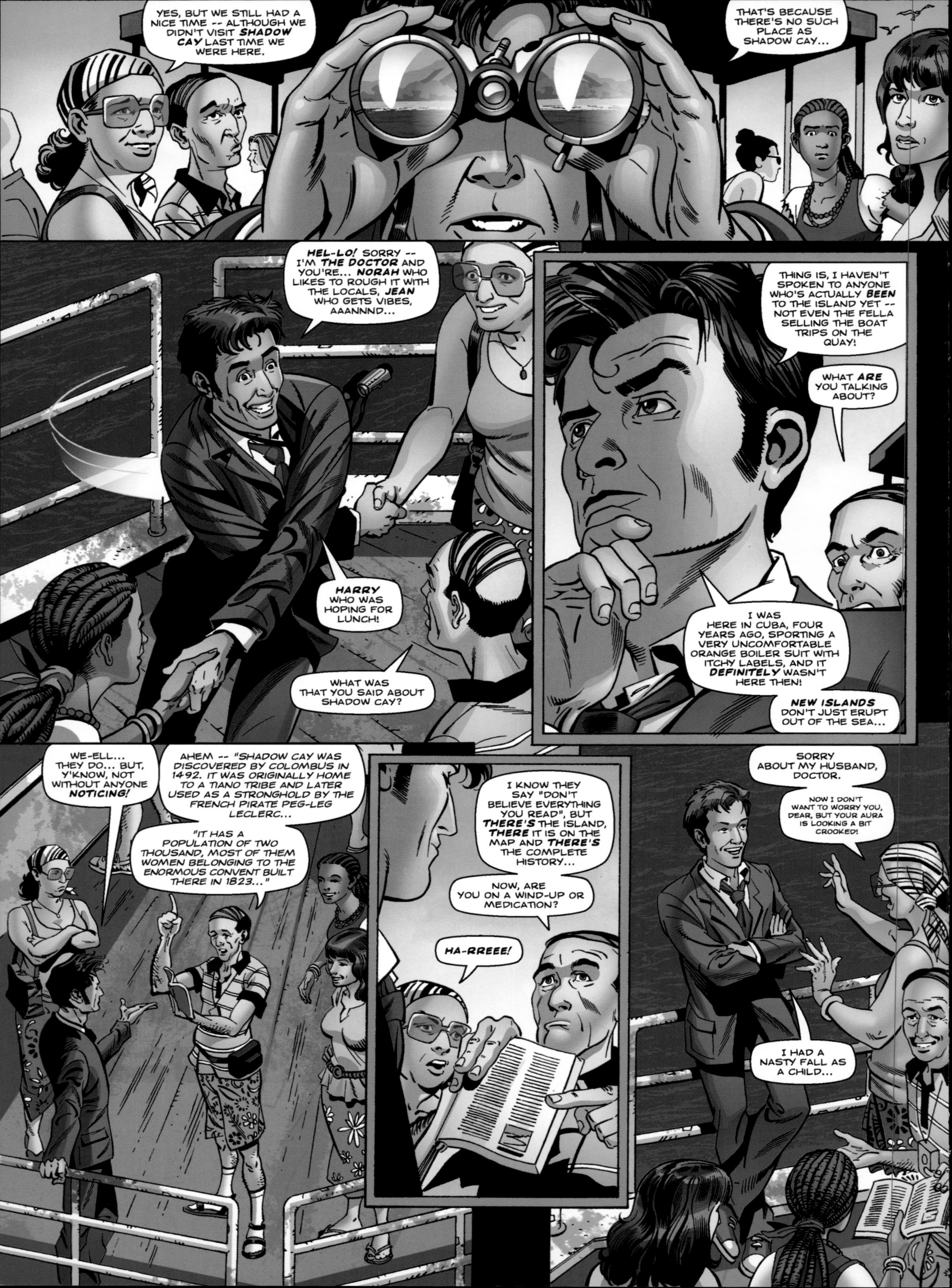

YES, BUT WE STILL HAD A NICE TIME -- ALTHOUGH WE DIDN'T VISIT SHADOW CAY LAST TIME WE WERE HERE.
THAT'S BECAUSE THERE'S NO SUCH PLACE AS SHADOW CAY...
HEL-LO! SORRY -- I'M THE DOCTOR AND YOU'RE... NORAH WHO LIKES TO ROUGH IT WITH THE LOCALS, JEAN WHO GETS VIBES, AAANNND...
HARRY WHO WAS HOPING FOR LUNCH!
WHAT WAS THAT YOU SAID ABOUT SHADOW CAY?
THING IS, I HAVEN'T SPOKEN TO ANYONE WHO'S ACTUALLY BEEN TO THE ISLAND YET -- NOT EVEN THE FELLA SELLING THE BOAT TRIPS ON THE QUAY!
WHAT ARE YOU TALKING ABOUT?
I WAS HERE IN CUBA, FOUR YEARS AGO, SPORTING A VERY UNCOMFORTABLE ORANGE BOILER SUIT WITH ITCHY LABELS, AND IT DEFINITELY WASN'T HERE THEN!
NEW ISLANDS DON'T JUST ERUPT OUT OF THE SEA...
WE-ELL... THEY DO... BUT, Y'KNOW, NOT WITHOUT ANYONE NOTICING!
AHEM -- "SHADOW CAY WAS DISCOVERED BY COLOMBUS IN 1492. IT WAS ORIGINALLY HOME TO A TIANO TRIBE AND LATER USED AS A STRONGHOLD BY THE FRENCH PIRATE PEG-LEG LECLERC...
"IT HAS A POPULATION OF TWO THOUSAND, MOST OF THEM WOMEN BELONGING TO THE ENORMOUS CONVENT BUILT THERE IN 1823..."
I KNOW THEY SAY "DON'T BELIEVE EVERYTHING YOU READ", BUT THERE'S THE ISLAND, THERE IT IS ON THE MAP AND THERE'S THE COMPLETE HISTORY...
NOW, ARE YOU ON A WIND-UP OR MEDICATION?
HA-RREEE!
SORRY ABOUT MY HUSBAND, DOCTOR.
NOW I DON'T WANT TO WORRY YOU, DEAR, BUT YOUR AURA IS LOOKING A BIT CROOKED!
I HAD A NASTY FALL AS A CHILD...

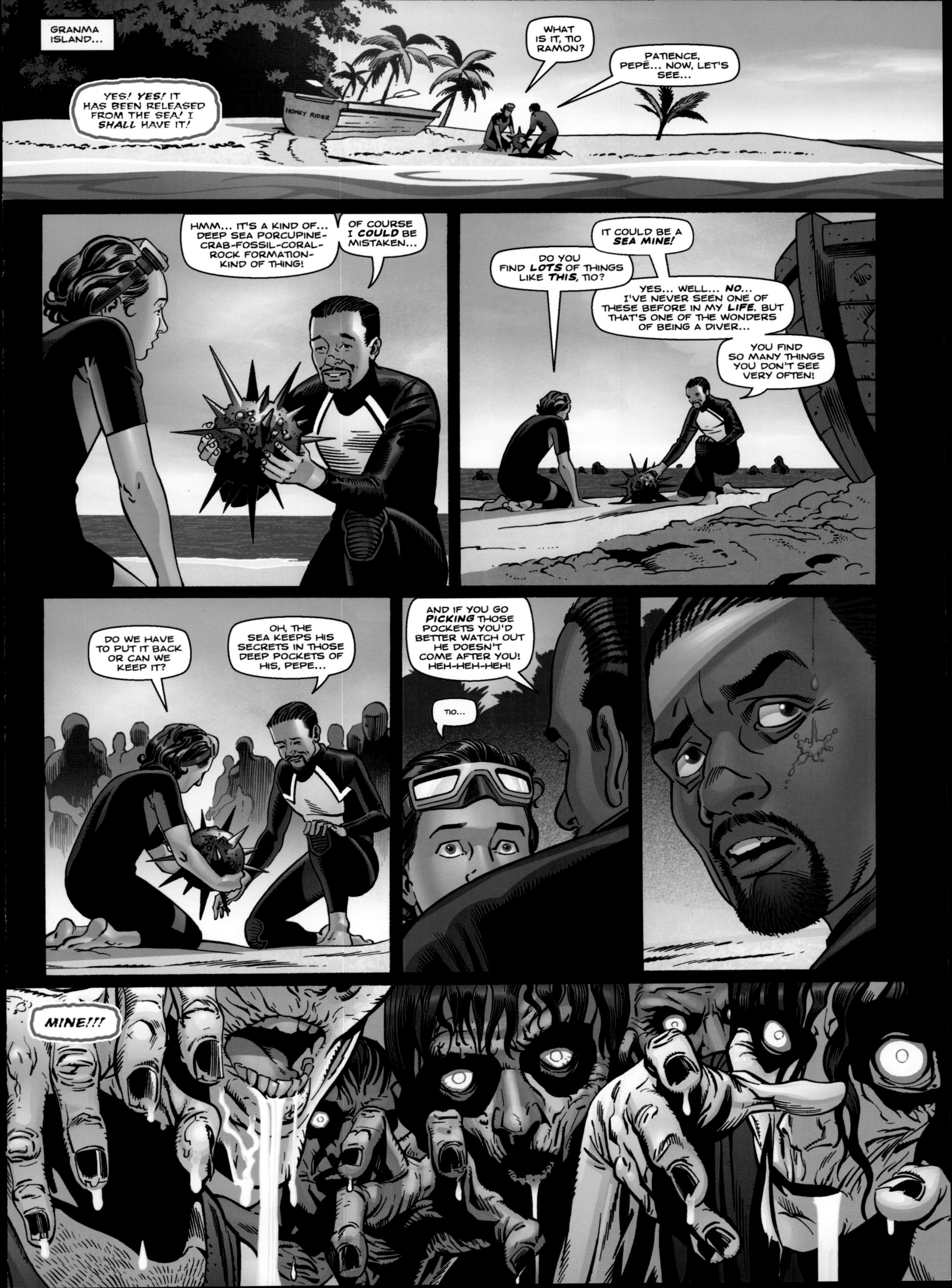
GRANMA ISLAND...
YES! YES! IT HAS BEEN RELEASED FROM THE SEA! I SHALL HAVE IT!
HONEY RIDER
WHAT IS IT, TIO RAMON?
PATIENCE, PEPÉ... NOW, LET'S SEE...
HMM... IT'S A KIND OF... DEEP SEA PORCUPINE-CRAB-FOSSIL-CORAL-ROCK FORMATION-KIND OF THING!
OF COURSE I COULD BE MISTAKEN...
IT COULD BE A SEA MINE!
DO YOU FIND LOTS OF THINGS LIKE THIS, TIO?
YES... WELL... NO... I'VE NEVER SEEN ONE OF THESE BEFORE IN MY LIFE. BUT THAT'S ONE OF THE WONDERS OF BEING A DIVER...
YOU FIND SO MANY THINGS YOU DON'T SEE VERY OFTEN!
DO WE HAVE TO PUT IT BACK OR CAN WE KEEP IT?
OH, THE SEA KEEPS HIS SECRETS IN THOSE DEEP POCKETS OF HIS, PEPE...
AND IF YOU GO PICKING THOSE POCKETS YOU'D BETTER WATCH OUT HE DOESN'T COME AFTER YOU! HEH-HEH-HEH!
TIO...
MINE!!!

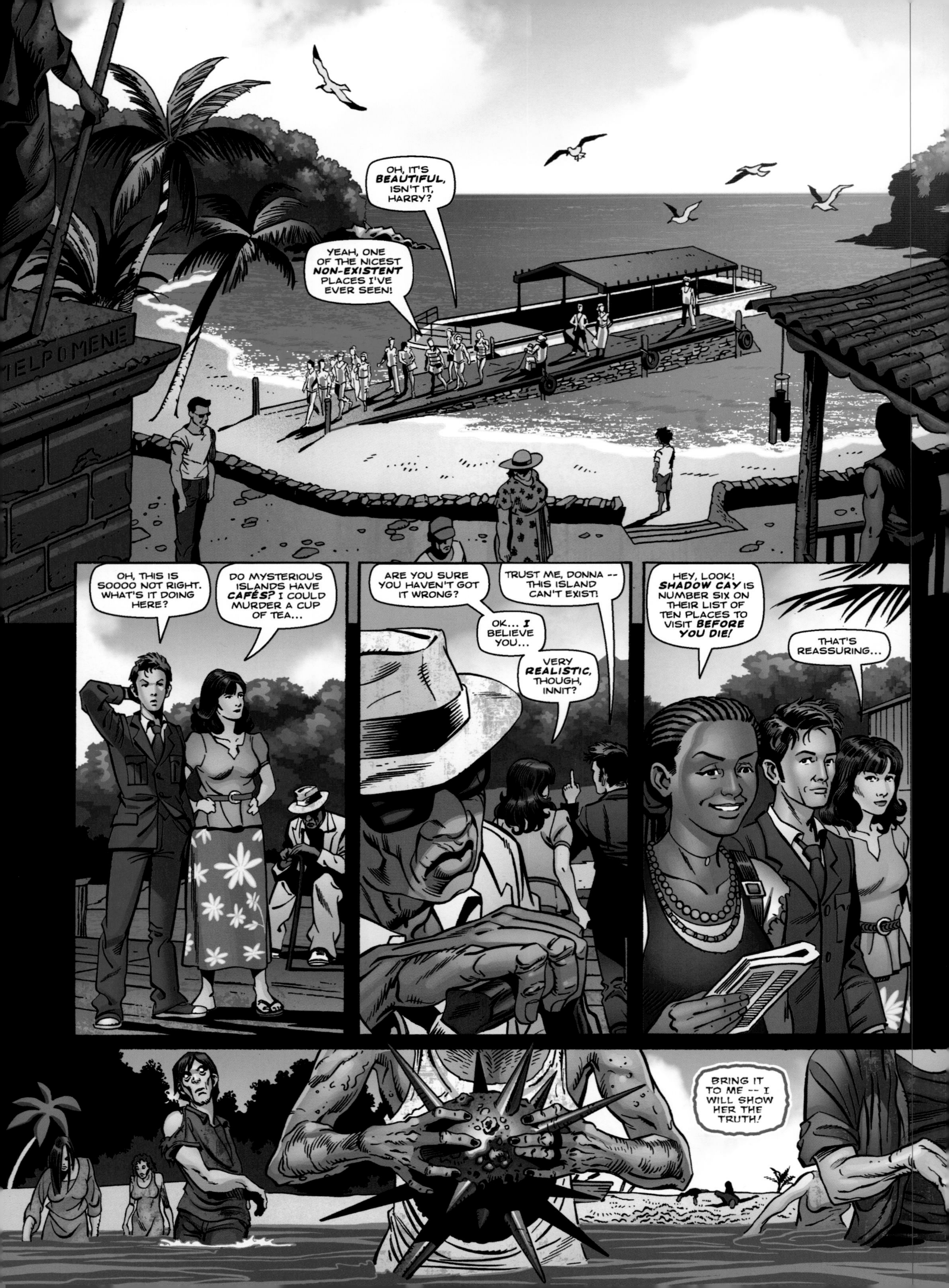
MELPOMENE
OH, IT'S BEAUTIFUL, ISN'T IT, HARRY?
YEAH, ONE OF THE NICEST NON-EXISTENT PLACES I'VE EVER SEEN!
OH, THIS IS SOOOO NOT RIGHT. WHAT'S IT DOING HERE?
DO MYSTERIOUS ISLANDS HAVE CAFÉS? I COULD MURDER A CUP OF TEA...
ARE YOU SURE YOU HAVEN'T GOT IT WRONG?
TRUST ME, DONNA -- THIS ISLAND CAN'T EXIST!
OK... I BELIEVE YOU...
VERY REALISTIC, THOUGH, INNIT?
HEY, LOOK! SHADOW CAY IS NUMBER SIX ON THEIR LIST OF TEN PLACES TO VISIT BEFORE YOU DIE!
THAT'S REASSURING...
BRING IT TO ME -- I WILL SHOW HER THE TRUTH!

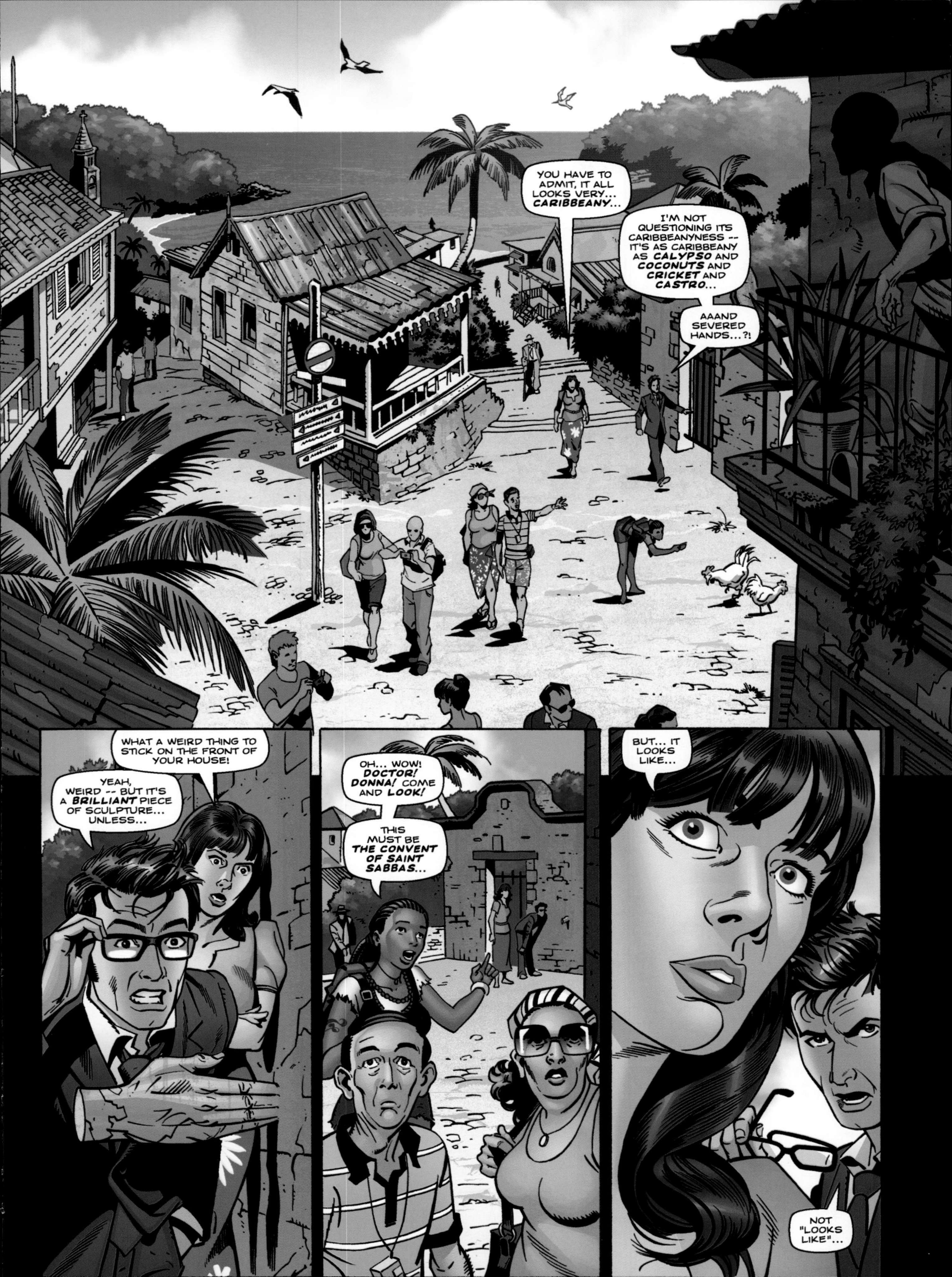
YOU HAVE TO ADMIT, IT ALL LOOKS VERY... CARIBBEANY...
I'M NOT QUESTIONING ITS CARIBBEANYNESS -- IT'S AS CARIBBEANY AS CALYPSO AND COCONUTS AND CRICKET AND CASTRO...
AAAND SEVERED HANDS...?!
WHAT A WEIRD THING TO STICK ON THE FRONT OF YOUR HOUSE!
YEAH, WEIRD -- BUT IT'S A BRILLIANT PIECE OF SCULPTURE... UNLESS...
OH... WOW! DOCTOR! DONNA! COME AND LOOK!
THIS MUST BE THE CONVENT OF SAINT SABBAS...
BUT... IT LOOKS LIKE...
NOT "LOOKS LIKE"...

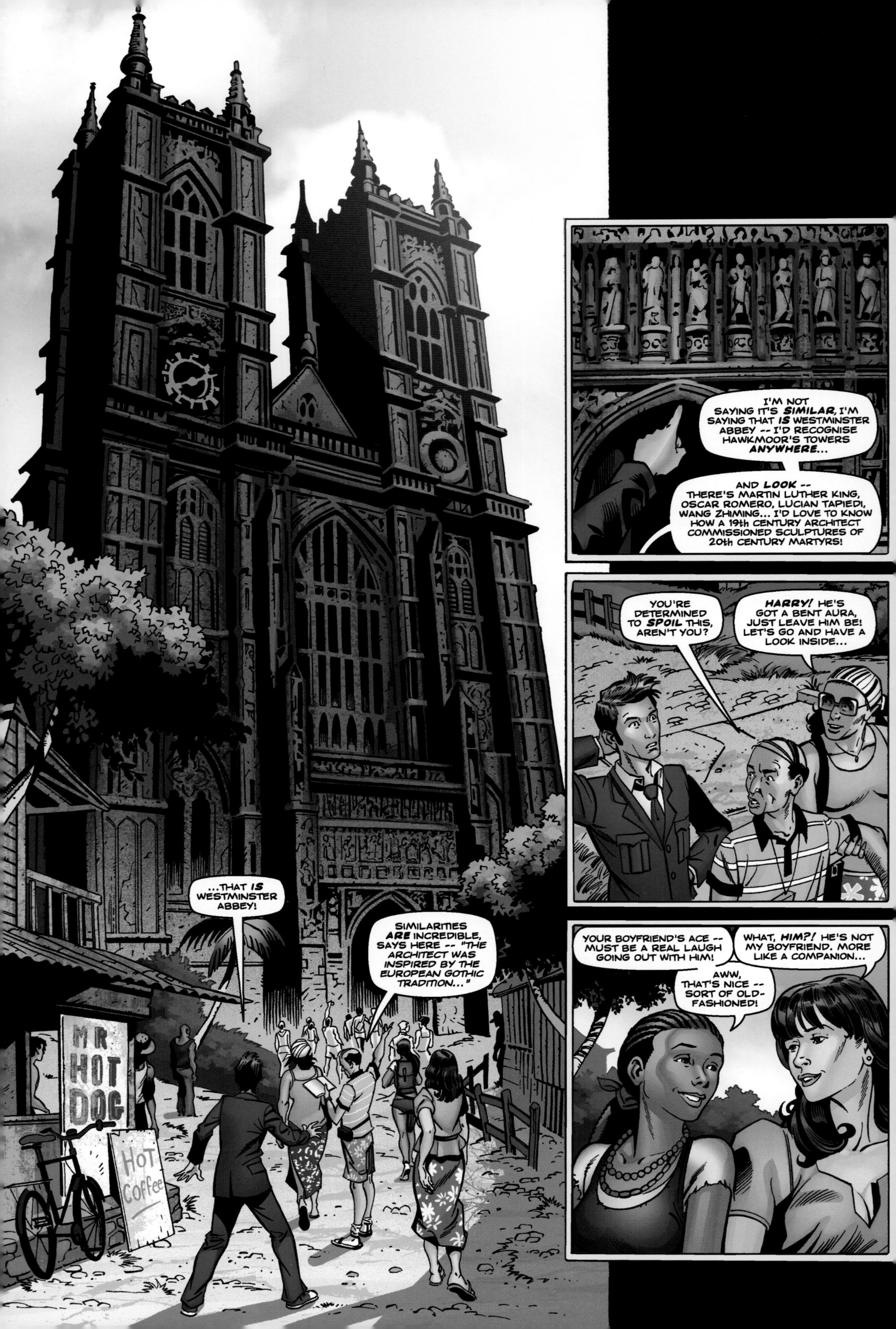
...THAT IS WESTMINSTER ABBEY!
SIMILARITIES ARE INCREDIBLE, SAYS HERE -- "THE ARCHITECT WAS INSPIRED BY THE EUROPEAN GOTHIC TRADITION..."
MR HOT DOG
HOT COFFEE
I'M NOT SAYING IT'S SIMILAR, I'M SAYING THAT IS WESTMINSTER ABBEY -- I'D RECOGNISE HAWKMOOR'S TOWERS ANYWHERE...
AND LOOK -- THERE'S MARTIN LUTHER KING, OSCAR ROMERO, LUCIAN TAPIEDI, WANG ZHIMING... I'D LOVE TO KNOW HOW A 19th CENTURY ARCHITECT COMMISSIONED SCULPTURES OF 20th CENTURY MARTYRS!
YOU'RE DETERMINED TO SPOIL THIS, AREN'T YOU?
HARRY! HE'S GOT A BENT AURA, JUST LEAVE HIM BE! LET'S GO AND HAVE A LOOK INSIDE...
YOUR BOYFRIEND'S ACE -- MUST BE A REAL LAUGH GOING OUT WITH HIM!
WHAT, HIM?! HE'S NOT MY BOYFRIEND. MORE LIKE A COMPANION...
AWW, THAT'S NICE -- SORT OF OLD-FASHIONED!

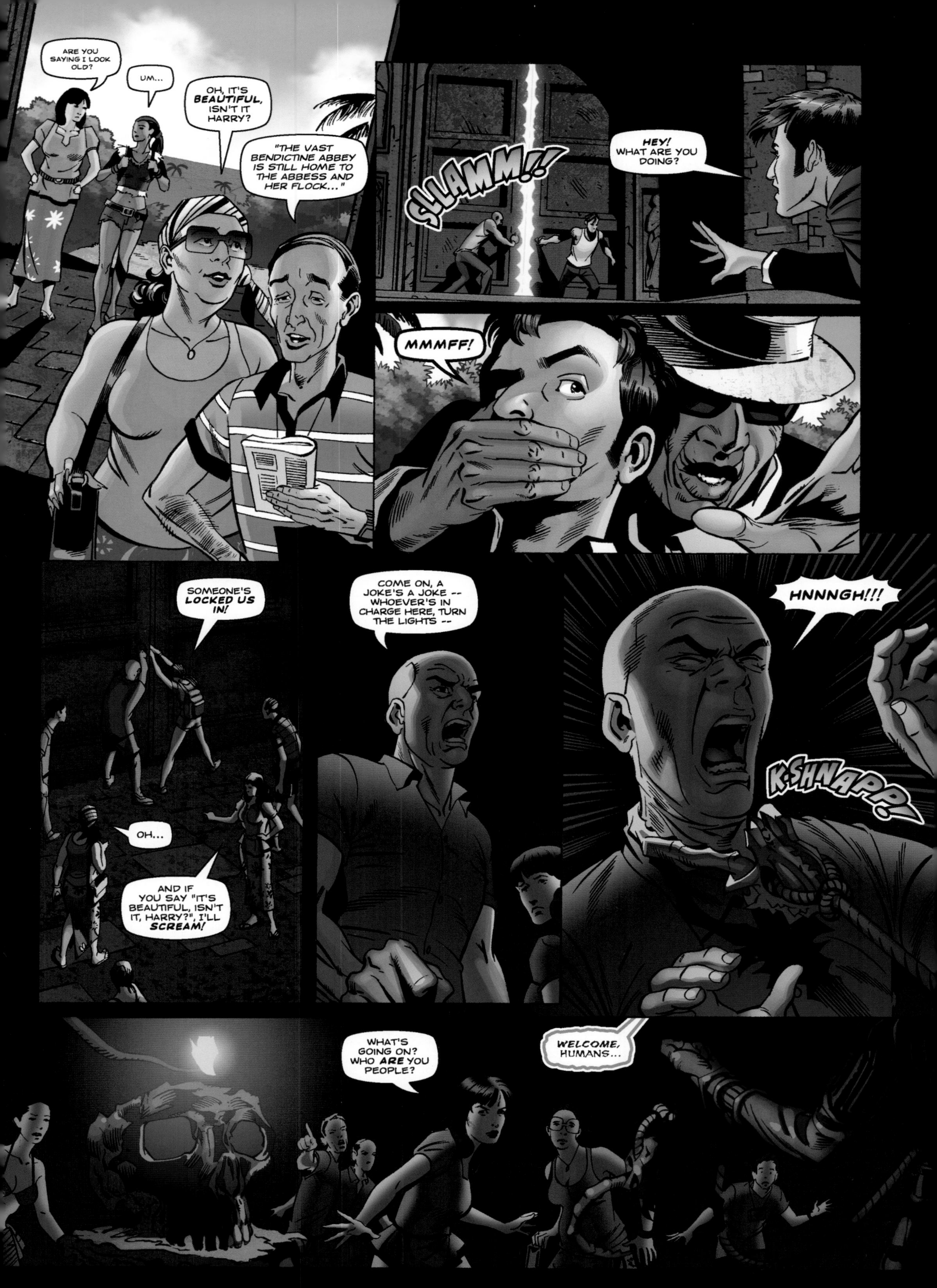
ARE YOU SAYING I LOOK OLD?
UM...
OH, IT'S **BEAUTIFUL**, ISN'T IT HARRY?
"THE VAST BENDICTINE ABBEY IS STILL HOME TO THE ABBESS AND HER FLOCK..."
SLLAMM!!
HEY! WHAT ARE YOU DOING?
MMMFF!
SOMEONE'S **LOCKED US** IN!
OH...
AND IF YOU SAY "IT'S BEAUTIFUL, ISN'T IT, HARRY?", I'LL **SCREAM!**
COME ON, A JOKE'S A JOKE -- WHOEVER'S IN CHARGE HERE, TURN THE LIGHTS --
HNNNGH!!!
K-SHNAPP!
WHAT'S GOING ON? WHO **ARE** YOU PEOPLE?
WELCOME, HUMANS...

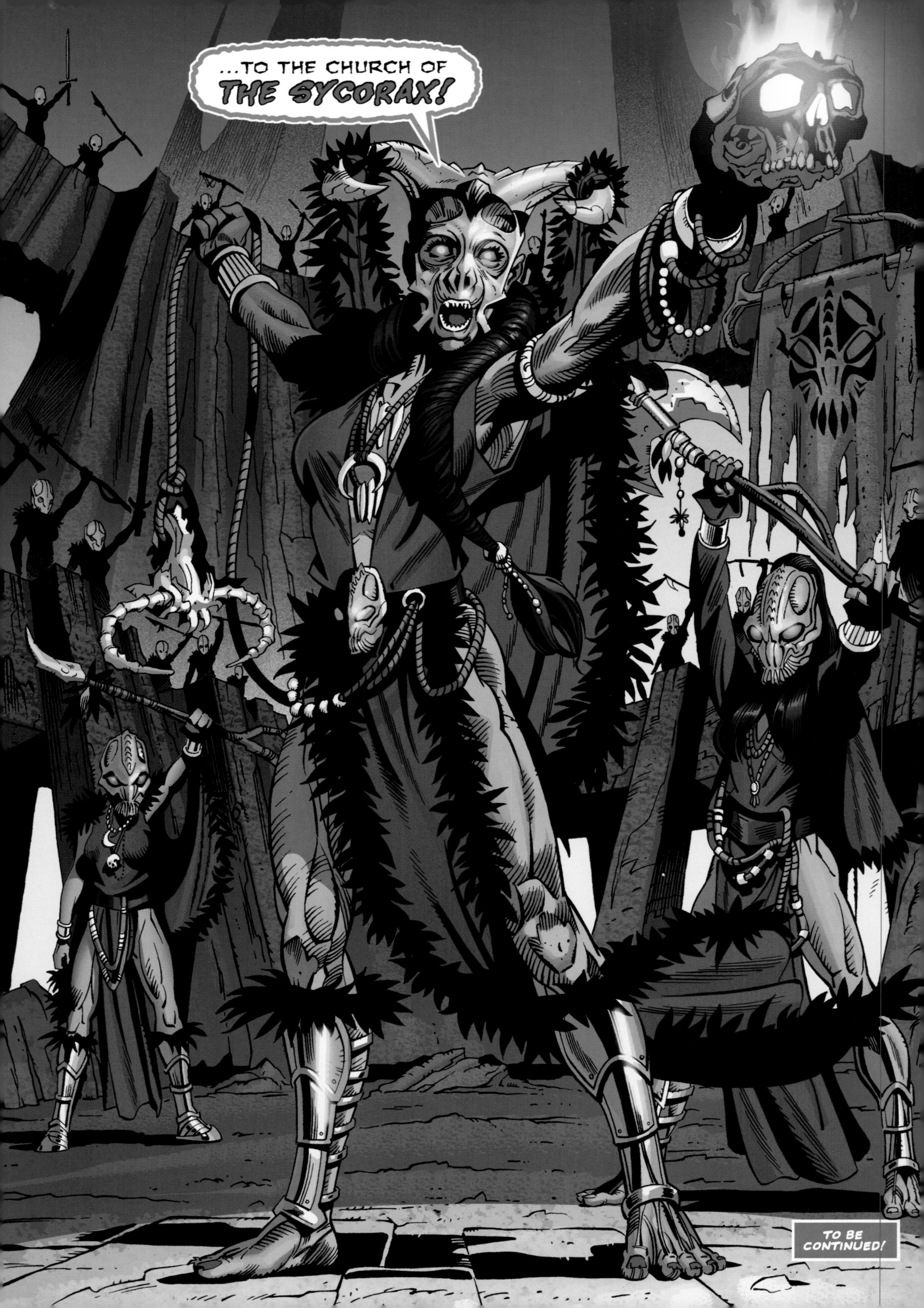
...TO THE CHURCH OF
THE SYCORAX!
TO BE CONTINUED!

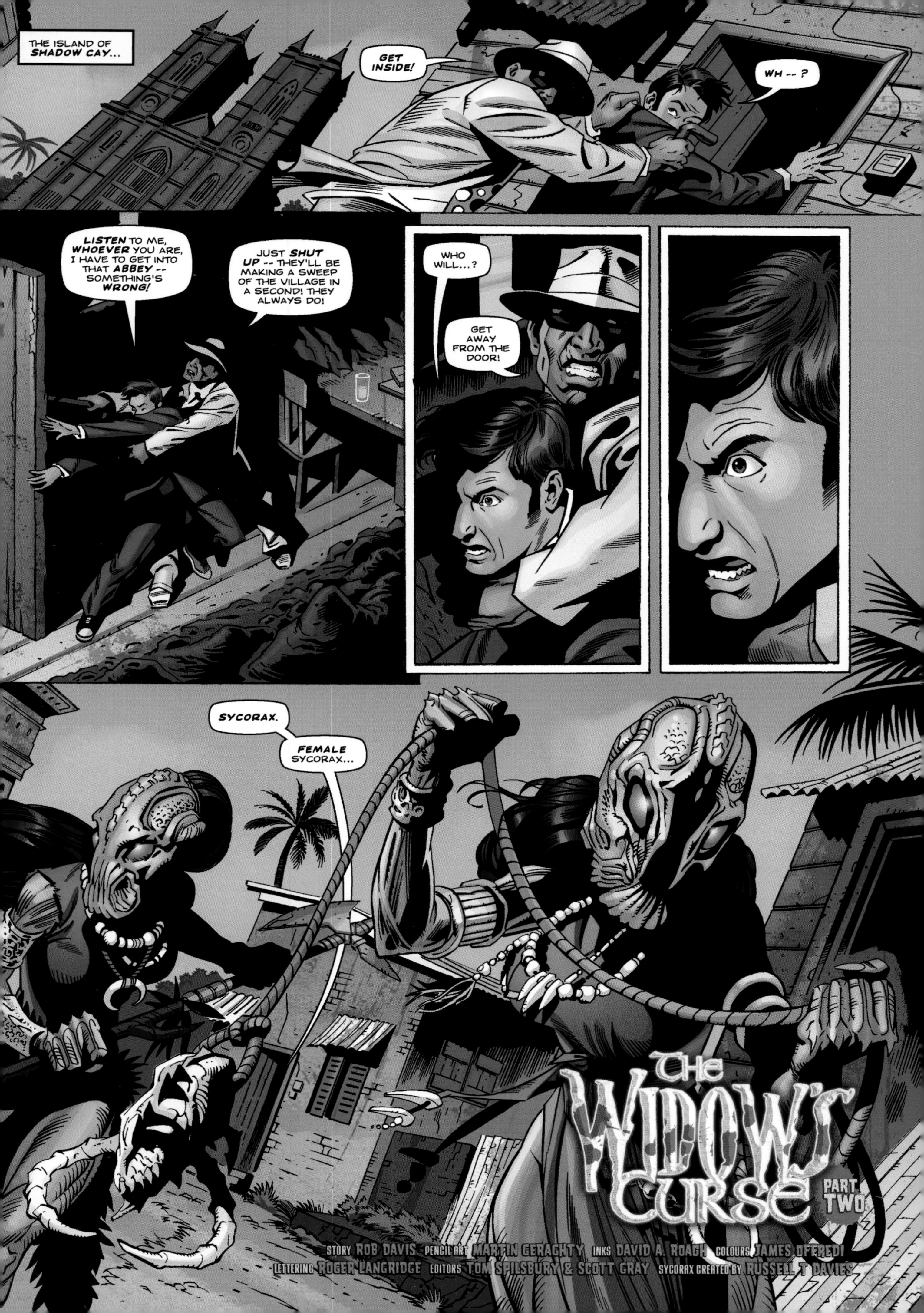
THE ISLAND OF SHADOW CAY...
GET INSIDE!
WH -- ?
LISTEN TO ME, WHOEVER YOU ARE, I HAVE TO GET INTO THAT ABBEY -- SOMETHING'S WRONG!
JUST SHUT UP -- THEY'LL BE MAKING A SWEEP OF THE VILLAGE IN A SECOND! THEY ALWAYS DO!
WHO WILL...?
GET AWAY FROM THE DOOR!
SYCORAX.
FEMALE SYCORAX...
THE WIDOW'S CURSE
PART TWO
STORY ROB DAVIS PENCIL ART MARTIN GERAGHTY INKS DAVID A. ROACH COLOURS JAMES OFFREDI
LETTERING ROGER LANGRIDGE EDITORS TOM SPILSBURY & SCOTT GRAY SYCORAX CREATED BY RUSSELL T DAVIES

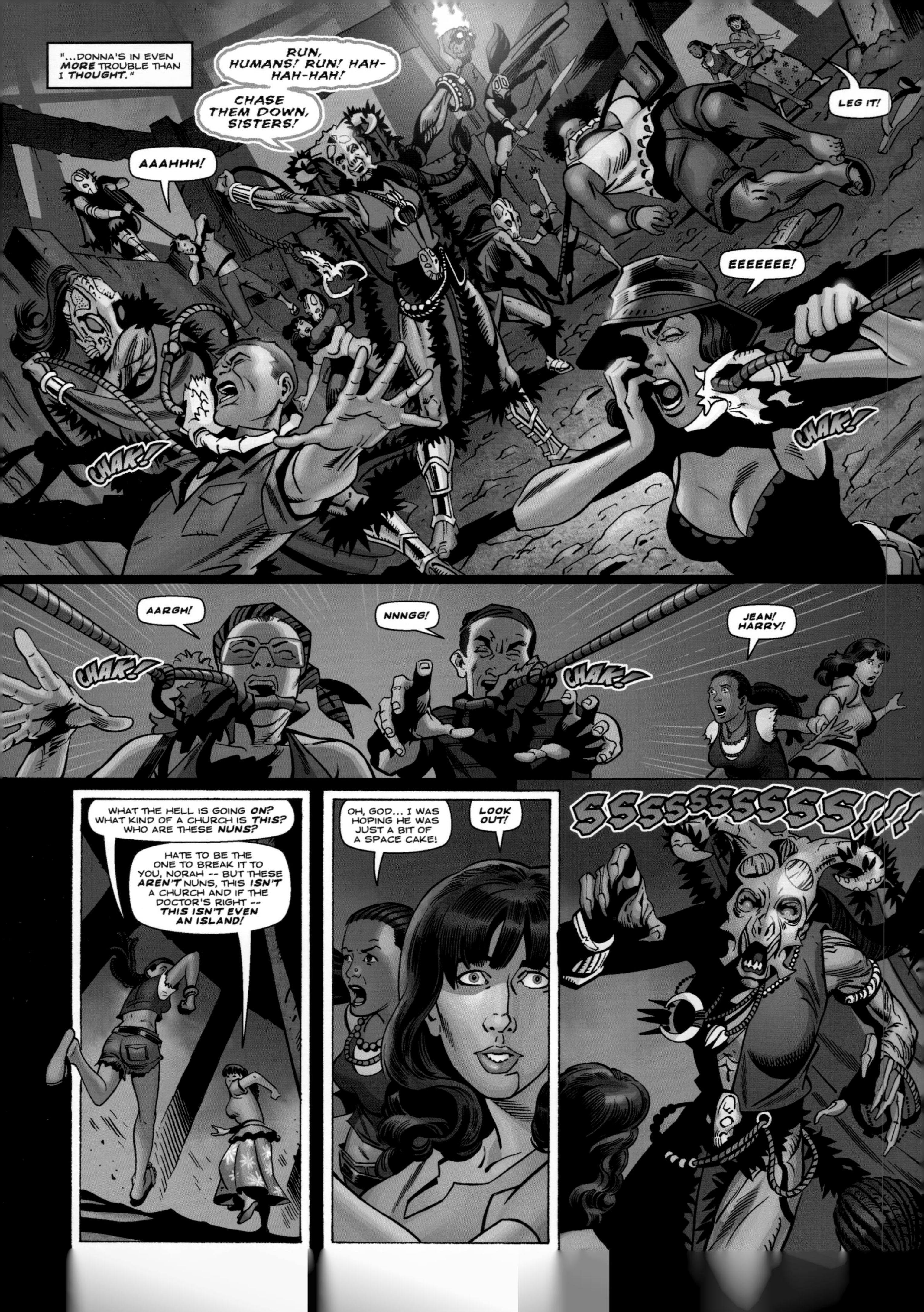
"...DONNA'S IN EVEN MORE TROUBLE THAN I THOUGHT."
RUN, HUMANS! RUN! HAH-HAH-HAH!
CHASE THEM DOWN, SISTERS!
LEG IT!
AAAHHH!
EEEEEEE!
CHAK!
CHAK!
AARGH!
NNNGG!
JEAN! HARRY!
CHAK!
CHAK!
WHAT THE HELL IS GOING ON? WHAT KIND OF A CHURCH IS THIS? WHO ARE THESE NUNS?
HATE TO BE THE ONE TO BREAK IT TO YOU, NORAH -- BUT THESE AREN'T NUNS, THIS ISN'T A CHURCH AND IF THE DOCTOR'S RIGHT -- THIS ISN'T EVEN AN ISLAND!
OH, GOD... I WAS HOPING HE WAS JUST A BIT OF A SPACE CAKE!
LOOK OUT!
SSSSSSSSSS!!!

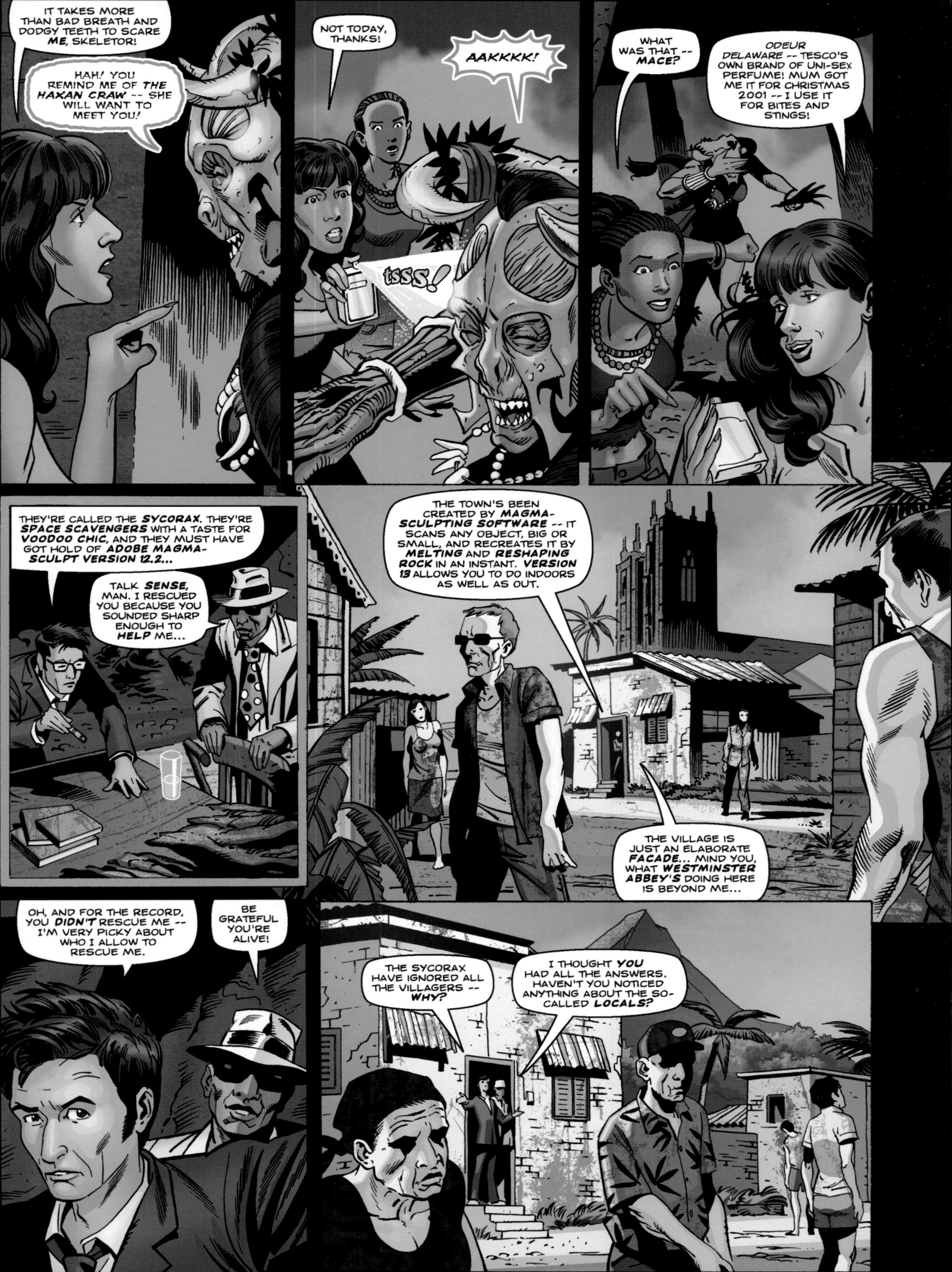
IT TAKES MORE THAN BAD BREATH AND DODGY TEETH TO SCARE ME, SKELETOR!
HAH! YOU REMIND ME OF THE HAXAN CRAW -- SHE WILL WANT TO MEET YOU!
NOT TODAY, THANKS!
AAKKKK!
tsss!
WHAT WAS THAT -- MACE?
ODEUR DELAWARE -- TESCO'S OWN BRAND OF UNI-SEX PERFUME! MUM GOT ME IT FOR CHRISTMAS 2001 -- I USE IT FOR BITES AND STINGS!
THEY'RE CALLED THE SYCORAX. THEY'RE SPACE SCAVENGERS WITH A TASTE FOR VOODOO CHIC, AND THEY MUST HAVE GOT HOLD OF ADOBE MAGMA-SCULPT VERSION 12.2...
TALK SENSE, MAN. I RESCUED YOU BECAUSE YOU SOUNDED SHARP ENOUGH TO HELP ME...
THE TOWN'S BEEN CREATED BY MAGMA-SCULPTING SOFTWARE -- IT SCANS ANY OBJECT, BIG OR SMALL, AND RECREATES IT BY MELTING AND RESHAPING ROCK IN AN INSTANT. VERSION 13 ALLOWS YOU TO DO INDOORS AS WELL AS OUT.
THE VILLAGE IS JUST AN ELABORATE FACADE... MIND YOU, WHAT WESTMINSTER ABBEY'S DOING HERE IS BEYOND ME...
OH, AND FOR THE RECORD, YOU DIDN'T RESCUE ME -- I'M VERY PICKY ABOUT WHO I ALLOW TO RESCUE ME.
BE GRATEFUL YOU'RE ALIVE!
THE SYCORAX HAVE IGNORED ALL THE VILLAGERS -- WHY?
I THOUGHT YOU HAD ALL THE ANSWERS. HAVEN'T YOU NOTICED ANYTHING ABOUT THE SO-CALLED LOCALS?

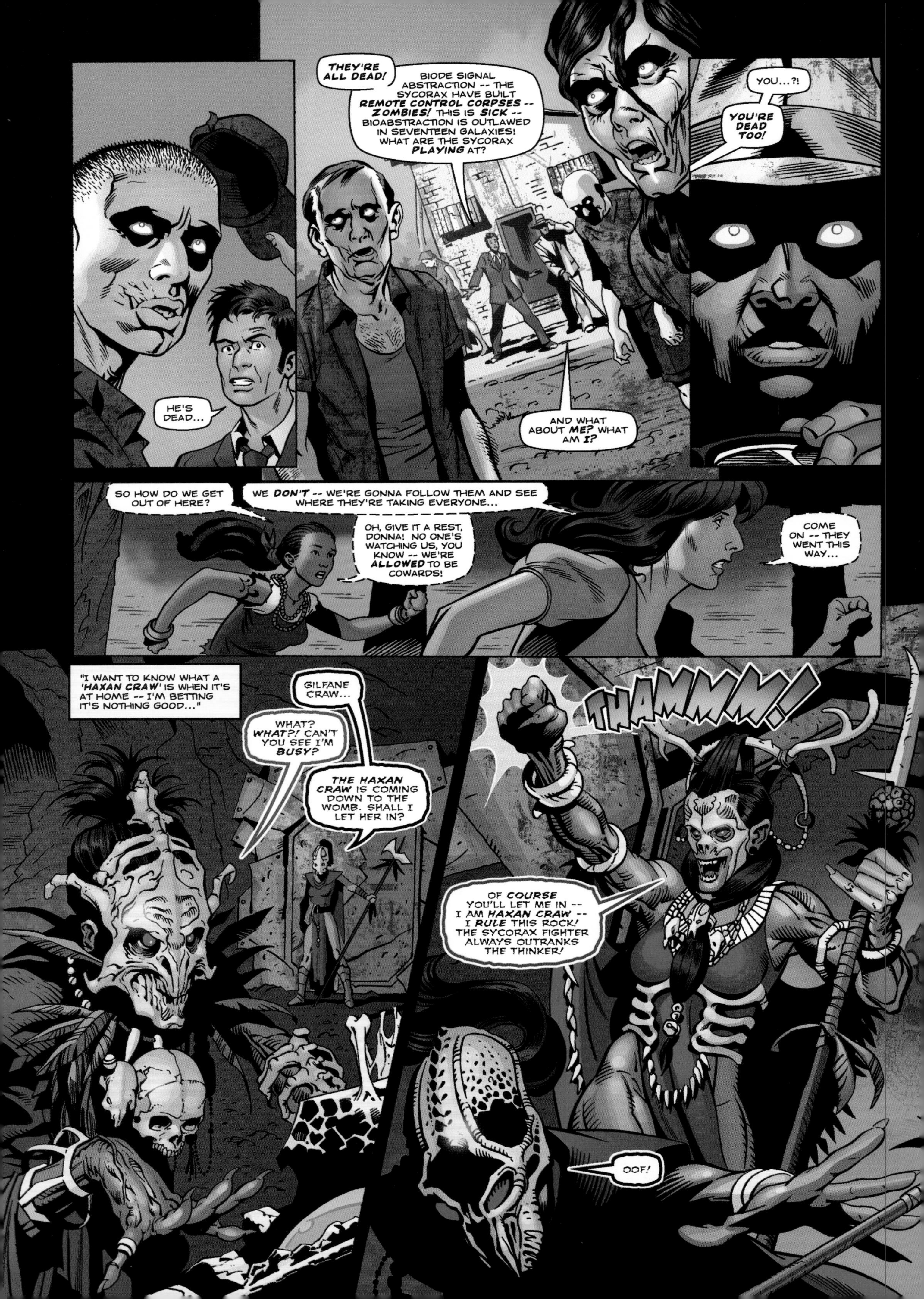
HE'S DEAD...
THEY'RE ALL DEAD!
BIODE SIGNAL ABSTRACTION -- THE SYCORAX HAVE BUILT REMOTE CONTROL CORPSES -- ZOMBIES! THIS IS SICK -- BIOABSTRACTION IS OUTLAWED IN SEVENTEEN GALAXIES! WHAT ARE THE SYCORAX PLAYING AT?
AND WHAT ABOUT ME? WHAT AM I?
YOU...?!
YOU'RE DEAD TOO!
SO HOW DO WE GET OUT OF HERE?
WE DON'T -- WE'RE GONNA FOLLOW THEM AND SEE WHERE THEY'RE TAKING EVERYONE...
OH, GIVE IT A REST, DONNA! NO ONE'S WATCHING US, YOU KNOW -- WE'RE ALLOWED TO BE COWARDS!
COME ON -- THEY WENT THIS WAY...
"I WANT TO KNOW WHAT A 'HAXAN CRAW' IS WHEN IT'S AT HOME -- I'M BETTING IT'S NOTHING GOOD..."
GILFANE CRAW...
WHAT? WHAT?! CAN'T YOU SEE I'M BUSY?
THE HAXAN CRAW IS COMING DOWN TO THE WOMB. SHALL I LET HER IN?
THAMMM!
OF COURSE YOU'LL LET ME IN -- I AM HAXAN CRAW -- I RULE THIS ROCK! THE SYCORAX FIGHTER ALWAYS OUTRANKS THE THINKER!
OOF!

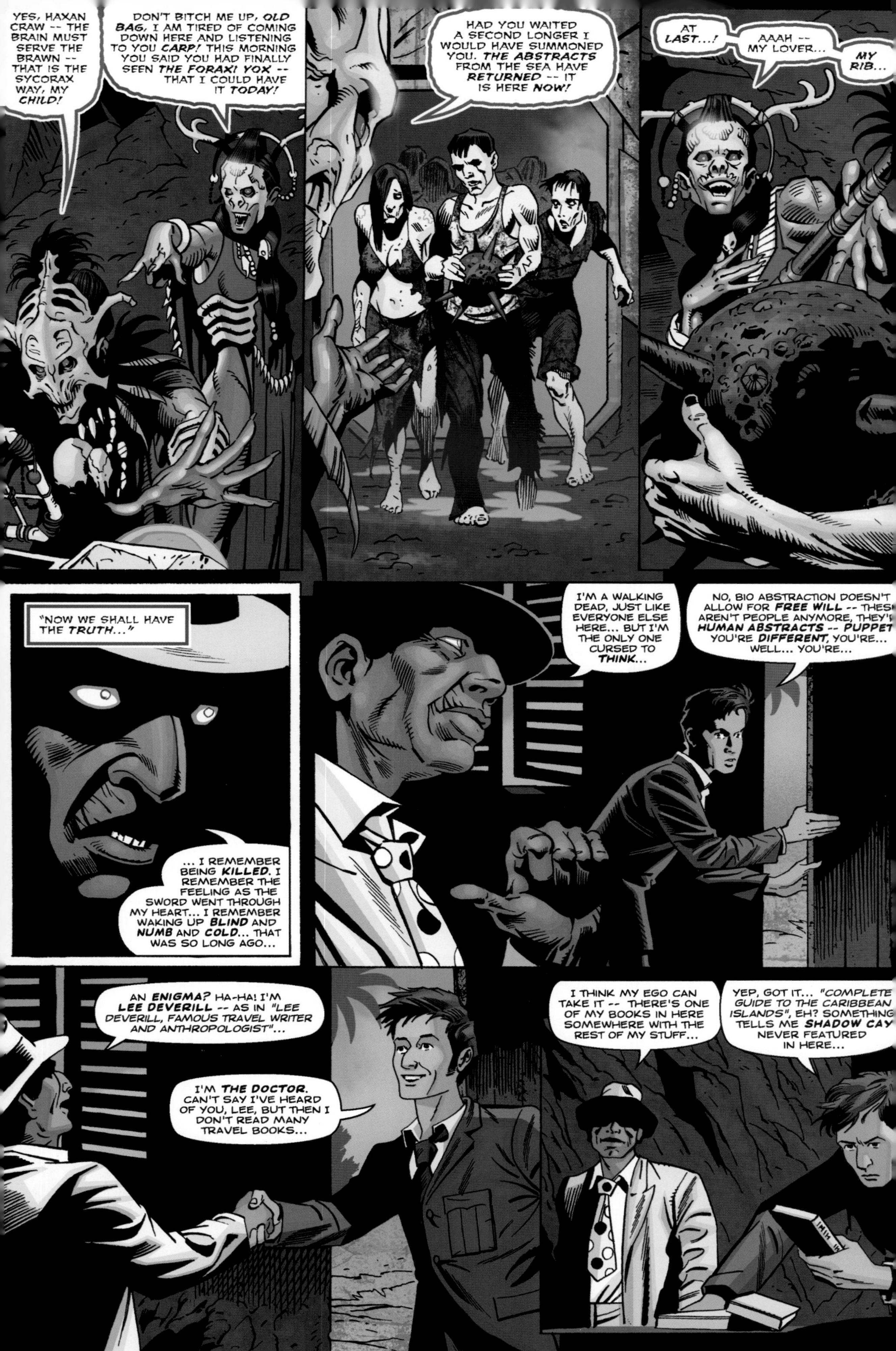
YES, HAXAN CRAW -- THE BRAIN MUST SERVE THE BRAWN -- THAT IS THE SYCORAX WAY, MY CHILD!
DON'T BITCH ME UP, OLD BAG, I AM TIRED OF COMING DOWN HERE AND LISTENING TO YOU CARP! THIS MORNING YOU SAID YOU HAD FINALLY SEEN THE FORAX! YOX -- THAT I COULD HAVE IT TODAY!
HAD YOU WAITED A SECOND LONGER I WOULD HAVE SUMMONED YOU. THE ABSTRACTS FROM THE SEA HAVE RETURNED -- IT IS HERE NOW!
AT LAST...!
AAAH -- MY LOVER...
MY RIB...
"NOW WE SHALL HAVE THE TRUTH..."
... I REMEMBER BEING KILLED. I REMEMBER THE FEELING AS THE SWORD WENT THROUGH MY HEART... I REMEMBER WAKING UP BLIND AND NUMB AND COLD... THAT WAS SO LONG AGO...
I'M A WALKING DEAD, JUST LIKE EVERYONE ELSE HERE... BUT I'M THE ONLY ONE CURSED TO THINK...
NO, BIO ABSTRACTION DOESN'T ALLOW FOR FREE WILL -- THES AREN'T PEOPLE ANYMORE, THEY'R HUMAN ABSTRACTS -- PUPPET YOU'RE DIFFERENT, YOU'RE... WELL... YOU'RE...
AN ENIGMA? HA-HA! I'M LEE DEVERILL -- AS IN "LEE DEVERILL, FAMOUS TRAVEL WRITER AND ANTHROPOLOGIST"...
I'M THE DOCTOR. CAN'T SAY I'VE HEARD OF YOU, LEE, BUT THEN I DON'T READ MANY TRAVEL BOOKS...
I THINK MY EGO CAN TAKE IT -- THERE'S ONE OF MY BOOKS IN HERE SOMEWHERE WITH THE REST OF MY STUFF...
YEP, GOT IT... "COMPLETE GUIDE TO THE CARIBBEAN ISLANDS", EH? SOMETHING TELLS ME SHADOW CAY NEVER FEATURED IN HERE...

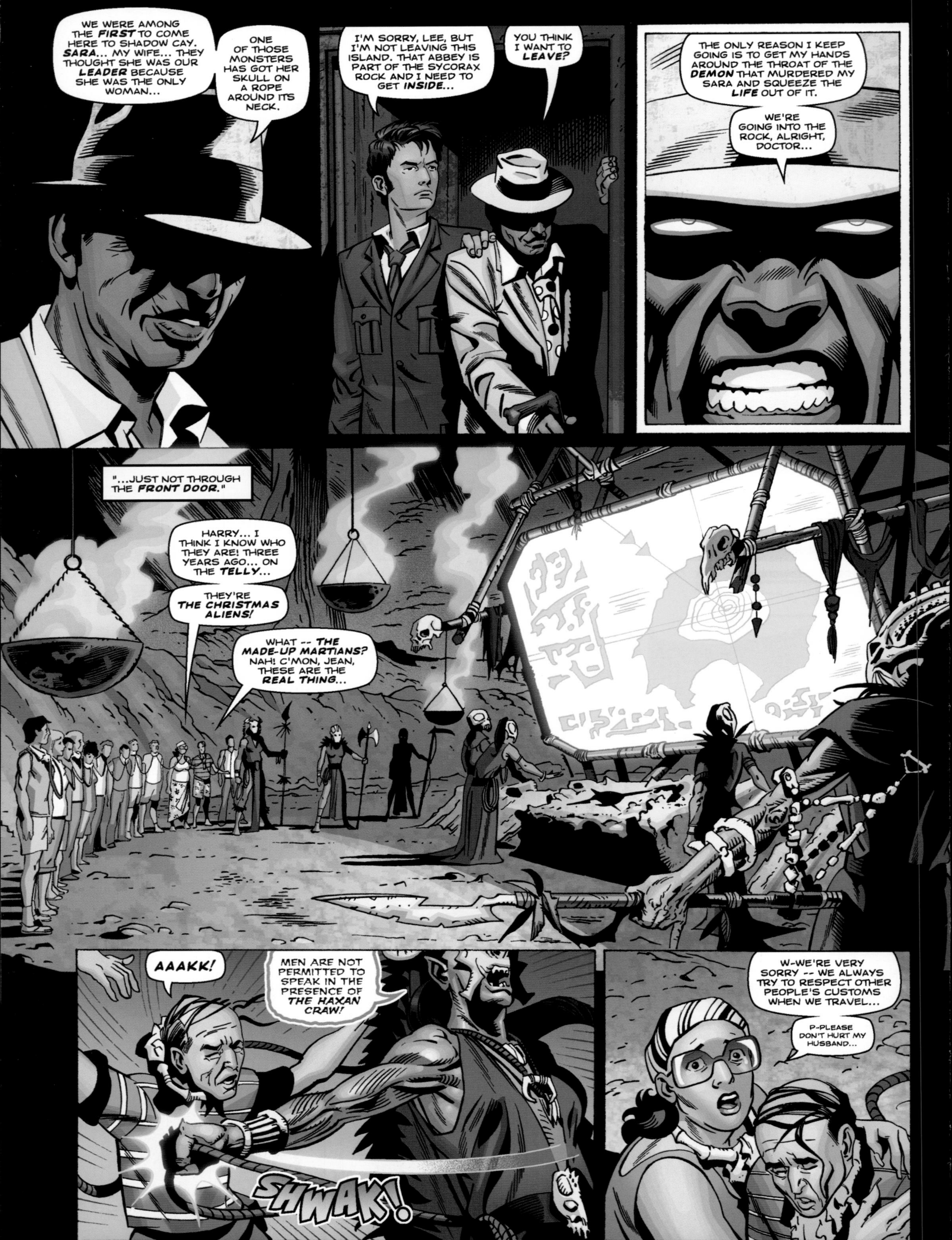
WE WERE AMONG THE FIRST TO COME HERE TO SHADOW CAY. SARA... MY WIFE... THEY THOUGHT SHE WAS OUR LEADER BECAUSE SHE WAS THE ONLY WOMAN...
ONE OF THOSE MONSTERS HAS GOT HER SKULL ON A ROPE AROUND ITS NECK.
I'M SORRY, LEE, BUT I'M NOT LEAVING THIS ISLAND. THAT ABBEY IS PART OF THE SYCORAX ROCK AND I NEED TO GET INSIDE...
YOU THINK I WANT TO LEAVE?
THE ONLY REASON I KEEP GOING IS TO GET MY HANDS AROUND THE THROAT OF THE DEMON THAT MURDERED MY SARA AND SQUEEZE THE LIFE OUT OF IT.
WE'RE GOING INTO THE ROCK, ALRIGHT, DOCTOR...
"...JUST NOT THROUGH THE FRONT DOOR."
HARRY... I THINK I KNOW WHO THEY ARE! THREE YEARS AGO... ON THE TELLY...
THEY'RE THE CHRISTMAS ALIENS!
WHAT -- THE MADE-UP MARTIANS? NAH! C'MON, JEAN, THESE ARE THE REAL THING...
AAAKK!
MEN ARE NOT PERMITTED TO SPEAK IN THE PRESENCE OF THE HAXAN CRAW!
SHWAK!
W-WE'RE VERY SORRY -- WE ALWAYS TRY TO RESPECT OTHER PEOPLE'S CUSTOMS WHEN WE TRAVEL...
P-PLEASE DON'T HURT MY HUSBAND...

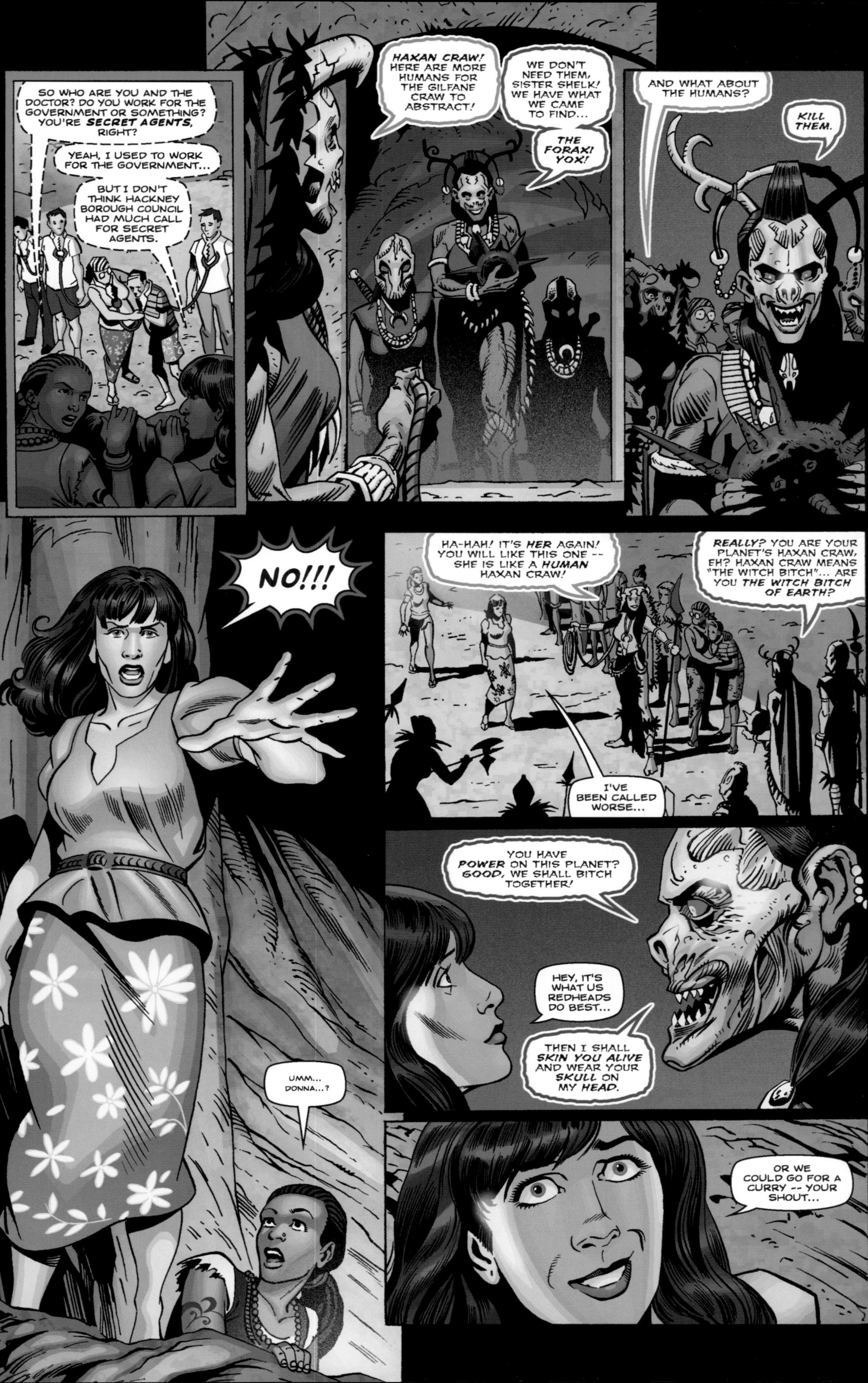
SO WHO ARE YOU AND THE DOCTOR? DO YOU WORK FOR THE GOVERNMENT OR SOMETHING? YOU'RE SECRET AGENTS, RIGHT?
YEAH, I USED TO WORK FOR THE GOVERNMENT...
BUT I DON'T THINK HACKNEY BOROUGH COUNCIL HAD MUCH CALL FOR SECRET AGENTS.
HAXAN CRAW! HERE ARE MORE HUMANS FOR THE GILFANE CRAW TO ABSTRACT!
WE DON'T NEED THEM, SISTER SHELK! WE HAVE WHAT WE CAME TO FIND...
THE FORAX! YOX!
AND WHAT ABOUT THE HUMANS?
KILL THEM.
NO!!!
UMM... DONNA...?
HA-HAH! IT'S HER AGAIN! YOU WILL LIKE THIS ONE -- SHE IS LIKE A HUMAN HAXAN CRAW!
REALLY? YOU ARE YOUR PLANET'S HAXAN CRAW, EH? HAXAN CRAW MEANS "THE WITCH BITCH"... ARE YOU THE WITCH BITCH OF EARTH?
I'VE BEEN CALLED WORSE...
YOU HAVE POWER ON THIS PLANET? GOOD, WE SHALL BITCH TOGETHER!
HEY, IT'S WHAT US REDHEADS DO BEST...
THEN I SHALL SKIN YOU ALIVE AND WEAR YOUR SKULL ON MY HEAD.
OR WE COULD GO FOR A CURRY -- YOUR SHOUT...

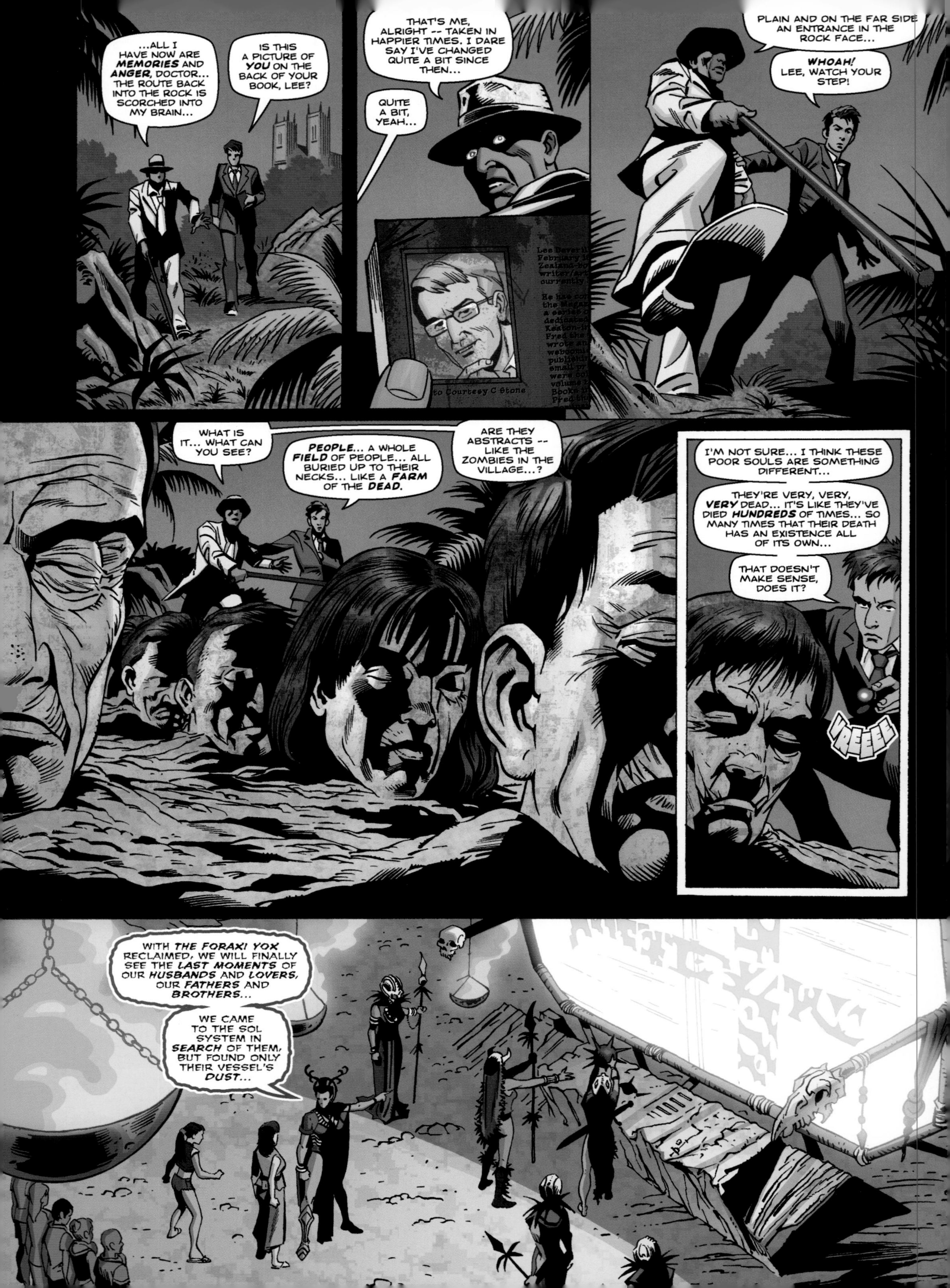

...ALL I HAVE NOW ARE **MEMORIES** AND **ANGER**, DOCTOR... THE ROUTE BACK INTO THE ROCK IS SCORCHED INTO MY BRAIN...
IS THIS A PICTURE OF **YOU** ON THE BACK OF YOUR BOOK, LEE?
THAT'S ME, ALRIGHT -- TAKEN IN HAPPIER TIMES. I DARE SAY I'VE CHANGED QUITE A BIT SINCE THEN...
QUITE A BIT, YEAH...
PLAIN AND ON THE FAR SIDE AN ENTRANCE IN THE ROCK FACE...
WHOAH! LEE, WATCH YOUR STEP!
WHAT IS IT... WHAT CAN YOU SEE?
PEOPLE... A WHOLE ***FIELD*** OF PEOPLE... ALL BURIED UP TO THEIR NECKS... LIKE A ***FARM*** OF THE ***DEAD***.
ARE THEY ABSTRACTS -- LIKE THE ZOMBIES IN THE VILLAGE...?
I'M NOT SURE... I THINK THESE POOR SOULS ARE SOMETHING DIFFERENT...
THEY'RE VERY, VERY, ***VERY*** DEAD... IT'S LIKE THEY'VE DIED ***HUNDREDS*** OF TIMES... SO MANY TIMES THAT THEIR DEATH HAS AN EXISTENCE ALL OF ITS OWN...
THAT DOESN'T MAKE SENSE, DOES IT?
VREEEE
*WITH **THE FORAXI YOX** RECLAIMED, WE WILL FINALLY SEE THE **LAST MOMENTS** OF OUR **HUSBANDS** AND **LOVERS**, OUR **FATHERS** AND **BROTHERS**...*
*WE CAME TO THE SOL SYSTEM IN **SEARCH** OF THEM, BUT FOUND ONLY THEIR VESSEL'S **DUST**...*

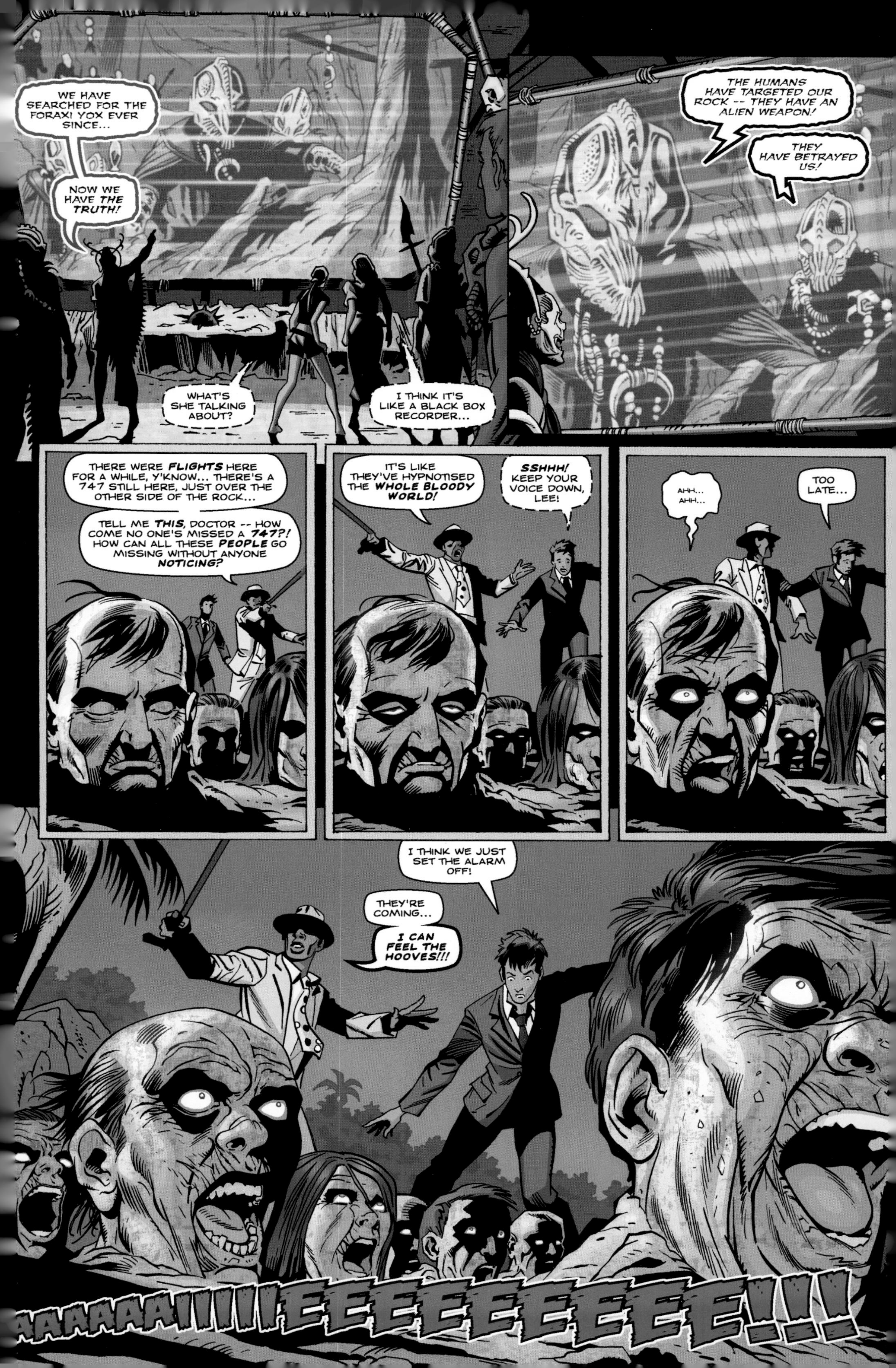
WE HAVE SEARCHED FOR THE FORAXI YOX EVER SINCE...
NOW WE HAVE THE TRUTH!
WHAT'S SHE TALKING ABOUT?
I THINK IT'S LIKE A BLACK BOX RECORDER...
THE HUMANS HAVE TARGETED OUR ROCK -- THEY HAVE AN ALIEN WEAPON!
THEY HAVE BETRAYED US!
THERE WERE FLIGHTS HERE FOR A WHILE, Y'KNOW... THERE'S A 747 STILL HERE, JUST OVER THE OTHER SIDE OF THE ROCK...
TELL ME THIS, DOCTOR -- HOW COME NO ONE'S MISSED A 747?! HOW CAN ALL THESE PEOPLE GO MISSING WITHOUT ANYONE NOTICING?
IT'S LIKE THEY'VE HYPNOTISED THE WHOLE BLOODY WORLD!
SSHHH! KEEP YOUR VOICE DOWN, LEE!
AHH... AHH...
TOO LATE...
I THINK WE JUST SET THE ALARM OFF!
THEY'RE COMING...
I CAN FEEL THE HOOVES!!!
AAAAAAIIIIIIEEEEEEEEEEE!!!

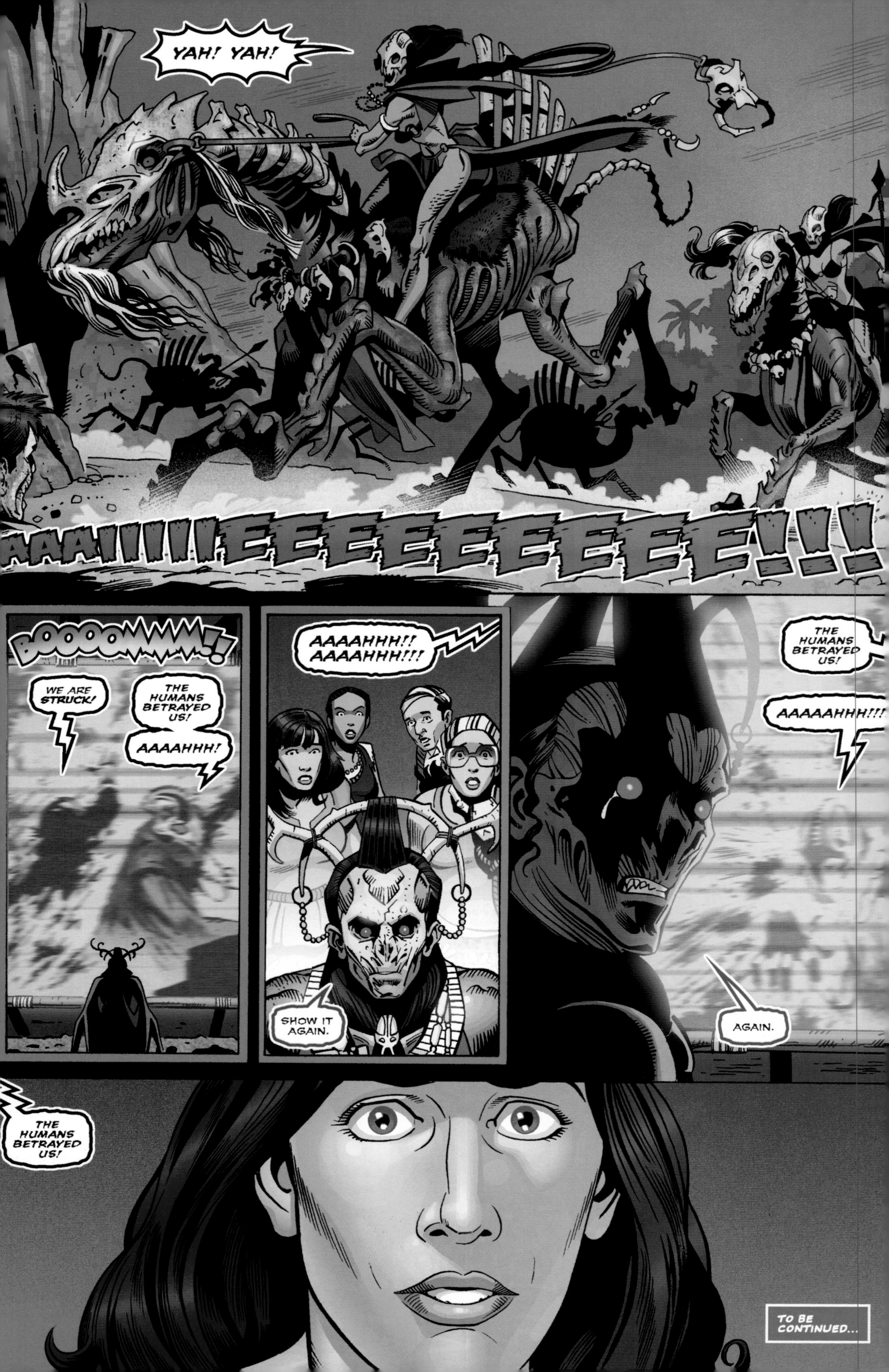
YAH! YAH!
AAAIIIIIEEEEEEEEEEE!!!
BOOOOMMM!!
WE ARE STRUCK!
THE HUMANS BETRAYED US!
AAAAHHH!
AAAAHHH!! AAAAHHH!!!
SHOW IT AGAIN.
THE HUMANS BETRAYED US!
AAAAAHHH!!!
AGAIN.
THE HUMANS BETRAYED US!
TO BE CONTINUED...

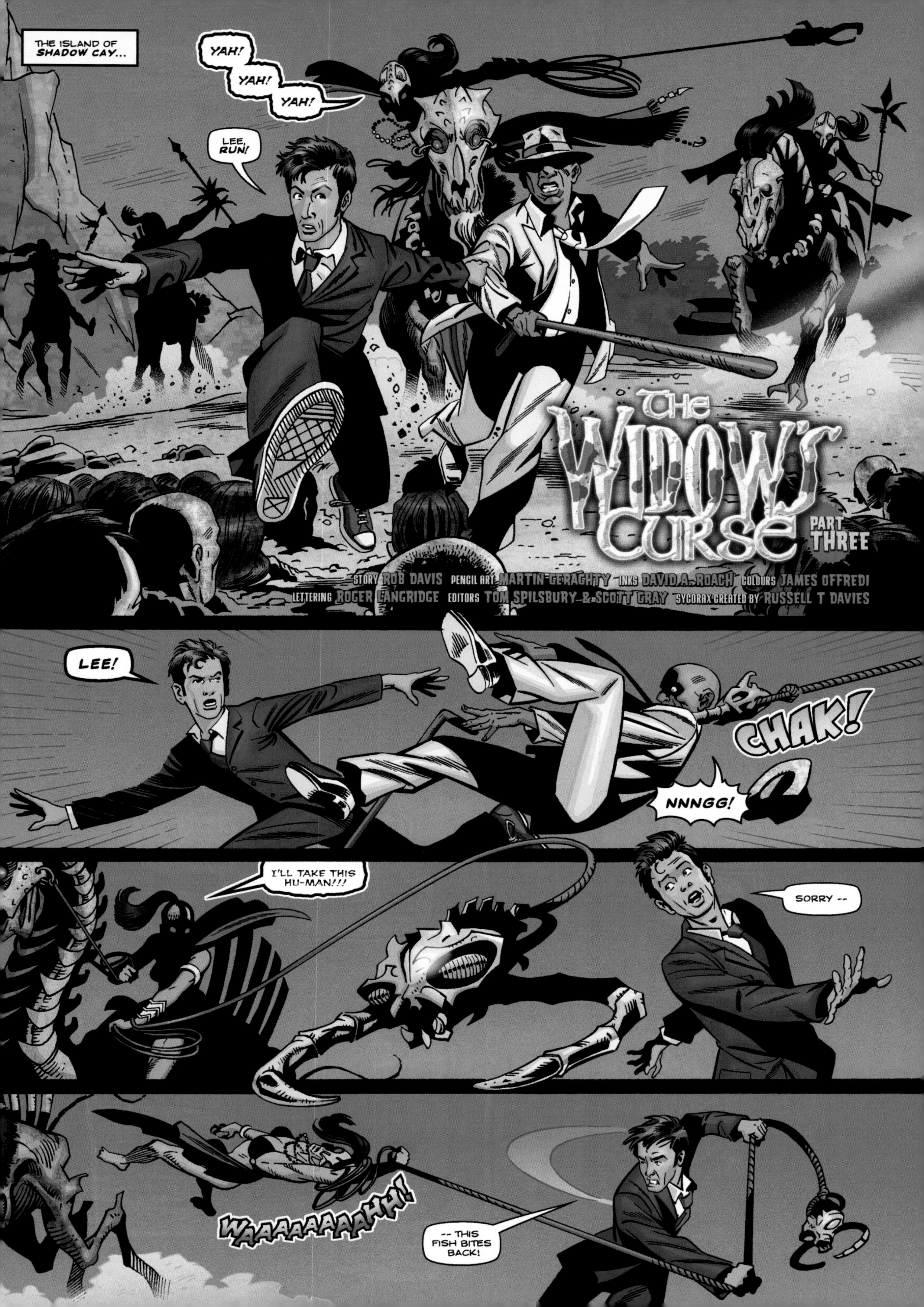
THE ISLAND OF SHADOW CAY...
YAH!
YAH!
YAH!
LEE, RUN!
THE WIDOW'S CURSE
PART THREE
STORY ROB DAVIS PENCIL ART MARTIN GERAGHTY INKS DAVID A. ROACH COLOURS JAMES OFFREDI
LETTERING ROGER LANGRIDGE EDITORS TOM SPILSBURY & SCOTT GRAY SYCORAX CREATED BY RUSSELL T DAVIES
LEE!
CHAK!
NNNGG!
I'LL TAKE THIS HU-MAN!!!
SORRY --
WAAAAAAAAHH!
-- THIS FISH BITES BACK!

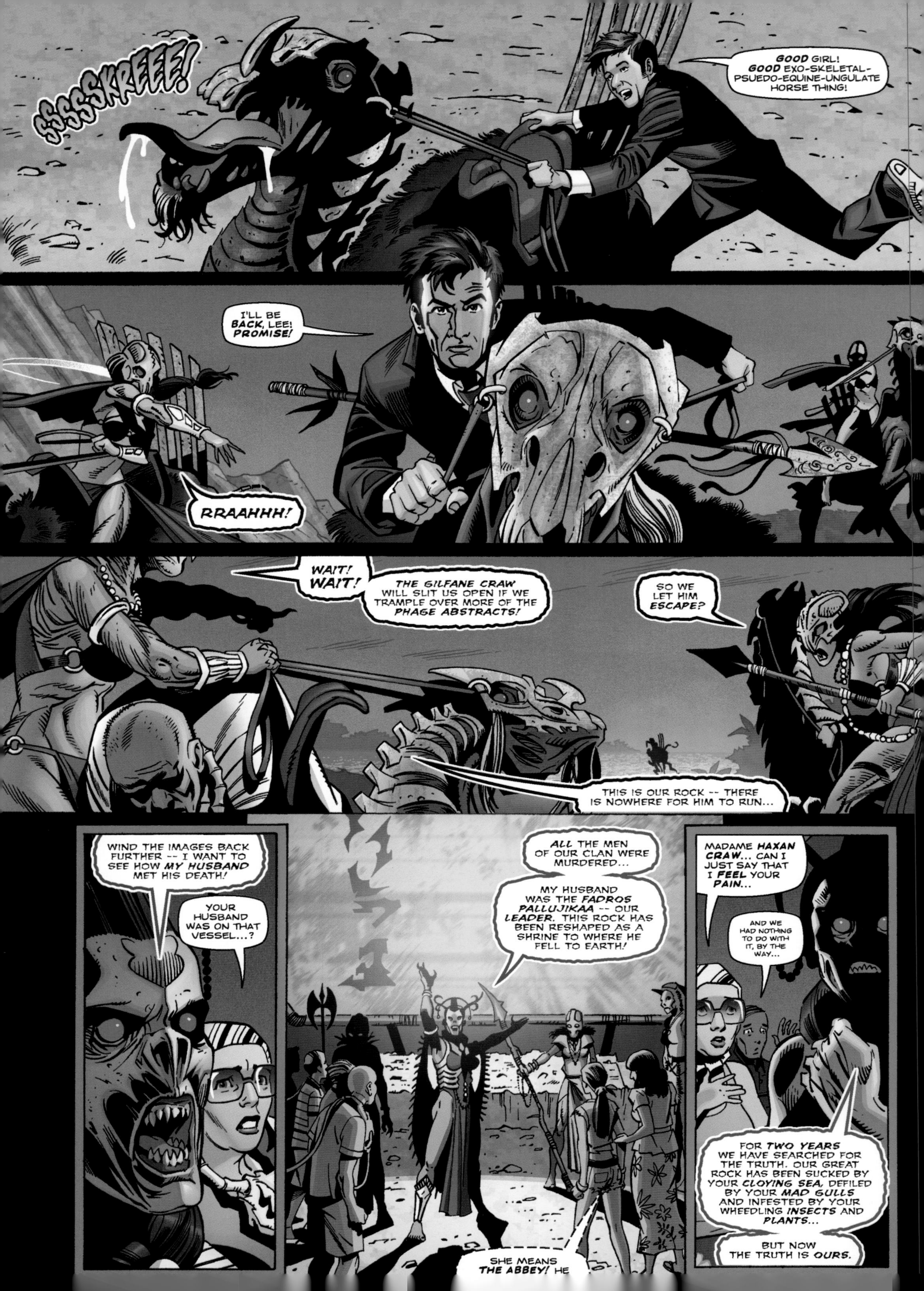

SSSSKREEE!
GOOD GIRL! GOOD EXO-SKELETAL-PSUEDO-EQUINE-UNGULATE HORSE THING!
I'LL BE BACK, LEE! PROMISE!
RRAAHHH!
WAIT! WAIT!
THE GILFANE CRAW WILL SLIT US OPEN IF WE TRAMPLE OVER MORE OF THE PHAGE ABSTRACTS!
SO WE LET HIM ESCAPE?
THIS IS OUR ROCK -- THERE IS NOWHERE FOR HIM TO RUN...
WIND THE IMAGES BACK FURTHER -- I WANT TO SEE HOW MY HUSBAND MET HIS DEATH!
YOUR HUSBAND WAS ON THAT VESSEL...?
ALL THE MEN OF OUR CLAN WERE MURDERED...
MY HUSBAND WAS THE FADROS PALLUJIKAA -- OUR LEADER. THIS ROCK HAS BEEN RESHAPED AS A SHRINE TO WHERE HE FELL TO EARTH!
SHE MEANS THE ABBEY! HE
MADAME HAXAN CRAW... CAN I JUST SAY THAT I FEEL YOUR PAIN...
AND WE HAD NOTHING TO DO WITH IT, BY THE WAY...
FOR TWO YEARS WE HAVE SEARCHED FOR THE TRUTH. OUR GREAT ROCK HAS BEEN SUCKED BY YOUR CLOYING SEA, DEFILED BY YOUR MAD GULLS AND INFESTED BY YOUR WHEEDLING INSECTS AND PLANTS...
BUT NOW THE TRUTH IS OURS.

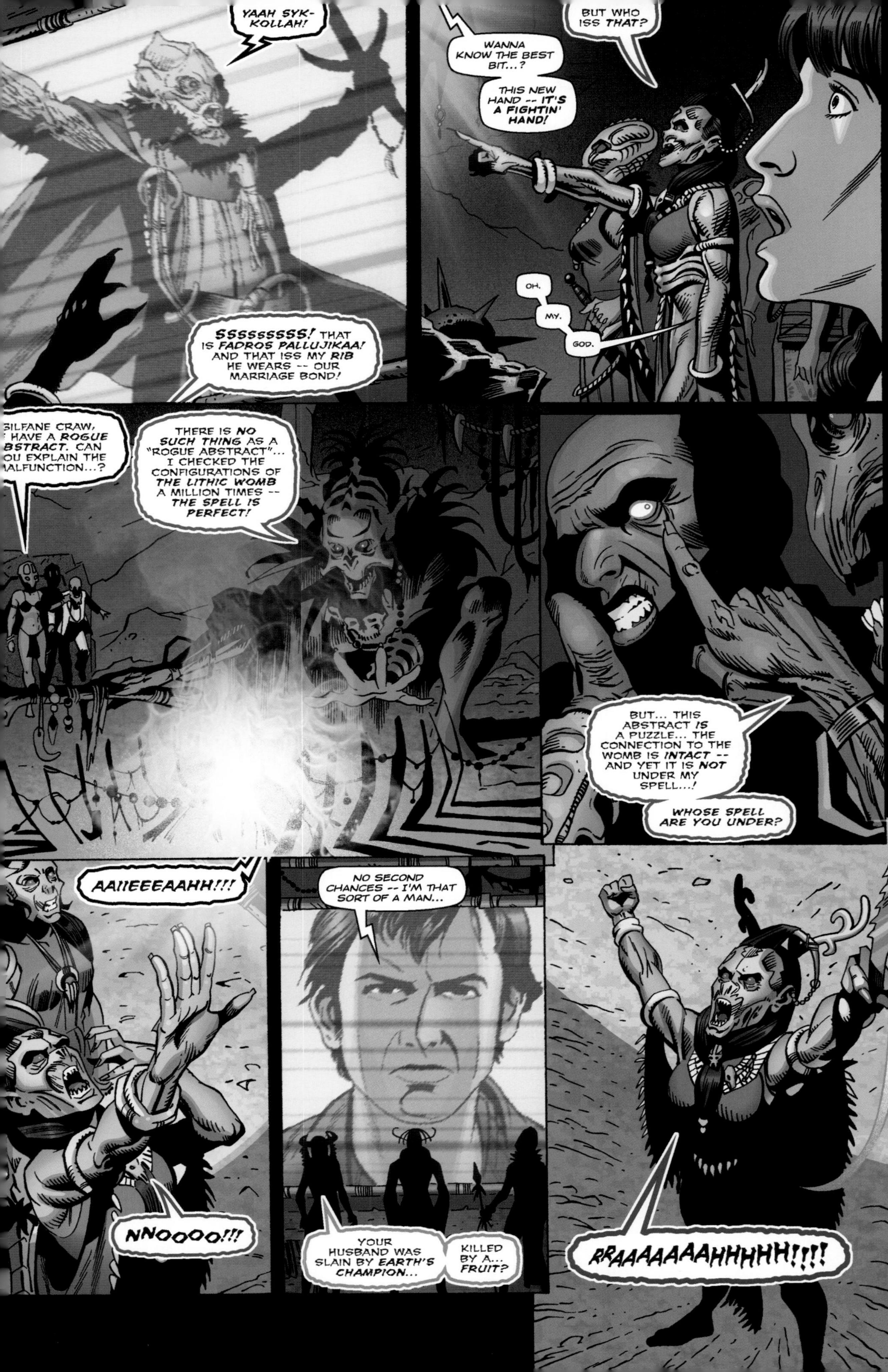
YAAH SYK-KOLLAH!
SSSSSSSSS! THAT IS FADROS PALLUJIKAA! AND THAT ISS MY RIB HE WEARS -- OUR MARRIAGE BOND!
BUT WHO ISS THAT?
WANNA KNOW THE BEST BIT...?
THIS NEW HAND -- IT'S A FIGHTIN' HAND!
OH.
MY.
GOD.
GILFANE CRAW, WE HAVE A ROGUE ABSTRACT. CAN YOU EXPLAIN THE MALFUNCTION...?
THERE IS NO SUCH THING AS A "ROGUE ABSTRACT"... I CHECKED THE CONFIGURATIONS OF THE LITHIC WOMB A MILLION TIMES -- THE SPELL IS PERFECT!
BUT... THIS ABSTRACT IS A PUZZLE... THE CONNECTION TO THE WOMB IS INTACT -- AND YET IT IS NOT UNDER MY SPELL...!
WHOSE SPELL ARE YOU UNDER?
AAIIEEEAAHH!!!
NNOOOOO!!!
NO SECOND CHANCES -- I'M THAT SORT OF A MAN...
YOUR HUSBAND WAS SLAIN BY EARTH'S CHAMPION...
KILLED BY A... FRUIT?
RRAAAAAAAHHHHHH!!!!!

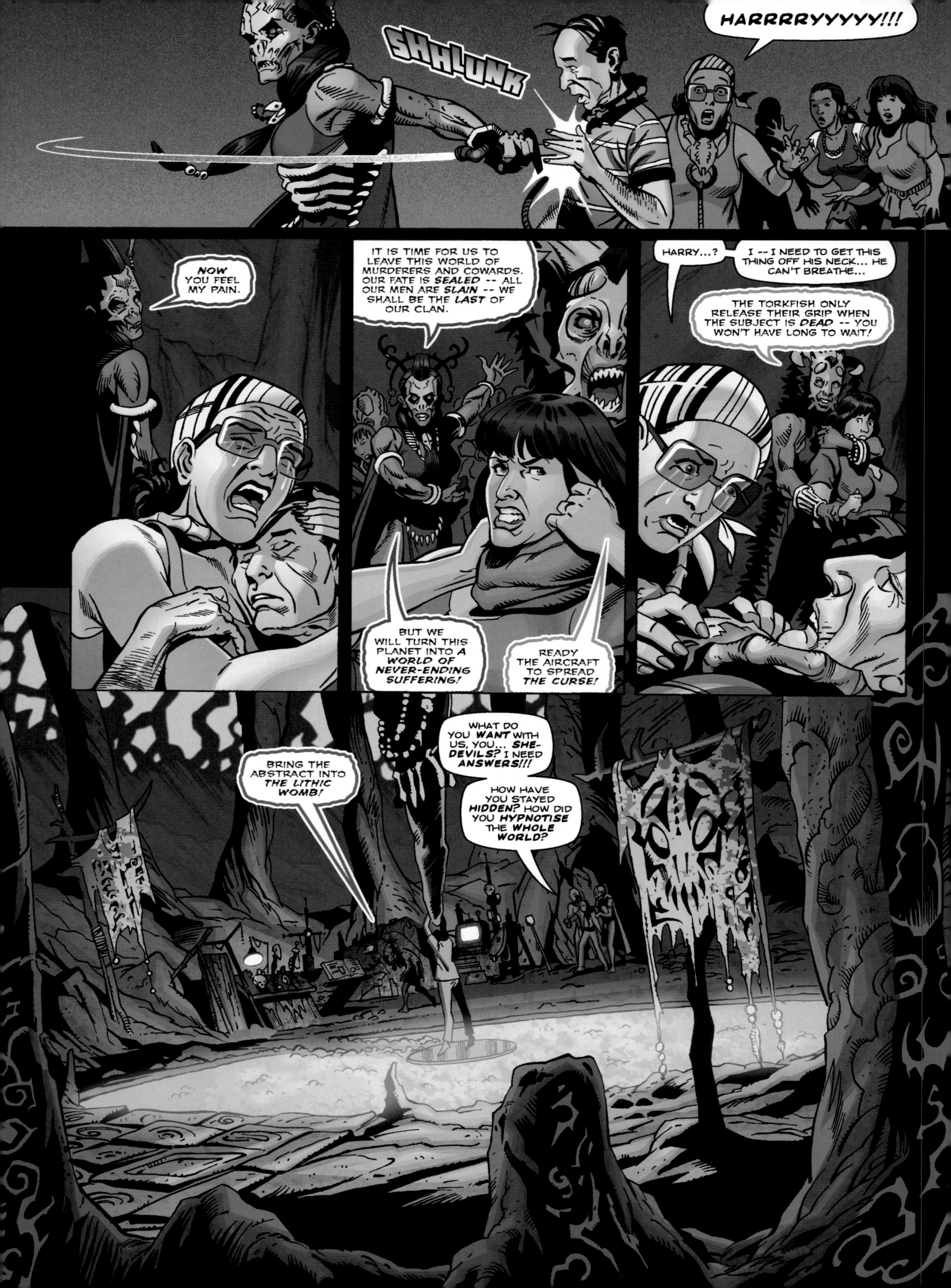

SHHLUNK
HARRRRYYYYY!!!
NOW YOU FEEL MY PAIN.
IT IS TIME FOR US TO LEAVE THIS WORLD OF MURDERERS AND COWARDS. OUR FATE IS SEALED -- ALL OUR MEN ARE SLAIN -- WE SHALL BE THE LAST OF OUR CLAN.
BUT WE WILL TURN THIS PLANET INTO A WORLD OF NEVER-ENDING SUFFERING!
READY THE AIRCRAFT TO SPREAD THE CURSE!
HARRY...?
I -- I NEED TO GET THIS THING OFF HIS NECK... HE CAN'T BREATHE...
THE TORKFISH ONLY RELEASE THEIR GRIP WHEN THE SUBJECT IS DEAD -- YOU WON'T HAVE LONG TO WAIT!
BRING THE ABSTRACT INTO THE LITHIC WOMB!
WHAT DO YOU WANT WITH US, YOU... SHE-DEVILS? I NEED ANSWERS!!!
HOW HAVE YOU STAYED HIDDEN? HOW DID YOU HYPNOTISE THE WHOLE WORLD?

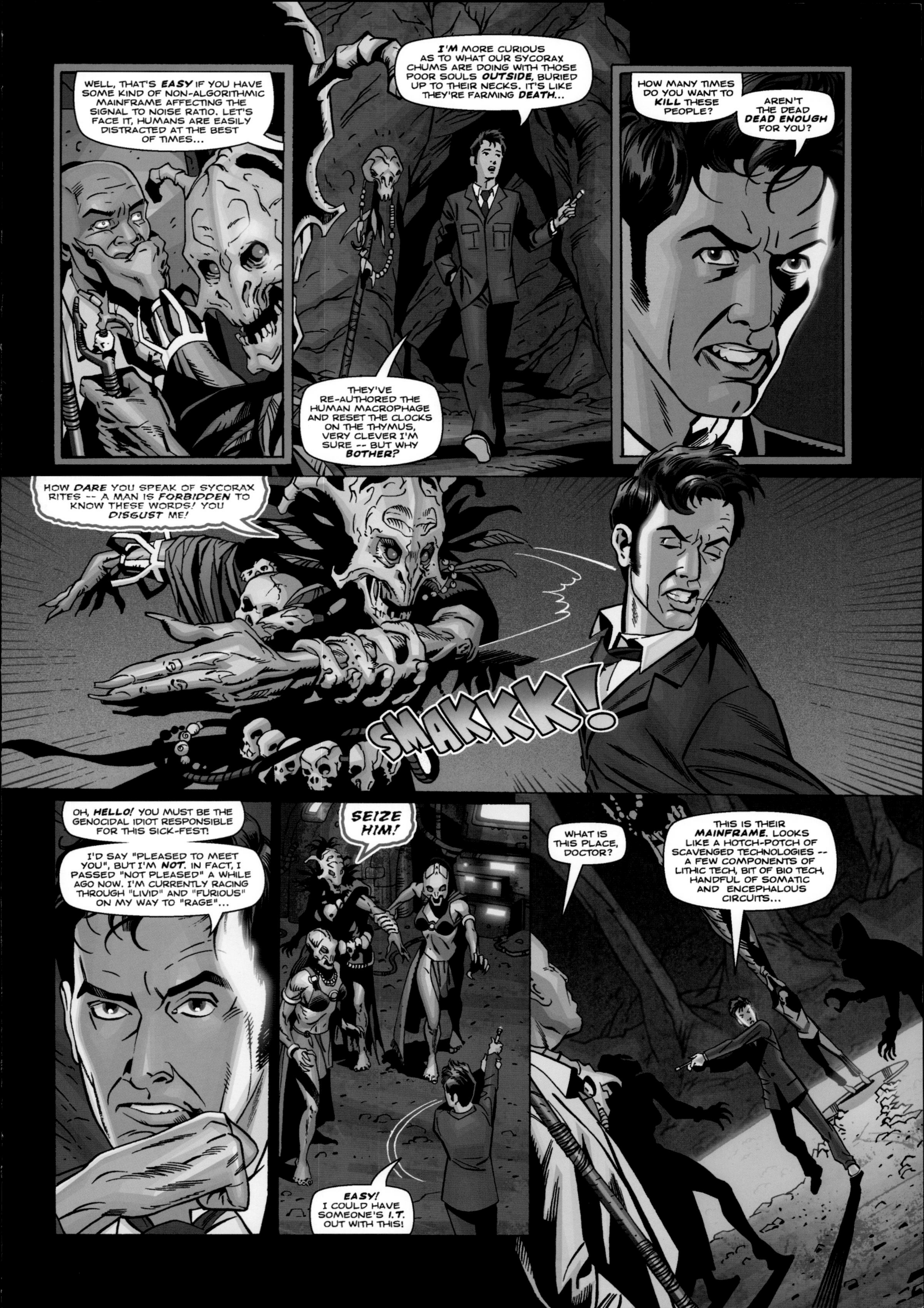
WELL, THAT'S EASY IF YOU HAVE SOME KIND OF NON-ALGORITHMIC MAINFRAME AFFECTING THE SIGNAL TO NOISE RATIO. LET'S FACE IT, HUMANS ARE EASILY DISTRACTED AT THE BEST OF TIMES...
I'M MORE CURIOUS AS TO WHAT OUR SYCORAX CHUMS ARE DOING WITH THOSE POOR SOULS OUTSIDE, BURIED UP TO THEIR NECKS. IT'S LIKE THEY'RE FARMING DEATH...
THEY'VE RE-AUTHORED THE HUMAN MACROPHAGE AND RESET THE CLOCKS ON THE THYMUS, VERY CLEVER I'M SURE -- BUT WHY BOTHER?
HOW MANY TIMES DO YOU WANT TO KILL THESE PEOPLE?
AREN'T THE DEAD DEAD ENOUGH FOR YOU?
HOW DARE YOU SPEAK OF SYCORAX RITES -- A MAN IS FORBIDDEN TO KNOW THESE WORDS! YOU DISGUST ME!
SMAKKK!
OH, HELLO! YOU MUST BE THE GENOCIDAL IDIOT RESPONSIBLE FOR THIS SICK-FEST!
I'D SAY "PLEASED TO MEET YOU", BUT I'M NOT. IN FACT, I PASSED "NOT PLEASED" A WHILE AGO NOW. I'M CURRENTLY RACING THROUGH "LIVID" AND "FURIOUS" ON MY WAY TO "RAGE"...
SEIZE HIM!
EASY! I COULD HAVE SOMEONE'S I.T. OUT WITH THIS!
WHAT IS THIS PLACE, DOCTOR?
THIS IS THEIR MAINFRAME. LOOKS LIKE A HOTCH-POTCH OF SCAVENGED TECHNOLOGIES -- A FEW COMPONENTS OF LITHIC TECH, BIT OF BIO TECH, HANDFUL OF SOMATIC AND ENCEPHALOUS CIRCUITS...

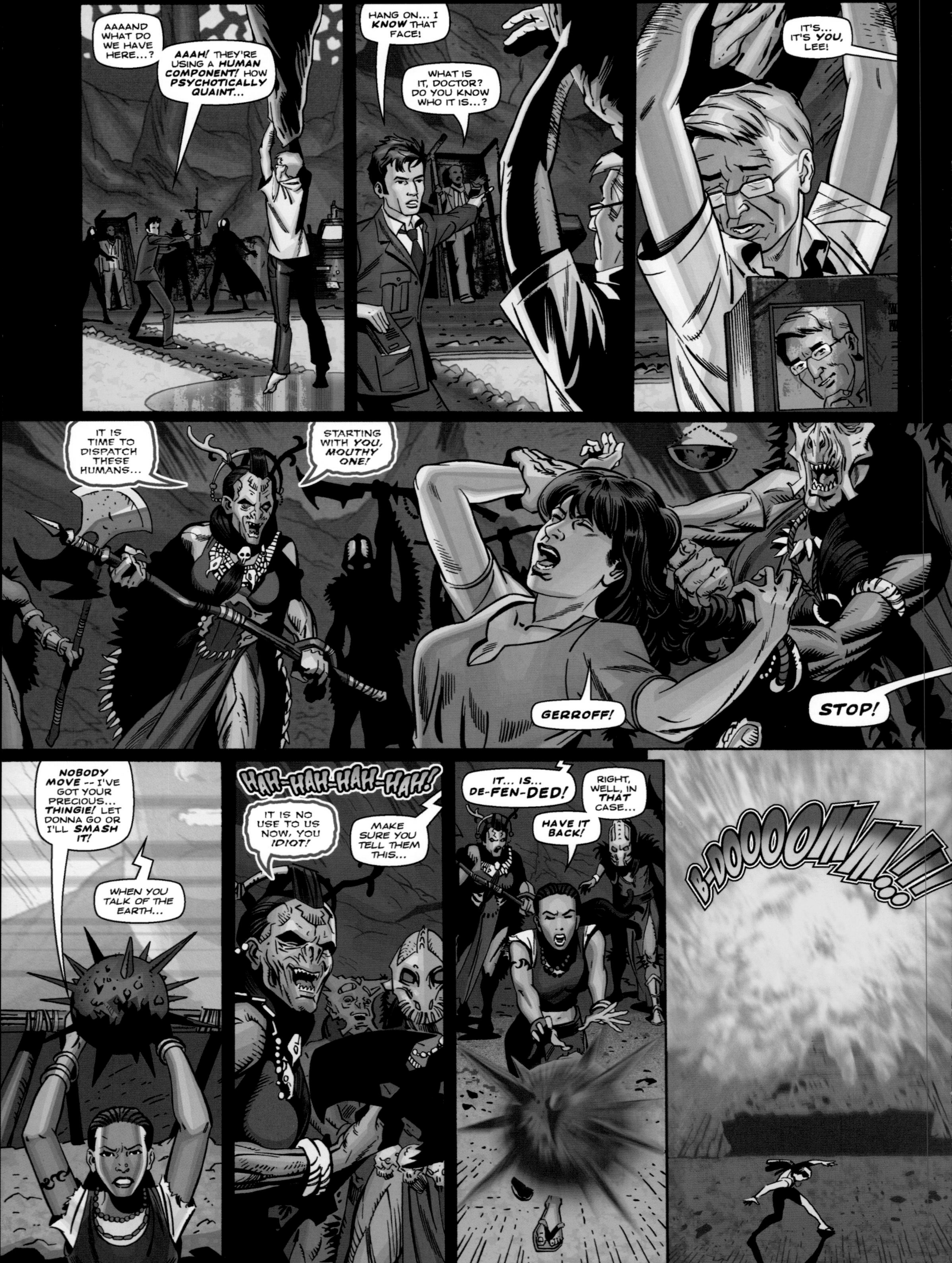
AAAAND WHAT DO WE HAVE HERE...?
AAAH! THEY'RE USING A HUMAN COMPONENT! HOW PSYCHOTICALLY QUAINT...
HANG ON... I KNOW THAT FACE!
WHAT IS IT, DOCTOR? DO YOU KNOW WHO IT IS...?
IT'S... IT'S YOU, LEE!
IT IS TIME TO DISPATCH THESE HUMANS...
STARTING WITH YOU, MOUTHY ONE!
GERROFF!
STOP!
NOBODY MOVE -- I'VE GOT YOUR PRECIOUS... THINGIE! LET DONNA GO OR I'LL SMASH IT!
WHEN YOU TALK OF THE EARTH...
HAH-HAH-HAH-HAH!
IT IS NO USE TO US NOW, YOU IDIOT!
MAKE SURE YOU TELL THEM THIS...
IT... IS... DE-FEN-DED!
RIGHT, WELL, IN THAT CASE...
HAVE IT BACK!
B-DOOOOOMM...!!!

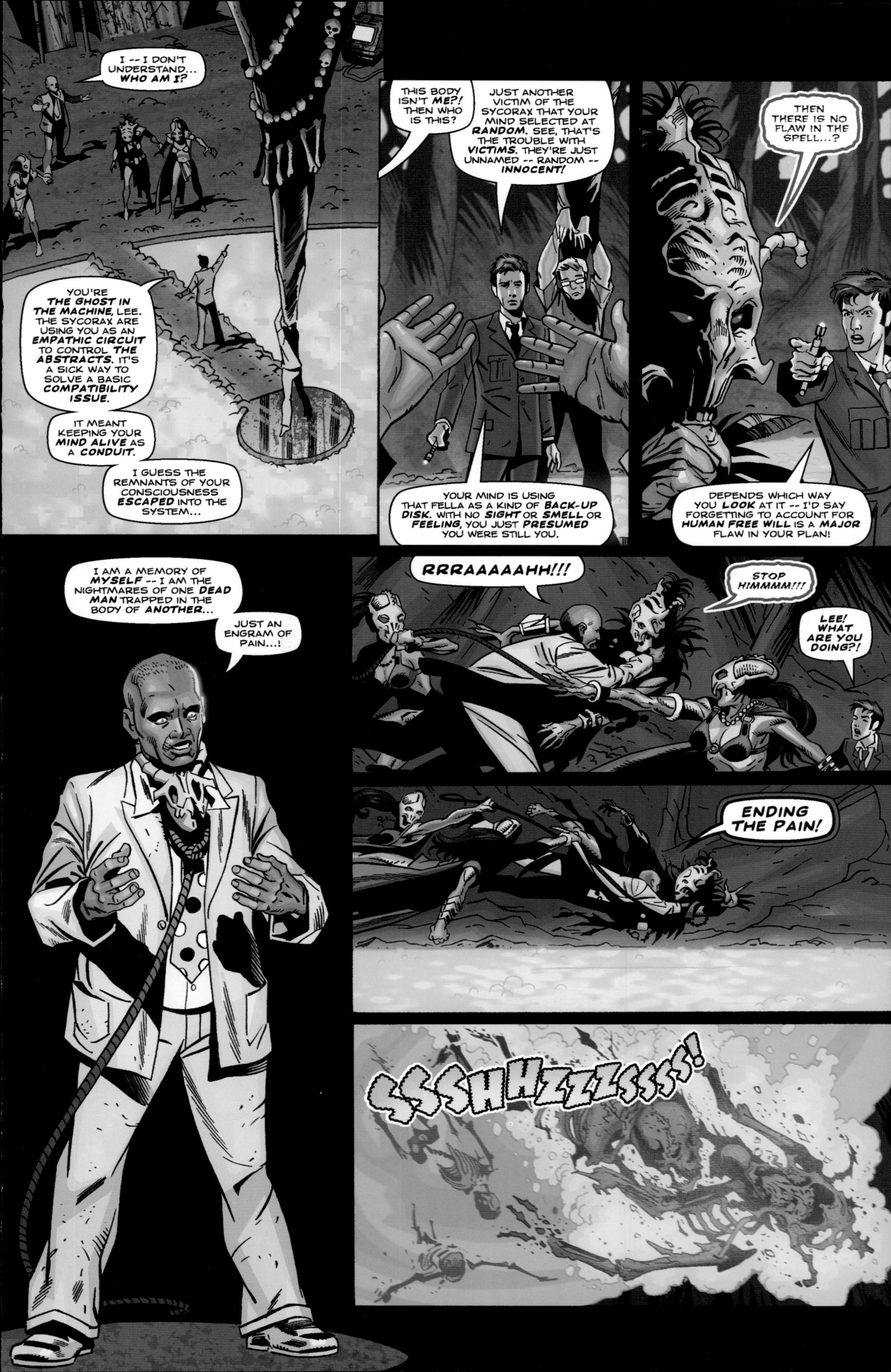
I -- I DON'T UNDERSTAND... WHO AM I?
YOU'RE THE GHOST IN THE MACHINE, LEE. THE SYCORAX ARE USING YOU AS AN EMPATHIC CIRCUIT TO CONTROL THE ABSTRACTS. IT'S A SICK WAY TO SOLVE A BASIC COMPATIBILITY ISSUE.
IT MEANT KEEPING YOUR MIND ALIVE AS A CONDUIT.
I GUESS THE REMNANTS OF YOUR CONSCIOUSNESS ESCAPED INTO THE SYSTEM...
THIS BODY ISN'T ME?! THEN WHO IS THIS?
JUST ANOTHER VICTIM OF THE SYCORAX THAT YOUR MIND SELECTED AT RANDOM. SEE, THAT'S THE TROUBLE WITH VICTIMS. THEY'RE JUST UNNAMED -- RANDOM -- INNOCENT!
YOUR MIND IS USING THAT FELLA AS A KIND OF BACK-UP DISK. WITH NO SIGHT OR SMELL OR FEELING, YOU JUST PRESUMED YOU WERE STILL YOU.
THEN THERE IS NO FLAW IN THE SPELL...?
DEPENDS WHICH WAY YOU LOOK AT IT -- I'D SAY FORGETTING TO ACCOUNT FOR HUMAN FREE WILL IS A MAJOR FLAW IN YOUR PLAN!
I AM A MEMORY OF MYSELF -- I AM THE NIGHTMARES OF ONE DEAD MAN TRAPPED IN THE BODY OF ANOTHER...
JUST AN ENGRAM OF PAIN...!
RRRAAAAAAHH!!!
STOP HIMMMM!!!
LEE! WHAT ARE YOU DOING?!
ENDING THE PAIN!
SSSHHZZZZSSSS!

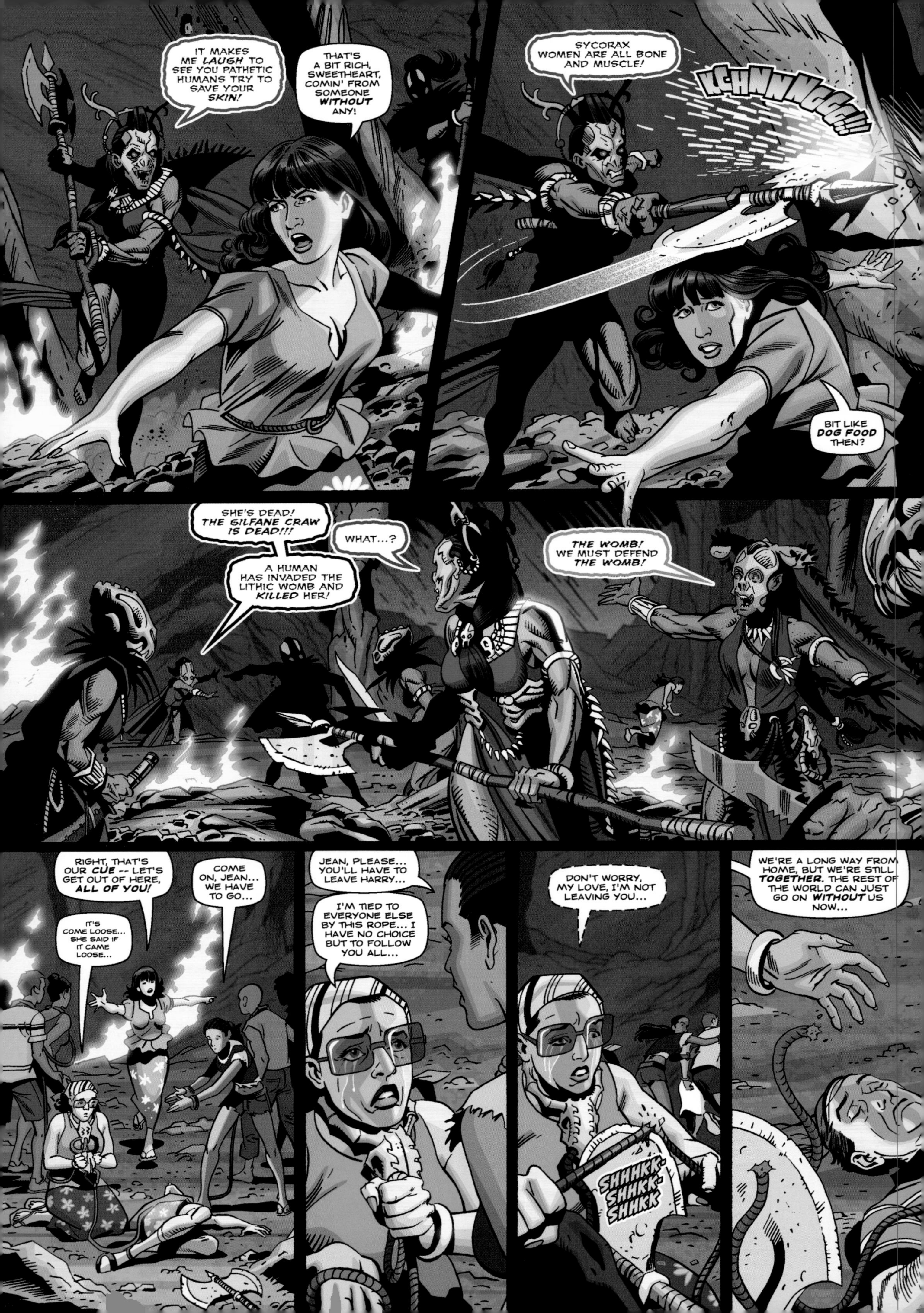
IT MAKES ME LAUGH TO SEE YOU PATHETIC HUMANS TRY TO SAVE YOUR SKIN!
THAT'S A BIT RICH, SWEETHEART, COMIN' FROM SOMEONE WITHOUT ANY!
SYCORAX WOMEN ARE ALL BONE AND MUSCLE!
KCHNNNGG!!!
BIT LIKE DOG FOOD THEN?
SHE'S DEAD! THE GILFANE CRAW IS DEAD!!!
WHAT...?
A HUMAN HAS INVADED THE LITHIC WOMB AND KILLED HER!
THE WOMB! WE MUST DEFEND THE WOMB!
RIGHT, THAT'S OUR CUE -- LET'S GET OUT OF HERE, ALL OF YOU!
COME ON, JEAN... WE HAVE TO GO...
IT'S COME LOOSE... SHE SAID IF IT CAME LOOSE...
JEAN, PLEASE... YOU'LL HAVE TO LEAVE HARRY...
I'M TIED TO EVERYONE ELSE BY THIS ROPE... I HAVE NO CHOICE BUT TO FOLLOW YOU ALL...
DON'T WORRY, MY LOVE, I'M NOT LEAVING YOU...
SHHHKK-SHHKK-SHHKK
WE'RE A LONG WAY FROM HOME, BUT WE'RE STILL TOGETHER. THE REST OF THE WORLD CAN JUST GO ON WITHOUT US NOW...

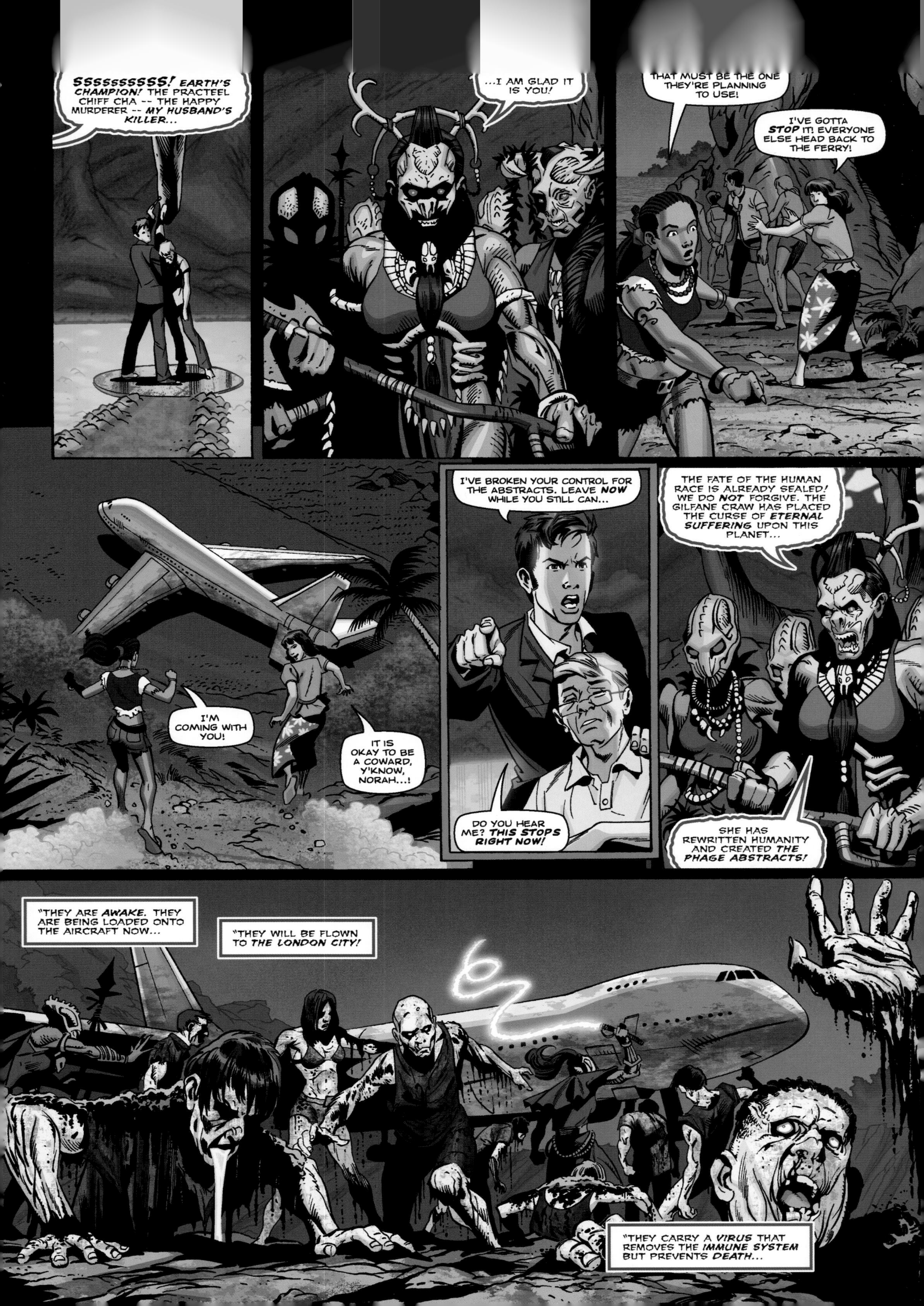
SSSSSSSSSS! EARTH'S CHAMPION! THE PRACTEEL CHIFF CHA -- THE HAPPY MURDERER -- MY HUSBAND'S KILLER...
...I AM GLAD IT IS YOU!
THAT MUST BE THE ONE THEY'RE PLANNING TO USE!
I'VE GOTTA STOP IT! EVERYONE ELSE HEAD BACK TO THE FERRY!
I'M COMING WITH YOU!
IT IS OKAY TO BE A COWARD, Y'KNOW, NORAH...!
I'VE BROKEN YOUR CONTROL FOR THE ABSTRACTS. LEAVE NOW WHILE YOU STILL CAN...
DO YOU HEAR ME? THIS STOPS RIGHT NOW!
THE FATE OF THE HUMAN RACE IS ALREADY SEALED! WE DO NOT FORGIVE. THE GILFANE CRAW HAS PLACED THE CURSE OF ETERNAL SUFFERING UPON THIS PLANET...
SHE HAS REWRITTEN HUMANITY AND CREATED THE PHAGE ABSTRACTS!
"THEY ARE AWAKE. THEY ARE BEING LOADED ONTO THE AIRCRAFT NOW...
"THEY WILL BE FLOWN TO THE LONDON CITY!
"THEY CARRY A VIRUS THAT REMOVES THE IMMUNE SYSTEM BUT PREVENTS DEATH...

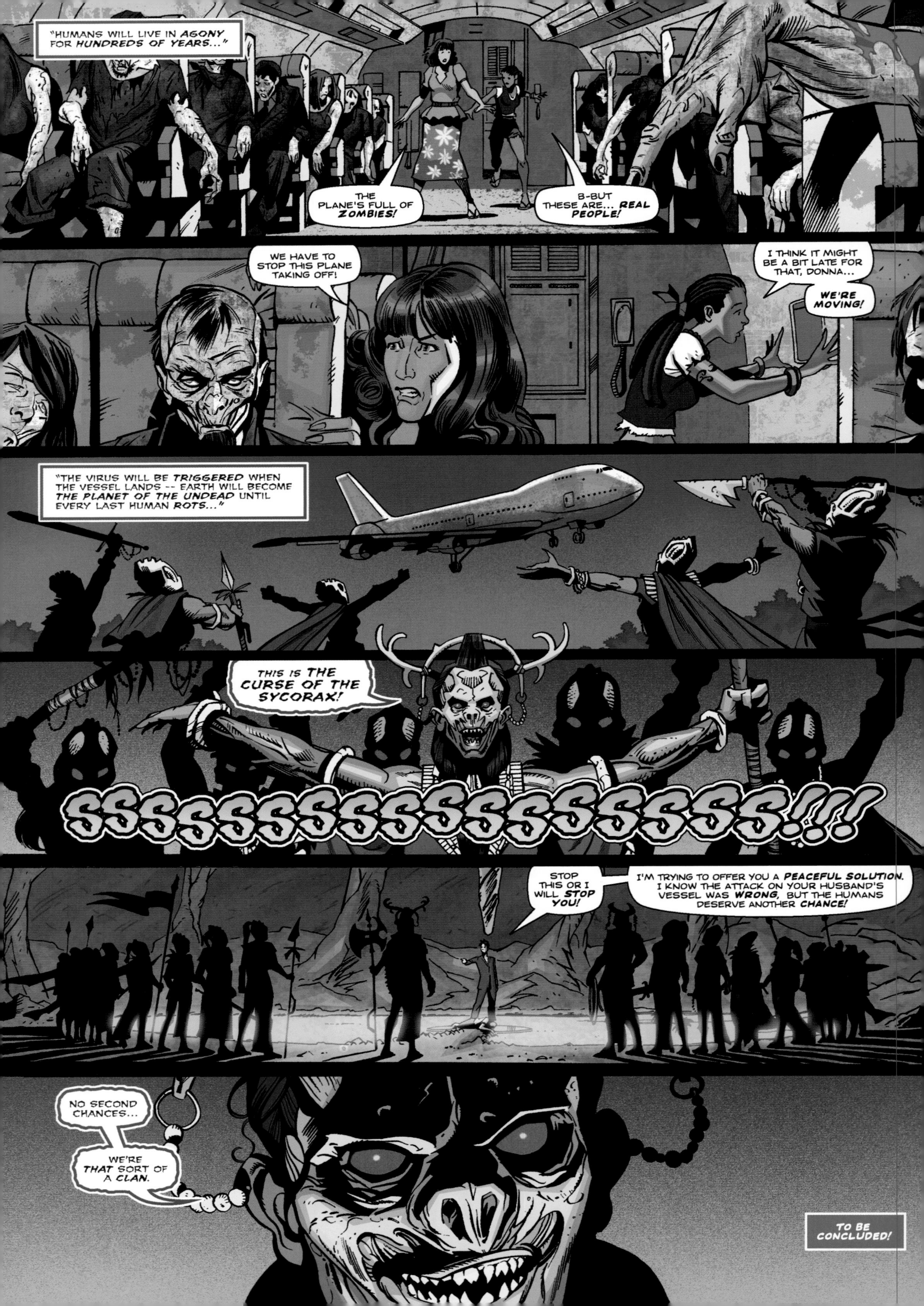
"HUMANS WILL LIVE IN AGONY FOR HUNDREDS OF YEARS..."
THE PLANE'S FULL OF ZOMBIES!
B-BUT THESE ARE... REAL PEOPLE!
WE HAVE TO STOP THIS PLANE TAKING OFF!
I THINK IT MIGHT BE A BIT LATE FOR THAT, DONNA...
WE'RE MOVING!
"THE VIRUS WILL BE TRIGGERED WHEN THE VESSEL LANDS -- EARTH WILL BECOME THE PLANET OF THE UNDEAD UNTIL EVERY LAST HUMAN ROTS..."
THIS IS THE CURSE OF THE SYCORAX!
SSSSSSSSSSSSSSSSSSS!!!
STOP THIS OR I WILL STOP YOU!
I'M TRYING TO OFFER YOU A PEACEFUL SOLUTION. I KNOW THE ATTACK ON YOUR HUSBAND'S VESSEL WAS WRONG, BUT THE HUMANS DESERVE ANOTHER CHANCE!
NO SECOND CHANCES...
WE'RE THAT SORT OF A CLAN.
TO BE CONCLUDED!

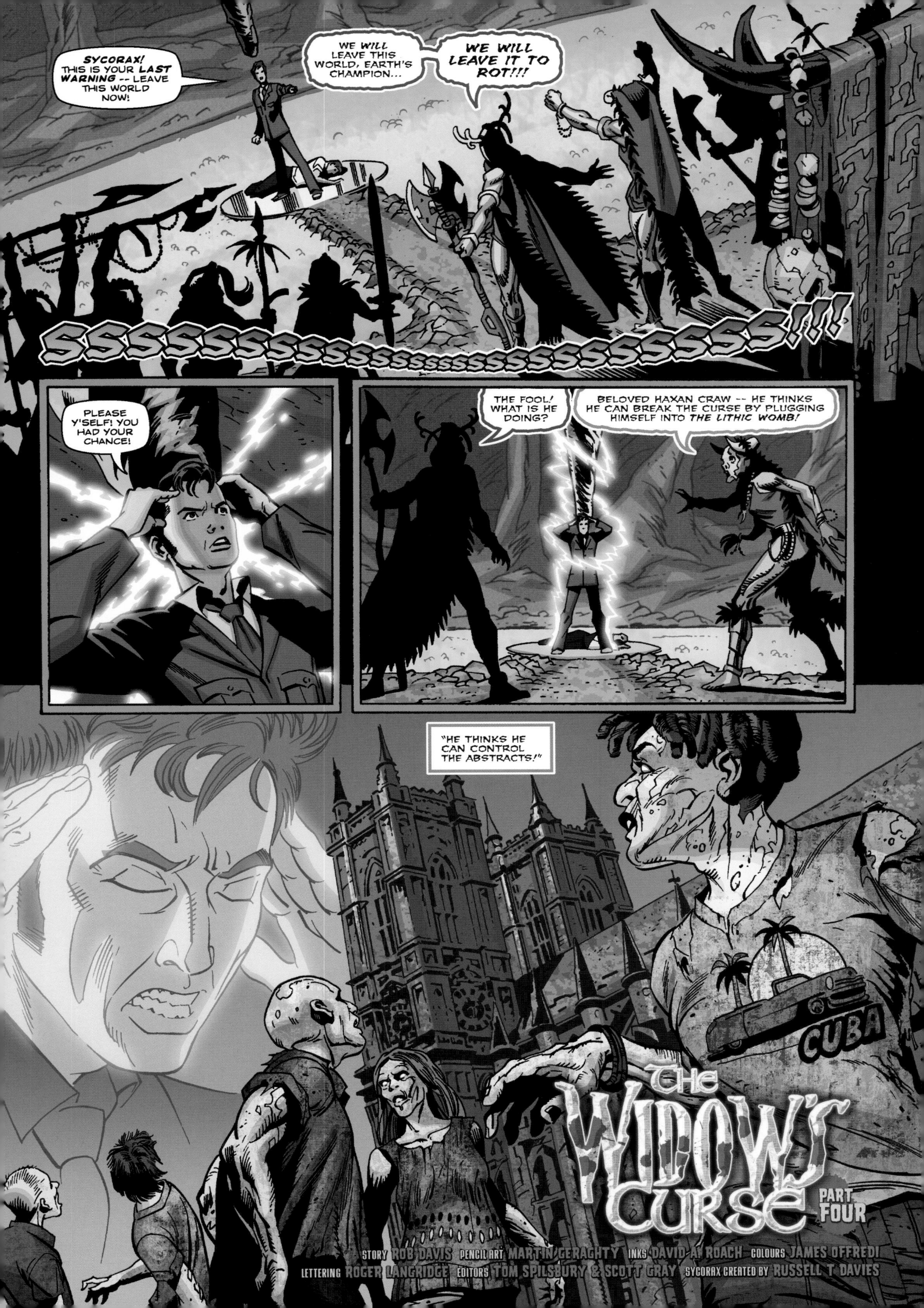
SYCORAX! THIS IS YOUR LAST WARNING -- LEAVE THIS WORLD NOW!
WE WILL LEAVE THIS WORLD, EARTH'S CHAMPION...
WE WILL LEAVE IT TO ROT!!!
SSSSSSSSSSSSSSSSSSSSSSSSSSSS!!!!
PLEASE Y'SELF! YOU HAD YOUR CHANCE!
THE FOOL! WHAT IS HE DOING?
BELOVED HAXAN CRAW -- HE THINKS HE CAN BREAK THE CURSE BY PLUGGING HIMSELF INTO THE LITHIC WOMB!
"HE THINKS HE CAN CONTROL THE ABSTRACTS!"
CUBA
THE WIDOW'S CURSE PART FOUR
STORY ROB DAVIS PENCIL ART MARTIN GERAGHTY INKS DAVID A. ROACH COLOURS JAMES OFFREDI
LETTERING ROGER LANGRIDGE EDITORS TOM SPILSBURY & SCOTT GRAY SYCORAX CREATED BY RUSSELL T DAVIES

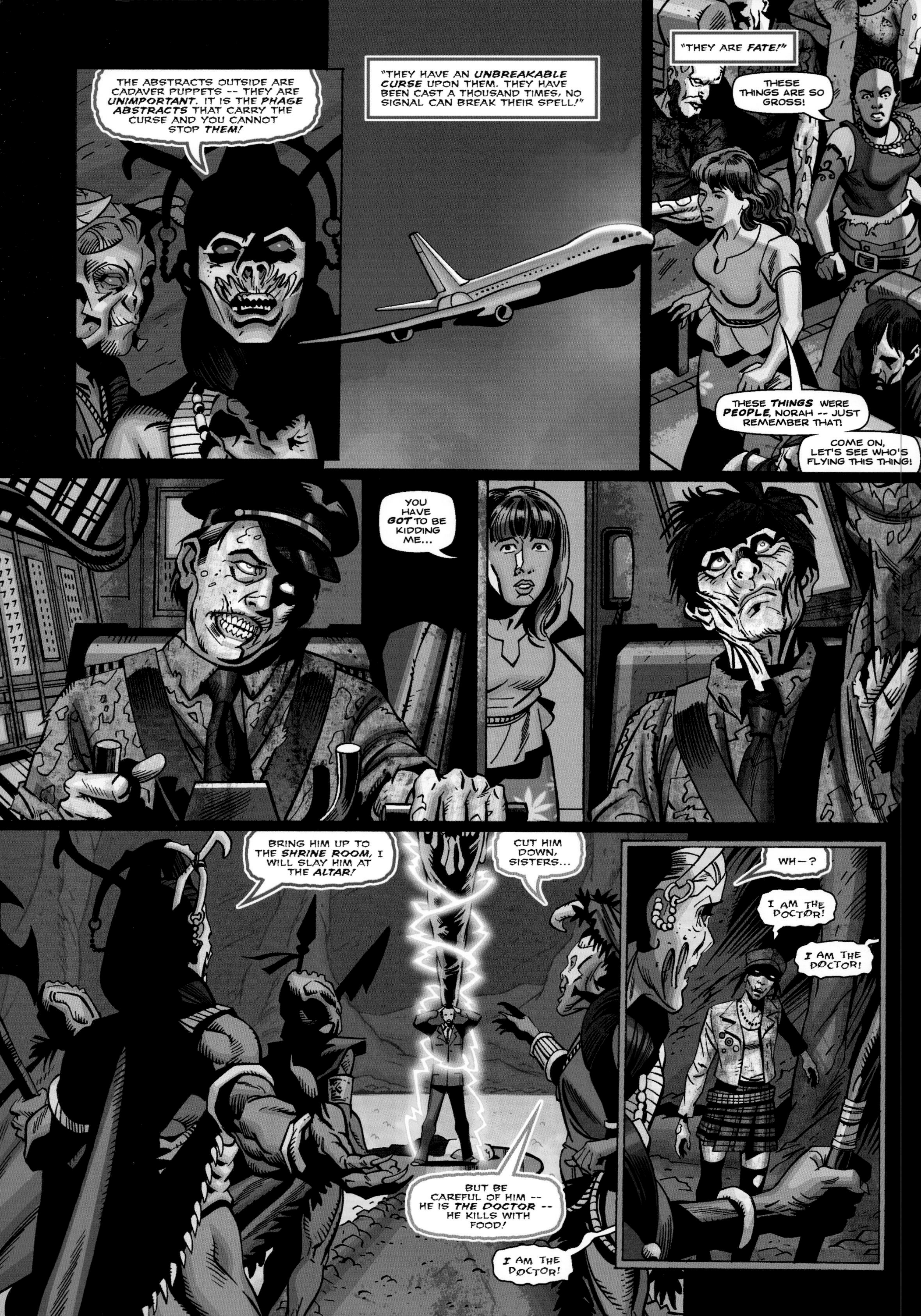
THE ABSTRACTS OUTSIDE ARE CADAVER PUPPETS -- THEY ARE UNIMPORTANT. IT IS THE PHAGE ABSTRACTS THAT CARRY THE CURSE AND YOU CANNOT STOP THEM!
"THEY HAVE AN UNBREAKABLE CURSE UPON THEM. THEY HAVE BEEN CAST A THOUSAND TIMES, NO SIGNAL CAN BREAK THEIR SPELL!"
"THEY ARE FATE!"
THESE THINGS ARE SO GROSS!
THESE THINGS WERE PEOPLE, NORAH -- JUST REMEMBER THAT!
COME ON, LET'S SEE WHO'S FLYING THIS THING!
YOU HAVE GOT TO BE KIDDING ME...
BRING HIM UP TO THE SHRINE ROOM, I WILL SLAY HIM AT THE ALTAR!
CUT HIM DOWN, SISTERS...
BUT BE CAREFUL OF HIM -- HE IS THE DOCTOR -- HE KILLS WITH FOOD!
I AM THE DOCTOR!
WH—?
I AM THE DOCTOR!
I AM THE DOCTOR!

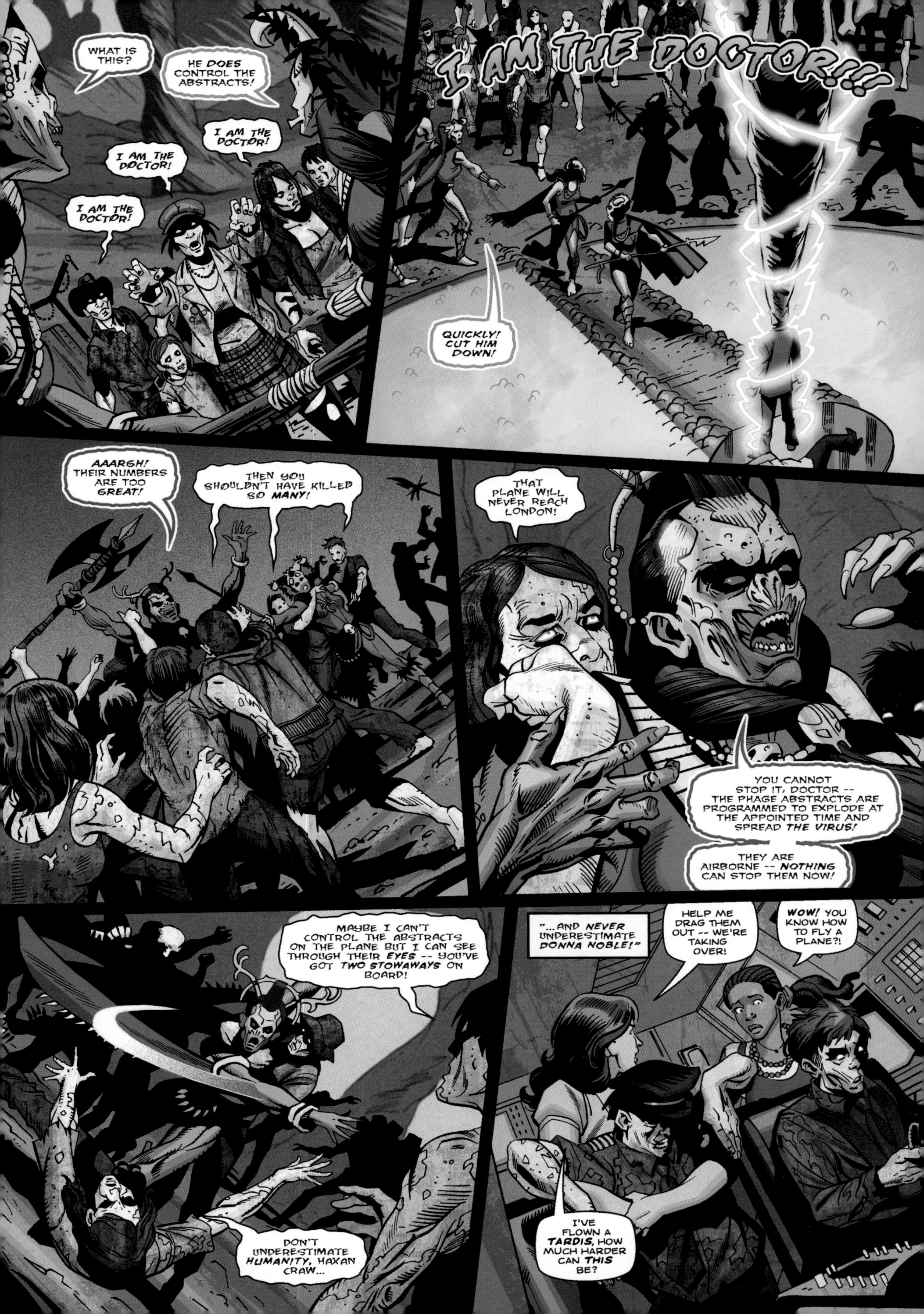
WHAT IS THIS?
HE DOES CONTROL THE ABSTRACTS!
I AM THE DOCTOR!
I AM THE DOCTOR!
I AM THE DOCTOR!
I AM THE DOCTOR!!!
QUICKLY! CUT HIM DOWN!
AAARGH! THEIR NUMBERS ARE TOO GREAT!
THEN YOU SHOULDN'T HAVE KILLED SO MANY!
THAT PLANE WILL NEVER REACH LONDON!
YOU CANNOT STOP IT, DOCTOR -- THE PHAGE ABSTRACTS ARE PROGRAMMED TO EXPLODE AT THE APPOINTED TIME AND SPREAD THE VIRUS!
THEY ARE AIRBORNE -- NOTHING CAN STOP THEM NOW!
MAYBE I CAN'T CONTROL THE ABSTRACTS ON THE PLANE BUT I CAN SEE THROUGH THEIR EYES -- YOU'VE GOT TWO STOWAWAYS ON BOARD!
DON'T UNDERESTIMATE HUMANITY, HAXAN CRAW...
"...AND NEVER UNDERESTIMATE DONNA NOBLE!"
HELP ME DRAG THEM OUT -- WE'RE TAKING OVER!
WOW! YOU KNOW HOW TO FLY A PLANE?!
I'VE FLOWN A TARDIS, HOW MUCH HARDER CAN THIS BE?

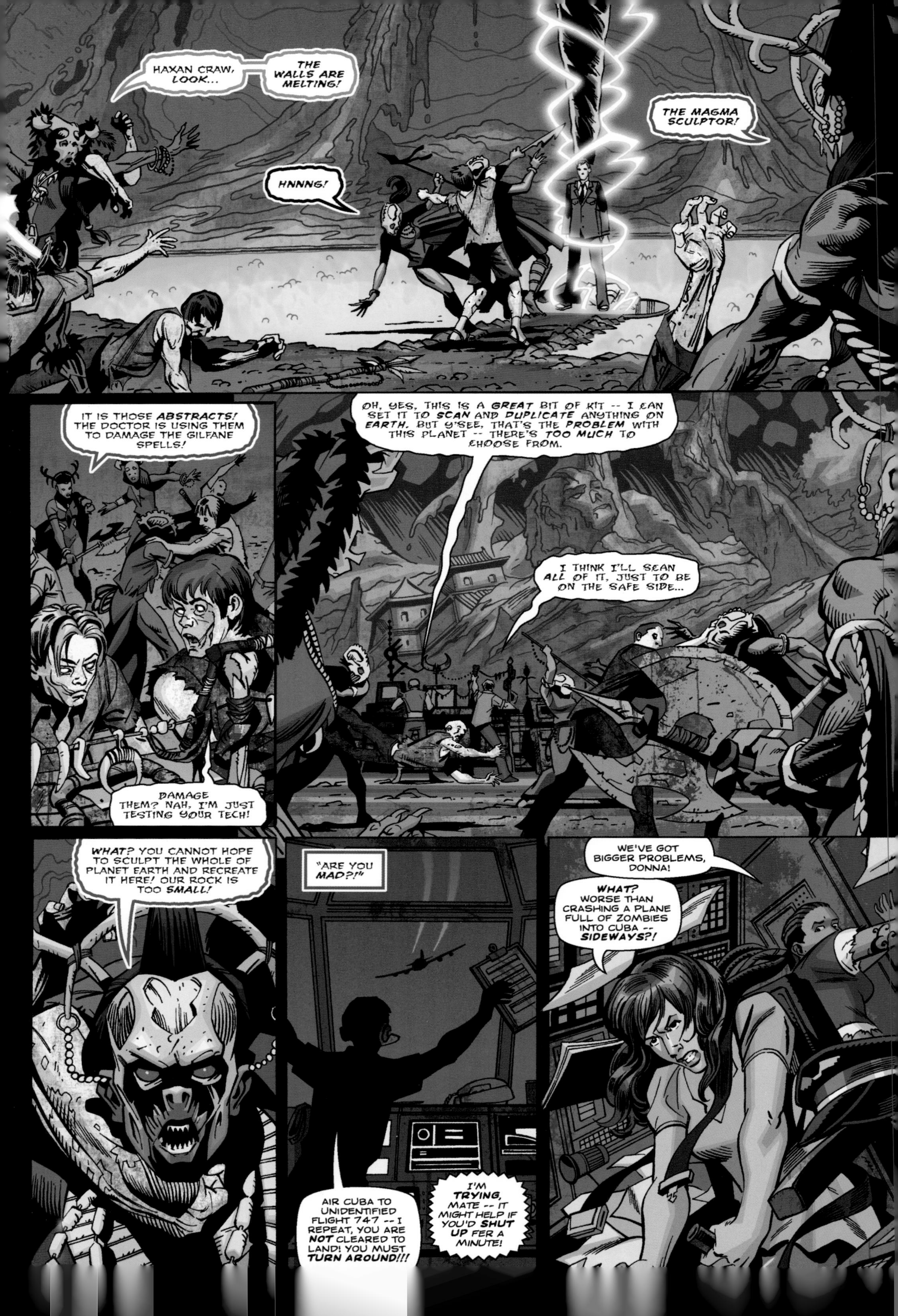

HAXAN CRAW, LOOK...
THE WALLS ARE MELTING!
HNNNG!
THE MAGMA SCULPTOR!
IT IS THOSE ABSTRACTS! THE DOCTOR IS USING THEM TO DAMAGE THE GILFANE SPELLS!
DAMAGE THEM? NAH, I'M JUST TESTING YOUR TECH!
OH, YES, THIS IS A GREAT BIT OF KIT -- I CAN SET IT TO SCAN AND DUPLICATE ANYTHING ON EARTH. BUT Y'SEE, THAT'S THE PROBLEM WITH THIS PLANET -- THERE'S TOO MUCH TO CHOOSE FROM.
I THINK I'LL SCAN ALL OF IT, JUST TO BE ON THE SAFE SIDE...
WHAT? YOU CANNOT HOPE TO SCULPT THE WHOLE OF PLANET EARTH AND RECREATE IT HERE! OUR ROCK IS TOO SMALL!
"ARE YOU MAD?!"
AIR CUBA TO UNIDENTIFIED FLIGHT 747 -- I REPEAT, YOU ARE NOT CLEARED TO LAND! YOU MUST TURN AROUND!!!
I'M TRYING, MATE -- IT MIGHT HELP IF YOU'D SHUT UP FER A MINUTE!
WE'VE GOT BIGGER PROBLEMS, DONNA!
WHAT? WORSE THAN CRASHING A PLANE FULL OF ZOMBIES INTO CUBA -- SIDEWAYS?!

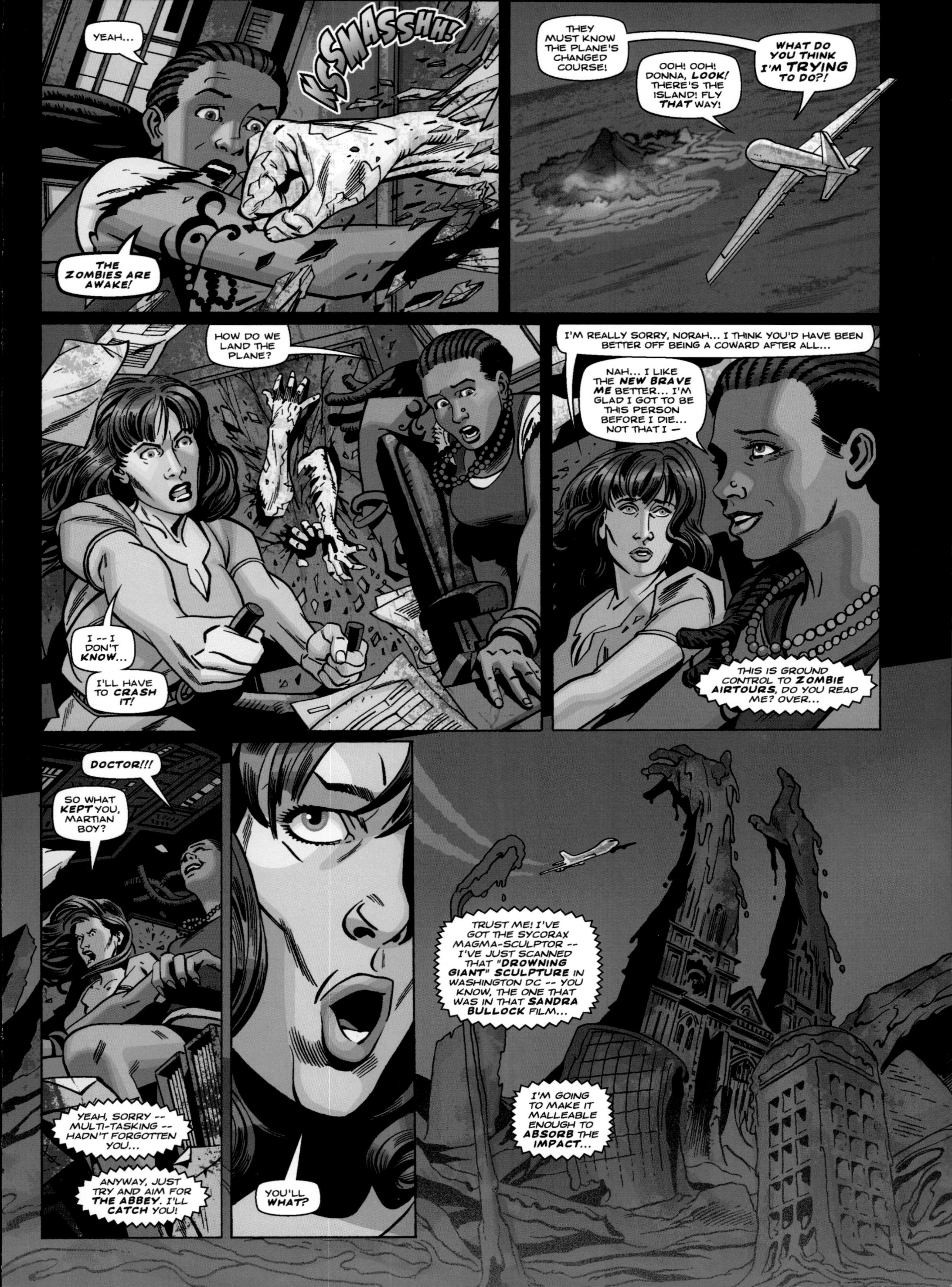
YEAH...
K'SMASSHH!
THE ZOMBIES ARE AWAKE!
THEY MUST KNOW THE PLANE'S CHANGED COURSE!
OOH! OOH! DONNA, LOOK! THERE'S THE ISLAND! FLY THAT WAY!
WHAT DO YOU THINK I'M TRYING TO DO?!
HOW DO WE LAND THE PLANE?
I -- I DON'T KNOW...
I'LL HAVE TO CRASH IT!
I'M REALLY SORRY, NORAH... I THINK YOU'D HAVE BEEN BETTER OFF BEING A COWARD AFTER ALL...
NAH... I LIKE THE NEW BRAVE ME BETTER... I'M GLAD I GOT TO BE THIS PERSON BEFORE I DIE... NOT THAT I —
THIS IS GROUND CONTROL TO ZOMBIE AIRTOURS, DO YOU READ ME? OVER...
DOCTOR!!!
SO WHAT KEPT YOU, MARTIAN BOY?
YEAH, SORRY -- MULTI-TASKING -- HADN'T FORGOTTEN YOU...
ANYWAY, JUST TRY AND AIM FOR THE ABBEY. I'LL CATCH YOU!
YOU'LL WHAT?
TRUST ME! I'VE GOT THE SYCORAX MAGMA-SCULPTOR -- I'VE JUST SCANNED THAT "DROWNING GIANT" SCULPTURE IN WASHINGTON DC -- YOU KNOW, THE ONE THAT WAS IN THAT SANDRA BULLOCK FILM...
I'M GOING TO MAKE IT MALLEABLE ENOUGH TO ABSORB THE IMPACT...

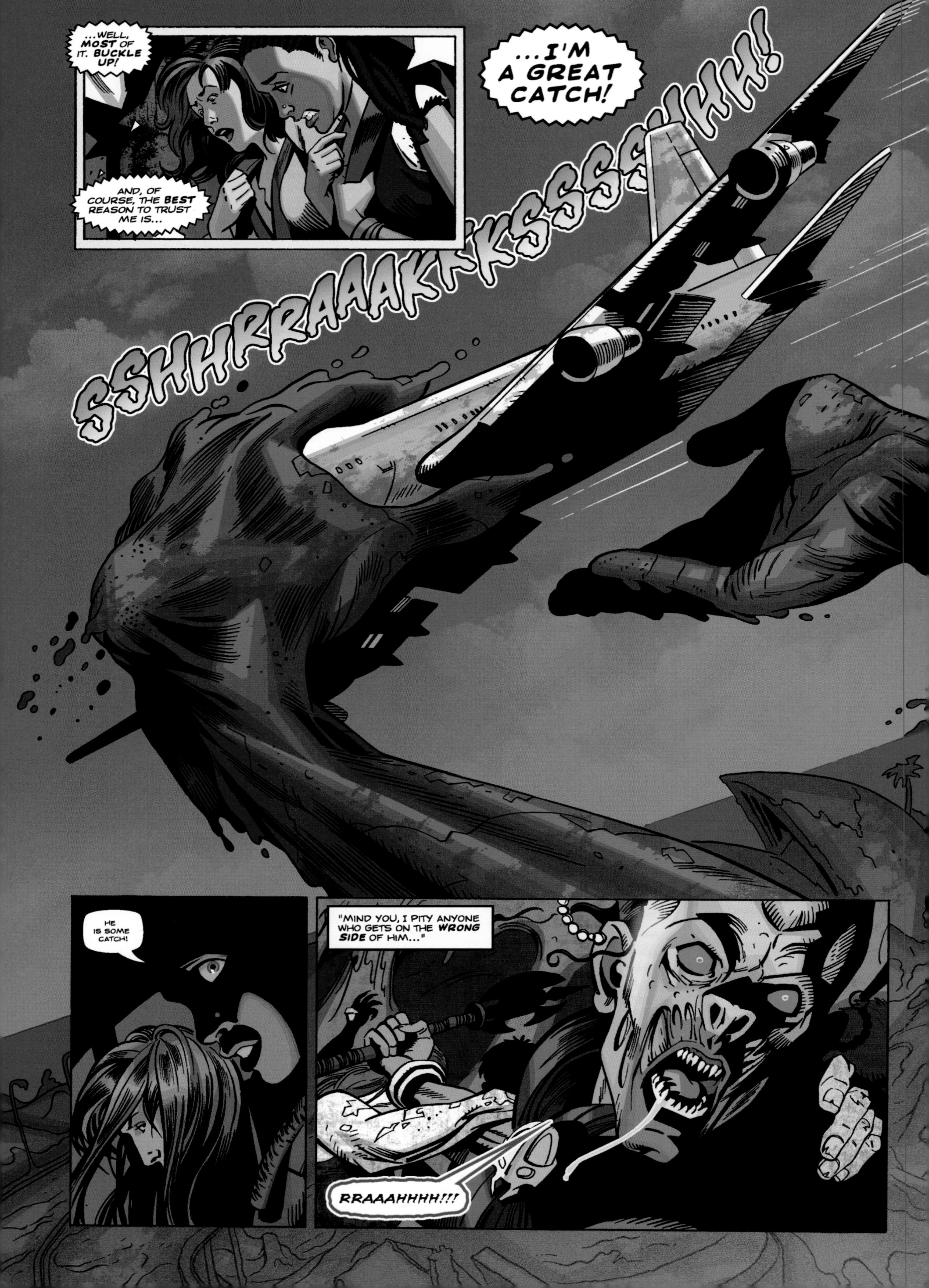

...WELL, MOST OF IT. BUCKLE UP!
AND, OF COURSE, THE BEST REASON TO TRUST ME IS...
...I'M A GREAT CATCH!
SSHHRRAAAKKKSSSSSHHH!
HE IS SOME CATCH!
"MIND YOU, I PITY ANYONE WHO GETS ON THE WRONG SIDE OF HIM..."
RRAAAHHHH!!!

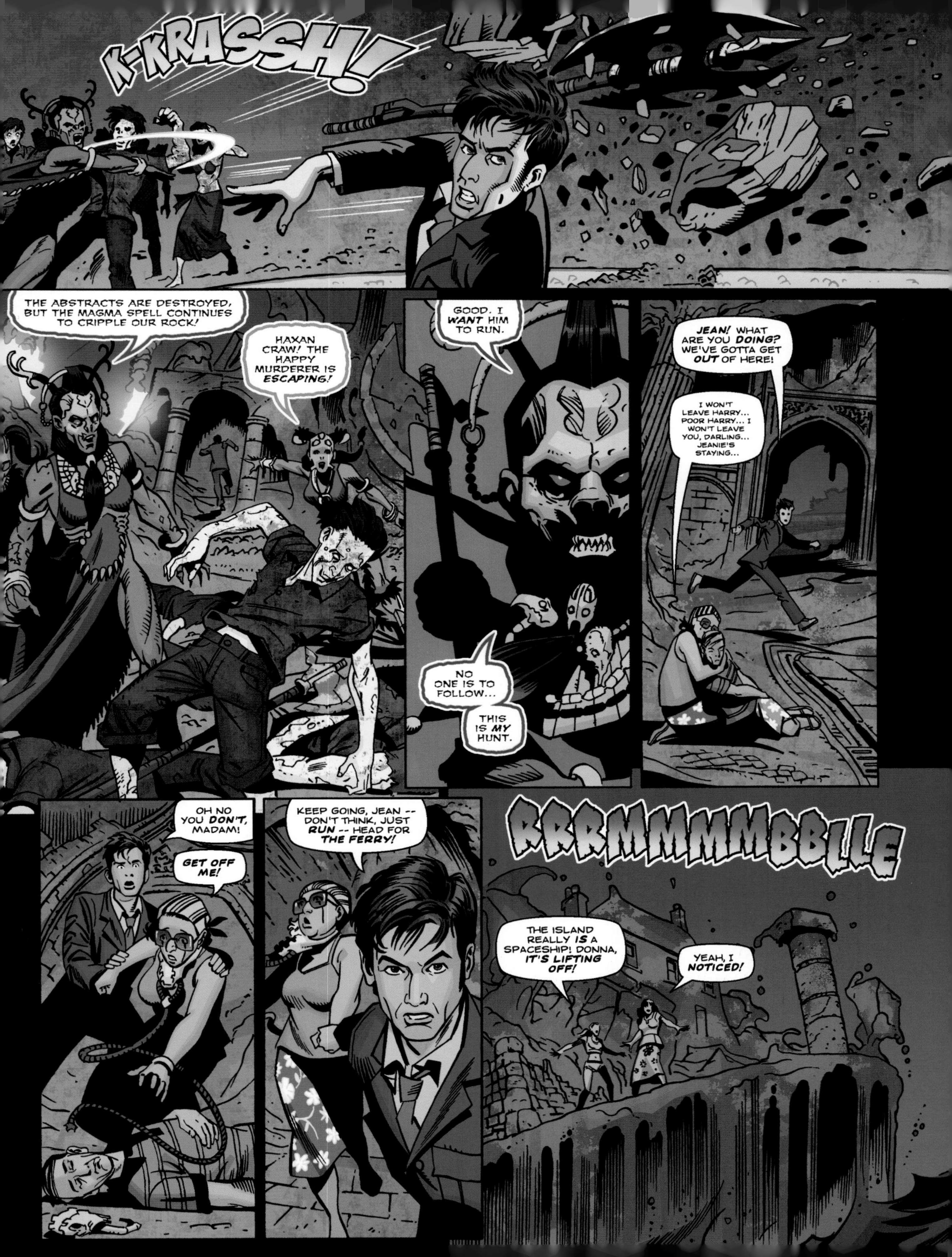
K-KRASSH!
THE ABSTRACTS ARE DESTROYED, BUT THE MAGMA SPELL CONTINUES TO CRIPPLE OUR ROCK!
HAXAN CRAW! THE HAPPY MURDERER IS ESCAPING!
GOOD. I WANT HIM TO RUN.
NO ONE IS TO FOLLOW...
THIS IS MY HUNT.
JEAN! WHAT ARE YOU DOING? WE'VE GOTTA GET OUT OF HERE!
I WON'T LEAVE HARRY... POOR HARRY... I WON'T LEAVE YOU, DARLING... JEANIE'S STAYING...
OH NO YOU DON'T, MADAM!
GET OFF ME!
KEEP GOING, JEAN -- DON'T THINK, JUST RUN -- HEAD FOR THE FERRY!
BRRRMMMMMBBLLE
THE ISLAND REALLY IS A SPACESHIP! DONNA, IT'S LIFTING OFF!
YEAH, I NOTICED!

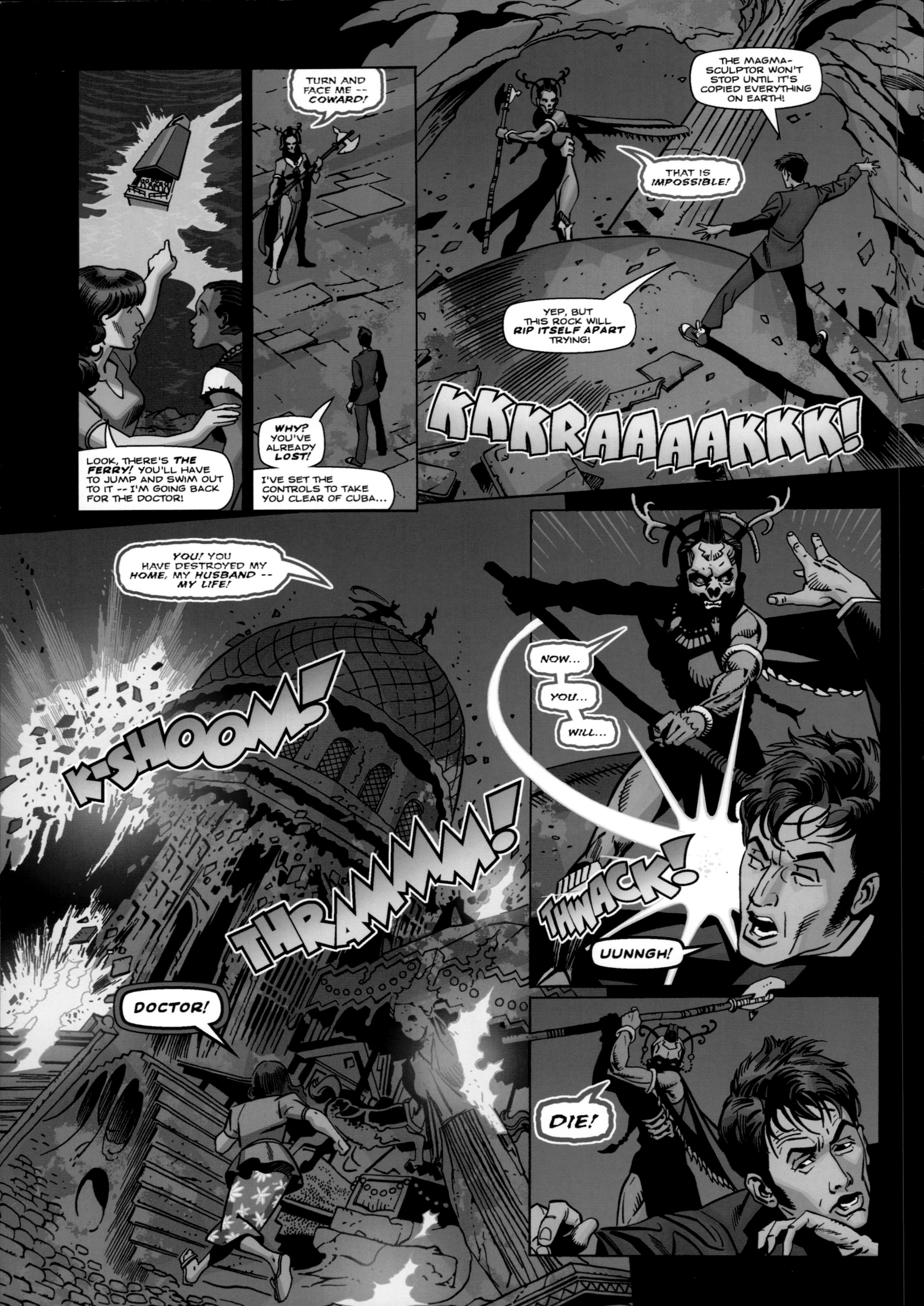
LOOK, THERE'S THE FERRY! YOU'LL HAVE TO JUMP AND SWIM OUT TO IT -- I'M GOING BACK FOR THE DOCTOR!
TURN AND FACE ME -- COWARD!
WHY? YOU'VE ALREADY LOST!
I'VE SET THE CONTROLS TO TAKE YOU CLEAR OF CUBA...
THE MAGMA-SCULPTOR WON'T STOP UNTIL IT'S COPIED EVERYTHING ON EARTH!
THAT IS IMPOSSIBLE!
YEP, BUT THIS ROCK WILL RIP ITSELF APART TRYING!
KKKRAAAAAKKK!
YOU! YOU HAVE DESTROYED MY HOME, MY HUSBAND -- MY LIFE!
K-SHOOM!
THRAMMM!
DOCTOR!
NOW...
YOU...
WILL...
THWACK!
UUNNGH!
DIE!

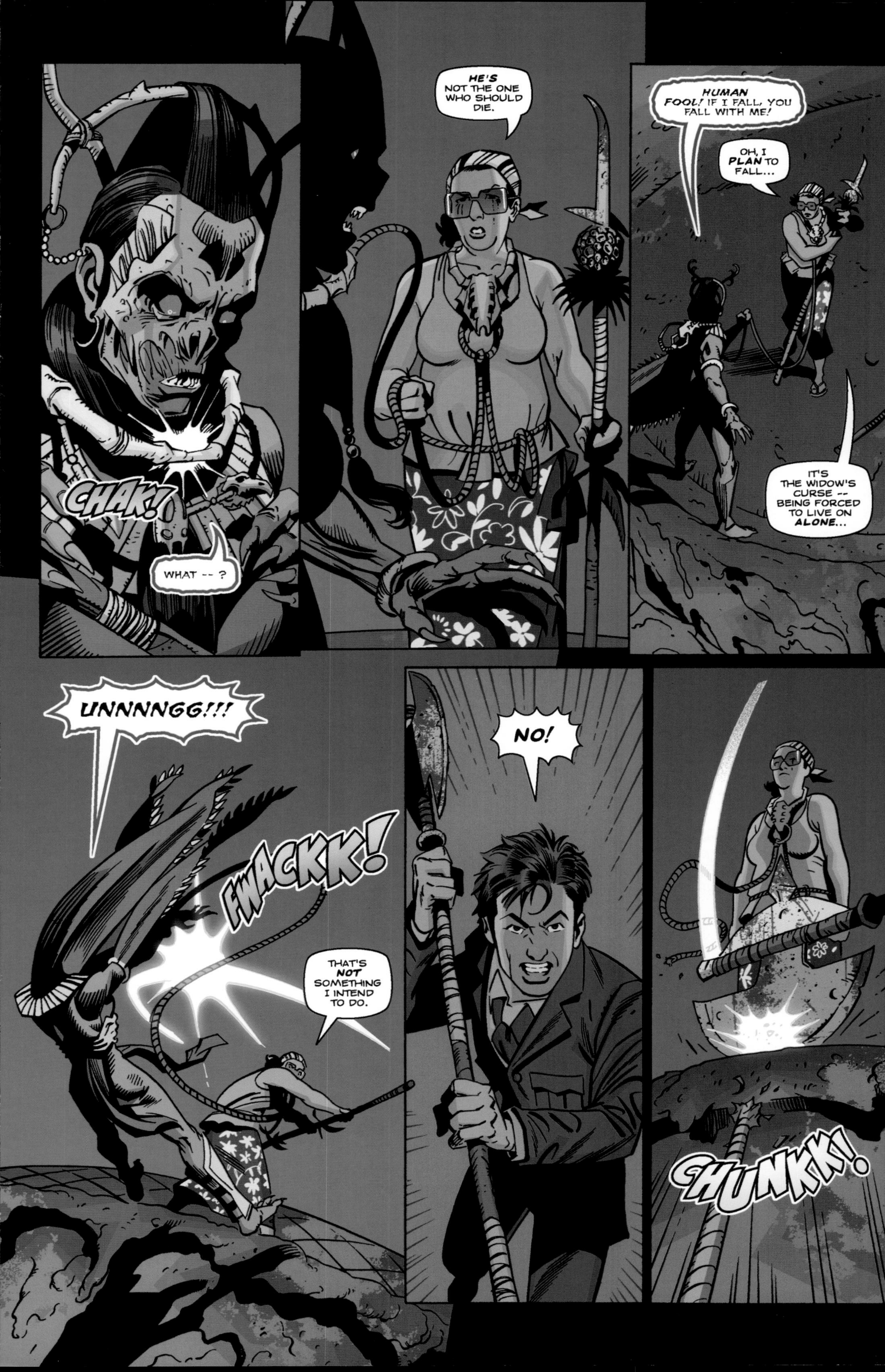
CHAK!
WHAT -- ?
HE'S NOT THE ONE WHO SHOULD DIE.
HUMAN FOOL! IF I FALL, YOU FALL WITH ME!
OH, I PLAN TO FALL...
IT'S THE WIDOW'S CURSE -- BEING FORCED TO LIVE ON ALONE...
UNNNNGG!!!
FWACKK!
THAT'S NOT SOMETHING I INTEND TO DO.
NO!
CHUNKK!

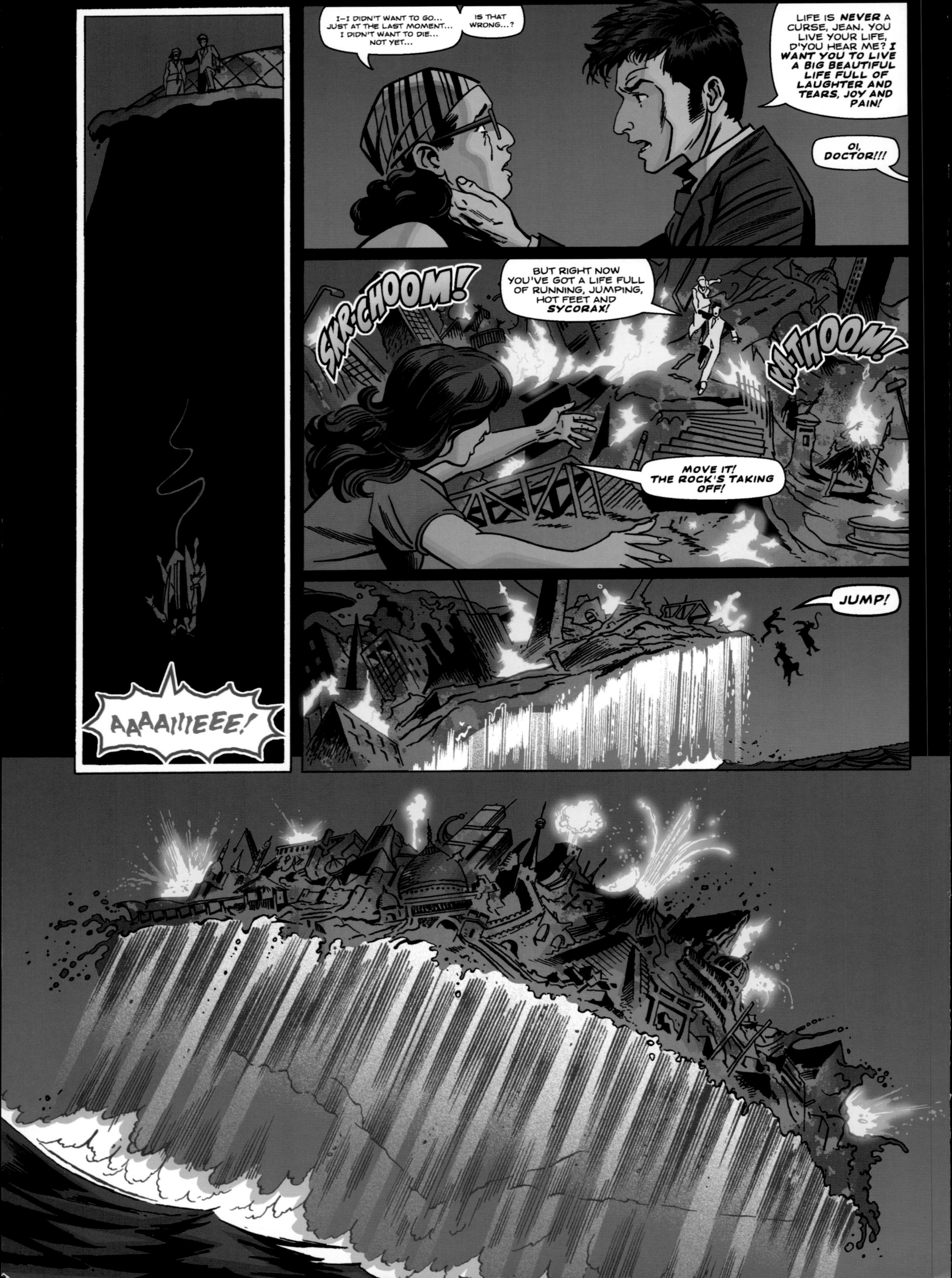
AAAAIIIIEEE!
I–I DIDN'T WANT TO GO... JUST AT THE LAST MOMENT... I DIDN'T WANT TO DIE... NOT YET...
IS THAT WRONG...?
LIFE IS NEVER A CURSE, JEAN. YOU LIVE YOUR LIFE, D'YOU HEAR ME? I WANT YOU TO LIVE A BIG BEAUTIFUL LIFE FULL OF LAUGHTER AND TEARS, JOY AND PAIN!
OI, DOCTOR!!!
SKR-CHOOM!
BUT RIGHT NOW YOU'VE GOT A LIFE FULL OF RUNNING, JUMPING, HOT FEET AND SYCORAX!
KA-THOOM!
MOVE IT! THE ROCK'S TAKING OFF!
JUMP!

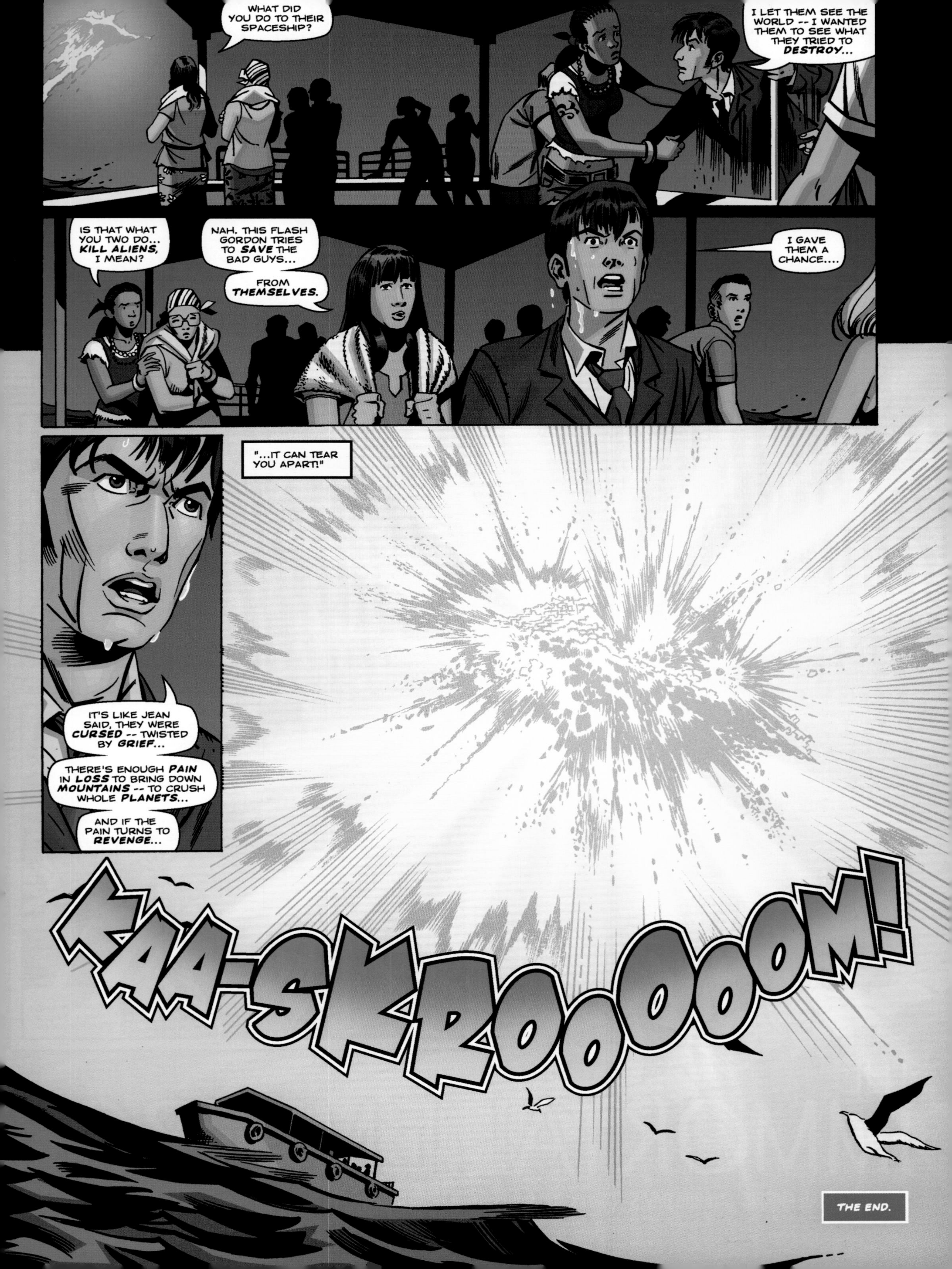
WHAT DID YOU DO TO THEIR SPACESHIP?
I LET THEM SEE THE WORLD -- I WANTED THEM TO SEE WHAT THEY TRIED TO DESTROY...
IS THAT WHAT YOU TWO DO... KILL ALIENS, I MEAN?
NAH. THIS FLASH GORDON TRIES TO SAVE THE BAD GUYS...
FROM THEMSELVES.
I GAVE THEM A CHANCE....
"...IT CAN TEAR YOU APART!"
IT'S LIKE JEAN SAID, THEY WERE CURSED -- TWISTED BY GRIEF...
THERE'S ENOUGH PAIN IN LOSS TO BRING DOWN MOUNTAINS -- TO CRUSH WHOLE PLANETS...
AND IF THE PAIN TURNS TO REVENGE...
KAA-SKROOOOOOM!
THE END.

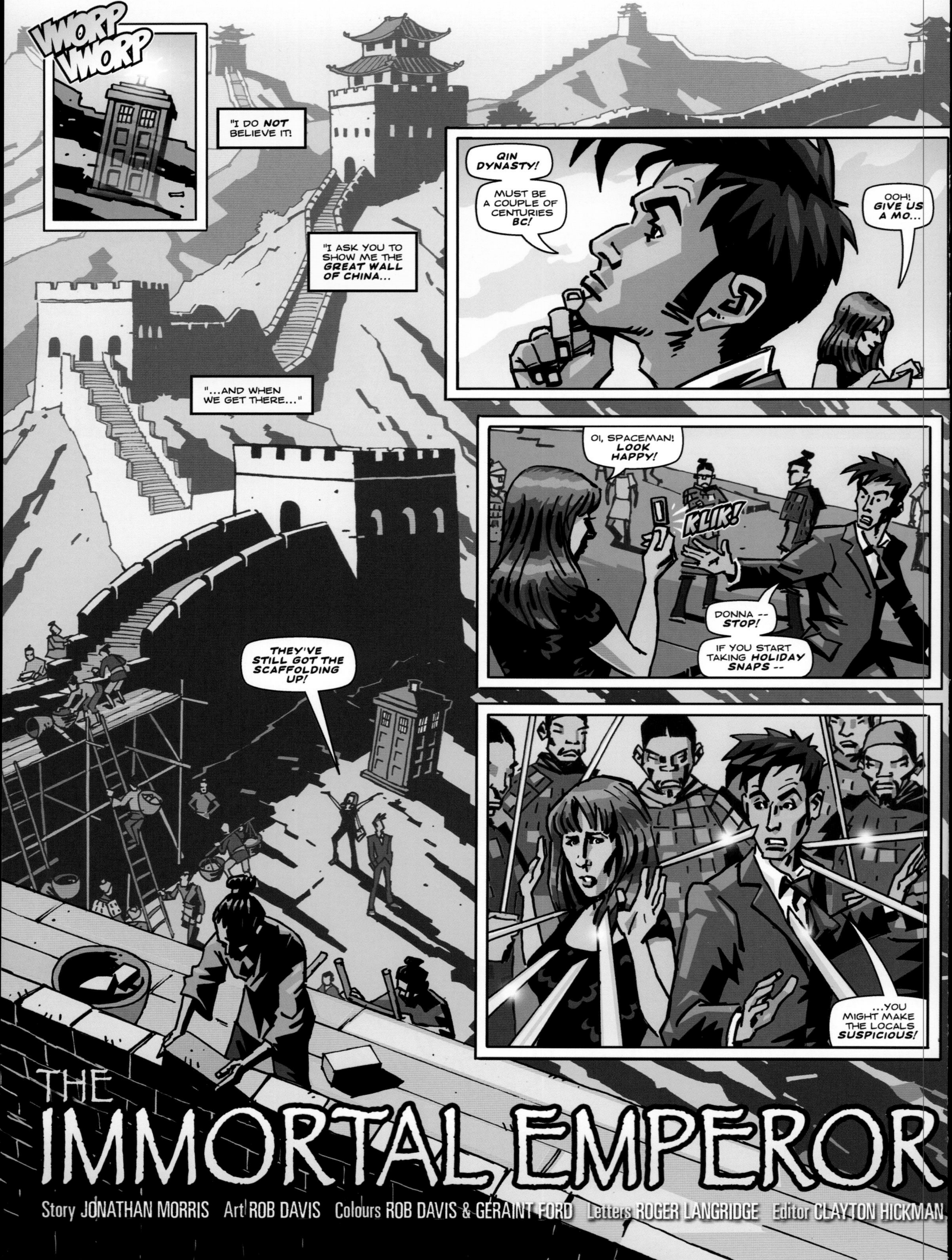

VWORP VWORP
"I DO NOT BELIEVE IT!
"I ASK YOU TO SHOW ME THE GREAT WALL OF CHINA...
"...AND WHEN WE GET THERE..."
THEY'VE STILL GOT THE SCAFFOLDING UP!
QIN DYNASTY!
MUST BE A COUPLE OF CENTURIES BC!
OOH! GIVE US A MO...
OI, SPACEMAN! LOOK HAPPY!
KLIK!
DONNA -- STOP!
IF YOU START TAKING HOLIDAY SNAPS --
...YOU MIGHT MAKE THE LOCALS SUSPICIOUS!
THE IMMORTAL EMPEROR
Story JONATHAN MORRIS Art ROB DAVIS Colours ROB DAVIS & GERAINT FORD Letters ROGER LANGRIDGE Editor CLAYTON HICKMAN

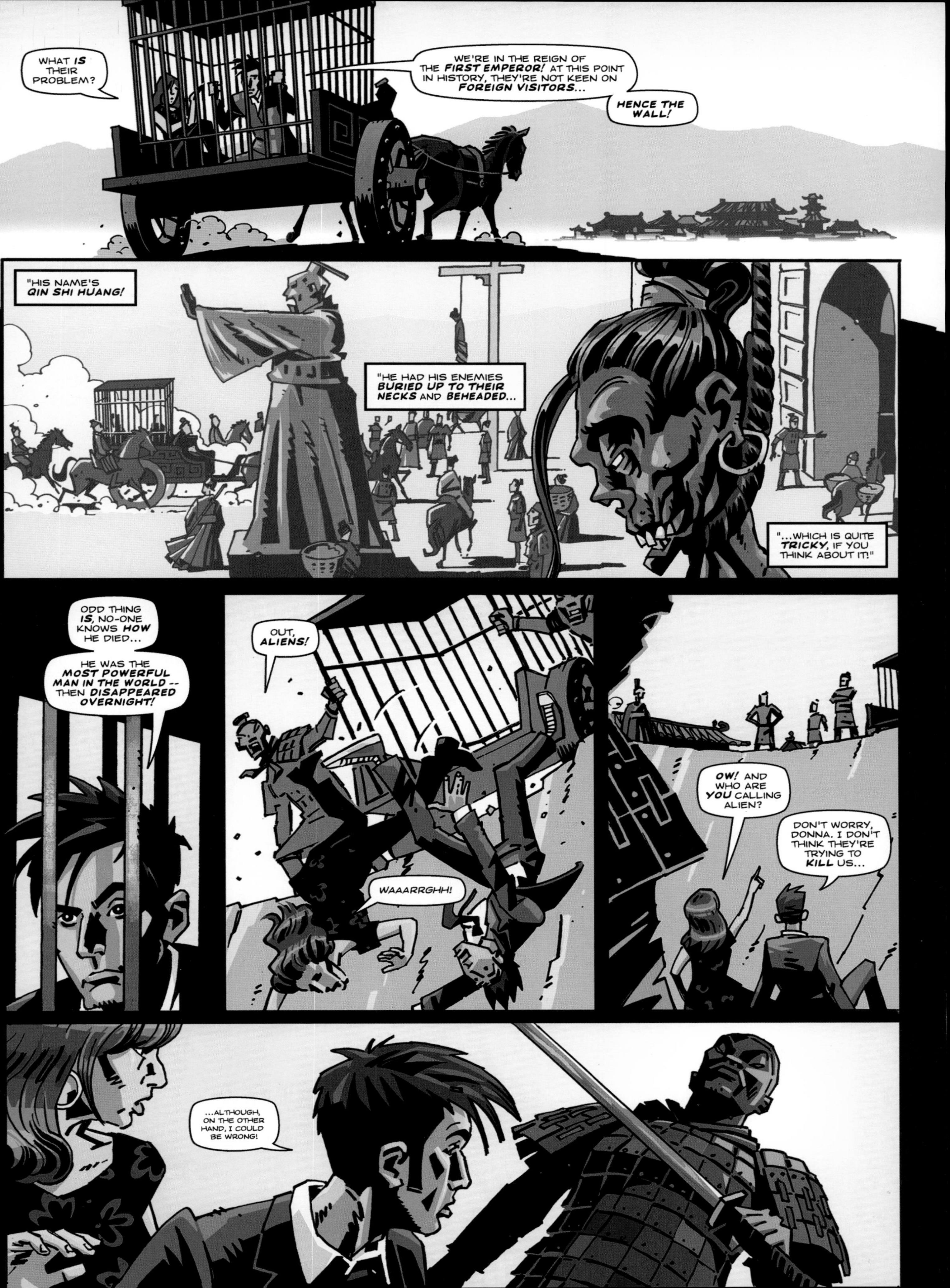
WHAT IS THEIR PROBLEM?
WE'RE IN THE REIGN OF THE FIRST EMPEROR! AT THIS POINT IN HISTORY, THEY'RE NOT KEEN ON FOREIGN VISITORS...
HENCE THE WALL!
"HIS NAME'S QIN SHI HUANG!
"HE HAD HIS ENEMIES BURIED UP TO THEIR NECKS AND BEHEADED...
"...WHICH IS QUITE TRICKY, IF YOU THINK ABOUT IT!"
ODD THING IS, NO-ONE KNOWS HOW HE DIED...
HE WAS THE MOST POWERFUL MAN IN THE WORLD -- THEN DISAPPEARED OVERNIGHT!
OUT, ALIENS!
WAAARRGHH!
OW! AND WHO ARE YOU CALLING ALIEN?
DON'T WORRY, DONNA. I DON'T THINK THEY'RE TRYING TO KILL US...
...ALTHOUGH, ON THE OTHER HAND, I COULD BE WRONG!

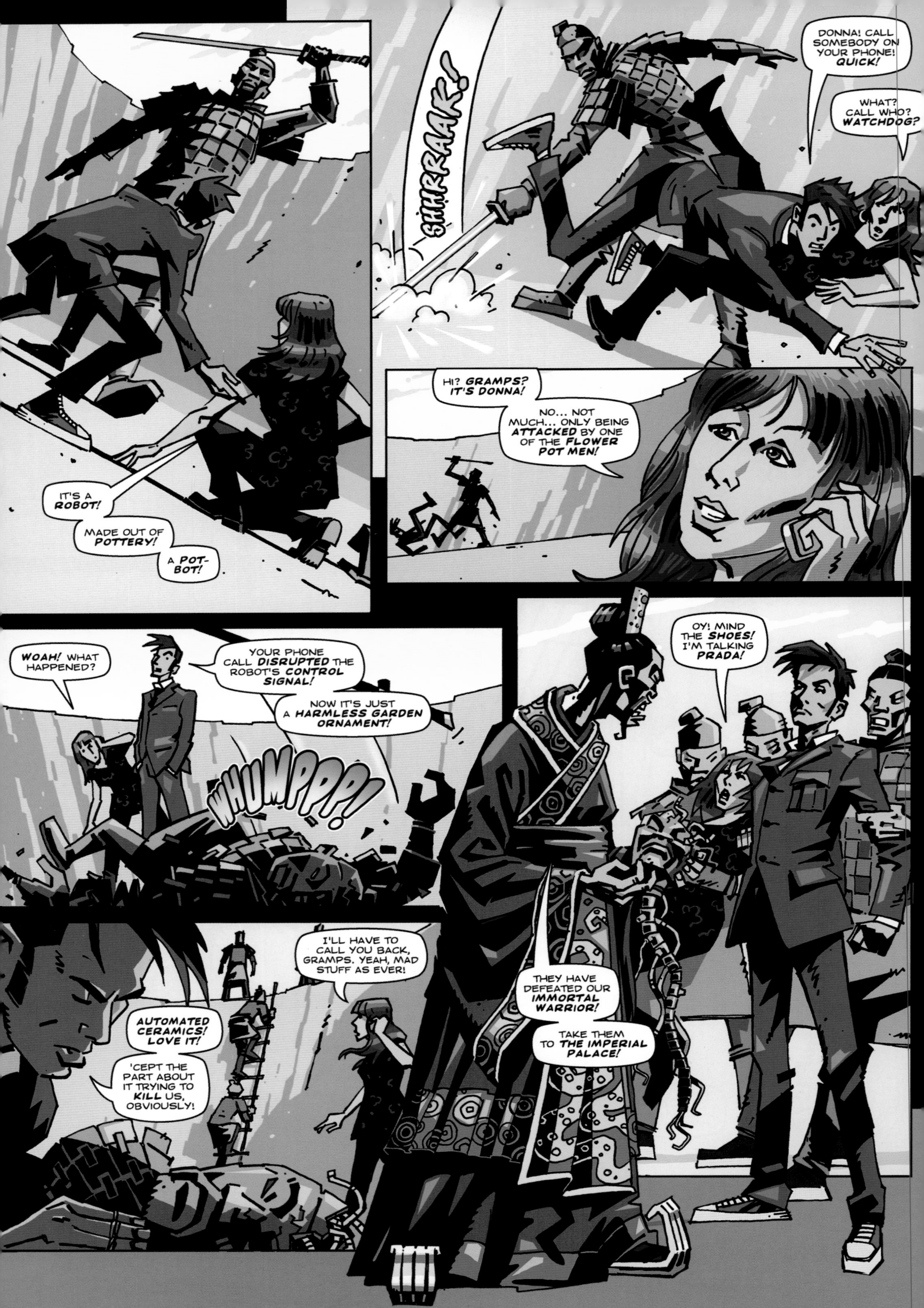

IT'S A ROBOT!
MADE OUT OF POTTERY!
A POT-BOT!
SHHRAAK!
DONNA! CALL SOMEBODY ON YOUR PHONE! QUICK!
WHAT? CALL WHO? WATCHDOG?
HI? GRAMPS? IT'S DONNA!
NO... NOT MUCH... ONLY BEING ATTACKED BY ONE OF THE FLOWER POT MEN!
WOAH! WHAT HAPPENED?
YOUR PHONE CALL DISRUPTED THE ROBOT'S CONTROL SIGNAL!
NOW IT'S JUST A HARMLESS GARDEN ORNAMENT!
WHUMPPP!
I'LL HAVE TO CALL YOU BACK, GRAMPS. YEAH, MAD STUFF AS EVER!
AUTOMATED CERAMICS! LOVE IT!
'CEPT THE PART ABOUT IT TRYING TO KILL US, OBVIOUSLY!
OY! MIND THE SHOES! I'M TALKING PRADA!
THEY HAVE DEFEATED OUR IMMORTAL WARRIOR!
TAKE THEM TO THE IMPERIAL PALACE!

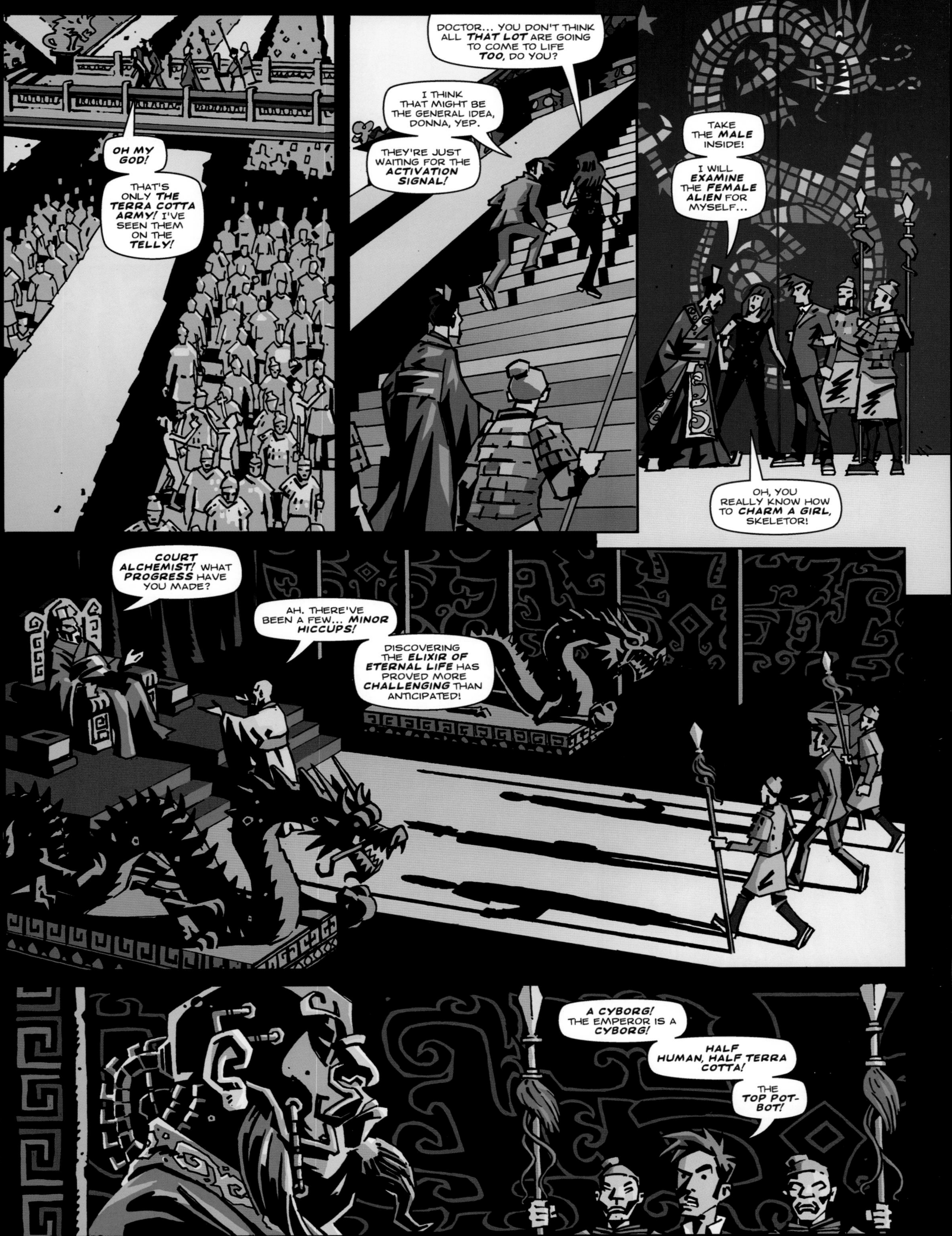
OH MY GOD!
THAT'S ONLY THE TERRA COTTA ARMY! I'VE SEEN THEM ON THE TELLY!
DOCTOR... YOU DON'T THINK ALL THAT LOT ARE GOING TO COME TO LIFE TOO, DO YOU?
I THINK THAT MIGHT BE THE GENERAL IDEA, DONNA, YEP.
THEY'RE JUST WAITING FOR THE ACTIVATION SIGNAL!
TAKE THE MALE INSIDE!
I WILL EXAMINE THE FEMALE ALIEN FOR MYSELF...
OH, YOU REALLY KNOW HOW TO CHARM A GIRL, SKELETOR!
COURT ALCHEMIST! WHAT PROGRESS HAVE YOU MADE?
AH. THERE'VE BEEN A FEW... MINOR HICCUPS!
DISCOVERING THE ELIXIR OF ETERNAL LIFE HAS PROVED MORE CHALLENGING THAN ANTICIPATED!
A CYBORG! THE EMPEROR IS A CYBORG!
HALF HUMAN, HALF TERRA COTTA!
THE TOP POT-BOT!

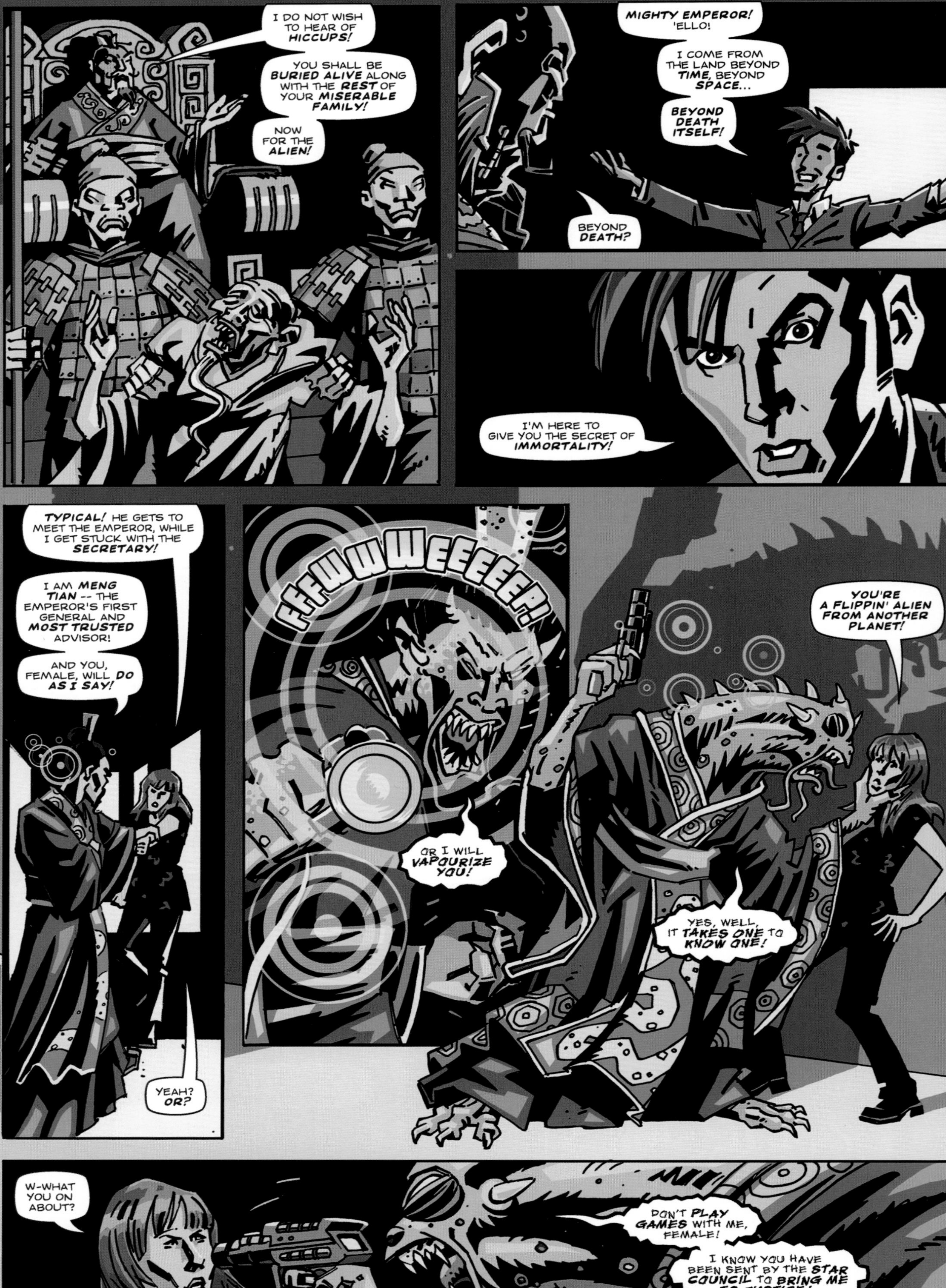
I DO NOT WISH TO HEAR OF HICCUPS!
YOU SHALL BE BURIED ALIVE ALONG WITH THE REST OF YOUR MISERABLE FAMILY!
NOW FOR THE ALIEN!
MIGHTY EMPEROR! 'ELLO!
I COME FROM THE LAND BEYOND TIME, BEYOND SPACE...
BEYOND DEATH ITSELF!
BEYOND DEATH?
I'M HERE TO GIVE YOU THE SECRET OF IMMORTALITY!
TYPICAL! HE GETS TO MEET THE EMPEROR, WHILE I GET STUCK WITH THE SECRETARY!
I AM MENG TIAN -- THE EMPEROR'S FIRST GENERAL AND MOST TRUSTED ADVISOR!
AND YOU, FEMALE, WILL DO AS I SAY!
YEAH? OR?
FFFWWWEEEEEP!
OR I WILL VAPOURIZE YOU!
YOU'RE A FLIPPIN' ALIEN FROM ANOTHER PLANET!
YES, WELL, IT TAKES ONE TO KNOW ONE!
W-WHAT YOU ON ABOUT?
DON'T PLAY GAMES WITH ME, FEMALE!
I KNOW YOU HAVE BEEN SENT BY THE STAR COUNCIL TO BRING ME TO JUSTICE!

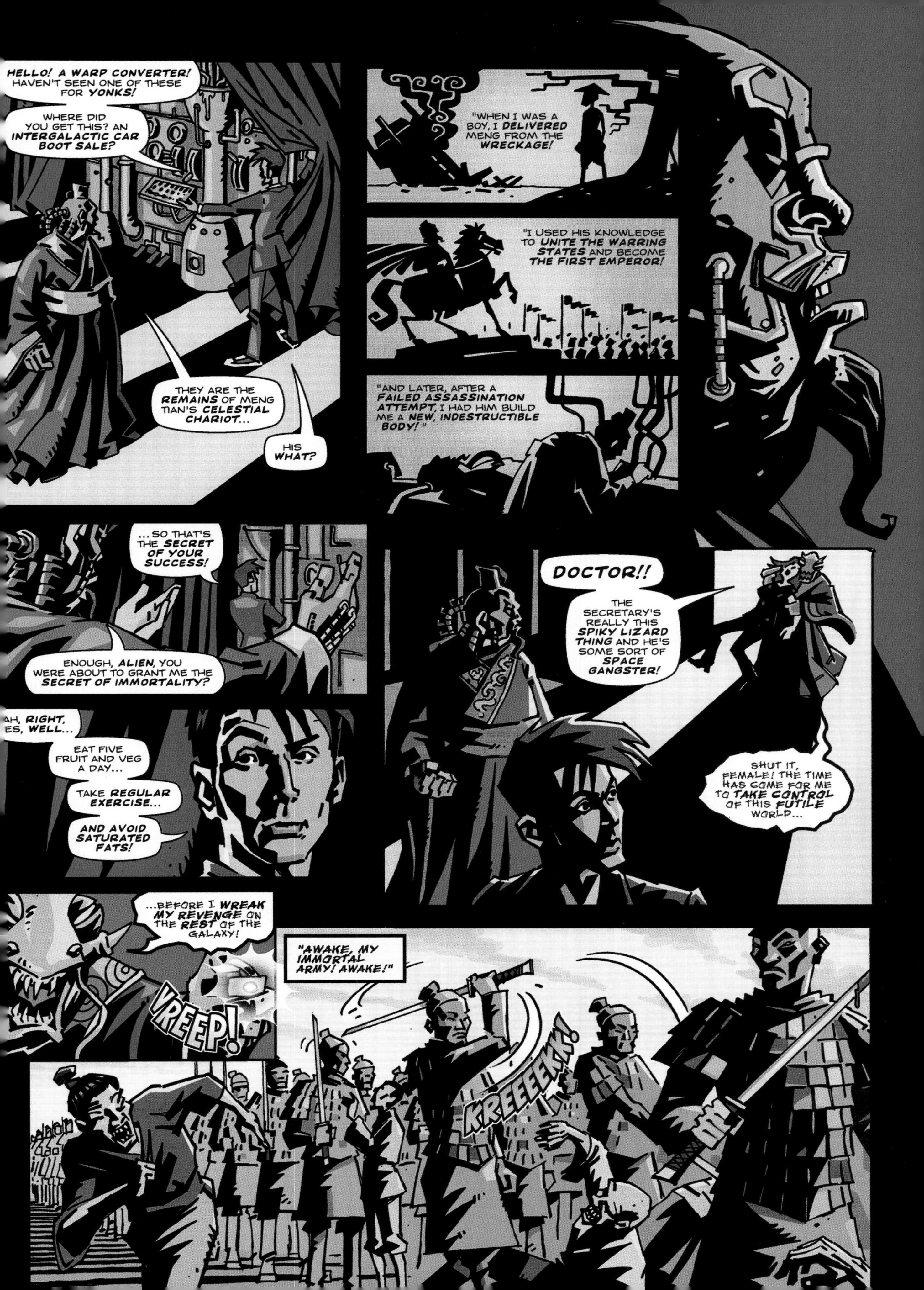

HELLO! A WARP CONVERTER! HAVEN'T SEEN ONE OF THESE FOR YONKS!
WHERE DID YOU GET THIS? AN INTERGALACTIC CAR BOOT SALE?
THEY ARE THE REMAINS OF MENG TIAN'S CELESTIAL CHARIOT...
HIS WHAT?
"WHEN I WAS A BOY, I DELIVERED MENG FROM THE WRECKAGE!
"I USED HIS KNOWLEDGE TO UNITE THE WARRING STATES AND BECOME THE FIRST EMPEROR!
"AND LATER, AFTER A FAILED ASSASSINATION ATTEMPT, I HAD HIM BUILD ME A NEW, INDESTRUCTIBLE BODY!"
...SO THAT'S THE SECRET OF YOUR SUCCESS!
ENOUGH, ALIEN, YOU WERE ABOUT TO GRANT ME THE SECRET OF IMMORTALITY?
AH, RIGHT, YES, WELL...
EAT FIVE FRUIT AND VEG A DAY...
TAKE REGULAR EXERCISE...
AND AVOID SATURATED FATS!
DOCTOR!!
THE SECRETARY'S REALLY THIS SPIKY LIZARD THING AND HE'S SOME SORT OF SPACE GANGSTER!
SHUT IT, FEMALE! THE TIME HAS COME FOR ME TO TAKE CONTROL OF THIS FUTILE WORLD...
...BEFORE I WREAK MY REVENGE ON THE REST OF THE GALAXY!
VREEP!
"AWAKE, MY IMMORTAL ARMY! AWAKE!"
KREEEEKK!

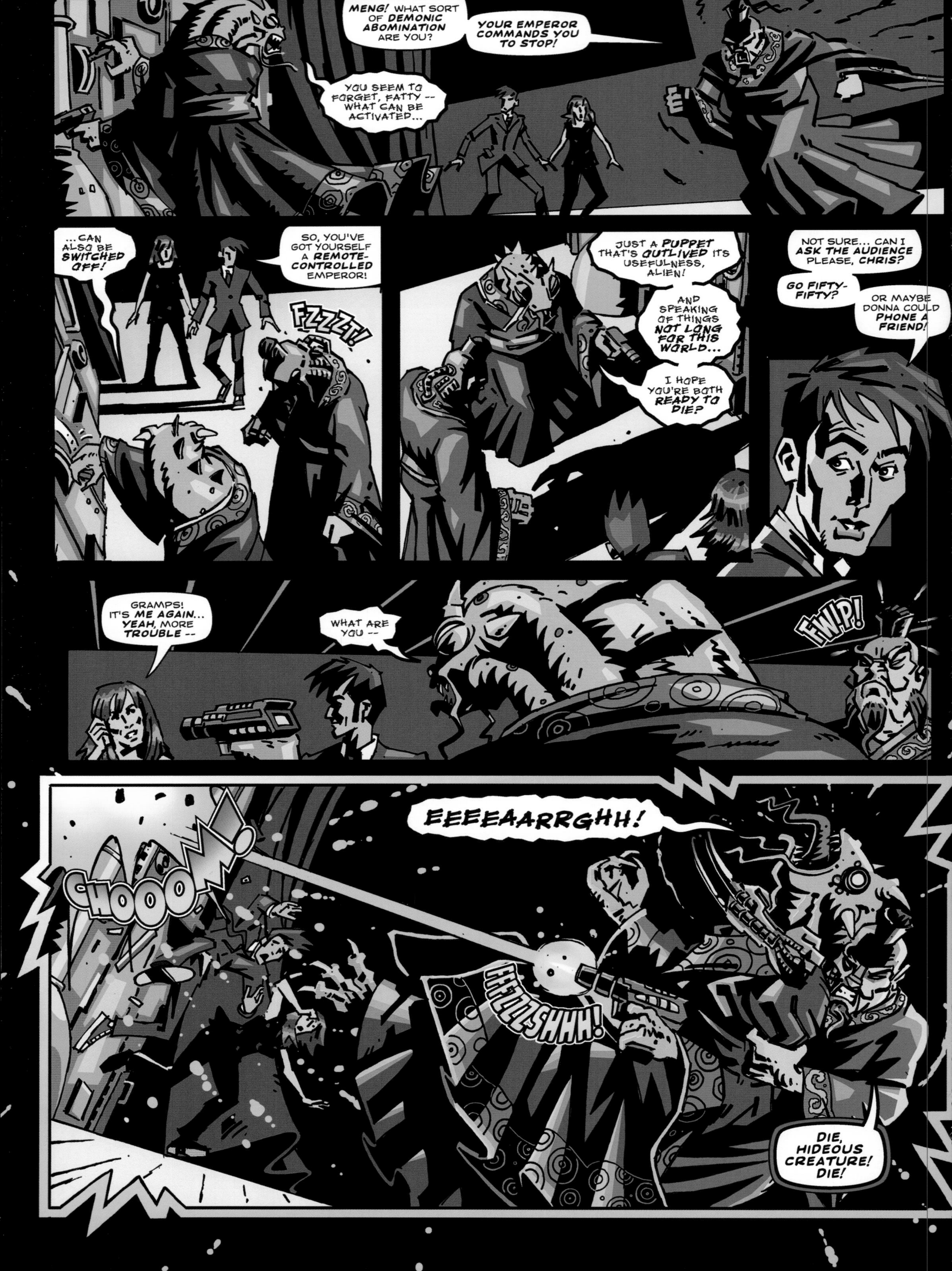
MENG! WHAT SORT OF DEMONIC ABOMINATION ARE YOU?
YOUR EMPEROR COMMANDS YOU TO STOP!
YOU SEEM TO FORGET, FATTY -- WHAT CAN BE ACTIVATED...
...CAN ALSO BE SWITCHED OFF!
SO, YOU'VE GOT YOURSELF A REMOTE-CONTROLLED EMPEROR!
FZZZT!
JUST A PUPPET THAT'S OUTLIVED ITS USEFULNESS, ALIEN!
AND SPEAKING OF THINGS NOT LONG FOR THIS WORLD...
I HOPE YOU'RE BOTH READY TO DIE?
NOT SURE... CAN I ASK THE AUDIENCE PLEASE, CHRIS?
GO FIFTY-FIFTY?
OR MAYBE DONNA COULD PHONE A FRIEND!
GRAMPS! IT'S ME AGAIN... YEAH, MORE TROUBLE --
WHAT ARE YOU --
FWIP!
EEEEAARRGHH!
CHOOOM!
FFZZZSHHH!
DIE, HIDEOUS CREATURE! DIE!

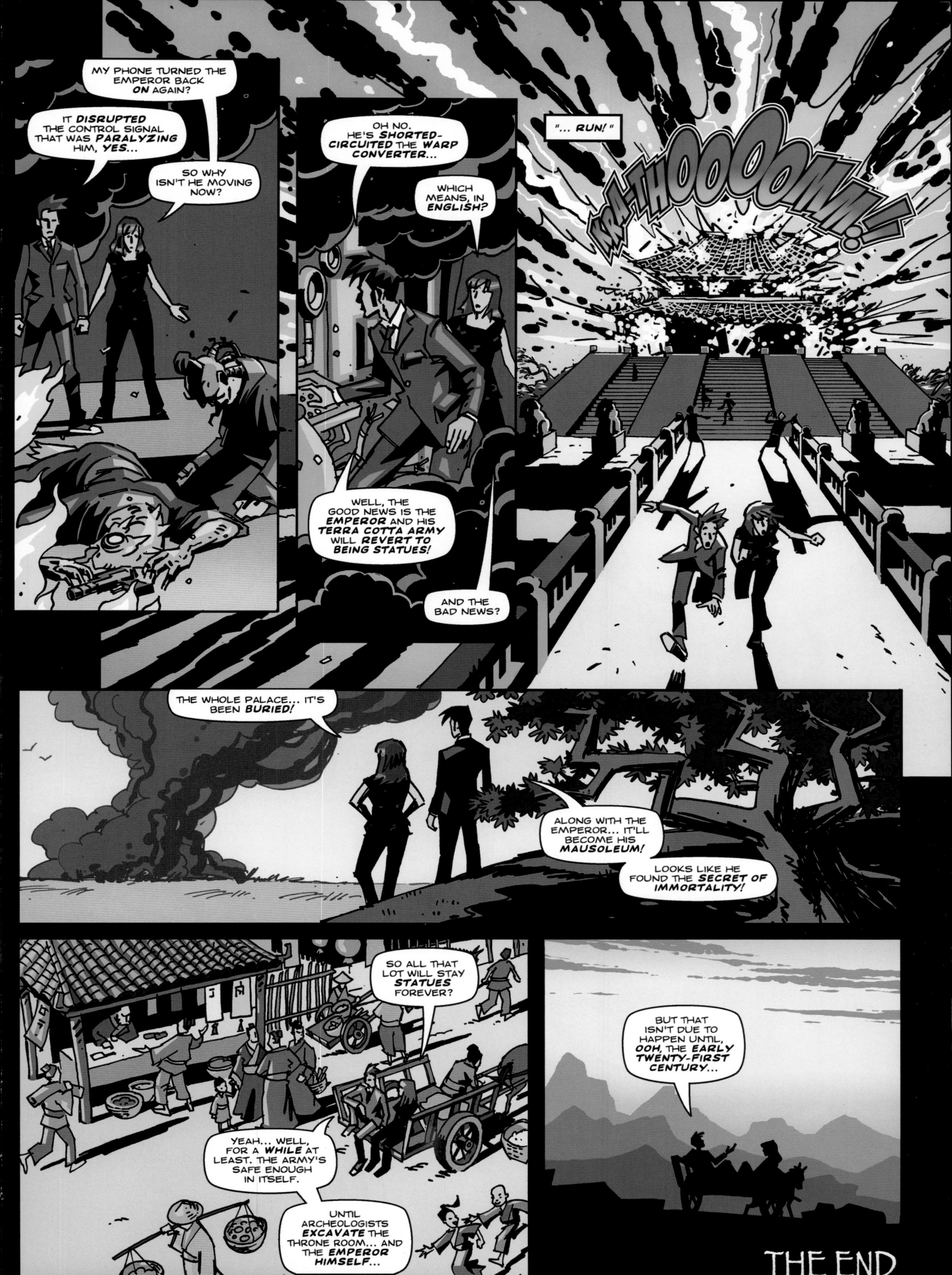
MY PHONE TURNED THE EMPEROR BACK ON AGAIN?
IT DISRUPTED THE CONTROL SIGNAL THAT WAS PARALYZING HIM, YES...
SO WHY ISN'T HE MOVING NOW?
OH NO. HE'S SHORTED-CIRCUITED THE WARP CONVERTER...
WHICH MEANS, IN ENGLISH?
WELL, THE GOOD NEWS IS THE EMPEROR AND HIS TERRA COTTA ARMY WILL REVERT TO BEING STATUES!
AND THE BAD NEWS?
"... RUN!"
KRA-THOOOOOMM!!
THE WHOLE PALACE... IT'S BEEN BURIED!
ALONG WITH THE EMPEROR... IT'LL BECOME HIS MAUSOLEUM!
LOOKS LIKE HE FOUND THE SECRET OF IMMORTALITY!
SO ALL THAT LOT WILL STAY STATUES FOREVER?
YEAH... WELL, FOR A WHILE AT LEAST. THE ARMY'S SAFE ENOUGH IN ITSELF.
UNTIL ARCHEOLOGISTS EXCAVATE THE THRONE ROOM... AND THE EMPEROR HIMSELF...
BUT THAT ISN'T DUE TO HAPPEN UNTIL, OOH, THE EARLY TWENTY-FIRST CENTURY...
THE END

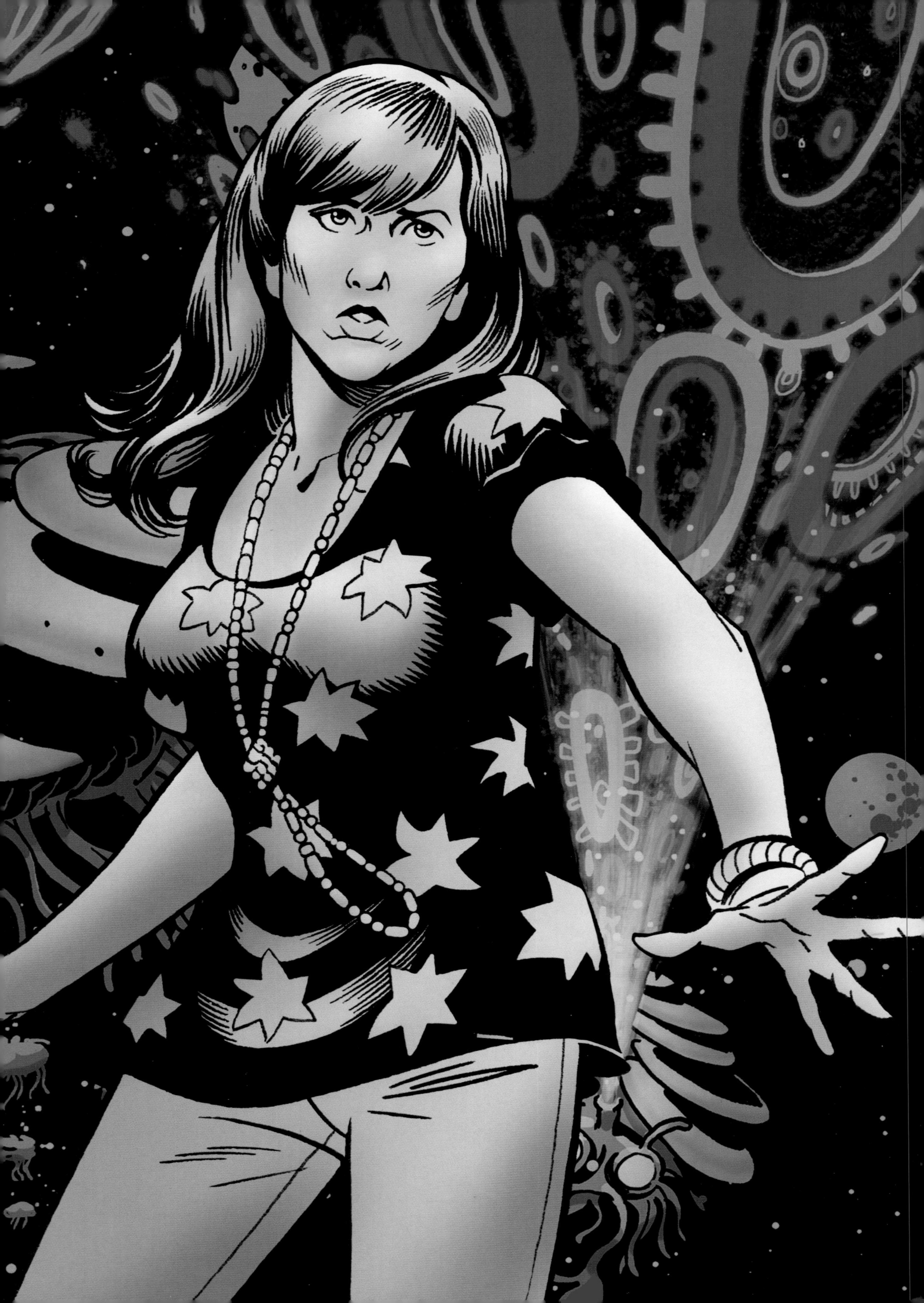

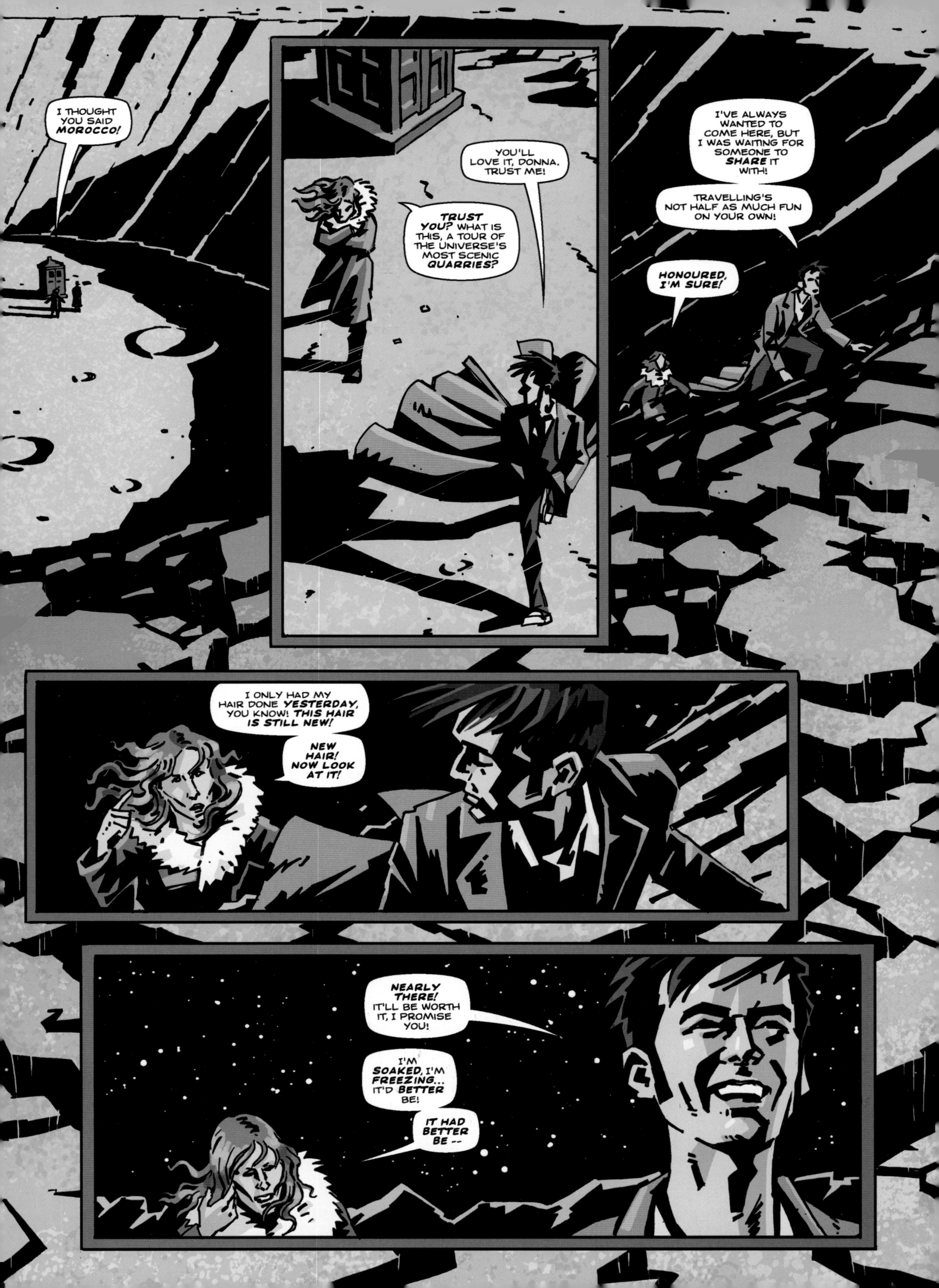

I THOUGHT YOU SAID MOROCCO!
YOU'LL LOVE IT, DONNA. TRUST ME!
TRUST YOU? WHAT IS THIS, A TOUR OF THE UNIVERSE'S MOST SCENIC QUARRIES?
I'VE ALWAYS WANTED TO COME HERE, BUT I WAS WAITING FOR SOMEONE TO SHARE IT WITH!
TRAVELLING'S NOT HALF AS MUCH FUN ON YOUR OWN!
HONOURED, I'M SURE!
I ONLY HAD MY HAIR DONE YESTERDAY, YOU KNOW! THIS HAIR IS STILL NEW!
NEW HAIR! NOW LOOK AT IT!
NEARLY THERE! IT'LL BE WORTH IT, I PROMISE YOU!
I'M SOAKED, I'M FREEZING... IT'D BETTER BE!
IT HAD BETTER BE --

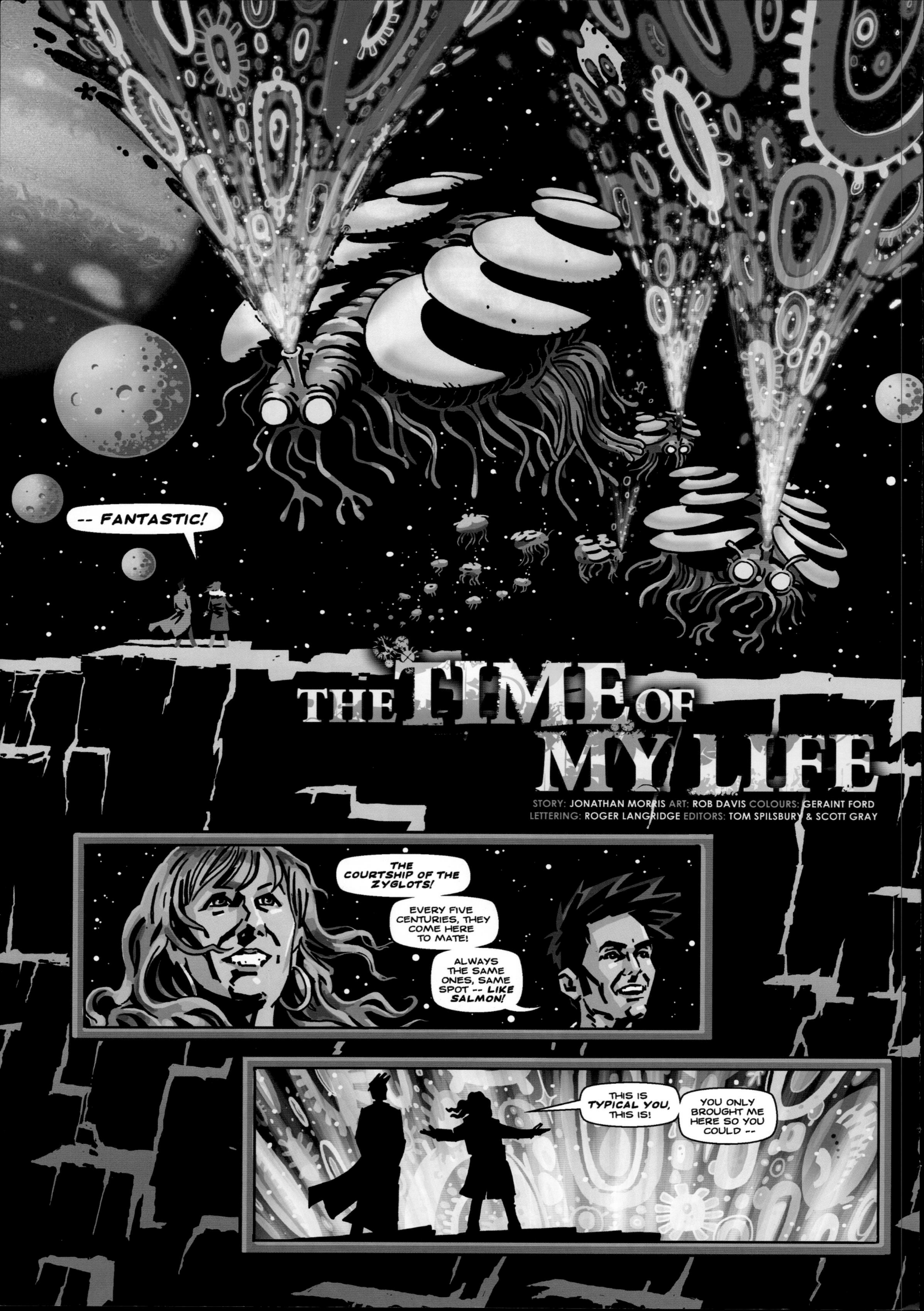
-- FANTASTIC!
THE TIME OF MY LIFE
STORY: JONATHAN MORRIS ART: ROB DAVIS COLOURS: GERAINT FORD
LETTERING: ROGER LANGRIDGE EDITORS: TOM SPILSBURY & SCOTT GRAY
THE COURTSHIP OF THE ZYGLOTS!
EVERY FIVE CENTURIES, THEY COME HERE TO MATE!
ALWAYS THE SAME ONES, SAME SPOT -- LIKE SALMON!
THIS IS TYPICAL YOU, THIS IS!
YOU ONLY BROUGHT ME HERE SO YOU COULD --

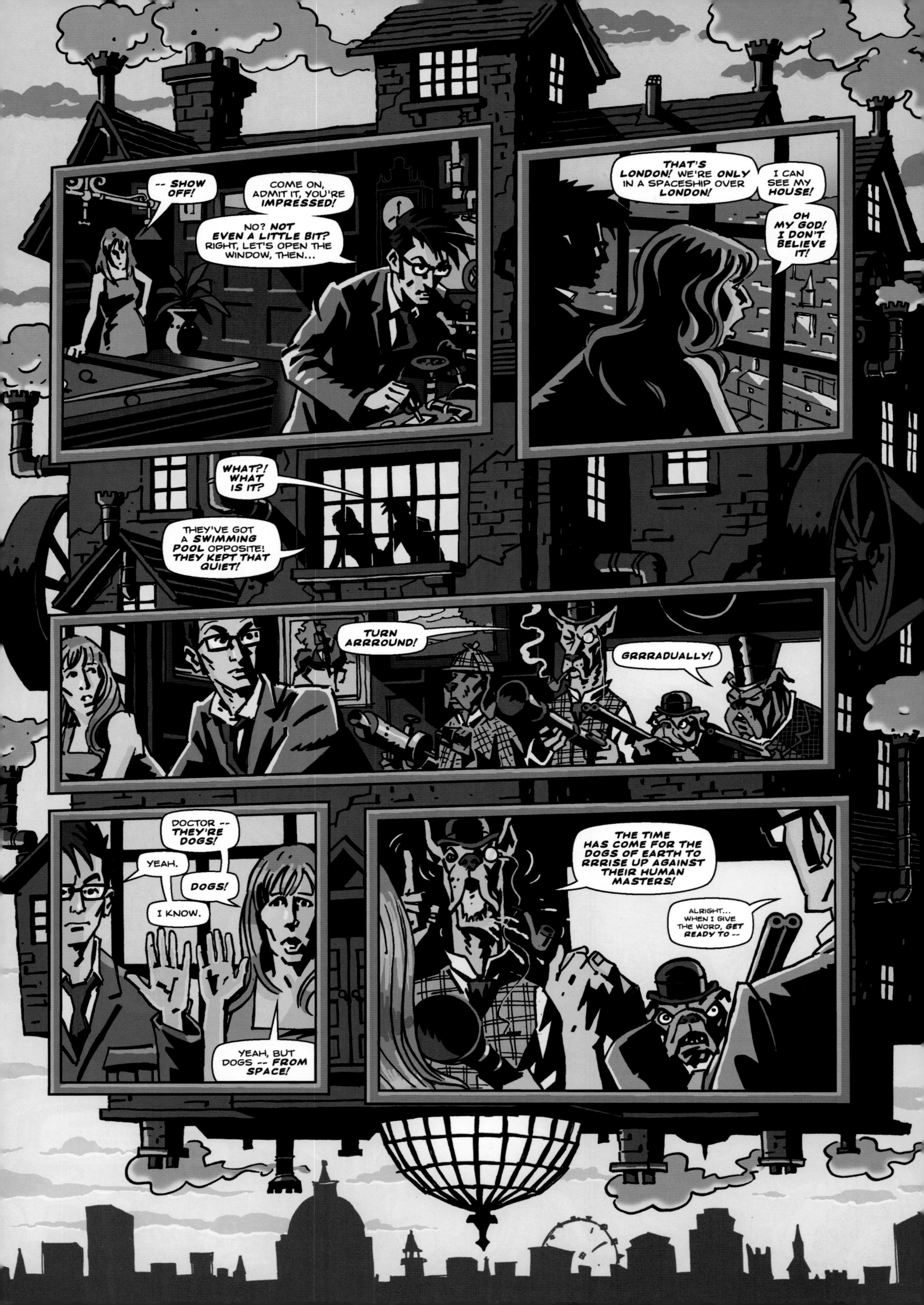
-- SHOW OFF!
COME ON, ADMIT IT, YOU'RE IMPRESSED!
NO? NOT EVEN A LITTLE BIT? RIGHT, LET'S OPEN THE WINDOW, THEN...
THAT'S LONDON! WE'RE ONLY IN A SPACESHIP OVER LONDON!
I CAN SEE MY HOUSE!
OH MY GOD! I DON'T BELIEVE IT!
WHAT?! WHAT IS IT?
THEY'VE GOT A SWIMMING POOL OPPOSITE! THEY KEPT THAT QUIET!
TURN ARRROUND!
GRRRADUALLY!
DOCTOR -- THEY'RE DOGS!
YEAH.
DOGS!
I KNOW.
YEAH, BUT DOGS -- FROM SPACE!
THE TIME HAS COME FOR THE DOGS OF EARTH TO RRRISE UP AGAINST THEIR HUMAN MASTERS!
ALRIGHT... WHEN I GIVE THE WORD, GET READY TO --

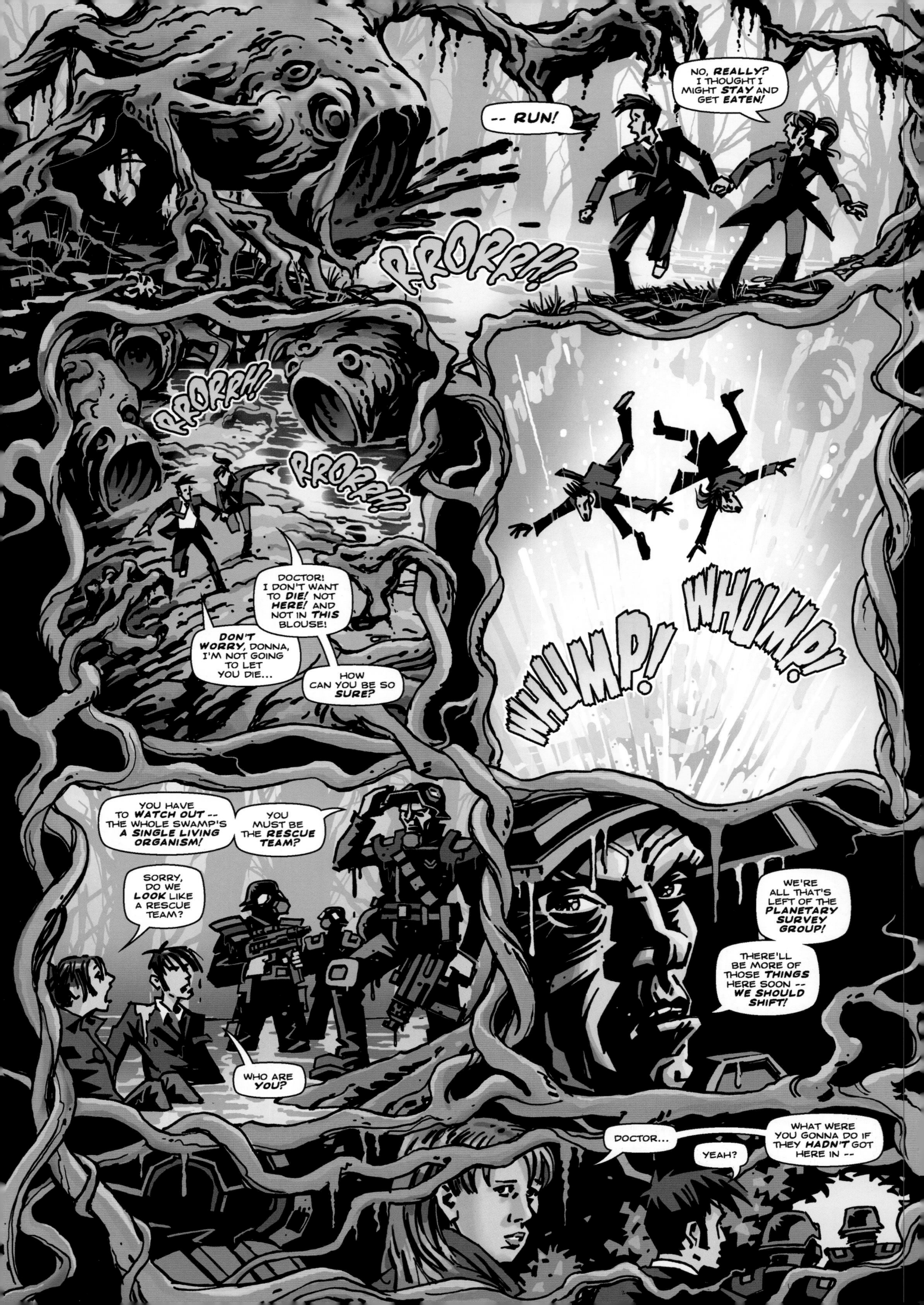
-- RUN!
NO, REALLY? I THOUGHT I MIGHT STAY AND GET EATEN!
RRORRH!
RRORRH!
RRORRH!
DOCTOR! I DON'T WANT TO DIE! NOT HERE! AND NOT IN THIS BLOUSE!
DON'T WORRY, DONNA, I'M NOT GOING TO LET YOU DIE...
HOW CAN YOU BE SO SURE?
WHUMP!
WHUMP!
YOU HAVE TO WATCH OUT -- THE WHOLE SWAMP'S A SINGLE LIVING ORGANISM!
YOU MUST BE THE RESCUE TEAM?
SORRY, DO WE LOOK LIKE A RESCUE TEAM?
WHO ARE YOU?
WE'RE ALL THAT'S LEFT OF THE PLANETARY SURVEY GROUP!
THERE'LL BE MORE OF THOSE THINGS HERE SOON -- WE SHOULD SHIFT!
DOCTOR...
YEAH?
WHAT WERE YOU GONNA DO IF THEY HADN'T GOT HERE IN --

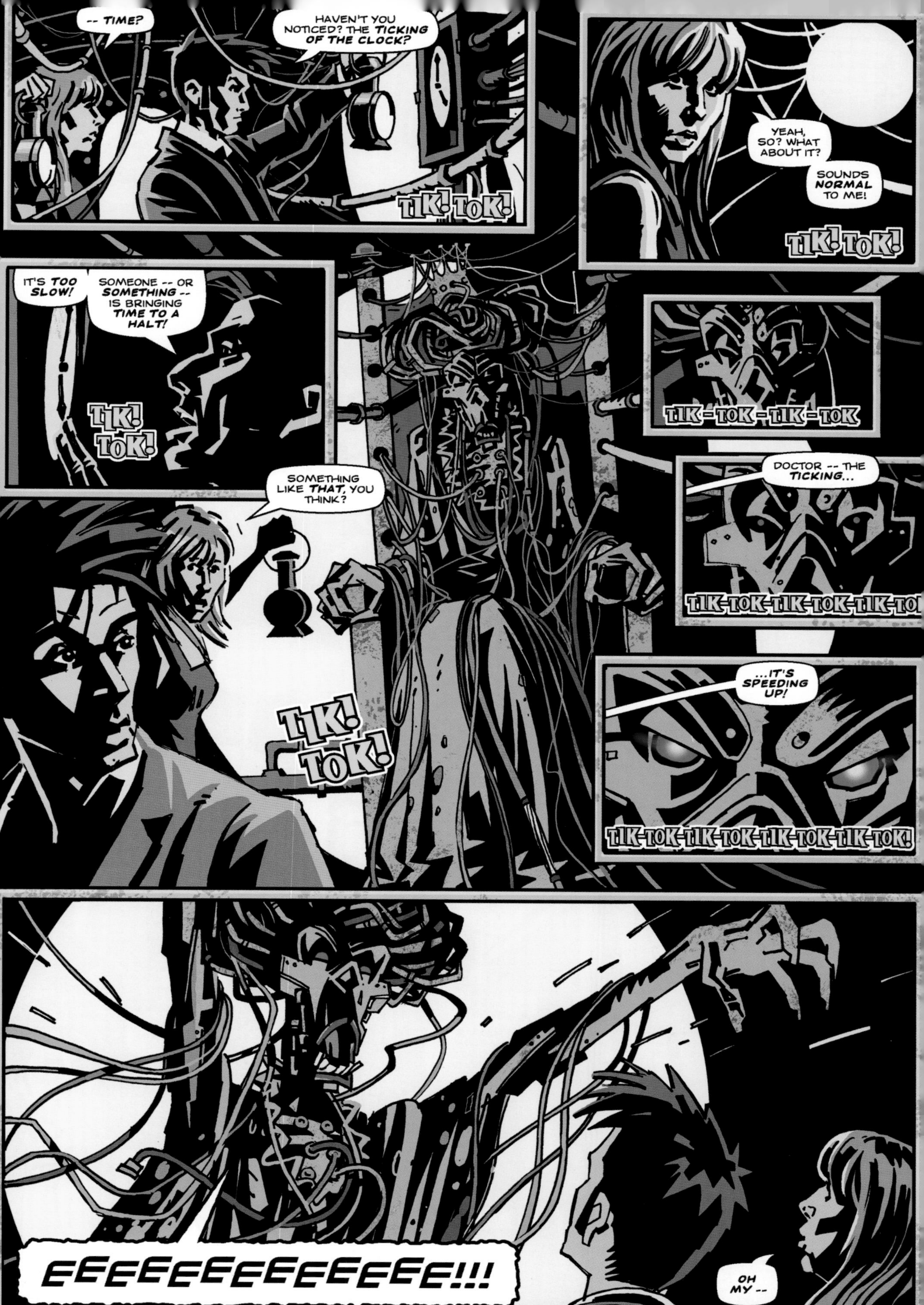
-- TIME?
HAVEN'T YOU NOTICED? THE TICKING OF THE CLOCK?
TIK! TOK!
YEAH, SO? WHAT ABOUT IT?
SOUNDS NORMAL TO ME!
TIK! TOK!
IT'S TOO SLOW!
SOMEONE -- OR SOMETHING -- IS BRINGING TIME TO A HALT!
TIK! TOK!
TIK - TOK - TIK - TOK
SOMETHING LIKE THAT, YOU THINK?
DOCTOR -- THE TICKING...
TIK-TOK-TIK-TOK-TIK-TOK
TIK! TOK!
...IT'S SPEEDING UP!
TIK-TOK-TIK-TOK-TIK-TOK-TIK-TOK!
EEEEEEEEEEEEEEE!!!
OH MY --

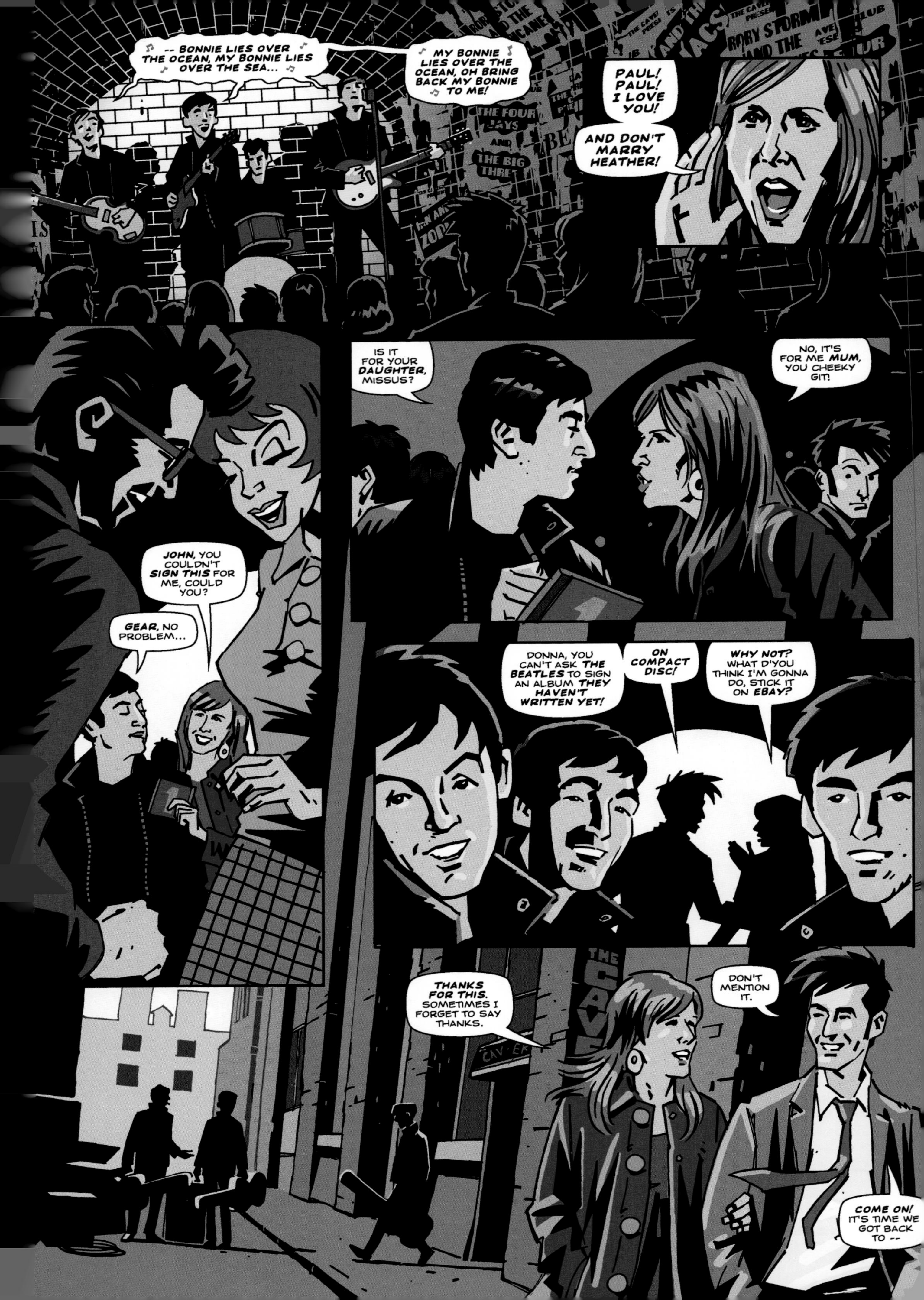
-- BONNIE LIES OVER THE OCEAN, MY BONNIE LIES OVER THE SEA...
MY BONNIE LIES OVER THE OCEAN, OH BRING BACK MY BONNIE TO ME!
PAUL! PAUL! I LOVE YOU!
AND DON'T MARRY HEATHER!
THE FOUR JAYS
AND
THE BIG THREE
JOHN, YOU COULDN'T SIGN THIS FOR ME, COULD YOU?
GEAR, NO PROBLEM...
IS IT FOR YOUR DAUGHTER, MISSUS?
NO, IT'S FOR ME MUM, YOU CHEEKY GIT!
DONNA, YOU CAN'T ASK THE BEATLES TO SIGN AN ALBUM THEY HAVEN'T WRITTEN YET!
ON COMPACT DISC!
WHY NOT? WHAT D'YOU THINK I'M GONNA DO, STICK IT ON EBAY?
THANKS FOR THIS. SOMETIMES I FORGET TO SAY THANKS.
DON'T MENTION IT.
COME ON! IT'S TIME WE GOT BACK TO --

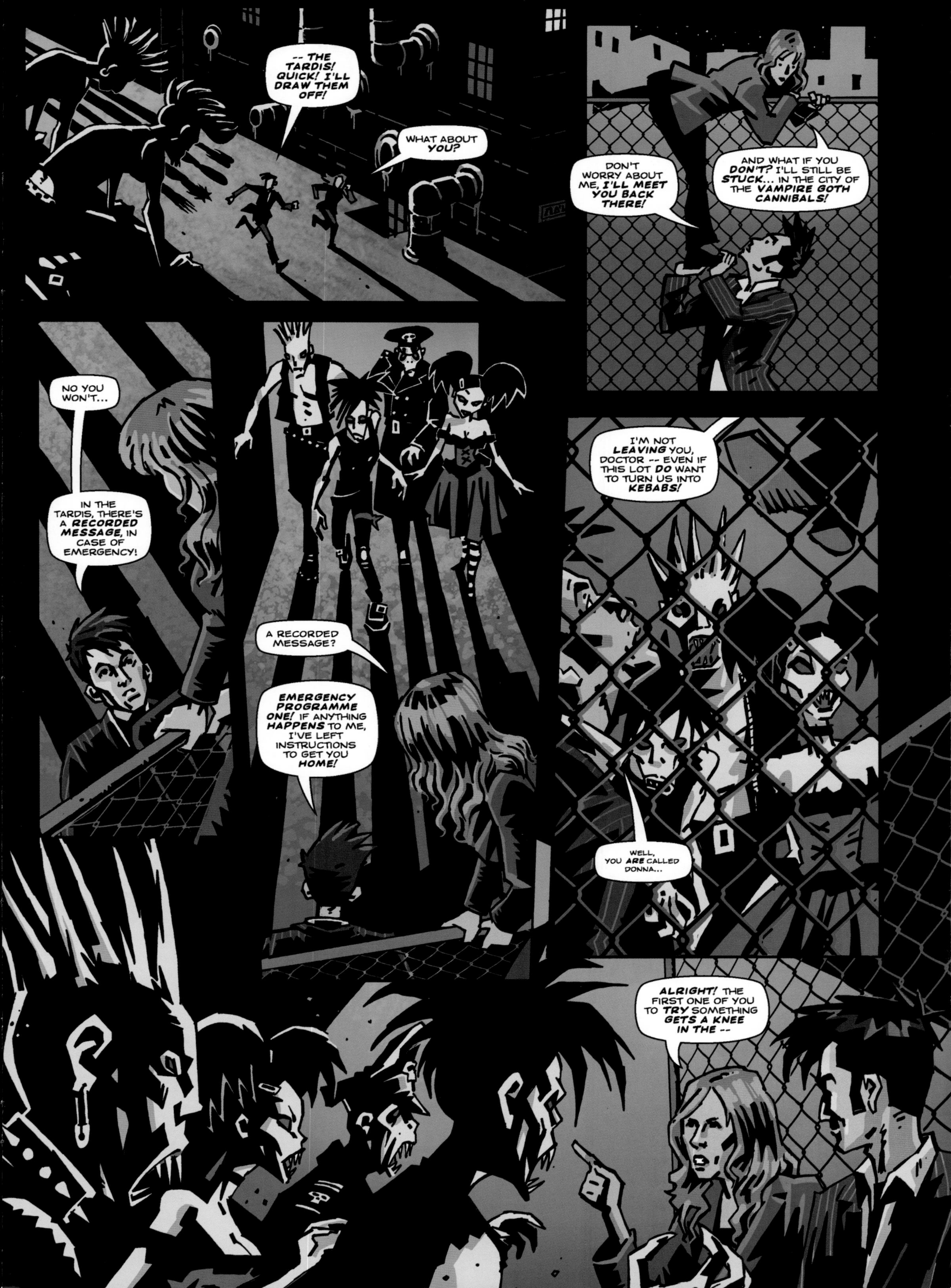
-- THE TARDIS! QUICK! I'LL DRAW THEM OFF!
WHAT ABOUT YOU?
DON'T WORRY ABOUT ME, I'LL MEET YOU BACK THERE!
AND WHAT IF YOU DON'T? I'LL STILL BE STUCK... IN THE CITY OF THE VAMPIRE GOTH CANNIBALS!
NO YOU WON'T...
IN THE TARDIS, THERE'S A RECORDED MESSAGE, IN CASE OF EMERGENCY!
A RECORDED MESSAGE?
EMERGENCY PROGRAMME ONE! IF ANYTHING HAPPENS TO ME, I'VE LEFT INSTRUCTIONS TO GET YOU HOME!
I'M NOT LEAVING YOU, DOCTOR -- EVEN IF THIS LOT DO WANT TO TURN US INTO KEBABS!
WELL, YOU ARE CALLED DONNA...
ALRIGHT! THE FIRST ONE OF YOU TO TRY SOMETHING GETS A KNEE IN THE --

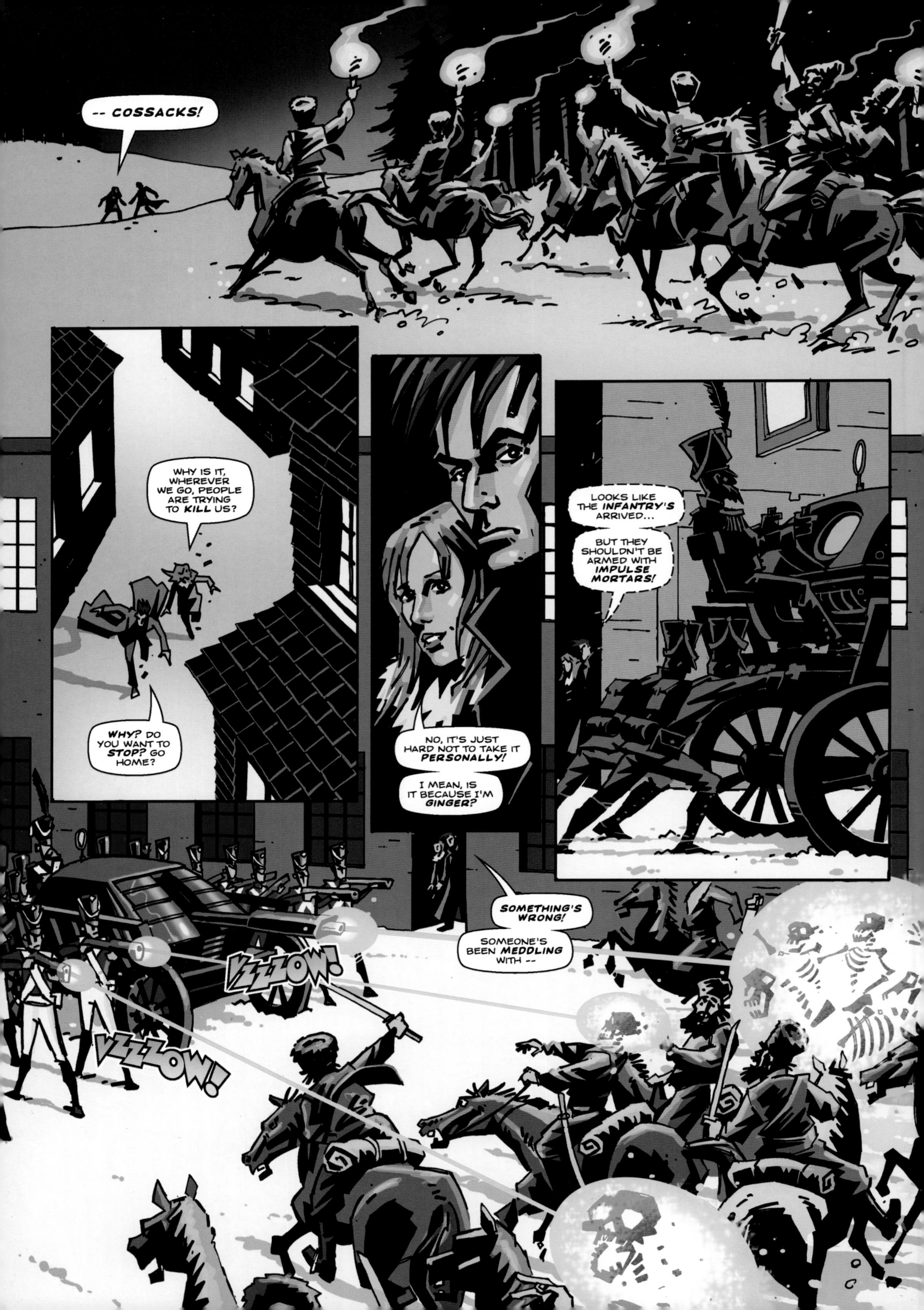
-- COSSACKS!
WHY IS IT, WHEREVER WE GO, PEOPLE ARE TRYING TO KILL US?
WHY? DO YOU WANT TO STOP? GO HOME?
NO, IT'S JUST HARD NOT TO TAKE IT PERSONALLY!
I MEAN, IS IT BECAUSE I'M GINGER?
LOOKS LIKE THE INFANTRY'S ARRIVED...
BUT THEY SHOULDN'T BE ARMED WITH IMPULSE MORTARS!
SOMETHING'S WRONG!
SOMEONE'S BEEN MEDDLING WITH --
VZZZOW!
VZZZOW!

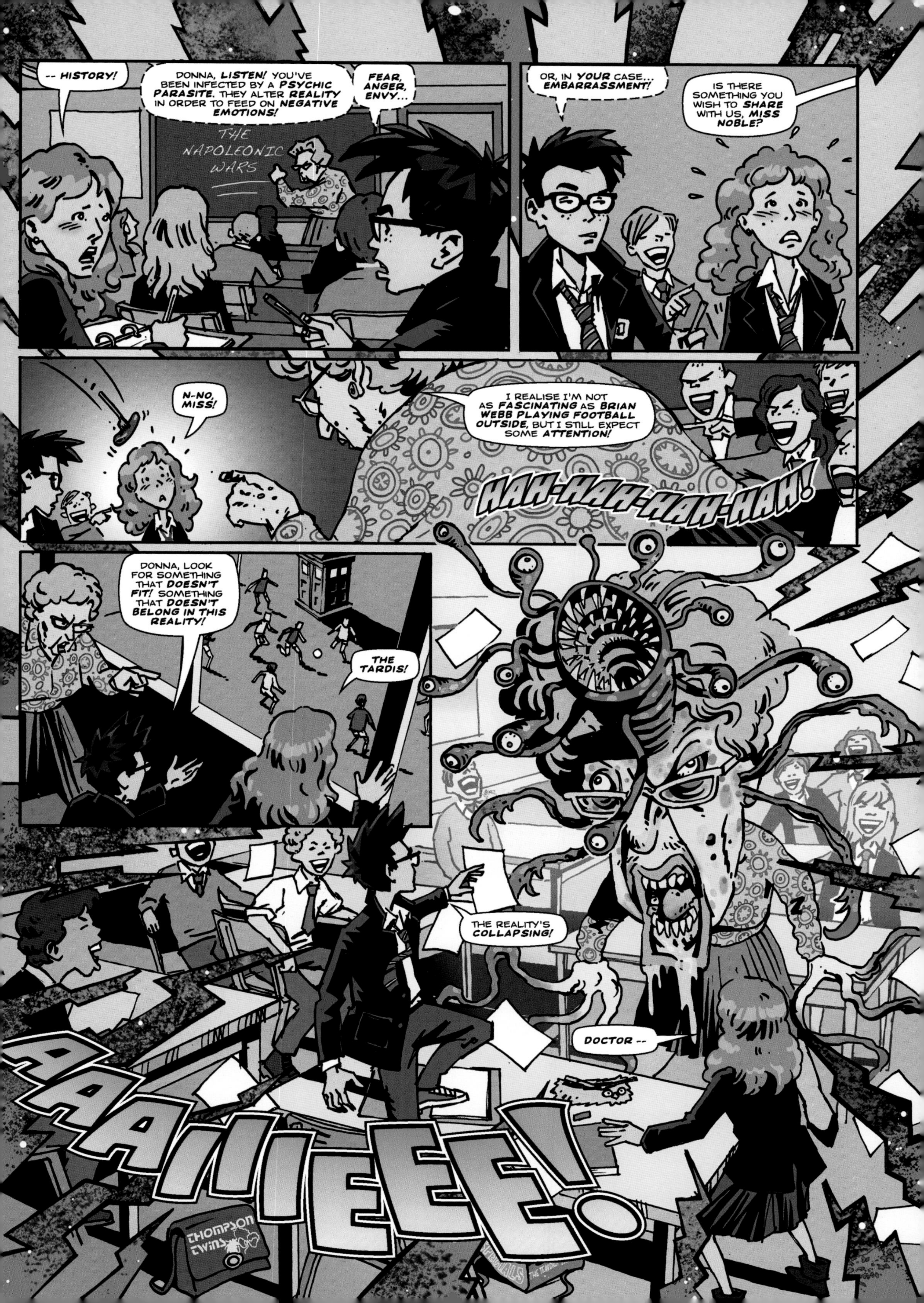
-- HISTORY!
DONNA, LISTEN! YOU'VE BEEN INFECTED BY A PSYCHIC PARASITE. THEY ALTER REALITY IN ORDER TO FEED ON NEGATIVE EMOTIONS!
FEAR, ANGER, ENVY...
THE NAPOLEONIC WARS
OR, IN YOUR CASE... EMBARRASSMENT!
IS THERE SOMETHING YOU WISH TO SHARE WITH US, MISS NOBLE?
N-NO, MISS!
I REALISE I'M NOT AS FASCINATING AS BRIAN WEBB PLAYING FOOTBALL OUTSIDE, BUT I STILL EXPECT SOME ATTENTION!
HAH-HAH-HAH-HAH!
DONNA, LOOK FOR SOMETHING THAT DOESN'T FIT! SOMETHING THAT DOESN'T BELONG IN THIS REALITY!
THE TARDIS!
THE REALITY'S COLLAPSING!
DOCTOR --
AAAIIIEEE!
THOMPSON TWINS

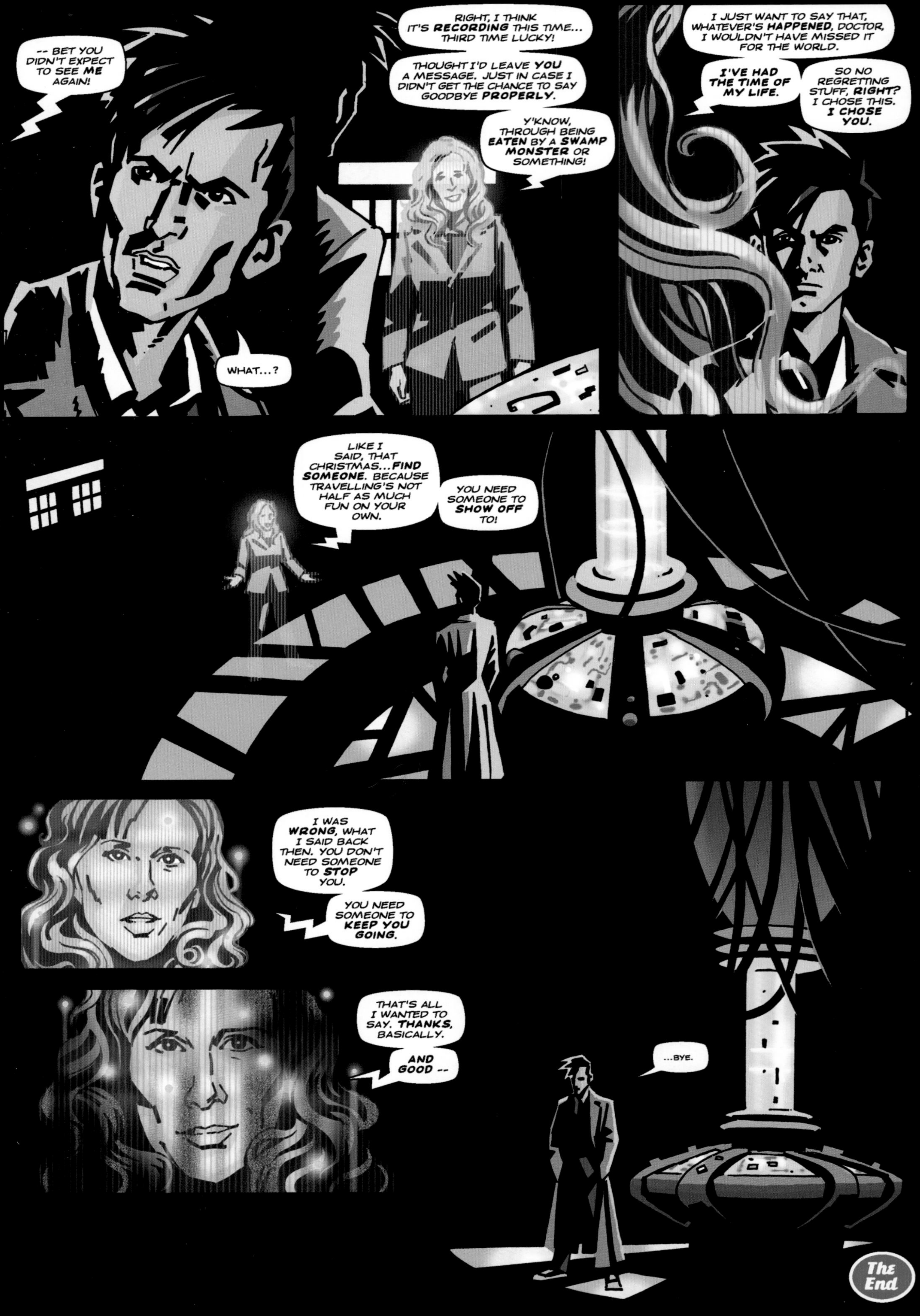
-- BET YOU DIDN'T EXPECT TO SEE ME AGAIN!
WHAT...?
RIGHT, I THINK IT'S RECORDING THIS TIME... THIRD TIME LUCKY!
THOUGHT I'D LEAVE YOU A MESSAGE. JUST IN CASE I DIDN'T GET THE CHANCE TO SAY GOODBYE PROPERLY.
Y'KNOW, THROUGH BEING EATEN BY A SWAMP MONSTER OR SOMETHING!
I JUST WANT TO SAY THAT, WHATEVER'S HAPPENED, DOCTOR, I WOULDN'T HAVE MISSED IT FOR THE WORLD.
I'VE HAD THE TIME OF MY LIFE.
SO NO REGRETTING STUFF, RIGHT? I CHOSE THIS. I CHOSE YOU.
LIKE I SAID, THAT CHRISTMAS...FIND SOMEONE. BECAUSE TRAVELLING'S NOT HALF AS MUCH FUN ON YOUR OWN.
YOU NEED SOMEONE TO SHOW OFF TO!
I WAS WRONG, WHAT I SAID BACK THEN. YOU DON'T NEED SOMEONE TO STOP YOU.
YOU NEED SOMEONE TO KEEP YOU GOING.
THAT'S ALL I WANTED TO SAY. THANKS, BASICALLY.
AND GOOD --
...BYE.
The End

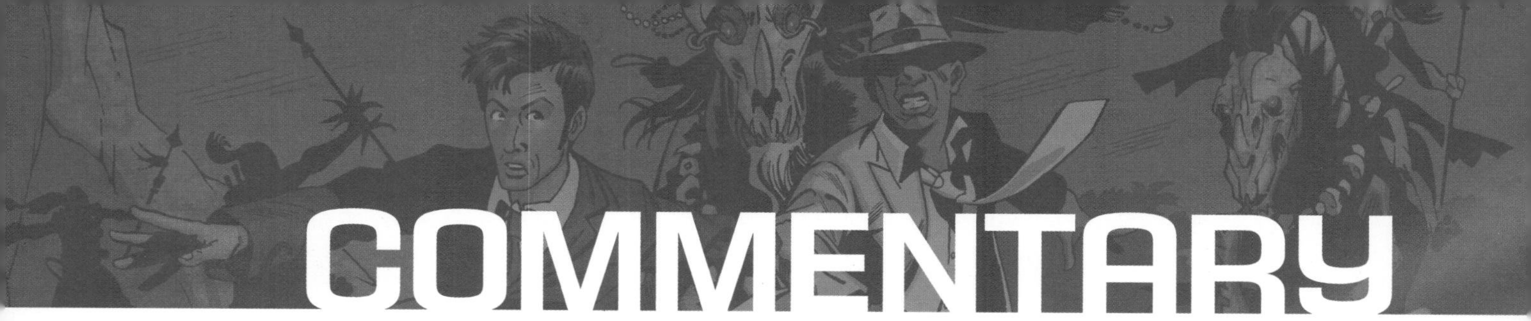

COMMENTARY

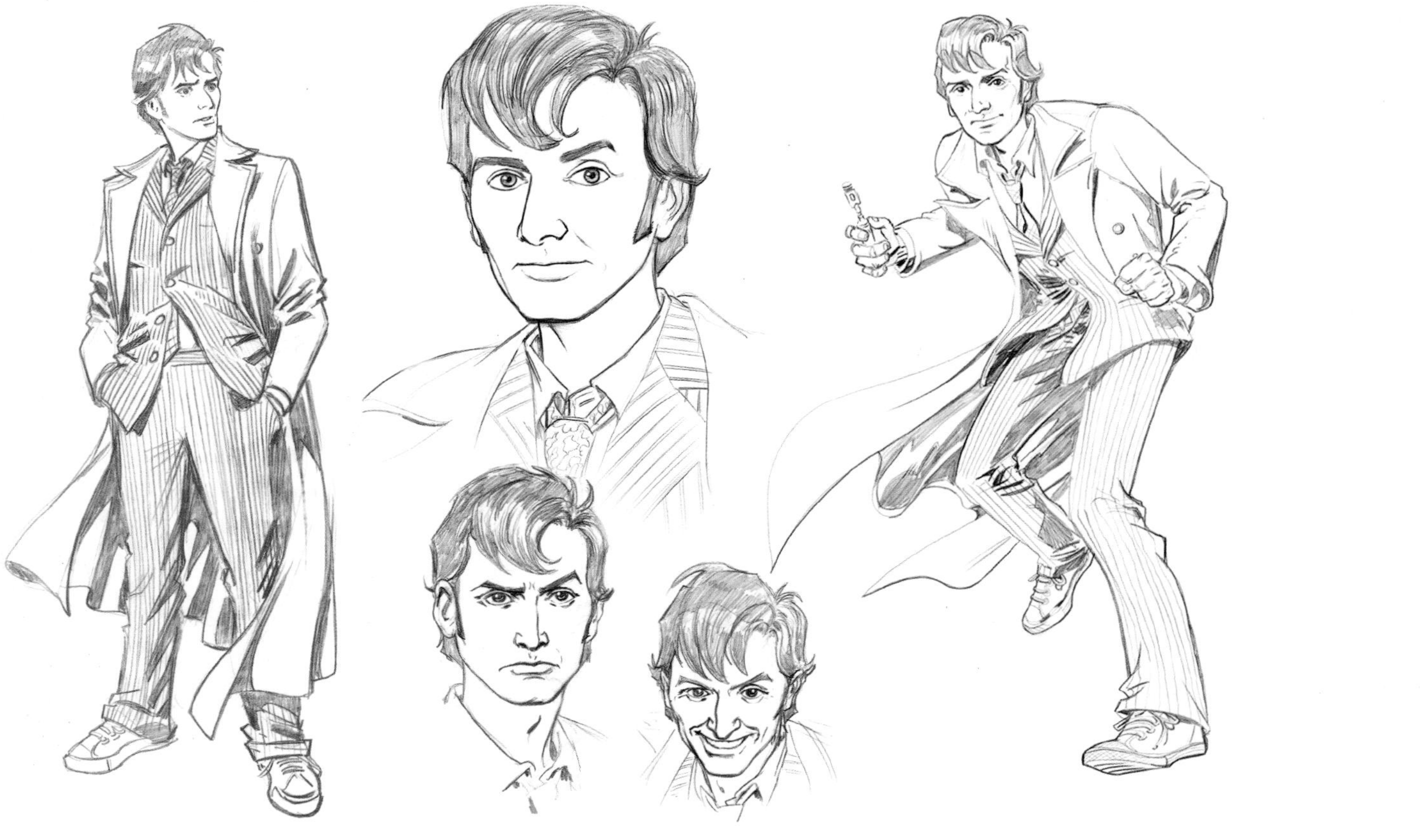

Mike Collins' original test artwork of the Tenth Doctor.

INTRODUCTION

Ah, the dying days of a regime. Statues toppled, desks tidied, longer lunch breaks. Yes, the first two-thirds of this volume collect *my* final strips as editor of **DWM**. Well, they're not my strips *per se*. I just worked on them a bit. You can hear from the real talent in the following commentary section. But this is my introduction, so I'm starring in it!

It's a funny thing, but once Rose departed the pages of **DWM**, the strip began to regain a certain feel we'd lost a bit with the Eighth Doctor's departure. A kind of weird, mad, odd loveliness that has been a vital part of many of the best *Doctor Who* comic strips. I think a lot of that came from us finding a small set of writers who really *got* the **DWM** strip, its history, and the variety of things it could do really well. It's not just a case of sticking the TV show into eight panels per page, there's a weird alchemy to it. And with Rob Davis and Dan McDaid – plus the steady guiding hand of Scott Gray – I think we started again on a road that stretched behind us to the first comic strip adventures of the Eighth Doctor, and then, much further back, to the classic tales of **Doctor Who Weekly**.

But when I look back on this period I'm also struck by the roads we *didn't* travel. The strips that never were. I might just be an old nostalgic, but these are stories we debated, laughed about, got excited about – but which never came to pass. I can clearly recall the lunch meetings where Scott outlined his multi-Doctor idea. The Tenth Doctor meeting the Eighth Doctor and Destrii on a desolate planet in an end-of-part-one splash page that would have been a hell of a cliffhanger. And then desperately having to hide the fact that... no. I won't spoil it. It's still a great idea. Who knows, it might happen one day.

But enough of what we didn't see, back to what we did. And I couldn't have been more pleased with my last set of **DWM** commissions. Mad fantasy, historical horror and wild soup chases. Yep, that's what the *Doctor Who* comic strip does best. And I really did see some of the best of the strip brought to life during my time at the magazine.

I don't think anyone could be unhappy with having their name on strips like *Children of the Revolution*, *Oblivion*, *The Land of Happy Endings*, *The Flood*, *The Cruel Sea*, *The Lodger* and *The Woman Who Sold the World*. Oh, and all the other ones too, now I think of it! I'm certainly not unhappy. In fact, as the most consistently fun and challenging aspect of the most consistently fun and challenging job in the world, I'm gobsmacked at how lucky I was to be allowed to work on these strips.

To all the brilliant people who brought these stories to life, I owe an enormous debt. And it's their sheer talent which still informs the strip to this day. Only now I get the pleasure of sitting down every four weeks without the faintest idea what's going to happen. That's still a thrill for me, and I hope for all of you, too. Thanks for reading. And here's to the next 30 years of **DWM** comics.

CLAYTON HICKMAN
SEPTEMBER 2009

THE WOMAN WHO SOLD THE WORLD

ROB DAVIS WRITER
I pitched this story to the magazine around Christmas 2005. I had been an occasional **DWM** buyer since the mid 1980s, but started buying regularly in the build-up to *Rose*. Looking at the Ninth Doctor strips I had a craving for the kind of towering fantasy epic that Steve Parkhouse and Dave Gibbons would produce. I wanted to tie the vast and fantastical to more mundane, everyday domestic realities. The style of the TV series almost demanded as much, anyway. Rather than base the story on Earth to get those aspects, I let everyday concerns become the themes of the story.

A lot of it reflected the stuff I was dealing with on a day-to-day basis – trying to manage debts, sitting in a queue on the phone to the bank, deciding which DVDs and games were suitable for my son and when to say no – I guess I was trying to take some responsibility for my past and my son's future. And with the small stuff it related to broader issues about freedom and responsibility. Somehow this all got boiled down to make a soup of enslaved computers, unwittingly genocidal children, flying chairs and brass robot Prime Ministers. I think the idea for the winged chair came from Enid Blyton's *Wishing Chair* books.

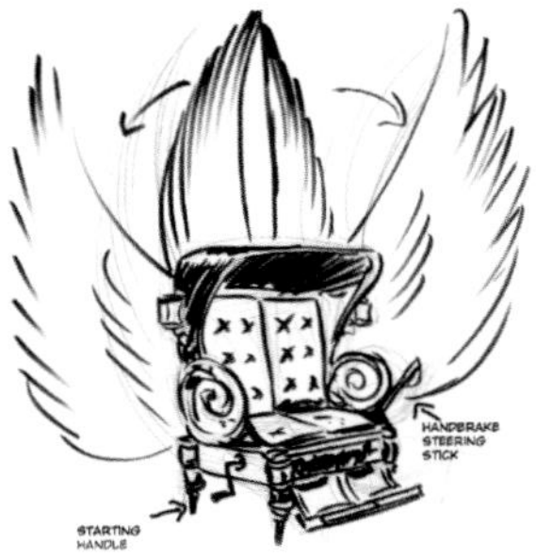
HANDBRAKE STEERING STICK
STARTING HANDLE

This spread: Writer Rob Davis provided sketches for how he imagined Sweetleaf and Sugarpea to look.

Loam, as the name suggests, is an alternative Earth. A version of Earth where the planet is mortgaged to cover a massive loan that allows the government of Loam to take their world from the dawn of the industrial revolution to futurist technologies and beyond in a single generation. Loam is a kind of well polished Steampunk world, which Mike Collins did a brilliant job in bringing to life. He must have exhausted himself putting in the details I asked for – I love the paintings of Sugarpea and Brassneck on the walls of the museum, the architecture of Loam and some of the tiny details like the coal-powered car at the foot of a High Goliax and the knight on the two-legged steed in the museum.

Loam has its own Margaret Thatcher-style ex-PM, retired from office and living with her lesbian lover in peace. Any resemblance to the Iron Lady was never meant to be flattering. She regrets some of the things she's done, and in the face of seeing her world destroyed, has the chance to put them right.

Showing the intimacy of a relationship between two old women could have been tricky, but their playful and almost interchangeable names for each other do the job instead. I wanted that to be how we knew them – not as ex-Prime Minister and companion, but as lovers – Sugarpea and Sweetleaf.

Their real names were Hellyer and Crowsdell, named after two bickering but likeable regulars on the *Outpost Gallifrey* forum.

The scary part about writing this story was that I had no idea what Sugarpea was up to. Her mission in the flying chair was just going to be a McGuffin, but Clay wanted it to be crucial to the story. I was over halfway through writing it, Mike had started drawing it, and I still didn't know myself what she was planning. Then, by chance, I came across an article on 'odious debt' – this was much better than her having a weapon to defeat the Krib; she could use the system of government and sacrifice herself for the cause. She became personally responsible for her actions as Prime Minister.

Clay wanted me to kill one of them (apparently this was because he liked them so much!), so I made the penalty for Sugarpea's actions death and then had her Brass *doppelgänger* do the deadly deed.

I think Part One was drawn before we had a title. It was called *Mind of a Child* when I first started, then I gave Clay and Scott a list of names to choose from. These included *Hex Life* (which became the title of Sugarpea's autobiography), *The Coal-Fire Heart* and *The Woman Who Sold the World*, which is a variation on the title of the David Bowie song.

MIKE COLLINS ARTIST
The Woman Who Sold the World is one of my favourite Tenth Doctor strips. I've said elsewhere that to me *Doctor Who* always has an air of Victorian Scientific

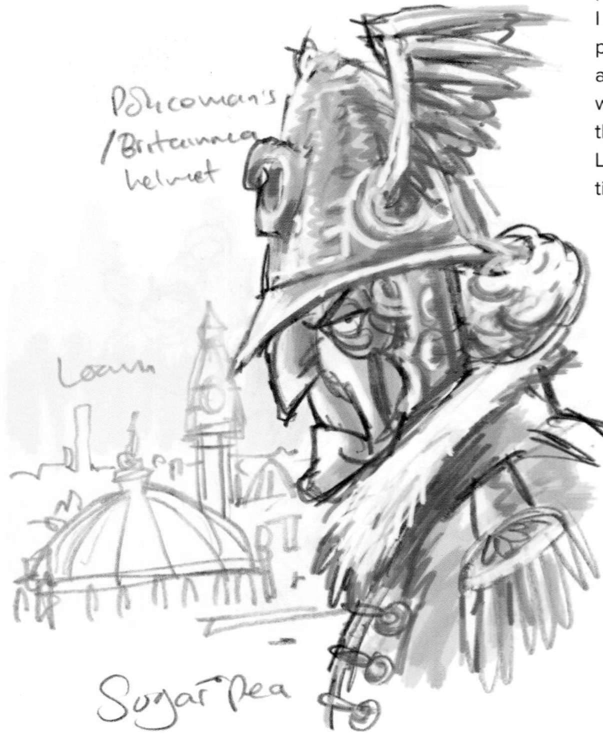
Policeman's /Britannia helmet
Loam
Sugarpea

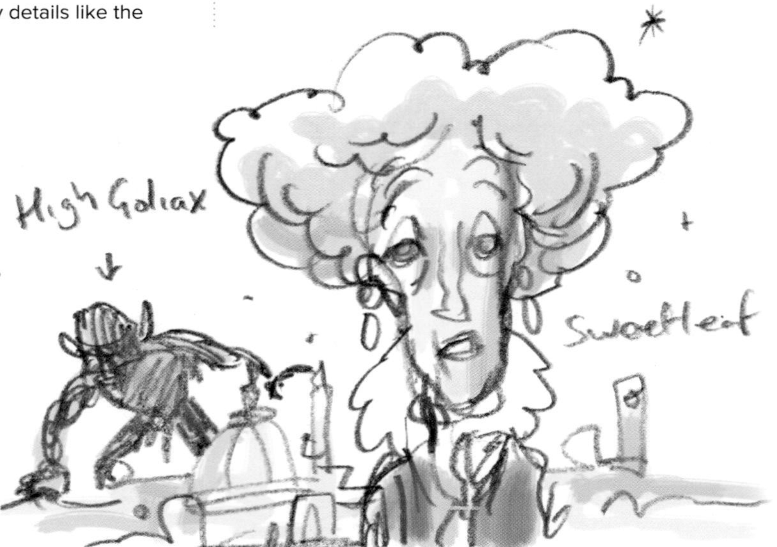
High Goliax
Sweetleaf

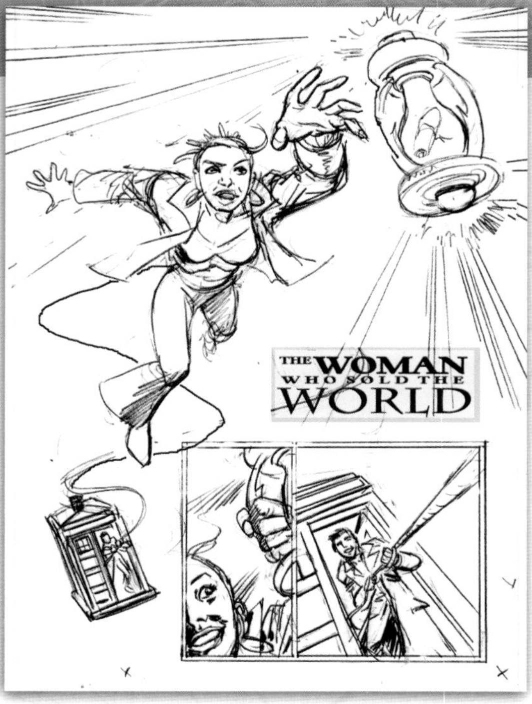
THE WOMAN WHO SOLD THE WORLD

Left: The rough artwork for Martha's comic strip début in **The Woman Who Sold the World.** Art by Mike Collins.

Romance and Rob's script hit all those beats I love so much. Not an easy script to draw, but that's not a bad thing at all. It made me think big and draw bigger.

Some of the design sensibilities actually spread across from an epic I was intending to write and draw for Martha that we could never break as a story, frustratingly. My mind, though, was in the right place – all very, very British Empire in Space vibes – to approach this Steampunk Marvel. I know the lead character was meant to be a satire of Margaret Thatcher (and as such gets off way too lightly in my reckoning) but I was immediately struck by the idea that the lesbian couple at the centre of the story (written *ages* before the TV episode that featured a similar pairing, dontcha know) were actually Margot and Barbara from *The Good Life*. For the sake of Panini's lawyers' blood pressure, I never actually drew them as such but that was what was going on in my mind as I doodled away.

The last episode, which has some of James' most gorgeous colours ever, was done in a crazed rush as my family holiday honed into view, crashing into my pencilling deadlines. I ended up working through the night, ironically, watching *The Iron Giant* as I drew. Hopefully there's no drop in quality, despite my welcoming the dawn from my drawing table.

I fell behind because I had, frankly, created a monster on this strip… by imagining the city as some Byzantium amalgam of Ancient Rome and eighteenth-century Paris (with touches of Greek and Eastern design) I managed to double the line count on each page we saw a cityscape. Those pages actually weigh more than others I've drawn.

It became a masochistic challenge to see if I could maintain that level of detail… in the Grand Concourse scenes (very much NYC's Grand Central Station re-imagined by Albert Speer), I decided to do as many detailed figures as I could in the throng. I snuck in Thor and Doctor Strange, and – God bless him – James coloured in their costumes. Now go back, and wreck your eyes trying to find them….

CLAYTON HICKMAN EDITOR

I remember being very excited by this strip, which probably wasn't great news for Rob as it meant I put him through a whole wholesaler's worth of hoops to make it as perfect as I always saw it in my mind. Actually that wasn't as awful as it sounds, as it was brilliant from the start – we just worked hard to make it even better.

I think it was around this time that we'd started cleaning up the Sixth Doctor's strips for their own graphic novel collection. Rob's story really brought to mind the mad-but-marvellous settings and characters of those halcyon Steve Parkhouse tales, while his dialogue was some of the best I'd ever seen. More than anything it just had an unashamed 'This Is The *Doctor Who* Comic Strip!' stamp which made me grin.

I was so in love with those cantankerous old alien lesbians, Sugarpea and Sweetleaf, that I cajoled Rob into making them much more central to the story. Much as I adored the giant metal men, the corpulent bankers and the twisted kiddies that Rob had also created, those two ladies in their flying chair seemed like the heart and soul of the story. I actually got teary when Sweetleaf finally realised that her life-long partner had sacrificed herself to save the planet. I never claimed to be manly.

More obviously, this was the very first comic strip to feature the adorable Martha Jones, so we made sure she had her very own splash page at the beginning, and we thought spacewalking on a bit of old twine to recover a message in a bottle was a suitably fun way of introducing her to the strip. Mike Collins did us proud with that imagery – in fact he did us proud with the whole strip. The detail in some of those dizzying high-angle cityscapes is simply astonishing.

One of my other strong memories of the story was how pedantic Scott Gray became about the strange jargon spouted by the kids who controlled the High Goliax. I don't think either Rob or I were all that precise about it, but Scott was incredibly on the ball and, should you ever meet him in real life, buy him a drink and I bet you he could explain exactly what a Flapperd Howw is. I'm not sure that I dare…

Below: The pencil rough for page 7 of **Bus Stop.** Art by John Ross.

BUS STOP

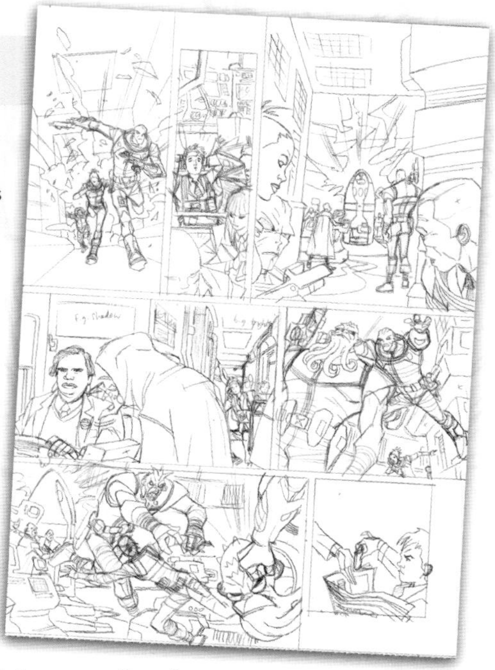

ROB DAVIS WRITER

Bus Stop was written in 2005 and pitched to **DWM** at the same time as *The Woman Who Sold the World*. The idea was to look at *Doctor Who* from outside – through the eyes of a 'not-we'. The TV series had gone from being one of the least cool things on Earth, associated with anoraks and personal hygiene issues, to the coolest thing on the box. I wanted to write a short story that reflected this and demonstrated how the 'not-we' have been missing out all along. I liked the idea of taking the *Rosencrantz and Guildenstern Are Dead* approach to a *Doctor Who* story, so we get a tiny glimpse of the big adventure through the perspective of an insignificant background character. And I also wanted

This spread:
More pencil art
from **Bus Stop**.
Art by John Ross.

to present the Doctor with a travelling companion who didn't think he was in the least bit amazing; in fact someone who ignored him as much as possible. I used the simple idea of a man on a London bus who feels persecuted by the 'weirdos' who sit next to him on his way home from work. Cue the arrival of the Doctor.

Clay loved the story from the off, but Scott wasn't convinced. I think he was concerned that we were laughing at the Doctor and setting up a McGuffin plot about Mars that didn't make sense. Scott changed the title to *The Wild Soup Chase* (a line from the story), but Clay overruled and the title was changed back. In the end I actually wrote out a synopsis for a hypothetical four-part adventure called *The Time Assassins* [see box, below] in which the events of *Bus Stop* feature as the

later section of Part Four to convince Scott. It was a bit tongue in cheek, but **DWM** ran the story as I wanted it and for that I am eternally grateful.

John Ross (of *Doctor Who Adventures* fame) did the art and did a wonderful job. I love the panel where the assassin says "Where is the Mayor of Earth?" Sums up the whole story.

It was pointed out to me a while later that some cheeky scallies had adapted the script, filmed it and put it up on YouTube. Have to admit, I was rather made up with that.

CLAYTON HICKMAN EDITOR
I don't think I've ever had more trouble with a comic strip than I had over *Bus Stop*. Over the seven years I was working with Scott Gray on the **DWM** strip, we almost never seriously disagreed. I mean, yes, the odd sulk from one of us now and again over some menial little point, but by and large we were of a like mind, and basically I trusted Scott absolutely. The man is, after all, a solid gold, 100%, hands-down comics genius.

Except he didn't really like *Bus Stop*. And I absolutely loved it! Again Rob's story and dialogue sang with the cheek and cleverness of the best *Doctor Who*, and this time he seemed to be channelling the early days of **Doctor Who Weekly** – specifically the poor fellow on board the bus that the Fourth Doctor and the Wrarth Warriors catch during *The Star Beast* ("Please don't let them sit next to me…").

I just wanted to get straight on and get the strip underway. Scott was very hesitant. I think he thought the backstory was confusing and silly and he just couldn't see what I saw in it. And as Scott was my co-editor I wasn't about to wave my magazine editor's credentials around and override him. No! He had to be coaxed! Bless Rob, he did everything we asked of him to help convince Scott that the strip would really work in print, nobody would be confused and nobody would seriously think we were just taking the piss. And, lord love him, Scott eventually let me have my way.

THE TIME ASSASSINS

The assassins aren't overly happy at the effect that time travel has had on them, however their own immediate plight has focused their minds and made them even more driven to complete their masterplan!

Two mutated assassins go all the way back to 2007 to kill the Mayor of London, they have a DNA Bio-scanner and an A to Z to help them locate him, as their local knowledge is limited.

As the lab empties the Doc, Martha, Moloch and Lithops creep in. Moloch disables the remaining mutant and the Doctor uses the machine to follow the assassins back in time and prevent the assassination.

The time machine sends the Doctor back to the 21st century and lets out a screaming, groaning noise, like someone running their fingernails down the blackboard of time whilst…

… groaning. The noise alerts the Elysium Popular front and Martha, Moloch and Lithops have to scarper.

The Doctor gets to the mayor before the assassins, he convinces the Mayor to hide then makes a 'Mayor soup' using some of the Mayor's hair and skin and adding some water, salt, fat etc and keeping it all at body temperature in a flask. Next the Doctor smashes up the Mayor's freeview box and numerous other electrical appliances to construct a machine that will convince the assassins scanners that the Doctor and soup are the Mayor and mean that they will target him instead.

With the Mayor safe the Doctor buys a travelcard and proceeds to ride the 5a bus in order to lead the assassins further away from the mayor. On board the bus, the Doctor borrows a phone and calls Martha. With the Doctor's mission complete, Martha, Moloch and Lithops return to the lab to bring the Doctor back. They battle the mutants and take control of the time machine.

Once back on Mars, the Doctor rigs the time machine to explode, he doesn't trust anyone with it, including Lithops.

The Elysium Popular Front are all arrested and the Doctor and Martha stroll happily away.

Or something like that…

And then the real trouble started...

We went for an established and very brilliant artist to draw *Bus Stop*, and I think I'm right in saying it would have been his first ever crack at the **DWM** strip. We'd all been bowled over by his previous work, and thought he'd fit *Doctor Who* like a glove. But things just didn't work out. The roughs he supplied were very rough and didn't really give us a good enough idea of what the finished artwork would be like. But we went ahead and trusted to providence. Sadly, I don't think providence had a very high opinion of us at that time. The pages we received just didn't do the script – or the artist himself – justice. The layouts were strange, the wrong things had been highlighted and a fun little story just fell completely flat. I worried, in fact, that Scott had been right all along.

But I persevered. I asked the artist for changes. He wasn't happy. Not happy at all. I think he'd been used to editors just minding their own business and not sticking their fat noses in. But that wasn't how **DWM** worked. We considered just pressing on, but I was increasingly miserable. I knew *Bus Stop* could work, but this artwork was just plain wrong for the story. Eventually I just bit the bullet. I paid the artist off for the work he had done, but said I was sorry, it just wasn't working. He was even more not happy. I doubt I'm on his Christmas card list.

Scott would have been well within his rights to shake his head, say 'Told you so,' and crack on with the next story. But he didn't. Because he is not only a genius, but a completely lovely man. We'd started, so we'd damn well finish! He made a call to our old friend John Ross, who'd done some fabulous work with us in the past, but was now up to his eyeballs with 16 pages of strip every month for *Doctor Who Adventures*. This time providence gave us a break – John loved the script and would, somehow, find the time to fit it in. Hallelujah!

And from the moment we received John's roughs, everything just slotted into place. By the time we had his finished artwork, so brilliantly coloured by James Offredi, even Scott could see what I'd been going on about all this time. *Bus Stop* worked! It was fun, it was clever, it was silly, it was mad.

And I'm very, very proud of it.

THE FIRST

DANIEL McDAID WRITER

The First pretty much came about as an act of desperation. I'd had my first ever, ever pitch to **Doctor Who Magazine** (a daffy little runaround in a library, with a reality-altering protagonist and a conspicuously bulbous-headed Doctor) shot down for being a bit too much like other stuff the mag had recently run (not to mention *The Mind Robber*). So I was feeling a bit despondent. "Don't worry," says Mr Clay, down the phone, "We're sure you have *lots* of other ideas." Ideas? Pshaw, I've only been writing, drawing and generally *thinking* about *Doctor Who* for 20 years. *Of course* I've got ideas!

You can probably guess what's coming next: it turned out that – some iffy fanfic notwithstanding – I had nothing in the bank at all. So I looked around the flat for inspiration: *Doctor Who in an exciting adventure with Some Ferns. Doctor Who and the Mantelpiece of Doom*... The TV offered the possibility of *Doctor Who Meets Frasier*,

which was cute, but not quite right. Then I saw a book my girlfriend had picked up on a whim the day before: *Escape from the Antarctic*, by Ernest Shackleton. So I said "*Doctor Who Meets Shackleton*"... and *The First* was born.

After that, it was just a matter of plotting the thing out. I think most *Doctor Who* writers would agree that this is the hardest bit, but it wasn't too tricky (and was a positive breeze compared to some of the stories I've worked on). I went up a rather exciting blind alley, with an amnesiac Doctor turning up in the snow with a hand made of ice and Martha missing presumed dead at the hands of the Skith. After that, I settled down to something a bit more trad. Actually, it's not a million miles from perennial *Who* fave *The Caves of Androzani*: a bunch of pioneering types out in the arse-end of nowhere come unstuck at the hands of a barely glimpsed monster. The Doctor arrives and tries to take charge of the situation... but falls foul of Captain Chellak – er, Ernest Shackleton. It's a classic, inherently workable structure, one that had been refreshed and revived thanks to the modern TV series hardly ever using it... and you'd be a fool to mess with it.

Having said that, I still had a good go. The ending was originally supposed to have the Doctor convincing the Mindcore that the Skith weren't so different to Shackleton and his men, and they should go in peace. As far as I was concerned, that's what the Doctor did: he was benign, rational – reasonable. He certainly didn't solve the plot by blowing up the bad guys. So I was pretty aghast when Clay and Scott asked for a massive explosion at the end, cos "that's what *Doctor Who* does." Is it, my friends? IS IT? Well let me tell you... oh wait. *Pyramids of Mars*, *City of Death*, *The Caves of Androzani*, *The Curse of Fenric*, *Survival*, the TV Movie, almost everything from 2005 onwards... Pretty much any *Doctor Who* story worth its salt ends with the bad guy going up in smoke. Right you are, then.

So the Skith went out with a bang. Though not too much of a bang – cos in a canny act of writerly self-preservation, I sneakily saved the Mindcore to bring back for a rainy day...

Above and below: Pencil art from **The First** by Martin Geraghty.

MARTIN GERAGHTY ARTIST

I *knew* I was going to love drawing up my first comic strip for Dan when Scott told me the subject matter. Brilliant! A pseudo-historical! I already had a copy of the wonderful Ken Branagh TV movie of *Shackleton* on tape and being the research geek I am, hot-footed it down to Warrington Library to gather up two armfuls of visual reference of the real Ernest and his crew and any other books on Polar exploration I could find. It's surprisingly well-stocked on the subject matter. Surprisingly, given that Warrington's not seen a meaningful snowfall since about 1981.

It was a joy to draw and Part One is a personal favourite episode of mine as it exorcised my love of period horror, and all things Hammer.

As has become a time-honoured tradition in **DWM**, the outgoing editor gets to make a cameo in his last strip, so you can see the magazine's longest-serving editor to date, Clay Hickman, on the last page – doing some heavy lifting for a change!

Cheers, Clay!

CLAYTON HICKMAN EDITOR

The Ninth Doctor had bowed out of the **DWM** strip having met Shakespeare, and I bowed out of the **DWM** strip during another pseudo-historical, this time featuring Ernest Shackleton. Yeah, okay, so my departure wasn't quite as important as Chris', but I'm very pleased, after seven years' worth of comic strips with my name on them, that my last one was such a great, traditional *Doctor Who* story, boasting great monsters and a couple of real prickle-up-the-spine moments.

Dan was great to work with, and again his dialogue, understanding of comic structure, and eye for the little details that can make a good story great, made my job a real pleasure. Having Martin Geraghty on board also made the whole thing that bit more 'real' to me. Martin was a mainstay of the strip before and during my tenure, and just as he'd been there, being brilliant, when I started at **DWM**, I was very pleased that he was there, still being brilliant,

Above: The Doctor becomes part Skith! Below: An original and amended panel from Part 4 of **The First***. Art by Martin Geraghty.*

when I left. And I was really over the moon that I got my little editor's cameo – as had Gary Gillatt and Alan Barnes before me – in the final episode. Not that I had gone on and on and on about it to Tom and Scott for months before my departure or anything. Oh no, not me. I mean, who'd be that uptight and controlling...?

SUN SCREEN

JONATHAN MORRIS WRITER

Around the middle of February 2007 I put together two pitches for comic strips for the *Doctor Who Storybook*. The first of which was called *Sunscreen*.

The idea came about because I'd read a post from someone on the internet moaning about scientific inaccuracies in the TV series – their argument being that it was poor 'science-fiction'. I vehemently disagreed, but this person's wrongness inspired me to attempt a proper 'hard' science-fiction *Doctor Who* story, just to see if it could be done; a story where the situation, the threat, and the Doctor's means of overcoming it would all be based in scientific fact. So successful was I in achieving this that nobody ever noticed!

The idea for a solar shield was something I'd read about in *New Scientist*. It's actually a scientifically-sound concept, and is the subject of serious research by NASA. For more details, type 'space sunshade' into Wikipedia.

Looking back at the pitch, I don't think I had a clear idea of what the monsters should look like:

They are vampire bats, but more sinister – great billowing leathery wings like Dracula's cloak, skeletal bodies and faces like deep-sea fishes, ashen grey like moths, horrific and terrifying. The Doctor describes them as 'Silhouettes' – creatures that live in the shadows of the universe, in the areas of dark matter between galaxies. Creatures from the low-energy depths.

This was still the period where I'd write the comic strip and Clayton and Scott would re-write it for me – because I didn't have much idea what Martha would be like and because I was still doing things like asking the artist to fit six or seven panels on a page whilst requesting that they should all be 'really big':

Panel 3 (really big)

Now we're out in space, looking at the single greatest human achievement – the Great Solar Shield, commonly known as the 'Sunscreen'.

It is a vast structure three thousand miles in diameter – but because we're in space it's hard to get a sense of scale. It's a vast hexagon set inside a wheel, reinforced with a spider's web network of struts and access tubes.

At each of the six points of the 'hexagon' and also at the central hub, there are vast hexagonal plates. They are huge mirrors, held in place against the wheel by a network of taut wires. The mirrors are large enough and tessellate so they only have very small gaps between them.

It should look vast, and spectacular, and awe-inspiring.

Earth

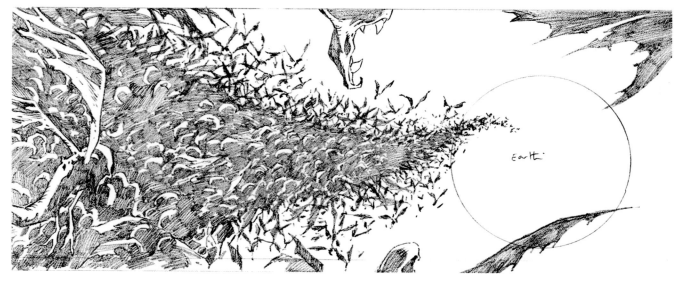

If possible we should get a sense of its scale and the sense that it is rotating about its central point.

At that central point is the 'control station', a space station embedded into the network of the wheel. It should look relatively tiny compared to the size of the structure, but we can make out it out because our viewpoint is nearby. The station should look very rough-and-ready, nuts and bolts – like an oil refinery.

The original draft also had the Doctor communicating with the silhouettes by telepathy and had Martha being paired off with a young chap called Hudson. The ending was also a little more... brutal.

PAGE EIGHT

Panel 1 (as big as we can manage)

And the Doctor's plan is in action... the shields of the sunscreen have been repositioned, each one tilted at an angle of forty-five degrees – though we can't really make this out, because it's all lost in a white burst of sunlight.

Emerging from that burst of light is a rainbow – like the cover of the Pink Floyd's Dark Side of the Moon, *or possibly circular and scattered, like a lens flare effect. It should be diffuse, transparent, but very brilliant and colourful.*

The Silhouettes are caught in space, writhing in agony, attempting to shield their eyes. But we can also see that their bodies are physically disintegrating, drying out and turning to dust – just as Hudson did earlier.

Panel 2

We're back in the control room. Tanaka looking at her computer. Martha grinning, grabbing the Doctor.

MARTHA: **YOU DID IT! WAHEY!**

TANAKA: THEY'RE **TOTALLY DUSTED! WOAH!**

When the script came back Clay and Scott had cut one or two panels from each page by combining the dialogue and events of adjacent panels. The original draft was a little dry and serious so I added quips like the 'biscuits in the scanner' – whilst some of the language was toned down, as I'd included lines like 'Not my cock-up!' and 'Shoot the sods!' It was also gently pointed out to me that it might be nice for Martha to have *some* dialogue at some point.

Draft two was delivered, Clay and Scott were happy, and so it was time for the script to be sent off to be approved by Gary Russell at the BBC. The merest formality, we all thought. We were wrong.

FROM: GARY RUSSELL
TO: CLAYTON HICKMAN
Sunscreen.

Eeeek. V V good in places but...

In so many ways, the set-up on a grimy broken down spaceship with a tired crew stationed near a sun, Martha going off with Hudson, psychic creatures... it's just Chris Chibnall's episode 7.

The Doctor's glee at killing the silhouettes is somewhat... off-message. Surely the Doctor would just zap 'em back to whichever Dark Time, primordial, not-at-all-Carrionite-similar home they came from rather than kill them.

Gary Russell

FROM: CLAYTON HICKMAN
TO: GARY RUSSELL
I did see some similarities with Chibber's story, but given that this is coming out months later, and it's our sun, not an alien sun, I wasn't unduly worried. Also, I was thinking Time-Flight/Night Flight To Nowhere *in my brain! :-)*

Just how different would it need to be to pass muster? You see, I really like the idea of it being about brave Earth pioneers trying to stop global warming in the usual rickety human way, so keeping the sun and the ricketiness of the station would be important to the story – if we changed Martha/Hudson and found something other than psychic energy needed to communicate with the monsters, would that be enough?

Above: Pencil art of the swarm from **Sun Screen** by Martin Geraghty.

Below: Pencils from **Sun Screen.** Art by Martin Geraghty.

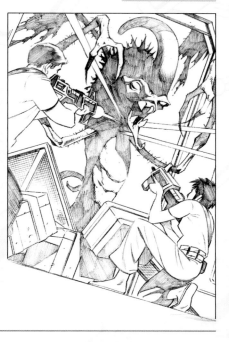

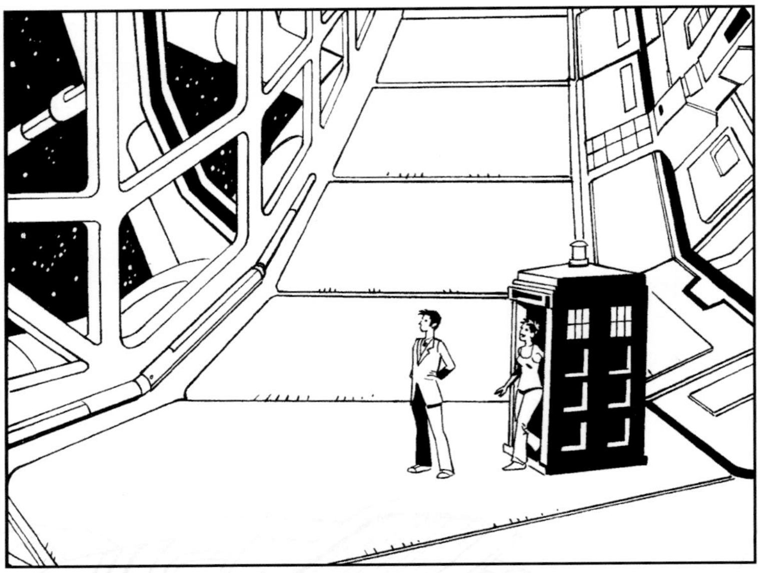

Above: 'An ultra-modern, super-efficient' space station. Art by Martin Geraghty.

The mass killing of what seem to be innocent, instinctive moth-monsters is a bit mean I guess – that can be changed, no worries.

C x

FROM: GARY RUSSELL
TO: CLAYTON HICKMAN
*I think I'd go for a real Stanley Kubrick/*Space 1999 *ultra-modern, super-efficient thing....[...] that'll move it away from Chibber's oil-tanker-in-space feel.*
Gary Russell

FROM: CLAYTON HICKMAN
TO: JONNY MORRIS
So, Jonny, me old mucker, let me know what you think. I don't think it needs to change the story massively, but removing the "human heroes"/"give us a hug"/"dangerous rickety old mission" elements would make it less derivative of The Satan Pit *and (although you'll have to take my work for it)* 42.

We will have to alter how the Doc deals with the monsters though.

Get in touch! Tell me what your brain tells you!
C x

FROM: JONNY MORRIS
TO: CLAYTON HICKMAN
Oh gosh. I am channelling Chris Chibnall. I'm off to put my head in a bucket of water. This happened last year with The Girl in the Fireplace*! This is why they should send me the scripts in advance. I try to predict what's going to happen next in* Doctor Who *and I KEEP ON GETTING IT RIGHT.*

Um. Right. Think.

Super-efficient station – no problem. Doesn't affect things either way.

Hudson – I sort of imagined him as Sawyer from Lost*. He can be an old git. He could be a butch lady. He could be a Dutch midget.*

We can cut the whole psychic thing, it's only mentioned in a couple of boxes. He could, ooh, send out a radio message, because they can detect radio waves. Peoples of the universe, your attention please...

*The character can say 'oh, the silhouettes have f***ed off' rather than being turned into dust. Seems a bit gutless to me, though – these galactic sods have killed someone by this point. No second chances!*

Virgin logo V good idea – I was thinking along similar lines myself!
Jonny

To be honest, and having seen and (immensely) enjoyed *42*, I'm not sure that *Sunscreen* would've been too similar had it been set in a 'rickety' oil refinery. After all, claustrophobic and rickety is much more *Doctor Who* than spacious and gleaming – it's also much more interesting to look at. God bless Clayton for sticking up for me! But then, the strip is perfectly marvellous as it stands. I can't help feeling, though, that in attempting to write 'hard science-fiction' I'd ended up placing an unnecessary constraint on my imagination.

MARTIN GERAGHTY ARTIST
So, a year on from *Opera of Doom* and another lovely little script thumps onto my doormat courtesy of Jonathan Morris – seemingly carving himself a very comfortable niche as the master of the *Who* one-shot strip at the time.

I'd already started to view these *Storybook* strips as continuing in the grand tradition of the World Distributors *Annual* comics of yesteryear (but considerably less bonkers, obviously – let's just say I wasn't expecting a return appearance by The Mongs anytime soon), so, as an affectionate nod to the first *Doctor Who* comic I ever read, I had the Doc and Martha drop the crew of the Solar Shield off in the same park that Jo Grant materialises in during *Dead on Arrival* from the 1975 *Doctor Who Annual*.

Comic Fanboy? Me?

CLAYTON HICKMAN EDITOR
Blimey! There's not much more I can add to that – other than the fact that I obviously wrote nicer emails than I remembered! It's a heck of a task to squish a whole story into just a handful of pages, and to tailor that story for a younger audience than our regular **DWM** readers (yes, I know *DWA* does it every week, but they're experts!). As Martin says, Jonny had carved himself a niche writing these *Storybook* strips, and it was always fun knocking ideas back and forth with him. Well, fun for me. Maybe less fun for poor Jonny!

More lovely stuff from Martin Geraghty in this one, naturally. But if I keep complimenting him he might put his rates up...

DEATH TO THE DOCTOR!

JONATHAN MORRIS WRITER
Death to the Doctor was a story I sent in, on-spec, in January 2007. I was so convinced that my idea was unturndownable that I wrote out the whole script and delivered it *fait accompli*. The thought had come about as an approach for a 'Doctor-lite' adventure (such as *Love & Monsters*) – why not tell a story from the monster's point of view? Start with a self-help group for defeated villains then kill them off, one-by one, in the manner of *The Ladykillers* or *Reservoir Dogs*. I took the Mexican-stand-off conclusion from the latter and toyed for a while with calling the strip *The Doctor-Killers* as a tribute to the former.

My other big influence were all those 'delegate' stories,

PFFFT

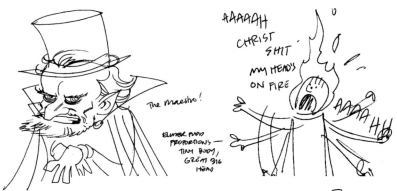

MARTHA: YOU GOT ALL THAT JUST FROM WAVING YOUR **SONIC SCREWDRIVER** ABOUT?

MARTHA (CONT'D): IS THERE ANYTHING IT **CAN'T** DO?

Panel 4
INT. ENTRANCE CORRIDOR.

The DOCTOR and MARTHA on the TARDIS threshold, taking one look back.

DOCTOR: SOMETHING **TERRIBLE** HAPPENED HERE, MARTHA... I CAN **FEEL** IT!

DOCTOR (CONT'D): WE SHOULD LEAVE...

Panel 5
INT. TARDIS CONSOLE ROOM

The DOCTOR is setting the controls as MARTHA watches doubtfully.

MARTHA: AND **THAT'S IT?** WE'RE **GOING?** THAT'S NOT LIKE YOU, NOT TO **INVESTIGATE-**

DOCTOR: THERE'S NO-ONE LEFT ALIVE... WE SHOULD LET THEM **REST IN PEACE**

Panel 6
INT. TARDIS CONSOLE ROOM

And, as the DOCTOR reaches for the dematerialisation control, he looks up, sadly, thoughtfully, a wanderer in eternity.

DOCTOR: AND BESIDES... I'VE GOT THE ODDEST FEELING THAT MY **REPUTATION** MAY HAVE **PRECEDED ME!**

THE END

When I was told that Roger Langridge would be drawing the artwork, initially I was a little worried – not because I'm not a massive fan of his work, because I am, but because, if a light-hearted story is paired with light-hearted artwork, it can sometimes end up feeling a bit too 'comedy'. When writing *Doctor Who* comic strips I always imagine them as drawn by John Ridgway. But my fears were unfounded and

The Maestro!
ELMER FUDD PROPORTIONS – TINY BODY, GREAT BIG HEAD
AAAAAH
CHRIST
SHIT
MY HEAD'S
ON FIRE
AAAAHH

Roger delivered a glorious piece of work which brought a lot of additional humour to the story but without losing what I will pretentiously call the 'integrity of the situation'. I couldn't have been more delighted – I love the aliens, the bits of dead fish, and in particular I love the spaceship which looks like two hairdryers stuck together.

The strip seemed to go down well – it won the **DWM** Award for the best comic strip of its year – and I'm particularly happy they found room for it in the issue with Kylie Minogue on the cover. And I still laugh at my own jokes when re-reading the story – I'm fascinated as to what Valis' plan to defeat the Doctor might've been – no doubt it would have been the most convoluted and implausible plan in the history of convoluted and implausible plans...

This page: More early doodles for the **Death to the Doctor!** villains by Roger Langridge.

ROGER LANGRIDGE ARTIST

Back on the *Who* bus again! *Death to the Doctor!* was one of those stories I get thrown from time to time by the good editors at *Who* Towers, a light-hearted excuse to draw lots of past Doctors. I guess it fits the readers' perception of me as a cartoonist, and I'm happy to play the role, but something I really liked about Jonathan Morris' script was that it wasn't just a bunch of daft gags strung together. Comedy tends to work best when it's just one element of a story contrasted against another, darker element – whether that's Buster Keaton's melancholy, Basil Fawlty's loveless marriage or, in the case of *Doctor Who*, something to give the kids nightmares. So Jonathan very nicely ticked that box. Kraarn of the Kraagaaron (did I spell that right?) is genuinely creepy, as is the setting – a decaying space base full of corpses. So that was something to get my teeth into.

What I really loved about Jonathan's script, though – and I wasn't expecting this from somebody I tend to think of as a verbal humorist – were the great visual ideas. Having pretend Hartnell-era baddie Questor be black and white, not just in the flashback but all the way through the strip, was inspired. The shiny studio floor in Questor's flashback, that was Jonathan's idea as well. The spaceship in the opening panel was another one – the script called for it to look like 'two hairdryers taped together'. Be careful what you ask for...

James Offredi's colouring here knocked my socks off. Just wanted to say. (Note to self: buy new socks.)

And I got to draw Christopher Eccleston, which was an added bonus – he was the only Doctor I hadn't drawn in the comic strip until then. Nice to complete the set. Now whenever anybody asks me which Doctors I've drawn in the strip, I can sneer, "All of them, my dear boy! All of them!" before I flounce away, maniacally cackling. Which is quite hard to do on a bus.

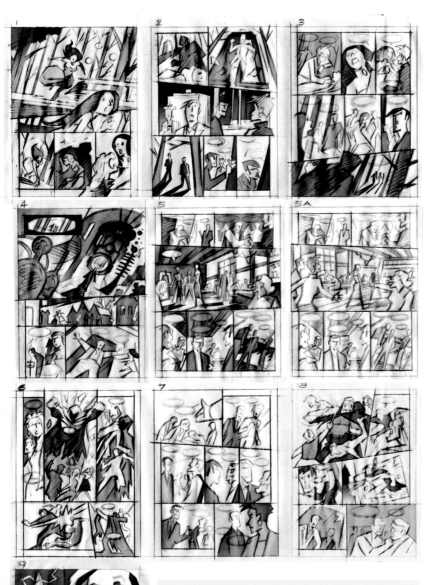

This spread:
Layout roughs
for **Universal
Monsters**. Art
by Adrian Salmon.

UNIVERSAL MONSTERS

IAN EDGINTON WRITER

Universal Monsters is my unashamed homage to some
of my absolute favourite *Doctor Who* episodes, namely
The Dæmons, *Horror of Fang Rock*, *Pyramids of Mars*,
The Talons of Weng-Chiang and, more recently, *Tooth
and Claw*.

As the title suggests, it's also a nod to the classic horror
films made by Universal Studios between the 1920s
and the 1960s, the gems for me being James Whale's
wonderfully atmospheric *Frankenstein* and *Bride of
Frankenstein*. I also couldn't resist adding just a touch of
Hammer to the proceedings. The Hammer horror movies
were the natural successor to the Universal films, carrying
the torch and tropes on for several decades more.

While ostensibly a science-fiction show, there is a strong
streak of horror that runs through certain episodes of
Doctor Who, yet typically the supernatural and mystical are
soon revealed to have a scientific, yet no less fantastical
origin. That's the same feel I wanted to convey here, to
depict a classic, almost clichéd, horror movie setting yet
with a twist.

There's the heaving-bosomed young woman being
pursed through the forest by some monstrous creature
– very Hammer! The isolated village living in the shadow
of the looming, ominous castle.

The quailing villagers, the immortal and enigmatic lord.
The lost young couple…

The next trick was to take all of these and to turn
them on their head, so that nothing what was quite as
it seemed, catching both the reader and the Doctor off
guard. So, the lost young couple became the Doctor
and Martha. The ageless lord was a clone, the hulking,
mute creature, a damaged cyborg and the poor, hapless
villagers, an army of genetically engineered warriors built
for blood and carnage.

It's not often you get to wrong-foot the Doctor, so it
was fun pulling the rug out from under him, then working
out how he'd put things right while the villagers were
snapping at his heels. It was also an interesting exercise
as a writer to give some depth to what, on the surface
at least seemed to be a cast of almost stereotypical
characters.

I wanted to take these classic clichés and do something
new with them, not just switch their roles around but
reveal that no one is entirely good nor evil and that it is
frighteningly easy to do the wrong thing for what you
imagine is the right reason, even for the Doctor. Ultimately.

ADRIAN SALMON ARTIST

Universal Monsters was a labour of love. I'd been a fan of
late night horror films, the Hammers and Universals as far
back as I can remember. To get the opportunity to draw
the Doctor and Martha in a gothic landscape like this was
brilliant! As Scott said to Ian: "Include any references to
Hammer you like, no matter how obscure – Ade will get it."

Viktor became my favourite character – he started off
in early designs very tall and lean but we realised he'd
need bulking up for his many action sequences. Cora
was described as the voluptuous Valerie Leon in the

script, but probably ended up more Jacqueline Pearce! Gideon was modelled after the brilliant Michael Ripper, the landlord of a million Hammer pubs and the Thane just popped out of my head. *American Werewolf in London* was the inspiration for the pub, though a couple of lads from Hammer's *Scars of Dracula* can be seen in the background supping ales. The Cyrene Khamirae were each individualised monsters, though the script asked for them to be a mixture of creatures. Realising they needed to be identifiable, I stuck with creating simpler monsters like Gideon the tigerman and Cora the reptilewoman.

The strip took upwards of six months plus to finish. Initially the pages were painted in grey wash before being scanned and digitally coloured – a laborious process that tested the patience of all concerned! I like to think the results were worth it.

THE WIDOW'S CURSE

ROB DAVIS WRITER

FROM: SCOTT GRAY DATE: 3 OCTOBER 2007
TO: ROB DAVIS

Dear Rob,

Hello! As I posted earlier, we want to get you thinking about the first Doctor/Donna story. And we have a brief for you! We want it to be four parts long. We want it to be mysterious at the start. We want it to be fast-paced and witty, look like a big-budget film and, of course, have some groovy monsters.

And we want the monsters to be the Sycorax!

We have permission from Russell to use them. But we're after a twist here – the Sycorax the Doctor met in The Christmas Invasion *were all male. And now they're all dead. But what if there's another tribe out there – a female one...? Yes! And they're deadlier than the blokes by far! Still with the same interesting voodoo magic/sci fi modus operandi, please (it's the thing that separates them from the usual alien invaders).*

One idea that might be a nice source of humour is the notion that the female Sycorax consider their gender to be naturally superior, so they assume Donna is the boss and the Doctor is her servant. Just a thought! But it's vital that Donna plays an important role in the story, of course – it's her comic strip début, after all!

Now, Gary Russell is already writing a Sycorax story for the upcoming Doctor Who *comic being published by IDW. We have to make sure there aren't any similarities with it. He's provided us with a story outline – here it is...*

"My Sycorax story is printing in Jan, so no clash. It's a space station/Sycorax ship setting, with a Sycorax hunting the Doctor to sell him on to hunters who like hunting the last example of a race. The Sycorax (singular in my story) is using a race of shapeshifters to a) capture creatures like the Doctor and b) sometimes to trick the hunters into thinking they've got rare creatures when they haven't. I saw the Sycorax a bit like the Collector in the Marvel Universe. At the end, his 'captives' wake up and we never see them presumably dismember his bony little hide!"

Okay, got all that? Avoid all of those elements – no space stations, shape-shifters, cosmic collectors or hunters! (I think we'd be fine with another Sycorax spaceship, though.)

We'd like Part One to have a mystery set-up that builds to a dramatic revelation of the Sycorax at the end of the chapter – a full-page reveal! As far as settings go, it's up to you – it could be present-day Earth (although if so, can we get away from England, please?) or a future setting on an alien planet (as long as we still have humans in peril).

Above: More pencil art from **Universal Monsters** by Adrian Salmon.

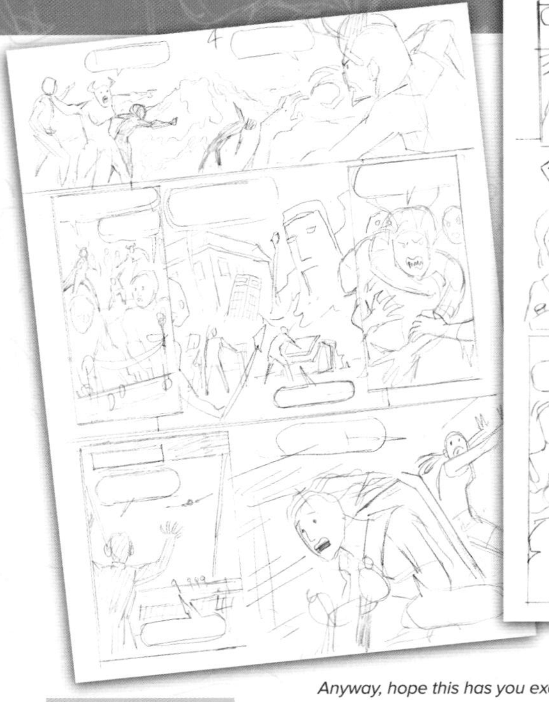

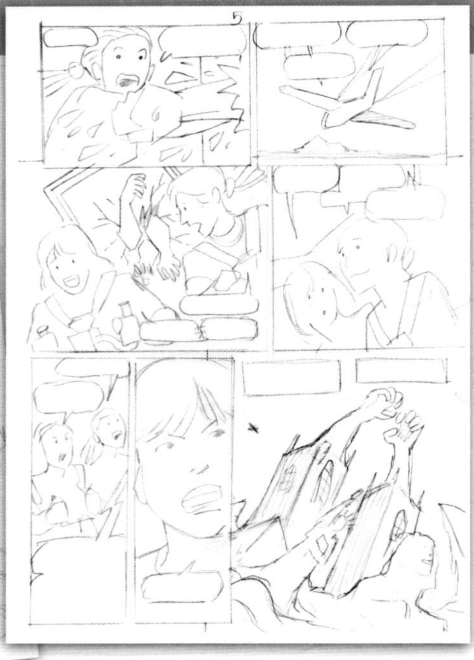

Above: Page layouts for **The Widow's Curse**. Art by Martin Geraghty.

Anyway, hope this has you excited. We're really looking forward to seeing what you come up with. If you want to ask us any questions, please post or phone!

Best, Scott.

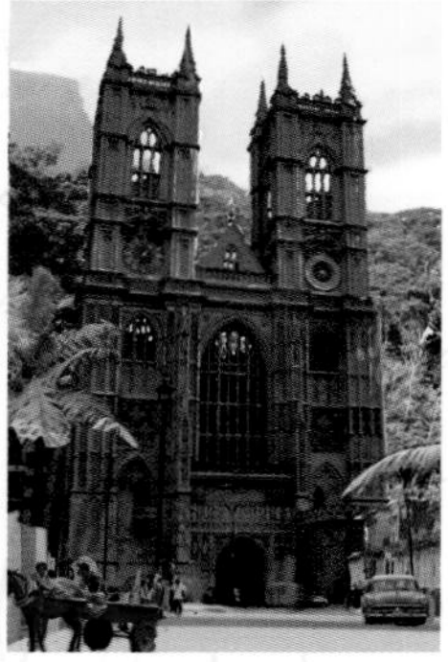

Above: An early Photoshopped mock-up image of how Westminster Abbey in the middle of the jungle would look.

Doctor Who stories are a bit like collages, most *Doctor Who* stories seem to have that aspect in their creation whether it's Victorian London torn up and pasted together with Chinese magic and gothic horror tropes or anything else that allows the Doctor to turn up and say "Hmm... something not right here..."

And that's how it was with *The Widow's Curse*. I had the brief from Tom and Scott, but needed a story and a location. Paste Westminster Abbey onto a made-up Caribbean Island and you have a mystery, fill it with Sycorax WAGS and you have a *Doctor Who* story in the making. I knew right from the original brief these Sycorax would be the bereaved wives and girlfriends of those seen in *The Christmas Invasion* and that they would be back for revenge. I also knew that the scenes from the end of *The Christmas Invasion* would become pivotal.

My first pitch was a case of 'throw it at the wall and see what sticks' (or in this instance 'throw it at Scott and Tom and see what sticks'!) As well as featuring Sycorax dentists and islanders with Steampunk masks it also had the scenes from *The Christmas Invasion* acted out by the Sycorax as a kind of primitive ritual, including one dressed in pyjamas and arriving in a cardboard box TARDIS doing the "No second chance" line. Scott pointed out, quite rightly, that we were missing a trick by having the Sycorax already know who the Doctor is and suggested that our Caribbean Sycorax WAGS should be trying to find out what happened to their menfolk as well as hatching a revenge plan. I had a new beginning and the plot fell into place from there on.

That collage I made of Westminster Abbey in the Caribbean stuck, but needed explaining. It was a carbuncle on the plot to begin with – the Sycorax had a technology they'd scavenged that allowed them to scan any object and instantly sculpt it from the rock of their ship, in this case they'd sculpted Westminster Abbey because that was where the corpse of the Sycorax leader, slain by the Doctor with a satsuma, had landed. Another idea I had from the beginning was to have a blind author who doesn't realise that he's in someone else's body and that his real body is being used as part of the Sycorax matrix. He became Lee Deverill, a combination of travel writer, human sacrifice and augmented technology. I wasn't entirely sure where these two ideas were going, but fortunately when I stuck them together they became the Doctor's *ad hoc* masterplan as he took Lee's place in the matrix and used the magma sculpting technology to destroy the Sycorax.

Another important aspect was that it would be Donna's first (and almost last) strip. She had to be central to the story and do something truly memorable. Flying a plane with Zombie passengers smashing down the door to get into the flight deck just seemed ideal. She also had Norah as a companion, allowing her to play the 'I'm-in-charge' Doctor role.

Scott and Tom insisted from the start that this story should be on a large scale and that included having a cast of characters. As well as Lee Deverill and the Sycorax – Haxan Craw, Gilfane Craw and Sister Shelka, we also had our three travellers – Norah, Jean and Harry. Once I decided that Harry would be the one to get it (this is *Doctor Who*, someone has to get killed!), it meant Jean would play a major role in tying the story together. I'd come up with the title, *The Widow's Curse*, by this point and widowing Jean allowed the theme of bereavement to come to the fore at the end of the story as the two Widows fight it out.

MARTIN GERAGHTY ARTIST

Thursday, 19th June, 2008

Dear Diary,

Finally finished the latest strip for **DWM** – and what a corker! A belting script from Rob Davis – full of action, spectacle, exotic locales – including a lovely reversal of the TV series' penchant for getting London Landmarks into a story... AND ZOMBIES! It is a truth, universally acknowledged, that if a comic strip artist doesn't love drawing zombies then he doesn't possess a pulse!

The reintroduction of the Sycorax race, creating a bona fide sequel that was logical and an intelligent expansion of their previous TV appearance, was just inspired!

Obviously, with all these elements in the mix, this is bound to be the finest Tenth Doctor/Donna strip to be committed to print. Oh yes...!

Thursday, 21st August, 2008

Dear Diary,

Just read *The Time of My Life* by Jonathan and Rob.

Bugger.

TOM SPILSBURY EDITOR

Scott and I had talked about using a TV monster in the strip for a while, and thought it would be nice to use something from a recent TV episode. Having briefly considered – and rejected – the likes of the Krillitanes or the Slitheen, we eventually went for the Sycorax... and fortunately for us, Russell T was more than happy for us to use them. The working title was *Curse of the Sycorax* – but we decided to change this to maintain the surprise at the end of Part One!

IMMORTAL EMPEROR

JONATHAN MORRIS WRITER

This story was pitched in February 2007 for the *Doctor Who Storybook* at the same time as *Sunscreen*; the Terracotta Army exhibition was due to arrive at the British Museum later that year. The idea of the Terracotta Army coming to life struck me as a very topical *Doctor Who*-ish idea; I'm surprised they didn't do it in the TV show (though the idea did eventually turn up in the third *Mummy* film). But, given the limit of eight pages, I couldn't find an interesting way of telling the story so it had both the exciting visuals of third-century China and the Terracotta Army in the present day – so I concentrated on the former.

For some inexplicable reason, when I re-submitted the story for the following years' *Storybook* I outlined it for seven pages. The plot was the same as the finished strip but with all the action of pages 2 and 3 taking place on a single page. The explanation of Meng Tian's identity was also significantly different (if rather conspicuously inspired by the story *The Talons of Weng-Chiang*!):

PAGE FIVE

Meng Tian is an arch-criminal from the future who has travelled back in time to evade capture. He used an experimental time machine which was one-way only. Now, with the Emperor as his puppet and an army at his command, he will be able to conquer the world and change history, thus preventing the 'Time Agents' who are after him from ever being born!

Meng questions Donna, and when she admits she is from the future, he is convinced that she and the Doctor are 'Time Agents'.

The Doctor, meanwhile, works out how Meng arrived here – there is a 'time rift' running through the Emperor's great chamber! A highly-unstable tear in the fabric of the universe. The Doctor discovers the futuristic-Steampunk machine that is being used to prevent the rift from closing. But why?

Returning, with Donna as his hostage, Meng orders the Emperor to activate his robot army. Meng is convinced more 'Time Agents' are on their way – which means he has to change history now, before they catch up with him.

This was ruled out because the TV series had established that nobody apart from the Time Lords had time travel, so instead Meng Tian became an alien (my thought being that he should look like a 'thorny devil' lizard).

The outline accepted, I wrote the strip in the same week as *The Time of my Life*. As with that story, I was guessing at Donna's character. By now Clayton had pointed out to me that I had eight pages, not seven. It went to a second draft, mainly due to clunkyness – originally Meng Tiang didn't appear until page 5.

While writing the story, I actually did some research, reading the excellent *The First Emperor of China* by Jonathan Clements. Whilst clearly there are some quite fundamental historical inaccuracies (things like me changing the manner of Qin Shi Huang's death and combining the locations of his palace and tomb) I'm quite proud of how many historical accuracies I managed to

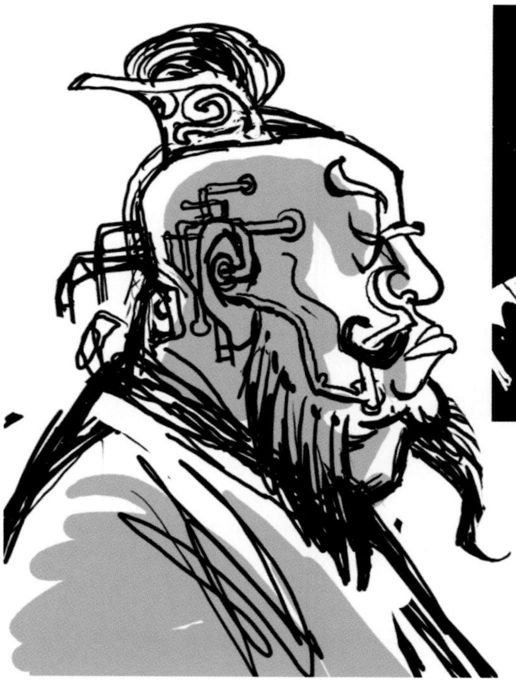

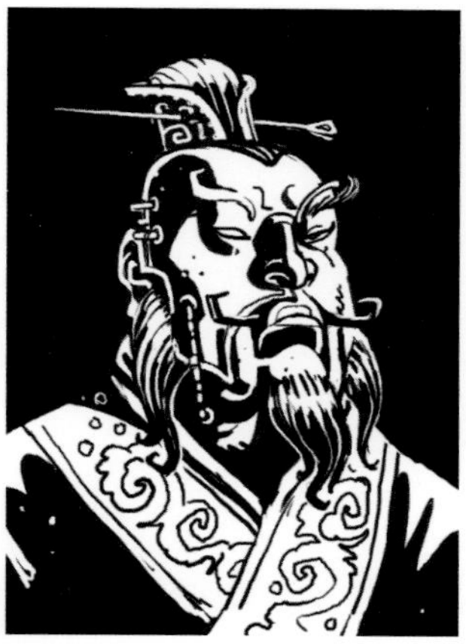

This page: Character designs from **The Immortal Emperor**. Art by Rob Davis.

sneak in. Qin was not only responsible for building the Great Wall and the Terracotta Army, he was obsessed with finding the secret of immortality, he was the victim of various assassination attempts, he surrounded his palace with giant statues of himself and there was even some business with a meteorite. As an example of my thoroughness, here's the description for one panel...

Panel 4 (LARGE)

A large shot of the throne room. The double doors are open and the Doctor is being brought in by two guards. Daylight streams in.

The walls are hidden beneath lush drapes and tapestries and burning braziers fill the gloomy chamber with smoke. There is a throne on a raised platform.

What is most impressive about the chamber is what lies in front of the throne – a huge map of China set into the floor, with the provinces marked out with rivers of liquid mercury. It's flat but has mountains and towns drawn upon it.

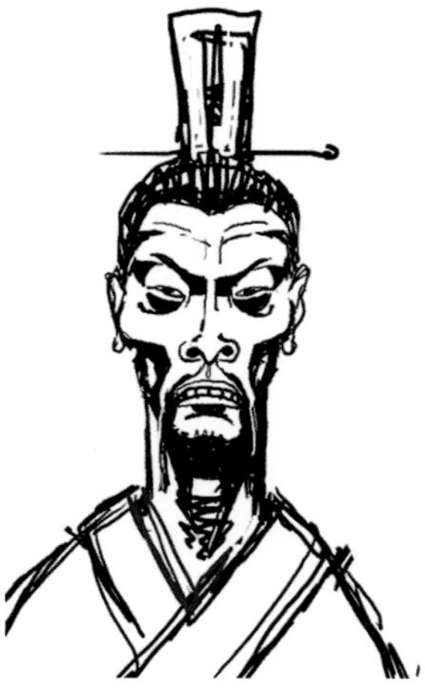

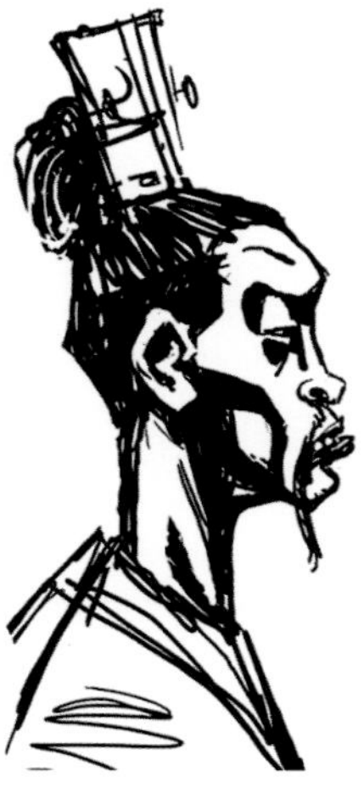

In the ceiling there are stars, so it seems the chamber opens onto the night sky. They are illuminated pearls and scattered in a stream like the milky way.

Everywhere in the chamber there is gold – jewelled statues of dragons and the emperor. (Concealed behind some drapes are some bulbous, golden, snake-like pipes, engines and machinery which will be revealed later on.)

… most of which was based on a contemporary description of the Emperor's tomb. Jonathan Clements was kind enough to look over the script, pointing out dreadful Jonny Morris anachronisms such as, er, 'Samurai swords'.

As with *The Time of my Life*, this was another Rob Davis masterpiece. It's rather beautiful; my only criticism is that eight pages isn't really enough – the story could easily have been extended to ten, or even 20 pages.

Oh, and Meng Tiang is on the run from the 'Star Council' – which, as I'm sure you know, were the same lot who were after Beep the Meep in *The Star Beast*!

CLAYTON HICKMAN EDITOR

My main memory of *Immortal Emperor* – aside from it being one of Jonny's easier rides as far as interference from me went! – is the amazing artwork that Rob Davis supplied to us. It was the first time I'd worked with Rob as an artist, though we'd obviously got to know each other well through *The Woman Who Sold the World* and *Bus Stop*. What I hadn't realised was that Rob brought his writer's rigour to bear even when he was in artist mode, and his insight and cleverness really made the script sparkle. He had some clever suggestions for layout, and for compressing panels while not losing the thrust of the plot or any of Jonny's better jokes.

It was the only Donna strip I edited, having vacated the editor's seat a while before, but Jonny's dialogue was brilliantly funny, and Rob's deceptively simple artwork really caught Catherine Tate, so I didn't feel I'd entirely missed out on the comic strip tenure of one of my very favourite companions.

Rob also managed to capture David Tennant's skinny, spiky Doctor in a few deft penstrokes, and his fantastic designs for the supporting cast really brought home to me what a talent he is. I do remember being unsure of some of the flat colours used for certain of the pages, and pestering him to add a few gradients here and there, but really I think I was just been pernickety. The strip is very beautiful and I really ought to learn to stop sticking my oar in!

THE TIME OF MY LIFE

JONATHAN MORRIS WRITER

FROM: TOM SPILSBURY DATE: 22 FEBRUARY 2008
TO: JONATHAN MORRIS

Hello Jonny. :)

I want to ask you if you'd be interested in taking on a comic strip commission?

It would be for Issue 399, and we're after a lovely one-part 10-page comic strip for Donna. By that point she's already going to have been written out of the TV series, (and she'll have only appeared in one other four-part DWM strip), so what we want is something lovely to celebrate her character. So it needs to be

funny, with Donna at the centre of things, but also with a nice poignant 'aaaaaah' moment at the end. Maybe the Doctor is remembering back to rest of the story, so it could have a final page a bit like The Land of Happy Endings? Something that makes people a little teary-eyed?

What do you think – are you interested? Shall we have a chat?

Tom x

My pitch was that the strip could be a series of one-page excerpts from untold Donna adventures – all of which would include memorable Donna moments which would link together in some ingenious but-yet-to-be-worked-out fashion. The final page would take place after Donna had left, with the Doctor seeing her 'if you are watching this, that means I am now dead' message.

As you'll see from the date on the email, this was before Donna's season of *Doctor Who* had been broadcast. So now, at last, the truth can be told; when I wrote this comic strip, I didn't know what would happen to Donna during her time with the Doctor and I didn't know how she would be written out. Oh, I had my suspicions, I had my educated guesses, but all I actually had to go on was Catherine Tate's performance as Donna in *The Runaway Bride*.

I don't think it shows; to me, the final page feels like a seamless epilogue to the conclusion of *Journey's End*. I wonder if people reading it thought it was put together at the last-minute or if I'd seen a copy of the script of her final story? But of course, Tom knew how Donna would be written and how she would be written out, so he would've let me know if I'd guessed incorrectly…

By the 8th of March I'd come up with a vague synopsis. The story was called *The Time of my Life*, after the song from *Dirty Dancing*, which struck me as a very Donna-ish movie. I did attempt to come up with a proper linking device but in the end decided to just link each story through the dialogue. It was a device I'd seen in another comic strip – I can't remember which one.

The original pitch was very close to the final story – the only differences being that the scene with the Polyglots took one page, that when Donna goes back to school it's because of a multi-dimensional giant cockroach, and that instead of the scene with the vampires, there was:

PAGE SIX

The Doctor and Donna are in a space prison – concrete, bleak and grim, like San Quentin. A cube-shaped panopticon where the Earth Empire sticks the Charles Mansons of the future.

Unfortunately, the Doctor and Donna's visit has coincided with a riot, which is also coinciding with a prison break, which is also coinciding with a space craft crashing into the side of the space station. All the maniacs have broken loose.

The other main difference was my original thought for the final page. For which I beg your forgiveness; it's excruciatingly embarrassing and would have left the emotional pudding well-and-truly over-egged.

PAGE TEN

BOX: THERE IS A DOOR IN THE TARDIS. A DOOR THAT IS RARELY OPENED.

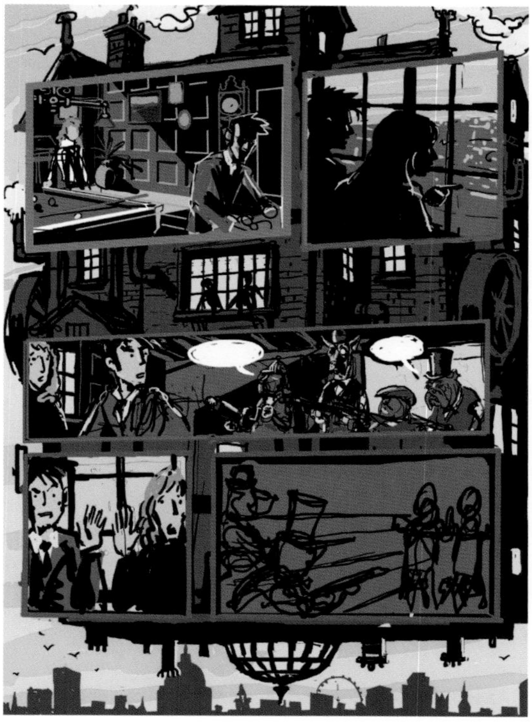

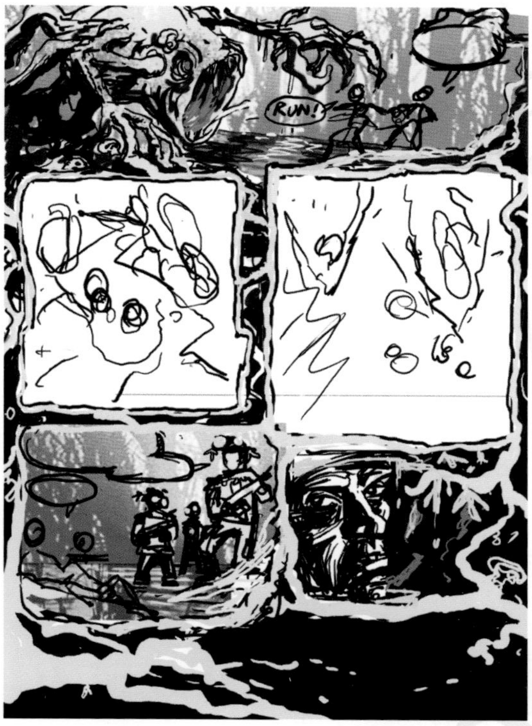
RUN!

This spread: Rob Davis' page designs for various segments of **The Time of My Life**.

BOX: BECAUSE IT LEADS TO THE ROOM WHERE THE MEMORIES ARE KEPT.

We see the room – it's a cross between the TARDIS console room and the cloister room. Ancient. Crumbling. Untidy, littered with junk, like an attic.

In the gloom there are holograms of the Doctor's past companions. Donna. Martha. Rose. And others... some we recognise, some we don't. More than we expect. Dozens. All like ghosts, caught in conversation, frozen.

The Doctor walks amongst them, into the darkness.

END

Gruesome, isn't it? Fetch the buckets! I'm always moaning about stories that end with portentous voice-overs and yet I end up writing the worst of them all.

Tom called me a few days later. The prison break would have to be changed because they were already planning a prison story. The cockroach would have to be changed because there was going to be a giant beetle in the TV series. And the final page would have to be changed because it was ghastly.

So I wrote a second outline, delivered on the 14th. The only other significant difference was that the Beatles section originally ended with the fab four being kidnapped by an alien memorabilia collector – it was felt that each page didn't necessarily have to include an extra-terrestrial menace.

In terms of the various stories, it was a case of me rummaging through my metaphorical bottom drawer for ideas which I'd never got around to using...

1) The Polyglots were included as a nod to the 80s comic strips in which they had featured (rush out and buy *Doctor Who: Voyager* if you haven't already). And at least one story should start with them landing in a quarry.

2) The aristocratic dogs were inspired by those paintings of dogs playing pool or poker in a gentleman's club. They were also an affectionate piss-take of the TV series' tendency to have aliens which are humans with animal heads (I'm still waiting for space sheep!). The plot was taken from an idea for a comic strip I'd submitted back in 2006:

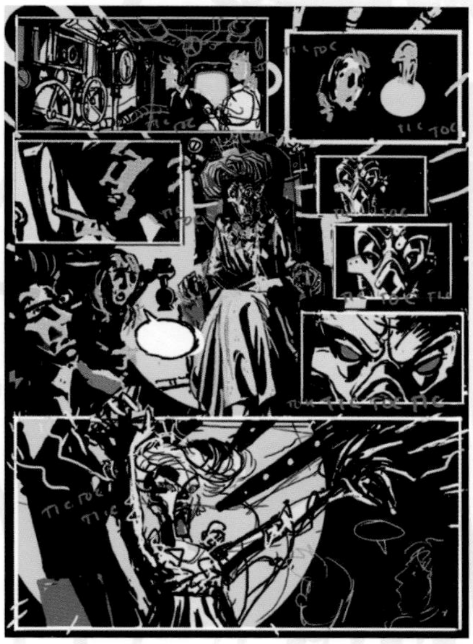

REVENGE OF THE SPIDERS

A spaceship arrives in orbit piloted by alien spiders. They have observed the Earth from afar and concluded that the spiders of Earth are being oppressed by the human race. Using communication satellites they set about reversing the status quo, directing a special beam down onto the Earth that will cause spiders to develop sufficient intelligence to 'rise up' against humanity.

Suddenly, everywhere in London, the spiders are out for blood! Thousands of them leap onto people, smothering them in webs. They swarm up out of plug holes. They only require humans for one thing – as repositories for their eggs.

The cliffhanger to Part One would be the Doctor and Rose locking themselves in a house as the streets outside are over-run. They seal themselves in, so no spiders can get at them. Then Rose opens her mouth – and spiders emerge!

How does the Doctor win? Well, just as you might kill a spider by using a magnifying glass and the sun's rays, the Doctor re-aligns the solar panels of a satellite to reflect the

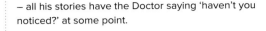

sun into the spider's alien spaceship. The spaceship begins to smoulder, so the alien spiders decide to vanish down a space/time wormhole. Better put a plug in it though, or they'll be back...

...a story which, after the events of *The Runaway Bride*, clearly wasn't going to be used anytime soon!

3) Another tribute to past strips – this time all those terribly macho **DWM** strips written in the late 80s by Dan Abnett about troopers investigating menaces on desolate alien worlds. Clearly he'd been to see *Aliens* one or two times!

4) A vague idea I'd had for a story which never got anywhere, the robot Miss Haversham was a result of a 'think of a spooky thing' exercise. The Doctor's 'haven't you noticed?' line is a Steven Moffat pastiche/tribute

This page: Character designs for Miss Haversham. Art by Rob Davis.

– all his stories have the Doctor saying 'haven't you noticed?' at some point.

5) I was determined that if anyone was going to write a story about the Doctor meeting The Beatles, it should be me. I can't quite believe they haven't done it in the TV series yet, to be honest. It would, quite literally, be fab. I had the Fab Four singing *My Bonnie* because it's one of the few songs they ever did which isn't in copyright. And they definitely did perform it at The Cavern.

6) A replacement for the 'prison break', this is a cod-*Buffy* load of old Goth.

7) Way back in 2000 I'd pitched a *Doctor Who* novel to BBC Books involving Napoleon attacking Moscow with nuclear bombs. That book never happened and I wrote *Anachrophobia* instead, but with *The Time of my Life* I finally had a chance to dust down the idea.

8) I'm slightly annoyed that I used the 'young Doctor and Donna' idea for one page of a comic strip as it would've made a good full-length story in its own right. They could even do it on TV with child actors. It would be amazing.
    Essentially, though, this was another tribute – this time to all those strips in the mid-90s where the Doctor would find himself in a virtual reality dimension, which would usually entail him floating through a sea of his dead companions' faces and flying chess pieces with the villain saying the lines, "Now you are in my reality, Time Lord, you play by my rules!" I wasn't really paying attention to the comic strips during the mid-90s but they seemed to do that an awful lot!

9) Donna's goodbye. This was the first thing I wrote. It flowed really easily. Because I had to be sure I was getting it right, this scene was written in full for the first synopsis and not a single comma ended up getting changed.
    If it was inspired by anything, it was the episode of *Star Trek* where Tasha Yar is killed by an oil slick monster and all the crew gather on the holodeck for her final message. It certainly *wasn't* inspired by the episode of *Torchwood* which had a similar ending – the strip was delivered on the 24th of March, before *Exit Wounds* was broadcast.
    Although I had *The Runaway Bride* to go on, I still had to guess at the 'new' Donna's personality. Plus, with comic strips, you have to caricature the dialogue slightly – make each Donna line so Donna-ish, make each Doctor line so Doctor-ish, in order to give a sense of the actors' voices. With Donna, I presumed she would be of the Russell T Davies 'cheeky and mouthy'-school, with the addition of Catherine Tate's very emphatic line delivery which means she tends to stress the last noun of each sentence.

    The finished strip went down extremely well and I received more kind comments than I knew what to do with. Which I suspect was partly due to the excellent timing, Tom's original idea for a 'poignant' strip, and partly due to the extraordinarily brilliant artwork by the extraordinarily brilliant Rob Davis. I can't praise his work highly enough. Each page looks like an excerpt from a different strip; the style of artwork changes and Geraint Ford gives each 'story' its own palette. I particularly love the frame with the Cossacks, it has so much energy, and the scene with young Doctor and Donna in a classroom which bears an uncanny similarity to the one I had in mind from my own schooldays. Plus there's the Thompson Twins satchel and the *Grange Hill* sausage... and those last few frames of Donna looking beautiful... oh, it's all just *glorious*. I was overjoyed when I received the proofs through the post – they were so good, I couldn't help looking through them again every day for the next month!

ROB DAVIS ARTIST
Jonny's script was all about stories, loads of untold stories, a perfect and painful tribute to Donna's fate as the companion who can't remember her time with the Doctor. As a comic strip companion she only featured in three strips, but thanks to *The Time of My Life* she gets an extra eight stories in one strip and a proper farewell scene. For most of the strip there is one story per page and to help make that work I wanted each page to have its own identity. Comic strip art isn't just about sequential storytelling, it can do things that other storytelling media like TV and books can't. I felt I needed to suggest more than you can fit into a handful of panels so I used themic layouts and different colour palettes for each page.

Here are the eight new adventures and that sad farewell.

1) The Polyglots. The mating ritual is art in nature – colours, patterns and exotic displays are par for the course in courtship and here the Zyglot wooing is represented by them ejaculating luminous psychedelic patterns into the ether. John Ridgway drew this as a kind of literal flowering – rendering the flowers as three-dimensional. I was after the patterns themselves – courtship as design – true to nature.

2) The aristocratic dogs. Jonny mentioned a floating Steampunk mansion in the script but hadn't actually asked for a picture of it. We had to see it, but there wasn't room for a giant house with six busy panels already on the page. I designed the page so that the original six panels fit inside a larger splash panel depicting the flying house... then realised how much extra work I'd given myself! I framed the five panels with gold frames as a nod to those dog paintings Jonny was thinking of, and for some reason I chose to set all the frames in perspective with the front of the house.

3) The swamp planet. After having fun with frames on the last page this time I went a step further. The line from the script that stuck with me was when the grim general type explains that the whole swamp is "a single living organism." This gave me the idea of making the page a single living organism – having the panels described by intertwined roots – everything that happens here is in the swamp's clutches! This page and its predecessor are the best examples of what I wanted to achieve: the periphery gives us a greater vision of the story without breaking the story's natural flow.

4) The brief for this page needed just three words: 'robot Miss Haversham'. How could I go wrong from there?! Lots of rusted cables and even some rusted panel boxes for good measure. I did a hatful of designs for Miss Haversham before I realised how small she'd be on the page and so I ended up using a much simpler design instead.

5) The Beatles. I inserted a Time Traveller's gag here... Jonny had Lennon asking if the signature was for Donna's daughter, seemed like the natural reply was "No, it's for me

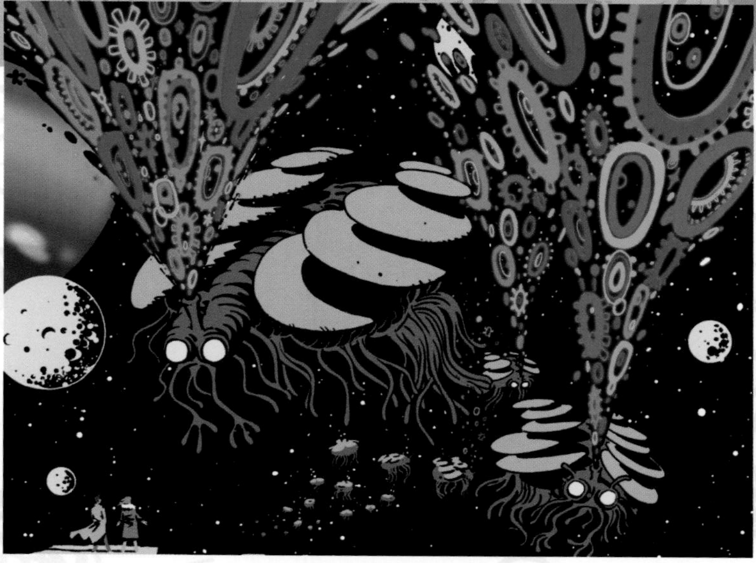

Above: The Polyglots make a comeback in **The Time of my Life**. Art by Rob Davis.

mum." Jonny wanted torn posters for the Mersey bands of the early Sixties like the Big Three and Ian and the Zodiacs to help give it a Cavern Club feel.

6) This page is a study in how to draw fences. Includes the lovely link line where Donna says "First one of you to try something gets a kick in the..." turn page: "COSSACKS!!"

7) I had intended to make the laser cannon in the last panel a giant Dalek's head which would have thrown up all sorts of questions. Don't know why I didn't, actually...

8) Geri has to get credit for rescuing this page with his colour work – I had produced rough colour guides for all the pages apart from this one and it wasn't working until Geri suggested making all the fantasy world black and white and everything real – the Doctor, Donna, TARDIS and alien virus – in colour. Brilliant idea, simple ideas are often the best. Jonny asked for a kind of giant moth/bat creature at the end, but I wanted to keep the teacher in the last panel and so I did a definitive 'bug-eyed monster' coming out of her head instead. (Also I couldn't think how to draw a giant moth/bat creature and I was running out of time!) Donna has The Thompson Twins Tipexed onto her school bag and the Doctor has a number of bands scrawled on his. The Doctor's bag is mostly hidden by the "AAAIIIEEE!" so here are those bands in full [see right]. Is this what a 12-year-old Tenth Doctor would have been listening to in 1982? I think so.

Below: Those bands in full – and the rough art of the final panel. Art by Rob Davis.

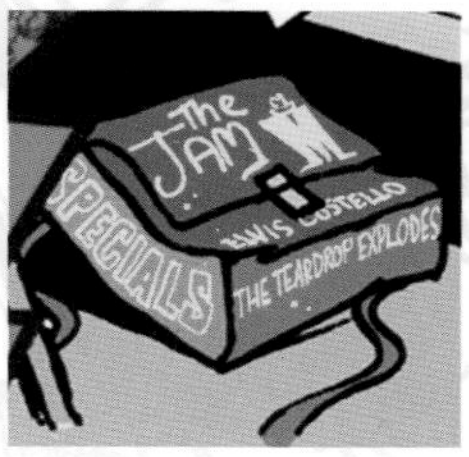
The JAM
SPECIALS
THE TEARDROP EXPLODES

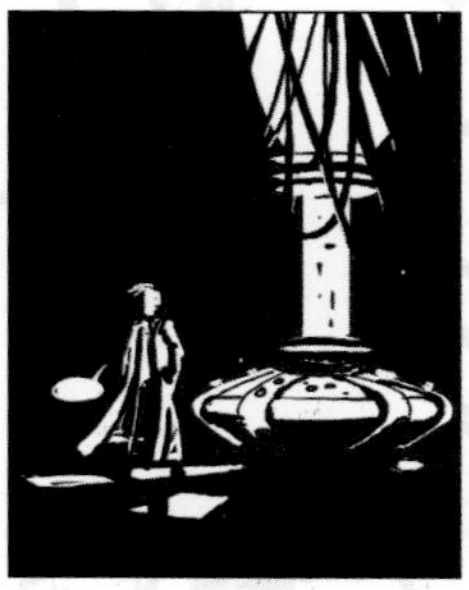

9) This was the first thing I drew as soon as I got the script. This page seemed to draw itself really. In fact my first rough for that last panel is almost identical to the final image.

TOM SPILSBURY EDITOR
It was a shame in a way, that we decided to write Donna out of the strip almost immediately, but Scott and I already had plans to introduce a new companion of our own, and sadly, that meant ditching Donna. It seemed sensible to start our new 'arc' in Issue 400, which left us with a gap for Issue 399. So it was fun to show all those 'strips that might have been', and given that we knew this would be published after the broadcast of *Journey's End*, we knew that anything we did would have an added air of poignancy. I was worried, for a while, about that final page, as we were effectively adding a new ending to Russell's story. Would he mind? Fortunately for us, he gave it the thumbs up. Of course, by then, we were deep into our plans for the next 21 issues of comic strip. But that's another story, for another time... ■

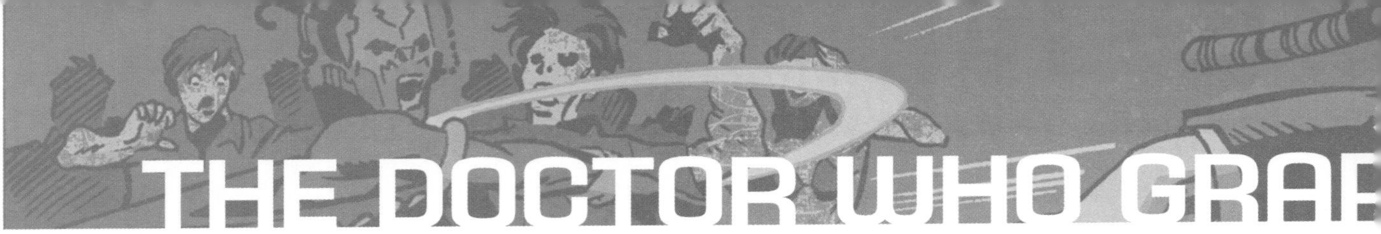
THE DOCTOR WHO GRAP

CLASSIC STRIP ADVENTURES

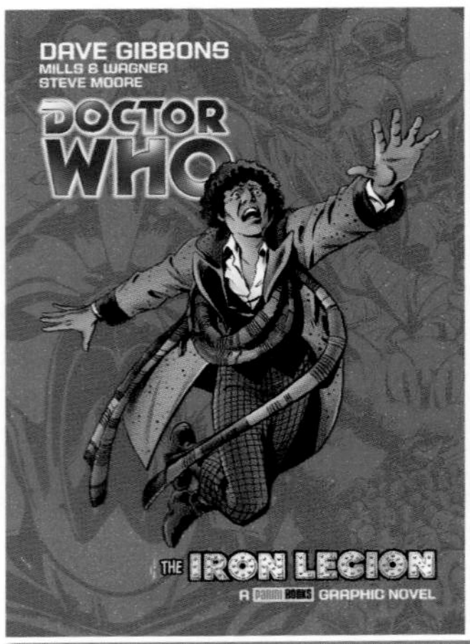
DAVE GIBBONS
MILLS & WAGNER
STEVE MOORE
DOCTOR WHO
THE IRON LEGION
A PANINI BOOKS GRAPHIC NOVEL

THE IRON LEGION

Containing 5 digitally restored Fourth Doctor stories: **THE IRON LEGION, CITY OF THE DAMNED, THE STAR BEAST, THE DOGS OF DOOM** and **THE TIME WITCH!**

Featuring work from **DAVE GIBBONS, PAT MILLS, JOHN WAGNER** and **STEVE MOORE**

164 pages | b&w softcover
£14.99 | $24.95
ISBN 1-9041 59-37-0

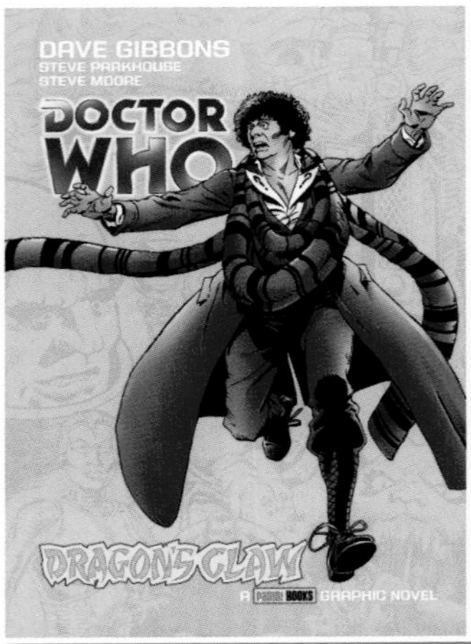
DAVE GIBBONS
STEVE PARKHOUSE
STEVE MOORE
DOCTOR WHO
DRAGON'S CLAW
A PANINI BOOKS GRAPHIC NOVEL

DRAGON'S CLAW

Containing 10 digitally restored Fourth Doctor adventures: **DRAGON'S CLAW, THE COLLECTOR, DREAMERS OF DEATH, THE LIFE BRINGER, WAR OF THE WORDS, SPIDER-GOD, THE DEAL, END OF THE LINE, THE FREE-FALL WARRIORS, JUNKYARD DEMON** and **THE NEUTRON KNIGHTS!**

164 pages | b&w softcover
£14.99 | $24.95
ISBN 1-9041 59-81-8

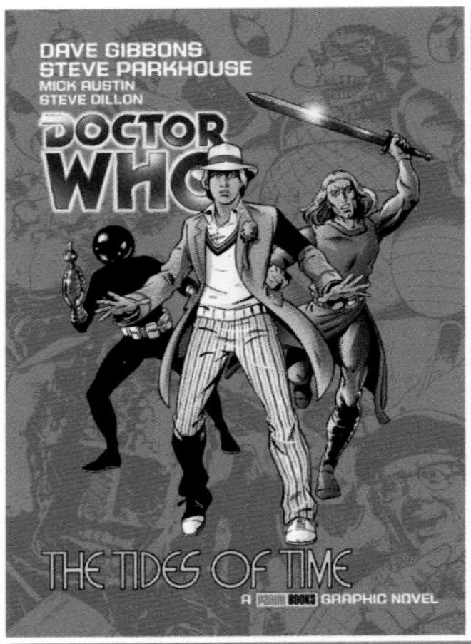
DAVE GIBBONS
STEVE PARKHOUSE
MICK AUSTIN
STEVE DILLON
DOCTOR WHO
THE TIDES OF TIME
A PANINI BOOKS GRAPHIC NOVEL

THE TIDES OF TIME

The Fifth Doctor's complete comic strip run: **THE TIDES OF TIME, STARS FELL ON STOCKBRIDGE, THE STOCKBRIDGE HORROR, LUNAR LAGOON, 4-DIMENSIONAL VISTAS** and **THE MODERATOR!**

Featuring art from **DAVE GIBBONS**

228 pages | b&w softcover
£14.99 | $24.95
ISBN 1-9041 59-92-3

THE COMPLETE EIGHTH DOCTOR

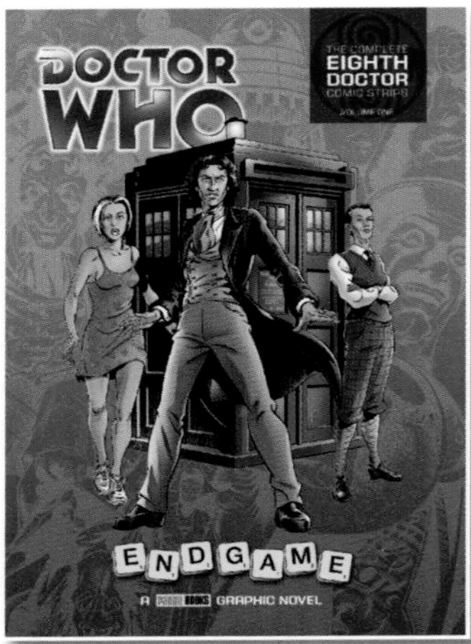
DOCTOR WHO
THE COMPLETE EIGHTH DOCTOR COMIC STRIPS
VOLUME ONE
ENDGAME
A PANINI BOOKS GRAPHIC NOVEL

ENDGAME

Volume One of the Eighth Doctor's complete comic strip adventures. Containing 8 digitally restored stories: **ENDGAME, THE KEEP, FIRE AND BRIMSTONE, TOOTH AND CLAW, THE FINAL CHAPTER, WORMWOOD, A LIFE OF MATTER AND DEATH** and **BY HOOK OR BY CROOK!**

PLUS a 16-page behind-the-scenes feature with unused story ideas, character designs and an authors' commentary on all strips!

228 pages | b&w softcover
£14.99 | $24.95
ISBN 1-9052 39-09-2

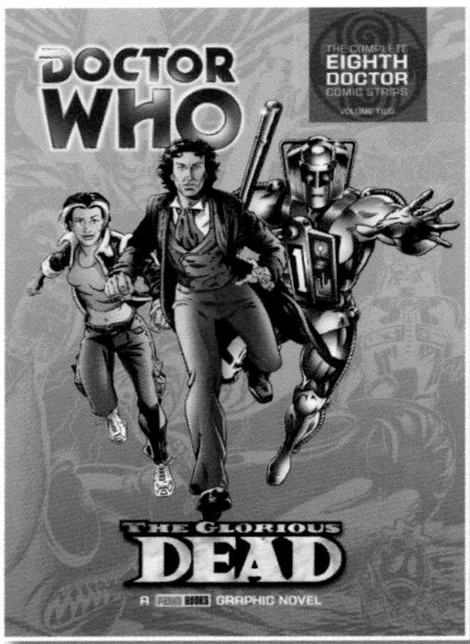
DOCTOR WHO
THE COMPLETE EIGHTH DOCTOR COMIC STRIPS
VOLUME TWO
THE GLORIOUS DEAD
A PANINI BOOKS GRAPHIC NOVEL

THE GLORIOUS DEAD

Volume Two of the Eighth Doctor's complete comic strip adventures. Containing 8 digitally restored stories: **THE FALLEN, UNNATURAL BORN KILLERS, THE ROAD TO HELL, COMPANY OF THIEVES, THE GLORIOUS DEAD, THE AUTONOMY BUG, HAPPY DEATHDAY** and **TV ACTION!**

PLUS a 6-page behind-the-scenes feature and two classic 1980s strips featuring Kroton the Cyberman: **THROWBACK** and **SHIP OF FOOLS!**

244 pages | b&w softcover
£15.99 | $26.50
ISBN 1-9052 39-44-0

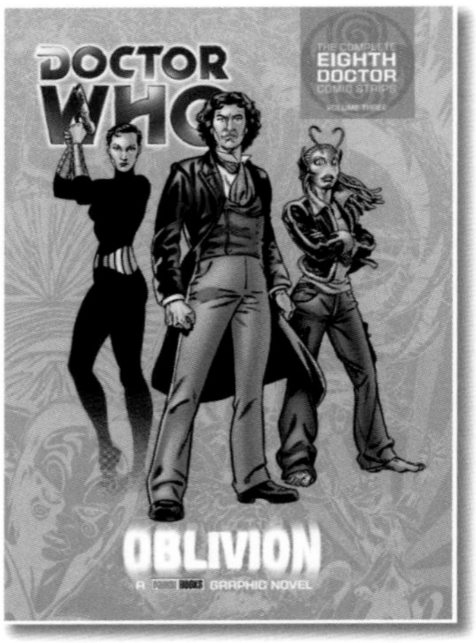
DOCTOR WHO
THE COMPLETE EIGHTH DOCTOR COMIC STRIPS
VOLUME THREE
OBLIVION
A PANINI BOOKS GRAPHIC NOVEL

OBLIVION

Volume Three of the Eighth Doctor's complete comic strip adventures. Containing 7 digitally restored stories: **OPHIDIUS, BEAUTIFUL FREAK, THE WAY OF ALL FLESH, CHILDREN OF THE REVOLUTION, ME AND MY SHADOW, UROBOROS** and **OBLIVION!**

PLUS a massive 22-page behind-the-scenes feature, bonus strip **CHARACTER ASSASSIN** and a newly-extended conclusion to Dalek strip **CHILDREN OF THE REVOLUTION!**

228 pages | full colour softcover
£15.99 | $26.50
ISBN 1-905239-45-9

HIC NOVELS COLLECTION

JOHN RIDGWAY
STEVE PARKHOUSE
ALAN McKENZIE
DOCTOR WHO
VOYAGER

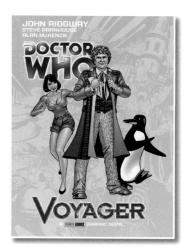

VOYAGER

Volume One of the Sixth Doctor's comic strip adventures containing 7 digitally restored adventures: **THE SHAPE SHIFTER, VOYAGER, POLLY THE GLOT, ONCE UPON A TIME LORD, WAR-GAME, FUNHOUSE** and **KANE'S STORY/ABEL'S STORY/THE WARRIOR'S STORY/FROBISHER'S STORY**!

172 pages | b&w softcover
£15.99 | $31.95
ISBN 978-1-905239-71-9

JOHN RIDGWAY
GRANT MORRISON
JAMIE DELANO
DOCTOR WHO
THE WORLD SHAPERS

THE WORLD SHAPERS

Volume Two of the Sixth Doctor's comic strip adventures containing the following digitally restored adventures: **EXODUS, REVELATION!, GENESIS!, NATURE OF THE BEAST, TIME BOMB, SALAD DAZE, CHANGES, PROFITS OF DOOM, THE GIFT** and **THE WORLD SHAPERS**!

188 pages | b&w softcover
£15.99 | $31.95
ISBN 978-1-905239-87-0

DOCTOR · WHO
A COLD DAY IN HELL!

A COLD DAY IN HELL!

Volume One of the Seventh Doctor's comic strip adventures containing 11 complete stories: **A COLD DAY IN HELL!, REDEMPTION!, THE CROSSROADS OF TIME, CLAWS OF THE KLATHI! CULTURE SHOCK!, KEEPSAKE, PLANET OF THE DEAD, ECHOES OF THE MOGOR!, TIME AND TIDE, FOLLOW THAT TARDIS!** and **INVADERS FROM GANTAC!**!

PLUS an introduction and commentary by former strip editors **Richard Starkings** and **John Freeman**

188 pages | b&w softcover
£15.99 | $31.95
ISBN 978-1-84653-410-2

DOCTOR WHO
EIGHTH DOCTOR
THE FLOOD

THE FLOOD

Volume Four of the Eighth Doctor's complete comic strip adventures. Containing 8 digitally restored stories: **WHERE NOBODY KNOWS YOUR NAME, THE NIGHTMARE GAME, THE POWER OF THOUERIS!, THE CURIOUS TALE OF SPRING-HEELED JACK, THE LAND OF HAPPY ENDINGS, BAD BLOOD, SINS OF THE FATHERS** and **THE FLOOD**!

PLUS a massive 28-page behind-the-scenes feature, and a newly-extended conclusion to **THE FLOOD!**

228 pages | full colour softcover
£15.99 | $26.50
ISBN 978-1-905239-65-8

THE TENTH DOCTOR

DOCTOR · WHO
THE BETROTHAL OF SONTAR

THE BETROTHAL OF SONTAR

Volume One of the Tenth Doctor's complete comic strip adventures from the pages of **DWM**. Containing 8 complete stories: **THE BETROTHAL OF SONTAR, THE LODGER, F.A.Q., THE FUTURISTS, INTERSTELLAR OVERDRIVE, OPERA OF DOOM!, THE GREEN-EYED MONSTER** and **THE WARKEEPER'S CROWN**!

PLUS a massive 15-page behind-the-scenes feature, including commentaries from the writers, artists and editors, cut scenes, pencil art, design sketches, and much, much more!

180 pages | full colour softcover
£15.99 | $31.95
ISBN 978-1-905239-90-0

ALL OF THESE TITLES ARE AVAILABLE NOW FROM ALL GOOD BOOKSHOPS, SPECIALIST COMIC SHOPS AND ONLINE RETAILERS!

Panini BOOKS

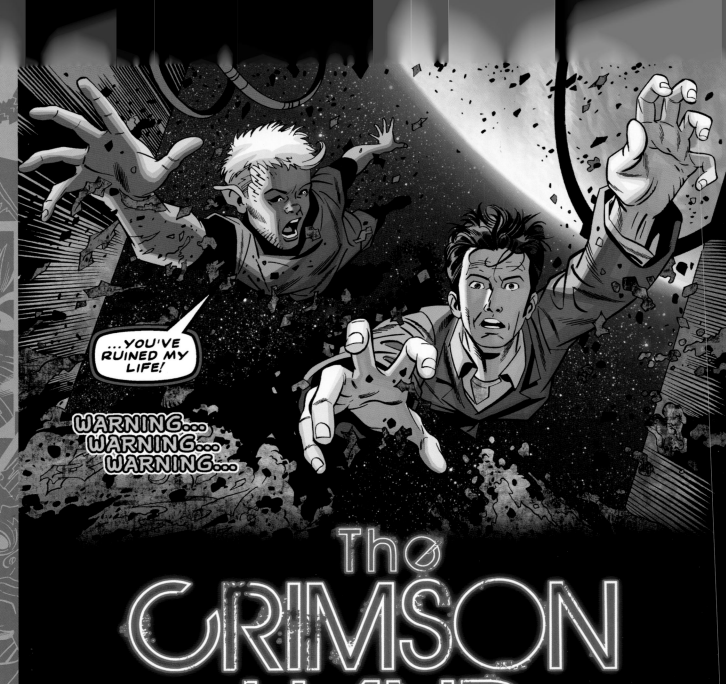

...YOU'VE RUINED MY LIFE!

WARNING... WARNING... WARNING...

The CRIMSON HAND

A PANINI BOOKS GRAPHIC NOVEL

THE DOCTOR MEETS A NEW COMPANION IN THE SHAPE OF MISS MAJENTA PRYCE – IN THE THIRD COLLECTED VOLUME OF STRIPS FEATURING THE TENTH DOCTOR, FROM THE PAGES OF **DOCTOR WHO MAGAZINE**!

FEATURING NINE THRILLING STORIES: **HOTEL HISTORIA, THINKTWICE, THE STOCKBRIDGE CHILD, MORTAL BELOVED, THE AGE OF ICE, THE DEEP HEREAFTER, ONOMATOPOEIA, GHOSTS OF THE NORTHERN LINE** AND **THE CRIMSON HAND**, ALL REPRINTED IN THEIR ORIGINAL EPISODIC FORMAT. PLUS EXCLUSIVE BONUS FEATURES, SKETCHES AND COMMENTARIES FROM THE WRITERS, ARTISTS AND EDITORS!

FEATURING ART FROM **MARTIN GERAGHTY, MIKE COLLINS, ROB DAVIS, SEAN LONGCROFT, DAVID A ROACH** AND **PAUL GRIST**. PLUS STUNNING COLOURS FROM **JAMES OFFREDI**, AND STORIES FROM **DANIEL McDAID**!

260 pages | full colour softcover | released Spring 2010

where lots of different alien races get together – in particular, the motley assortment we encounter in the second episode of *The Daleks' Master Plan*. As it would be a 'comedy', the villains should be the most hapless and ineffectual bunch possible; a gang of z-list baddies that the Doctor had defeated without even trying.

I'm not sure what happened next. I know Clayton quite enjoyed the strip but wasn't keen on the flashbacks – in the first draft, the 'crystal of consciousness' was with the Tenth Doctor and Martha and the 'banana' was with the Tenth Doctor and Rose, as I wasn't sure we were allowed to use 'past' Doctors.

Nothing happened with the strip until September, when Tom Spilsbury (who had taken over from Clayton as editor of **DWM**) asked for a second draft. Unlike Clayton, he loved the flashbacks – and wanted more of them, but with old Doctors and companions! I was only too happy to oblige.

As an experiment, I wrote the second draft using the Final Draft programme – it doesn't have a 'comic strip' setting so it feels like you're writing a movie...

PAGE ONE

Panel 1

A large panel showing a desolate alien landscape. It resembles BRYCE CANYON but even more twisted and organic, as though the rocks and mountains are petrified corals. We should get a sense of how inhospitable this world is – the peaks are jagged and there are bubbling pools of lavas.

Soaring overhead is a battered spacecraft. It's design is peculiar – it looks as though someone has designed a spacecraft to look like TWO HAIRDRYERS STUCK TOGETHER but with huge glowing engines. The ship is heavily armed and battle-scarred. Seriously military.

We can also see the building the ship is bound for – a colony station. It is the sort of place that would normally consist of a cluster of habitation domes. The architecture resembles a half-

buried GRAPEFRUIT SQUEEZER. With aerials and sensor dishes, and access tubes linking it to other grapefruit squeezers.

BOX ONE (COMPUTER):	**WARNING! RESEARCH BASE TRURO IS UNDER STRICT QUARANTINE DUE TO AN OUTBREAK OF GALACTIC PLAGUE!**
BOX TWO (COMPUTER):	**DO NOT APPROACH... ON PAIN OF DEATH!**

I had great fun making up the various aliens:

Panel 3
INT. ENTRANCE CORRIDOR.

An airlock door has opened like a camera iris to reveal a silhouette – this is VALIS. When we see him more clearly he is cowled in robes like the GHOST OF CHRISTMAS YET TO COME. He should look scary and enigmatic.

He is being greeted by another alien, a humanoid, called KRAARN. KRAARN is wearing a dark space-suit uniform. His skin is mottled and glowing like lava. His head is bald, and resembles a leering skull. He is totally creepy.

Above: Zargath lets rip. Art by Roger Langridge.

The 'lava' aspect was dropped, as it would be too similar to the monsters from *The Fires of Pompeii*.

PAGE TWO

Panel 1
INT. MEETING ROOM.

The lights go on to reveal the purpose of this meeting. Seven ALIENS have gathered – four sitting, three standing. The three standing are KRAARN, BOLOG and ZARGATH, each one announcing themselves to the gathering. The seated aliens are QUESTOR, PLINK, VALIS and THE MENTOR.

From left to right: Kraarn, Valis, Questor and Plink. Art by Roger Langridge.

It's a SUPPORT GROUP FOR DEFEATED DOCTOR WHO ALIENS. A sort of 'antagonists anonymous'!

We've already met KRAARN and VALIS. The other aliens are: BOLOG – BOLOG is short, dumpy, green, lizard-like and wearing a baggy spacesuit. A cross between MARK BENTON and an IGUANA. He should resemble the most unconvincing sort of man-in-a-rubber-suit-type of monster.

ZARGATH – ZARGATH is half human, half ANGLER FISH. He has the jagged teeth of an angler fish and a little light bulb dangling at the front. He should resemble a STAR TREK-style monster based around prosthetic make-up.

QUESTOR – QUESTOR looks like something from THE SPACE MUSEUM ie an extremely cheap 1960's monster. He is wearing overalls with a tin foil 'lightning' design, false eyebrows and a Beatles wig. A frond of seaweed is stuck to his chin. His translation unit looks like an AIR FRESHENER. It's important he's rendered ONLY IN BLACK, WHITE and GREY.

PLINK – PLINK has an all-over body space suit, so his face – whatever that might be – is obscured by a breathing mask and a visor with three-eye holes. His space suit is very 80s, very BLAKE'S 7 – gold-braided with shoulder-pads.

THE MENTOR – A low-rent Master. A man in his sixties who has gone to seed. Balding with a comb-over. Rotund with the tired-eyed look of someone who's had too many gin and tonics. His sinister black outfit is tight around his gut, emphasizing his beer belly.

Above: Bolog and Questor look for the Doctor. Art by Roger Langridge.

Below: The original sketch for the Mentor. Bottom right: Roger Langridge's first sketches for Bolog and Zargath.

For some inexplicable reason I also decided that Questor should have an Irish accent (the 'sweet Bejayus' line was a typo).

In terms of the past Doctors, I went for the Eighth Doctor and his comic-strip companion Izzy, the Fourth with his TV companions Romana and K9, the Ninth with Rose, the Sixth with his comic-strip companion Frobisher the penguin, the Third with the Brigadier and Jo Grant and the First with TV companions Dodo and Steven. I remember Tom Spilsbury suggesting it might be fun to just have comic strip companions and to have the Fourth Doctor with Sharon and the First Doctor with John and Gillian. Thankfully we decided against it.

There were only a few changes to the second draft. I'd overstepped a line by making Plink's last words 'What the f-'? And, whilst the following was intended as affectionate teasing, it could've been misinterpreted as an attack on the TV series:

PAGE THREE

Panel 3
INT. MEETING ROOM.

Two aliens are comparing notes – THE MENTOR and QUESTOR – both with

'whatever' expressions. The other DELEGATES (if visible) are nodding sagely or have 'that's so true' looks.

THE MENTOR: HIM AND HIS **BLOODY SONIC SCREWDRIVER!** IS THERE ANYTHING IT CAN'T DO?

QUESTOR: I KNOW – IF YOU ASK ME, IT'S, LOIKE, **TOTALLY UNFAIR!**

PAGE FIVE

Panel 2
INT. TUNNEL TOWARDS THE LIFT SHAFT.

BOLOG and QUESTOR are making their way down another tunnel, heading towards the waiting lift. Both are armed with business-like guns. The corridor is gloomy – things could be lurking in the darkness!

BOLOG: BUT HOW DID HE GET PAST THE **SECURITY PROTOCOLS?**

QUESTOR: HE PROBABLY USED THAT THERE **SONIC SCREWDRIVER** OF HIS!

The 'living jungle of Tropicalus' was Tom's idea, I think, as was the final line of the story – as I'd written it, it ended on a rather flat note:

PAGE NINE

Panel 3
INT. ENTRANCE CORRIDOR.

The DOCTOR and MARTHA are now looking over some computer panels. The DOCTOR is examining them using his sonic screwdriver.

DOCTOR: THIS WIRING IS **CENTURIES OLD... DANGEROUS STUFF,** CAN CAUSE **FREAK POWER SURGES** IF YOU'RE NOT CAREFUL!

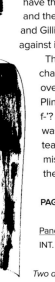